GREAT ATHLETES

GREAT ATHLETES

Volume 7
Sarazen–Unseld
Indexes

Edited by
The Editors of Salem Press

Special Consultant
Rafer Johnson

SALEM PRESS, INC.
Pasadena, California   Hackensack, New Jersey

Editor in Chief: Dawn P. Dawson

Managing Editor: R. Kent Rasmussen   *Research Supervisor:* Jeffry Jensen
Manuscript Editor: Lauren Mitchell   *Acquisitions Editor:* Mark Rehn
Production Editor: Cynthia Beres   *Page Design and Layout:* James Hutson
Photograph Editor: Philip Bader   *Additional Layout:* William Zimmerman
Assistant Editors: Andrea Miller   Eddie Murillo
Elizabeth Slocum

Cover Design: Moritz Design, Los Angeles, Calif.

Library of Congress Cataloging-in-Publication Data
Great athletes / edited by the editors of Salem Press ; Rafer Johnson, special consultant.—Rev.
    p. cm.
Includes bibliographical references and index.
ISBN 1-58765-007-X (set : alk. paper) — ISBN 1-58765-008-8 (v. 1 : alk. paper) —
ISBN 1-58765-009-6 (v. 2 : alk. paper) — ISBN 1-58765-010-X (v. 3 : alk. paper) —
ISBN 1-58765-011-8 (v. 4 : alk. paper) — ISBN 1-58765-012-6 (v. 5 : alk. paper) —
ISBN 1-58765-013-4 (v. 6 : alk. paper) — ISBN 1-58765-014-2 (v. 7 : alk. paper) —
ISBN 1-58765-015-0 (v. 8 : alk. paper)
    1. Athletes—Biography—Dictionaries. I. Johnson, Rafer, 1935-   . II. Salem Press

GV697.A1 G68 2001
796′.092′2—dc21

2001042644

First Printing

Contents

page

page

GREAT ATHLETES

GENE SARAZEN

Sport: Golf

Born: February 27, 1902
Harrison, New York
Died: May 13, 1999
Naples, Florida

Early Life

Eugenio Saraceni was born February 27, 1902, in Harrison, New York. His father had been forced by financial need to abandon his studies in Rome for the priesthood. Instead, he emigrated to the United States and worked as a carpenter. He always regretted his failure to pursue his scholarly career and was a bitter and unhappy man.

As a result, he and Gene had a poor relationship. Gene worked as a caddy at local golf clubs but did not take up the game seriously until the conflict with his father worsened. This further break took place after the entry of the United States into World War I in 1917. Gene's father secured a job for him at a local shipyard after urging him to quit school.

In part because of the hard labor required, Gene developed pneumonia. After his recovery, he abandoned his job and decided to become a professional golfer, much to his father's displeasure.

The Road to Excellence

Gene Sarazen (he adopted this name after turning professional) had a number of qualities that marked him for greatness. He was aggressive and cocky with a fierce will to win. He was capable of spectacular shot-making under pressure.

His golf matched his temperament. He punched his shots so that they had a low trajectory, enabling him in large part to ignore unfavorable wind condi-

tions. Although only 5 feet 6 inches tall, he was immensely strong, and his fast hand action enabled him to generate highly powerful shots. His best clubs were the fairway woods, in the use of which he became one of the two or three best of all time.

Putting was not his forte, but Gene's method of dealing with this weakness was characteristic. He spent hours practicing this aspect of his game until, far from being a weakness, it became a real weapon in his arsenal.

MAJOR CHAMPIONSHIP VICTORIES

1922-23, 1933	PGA Championship
1922, 1932	U.S. Open
1932	British Open
1935	The Masters
1954, 1958	PGA Seniors Championship

OTHER NOTABLE VICTORIES

1925	Metropolitan Open
1927-28, 1939	Metropolitan PGA Championship
1927, 1929, 1931, 1933, 1935, 1937	Ryder Cup team
1930	Western Open
1934	Hawaiian Open
1936	Australian Open
1954	International Seniors

The Emerging Champion

Gene emerged as a major presence in golf in 1922. In that year, he won the United States Open, held at the difficult Skokie course near Chicago. How he won the tournament exemplifies his personality. He made a study of the course in the week preceding the event and memorized the contours of the greens. As a result, he was among the tournament's leaders after three rounds, a position he had never before attained in the Open.

The young player, undaunted by the Open's prestige, proceeded to play the last round in aggressive fashion; he finished with a 69, a good enough score to win the tournament outright. He avoided a playoff by a daring approach to the last green.

In the same year, Gene won the Professional Golfers' Association (PGA) Championship. The PGA was at that time a match play event, in which golfers faced each other head-to-head, and Walter Hagen was generally regarded as the greatest of all match players. Gene showed himself immune to the pressure and dispatched Hagen, a feat he repeated in an arranged match for the "World's Golf Championship."

In 1923, Gene's game slumped, and he finished poorly in the United States Open. He revived by the time of the PGA and again defeated Hagen in the final. Gene now appeared set for a long reign at golf's pinnacle, but the remainder of the 1920's proved a disappointment. He did not win any other major titles in that decade.

In part, the reason for his fall was precisely the source of his strength. His aggressive game some-

times got out of control. In the 1928 British Open, he missed a chance to win by ignoring the advice of his experienced caddy, Skip Daniels. He attempted a risky shot that failed, and his 7 on the hole cost him the tournament.

Continuing the Story

Gene's way of coping with his slump showed his immense dedication. In spite of his success—his slump was by most golfers' standards a period of great success—he decided to revamp his game completely. He had come to adopt an outside-in trajectory on his swing that, he believed, was responsible for inadequate control of the club. He thought that an inside-out swing was more suited to his game and embarked on the endless hours of practice required to alter his swing.

Gene also endeavored to improve his play in sand bunkers. To this end, he invented a new golf club, the sand wedge, which proved much more efficient than the earlier niblick and soon became a standard item.

In the 1932 British Open, Gene again had Skip Daniels as his caddy. This time he followed his adviser's suggestions and triumphed in the tournament. He also won the United States Open that year, doing so by one of his come-from-behind charges.

His most famous victory took place in the 1935 Masters. As the tournament neared its end, Gene found that he needed to birdie three of the last

RECORDS AND MILESTONES

First player to win all four major (Grand Slam) golf tournaments
Placed second in the British Open (1928), third (1931, 1933)
Placed second in the U.S. Open (1934, 1940), third (1926)

HONORS AND AWARDS

1932	Associated Press Male Athlete of the Year
1940	Inducted into PGA Hall of Fame
1965	GWAA Richardson Award
1974	Inducted into PGA/World Golf Hall of Fame
1984	Charlie Bartlett Award
1988	Old Tom Morris Award

four holes in order to secure a tie with Craig Wood, who had already finished his round. On the fifteenth hole, Gene used his skill with fairway woods to full effect. He sank his second stroke, a 250-yard shot to green, giving him a double-eagle 2 on the par 5 hole. This was sufficient to give him his tie with Wood, who he bested in the playoff.

An unusual feature of Gene's game was his longevity as a topflight golfer. In 1940, he tied for the United States Open with Lawson Little. Although he lost the playoff, his achievement was remarkable. He was thirty-eight years old at the time, in golf a quite advanced age.

Perhaps even more amazing was his performance in the 1958 British Open. He finished only 10 strokes behind the winner. He ended in a tie for sixteenth place with Bobby Locke, the previous year's victor. Gene also became the only player older than sixty to make the cut at the Masters.

Summary

Gene Sarazen became one of the greatest golfers of the 1920's and 1930's by a combination of aggressive temperament and physical ability. His strength and speed enabled him to risk shots that other golfers dared not attempt. He played best when under pressure, and his dashing style gained him wide publicity as well as seven major championships.

Bill Delaney

Additional Sources:

Grimsley, Will. *Golf: Its History, People, and Events.* Englewood Cliffs, N.J.: Prentice-Hall, 1966.

Porter, David L., ed. *Biographical Dictionary of American Sports: Outdoor Sports.* Westport, Conn.: Greenwood Press, 1988.

Sarazen, Gene, and Herbert W. Wind. *Thirty Years of Championship Golf: The Life and Times of Gene Sarazen.* New York: Prentice-Hall, 1950. Reprint. London: A & C Black, 1990.

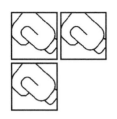

FELIX SAVON

Sport: Boxing

Born: September 27, 1967
San Vincente, Cuba

Early Life

Felix Savon was born in San Vincente, Cuba, just eleven miles from the United States Navy base at Guantanamo. The son of peasants who later divorced, he grew up with few luxuries.

Felix began competing in sports at an early age, running track with his four sisters. In the fall of 1981 his sister, Maure, was accepted to a prestigious sports school in Guantanamo. Though Felix also wanted to attend, there were no spots open there for boys. Remaining at home, he participated in both track and rowing.

By midterm in 1981, several boys had left the school, creating the precious opening Felix needed. The boxing coach came to his house, offering him entry to the school. Felix was happy to compete in any sport, and boxing was chosen for him. Weeks later, when he returned home for a visit, his mother saw that his hands were bruised and swollen. She wanted to pull him out of the school and threatened him that he would not be welcome to return home if he continued boxing. Felix tried to reassure her and eventually returned to school. Some months later his father also tried to get him to leave school. Officials told his father that Felix could only leave if his mother insisted, since he was living with her. His mother did not insist, and Felix was able to stay. That year he won a gold medal in the 1981 School Games.

The Road to Excellence

In 1983 and 1984 Felix began to assert his dominance in Cuban boxing when he was twice awarded the Cuban Junior National Championship. By 1986 his presence was being felt outside of Cuba. That year the nineteen-year-old dominated the heavyweight division and won the world championship crown. He followed up those wins with gold medals at the Pan-Am and World Cup Championships in 1987.

His constant training and rigorous regimen pointed him toward the 1988 Olympics, where Felix was predicted to be the heavyweight champion. At 6 feet, 4 inches and 201 pounds, he seemed assured of the title. Cuba, however, chose to boycott the

Cuban boxer Felix Savon in March, 1996.

AP/Wide World Photos

Olympics that year, denying Felix his gold. He later had the chance to prove himself when he beat United States gold medalist Ray Mercer in a dual meet in Atlantic City, New Jersey. He may not have won the gold for his country, but he did prove that he was the heavyweight champion.

Many thought that twenty-two-year-old Felix should turn professional, but he refused. Although he made only 120 pesos per month boxing, supplemented by an additional 140 doing odd jobs at the sports school, he insisted that he boxed because he loved the sport and wanted to represent his country, not because he was interested in making money.

Between the 1988 and the 1992 Olympics, Felix added to his heavyweight titles, winning the World Championships in both 1989 and 1991. In 1990 he also added wins at the Goodwill Games and the World Championships Challenge. In 1991 he added a second Pan-American Games to his list of victories.

The Emerging Champion

At twenty-four, Felix had his first chance to win Olympic gold at the games in Barcelona. In his early rounds he often appeared awkward, and he struggled in his quarterfinal round with American Danell Nicholson. By the third round it looked as if Felix would be eliminated until suddenly he landed a series of blows. He was unable to finish Nicholson, but prevailed on points, winning 13 to 11. He had none of these problems in his final round when he defeated Nigeria's David Izonritei, 14 to 1. It was a difficult series of matches; however, Felix emerged undefeated and won the gold medal.

Again he received offers to turn professional, and again he ignored them. Instead, he returned to Cuba to resume his training. The years following the 1992 Olympics were more of the same for Felix. Among his many victories were the 1993 World Championships, the 1994 Goodwill Games, the 1995 Pan-American Games, and the 1995 World Championships. His trip to Atlanta for the 1996 Olympics added another gold medal to his many wins. With two Olympic gold medals, he was now chasing his fellow countryman Teofilo Stevenson's three straight Olympic gold medals.

In 1997 and 1998, Felix proved himself to be the undisputed champion by again winning the

MAJOR CHAMPIONSHIPS		
Year	Competition	Place
1985	World Junior Championships	1st
1986	World Championships	1st
1987	Pan-American Games	1st
1989	World Championships	1st
1990	Goodwill Games	1st
1991	Pan-American Games	1st
	World Championships	1st
1992	Olympic Games	Gold
1993	World Championships	1st
1994	World Goodwill Games	1st
1995	Pan-American Games	1st
	World Championships	1st
1996	Olympic Games	Gold
1997	World Championships	1st
1998	Goodwill Games	1st
1999	World Championships	2d
2000	Olympic Games	Gold

World Championships and the Goodwill Games. In 1999, for the first time, Felix began showing his age but nevertheless brought home the silver medal from the 1999 World Championships.

Continuing the Story

Despite the defeat, Felix focused all of his attention on the upcoming 2000 Olympics in Sydney, Australia. He hoped to be able to tie Stevenson's record of three Olympic gold medals. His quarterfinal match was greatly anticipated. Felix was pitted against defending world champion Michael Bennett of the United States. The anticipation did not match the fight, however, and Felix won easily. The fight was called three seconds before the end of the third round because Felix was already winning by 15 points. He also won his semifinal match, but received a cut under his left eye.

In the final match, he struggled against Russian Sultanhmed Ibzagimov. With only 14 seconds left in the fight, a blow from his opponent reopened the cut under Felix's eye. The referee stopped the fight in order to examine Felix. After the referee allowed the fight to cotinue, Felix evaded the Russian until the final bell was rung. He won, receiving a 20 to 12 judgement.

Felix's wife and five children, including his twin daughters, watched him on television, as did the rest of Cuba. In Sydney he tied Stevenson's record with his own three consecutive gold medal wins. If Cuba had not boycotted the 1988 games, Felix could possibly have surpassed his idol by winning four gold medals.

Summary

During his impoverished childhood, Felix Savon had no idea that he would become a treasure in his Cuban homeland. Though not a polished fighter, he was powerful and driven. Throughout his career he refused offers to turn professional, once saying, "I do not like professional boxing. There is a tremendous difference between Olympic-style and professional boxing. In the professional ranks the athlete is not protected at all, they don't take care of him at all, and of course the main interest is earning money. It's a very dirty sport. In Olympic-style boxing, the amateur sport is very clean and it's truly something that is good for the athlete." With that attitude, he established himself as a heavyweight icon both inside and outside of Cuba.

Deborah Service

Additional Sources:

Blaudschun, Mark. "Savon's Superiority Shines Through in Bennett Battle." *Boston Globe*, September 27, 2000, p. G5.

Hummer, Steve. "Cuban Ends Bennett's Story." *The Atlanta Journal-Constitution*, September 27, 2000, p. F5.

Myslenski, Skip. "Boxer Savon Grows into Legendary Figure in Cuba." *Chicago Tribune*, August 14, 1991, p. 41.

"Slight Heavies." *Sports Illustrated* 77, no. 7 (August 17, 1992): 56.

"The Summer Olympics/The Ones to Beat," *Time* 156, no. 11 (September 11, 2000): 84.

TERRY SAWCHUK

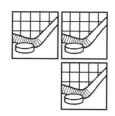

Sport: Ice hockey

Born: December 28, 1929
Winnipeg, Manitoba, Canada
Died: May 31, 1970
Mineola, New York

Early Life

Terrance Gordon Sawchuk was born on December 28, 1929, in the city of Winnipeg, Manitoba, Canada. His father, a tinsmith, worked hard to support the family, but everyone had to contribute. A busy childhood saw Terry working at odd jobs at the age of fourteen. The money he earned from work at the local foundry and a sheet metal company was usually taken home and handed over to his mother. She, in turn, gave Terry his allowance out of his earnings.

Throughout all of this, Terry still found time to play hockey. He started playing goal early in life mainly because his brother Michael, seven years his senior, played goal for his school and Terry naturally fell into the pads and into playing the goalkeeper. The local league he played in was sponsored by the Detroit Red Wings, so there was no shortage of scouts to gauge his progress. By the age of fifteen, he was playing Junior League for the Winnipeg Rangers, where the maximum age limit was twenty years old.

Terry Sawchuk of the Detroit Red Wings in 1959.

The Road to Excellence

Terry played one season for Detroit's farm club in Windsor, Ontario, and then, at the age of seventeen, turned professional. His first professional club, the Omaha Knights of the United States Hockey League, was far from home, but Terry did well and adjusted to the life of a profes-sional hockey player. In 1947, his first year at Omaha, Terry was named Rookie of the Year. This performance prompted a promotion, and the following season Terry found himself playing for Indianapolis of the American Hockey League. At this higher league, the competition was tougher and gradually prepared the young goalkeeper for future duty in the big leagues.

STATISTICS

Season	GP	W	L	T	GAA	PIM
1949-50	7	4	3	0	2.29	0
1950-51	70	44	13	13	1.99	2
1951-52	70	44	14	12	**1.90**	2
1952-53	63	32	15	16	**1.90**	5
1953-54	67	35	19	13	1.94	0
1954-55	68	28	24	26	1.96	0
1955-56	68	22	33	13	2.66	**20**
1956-57	34	18	10	6	2.38	14
1957-58	70	29	29	12	2.96	**39**
1958-59	67	23	36	8	3.12	**12**
1959-60	58	24	20	14	2.69	**22**
1960-61	37	12	16	8	3.05	8
1961-62	43	14	21	8	3.33	12
1962-63	48	23	16	7	2.48	**14**
1963-64	53	24	20	7	2.60	0
1964-65	36	17	13	6	2.56	**24**
1965-66	27	10	11	4	2.96	12
1966-67	28	15	5	4	2.81	2
1967-68	36	11	14	6	3.07	0
1968-69	13	3	4	3	2.62	0
1969-70	8	3	1	2	2.91	0
Totals	971	**435**	337	188	2.50	188

Notes: Boldface indicates statistical leader. GP = games played; W = wins; L = losses; T = ties; GAA = goals against average; PIM = penalties in minutes

It was two seasons later, during the 1950-1951 season, that Detroit goalie Harry Lumley was injured and Terry was called up to replace him. Terry finished the season in fine fashion, allowing only 16 goals in seven games. The following season, Detroit traded Lumley and Terry became the number one goalie on the team. The fans backed Terry as the number one goalie, amazed at the results he got from the unorthodox, crouching style that he brought to the position of keeper. He claimed that his low crouch helped him see the puck and the play better. This style and his lightning quickness were to win Terry and his teammates many awards over the following seasons.

The Emerging Champion

It was during this season, officially his rookie year, that Terry barely missed earning the Vezina Trophy, awarded to the goalie who allows the fewest goals per game over the course of the season. As it turned out, Terry was the unanimous selection for the Calder Trophy, which is awarded to the best rookie. The next season, instead of suffering the sophomore jinx, Terry came back with even a better season than his rookie year. He lowered his goals against average to 1.90 and had

twelve shutouts while capturing the Vezina Trophy. His team went on to win the Stanley Cup, given to the league champions.

During the early 1950's, Terry was at the top of his game and was recognized as the premier goalie in the league. In one memorable game against the Montreal Canadiens, his Detroit team was outshot 43-12, yet managed to win the game by a score of 3-1. Most of the action during the game occurred in the Detroit zone, yet the Flying Frenchmen from Montreal were stymied on every attempt. Terry seemed to love playing the Canadiens and, in spite of the nervous disorders that plagued him throughout his career, he played his best against Montreal.

Terry would go on to play in 971 regular season games, 106 Stanley Cup games, and win the championship three times with Detroit and once after he was traded to Toronto. He also captured three Vezina Trophies with Detroit and shared one with Johnny Bower while in Toronto. He ended his career with 103 shutouts.

Continuing the Story

While all these good things were happening to Terry on the ice, his life away from hockey was usually a disaster. Two of his brothers died early

NHL RECORDS

Most wins, 435
Most shutouts, 103
Most shutouts in one Stanley Cup Playoffs, 4 (1952) (record shared)
Lowest GAA in one Stanley Cup Playoffs, 0.63 (1952)

HONORS AND AWARDS

1951	Calder Memorial Trophy
1952-53, 1955, 1965	Vezina Trophy
1971	Lester Patrick Award Inducted into Hockey Hall of Fame
1975	Inducted into Canada's Sports Hall of Fame

in life, before they had a chance to see Terry play professionally. He was a moody man of extreme peaks and depths in his emotions. He had more than his share of injuries, illness, accidents, operations, and personal problems. His playing weight jumped between 146 pounds and 228 pounds, depending on the nature of Terry's emotional state. He took his life very seriously and when things did not go well, Terry took to drinking, which only worsened the other problems.

Throughout all of this there was one constant in Terry's life, and that was hockey. His drive and determination to get back into the game helped him to overcome some injuries that would have ended the careers of less strong-willed men. Eventually, the stress of life became so extreme that Terry had to quit hockey for a while. A trade that separated his family took a further toll on his mental condition. A series of strange, but serious injuries kept occurring, interrupting a brilliant career. Finally, while horsing around with a fellow teammate at a barbecue, Terry fell and suffered fatal injuries. The final ruling was that his death was accidental.

Summary

In spite of the great talent Terry Sawchuk possessed, he was a troubled man. Even though he received the cheers of the fans and the high salary of a star player, life was not complete. There were so many external disturbances that one has to wonder just what type of career Terry might have had if he had not been so troubled. In any case, his love of the game and determination took him all the way from the outdoor rinks of Winnipeg to the Hockey Hall of Fame. His crouched-over style revolutionized the art of goalkeeping and his records reflect nothing but greatness.

Carmi Brandis

Additional Sources:

Dryden, Steve, and Michael Ulmer, eds. *The Top 100 NHL Hockey Players of All Time.* Toronto: McClelland & Stewart, 1998.

Dupuis, David M. *Sawchuk: The Troubles and Triumphs of the World's Greatest Goalie.* Toronto: Stoddart, 1998.

Hunter, Douglas. *A Breed Apart: An Illustrated History of Goaltending.* New York: Viking, 1995.

Kendall, Brian. *Shutout: The Legend of Terry Sawchuk.* Toronto: Viking, 1996.

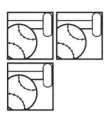

STEVE SAX

Sport: Baseball

Born: January 29, 1960
Sacramento, California

Early Life

Stephen Louis Sax was born in Sacramento, California, on January 29, 1960. His parents, John and Nancy Jane Sax, reared Steve, his older brother and best friend, David, and three sisters (Tammy, Dana, and Cheryl) on a farm in West Sacramento.

As a young boy, Steve performed typical farm chores such as milking cows and baling hay. Like most children, he preferred doing things other than chores such as playing the drums or playing baseball, especially with his brother. In order to have more time to play, Steven often hurried, literally running to finish his chores. While he was very fast, the job was often not done properly. His father, who was his mentor and greatest influence, would then make Steve redo the chores until he finished them properly. Later, Steven applied this way of thinking to playing baseball.

The Road to Excellence

Steve's love for baseball began early, and by age six he knew he wanted to be a major leaguer. He was a fan of the San Francisco Giants and Willie Mays, but the major league player he admired most was Pete Rose. Steve was inspired by Pete's enthusiasm and aggressiveness. He wanted to imitate the way his hero always ran out the bases, even when put on first base after four balls.

In 1974, Steve began attending James Marshall High School in West Sacramento. In his junior year, he earned All-American, All-State, and All-City honors and was selected the league's most valuable player. In his senior year, he was named the league's most valuable player again, and before his graduation in June, 1978, he had set four school baseball records.

Steve's professional career began on June 6, 1978, when he signed with Dodger scout Ronnie King. He was sent to Lethbridge, Canada (a Dodger farm team). His brother David joined him after a few days and the Sax brothers be-

Chicago White Sox second baseman Steve Sax fields a ground ball during a game at Comiskey Park in 1992.

2454

STATISTICS

Season	GP	AB	Hits	2B	3B	HR	Runs	RBI	BA	SA
1981	31	119	33	2	0	2	15	9	.277	.345
1982	150	638	180	23	7	4	88	47	.282	.359
1983	155	623	175	18	5	5	94	41	.281	.350
1984	145	569	138	24	4	1	70	35	.243	.304
1985	136	488	136	8	4	1	62	42	.279	.318
1986	157	633	210	43	4	6	91	56	.332	.441
1987	157	610	171	22	7	6	84	46	.280	.369
1988	160	632	175	19	4	5	70	57	.277	.343
1989	158	651	205	26	3	5	88	63	.315	.387
1990	155	615	160	24	2	4	70	42	.260	.325
1991	158	652	198	38	2	10	85	56	.304	.417
1992	143	567	134	26	4	4	74	47	.236	.317
1993	57	119	28	5	0	1	20	8	.235	.303
1994	7	24	6	0	1	0	2	1	.250	.333
Totals	1,769	6,940	1,949	278	47	54	913	550	.281	.358

Notes: GP = games played; AB = at bats; 2B = doubles; 3B = triples; HR = home runs; RBI = runs batted in; BA = batting average; SA = slugging average

came teammates. In 1979, Steve reported to Clinton, Iowa, in the Midwest League. In 1980, he went to Vero Beach, where he won Florida State League All-Star honors. In 1981, he was sent to San Antonio. He led the Texas League with a .364 batting average and was named most valuable player. He also received Texas League and Topps National Association All-Star honors. During his minor league career, he was a shortstop, a third baseman, and an outfielder before settling on second baseman.

On August 18, 1981, Steve joined the Dodgers, replacing injured second baseman Davey Lopes. That day, he had his first major league hit; five days later, he hit his first major league home run. As a result of his contributions, Steve was placed on the Dodger roster for the 1982 season.

The Emerging Champion

The twenty-two-year-old rookie was a catalyst for the 1982 Dodgers. With Steve's help, the team finished one game out of first place in the National League West. During his first full major league season, Steve walked 49 times, led the Dodgers with 180 hits and 88 runs scored, set a Dodger rookie record by stealing 49 bases, and was the only rookie named to the National League All-Star team. He was also named to the United Press International and Topps Manager Rookie All-Star teams. Because of his outstanding performance, he received the Rookie of the Year Award.

Steve's road to continued success was not an easy one, however. His second year in the majors was a disappointment defensively. For three months, he had a mental block that contributed to 26 throwing errors. A lesser man might have crumbled, but not Steve Sax. Instead, he prayed and listened to his father's advice that with time, it would pass. Because his problem was more mental than physical, by August, it was gone. He was errorless for the last thirty-eight games of the season. Nevertheless, Steve led the National League that year with 30 errors. He lived with the reputation for being wild until the 1990 season, when at last he was given credit for his defensive capabilities. Ironically, 1983 was outstanding for Steve offensively.

One of Steve's finest years came in 1986. He led the Dodgers with a .332 batting average, hit his first grand slam, and received the National League second baseman Silver Slugger Award. He was also named the National League Player of the Month (September) for hitting in twenty-five straight games and for committing only 16 errors in 815 chances. Steve also had a good year personally in 1986. On October 21, he married Debbie Graham. They had two children, Lauren and John.

Continuing the Story

Steve's career was impressive because he cared about being a winner. He was an excellent leadoff hitter and a good bunter. He ran fast and knew how to get into position to catch the ball when it was hit in his direction. He became known for sliding in the outfield grass, grabbing the ball, and throwing out the runner. He was enthusiastic and very aggressive.

At times, he was perhaps a little too aggressive. In 1982, he was thrown out 19 times while trying to steal bases, and in 1983, he led the National League in failed steals (30). He had to overcome his greatest weakness—hurrying to get the job done and thus making errors.

From 1982 to 1988, Steve was a leader for Los Angeles. He led the team for four or more years in games played, at bats, hits, and stolen bases. Steve also helped the Dodgers in postseason play. They were in four National League Championship Series: 1981, 1983, 1985, and 1988.

Steve helped the Dodgers into two World Series, in 1981 and 1988. Steve's involvement in the 1981 Series victory over the New York Yankees was limited to one at bat as a pinch hitter. In the 1988 Series victory over the Oakland Athletics, Steve excelled with a .300 batting average, led the club with 20 at bats, hit safely in all five games, and had no errors.

On November 2, 1988, Steve was granted free agency. Much to his surprise, he could not negotiate a favorable contract with Los Angeles. On November 23, 1988, Steve signed a three-year contract with the New York Yankees.

In 1989, Steve led the American League and set a Yankee single-season record for singles, with 171. Steve also led the Yankees in batting averages, hits, runs, and stolen bases.

Steve participated in several All-Star games. He played on the 1982, 1983, and 1986 National League All-Star teams. In 1989 and 1990, he was elected to the American League All-Star team. Following one of his best hitting seasons of his career, Steve was traded from New York to the White Sox in early 1992. He lost his starting job at second base in 1993, playing only fifty-seven games that season. Following a seven-game season with Oakland in 1994, Steve retired from baseball. He later began a successful career in television broadcasting.

Summary

Steve Sax believed strongly in the work ethic. Giving 100 percent of himself was always important to him. At a time when many athletic heroes were in the news for drug and substance abuse, Steve was a positive role model for millions of young people. His persistence and determination to excel inspired America's youth.

Victoria Reynolds

HONORS AND AWARDS	
1982	United Press International National League All-Star Team
	National League Rookie of the Year
	Topps Manager Rookie All-Star Team
1982-83, 1986	National League All-Star Team
1986	*Sporting News* National League All-Star Team
	National League Silver Slugger Award
	Sporting News Silver Slugger Team
1989-90	American League All-Star Team

Additional Sources:

Sax, Steve, with Steve Delsohn. *Sax!* Chicago: Contemporary Books, 1986.

GALE SAYERS

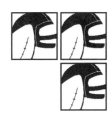

Sport: Football

Born: May 30, 1943
Wichita, Kansas

Early Life

Gale Eugene Sayers was born on May 30, 1943, in Wichita, Kansas, the second son of Roger and Bernice Sayers. Sayers's father was an automobile mechanic who moved his family from Wichita to Speed, Kansas, in 1950 for a short time, then to Omaha, Nebraska, where Gale grew up. His mother named him Gale because she was expecting a girl and had no boy's names picked out. His older brother Roger became an outstanding sprinter at the University of Nebraska at Omaha, and many expected Gale, who was also blessed with outstanding speed, to emulate him.

The Road to Excellence

It was apparent to Gale's coaches that his major talent was carrying a football. He starred at Omaha Central High School to such a degree that by his senior year college recruiters from around the nation were at his door almost night and day. He chose the University of Kansas over other schools such as the Universities of Nebraska and Notre Dame, primarily because he was impressed with the Kansas coach, Jack Mitchell. In 1962, Gale made the varsity team and immediately demonstrated the skills that have led several historians of the game to call him the greatest running back of all time.

In his sophomore year at Kansas, Sayers averaged 7.2 yards per carry and gained 1,125 yards. His performance led to his selection as All-Big Eight running back. During his junior and senior seasons, Sayers was a unanimous choice for All-American honors. His performance during his career at Kansas had professional teams drooling to sign Sayers after the 1964 season.

In 1965 the rivalry between the American (AFL) and National Football Leagues (NFL) was at its height. Sayers was desperately pursued by the Chicago Bears of the older NFL and the Kansas City Chiefs of the AFL. Sayers finally signed a four-year

Chicago Bears halfback Gale Sayers in 1965.

STATISTICS

Season	GP		Rushing					Receiving		
		Car.	Yds.	Avg.	TD	Rec.	Yds.	Avg.	TD
1965	14	166	867	5.2	22	29	507	17.5	6
1966	14	229	**1,231**	5.4	8	34	447	13.1	2
1967	13	186	880	4.7	7	16	126	7.9	1
1968	9	138	856	6.2	2	15	117	7.8	0
1969	14	236	**1,032**	4.4	8	17	116	6.8	0
1970	2	23	52	2.3	0	1	−6	−6.0	0
1971	2	13	38	2.9	0	0	0	0.0	0
Totals	68	991	4,956	5.0	47	112	1,307	11.7	9

Notes: Boldface indicates statistical leader. GP = games played; Car. = carries; Yds. = yards; Avg. = average yards per carry *or* average yards per reception; TD = touchdowns; Rec. = receptions

contract with the Bears for the then-substantial salary of $25,000 per year plus a $50,000 signing bonus. Before he ever played a professional football game professional coaches were already comparing him favorably with the great Cleveland running back Jim Brown.

The Emerging Champion

Sayers did not disappoint the coaches or the fans. His rookie year of 1965 was nothing short of spectacular. Bears owner George Halas insisted on bringing him along slowly, so Sayers did not start in the Bears backfield until the third game of the season. Sayers then led his team to nine victories in their last ten games, setting a number of Bears and NFL records along the way. The NFL records included most touchdowns in a game (6, shared with Dub Jones of Cleveland and Ernie Nevers of the Chicago Cardinals) and most touchdowns in a season (22). It surprised no one when the league named Sayers its Rookie of the Year for 1965.

Despite playing on a sub-par Chicago team in 1966 and 1967 (the Bears finished 5-7-2 and 5-8-1, respectively), Sayers continued to excel. He led the league in 1966 with 1,231 yards rushing and 2,440 all-purpose yards, a league record. His 880 yards rushing in 1967 placed him third in the league, despite his first football injury, a sprained ankle, which slowed him throughout the year.

In the ninth game of the 1968 season, with Sayers having averaged more than 100-yards-per-game rushing to that point, he suffered a serious knee injury. The injury ended his season and threatened to end his career. Sayers was helped through a difficult rehabilitation by Brian Piccolo, his roommate on Bears road trips. Piccolo and Sayers both joined the Bears in 1965 to compete for the same job at running back. Despite a heated rivalry, the two men became close friends, ultimately becoming the first interracial roommates in Bears history. With Piccolo's help, Sayers was ready to start the 1969 season.

To the delight of Sayers and Piccolo, both men started in the Bears backfield at the begin-

NFL RECORDS

Most touchdowns from kickoff returns, 6 (record shared)
Highest average yards per kickoff return, 30.6
Most touchdowns in a game, 6, 1965 (record shared)

HONORS AND AWARDS

1963	All-Big Eight Conference Team
1964-65	Consensus All-American
1965	United Press International NFL Rookie of the Year Bell Trophy
1965-70	NFL All-Pro Team
1966-68, 1970	NFL Pro Bowl Team
1967-68, 1970	NFL Pro Bowl Player of the Game, co-recipient
1970	NFL All-Pro Team of the 1960's Halas Trophy
1975	Inducted into Black Athletes Hall of Fame
1977	Inducted into Pro Football Hall of Fame Inducted into College Football Hall of Fame

ning of the season. In November, tragedy struck. Piccolo was diagnosed as having cancer, and was hospitalized. Sayers went on to have another outstanding season, but Piccolo died in June the following year. Sayers had just received the Halas Trophy, awarded each year to the most courageous player in the NFL, when he heard of his friend's death. He traveled to Chicago, taped Piccolo's name over his own on the trophy, and gave it to his friend's wife. This story is poignantly told in what many critics consider the best football movie ever made, *Brian's Song* (1970).

Continuing the Story

In the third game of the 1970 season, Sayers seriously injured ligaments in his other knee. Despite efforts at rehabilitation, Sayers was never able to come back from this second knee injury. His meteoric career in football was over.

Sayers went on to a successful fourteen-year career in athletic administration before entering private business as an executive in 1986.

Summary

Gale Sayers was perhaps the most explosive runner in football history, combining speed and power with the uncanny ability to change speed and direction almost instantly. Along with his prowess on the gridiron, he will be remembered for his relationship with Brian Piccolo, and the lessons both men learned and taught the world about racial relationships and human courage.

Paul Madden

Additional Sources:

Berger, Phil. *Great Running Backs in Pro Football.* New York: J. Messner, 1970.

Hahn, James, and Lynn Hahn. *Sayers!: The Sports Career of Gale Sayers.* Mankato, Minn.: Crestwood House, 1981.

King, Peter. "Inside the NFL: 1925-1975." *Sports Illustrated* 83, no. 14 (October 2, 1995): 63-65.

May, Julian. *Gale Sayers, Star Running Back.* Mankato, Minn.: Crestwood House, 1973.

DOLPH SCHAYES

Sport: Basketball

Born: May 19, 1928
New York, New York

Early Life

Adolph Schayes was born on May 19, 1928, in the Borough of the Bronx in New York City. His parents, Carl and Tina Schayes, emigrated from Romania to the United States in the early 1920's. Dolph was the second of their three sons.

With other young people in his New York neighborhood, Dolph attended Public School 91 and Creston Junior High School. He and his friends formed their own clubs and challenged other groups of boys to games of football, baseball, and basketball. They played basketball more often than other sports because nearly every school had outdoor basketball courts, while it was necessary to travel miles to reach a park that had the space to play football and baseball.

The Road to Excellence

Dolph entered DeWitt Clinton High School in 1942. As a 6-foot 5-inch sophomore, he became a member of the basketball team. Despite being the ideal height for a high school center, he played all positions. That enabled him to develop the skills needed to be a versatile player.

In 1944, several universities offered Dolph scholarships. He accepted one from New York University (NYU), which was located a few blocks from his home.

He became a student at NYU in February, 1945, and immediately became a starter on the basketball team. At the age of sixteen, he found himself matched against many older, stronger, and more experienced athletes. The tough competition against these men enabled him to improve his playing skills.

During the summers while he attended college, Dolph worked at resorts in New York State's Catskill Mountains. He played basketball in summer leagues organized by the resorts.

In 1948, NYU competed in the finals of the National Invitational Tour-

Dolph Schayes of the Syracuse Nationals (right) makes a shot in a 1959 game.

STATISTICS

Season	GP	FGM	FG%	FTM	FT%	Reb.	Ast.	TP	PPG
1948-49	63	272	—	267	.724	—	—	811	12.8
1949-50	64	348	.385	376	.774	—	259	1,072	16.8
1950-51	66	332	.357	457	.752	**1,080**	251	1,121	17.0
1951-52	63	263	.355	342	.807	773	182	868	13.8
1952-53	71	375	.367	512	.827	920	227	1,262	17.8
1953-54	72	370	.380	488	.827	870	214	1,228	17.1
1954-55	72	422	.383	489	.833	887	213	1,333	18.5
1955-56	72	465	.387	542	.858	891	200	1,472	20.4
1956-57	72	496	.379	625	.904	1,008	229	1,617	22.5
1957-58	72	581	.398	629	**.904**	1,022	224	1,791	24.9
1958-59	72	504	.387	526	.864	962	178	1,534	21.3
1959-60	75	578	.401	533	**.892**	959	256	1,689	22.5
1960-61	79	594	.372	680	.868	960	296	1,868	23.6
1961-62	56	268	.357	286	**.896**	439	120	822	14.7
1962-63	66	223	.388	181	.879	375	175	627	9.5
1963-64	24	44	.308	46	.807	110	48	134	5.6
Totals	1,059	6,135	.380	6,979	.844	11,256	3,072	19,249	18.2

Notes: Boldface indicates statistical leader. GP = games played; FGM = field goals made; FG% = field goal percentage; FTM = free throws made; FT% = free throw percentage; Reb. = rebounds; Ast. = assists; TP = total points; PPG = points per game

nament. Dolph received the Haggerty Award for the best New York City collegiate player. He graduated with a degree in aeronautical engineering.

When Dolph finished college, professional basketball was not the popular sport it became in the 1950's and 1960's. In 1948, two leagues existed, the National Basketball League (NBL), organized in 1937, and the Basketball Association of America (BAA), founded in 1946. The New York Knickerbockers of the BAA and the Syracuse (New York) Nationals of the NBL both offered Dolph a contract. He signed to play for the Nationals, or Nats, as they were popularly known. Dolph was only twenty years old.

The Emerging Champion

In the fall of 1948, Dolph moved to Syracuse to begin his long career with the Nats. He was chosen Rookie of the Year for the 1948-1949 season. By the fall of 1949, the BAA and the NBL merged and founded the National Basketball Association (NBA).

During the 1950's, Dolph emerged as an NBA star. For twelve consecutive years, he was selected for the first or second NBA All-Star team. He was the league's leading rebounder in 1951 and the leader in foul-shooting accuracy in 1958, 1960, and 1962. The Nats played well together, qualifying for the league playoffs most years

and winning the 1954-1955 NBA championship.

As in high school and college, Dolph proved to be a multitalented player who improved as the years passed. He played the forward position for the Nats and showed he could make goals from close to the basket or from far away. Sportswriters often commented on his ability to shoot a high arcing set shot. He was a fine rebounder and an excellent foul shooter.

Dolph worked hard to improve his skills. He studied other players to see what made them successful and copied their techniques. To improve his foul-shooting accuracy, he practiced with a fourteen-inch-diameter hoop, which he fitted inside the regulation eighteen-inch-diameter one. When he broke his right wrist in 1952, he learned to shoot left-handed. When he broke his left wrist in 1954, he worked to improve his one-handed shots and participated in the playoffs wearing a cast. Dolph came back to play after fracturing his cheekbone in 1961 and after suffering a knee injury in 1962.

Continuing the Story

At the end of the 1962-1963 NBA season, the Syracuse Nationals were sold to a group of Philadelphia businessmen. The team was renamed the Philadelphia 76ers. Dolph went to Philadelphia and became the player-coach of the team.

After the 1963-1964 season, Dolph retired as a player. He coached the 76ers during the 1964-1965 and 1965-1966 seasons. He was named NBA Coach of the Year for 1965-1966. Following the season, however, the 76ers' owners decided to hire a new coach. Dolph then became Supervisor of Officials for the NBA.

In 1970, a new coaching opportunity arose. The NBA added teams and Dolph became the coach of the new Buffalo (New York) Braves. He served as coach during the 1970-1971 season and for one game of the 1971-1972 season. Braves owners, disappointed by the team's performance the previous year and a loss on opening night, replaced Dolph with another coach. This ended his long association with professional basketball.

Dolph returned to Syracuse. While playing for the Nats, he had started a real estate development and management business. He now built this into a very successful firm.

Dolph married Naomi Gross in 1951. They are the parents of four children, Debra, Carrie, David, and Daniel. Dan, the youngest, followed in his father's footsteps. After playing college basketball at Syracuse University, he went on to become a professional basketball player in the NBA.

Summary

Dolph Schayes became an outstanding player because he loved the sport and worked hard to develop his skills. He was dedicated to learning all he could about the sport and applying it when he played.

Away from the basketball court, he applied the same kind of effort to whatever he did. As a result, Dolph became a respected businessman and community member as well as a professional basketball player.

Ann M. Scanlon

Additional Sources:

D'Alessandro, Dave. "Players for All Seasons." *The Sporting News* 214, no. 14 (April 6, 1992): 20-23.

Groliers Educational Corporation. *Pro Sports Halls of Fame.* 8 vols. Danbury, Conn.: Groliers Educational Corporation, 1996.

Hickok, Ralph. *A Who's Who of Sports Champions.* Boston: Houghton Mifflin, 1995.

LaBlanc, Michael L., and Mary K. Ruby, eds. *Professional Sports Team Histories: Basketball.* Detroit: Gale, 1994.

HONORS AND AWARDS

1948	Haggerty Award
1949	National Basketball League (NBL) Rookie of the Year
1950-61	All-NBA Team
1951-62	NBA All-Star Team
1966	NBA Coach of the Year
1970	NBA 25th Anniversary All-Time Team
1972	Inducted into Naismith Memorial Basketball Hall of Fame
1977	Inducted into International Jewish Hall of Fame
1987	Inducted into Syracuse Sports Hall of Fame
1988	Inducted into New York University Hall of Fame
1990	Inducted into New York City Basketball Hall of Fame

VITALY SCHERBO

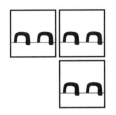

Sport: Gymnastics

Born: January 13, 1972
Minsk, Byelorussia, U.S.S.R. (now
Belarus)

Early Life

Vitaly Vitediktovich Scherbo was born to former acrobats in Minsk, Belarus (then part of the Soviet Union), on January 13, 1972. His mother brought him to the gym for the first time at the age of seven, where he impressed coach Leonid Vydritsky by doing fifteen pull-ups at his first practice.

Vitaly Scherbo performs on the rings at the 1992 Olympics. He won in this and four other events at the Games.

Vitaly's early training followed proven Soviet methods, focusing on strength, flexibility, dance (for body alignment and rhythm), and basic skills, and his considerable talent bloomed. He won his first competition and later made the Soviet junior national team. The promising gymnast developed under the guidance of his coach, Sergei Shinkar, and other expert teachers for three years.

The Road to Excellence

Vitaly's success as a junior won him a spot on the senior national team in 1988, though the outside world had yet to hear of him. By 1989, the Soviet national coaches thought enough of Vitaly to take him along to the World Championships in Stuttgart, Germany, as a reserve. Though the seventeen-year-old did not compete, he and his fellow alternate impressed the experts during training. Here was the new generation.

Vitaly made his international debut at Japan's well-regarded Chunichi Cup competition in November of 1989. He finished fourth but won the vault with his unique version of the Yurchenko, a vault normally done by women. The vault, more dangerous and more difficult for men, had just been allowed, and few dared to exploit it. Vitaly blithely added an extra twist—and even did his double twist better than anyone else's single twist.

At the European Championships the following spring, Vitaly was again the talk of the meet. He executed state-of-the-art skills with amazing sureness. In addition to his spectacular vault, Vitaly set a new trend on rings, crossing and uncrossing the cables in the course of his routine. He took home three European titles (for floor exercise, vault, and high bar) and established a formidable reputation in the gymnastics world. Still, he had yet to win a major all-around title.

2463

The Emerging Champion

Seattle's 1990 Goodwill Games belonged to Vitaly. He competed like a veteran, winning the all-around, vault, and high bar. Moreover, the young athlete could relate to the crowd. When his flawless vault received a 10.0, Vitaly had the nerve to hop up on the podium for an extra bow—a radical departure from the stoicism Westerners expected from Soviet athletes.

While his 5-foot 6-inch, 136-pound frame was considered large for a gymnast, Vitaly felt his size worked to his advantage, giving him better balance for landings. Indeed, he was a master of the "stick," gymnasts' term for a perfect landing. Otherwise, his physical attributes were nearly perfect for the sport. He was strong, quick, graceful (thanks to that early ballet training), and confident.

As phenomenal as Vitaly's assets were, he was not invincible. He suffered narrow losses to teammates Valery Belenky at the 1990 World Cup and Grigori Misiutin (ironically, the other alternate in Stuttgart) at the 1991 World Championships. Moreover, though Vitaly began the Olympic year of 1992 with his first world titles (for pommel horse and rings) at the first Individual-Event Worlds in Paris, he experienced yet another setback at the European Championships, where a fall from the high bar left him third—and determined.

Despite the domestic turmoil caused by the dissolution of the Soviet Union, the former Soviet team, together one last time for the Olympics as the Unified Team, arrived in Barcelona for the Summer Olympics well prepared. In training, Vitaly looked invincible, and in competition he proved it, leading his team to its final gold medal.

MAJOR CHAMPIONSHIPS					
Year	Competition	Event	Place	Event	Place
1989	Chunichi Cup	All-Around	4th	Vault	1st
1990	European Championships	All-Around	5th	Floor exercise	1st
		High bar	1st	Vault	1st
	Goodwill Games	All-Around	1st	Floor exercise	2d
		High bar	1st	Parallel bars	6th
		Team	1st	Vault	1st
	World Cup	All-Around	2d	Floor exercise	1st
		Vault	1st	Rings	3d
		Parallel bars	4th	Pommel horse	7th
		Horizontal bar	5th		
1991	World Championships	All-Around	2d	Floor exercise	2d
		High bar	3d	Parallel bars	8th
		Team	1st	Vault	2d
1992	Olympic Games	All-Around	Gold	Floor exercise	6th
		Parallel bars	Gold	Pommel horse	Gold
		Rings	Gold	Team	Gold
		Vault	Gold		
	World Championships	Floor exercise	2nd	Pommel horse	1st
		Rings	1st		
	European Championships	All-Around	3d	Pommel horse	1st
		Vault	1st	Floor exercise	2d
1992	European Championships	Rings	2d	Parallel bars	2d
1993	World Championships	All-Around	1st	Floor exercise	2d
		High bar	4th	Parallel bars	1st
		Pommel horse	8th	Vault	1st
	Chunichi Cup	All-Around	3d	Vault	1st
		Floor exercise	2d	Parallel bars	2d
		Pommel horse	3d		
	World University Games	All-Around	1st	Vault	1st
		Horizontal bar	3d	Parallel bars	2d
1994	European Championships	Horizontal bar	2d	Vault	1st
	World Championships	All-Around	3d	Floor exercise	1st
		Horizontal bar	1st	Vault	1st
		Pommel horse	6th	Team	4th
1995	World University Games	All-Around	3d		
	World Championships	All-Around	2d	Floor exercise	1st
		Parallel bars	1st	Vault	3d
		Horizontal bar	5th		
1996	European Championships	All-Around	2d	Floor exercise	1st
		Parallel bars	1st	Vault	1st
		Horizontal bar	3d		
	Olympic Games	All-Around	Bronze	Team	4th
		Parallel bars	Bronze	Vault	Bronze
1996	Olympic Games	Horizontal bar	Bronze	Floor exercise	7th
	World Championships	Floor exercise	1st	Parallel bars	2d
		Horizontal bar	3d	Vault	4th

Although the scores were close during the all-around competition, Vitaly performed at the peak of his powers and triumphed. The Olympic all-around gold medal was his at last. He continued his gold rush through the finals, where he won four of the five events for which he had qualified: pommel horse, rings, vault, and parallel bars.

Continuing the Story

"At the very least, I want to win the Olympic Games," Vitaly had stated in 1990. He was true to his word, winning six of a possible eight gold medals. As the most-decorated athlete of the 1992 Olympic Games, he brought men's gymnastics to world attention, lending credence to the claim that the Olympic all-around champion in gymnastics is truly the world's greatest athlete.

Life turned upside down for former Soviet athletes after the Games. Capitalism and crime rose in Belarus. Vitaly himself was robbed twice, once by a former teammate. With his medals safely ensconced at his mother's house, he left for tours in the United States to earn that new marvel, hard Western currency. Yet he was unable to use his new wealth back home; there was nothing to buy. Vitaly spent most of 1993 in the United States, living and training at Pennsylvania State University. He married Irina Tchernilevskaya, and his baby daughter, Kristina, was born in late February.

The demands of domestic life and earning a living took a toll on Vitaly's gymnastics, but though he was not in top form, he won the World Championships in April and the World University Games in July, 1993, between the two meets adding five more gold medals, two silver, and one bronze to his already impressive collection.

Although Vitaly would not win another world all-around title, he continued to compete at the top levels for another three years. His routines were always impressive, his tricks difficult, his attitude vibrant and flamboyant, and his showmanship unmatched. At the 1994 World Championships, he was third in the all-around competition but took first in floor exercise, vault, and high bar. The following year, he moved up to second in the all-around, with first-place finishes in the floor exercise and parallel bars and a third in vault.

Vitaly's last full year of competition was 1996. At the age of twenty-four, he represented Belarus at the Atlanta Olympic games, and he was again a crowd favorite. He took home a bronze medal in the all-around, made four of the six event finals, and medaled in three of them. He earned his last world gold medal in the floor exercise of the 1996 World Championships. Vitaly ended his career with a staggering thirty-three world and Olympic medals, eighteen of which were gold.

Vitaly is a true gymnastics legend. He was the last great Soviet gymnast from a dynasty of perfectly trained, disciplined, world-dominating gymnasts. He was a leader into the new world of crowd-pleasing performances, with an eye toward a professional future. After retiring, Vitaly enjoyed touring with exhibitions. He made his home in Las Vegas, Nevada, with his wife and daughter. There, he started his own gymnastics school, the Vitali Scherbo School of Gymnastics.

Summary

The Soviet gymnastics dynasty began after World War II and endured for more than forty years, challenged but rarely defeated. Vitaly Scherbo was the last and best of a long line of champions, and he became one of the first athletes to exploit the new world of professionalism in Olympic sports. Along the way, he raised both the level and profile of gymnastics.

Nancy Raymond

Additional Sources:

Bhattacharji, Alex, and Bob Der. "Vitaly Is Scherbo-Charged!" *Sports Illustrated for Kids*, July, 1996, 52.

Eskenazi, Gerald. "On Scherbo's Night, Dimas Also Sparkles." *The New York Times*, August 8, 1992, p. C1.

Frey, Jennifer. "For Scherbo, a Change of Perspective: After '92 Gold Rush, Wife's Near-Fatal Accident Almost Derailed Return." *The Washington Post*, July 23, 1996.

Richards, Gabby. "For Olympic Star Scherbo, the Games Go On and On." *The Washington Post*, July 10, 1993, p. C1.

Scherbo, Vitaly. "Ready for the Defense." Interview by Dwight Normile. *International Gymnast*, October, 1995, 24.

"Scherbo Will Retire in August." *The Washington Post*, April 21, 1996.

HONORS AND AWARDS

1990	Master of Sport of International Class
1992	Trans World Sport Award: Best Athlete in the World
1993	France Telecom Award Jesse Owens International Trophy

MAX SCHMELING

Sport: Boxing

Born: September 28, 1905
Klein Luckow, Uckermark, Germany

Early Life

Maximilian Adolph Otto Siegfried Schmeling was born September 28, 1905, in Klein Luckow, Uckermark, Germany, about seventy miles north-west of Berlin. His father was a pilot with a major steamship line and, soon after Max was born, moved his family to Hamburg, Germany's largest port city, so he could visit them more easily when he came home. Max Schmeling was nine when war broke out in 1914. His father lost his job; the family suffered greatly, often coming close to starving because of the blockade of the city. Thirteen years old when the war ended in 1918, Max had to find work because there was no money to continue his education.

As far back as he could remember, Max Schmeling had wanted to be a boxer. At the time he was born, boxing was prohibited in Germany, but Max's father often talked about it and told his son that the English were the pioneers in the sport, having invented the rules. Therefore, in 1922, Max decided to leave Hamburg. With no money and trusting to luck, he managed to get to Düsseldorf in the German Rhineland, then under English occupation.

The Road to Excellence

According to Max, luck and hard work enabled him to become a champion. With no training in boxing but with a strong body, a good mind, and great enthusiasm, Max persuaded a merchant who was also a boxing enthusiast to give him a room and money to train. From 1924 on, Max devoted his life to boxing. Jack Dempsey, the American champion, whom Max resembled, be-

came his model. He managed to see several films of Dempsey and carefully studied his techniques. Dempsey visited Germany in 1924, and Max managed to spar with him, an experience he never forgot.

His promoter went bankrupt in 1926, and Max lost all his savings. By chance or luck, he met Max Machon, a boxing manager from Berlin, who told Max that only in the capital could he

Courtesy of Amateur Athletic Foundation of Los Angeles

RECOGNIZED WORLD HEAVYWEIGHT CHAMPIONSHIPS

Date	Location	Opponent	Result
June 12, 1930	New York City, N.Y.	Jack Sharkey	4th-round win by foul
July 3, 1931	Cleveland, Ohio	Young Stribling	15th-round technical knockout
June 21, 1932	Long Island City, N.Y.	Max Schmeling (Jack Sharkey, winner)	15th-round split decision
June 22, 1938	New York City, N.Y.	Max Schmeling (Joe Louis, winner)	1st-round knockout

make a name for himself in boxing. When he arrived in Berlin, Max did not even have enough money for car fare. Luck came his way again when he met Arthur von Bülow, the editor of the magazine *Boxsport,* who agreed to pay for the young man's continued training.

The Emerging Champion

Machon joined Max in Berlin, and together, Machon and von Bülow changed Max's life. After training up to fourteen hours a day, Max knocked out Max Diechmann on August 24, 1926, to become Germany's light heavyweight champion. Max became the German heavyweight champion in 1928.

Because he now had enough money, Max invited his widowed mother to live with him. He also worked on improving his mind. Berlin was the cultural capital of Europe at the time, and Max managed to meet leading writers and artists who liked the attractive young boxer. Although Max learned from them, his boxing career always came first. He was in bed by ten o'clock every night; he never touched alcohol, tobacco, or other drugs.

Although now well-known in Europe, Max knew that he would have to go to the United States to make money. He had studied American boxing techniques and knew them to be more brutal and dangerous than European methods, but was prepared to take the risk.

Max, together with von Bülow and Machon, arrived in New York in 1930, but he could find no one to arrange the kind of match he wanted until he met Joe Jacobs, a fast-talking, streetwise native New Yorker who agreed to become his American manager. Jacobs arranged a match with Jack Sharkey, the American champion. Before any match, Max always tried to learn as much as possible about his opponent. He knew Sharkey had bad nerves and would do rash things. Max won

the match on a disqualification to become the world champion, but it was a crown without real meaning. Max truly won the world championship when he knocked out Young Stribling in 1931 in Cleveland, Ohio.

Continuing the Story

In 1932, Max lost the heavyweight crown to Sharkey on points. Many, including Jacobs, disputed the decision, but Max good-naturedly accepted it.

Back in Germany in 1933, Max married the film actress Anny Ondra. Although nonpolitical, Max was disturbed by the Nazi takeover of power and the violent anti-Semitism. Unlike many of his artist friends, however, Max decided to stay in Germany.

Max returned to America in 1936 and reached the high point of his boxing career. On June 19, he defeated Joe Louis, who was to become world heavyweight champion the following year and is considered perhaps the greatest boxer at his weight in ring history. As with Sharkey, Max said

STATISTICS

Bouts, 70
Knockouts, 38
Bouts won by decision, 15
Bouts won by fouls, 3
Knockouts by opponents, 5
Bouts lost by decision, 5
Draws, 4

HONORS AND AWARDS

| 1930 | *Ring* magazine Merit Award |
| 1970 | Inducted into *Ring* magazine Boxing Hall of Fame |

MILESTONES

Awarded the Golden Ribbon of the German Sports Press Society
Named an honorary citizen of Los Angeles

2467

his victory was the result of his having studied Louis's boxing techniques.

Max was embarrassed when the Nazis attempted to turn his victory into proof of black inferiority. The return bout, held before seventy thousand spectators in Yankee Stadium in New York, on June 22, 1938, was billed as the greatest event in boxing history. Grossing more than a million dollars, a huge sum during the Depression in America, it was both racially and politically motivated. The Nazis were so hated that Max had to be escorted to the ring under guard.

Determined to defend both America and his race, Louis attacked Max with unrelenting fury, knocking him out within two minutes and 4 seconds of the first round.

Max was seriously injured from the bout and was never again the same fighter, although he won the European heavyweight boxing championship in 1939.

Max was drafted into the German army and served as a parachutist. After Germany's defeat in 1945, he found himself penniless when his home and property were confiscated. Although more than forty years old, he attempted a boxing comeback, without success, but managed to set himself up in business. Outgoing and friendly, the former heavyweight champion would remain a popular and respected figure with both Germans and Americans.

Summary

Max Schmeling's long and distinguished career in boxing was proof that intelligence and a sense of fair play are as essential as a strong body to becoming a success. Max helped to raise boxing from a brutal, often illegal pastime to a respected sport. Some boxing experts rank Max Schmeling among the top ten heavyweight fighters in modern ring history.

Nis Petersen

Additional Sources:

Cox, James A. "The Day Joe Louis Fired Shots Heard 'Round the World." *Smithsonian* 19, no. 8 (November, 1988): 170-187.

Mee, Bob. *Boxing: Heroes and Champions.* Edison, N.J.: Chartwell Books, 1997.

Schmeling, Max, and George B. von der Lippe. *Max Schmeling: An Autobiography.* Chicago: Bonus Books, 1998.

Weisbord, Robert, and Norbert Hedderich "Max Schmeling: Righteous Ring Warrior?" *History Today* 43 (January, 1993): 36-41.

JOE SCHMIDT

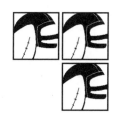

Sport: Football

Born: January 18, 1932
　　　　Mount Oliver, Pennsylvania

Early Life

Joseph Paul Schmidt, the youngest son of a bricklayer, was born on January 18, 1932, in Mount Oliver, a suburb of Pittsburgh, Pennsylvania. One of the Schmidt brothers died in a fall from a tree before Joe was born, and another brother was killed by a sniper's bullet in France during World War II. His brother John played football at Carnegie Tech University (later called Carnegie-Mellon) before the war and played for the Pittsburgh Steelers in 1940.

When Joe was fourteen years old, he played tackle on sandlot football teams with older boys and even grown men. At Brentwood High School, he starred at fullback. Many colleges across the nation tried to recruit him upon his graduation in 1949, but Joe decided to stay close to home and entered the University of Pittsburgh.

The Road to Excellence

Pittsburgh had been a power in college football during the 1930's, but by the time Joe arrived, the program was not going well. In Joe's four years, the Panthers had four head coaches. Despite the changes and a nagging series of injuries, Joe excelled as a defensive linebacker. In his senior year, 1952, he was elected captain.

The high point of his college career came that year, when he returned an intercepted pass 60 yards to help upset the University of Notre Dame, 22-19, at South Bend, Indiana. The International News Service (INS) named him to its 1952 All-America team, and he was selected to play in the postseason North-South and Senior Bowl All-Star games.

The injuries that had so often kept Joe on the sideline at Pittsburgh also made professional teams leery of him. They feared he was too injury-prone to succeed in the National Football League (NFL). A Detroit Lions scout watched Joe play in the Senior Bowl and recommended him to Lions coach Raymond Parker. Detroit selected him in the seventh round of the 1953 draft.

The Lions were a close-knit team that had won the NFL championship the previous year. They did not take kindly to raw rookies who had not yet proven themselves in battle. Although Joe impressed Parker in training camp, he sat on the bench through the early season games. Then, at midseason, a veteran linebacker was injured and Joe got his chance to play. Once he got into the lineup, he played so well that there was no getting him out. He was a starting linebacker in the championship game when the Lions won their second straight NFL title. The next season, the Associated Press named him to its All-NFL team.

The Emerging Champion

After two straight NFL crowns, the Lions lost the 1954 championship Game and fell to last place in their division in 1955. Parker decided on a big change in his defense.

In college and in his first few years with the Lions, Joe played an outside linebacker, usually one of two with five linemen up front—a 5-2 defense. Several NFL teams were beginning to use a new defense, however, with four front linemen and three linebackers. The 4-3 required an unusually versatile middle linebacker. He had to be strong enough to move into the line and stop running plays up the middle, quick and agile enough to evade 250-pound blockers and run down plays to the outside, and fast enough to drop back and help cover pass receivers. Above all, as the key man in the defense, he had to be a master at reading plays so he would not be caught out of position and allow a long gain. Parker decided he had the perfect candidate in Joe.

From the moment Joe moved into the middle, he was regarded as the NFL's best middle linebacker. At 6 feet and 218 pounds, he was smaller than most who played the position, but his enthusiasm, superior quickness, sure tackling, and uncanny ability to anticipate where the next play would go made him a sensation. Many mistakenly believed he invented the middle linebacker position, but the truth was that he simply played it better than anyone ever had before.

With Joe setting new standards in the middle of the defense, Detroit challenged for the divi-

HONORS AND AWARDS	
1952	All-American
1953	Senior Bowl All-Star Team North-South All-Star Team
1954-62	Associated Press All-NFL Team
1955-63	NFL Pro Bowl Team
1956-59, 1961-62	United Press International All-NFL Team
1960	Associated Press NFL Co-Player of the Year
1963	NFL All-Pro Team of the 1950's
1973	Inducted into Pro Football Hall of Fame Uniform number 56 retired by Detroit Lions
2000	Inducted into College Football Hall of Fame

sion title in 1956. In 1957, the year he was named team captain, Detroit won another NFL championship.

Continuing the Story

After their 1957 championship, the Lions went through several seasons in which they came close to winning another title but fell just short. No one could blame the sure-tackling Joe. In four different seasons, his teammates voted him the team's most valuable player. Joe was named All-NFL nine straight seasons and played in nine straight Pro Bowls.

Although he was known for spectacular, teeth-rattling tackles, Joe was at the same time a steady player who gave the game his all on every play. Because he was responsible for calling out defensive signals, he spent hours reviewing opponents' game films. His meticulous study made him a wizard at knowing just when to call for a blitz of the passer. When opponents chose to run, as one player said, "He was always in the way."

Joe retired after the 1965 season but stayed with the Lions as an assistant coach. In 1967, he was named head coach. The following year, he appeared as himself in the film *Paper Lion*, in which Alan Alda starred as a journalist pretending to be a rookie quarterback in the Lions' training camp.

Over six years, he produced a winning record, 43-34-7, but the Detroit media were not satisfied. They wanted another championship and often criticized Joe harshly. After the 1972 season Joe resigned to enter business because he did not want to subject his family to further media abuse. Joe continued in business for some time and retired in the late 1990's.

In 1973 Joe was inducted into the Pro Football Hall of Fame. In 2000 Joe was inducted into the College Football Hall of Fame. At the September 16, 2000, Pitt-Penn State game at Three Rivers Stadium in Pittsburgh, Joe's alma mater, the University of Pittsburgh, honored him.

Summary

During his thirteen-year NFL career, Joe Schmidt changed the way pro football was played. He developed the role of middle linebacker into the dominant defensive position. His leadership, strength, quickness, and ability to read opponents' offenses set the standard for later outstanding middle guards like Sam Huff, Ray Nitschke, and Jack Lambert. In 1973, he was named to the Pro Football Hall of Fame.

Bob Carroll

Additional Sources:

Anderson, Dave. *Great Defensive Players of the NFL.* New York: Random House, 1967.

Attner, Paul. "NFL: Football's One Hundred Greatest Players—Better than All The Rest." *The Sporting News* 223 (November 8, 1999): 58-59, 62.

Barber, Phil. "NFL: Football's One Hundred Greatest Players—The Hit Men." *The Sporting News* 223 (November 1, 1999): 12-16.

Pro Football Hall of Fame. http://www.profootballhof.com.

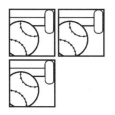

MIKE SCHMIDT

Sport: Baseball

Born: September 27, 1949
Dayton, Ohio

Early Life

Michael Jack Schmidt was born to Jack and Lois Schmidt on September 27, 1949, in Dayton, Ohio. While growing up in Dayton, he attended public schools and participated in youth league baseball, football, and basketball. Like many children, he often dreamed of becoming a professional athlete.

Mike attended Fairview High School in Dayton, where he continued to play baseball, basketball, and football. He was a good athlete in high school but did not display the kind of talent that one would associate with future greatness. He was not even considered the best player on his high school baseball team and, at the time of his high school graduation, did not receive a college athletic scholarship.

The Road to Excellence

In 1967, Mike enrolled at Ohio University to begin a major in business administration. He became a member of the university's baseball team and focused on developing his baseball skills and fundamentals. He soon began to blossom into a good baseball prospect. He became Ohio University's starting shortstop his sophomore year and helped to lead his team to conference championships in 1969, 1970, and 1971, and to the 1970 College World Series. Twice he won college All-American honors.

In the 1971 major league free agent draft, Mike was drafted in the second round by the Philadelphia Phillies. The Phillies felt he lacked the range to play shortstop and would be better suited to play third base. Shortly thereafter, he was signed to a professional contract and was assigned to a Philadelphia minor league farm club in Reading, Pennsylvania, where he hit only .211.

In 1972, he was assigned to Philadelphia's top farm club in Eugene, Oregon. There he hit 29 home runs and displayed the raw power that the Phillies had hoped would develop.

In 1973, Mike was placed on the Philadelphia roster and his dream of playing in the

Mike Schmidt rounds the bases in a 1981 game.

AP/Wide World Photos

STATISTICS

Season	GP	AB	Hits	2B	3B	HR	Runs	RBI	BA	SA
1972	13	34	7	0	0	1	2	3	.206	.294
1973	132	367	72	11	0	18	43	52	.196	.373
1974	162	568	160	28	7	**36**	108	116	.282	**.546**
1975	158	562	140	34	3	**38**	93	95	.249	.523
1976	160	584	153	31	4	**38**	112	107	.262	.524
1977	154	544	149	27	11	38	114	101	.274	.574
1978	145	513	129	27	2	21	93	78	.251	.435
1979	160	541	137	25	4	45	109	114	.253	.564
1980	150	548	157	25	8	**48**	104	**121**	.286	**.624**
1981	102	354	112	19	2	31	**78**	**91**	.316	**.644**
1982	148	514	144	26	3	35	108	87	.280	**.547**
1983	154	534	136	16	4	**40**	104	109	.255	.524
1984	151	528	146	23	3	**36**	93	**106**	.277	.536
1985	158	549	152	31	5	33	89	93	.277	.532
1986	160	552	160	29	1	**37**	97	**119**	.290	.547
1987	147	522	153	28	0	35	88	113	.293	.548
1988	108	390	97	21	2	12	52	62	.249	.405
1989	42	148	30	7	0	6	19	28	.203	.372
Totals	2,404	8,352	2,234	408	59	548	1,506	1,595	.267	.527

Notes: Boldface indicates statistical leader. GP = games played; AB = at bats; 2B = doubles; 3B = triples; HR = home runs; RBI = runs batted in; BA = batting average; SA = slugging average

major leagues was realized. This dream quickly vanished into a nightmare as Mike had a disastrous season, hitting only .196. After the season, Philadelphia manager Danny Ozark remarked, "I'd trade Schmidt for a load of pumpkins."

Luckily for Philadelphia, they did not give up on Mike, nor did he give up on himself. Mike played winter ball in Puerto Rico, determined as ever to work hard and improve his baseball skills.

The Emerging Champion

Mike's hard work and determination paid off the very next season. In 1974, he led baseball's National League with 36 home runs and had a .282 batting average. He was on his way to establishing himself as a great all-around third baseman.

While playing at the Astrodome in Houston, Texas, Mike crushed a fastball that traveled 329 feet from the plate and 117 feet into the air to hit a speaker hanging from the Astrodome's roof. The ball fell to the playing field and was ruled a single. Undoubtedly, this is one of the longest singles in the history of the game.

In 1975 and 1976, Mike continued his home-run production, hitting 38 home runs in each of those years. In a game against the Chicago Cubs on July 17, 1976, Philadelphia rallied from 11 runs down to beat Chicago in a 10-inning game by the score of 18 to 16. While the comeback itself was amazing, it was Mike's 4 home runs in the game that dominated the sports section of many newspapers the following day.

Mike suffered an off-year in 1978, hitting only 21 home runs for the Phillies. In 1979 and 1980, he returned to form, hitting 45 home runs in 1979 and a career high of 48 home runs in 1980.

Continuing the Story

Mike's home-run production continued into the 1980's, and he consistently earned the distinction of being the premier power hitter of the 1970's and 1980's. His career total of 548 home runs places him into the elite "500 club" and ranks him on the all-time home-run list ahead of such baseball greats as Mickey Mantle, Ted Williams, and Willie McCovey.

Although hitting is what Mike did best, he was a great defensive third baseman. Mike won a total of ten National League Gold Glove Awards for excellence in fielding. He also won the National League most valuable player (MVP) award in 1980, 1981, and 1986. Mike helped the Phillies to five National League Championships and two appearances in the World Series. In the 1980 World Series, he teamed with baseball greats Pete Rose,

2473

HONORS AND AWARDS

1974, 1976-77, 1979-84, 1986-87, 1989	National League All-Star Team
1976-84, 1986	National League Gold Glove Award
1980	World Series most valuable player
1980-81, 1986	National League most valuable player
1981	Seagram's Seven Crowns of Sports Award
1983	Voted the "Greatest Philadelphia Phillies Player Ever"
1995	Inducted into National Baseball Hall of Fame
1999	MLB All-Century Team Uniform number 20 retired by Philadelphia Phillies

Throughout his great career, Mike was popular with the fans, the media, and his teammates. In 1983, Philadelphia fans voted him the greatest Phillies player ever. After his retirement from baseball, Mike lived in Philadelphia with his wife, Donna, and two children, Jessica and Jonathan. He became a Philadelphia restaurant owner and a television broadcaster for baseball games.

Steve Carlton, and others to bring the Philadelphia Phillies and their fans the first World Championship in the history of the franchise. Mike was named the World Series most valuable player, a highlight in his career. During his career, he was named to twelve National League All-Star teams and elected a starter nine times.

In 1988, Mike suffered a serious shoulder injury that forced him to miss the final third of the season. He returned briefly to the playing field in 1989 but felt that his injury had not sufficiently healed to continue playing and decided to retire. Despite his retirement, baseball fans honored Mike's outstanding career by electing him to the starting line-up of the National League All-Star team. In 1995, his first year of eligibility, Mike was elected to the Hall of Fame with 444 out of 460 votes. He also received the highest number of votes among third basemen in his selection for major league baseball's All-Century team in 1999.

Summary

A fierce competitor and acknowledged leader, Mike Schmidt proved the importance of hard work and perseverance. Mike had one of the finest careers in the history of the game. He is recognized by teammates, opponents, and fans as a complete ballplayer.

At his retirement in May 29, 1989, Mike either held or shared fourteen major league records, twenty-four Philadelphia Phillies career records, and eleven Philadelphia Phillies season records.

Thomas R. Garrett

Additional Sources:

Kashatus, William C. *Mike Schmidt: Philadelphia's Hall of Fame Third Baseman.* Jefferson, N.C.: McFarland, 2000.

Schmidt, Mike, with Barbara Walder. *Always on the Offense.* New York: Atheneum, 1982.

Westcott, Rich. *Mike Schmidt.* New York: Chelsea House, 1995.

PETRA SCHNEIDER

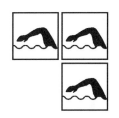

Sport: Swimming

Born: January 11, 1963
     East Berlin, East Germany

Early Life

Petra Schneider was born on January 11, 1963, in what was then East Berlin in the now defunct German Democratic Republic. When the Iron Curtain was down over Eastern Europe, it was almost impossible to find out what a young East German athlete's life was like. That country's young female swimmers, the world's best, dominated world records and Olympic swimming. One of these swimmers was Petra Schneider, who grew to 5 feet 5 inches and 119 pounds.

The Road to Excellence

Petra Schneider was queen of the four-stroke individual medley, and many consider that she was the best woman swimmer in the world by the measure of her winning performances between 1979 and 1984. She began as one of the East German wonder kids of the Karl Marx State Swim Club in East Berlin, and her first big meet was the World Championships held in Hitler's old 1936 Olympic pool in West Berlin. The pool was refurbished for this occasion, the first World Championship competition in Berlin in forty years since World War II. It was 1978, and Petra won a third-place bronze medal in the 400-meter individual medley and placed fifth in the 200-meter individual medley. Both events were won by the American Tracy Caulkins, who led the United States to a surprise victory over the East German girls.

The Emerging Champion

Petra Schneider would never lose an individual medley race in international competition to anybody other than Tracy Caulkins in her swimming career. Caulkins beat Petra in the 1981 United States International Meet, but Petra beat Tracy in most of the other international meets from 1979 on. Petra's middle- and long-distance freestyle performances were only slightly less sensational, and she frequently won in the longer breaststroke races.

In the record book and by popular acclaim, Petra was the greatest woman swimmer in the world before, during, and after the 1980 Moscow Olympics. Not only did she win the 400-meter individual medley,

STATISTICS

Year	Competition	Event	Place	Time
1978	World Championships	400-meter individual medley	3d	4:48.56
1980	Olympic Games	400-meter individual medley	Gold	4:36.29 WR, OR
		400-meter freestyle	Silver	—
1981	European Championships	200-meter individual medley	3d	2:12.64
		400-meter individual medley	1st	4:39.30
1982	World Championships	400-meter freestyle	2d	4:10.08
		800-meter freestyle		8:36.27
		200-meter individual medley	1st	2:11.79
		400-meter individual medley	1st	4:36.10 WR
1983	European Championships	400-meter individual medley	2d	4:40.34

Notes: OR = Olympic Record; WR = World Record

swimming's most all-around event, at the 1980 Olympics, but she repeated this feat at the 1982 World Championships and won the 200-meter individual medley also. In the 1980 Moscow Olympics, she also won a silver medal in the 400-meter freestyle event.

Petra was cheated out of beating the whole world in the pool because of politics. First, the United States swimmers were kept out of the Moscow Games as a protest to the Soviet invasion of Afghanistan; the Soviets reciprocated by boycotting the Los Angeles Olympics four years later. Thus, Petra Schneider and her United States rival Tracy Caulkins never faced each other in an Olympic Games.

After the Moscow Olympics, Petra dominated the first five United States Internationals, usually winning her specialty individual medley events. She held the world's best time in the 800-meter freestyle, 1,500-meter freestyle, and 200-meter individual medley in addition to her patented 400-meter individual medley.

Continuing the Story

Swimming World magazine elected Petra the 1980 and 1982 World Swimmer of the Year, and she was European Swimmer of the Year in 1979 and 1980. In 1980, Petra brought down the world record for the 400-meter individual medley to 4 minutes 39.96 seconds at Leningrad in March, to 4 minutes 38.44 seconds at Magdeburg, East Germany, in May,

and more than 2 seconds lower, to 4 minutes 36.29 seconds, at the Moscow Olympics in July. Two years later, at the World Championships in Ecuador, she reduced her 400-meter individual medley to 4 minutes 36.10 seconds.

Petra credited her coach, Eberhard Mothes, with keeping her interest in swimming at a high level. Mothes, Petra said, "never failed to come up with something interesting or challenging in the course of the work. I am the kind of person who likes being challenged and expected to achieve as much as I possibly can." When asked, at the United States Internationals in 1982, if she felt tired after coming so far to swim four great long-distance races, she quipped, "Why should I feel tired? Races are not something you should sleep in. You can sleep at home."

Summary

Petra Schneider was the most outstanding swimmer of the 1980 Moscow Olympics, which was boycotted by the Americans, and a many-time champion of the United States International Meets. She was inducted into the International Swimming Hall of Fame in Fort Lauderdale, Florida, in 1989.

Buck Dawson

Additional Sources:

Levinson, David, and Karen Christenson, eds. *Encyclopedia of World Sport: From Ancient Times to Present.* Santa Barbara, Calif.: ABC-CLIO, 1996.

Wallechinsky, David. *The Complete Book of the Olympics.* Boston: Little, Brown and Company, 1991.

RECORDS

Set 4 world records and 8 European records in the 200-meter and 400-meter individual medley

HONORS AND AWARDS

1979-80	European Swimmer of the Year
1980, 1982	*Swimming World* magazine World Swimmer of the Year
1989	Inducted into International Swimming Hall of Fame

DON SCHOLLANDER

Sport: Swimming

Born: April 30, 1946
      Jacksonville, Florida

Early Life

If ever there was a boy destined from birth to be a swimmer, it was Donald Arthur Schollander, born April 30, 1946, in Jacksonville, Florida. Don's mother, Martha Dent Perry Schollander, was the swimming stand-in for Maureen O'Sul-livan's Jane in the Tarzan movies opposite Johnny Weissmuller.

Don's uncle, Newt Perry, who taught Don to swim at his swim school in Silver Springs, Florida, was the underwater consultant for the water scenes in the Tarzan movies, which were shot at Silver Springs. Despite the fact that these events occurred before Don was born, Martha and Newt were influenced enough by Johnny Weissmuller to dream that Don would also be an Olympic champion some day.

The Road to Excellence

The Schollanders moved to Lake Oswego, Oregon, where Don started swimming seriously with the famous Multnomah Athletic Club of Portland. He was coached there by Phill Hansel, and then Walt Schlueter, who helped Don to develop the perfect freestyle stroke. Don became an almost instant success as an age-group swimmer, monopolizing the record book for the ten-and-under, eleven-and-twelve, and thirteen-and-fourteen age-group classes.

When he was ready for senior swimming, his mother determined that her son must go south to the Santa Clara Swim Club to swim with George Haines and the largest collection of national champions, both high school and Amateur Athletic Union (AAU) club swimmers. Don made the move and became in a short time the best freestyler at all distances from 100 yards to the mile. His competition was his own club teammate, Steve Clark, an amazing sprinter. Don had been trained to hold his stroke and keep his rhythm regardless of the distance; hence he won his 100-meter races in the final 10 meters,

Don Schollander in a 1963 swim meet.

AP/Wide World Photos

2477

never breaking stroke no matter how far behind in the early lengths of his race. He was allowed to break his stroke rhythm only when pushing off the wall for the final length, where he could all-out sprint home to the finish line.

The Emerging Champion

By age nineteen, Don was the toast of the sporting world. He was elected World Athlete of the Year after winning a record four gold medals at the 1964 Tokyo Olympics. Don received 138 first-place votes and 459 points to 14 firsts and 134 points for runner-up Johnny Unitas, the All-Pro quarterback of the National Football League. No swimmer had won the poll in its thirty-four-year history and no athlete in any sport had won it by such an overwhelming margin.

One of Don's reward trips after the Olympics included a trip to Sweden, where he was met by

an age-group swimming champion from that country by the name of Carl Gustav. Carl would soon become the King of Sweden, perhaps the highest rank ever attained by a swimmer.

Don was the first man in the world to break 2 minutes for the 200-meter freestyle, on July 7, 1963. Perhaps his most amazing performance, however, was as a Yale freshman, when he swam the 200-yard freestyle in 1 minute 41.7 seconds in the spring of 1965 at the AAU Indoor Championships. His time was .7 second faster than the world record set by Yale's 200-yard freestyle relay team in 1917. It is a dramatic illustration of the improvement in swimming times, training, and techniques in less than fifty years.

In preparing him for the 1964 Olympic trials and Games, Don's coach, George Haines, felt Don could win any freestyle event for which he trained. The middle distances were his forte, but Haines felt it would be difficult to prime Don for both the 100-meter sprint and 1,500-meter distance races at the same time, even though he had won and set records at both distances on several occasions. The coach picked the 100-meter event. Although Don was not a sprinter, he had an almost perfect stroke, and the 100-meter distance was long enough for this good stroking to pay off in a come-from-behind victory. Don's best distance at the time was the 400-meter race, and he also swam on two of the United States' gold-medal, world-record-breaking freestyle relays, something he might not have been able to do had he primed for the 1,500-meter event. No swimmer before Don had ever won four gold medals in one Olympics.

Continuing the Story

Don swam through his college days at Yale. He could not train as hard and long as he had during his high school years as a young phenomenon, but he continued his mastery of the middle-distance

MAJOR CHAMPIONSHIPS

Year	Competition	Event	Place	Time
1962	AAU Outdoor Championships	200-meter freestyle	1st	2:00.4
1963	Pan-American Games	400-meter freestyle	2d	4:23.3
	AAU Outdoor Championships	200-meter freestyle	1st	1:59.0
		400-meter freestyle	1st	4:17.7
	AAU Indoor Championships	200-yard freestyle	1st	1:44.4
1964	Olympic Games	100-meter freestyle	Gold	53.4 OR
		400-meter freestyle	Gold	4:12.2 WR, OR
		4×100-meter freestyle relay	Gold	3:33.2 WR, OR
		4×200-meter freestyle relay	Gold	7:52.1 WR, OR
	AAU Outdoor Championships	100-meter freestyle	1st	54.0
		200-meter freestyle	1st	1:57.6 WR
		400-meter freestyle	1st	4:12.7
	AAU Indoor Championships	200-yard freestyle	1st	1:42.6
		500-yard freestyle	1st	4:44.5
1965	AAU Indoor Championships	200-yard freestyle	1st	1:41.7 WR
1966	AAU Outdoor Championships	100-meter freestyle	1st	53.5
		200-meter freestyle	1st	1:56.2 WR
		400-meter freestyle	1st	4:11.6 WR
	AAU Indoor Championships	200-yard freestyle	1st	1:42.8
1967	Pan-American Games	200-meter freestyle	1st	1:56.01
		4×100-meter freestyle relay	1st	3:34.08
		4×200-meter freestyle relay	1st	8:00.46
	AAU Outdoor Championships	100-meter freestyle	1st	53.3
		200-meter freestyle	1st	1:55.7 WR
	AAU Indoor Championships	200-yard freestyle	1st	1:41.2
1968	NCAA Championships	200-yard freestyle	1st	1:42.04
		4×100-yard freestyle relay	1st	3:04.09
		4×200-yard freestyle relay	1st	6:50.77
	Olympic Games	200-meter freestyle	Silver	1:55.8

Note: OR = Olympic Record; WR = World Record

freestyle. He was undefeated in the 200-yard and 200-meter freestyle until finally beaten by Michael Wendon of Australia in his last race at the 1968 Mexico Olympics.

Don's life after swimming included writing a best-selling book, *Deep Water* (1971), and working as a Wall Street stockbroker, a television color commentator, and ultimately a Lake Oswego businessman in his Oregon hometown.

Summary

Don Schollander was the first great male swimmer coming out of what is now known throughout the world as age-group swimming. He was among the most celebrated athletes in the world before he entered college at Yale University. He went on to break many records at Yale and continued to set records up to the 1968 Olympics. He wrote a best-selling book, was a success on Wall Street, and ultimately settled into a relatively quiet life in his hometown. As Kim Chapman wrote, "He has turned into the rarest of swimming heroes—the champion who ages with grace and dignity and, despite the inevitable challenges, with considerable success." His adjustment from being a youthful celebrity to the much longer climb to success in business has been an example for all swimmers who have followed him.

Buck Dawson

RECORDS
First man in the world to break 2 minutes for the 200-meter freestyle (1963)
First swimmer to win four gold medals at an Olympic Games (1964)
Broke several U.S. and world freestyle records in the early 1960's

HONORS AND AWARDS	
1964	Sullivan Award
	Lawrence J. Johnson Award
	Associated Press Male Athlete of the Year
	U.S. Athlete of the Year
	World Athlete of the Year
1965	Inducted into International Swimming Hall of Fame
1983	Inducted into U.S. Olympic Hall of Fame

Additional Sources:

Devaney, John. *Great Olympic Champions.* New York: Putnam, 1967.

Edelson, Paula. *Superstars of Men's Swimming and Diving.* Philadelphia, Pa.: Chelsea House, 1999.

Hickok, Ralph. *A Who's Who of Sports Champions.* Boston: Houghton Mifflin, 1995.

Schapp, Dick. *An Illustrated History of the Olympics.* New York: Alfred A. Knopf, 1975.

Schollander, Don, and Duke Savage. *Deep Water.* New York: Crown, 1971.

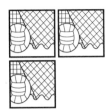

SCOTT SCHULTE

Sport: Water polo

Born: April 19, 1959
Orange, New Jersey

Early Life

Scott Schulte was born on April 19, 1959, in Orange, New Jersey. Like many outstanding swimmers, he began competitive swimming while in grade school and enjoyed considerable success with a fluid, powerful stroke that enabled him to be among the best in his age group in northern New Jersey.

While continuing to swim competitively, he also started playing water polo when he was in the eighth grade, beginning a career that has seen him become perhaps the finest non-Californian to play the sport in the United States.

The Road to Excellence

After being introduced to water polo, Scott continued to play in high school at Montclair Kimberley Academy in Montclair, New Jersey, and led his team to one Eastern Interscholastic championship and to two second-place finishes in the Eastern championship tournament. He was named to the All-East team following all four of his high school years and, as a senior, was the most valuable player in the Eastern championships and was on the Junior All-American First Team.

Scott was also an outstanding swimmer, and the combination of his swimming and water polo talents attracted the attention of many college coaches who wanted him to attend their schools. If his only interest in attending college had been in playing water polo, he might have gone to California, whose schools dominate the national collegiate championships every year and where the sport has achieved its greatest popularity in the United States.

He was interested, however, in academics as well as swimming and water polo, and he selected Bucknell University, a relatively small, private university (with thirty-two hundred students) located in Lewisburg in central Pennsylvania. Bucknell, under Coach Dick Russell, had just moved its water polo program from a "club" to a "var-

STATISTICS

Season	GP	Ast.	Pts.
1977	154	62	216
1978	127	50	177
1979	121	56	177
1980	184	88	272
Totals	586	256	842

Notes: G = goals; Ast. = assists; TP = total points

sity" sport, and Scott Schulte knew that he would be playing on the school's first varsity team in the sport.

What he might not have known, and what certainly most water polo fans in the East did not know, was that he would so dominate the sport during his four years at Bucknell that the school would gain immediate national attention.

The Emerging Champion

It did not take Scott long to demonstrate his talents, and his play and leadership helped to make Bucknell the dominant water polo team in the East during his four years at the school. In his freshman year, he scored 154 goals and assisted on 62 others, leading Bucknell to a 28-5 record, a victory at the Eastern championship, and its first appearance ever in the National Collegiate Athletic Association (NCAA) tournament. The Bisons finished seventh in the national competition, but Scott was the leading scorer with 14 goals.

That was the beginning of a spectacular career. He also led the Bisons in scoring in each of his next three years on campus and finished his career with 586 goals and 256 assists. Bucknell had a combined 114-15-3 record in his four years. The goal total set a national collegiate record for the blond, muscular young man who, at 6 feet 1 inch, is somewhat shorter than most of the big scorers at the California schools.

Scott also led Bucknell to three more Eastern champion-

ships and three more appearances in the NCAA Championship Tournament. He was named to the All-East First Team for four straight years, was named to the NCAA All-American squad and the Amateur Athletic Union All-American team as a junior and senior, and was the leading scorer in the NCAA Tournament in 1978, 1979, and 1980, as he had been as a freshman in 1977. In November of his senior season, he received special national recognition by appearing in the "Faces in the Crowd" section of *Sports Illustrated* magazine.

His unique position in college water polo is demonstrated by the fact that the 50 goals he scored in four NCAA Tournaments is the all-time career record, and by the fact that he was the only non-Californian among the thirty-one members of the All-American squad in 1980. He was also the only non-Californian among the twenty-five members of the National Training squad that year.

It is unlikely that Scott's water polo scoring records will soon be broken at Bucknell, and he certainly will not be forgotten. He was the Outstanding Athlete in his senior class and was elected to the school's Athletic Hall of Fame in 1986, five years after he graduated with a bachelor of science degree in business administration. His teammates also honored him by establishing the Scott Schulte Award, which is given each year

NCAA RECORDS

Most goals in NCAA Championship Tournament competition, 50

HONORS AND AWARDS

1973-76	Scholastic All-East Team
1977-80	Eastern Championship Team
1977-80	Collegiate All-East Team
1979-80	NCAA All-American
1979-85	AAU All-American
1980-84	U.S. National Team
1981	Christy Mathewson Award (outstanding Bucknell University senior athlete)
1981, 1984	Indoor Nationals most valuable player
1986	Inducted into Bucknell University Athletic Hall of Fame
1990	U.S. Olympic Festival silver medalist (total of five silver and four bronze medals won in Olympic Festival competition)

to "the individual who contributes the most to Bucknell water polo."

Continuing the Story

Most college athletes in sports that are not played on the professional level stop competing on a national level when they leave college, but Scott continued to play water polo with the best players in the country. He competed for the New York Athletic Club in the indoor and outdoor national championships and for the East team at the Olympic Festival.

From 1980 through 1984, he was a member of the U.S. national team, and from graduation through 1990, he played in nine Olympic Festivals. In 1990, nearly two decades after he took up the sport, Scott tied for the scoring lead at the festival as his team won the silver medal. In all, he played on teams that placed second five times and third four times at the festival. He was the most valuable player at the Indoor Nationals in 1981 and 1984. Scott remained active in the New York Athletic Club as coach of the senior men's water polo team.

Summary

Married in September, 1984, to his Bucknell sweetheart, the former Dana Smith, Scott Schulte combined success in business with athletic success. A resident of Wyckoff, New Jersey, he would become an investment broker and first vice president of Prudential-Bache Securities. He also continued to demonstrate why some observers called him "the greatest player in Eastern collegiate history." Speaking of the sport that he has done a great deal to popularize in the East, he has said, "Water polo continues to add many highlights and travel to my life."

Brad Tufts

Additional Sources:

Levinson, David, and Karen Christenson, eds. *Encyclopedia of World Sport: From Ancient Times to Present.* Santa Barbara, Calif.: ABC-CLIO, 1996.

Mallon, Bill, and Ian Buchanan. *Quest for Gold: The Encyclopedia of American Olympians.* New York: Leisure Press, 1984.

Wallechinsky, David. *The Complete Book of the Olympics.* Boston: Houghton Mifflin, 1991.

MICHAEL SCHUMACHER

Sport: Auto racing

Born: January 3, 1969
Hürth-Hermülheim, Germany

Early Life

Michael Schumacher was born to a middle-class family in Hürth-Hermülheim, Germany, on January 3, 1969. His father, Rolf, started Michael on his career path without realizing it, when he added a motor to his son's pedal car. After Mi-

Michael Schumacher celebrates after winning the Formula One Pacific Grand Prix in 1994.

chael crashed into a light pole, his father decided he should drive on a track, so Michael became a member of the local go-kart club at the age of four.

At first he go-karted just for fun, but as young Michael's love of racing and skill developed, it became a more serious hobby. By 1984, he had become the German junior champion at age 15. He was champion again the next year and finished second in the World Junior Championships at Le Mans, France. In 1987 he dominated the German Championships and also won the European Championships.

The Road to Excellence

Michael made the jump in 1988 to racing Formula König cars, which are considered the first step in single-seaters. He won nine of the ten races he entered in his first year. At the same time he finished second in a series for the faster Formula Ford cars. His dazzling performance brought him to the attention of Willi Weber, who immediately signed Michael to drive his Formula Three car. When Weber, who would guide Michael's career for the next ten years, became his manager, Michael began to think that his hobby could become a profession.

In 1990, his second year in Formula Three, Michael won the championship and Weber moved him into the next phase of his career, placing him on the Mercedes Group C sports-car team. This became the final course in Michael's professional racing education.

In the summer of 1991 the Jordan Formula One team needed a substitute driver for the Belgian Grand Prix. Weber arranged for Michael to fill the seat, and Michael surprised observers by qualifying seventh on one of Formula One's most challenging tracks. In the race itself he went out with mechanical problems on the first lap, but he was already recognized as a future star.

FORMULA ONE AND OTHER VICTORIES

Year	Series	Place
1984	German Junior Karting	1st
1985	German Junior Karting	1st
1986	European Karting	3d
1987	German Karting	1st
	European Karting	1st
1988	German Formula König	1st
1989	German Formula Three	3d
1990	World Endurance	—
1991	German Formula Three	1st
	World Endurance	—
	Formula One debut	—
1992	World Formula One	3d
1993	World Formula One	4th
1994	World Formula One	1st
1995	World Formula One	1st
1996	World Formula One	3rd
1997	World Formula One	—
1998	World Formula One	2d
1999	World Formula One	5th
2000	World Formula One	1st

The Emerging Champion

Michael jumped right into the middle of Formula One controversy and politics as the Jordan team and the Benetton team, for whom he had also driven, argued over his contract. Characteristically, Michael ignored the legal arguments and the interpersonal politics and concentrated on his driving; Benetton eventually won his contract.

Just one year after his debut, Michael got his first win at the Belgian Grand Prix and then continued on to place third in the championship for 1992. In 1993 he finished fourth, behind Alain Prost, Ayrton Senna, and Damon Hill. A verbal feud that had developed the previous year between Michael and three-time world champion Senna continued, demonstrating Michael's confidence and his growing skill in the mind-games often played among rival drivers.

Events of 1994 made it a tumultuous year for Michael and Formula One racing as a whole. At the Grand Prix of San Marino, rookie Roland Ratzenberger was killed in a crash during a qualifying race. The next day, Ayrton Senna crashed and was killed in the early laps of the race. Michael went on to win the race, not knowing until after the finish that Senna had died. After several pensive days, Michael decided that racing was important enough to him to continue, and he won his next race, at Monaco. He also took over leadership of the Formula One Racing Drivers Association and campaigned for greater safety measures. In Spain he finished second while being stuck in fifth gear for much of a race, and in doing so he became, in the minds of many, the new Senna, the new top racing driver.

The difficult season continued. Michael was disqualified from four races for technical reasons. A war of words raged in the press between Michael and a new rival, Damon Hill. Finally the championship came down to the last race, in Australia; though Michael collided with Hill in what many thought was a deliberate crash, Michael won the race and became world champion by one point. In 1995 he equaled Nigel Mansell's record of nine wins in one season and took the championship again, becoming the youngest-ever two-time champion.

Continuing the Story

At the age of twenty-six, Michael had reached the top of his sport and could only find continuing challenge by moving to another team. He accepted an offer of $25 million a year from the famous Ferrari team and became one of the highest-paid athletes in the world. Ferrari had not won a championship since 1979 and hoped Michael's skill and leadership would bring them back to the front. In 1996 Michael battled Hill and newcomer Jacques Villeneuve to give Ferrari a third-place finish. The following year Michael was contending for the championship, with five wins, when he crashed into leader Villeneuve in the final race. Michael's aggressive style failed him this time. The Formula One governing board ruled the crash deliberate and stripped Michael of his points for the year, taking away his second place in the world championship.

Michael came back in 1998 and finished second again, behind the superior McLaren car of Mika Häkkinen. A brake failure in Michael's car at the 1999 British Grand Prix sent him into the tire barrier, then to the hospital with a broken leg. He was out for seven races but returned to finish second at the race in Malaysia.

In 2000 Michael won five of eight races, then alowed Häkkinen to pass him in the standings. Häkkinen, however, was among the first to congratulate Michael when, at Suzuka, Japan, Michael won his third world championship. It was the first win for the Ferrari team in twenty-one years. With three world titles, Michael joined five other drivers in the all-time career list in Formula One.

Summary

Michael Schumacher earned his racing reputation with hard work, determination, and natural skill, in a sport where costs are formidable and some competitors "buy a ride" with their personal wealth.

Michael stormed his way through go-kart racing, the beginning formula cars, and sports cars before he amazed the Formula One world with his talent and maturity. His self-confidence—some might say arrogance—and aggressive style landed him in trouble more than once, but no one could deny his skill as a racer. He fairly earned the title of world champion as well as his reputation as the best driver of his generation.

Joseph W. Hinton

Additional Sources:

Allsop, Derek. *Michael Schumacher: Formula for Success.* Osceola, Wis.: Motorbooks International, 1996.

Collings, Timothy. *Schumacher: The Life and Times of the New Formula One Champion.* Osceola, Wis.: Motorbooks International, 1996.

Hilton, Christopher. *Michael Schumacher: Defending the Crown.* Osceola, Wis.: Motorbooks International, 1995.

Sparling, Ken. *Michael Schumacher.* Willowdale, Ont.: Firefly Books, 1999.

ARNOLD SCHWARZENEGGER

Sport: Bodybuilding

Born: July 30, 1947
Graz, Austria

Early Life

Arnold Alois Schwarzenegger was born on July 30, 1947, in the Austrian town of Graz, and he grew up in the village of Thal, located just a few miles from his birthplace.

Arnold's father, Gustav, was Thal's chief of police and a champion athlete in his own right.

AP/Wide World Photos

Gustav and his wife, Aurelia, together with Arnold and his older brother, Meinhard, formed a close-knit family.

The biggest influence in Arnold's early life was his father. Gustav was a strict disciplinarian who demanded total obedience from his sons. Arnold undoubtedly applied the lessons of strictness and duty that he learned from his father to his training as a bodybuilder. It was Gustav who forced him to be goal oriented.

Arnold had been a sickly child, but under his father's stern orders, the boy began playing several sports. Eventually, Arnold settled on soccer, and, because of the strenuous exercise this entailed, his health gradually improved to the point where he became a very good player.

The Road to Excellence

Even from an early age, Arnold was an ambitious person. "From the time I was ten years old," he told an interviewer in 1977, "I wanted to be the very best in something." When he was fifteen, he discovered what he would be the very best in: bodybuilding.

Originally, Arnold began working out in order to improve his leg strength so that he could be a better soccer player, but soon he discovered that his body responded dramatically to the new exercises. The young athlete found that his muscles grew rapidly, and he delighted in adding the new bulk to his body.

Arnold began to train obsessively six days a week for several hours at a time. When he was not at the gym, Arnold would travel into Graz to see gladiator movies starring muscular heroes like Steve Reeves and Reg Park. He daydreamed of leaving Austria and coming

MAJOR CHAMPIONSHIPS

Year	Competition	Place
1966	Mr. Europe	1st
	International Powerlifting Championship	1st
	NABBA Amateur Mr. Universe	2d
1967	NABBA Amateur Mr. Universe	1st
1968-70	NABBA Professional Mr. Universe	1st
1968	IFBB Mr. Universe	2d
1969	IFBB Mr. Universe	1st
	Mr. Olympia	2d
1970	Mr. World	1st
1970-75, 1980	Mr. Olympia	1st

to America, where he would become a physique champion and perhaps a film star, too.

After high school and a brief stint in the Austrian army, nineteen-year-old Arnold moved from Thal to Munich, Germany. There he found a job managing a gymnasium, but he continued to work out regularly. While in Germany, Arnold developed many of his most important innovations in bodybuilding. Breaking up the workout into morning and evening sessions was termed the "split routine," and overdoing an exercise so as to get past the pain barrier and on to bigger muscles was called "muscle shock." The "Austrian Oak," as he was nicknamed by his friends, was beginning to be a force in the bodybuilding world.

The Emerging Champion

In Munich, Arnold began entering and winning contests. Far from being male beauty contests, bodybuilding competitions are designed to judge the best-developed physiques as carefully and impartially as possible. There are three phases to a contest, only one of which is seen by the public. The first two sessions take place privately on the day of the contest. The judges look for overall proportion as well as for muscle mass and definition. The public sees only the final posing after the compulsory phase has been completed. All bodybuilders, even stars like Arnold, must compete under the same rules.

In 1966, Arnold was judged Best Built Man of Europe and Mr. Europe and came in second in the amateur division of the Mr. Universe com-

petition in London. The following year, he captured first place in the amateur Mr. Universe, and in 1968, he returned to win the coveted professional division Mr. Universe.

Also in 1968, Arnold was invited by publisher and businessman Joe Weider to come to America and compete in a number of competitions, including the Mr. Olympia contest, often called the "superbowl of bodybuilding."

Unfortunately, Arnold was not victorious in his first Mr. Olympia (he placed second), but fired by a new enthusiasm, the Austrian Oak came back in 1970 and captured the title. From then on, Arnold vaulted from one victory to another. Eventually, he claimed seven Mr. Olympia victories, a record that was only eclipsed by Lee Haney in 1991.

Continuing the Story

Arnold's last Mr. Olympia win came in 1980, and after that victory, he decided to retire from bodybuilding competition. There was no trouble about finding something to do, however.

From the time he was a boy in Austria, Arnold had dreamed of starring in films. This dream became a reality when he appeared in a low-budget film in 1970, but it was not until 1976, when he appeared in *Stay Hungry,* that his cinematic career took off.

The Austrian bodybuilder has been busy at the studios ever since. *Conan the Barbarian* (1982) proved to be Arnold's first big hit, but it was followed by other even bigger successes. With each new film, Arnold has tried to play different types of characters. His first role as a villain came in 1984, when he played the murderous cyborg in *The Terminator.* In 1988, Arnold starred in his first comedy, *Twins,* and two years later, he portrayed an elementary school teacher in *Kindergarten Cop* (1990). Arnold's career as a film star has been as triumphant as his athletic career.

With later film such as *True Lies* (1994), *Junior* (1995), and *Batman and Robin* (1997), Arnold secured his position as one of Hollywood's top box-

HONORS AND AWARDS

1966	Named Best Built Man of Europe

office draws. He even added directing to his growing list of accomplishments with television movie.

A staunch Republican, Arnold was appointed by President George Bush in 1990 as chairman of the President's Council of Physical Fitness and Sports. Arnold remained an outspoken advocate for physical fitness.

Summary

The Austrian Oak came to America and made his fortune, and for this he is grateful. In 1983, Arnold Schwarzenegger confirmed his love for his adopted country by becoming a United States citizen. Three years later, he cemented a relationship of a different sort by marrying Maria Shriver, the newscaster-niece of former President John F. Kennedy.

True to his early wish, Arnold Schwarzenegger has become "the very best" in not just one, but in a variety of areas. Arnold has lived the American dream: He has risen from obscurity to fame and fortune.

David Chapman

Additional Sources:

Andrews, Nigel. *True Myths: The Life and Times of Arnold Schwarzenegger.* New York: Carol Group, 1996.

Green, Tom. *Arnold!* New York: St. Martin's Press, 1987.

Lipsyte, Robert. *Arnold Schwarzenegger, Hercules in America.* New York: HarperCollins, 1993.

Schwarzenegger, Arnold. *The New Encyclopedia of Modern Bodybuilding.* New York: Simon & Schuster, 1999.

Torres, John Albert. *Fitness Stars of Bodybuilding: Featuring Profiles of Arnold Schwarzenegger, Lou Ferrigno, Ronnie Coleman, and Lenda Murray.* Bear, Del.: Mitchell Lane, 2001.

DAVE SCOTT

Sport: Triathlon

Born: January 4, 1954
Woodland, California

Early Life

David Forshee Scott was born on January 4, 1954, in Woodland, California, to Verne H. Scott, a civil engineering professor, and Dorothy J. (Forshee) Scott. As one of three children, Dave learned to appreciate family activities, which included sports such as swimming. Growing up in Northern California, he also spent many hours in the vast wilderness of the region.

Dave went to Davis High School, where he excelled at water polo, swimming, and basketball. He was named an All-American in water polo, be-

Courtesy Dave Scott

coming the first All-American at Davis High School in any sport. After high school, Dave decided to attend the University of California at Davis, where his father taught civil engineering. He majored in physical education and exercise physiology.

The Road to Excellence

Dave continued to participate in water polo and swimming at Davis. During his college career, he earned All-American honors in swimming and made the All-Conference team twice in water polo. Dave also played in two National Collegiate Athletic Association (NCAA) water polo championships.

After graduation in 1976, he became the head coach for the Davis Aquatic Masters program. He had started with the program in 1974, when it had merely eleven members. Dave remained the head coach of the program until 1981; by that year, the membership had swelled to 425, making it the largest Aquatic Masters program in the United States. There were times when Dave was coaching and counseling as many as four hundred people a day. In addition to the exercise Dave would get at work, he liked to go on long runs during his free hours.

Dave was an enthusiastic spokesman for the virtues of physical fitness. He would participate in clinics and speak at club meetings and seminars. Dave had found an outlet for inspiring others to take physical fitness seriously, but he also needed some competitive outlets that would challenge himself. He began entering long-distance swimming events, including the 2.4-mile Hawaiian Open Water Swim at Waikiki. Dave won the Waikiki event in 1978 and 1979. At the 1978 awards ceremony, he was asked to compete in the newly created Ironman Triathlon event. The Ironman consisted of a 2.4-mile swim, a 112-mile bike ride, and a 26.2-mile run, each com-

MAJOR CHAMPIONSHIPS

1980,1982-84,1986-87	Hawaii Ironman Triathlon
1982	Hanover Hamptons Triathlon
	Southhampton Triathlon
	USTS Portland Triathlon
	USTS San Diego Triathlon
	USTS Seattle Triathlon
1983,1986	Gulf Coast Triathlon
1985,1989	Japan Ironman Triathlon
1985,1989	USTS Miami Triathlon
1988	USTS Houston Triathlon
1989	USTS Phoenix Triathlon

pleted one right after the other in a single day. The first Ironman had been held in 1978. Dave was intrigued by the thought of competing, and in 1979, he set out to train for the Ironman.

The Emerging Champion

Dave felt confident of his ability to handle the swimming portion of the Ironman, but he was less sure of his cycling and running skills. With the help of friends, Dave pushed himself until he felt confident that he could complete all three sections of the triathlon. In addition to physical training, he experimented with a special diet, high in complex carbohydrates but low in fat. Since the triathlon was such a new event, there had not been any studies done that could tell Dave how to train. The 6-foot 160-pound athlete took it upon himself to test the limits of what one person could physically do. Dave was going to adapt both his mind and body in order to complete a superhuman task.

In 1980, Dave competed in his first Ironman. He surprised everyone but himself by not only winning the event but also setting a new record time of 9 hours, 24 minutes, and 33 seconds. He shattered the old record by almost 2 hours. His workouts, which had lasted up to nine hours a day, had paid off. Yet beyond the intense training, it had been Dave's passion to excel that had made him a champion.

Injuries forced Dave to miss the 1981 Ironman, but he was in prime shape for 1982. Whereas the 1980 Ironman competition was not billed as a world championship, the 1982 competition was, and the competition was renamed the Ironman Triathlon World Championship. The event had also been moved from the early part of the year to October and was now held at Kono, Hawaii. The changes did not seem to affect Dave, who won easily, setting a new record with a time of 9 hours, 8 minutes, and 23 seconds.

Continuing the Story

Dave has been called the ultimate triathlete. In addition to 1980 and 1982, Dave went on to capture the Ironman title in 1983, 1984, 1986, and 1987. In 1984, he became the first to finish the Ironman in less than 9 hours. The first Ironman in 1978 attracted merely fifteen competitors, but by the 1990's, the Ironman was drawing nearly 1,500 triathletes. Competition had become so fierce that triathletes had to qualify for the world championship at Kono by doing well at other events.

Dave's principal rival during the late 1980's was Mark Allen. In 1986 and 1987, Dave prevailed at the Ironman, but in 1989 Allen won the first of his many Ironman championships. The 1989 race is considered one of the most dramatic duels in triathlon history. Dave finished with a remarkable time of just over 8 hours and 10 minutes, but Allen's time was 58 seconds faster. In 1989, moreover, Dave began to suffer from various injuries, including a painful knee condition, and in the summer of 1991, he retired from competition. Dave came out of retirement to compete in the Hawaii Ironman Triathlon two more times, in 1994 and 1996, finishing in second place overall and fifth overall, respectively

He devoted himself to coaching, lecturing, conducting clinics, and writing, and he was able to spend more time with his wife, Anna, and their children. He also appeared as a commentator and analyst for triathlon competitions on several networks in the United States and Canada. For

HONORS AND AWARDS

1982	*City Sports* magazine Athlete of the Year
1987	*Triathlete* magazine Outstanding Performance Award
1987-88	*Triathlon Today* All-American
1993	Ironman Hall of Fame
1999	*Triathlete* magazine Hall of Fame

his extraordinary accomplishments, Dave was the first inductee of the newly established Ironman Hall of Fame in 1993.

Summary

Dave Scott combined intense training habits, a strict diet, and an iron will to become the first great triathlete. He helped to bring triathlons to the attention of the public, transforming the competitions from the hobby of a few fitness fanatics into a worldwide sport.

Jeffry Jensen

Additional Sources:

Brant, John. "Iron Master." *Runner's World* 30, no. 5 (1995).

Davis, Logan. "Iron Man." *Men's Health* 10, no. 2 (1995).

Mallon, Bill, and Ian Buchanan. *Quest for Gold: The Encyclopedia of American Olympians.* New York: Leisure Press, 1984.

Scott, Dave, with Liz Barrett. *Dave Scott's Triathlon Training.* New York: Simon & Schuster, 1986.

Wallechinsky, David. *The Complete Book of the Olympics.* Boston: Little, Brown and Company, 1991.

MIKE SCOTT

Sport: Baseball

Born: April 26, 1955
Santa Monica, California

Early Life

Michael Warren Scott was born on April 26, 1955, in Santa Monica, California, a beachfront community in the southern part of the state.

Life there was ideal for a young athlete like Mike Scott. The weather was nice almost every day of the year, leaving children free to play outdoors all the time. Mike, who was always tall for his age, was known as quite a basketball player.

He also found that his height and strong arm enabled him to throw the ball faster than most kids his age, so he gravitated toward baseball and the pitcher's mound.

The Road to Excellence

Mike's baseball career got off to a slow start. Unlike most players who show promise early, Mike was not drafted out of high school. The New York Mets finally picked him in the second round of the June, 1976, draft, after his junior year at Pepperdine University in Malibu, California.

Mike had some good years in the minors but went only 14-27 for the Mets before they traded him to Houston in 1982.

Mike showed signs of promise shortly after the trade. In 1983, he won 10 of 16 decisions. After the 1984 season, he discovered the pitch that catapulted him to stardom.

Former major leaguer Roger Craig taught Mike how to throw the split-fingered fastball during that winter of 1984. Craig, who was out of baseball at the time, spent more than a week with Scott, teaching him the new pitch.

The split-fingered fastball is held with the fingers spread out across the ball but uses the same motion as a fastball. It travels just as quickly as a fastball but breaks sharply downward as it reaches the plate. Mike's big hands helped him to grip the ball properly for the pitch.

With the new weapon in his arsenal, Mike became one of the best pitchers in baseball. In 1985, he won eighteen games, the most on the Houston staff.

Mike Scott in 1989.

STATISTICS

Season	GP	GS	CG	IP	HA	BB	SO	W	L	S	ShO	ERA
1979	18	9	0	52.0	59	20	21	1	3	0	0	5.37
1980	6	6	1	29.0	40	8	13	1	1	0	1	4.34
1981	23	23	1	136.0	130	34	54	5	10	0	0	3.90
1982	37	22	1	147.0	185	60	63	7	13	3	0	5.14
1983	24	24	2	145.0	143	46	73	10	6	0	2	3.72
1984	31	29	0	154.0	179	43	83	5	11	0	0	4.68
1985	36	35	4	221.2	194	80	137	18	8	0	2	3.29
1986	37	37	7	275.1	182	72	**306**	18	10	0	5	**2.22**
1987	36	36	8	247.2	199	79	233	16	13	0	3	3.23
1988	32	32	8	218.2	162	53	190	14	8	0	5	2.92
1989	33	32	9	229.0	180	62	172	**20**	10	0	2	3.10
1990	32	32	4	205.2	194	66	121	9	13	0	2	3.81
1991	2	2	0	7.0	11	4	3	0	2	0	0	12.86
Totals	347	319	45	2,065.9	1,858	627	1,469	124	108	3	22	3.54

Notes: Boldface indicates statistical leader. GP = games played; GS = games started; CG = complete games; IP = innings pitched; HA = hits allowed; BB = bases on balls (walks); SO = strikeouts; W = wins; L = losses; S = saves; ShO = shutouts; ERA = earned run average

The Emerging Champion

The next season, he kept right on winning. He won eighteen games again in 1986, leading the league in earned run average and strikeouts. On September 25, he pitched a no-hitter against the San Francisco Giants, whose manager at the time was Roger Craig—the same man who had taught Mike the new pitch.

He finally helped the Astros become a winner. The team won its division and qualified for the playoffs. In the league Championship Series, Mike started and won two games against his old team. He was rested and ready to pitch in the seventh and final game of the series when the Mets rallied to capture the pennant in six games.

Opposing hitters were so baffled by Mike's new pitch that some charged he was using illegal means to make the ball behave so strangely. Mike was never charged with any wrongdoing, however. He just kept getting the hitters out.

Mike always remained level-headed, despite the tremendous success he enjoyed during the second half of the 1980's. He never let that success change him. He remembered all too well those years in which he struggled to make it as a big league pitcher. He realized that he was fortunate to be able to turn around his baseball career, and he remained as even-tempered and easygoing as ever.

Even in the best of years, the Astros were not a strong-hitting team, which meant that Mike often did not get much run support. The Astros were unable to win anything more than the divisional title while Mike was with them during the 1980's, but he never complained or demanded to be traded. He was happy that he had found some personal success and appreciated the Astros having stood by him during those difficult early years.

Continuing the Story

After Mike found the formula, he was determined to make it work. He knew what opposing players were saying and he was determined to prove them wrong. Mike wanted to show that he and the split-fingered fastball were no fluke, and that he could become a consistent winner with his new, perfectly legal, pitch.

He continued to keep National League hitters off-stride for the rest of the 1980's and into the 1990's. He won fifty games in the three years after his remarkable 1986 season, and in 1989, he fi-

HONORS AND AWARDS

1986	National League Cy Young Award
	National League Championship Series most valuable player
1986-87, 1989	National League All-Star Team

nally achieved the one goal that had escaped him. That season, Mike went 20-10, reaching the magical twenty-win plateau for the first time in his career. He was the only National League pitcher to win twenty and one of only three pitchers in baseball to win that many games that season.

Mike had struggled to achieve stardom throughout his career, and the honors and awards did not come to him until after he turned thirty, a time when many athletes, especially pitchers, begin to think about retirement.

Mike kept trying to get better, however, and his persistence paid off. He learned a new technique and worked hard to perfect it, and that persistence paid off for Mike and the Astros. Mike retired from baseball in 1991.

Summary

Many people, including so-called baseball experts, had written off Mike Scott. They said he would never be a great major league pitcher. Mike kept working, however, trying new things to help himself, and found what he was looking for. His new pitch, the split-fingered fastball, would prove to be effective in getting the hitters out. National League batters wish that Mike had never learned how to throw it.

John McNamara

Additional Sources:

Fimrite, Ron. "No Wonder He's Hot." *Sports Illustrated* 66 (January 12, 1987): 92-102.

Hickok, Ralph. "Scott, Mike." In *A Who's Who of Sports Champions.* Boston: Houghton Mifflin, 1995.

STEVE SCOTT

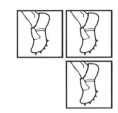

Sport: Track and field (middle-distance runs)

Born: May 5, 1956
Upland, California

Early Life

Steve Scott was born on May 5, 1956, in Upland, California, about thirty miles east of Los Angeles. Southern California's warm year-round climate and many track and field facilities make it a mecca for young runners, and it was natural for Steve to develop his running prowess there.

Unlike many distance runners, who are thin or even frail-looking, Steve was tall and well-built. He was a talented athlete in other sports as well, but he said that after once pitching 11 consecutive balls in a baseball game he knew that he should concentrate on running.

The Road to Excellence

Steve starred as a middle-distance runner at Upland High School, recording a best time of 1 minute 52 seconds in the 880-yard run. By the time he was graduated from high school, Steve had won the silver medal in the California state high school 880-yard championship.

Steve wanted to attend a college near his home with a track program that he liked. He chose the University of California at Irvine, where he enjoyed running in the school's mustard-colored track vests emblazoned with the bold letters "UCI."

In 1975, his freshman year, Steve won the National Collegiate Athletic Association (NCAA) Division II 1-mile title, recording times of 4 minutes 9.7 seconds in the mile and 3 minutes 47.5 seconds in the 1,500-meter run. One year later,

Runner Steve Scott after winning a 1988 mile race.

Steve won his second Division II mile title and cut his time in the 1,500 meters to 3 minutes 40.4 seconds.

As a twenty-year-old, Steve was relatively young and lacked the depth of racing experience to appear as a strong contender for a spot on the U.S.

Olympic team for the 1976 Games in Montreal. Nonetheless, he trained hard for the 1976 Olympic trials, where he progressed through the preliminary rounds to earn a spot in the finals. Competing in the 1,500-meter final, though, Steve finished seventh, and he was not selected for the U.S. team. Still, he had done well, and he remarked that "it was exciting just to be there."

The Emerging Champion

In early 1977, Steve moved from the college ranks up to world-class status. At an indoor 1-mile race in San Diego, Steve competed against many of the world's best runners, including prerace favorites John Walker of New Zealand, who was the 1976 Olympic champion, Eamonn Coghlan of Ireland, and Wilson Waiqwa of Kenya. Steve later remembered, "I was really relaxed about the race. I'd had a good week of workouts, and there was no pressure on me. I even fell asleep in the car on the way to the race."

There was much press speculation that Walker was planning an attempt on the world 1-mile record in the race. The Olympic champion was not impressive, though, and in the final lap Steve went into the lead. Though Wilson Waiqwa

passed Steve at the finish line, Steve had run the mile in just 3 minutes 56.5 seconds. By finishing in second place ahead of so many world-class athletes, Steve had shown that he was one of the world's elite runners.

Steve's time at San Diego was the sixth-best indoor performance ever by an American, and his youth and promise made track experts optimistic about his prospects. Steve was seen as his country's leading miler and a possible contender for the 1980 Olympics.

1977 continued to be a rewarding year for Steve. In a race in Jamaica in May, he defeated Great Britain's Steve Ovett and Tanzania's Filbert Bayi over 1,500 meters. In the NCAA championships that year, however, Steve lost again to his nemesis, Wilson Waiqwa, who was competing for the University of Texas-El Paso. A few weeks later at the Amateur Athletic Union championships, though, Steve ran the 1,500 meters in 3 minutes 37.3 seconds, beating Waiqwa by inches for his first victory over the African runner in six meetings. Steve's consistent performances had established him as one of the favorites for the gold medal at the 1980 Olympics.

However, at the 1980 Olympics, a British runner named Sebastian Coe won the 1,500 meters without even having to face Steve. In response to the Soviet Union's invasion of Afghanistan, U.S. President Jimmy Carter had convinced the U.S. Olympic Committee to boycott the 1980 Games, which were held in Moscow. For Steve, the boycott was a disappointment, depriving him of his best chance at an Olympic medal.

Continuing the Story

By the time of the 1984 Olympics in Los Angeles, Steve was twenty-eight years old, but he was still a highly regarded runner. He ran the 1,500 meters in 3 minutes 41.02 seconds in the preliminary round and advanced to the semifinals, where his time of 3 minutes 35.71 seconds was good enough

STATISTICS

Year	Competition	Event	Place	Time
1977	U.S. Nationals	1,500 meters	1st	3:37.3
1978	U.S. Nationals	1,500 meters	1st	3:38.8
1979	U.S. Nationals	1,500 meters	1st	3:36.4
	USA/Mobil Indoor Championships	1 mile	1st	4:01.4
1981	U.S. Nationals	1,500 meters	2d	3:35.5
	USA/Mobil Indoor Championships	1 mile	1st	3:57.3
1982	U.S. Nationals	1,500 meters	1st	3:34.92
1983	World Championships	1,500 meters	2d	3:41.87
1984	Olympic Games	1,500 meters	10th	3:39.86
	USA/Mobil Indoor Championships	1 mile	1st	4:00.06
1985	U.S. Nationals	1,500 meters	2d	3:39.61
1986	U.S. Nationals	1,500 meters	1st	3:42.41
1987	Pan-American Games	1,500 meters	3d	3:47.76
	U.S. Nationals	1,500 meters	2d	3:44.10
1988	Olympic Games	1,500 meters	5th	3:36.99
1989	USA/Mobil Indoor Championships	3,000 meters	1st	7:53.69
1990	USA/Mobil Indoor Championships	1 mile	Tied for lead	3:57.35

for second place and a spot in the finals. In the finals, though, Steve slipped to a time of 3 minutes 39.86 seconds and finished in tenth place. Once again he had missed an Olympic medal.

Consistency was one of Steve's strengths, though, and he was again a member of the U.S. team for the 1988 Olympics in Seoul, South Korea. Again Steve progressed to the semifinals, where he won his race with a time of 3 minutes 38.20 seconds, and again he finished out of the medals in the final round, running a time of 3 minutes 36.99 seconds and finishing fifth. Peter Rono of Kenya won the race in a time of 3 minutes 35.96 seconds, so over the 1,500-meter distance, Steve missed the gold medal by just over a second.

Summary

Steve Scott never won an Olympic title, and he even had to be content with watching his great rival, John Walker, become the first runner to complete one hundred 1-mile races in sub-4-minute times. Nevertheless, Steve established himself as a premier athlete during a career that lasted

---

RECORDS

World indoor record at 2,000 meters in 1981 (4:58.6)
Two American indoor records in 1981: 1,500 meters (3:36.0), 1 mile (3:51.8)
American indoor record at 3,000 meters in 1989 (7:39.94)
American record at 1,500 meters in 1979 (3:36.4)

---

from the 1970's into the 1990's. Among his contemporaries, only Walker ran so long and so well.

Scott A. G. M. Crawford

Additional Sources:

Bateman, Hal. *United States Track and Field Olympians, 1896-1980*. Indianapolis, Ind.: The Athletics Congress of the United States, 1984.

Hickok, Ralph. *A Who's Who of Sports Champions*. Boston: Houghton Mifflin, 1995.

Scott, Steve, with Marc Bloom. *The Miler: America's Legendary Runner Talks About His Triumphs and Trials*. New York: Macmillan USA, 1997.

Wallechinsky, David. *The Complete Book of the Olympics*. Boston: Little, Brown and Company, 1991.

Watman, Mel. *Encyclopedia of Track and Field Athletics*. New York: St. Martin's Press, 1981.

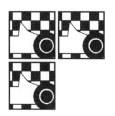

WENDELL SCOTT

Sport: Auto racing

Born: August 28, 1921
　　　Danville, Virginia
Died: December 23, 1990
　　　Danville, Virginia

Early Life

Wendell Scott was the founding father of African American stock car racing. He was born on August 28, 1921, in Danville, Virginia, and studied at Danville High School, leaving after eleventh grade. He did not perform especially well in

Courtesy of Betty Carlan/International Motor Sports Hall of Fame

athletics or academics but played baseball enthusiastically. Baseball would remain a lifelong interest.

During World War II, Wendell served in the U.S. Army from 1942 to 1945 and saw military service in Cheyenne, Wyoming, and Europe. An able mechanic, Wendell ended his war service in charge of a convoy of trucks. Many successful National Association for Stock Car Auto Racing (NASCAR) drivers bloomed under the same sort of apprenticeship. Wendell joined Grand National racing in 1961 at Spartanburg, South Carolina.

The Road to Excellence

Wendell's initial success came in 1959, when he won the Sportsman Racing Championship at Southside Speedway in Richmond, Virginia. The same year, he captured the Virginia Championship for portsman stock car drivers. During his early years, Wendell struggled for the financial backing necessary to turn out a competitive racing machine. In one race, he endured the frustration of a broken seat and gas pedal.

During the 1961 racing season, Wendell ranked thirty-second in national point standings. The next year, he demonstrated his true racing form. At the wheel of a 1961 Chevrolet, he started forty-one races and finished among the top ten on seventeen occasions. In 1963, Wendell started forty-seven races with fifteen top-ten finishes. Wendell still drove his faithful 1961 Chevrolet, logging 6,163.4 miles in competitive racing. He recorded his only 1963 NASCAR victory in a Jacksonville, Florida, race. His next-best performance that year came in a fifth place at Spartanburg, South Carolina.

The Emerging Champion

In 1964, Wendell began the season in a 1962 Chevrolet. Halfway through the season, Wendell opted for a 1963 Ford and immediately enjoyed greater success. With the Ford, he generated greater acceleration and started being a "charger." He finished sixth in the Grand National standings in 1966, earning $16,780 in forty-five starts, finishing three times among the top five, and ranking seventeen times in the top ten. For many years, he occupied the spotlight as the only African American driver on the circuit.

Like many auto racers, Wendell possessed superstitions. He never wore green or allowed green coloring on his automobile or allowed peanuts to be consumed in his pits or garage area. He did experience some prejudice as a black racer but never let it affect him.

Wendell launched his racing career just as NASCAR began to achieve momentum as a sport. The Daytona International Speedway opened in 1959, while speedways opened at Atlanta, Georgia, and Charlotte, North Carolina, in 1960. The 1961 Firecracker 400 race at Daytona Beach, Florida, was televised, signifying national coverage for the sport.

Continuing the Story

Wendell's best NASCAR season came in 1969, when he finished eleven times in the top ten and collected $27,542 in prize money. In May, 1973, Wendell was involved in a nineteen-vehicle wreck during the Talladega race. Wendell's 1971 Mercury was demolished, and he suffered the first serious injuries of his racing career. He ended up with three fractured ribs, two fractures in the pelvic girdle, a fractured right knee, two fractures of the left knee, a fractured leg, and an arm laceration that necessitated sixty stitches.

Wendell died on December 23, 1990, at age sixty-nine, having suffered from spinal cancer, bilateral pneumonia, high blood pressure, and kidney ailments. He frequently described himself as an aging pugilist: "I guess I'm like a washed-up prize fighter. He knows it's the last round, and he knows he's beat, but he keeps trying to land that knockout punch." At his Danville, Virginia, fu-

RACING RECORD	
1959	Sportsman Racing Championship —Richmond, Virginia Virginia Championship (auto drivers sportsmen)
1962	Raced forty-one times, seventeen top-ten finishes
1963	Raced forty-seven times, fifteen top-ten finishes NASCAR win in Jacksonville, Florida
1966	Raced forty-five times, seventeen top-ten finishes
1969	Eleven top-ten finishes

neral, many NASCAR drivers paid respects to the pioneer racer who started over five hundred Grand National races and finished among the top five twenty times.

Summary

In 1977 the film *Greased Lightning* reprised Wendell Scott's life, career, successes, and setbacks. Wendell's life is an example of how hard it was for any NASCAR racer, white or black, to succeed. It is of real sociocultural significance that Wendell's successful years, in the late 1960's, occurred during the era of the Civil Rights movement, Martin Luther King, Jr.'s prominence and death, and racial tensions that threatened to pull America into major social disorder. Wendell battled to survive as a lone black driver in a culture of racial discrimination and segregation. As there were no African American drivers on the NASCAR circuit even at the start of the twenty-first century, Wendell's accomplishments seem all the more admirable.

Scott A. G. M. Crawford

Additional Sources:

Black American Racers Association. *Black Racers Yearbook 1974: Official Annual of the Black American Racers Association.* Trenton, N.J.: The Association, 1974.

Rooney, John F., and Richard Pillsbury. *Atlas of American Sport.* New York: Macmillan, 1992.

Zucker, Harvey M., and Lawrence J. Babich. *Sports Film: A Complete Reference.* Jefferson, N.C.: McFarland, 1987.

BRIANA SCURRY

Sport: Soccer

Born: September 7, 1971
Minneapolis, Minnesota

Early Life

Briana Scurry, the youngest of nine children born to Earnest and Robbie Scurry, grew up in Dayton, Minnesota, a predominantly white suburb of Minneapolis. The Scurry family was one of the few African American families to live in Dayton, a small, farming community of two thousand people.

Briana was a soft-spoken child, and one of her hobbies was painting model airplanes. In junior high and high school, she had aspirations of becoming a lawyer.

During her school years, Briana enjoyed playing many sports including basketball, softball, floor hockey, karate, football, and soccer. In fourth grade she began her soccer career; throughout her youth she played for the "Minneapolis Kickers." Briana continued her participation in sports through high school, where her sports honors included being named an All-State power forward in basketball and an all-American soccer player. In 1989, her high school soccer team won the Minnesota championship: Briana was named the state's top athlete.

The Road to Excellence

From Minnesota, Briana traveled east to attend the University of Massachusetts (UMASS). At UMASS she was a goalkeeper on the women's soccer team. Her coach, whom she credited with molding her into a goalkeeper, was Jim Rudy. Briana played for UMASS from 1990 to 1993. In 1992, she participated in the Boston Soccer-Fest All-Star Tournament. There she received the notice of the United States women's soccer coach, Anson Dorrance, and the goalkeeper coach, Tony DiCicco. In 1993 the UMASS team lost, 4-1, to the Dorrance-coached University of North Carolina team in the National

Briana Scurry celebrates after blocking a shot in the 1999 women's World Cup final, which the United States won.

AP/Wide World Photos

2500

NATIONAL TEAM STATISTICS

Year	Record	GP	GAA	ShO
1994	11-1-0	12	0.42	7
1995	11-2-2	15	0.74	9
1996	15-1-1	17	0.66	8
1997	10-1-0	11	0.69	7
1998	15-1-2	18	0.50	12
1999	17-2-1	20	0.66	11
2000	0-0-4	4	1.19	0
Totals	79-8-10	97	0.63	54

Notes: GP = games played; GAA = goals against average; ShO = shutouts

Collegiate Athletic Association (NCAA) Division I final. Briana's UMASS record boasted 37 shutouts in 65 starts, with 0.56 goals against average; Briana had allowed fewer than one goal per game to get by her. She was invited to the national team camp.

The Emerging Champion

Briana was named the starting goalkeeper for the U.S. Women's World Cup soccer team in 1994. She held that position until 2000. Her debut as their goalkeeper was in the U.S.-Portugal game on March 16, 1994. The final score was 5-0, one of many shutouts for Briana. In 1995, Briana started five of six games in the World Cup; the U.S. team finished third. In 1996, Briana started every game of the Olympics. When the U.S. team won the gold medal, Briana followed through on a promise and ran naked through the streets of Athens, Georgia, in celebration.

Continuing the Story

The 1999 women's World Cup soccer tournament was a three-week, sixteen-team, thirty-two-match tournament. On July 10, 1999, a record-size crowd for a women's sporting event (90,185) gathered at the Rose Bowl in Pasadena, California, to witness the first women's World Cup soccer match played in the United States. Forty million television viewers tuned in to see the most-watched soccer match in the history of network television. The fans saw ninety minutes of regulation scoreless soccer, two fifteen-minute periods of sudden-death overtime, and ten minutes of penalty kicks. Briana stopped China's third penalty kick by Liu Ying; then the U.S. fifth

kicker, midfielder Brandi Chastain, kicked a penalty kick that gave the Americans a 5-4 victory. Briana's save was said to be the biggest of the World Cup.

The team was on the cover of *Time, Newsweek, Sports Illustrated,* and *People,* all in one week, only the second time one event made all four covers. In December, 1999, the team was named Sportswomen of the Year by *Sports Illustrated for Women,* which said, "Their character and performance symbolizes the ideals of sportsmanship." In 2000, the team completed a twelve-match "victory tour" to raise awareness of women's soccer and make plans to form a professional league in 2001. As expected, the victory tour had record attendance.

Fans who saw them play were again rewarded when the U.S. team captured the silver medal in the 2000 Olympics in Sydney. In those games Briana played backup goalkeeper, after having developed a severe case of shin splints which forced her to miss four months of play earlier in the year. She was replaced on the U.S. team by Siri Mullinax as starting goalkeeper.

Briana has made appearances on *The Tonight Show with Jay Leno, Late Show with David Letterman,* and *The Rosie O'Donnell Show.* She signed endorsement deals with Pepsi cola and Allstate Insurance. She has been featured at store openings, signed countless autographs, and traveled extensively. "It's been a great ride," she said. "There are times when it gets a bit much, but you can't deny the smiles on the kids' faces. That in itself makes it all worthwhile."

Summary

Briana Scurry began playing soccer as a young girl in Minnesota. She kept at it while participating in a variety of other sports. From Minnesota, she went on to become a strong goalkeeper for

WORLD CUP STATISTICS

Year	Record	GP	GAA	ShO
1995	3-1-1	5	0.81	2
1999	5-0-1	6	0.47	4
Totals	8-1-2	11	0.62	6

Notes: GP = games played; GAA = goals against average; ShO = shutouts

the UMASS women's soccer team. After she finished college she was recruited as goalkeeper for the U.S. Women's World Cup soccer team and was hailed as the hero of the seminal 1999 women's World Cup, the series which drew the most widespread attention to women's soccer of any games to date. A two-time Olympic medalist, Briana was widely recognized as a role model for sports-minded women and girls.

Betsy L. Nichols

HONORS, AWARDS, AND RECORDS

1989	Minnesota State Soccer Champions, Anoka High School Minnesota's Top Athlete
1992	Boston Soccer-Fest All-Star Team
1993	NCAA Women's Soccer Final, Division I, UMASS vs. UNC, lost 4-1
1994	U.S. Women's World Cup Soccer Team, starter goalkeeper
1995	3d place win with U.S. Women's World Cup Soccer Team
1996	Gold Medal with U.S. Women's Olympic Soccer Team
1999	1st place win with U.S. Women's World Cup Soccer Team
2000	Silver Medal with U.S. Women's Olympic Soccer Team

OLYMPIC GAMES STATISTICS

Year	Record	GP	GAA	ShO
1996	4-0-1	5	0.60	2
2000	0-0-0	0	—	—
Totals	4-0-1	5	0.60	2

Notes: GP = games played; GAA = goals against average; ShO = shutouts

Additional Sources:

Bamberger, Michael. "Dream Come True." *Sports Illustrated* 91, no. 24 (December 20, 1999): 46-60.

Caparez, Dean. "Akers and Scurry Take out Brazil." *Soccer America* 54, no. 28 (July 19, 1999): 8-9.

Christopher, Matt. *In the Goal with Briana Scurry.* Boston: Little, Brown, 2000.

Luder, Bob. "Life in the Whirlwind of Celebrity." *Soccer America* 54, no. 42 (October 25, 1999): 27.

Stewart, Mark. *Briana Scurry, Super Saver.* New York: Children's Press, 2000.

Wahl, Grant. "Out of This World." *Sports Illustrated* 91, no. 3 (July 19, 1999): 38-43.

BOB SEAGREN

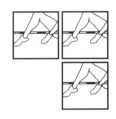

Sport: Track and field (pole vault)

Born: October 17, 1946
      Pomona, California

Early Life

Robert Lloyd Seagren was born in Pomona, California, on October 17, 1946. The Seagrens were an athletic California family; Bob's father, Arthur, hoped that Bob would be a baseball player. Like his older brother Arthur Jr., however, Bob was attracted to track and field athletic competition, particularly pole-vaulting.

Bob was a sixth-grader in the Pomona public schools when he first tried pole-vaulting. A local carpet merchant allowed neighborhood children to take the bamboo poles that had been used to store rugs for backyard play. Bob and his friends used them as vaulting poles and as cross-bars for their vaulting practice.

Bob would ride from a garage roof to the roof of a shed to get practice holding and balancing himself on the poles. Innovative and determined, Bob and his brother vaulted over a wall,

Bob Seagren in 1966.

2503

POLE VAULT STATISTICS

Year	Competition	Place	Height
1966	National AAU Outdoor Championships	1st	17'
	National AAU Indoor Championships	1st	17' ¼"
1967	Pan-American Games	1st	16' 1"
	NCAA Outdoor Championships	1st	17' 4"
	NCAA Indoor Championships	1st	17' ¼"
	National AAU Indoor Championships	1st	17' ¾"
1968	Olympic Games	Gold	17' 8½" OR
1969	NCAA Outdoor Championships	1st	17' 7"
	National AAU Outdoor Championships	1st	17' 6"
1970	National AAU Outdoor Championships	1st	17' 2"
	National AAU Indoor Championships	1st	17' 0"
1972	Olympic Games	Silver	17' 8½"

Note: OR = Olympic Record

using an abandoned, sunken-in bomb shelter, stuffed with weeds and lawn clippings, as a makeshift "pit" for soft landings.

The Road to Excellence

By the time he was twelve, Bob had vaulted 6 feet 1 inch. When he was a tenth-grader, he had cleared 10 feet. At the end of his high school career, he was close to clearing 16 feet and finally did at a meet in April, 1965. He knew that he had the potential to be a world-class pole-vaulter and was hoping for a chance at the Olympics. Because he needed more focused training and sanctioned competition, he decided to attend college.

Bob wanted to attend the University of Southern California (USC), a premier institution for track athletes, but his high school grades were too low. The coaching staff at USC suggested that he enroll at a junior college to work on academics while continuing to train and compete when he could.

Bob eventually attended two different junior colleges, Mount San Antonio and Glendale, both in California. While at an American Athletic Union competition in San Diego, he met John Pennel, the first pole-vaulter to clear 17 feet. Bob and John became close friends and shared an apartment in Glendale.

The two athletes attended track meets together, graded the competition, and watched films of themselves and other successful vaulters in action. Every bit of information they could glean from their study was put into action in their own preparation for future competition.

The Emerging Champion

In March, 1966, Bob began a quick rise to the top of American pole-vaulting, becoming the first vaulter to clear 17 feet indoors at a meet in New Mexico. Two weeks later, he set a new world record at the Knights of Columbus meet at Cleveland, Ohio, crossing the bar at 17 feet, ¾ inch.

The track and field establishment was abuzz with excitement over this new phenomenon, who planned to enroll at USC in fall, 1966. On May 15, 1966, Bob set a new world record at an outdoor meet in Fresno, California, vaulting 17 feet 5½ inches. The record stood only long enough for Bob's friend John Pennel to retake it, vaulting 17 feet 6¼ inches in the same meet.

This friendly rivalry continued when, a month later, Bob reclaimed the outdoor record in Sacramento, California, with a vault of 17 feet, 7 inches. Bob earned a gold medal in the pole-vault event of the Pan-American Games in 1967.

Continuing the Story

Bob's remarkable string of vaulting successes continued into 1968 as he began to ready himself

RECORDS AND MILESTONES

World records: 1966 outdoor (17' 5½"), 1966 (17' ¾"), 1967 outdoor (17' 7"), 1968 (17' 9") 1968 indoor (17' 4¼") 1972 (18' 5¾")

Equaled or bettered world outdoor records six times (1966-72)

Set eight world indoor records during his career

Winner, 1973 ABC World Superstars competition

Winner, 1977 ABC World Superstars competition

HONORS AND AWARDS

1966	Dieges Award
1967	*Track and Field News*, Indoor Athlete of the Year
1986	Inducted into National Track and Field Hall of Fame

for the Olympic team. He placed first in seven of nine indoor meets, including the famous Milrose Games in New York, where he extended his own indoor record, vaulting 17 feet 4¼ inches.

Bob enjoyed these victories, but his eye was on Olympic gold and the records held by American Bob Richards, who reigned as an Olympic champion in the 1950's, winning two consecutive gold medals and numerous international championships. After Bob graduated from USC in 1968, the Olympics had his full attention.

In his first Olympic competition in 1968 in Mexico City, Bob won with great flair. Passing up the early competition until the bar had reached 17 feet 6¾ inches, Bob hoped to place psychological pressure on his opponents while avoiding "misses" in his own record.

He made that height easily, but four others did also, including his old friend, John Pennel. When the bar was raised to 17 feet 8½ inches, he missed his first attempt but made his second, as did two competitors from West and East Germany. When the bar was raised another 2 inches, all three finalists failed and Bob was declared the winner on the basis of his fewer misses.

Hoping to repeat his success in the 1972 Olympics, Bob spent the intervening years dueling with other vaulters, extending, losing, and then reclaiming his indoor and outdoor world records. He met disappointment, however, in the Munich Olympics, when the brand of pole he was accustomed to using was banned the night before the competition began. Using a pole that he was not used to, Bob cleared only 17 feet, 8½ inches, good enough for the silver but not the gold.

Bob recovered from the disappointment and eventually became one of the charter members of the short-lived professional track and field organization known as the International Track Association (ITA). In 1973, he won the first-ever World Superstars competition sponsored by the ABC television network, defeating athletes from various professional sports in a variety of decathlon-like events. He repeated as the winner of the Superstars competition in 1977 against an array of American and international sports stars.

After four years of competition, the ITA eventually folded, and Bob pursued a career in acting and as a business executive for a running shoe company. Bob was elected to the National Track and Field Hall of Fame in 1986.

Summary

Although Bob Seagren did not equal Bob Richards's Olympic gold medal success, he more than surpassed Richards in breaking and holding American and international outdoor and indoor pole-vaulting records. He equaled or bettered the world outdoor record six times between 1966 and 1972 and set a world indoor record eight times during his career. He is rightly regarded as one of America's greatest track and field athletes.

Bruce L. Edwards

Additional Sources:

Bateman, Hal. *United States Track and Field Olympians, 1896-1980.* Indianapolis, Ind.: The Athletics Congress of the United States, 1984.

Hickok, Ralph. *A Who's Who of Sports Champions.* Boston: Houghton Mifflin, 1995.

Wallechinsky, David. *The Complete Book of the Olympics.* Boston: Little, Brown and Company, 1991.

Watman, Mel. *Encyclopedia of Track and Field Athletics.* New York: St. Martin's Press, 1981.

TOM SEAVER

Sport: Baseball

Born: November 17, 1944
Fresno, California

Early Life

George Thomas Seaver was born on November 17, 1944, in Fresno, California. Tom began Little League baseball at the age of nine, and at twelve pitched a no-hitter while being the leading hitter for his team. Despite this brilliant beginning, Tom did not grow as fast as his teammates, and soon lacked the size and strength to compete on the basis of sheer talent. To compensate, Tom began the habits that would last a lifetime. He studied the art of pitching and learned every pitch he could to succeed, even though he could not throw as hard or as fast as the other pitchers. Finally, after a period of manual labor and a hitch in the Marine Corps, Tom finally had the size, strength, and knowledge to pursue his dream of a major league career.

The Road to Excellence

At each step of the way, Tom had to prove that he deserved a chance to play major league baseball. He played outstanding baseball at Fresno City College and in an amateur summer league in Alaska to earn a scholarship at the University of Southern California (USC).

At USC, he finally attracted the attention of professional scouts. He was eventually offered a contract by the Atlanta Braves, led by his hero, Hank Aaron, who would eventually break Babe Ruth's home-run record.

Tom was heartbroken when this contract was declared invalid by the commissioner of baseball. Tom had signed the contract after the start of the USC baseball season, not knowing that this was a violation of the rules of both professional and amateur baseball. Tom could not play for the Atlanta Braves, nor could he return to USC, because he had already signed a professional contract. Tom appealed directly to the commissioner of baseball, who agreed to hold a lottery for the rights to sign Tom among any of the teams who would agree to match the original terms of the Atlanta Braves. Tom listened over the telephone as he learned that he had been selected by the New York Mets.

Courtesy of the New York Mets

STATISTICS

Season	GP	GS	CG	IP	HA	BB	SO	W	L	S	ShO	ERA
1967	35	34	18	251.0	224	78	170	16	13	0	2	2.76
1968	36	35	14	278.0	224	48	205	16	12	1	5	2.20
1969	36	35	18	273.1	202	82	208	25	7	0	5	2.21
1970	37	36	19	291.0	230	83	**283**	18	12	0	2	**2.81**
1971	36	35	21	286.0	210	61	**289**	20	10	0	4	**1.76**
1972	35	35	13	262.0	215	77	249	21	12	0	3	2.92
1973	36	36	18	290.0	219	64	**251**	19	10	0	3	**2.08**
1974	32	32	12	236.0	199	75	201	11	11	0	5	3.20
1975	36	36	15	280.0	217	88	**243**	**22**	9	0	5	2.38
1976	35	34	13	271.0	211	77	**235**	14	11	0	5	2.59
1977	33	33	19	261.1	199	66	196	21	6	0	7	2.58
1978	36	36	8	260.0	218	89	226	16	14	0	1	2.87
1979	32	32	9	215.0	187	61	131	16	6	0	**5**	3.14
1980	26	26	5	168.0	140	59	101	10	8	0	1	3.64
1981	23	23	6	166.0	120	66	87	**14**	2	0	1	2.55
1982	21	21	0	111.1	136	44	62	5	13	0	0	5.50
1983	34	34	5	231.0	201	86	135	9	14	0	2	3.55
1984	34	33	10	236.2	216	61	131	15	11	0	4	3.95
1985	35	33	6	238.2	223	69	134	16	11	0	1	3.17
1986	28	28	2	176.1	180	56	103	7	13	0	0	4.03
Totals	656	647	231	4,780.8	3,971	1,390	3,640	311	205	1	61	2.86

Notes: Boldface indicates statistical leader. GP = games played; GS = games started; CG = complete games; IP = innings pitched; HA = hits allowed; BB = bases on balls (walks); SO = strikeouts; W = wins; L = losses; S = saves; ShO = shutouts; ERA = earned run average

The New York Mets represented both a risk and a wonderful opportunity for Tom. The Mets were by far the worst team in baseball every year since they had joined the National League as an expansion team in 1962. The roster was full of young players with talent but without experience and aging veterans long past their prime.

The Emerging Champion

The Mets proved to be Tom's quickest route to the majors. The team desperately needed new quality players and could bring Tom up to the majors as soon as he was ready. After only one season in the minor leagues, Tom Seaver was a New York Met.

Tom earned the nickname "Tom Terrific" in his very first year with the Mets. In 1967, he won sixteen games, pitched in the All-Star game, and was Rookie of the Year for a team that finished dead last and won only sixty-one games. In 1968, he again won sixteen games for a last-place team. That year, he struck out more than 200 batters, which he would do for the next nine years in a row.

In 1969, Tom led the Mets throughout the most improbable season of all. The Mets stunned the world by winning the National East Division,

the playoffs, and the World Series itself. Tom won twenty-five games during the regular season plus key victories in the playoffs and World Series. He was honored with the Cy Young Award as the finest pitcher in the National League.

The exceptional performance continued. Tom routinely won twenty games or more and often led the National League in both strikeouts and earned run average. In 1973, he led the Mets to the second National League pennant in their short history and won the Cy Young Award as the outstanding pitcher in the National League. Following a disappointing season in 1974, he again won the Cy Young in 1975 for a remarkable third time.

Continuing the Story

Tom Seaver had become the symbol of the Mets to most of the baseball world. In 1977, that world was shocked when the Mets traded Tom to the Cincinnati Reds. As a part of the Cincinnati Reds, Tom joined an elite organization with its own proud tradition of winning. In his years with the Reds, Tom pitched the first no-hitter of his professional career in 1978, led the Reds to the National League Western Division title in 1979, and won the National League Comeback Player

HONORS AND AWARDS

1967	National League Rookie of the Year
1967-73, 1975-78, 1981	National League All-Star Team
1969	Associated Press Male Athlete of the Year *Sports Illustrated* Sportsman of the Year *Sporting News* Man of the Year Hickok Belt
1969, 1973, 1975	National League Cy Young Award
1981	National League Comeback Player of the Year
1992	Inducted into National Baseball Hall of Fame Uniform number 41 retired by New York Mets

of the Year award in 1981 with a record of fourteen wins and only two losses in a season delayed and shortened by a players' strike.

Tom Terrific eventually returned to the New York Mets, but only for one year. At the end of the season, the Mets failed to protect him on their roster of major league players, and the Chicago White Sox claimed the talented but aging pitcher. In his years with the White Sox, Tom remained the ace of their pitching staff, consistently winning games as he approached, and passed, his fortieth birthday. He substituted cunning and guile for the pure physical talents he had once possessed. His knowledge of the game and ability to adapt as a pitcher earned him the longevity necessary to win more than three hundred games, strike out more than 3,600 batters, and assure him a place in the National Baseball Hall of Fame.

Tom even left the game a winner. Toward the end of his final season in 1986, he left Chicago to join the Boston Red Sox and helped pitch his final team to the American League pennant and the chance to face, of all teams, the New York Mets in the World Series. Tom was elected to baseball's Hall of Fame in 1992 by an overwhelming majority of 425 out of 430 votes. He finished his career in baseball with a lifetime 2.86 earned run average and in third place on the all-time strikeout leaders list.

Summary

Tom Seaver studied every aspect of the game and its players and adjusted his pitching to remain effective at each level of competition. Tom's success was a function of this never-ending learning and development. His love and knowledge of the game comes through in the six books about baseball he has written, his work as a player, and later, as a sports announcer. Tom Terrific was one of the most perfect students the game has ever known.

Spencer Weber Waller

Additional Sources:

Schlossberg, Dan. "Tom Seaver: Perfection Was His Goal." *Baseball Digest* 58, no. 3 (1999).

Schoor, Gene. *Seaver: A Biography.* Chicago: Contemporary Books, 1986.

Seaver, Tom, with Lee Lowenfish. *The Art of Pitching.* New York: Hearst Books, 1984.

Seaver, Tom, with Herb Resnicow. *Beanball.* New York: Morrow, 1989.

VIC SEIXAS

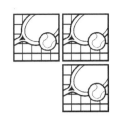

Sport: Tennis

Born: August 30, 1923
Philadelphia, Pennsylvania

Early Life

Elias Victor Seixas, Jr., was born August 30, 1923, in Philadelphia, Pennsylvania. Vic's father, of Portuguese descent, operated a plumbing and heating supply business in Philadelphia.

Although Vic began playing tennis when he was very young, his early life does not much resemble that of most sports champions. After graduation as an honor student from high school, he enlisted in 1942 in the Army Air Force. He served from 1942 to 1946 as a test pilot and flight instructor.

After his discharge from the Air Force, he attended the University of North Carolina, majoring in business administration. He played on the school tennis team and won awards for his combination of scholarship and athletic ability. After his graduation, he joined the family business.

The Road to Excellence

Unlike most outstanding athletes, Vic did not display extraordinary ability when he was very young. Although he played tennis both in school and as a pastime throughout his high school and college years, he did not practice the game with single-minded intensity. Further, he did not come under the wing of a first-rate coach who could have guided him toward success.

Vic's rise to the top was sudden and unexpected. He found that his tennis ability rose dramatically after he was graduated from college. Taking advantage of the change, Vic began to enter important tournaments and soon established himself as a major presence.

Vic Seixas in 1949.

Vic's sudden blossoming, although unusual in its mode, does have an explanation. His quickness and intelligence fitted him for the style of play that came into fashion just after the end of World War II in 1945. During the 1920's, most players tended to remain at the baseline. Long rallies were the order of the day, and the key to success lay in swift and accurate ground strokes.

2509

The new style was different. Pioneered by Jack Kramer, it placed much less emphasis on baseline play. Instead, a player would rush the net following service. He would attempt to put away his opponent's return with a quick volley. Points were scored much more rapidly than before, and the new method proved popular with the fans. Although defenders of the old approach such as Bill Tilden lamented that the skill had gone out of the game, their protests were of no avail. Few players of the immediate post war period had the ground strokes needed to combat the new technique.

Vic and the new style were made for each other. He was very skilled at volleying, and his knowledge of tennis strategy enabled him to place his shots so that returning them was extremely difficult.

The Emerging Champion

Vic entered Wimbledon in 1950, when he was only twenty-seven. Although he did not win the tournament, he aroused wide attention by defeating the great Australian player John Bromwich in the quarterfinals. Vic made the quarterfinals or semifinals of nearly every tournament he entered that year.

In 1951, Vic's game was even better. He reached the finals of the U.S. National Championship at Forest Hills. There, he suffered a setback. He lost in the finals to the Australian Frank Sedgman, who had unusual strength and won the match by overpowering Vic.

Vic was not one to take defeat lightly. He visited Australia in 1951, in preparation for the Davis Cup. He astonished the Australians by defeating Sedgman to win the New South Wales Championship. However, in the Davis Cup challenge round, he again met defeat at the hands of the powerful Australian.

Vic was never able to establish his superiority over the great Australian players of the early 1950's,

who, besides Sedgman, included Ken Rosewall and Lew Hoad. But he usually gave as good as he got, and his record in many years of Davis Cup play was outstanding.

Continuing the Story

The patterns that emerged at the start of Vic's amateur career continued throughout the early 1950's. As he gained more experience, his skill at volleying and his breakneck rushes of the net made him one of the world's best players in the 1950's.

His chief rival in the United States was Tony Trabert, a younger player who eventually supplanted Vic as the best player in the United States. Vic and Trabert played many close matches, and Vic usually held his own. He won the U.S. National Championship in 1954 and Wimbledon in 1953.

Vic did not let his rivalry for singles honors with Trabert stop him from joining his erstwhile foe as a doubles partner. Both of them were highly intelligent and mastered the intricacies of doubles play without difficulty. During the years

MAJOR CHAMPIONSHIP VICTORIES AND FINALS

1951, 1953	U.S. National Championship finalist
1952, 1954	U.S. National Championship doubles (with Mervyn Rose; with Tony Trabert) Wimbledon doubles finalist (with Eric Sturgess; with Trabert)
1953	Wimbledon French Championship mixed doubles (with Doris Hart)
1953-56	U.S. National Championship mixed doubles (with Hart)
1953-56	Wimbledon mixed doubles (with Hart)
1953	French Championship finalist
1954	U.S. National Championship
1954-55	French Championship doubles (with Trabert)
1955	Australian Championship doubles (with Trabert)
1956	U.S. National Championship doubles finalist (with Hamilton Richardson)

OTHER NOTABLE VICTORIES

1949, 1954	U.S. Clay Court Championship doubles (with Sam Match; with Trabert)
1948	U.S. Hardcourt Championship doubles (with Ted Schroeder)
1952, 1954, 1957	Pacific Southwest Championship
1953	Italian Championship mixed doubles (with Hart)
1953, 1957	U.S. Clay Court Championship
1954	On winning U.S. Davis Cup team
1955, 1956	U.S. Indoor Championship doubles (with Trabert; with Sam Giammalva)
1976	Grand Masters Championship doubles (with Rex Hartwig)

HONORS, AWARDS, AND MILESTONES

1948	William M. Johnston Award
1951, 1954, 1957	Nationally ranked number one
1951-57	U.S. Davis Cup team
1952, 1964	U.S. Davis Cup team captain
1971	Inducted into National Lawn Tennis Hall of Fame

of their partnership, they established themselves as the world's best doubles team.

Their duals with the Australians were especially notable. Had it not been for Vic and Tony, the Australians would have been unstoppable during the early 1950's. Instead, Vic's volleying skill, quickness, and intelligence often enabled him to triumph over the physically stronger and more naturally gifted Australians.

Vic did not become a professional player; he continued his business career when his playing days were over.

Summary

Vic Seixas was one of several outstanding American players in the early 1950's, including Bill Talbert, Budge Patty, and Tony Trabert. He was definitely not a standard-model athlete. He became an outstanding player only after graduation from college and had as a youth played tennis just as a hobby. His quickness and volleying technique secured his rapid rise to the top, and he ranked as one of the world's best players in the early 1950's, in both singles and doubles.

Bill Delaney

Additional Sources:

Collins, Bud, and Zander Hollander, eds. *Bud Collins' Modern Encyclopedia of Tennis*. 3d ed. Detroit: Gale, 1997.

Grimsley, Will. *Tennis: Its History, People, and Events*. Englewood Cliffs, N.J.: Prentice-Hall, 1971.

Seixas, Vic, and Joel H. Cohen. *Prime Time Tennis*. New York: Charles Scribner's Sons, 1983.

MONICA SELES

Sport: Tennis

Born: December 2, 1973
Novi Sad, Yugoslavia

Early Life

Monica Seles was born on December 2, 1973, in Novi Sad, Yugoslavia. She is the daughter of Karolj and Esther Seles. Karolj has worked as a newspaper cartoonist and television director, while Esther has worked as a computer programmer. Monica has an older brother, Zoltan. Karolj gave Monica her first tennis racket when she was six years old. She played for a few weeks, but then she lost interest and stopped.

It was not until Zoltan won the Yugoslav junior championship two years later that Monica decided to play again. To encourage her not to lose interest, Karolj drew Monica's favorite cartoon characters—Tom and Jerry—on tennis balls. She would hit the balls as hard as she could. Her father would also put stuffed animals on the tennis court at which Monica could aim.

The Road to Excellence

Monica won the Yugoslav twelve-and-under championship when she was nine years old. While ten years old, in 1984, she won the European twelve-and-under championship, in Paris. Monica was named Yugoslavian Sportswoman of the Year in 1985 when she was merely eleven years old. She was the first individual under the age of eighteen to win this prestigious award. In the same year, Monica competed in the Orange Bowl twelve-and-under tournament, which is held in Miami, Florida. While there, she was spotted by the respected tennis coach Nick Bollettieri. Monica won the tournament, and Bollettieri was so impressed with this small girl who could hit the ball hard with two-handed shots on either side that he offered her a full scholarship to his Nick Bollettieri Tennis Academy in Bradenton, Florida.

Monica and her brother, Zoltan, moved to Bradenton in 1986. Her parents left their jobs, closed their two Novi Sad homes and their country vacation home, and moved to Bradenton to

Monica Seles volleys during the 1997 French Open.

concentrate on Monica's promising career. Always a perfectionist, Monica began practicing six hours a day. She was determined to be the best. It was hard for her and her family to adjust to life in Florida, but every member of the family was focused on helping Monica succeed, so the cultural shock of living in a new country became merely a minor challenge.

Karolj, Zoltan, and Bollettieri all played a part in molding Monica into a complete tennis player. Her father would concentrate on drills, while her brother would hit with her. Strategy was left to Bollettieri. Monica is left-handed, but she hits two-handed shots on both the forehand and backhand sides, which makes it necessary for her to be very quick so as to reach wide shots. She also would attempt to put the ball away as quickly as possible so as to avoid having to run down shots constantly. The harder Monica would hit the ball, the louder she would grunt. Grunting became a trademark of Monica's tennis game.

The Emerging Champion

Monica did not play any junior tournaments during this time at the tennis academy. It was decided to keep her unique style of play out of the public eye. That was difficult to do at the academy because of the number of children who either were visiting or who were part of a tennis program there. The Seles family wanted Monica to have complete privacy, whereas Bollettieri wanted to publicize his star pupil. Monica finally played in her first professional event in 1988. She won her first match in March of 1988 at the Virginia Slims of Florida, where she upset Helen Kelesi. The best result Monica had for the year was at a tournament in New Orleans. She reached the semifinals of the tournament by defeating Lori McNeil. Monica may not have won many matches yet, but she did serve notice to the tennis world that she was serious about her game and that in the very near future she would be winning more often than she would be losing.

Monica turned professional in February, 1989. She was finally ready to compete against the best in the game and not feel overmatched. Monica believed in hard work and was determined not to settle for being merely good; she was working toward being great. In 1989, Monica made solid strides toward the top of women's ten-

MAJOR CHAMPIONSHIP VICTORIES AND FINALS	
1990-92	French Open
1991-92	U.S. Open
1991-93, 1996	Australian Open
1992	Wimbledon finalist
1995-96	U.S. Open finalist
1998	French Open finalist

OTHER NOTABLE VICTORIES	
1989	Virginia Slims of Houston
1990	U.S. Hardcourt Championship German Open Lufthansa Cup
1990-91, 1997	Virginia Slims of Los Angeles
1990-92	Virginia Slims Championship
1990, 2000	Italian Open
1995-98	Canadian Open
1999-2000	Amelia Island
2000	Bronze Medal, Olympic women's tennis singles

nis. She won her first tournament at the Virginia Slims of Houston, where she defeated Chris Evert 3-6, 6-1, 6-4 in the final. At this tournament, Monica became the youngest player to reach the final of a Virginia Slims event.

Her best showing in a Grand Slam tournament was at the French Open, where she reached the semifinals. Monica took Steffi Graf to a third set before succumbing 6-3 in the final set. In the other Grand Slam events which she entered (Wimbledon and the U.S. Open), Monica reached the fourth round. By the end of the year, she had achieved a ranking of number six in the world, and she had grown to a height of 5 feet 9 inches. Monica had to practice even harder now so as to adjust her game to her added height.

Continuing the Story

Monica should have entered 1990 confident that it was merely a matter of time before she would win a major title, but growing so much made her struggle with her game in the early part of the year. Tension was also growing between Bollettieri and the Seleses. By March, though, her game was in fine form when she defeated Judith Wiesner 6-1, 6-2 to capture the Lipton International Players Championship. Soon after the tournament, the Seles family packed up and left the tennis academy for good. Monica won some important championships during the rest of the year, including the U.S. Hardcourt Championship, the Italian Open, the Virginia Slims Championship, and—most important of all—the French Open. She defeated Graf 7-6, 6-4 at the French Open in June to win her first Grand Slam singles title. Because of her strong play during the year, Monica was named by *Tennis* magazine as the Most Improved Player.

Monica tried her best to become Americanized. She modeled in such magazines as *Vogue, Seventeen,* and *Elle.* Being in the public eye at such a young age forced her to grow up rapidly. Under the circumstances, Monica matured in a remarkably graceful manner. Tennis remained the center of her world, though, and she finally made it to number one in the rankings after winning the 1991 Australian and French Opens.

After capturing the first two Grand Slam championships of the year, there was talk of Monica's possibly becoming the first player to win all four Grand Slam titles in a single year since Graf did it in 1988. However, Monica withdrew at the last minute from Wimbledon and went into seclusion. There were a number of ru-

mors concerning her physical condition, and experts and fans alike were puzzled by her behavior. A statement was finally issued in July, 1991, which said that "shin splints and a slight stress fracture" in her left leg had forced her to bow out of Wimbledon. Monica did recover from her injury, and she captured her third Grand Slam title of 1991 by defeating Martina Navratilova 7-6, 6-1 in the final of the U.S. Open.

During the early 1990's, Monica was a dominant force in women's tennis. She won three French Open singles titles in a row (1990-1992), three Australian Open singles titles in a row (1991-1993), and two U.S. Open singles titles in a row (1991-1992). In 1993, she was tragically stabbed in the back during the changeover of a tennis match in Hamburg, Germany, by an irate spectator. It would not be until 1995 that Monica felt physically and psychologically ready to compete again on the court. In 1996, she came back to win the Grand Slam singles title at the Australian Open. She was a finalist at the 1995 and 1996 U.S. Open and a finalist at the 1998 French Open.

Summary

Monica Seles, in a very short time, rose to the top of women's tennis. With her talent and strong work ethic, she became a powerful force in the game. Monica was one of the most important tennis stars of the 1990's.

Michael Jeffrys

HONORS, AWARDS, AND MILESTONES

1985, 1989	Yugoslavian Sportswoman of the Year
1989	Rolex Rookie of the Year
1990	*Tennis* magazine Most Improved Player
1991	Ranked number one in the world
1991-92	WTA Player of the Year Associated Press (AP) Female Athlete of the Year United Press International (UPI) International Athlete of the Year
1995-96, 1998-00	Federation Cup team
1995	*Tennis* magazine Comeback Player of the Year
1995, 1998	WTA Tour Comeback Player of the Year
2000	Flo Hyman Award

Additional Sources:

Layden, Joseph. *Return of a Champion: The Monica Seles Story.* New York: St. Martin's, 1996.

Rutledge, Rachel. *The Best of the Best in Tennis.* Brookfield, Conn.: Millbrook Press, 1998.

Schwabacher, Martin. "Monica Seles." In *Superstars of Women's Tennis.* Philadelphia: Chelsea House, 1997.

Seles, Monica, with Nancy Ann Richardson. *Monica: From Fear to Victory.* New York: HarperCollins, 1996.

FRANK SELVY

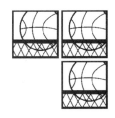

Sport: Basketball

Born: November 9, 1932
Corbin, Kentucky

Early Life

Franklin Delano (Frank) Selvy was born in Corbin, Kentucky, on November 9, 1932. He was named for Franklin Delano Roosevelt, who was inaugurated as president of the United States on the same day Frank was born. Frank was the third of seven children. His father was a coal miner and city worker. Young Frank grew up in the tough coal mining areas of south central Kentucky.

The Road to Excellence

Frank did not make his high school team as a freshman because he was considered too small. He persevered, however, and finally made the varsity as a junior. By the end of his senior year, he had grown to an even 6 feet tall. He was then chosen to play in a state All-Star game in which he played well against taller opponents. Yet because he had played at a smaller high school and was only of average height, he was ignored by recruiters from major colleges and universities, including the legendary University of Kentucky coach, Adolph Rupp. Consequently, Frank enrolled at Furman College in Greenville, South Carolina.

There he attracted national attention as a high-scoring guard. In his sophomore year, he starred in a memorable 73-72 upset of mighty Duke University. He scored 36 points in that game, half the total of the entire Duke team. In his junior year, he was a consensus National Collegiate Athletic Association (NCAA) Division I second-team All-American. That year, he scored 738 points for an average of 29.5 points per game. In his senior year, he was a consensus NCAA Division I first-team All-American. That year he scored more than 1,200 points with an incredible 41.7-points-per-game average.

In his greatest game, he scored 100 points against Newberry College, on February 13, 1954. This game was the first-ever televised game throughout South Carolina. Frank was playing before friends from his hometown of Corbin, Kentucky. His parents also were there. It was the only time they ever saw him play as a collegian or a professional. He scored 24 points in the first quarter of this game, 13 in the second quarter,

Basketball great Frank Selvy during his senior season at Furman University in 1954.

AP/Wide World Photos

STATISTICS

Season	GP	FGM	FG%	FTM	FT%	Reb.	Ast.	TP	PPG
1954-55	71	452	.378	444	.728	394	245	1,348	19.0
1955-56	17	67	.366	53	.746	54	35	187	11.0
1957-58	38	44	.263	47	.610	88	35	135	3.6
1958-59	68	233	.385	201	.767	248	96	667	9.8
1959-60	62	205	.393	153	.736	175	111	563	9.1
1960-61	77	311	.405	210	.727	301	246	832	10.8
1961-62	79	433	.420	298	.738	412	381	1,164	14.7
1962-63	80	317	.424	192	.714	288	281	826	10.3
1963-64	73	160	.378	78	.639	149	149	398	5.5
Totals	565	2,222	.394	1,676	.725	2,109	1,579	6,120	10.8

Notes: GP = games played; FGM = field goals made; FG% = field goal percentage; FTM = free throws made; FT% = free throw percentage; Reb. = rebounds; Ast. = assists; TP = total points; PPG = points per game

25 more points in the third quarter, and an unbelievable 38 points in the final quarter. His final 10 points came with less than 10 seconds to go in the game and his last points came from a shot from midcourt. Furman won the game 149-95. When Frank reflected on that game in 2000, he pointed out that he was much prouder of the victories he helped produce at Furman than of the 100 points he scored in one game.

Frank had other high-scoring games, including 63 points against Mercer College, 30 points against the University of South Carolina, and 42 points against Manhattan College. The latter game, in 1954, earned him the Metropolitan New York Basketball Writers Award as the outstanding college player to play in New York that season. When Frank left Furman after the 1954 season, he held twenty-four major college records and had scored 50 points or more on eight different occasions. During the 1953-1954 campaign, he had averaged an amazing 41.3 points per game. He is a member of the Furman Hall of Fame and the South Carolina Hall of Fame and was selected as a member of the Southern Conference's seventy-five-year anniversary team. In the mid-1990's, Frank was selected as one of the top one hundred players in NCAA history.

The Emerging Champion

Frank had grown to be 6 feet 3 inches tall and 180 pounds by the end of his college career. He could shoot layups with either hand and had a deadly hook shot. He also excelled on drives to the basket. He was best known for his one-

handed jump shot from outside the foul circle. Going straight up and holding the ball at arm's length, he would deliver the shot at the peak of his jump. Sometimes he would fake the shot and drive to the basket when his opponent left his feet. His jump shot was considered to be virtually unstoppable. With his fakes and hesitation moves, he drew many fouls from his opponents, and he was an outstanding free-throw shooter.

With such skills, Frank became one of the legendary scorers in major college basketball. In three varsity seasons, he scored 2,538 points for a 32.5-points-per-game average. He was the NCAA Division I scoring champion in 1953 and again in 1954. He was also the first player in NCAA Division I college basketball to score more than 1,000 points in a season (1953-1954), and he was the first to reach 2,000 points in a three-season career. Often overlooked was his 1953-1954 perfor-

NCAA DIVISION I RECORDS

Most free throws made in a season, 355 (1953-54)
Most points in a game, 100 (1954)
Most field goals in a game, 41 (1954)

HONORS AND AWARDS

1953-54	Consensus All-American
1954	Metropolitan New York Basketball Writers Award Overall first choice in the NBA draft
1955, 1961	NBA All-Star Team
1998	Named one of the top 100 players in NCAA history

mance of a record 355 free-throw points on a record 444 attempts. In his famous 100-point game, he scored on 41 field goals in 66 attempts for a 62.1 percent shooting average.

Frank was an honors student at Furman and received his degree in 1954. He was also a recognized leader on campus. He was active in many campus organizations and was a platoon leader and First Lieutenant in the college Reserve Officers' Training Corps program. He was also elected president of his senior class.

Continuing the Story

Frank was the first player chosen in the 1954 National Basketball Association (NBA) draft. When the Baltimore franchise folded in the fall of 1954, he was sent to Milwaukee, where he averaged 19.0 points per game in his rookie season. The franchise was then moved to St. Louis in 1955. Frank played there briefly before going into the armed services. He returned to St. Louis late in the 1957-1958 season. He was then traded to New York for the 1958-1959 season and moved on to the Syracuse-Minnesota team in 1959. Finally, in 1960 he joined the Los Angeles Lakers, where he played for the remainder of his professional career. Teamed in the Laker's backcourt with the famous Jerry West, Frank had his greatest season as a professional in 1961-1962, when he scored 1,164 points for a 14.7-points-per-game average. He also scored an additional 589 points in fifty-two playoff games (an 11.3-points-per-game average). He was selected to play in both the 1955 and 1961 NBA All-Star games. Before he retired after the 1963-1964 season, he had scored a total of 6,709 points as a professional in 617 regular season and playoff games.

Upon his retirement, he went into business in Greenville, South Carolina. When Wilt Chamberlain passed away in 1999, many writers recalled Chamberlain's 100-point game in the NBA, and in retrospect, Frank's 100-point collegiate game. When asked about Chamberlain's performance, Frank recalled one night when he shocked Chamberlain. The Lakers were playing Philadelphia, and Chamberlain and Frank were matched up for a jump ball. The 7-foot 1-inch Chamberlain did not think that Frank would even attempt jumping, so he stood still. To Chamberlain's surprise, Frank jumped and won the tap.

In 2000, a contest was held to select the greatest moments in the history of the Los Angeles Lakers. One of those moments involved Frank— the seventh game of the 1962 NBA championship series with the Boston Celtics. The Lakers had come back in the last minute of play to tie the score with 2 clutch field goals by Frank. He then took a memorable last-second shot that missed. Had he made that one, the Lakers would have claimed their first league title since moving to Los Angeles. The miss allowed the Boston Celtics to win an overtime victory for its fourth straight NBA title. Unfortunately, Frank is still labeled as the Bill Buckner of NBA championship play.

Summary

Frank Selvy is best known as the first NCAA Division I college basketball player to score 100 points in a game, the first to score more than 1,000 points in a season, and the first to score 2,000 points in a three-season career. At one time, he held twenty-one different individual scoring records as a collegiate player. He was never the dominating player in the NBA that he had been in college, but he is always remembered as a hardworking, steady, consistent team player who was not afraid to take his shot in crucial games. Popular with fellow students and his teammates, the handsome athlete parlayed his fame as a star basketball player into a later successful career in public relations.

Daniel R. Gilbert

Additional Sources:

Bjarkman, Peter C. *The Biographical History of Basketball.* Chicago: Masters Press, 1998.

Gutman, Bill. *The History of NCAA Basketball.* New York: Crescent Books, 1993.

Lace, William W. *The Los Angeles Lakers Basketball Team.* Berkeley Heights, N.J.: Enslow, 1998.

Thornley, Stew. *Basketball's Original Dynasty: The History of the Lakers.* Minneapolis, Minn.: Nodin Press, 1989.

AYRTON SENNA

Sport: Auto racing

Born: March 21, 1960
  São Paulo, Brazil
Died: May 1, 1994
  Bologna, Italy

Early Life

Ayrton Senna da Silva was born on March 21, 1960, in São Paulo, Brazil. He was the oldest son

Racer Ayrton Senna after winning the Monaco Formula One Grand Prix in 1992.

of Milton da Silva, a well-to-do São Paulo businessman. Ayrton grew up in a loving family environment. At the age of four, his father built him his first go-kart. When Ayrton started school, his father let it be known that if Ayrton did not have good monthly school reports, then he would not be allowed to use the go-kart for a month.

In July, 1973, Ayrton made his debut in his first go-kart race. He started in the 100-cubic-centimeter category. After racing in that category for several years, Ayrton decided that it was time to contend for the Kart World Championship. In 1977, the championship was held at Le Mans, France, and Ayrton finished a respectable sixth. He finished second in 1979 and 1980 and fourth in 1981. During his years of go-kart racing, Ayrton won the South American Championship twice (in 1977 and 1978) and the Brazilian Championship four times (in 1978, 1979, 1980, and 1981).

The Road to Excellence

After eight years of go-kart racing, Ayrton decided that it was time for him to try his hand at auto racing. Ayrton was a shy young man, but he was brimming with determination. In March, 1981, he competed in his first British Formula Ford 1600 car race, driving a Van Diemen RF80-Ford. His previous go-kart experience held him in good stead, and Ayrton had his first win in only his third race. By the end of the Formula Ford season, he had won twelve of his twenty races.

For all of his talent on the track, however, Ayrton was having difficulty understanding how the racing business functioned. It was necessary for him to find financing if he was to advance to more competitive circuits. Moreover, his marriage to his childhood

GRAND PRIX VICTORIES

1985	Portuguese Grand Prix
1985, 1988-91	Belgian Grand Prix
1986-88	Detroit Grand Prix
1986, 1989	Spanish Grand Prix
1987, 1989-93	Monaco Grand Prix
1988-89, 1991	San Marino Grand Prix
1988-90	German Grand Prix
1988, 1990	Canadian Grand Prix
1988, 1991-92	Hungarian Grand Prix
1988, 1993	British Grand Prix Japanese Grand Prix
1989	Mexican Grand Prix
1990-91	U.S. Grand Prix
1990, 1992	Italian Grand Prix
1991, 1993	Australian Grand Prix Brazilian Grand Prix

sweetheart, Liliane, was damaged by his racing frustrations. By the time the 1982 racing season began, Ayrton had overcome his doubts about continuing to race and had found the necessary funding, but his marriage was dissolved after only six months.

In 1982, Ayrton began racing in Formula Ford 2000 races, driving a Van Diemen RF82-Ford for Rushen Green Racing. He competed in both the British and European races, entering twenty-seven and winning twenty-one. Ayrton was graduated to British Formula Three races for the next season, driving for West Surrey Racing in a Ralt RT3-Toyota. Ayrton won the first nine races of the season and a total of 12 rounds of the British Formula Three Championship on his way to dethroning titleholder Martin Brundle. Racing experts were amazed by Ayrton's racing talent, as well as by his complete refusal to accept anything less than victory.

The Emerging Champion

With his Formula Three exploits, Ayrton had impressed various sponsors who wanted him to race for them in the top level of Formula One racing. After much thought, Ayrton decided to team up with Toleman Group Motorsport. He drove in his first Formula One competition on

March 25, 1984, at the Brazilian Grand Prix in Rio de Janeiro, driving a Toleman TG183B-Hart. Although Ayrton did not win a Grand Prix race during the 1984 season, he impressed larger and wealthier racing teams. Ayrton could not resist the chance to join John Player Team Lotus for the 1985 season, since Lotus could afford more sophisticated equipment. Driving a Lotus 97T-Renault, Ayrton won his first Grand Prix race in Portugal on April 21, 1985.

Ayrton's first year with Team Lotus was relatively successful; he won two races and finished fourth in Formula One world championship points. Ayrton, though, was disappointed with the results. He made it clear that for next season he was to be Team Lotus's number-one driver. Ayrton finished fourth again in world championship points in 1986 and third in 1987, however, and he came to the conclusion that he was never going to contend for the world championship unless he changed teams. For 1988, Ayrton joined the Honda Marlboro McLaren team. Alain Prost, a former world champion, also drove for McLaren, but Ayrton nevertheless captured his first Formula One championship by winning eight of the sixteen Grand Prix in which he was entered.

Continuing the Story

Ayrton and Prost were once again teammates for the 1989 season. Both were intense competitors, and relations between the two were not always civil. Ayrton was always an aggressive driver, and his racing tactics were sometimes questioned by those with whom he competed. In 1989, Prost won the championship, and Ayrton finished second. Prost was well liked by the media, whereas Ayrton had no interest in talking to the press. A deeply religious man, he remained close to his family and guarded his privacy. All of his energy was funneled into his racing. Ayrton found little or no time for the added commitments that came with being a world champion driver.

In 1990, Prost left the McLaren team and joined Ferrari. The two drivers again contended for the championship, but this time Ayrton won the title, and Prost had to settle for second place. Ayrton won his third world championship in 1991, while Prost finished a distant fifth. Nigel

HONORS AND AWARDS

1988, 1990-91	World Championship of Drivers
1994	Brazilian Grand Cross of Merit

Mansell captured the title in 1992, and Prost came back to win it in 1993, with Ayrton finishing second.

After the 1993 season, Prost announced his retirement; moreover, Mansell had left the Formula One circuit to race Indy cars. Ayrton was thus the odds-on favorite for the 1994 title. Early in the 1994 season, however, Ayrton was leading the field at the San Marino Grand Prix when his car left the course at full speed and crashed into a concrete wall. He was rushed to a nearby hospital, but his injuries were severe, and he was pronounced dead hours after the accident. The Brazilian government declared three days of national mourning in his honor, and hundreds of thousands of fans attended his funeral services in São Paulo. Even his most bitter rivals mourned him publicly, conceding that he had been one of the top drivers in Formula One history. His career total of forty-one Formula One victories left him second only to Prost.

Summary

Ayrton Senna combined remarkable racing technique with a fiery spirit to reach the top of Formula One competition. His untimely death was a major loss to auto racing.

Jeffry Jensen

Additional Sources:

Henry, Alan. *Ayrton Senna: One Year On.* Osceola, Wis.: Motorbooks International, 1995.

Hilton, Christopher. *Ayrton Senna: As Time Goes By.* Newbury Park, Calif.: Haynes, 1999.

_____. *Ayrton Senna: His Full Car Racing Record.* Sparkford, England: Patrick Stephens, 1995.

Rayment, Tim, Peter Windsor, and Steve Spence. "What Killed Ayrton Senna?" *Car and Driver* 43, no. 1 (July, 1997): 128-135.

Senna, Ayrton. *Ayrton Senna's Principles of Race Driving.* Osceola, Wis.: Motorbooks International, 1993.

BORIS SHAKHLIN

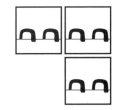

Sport: Gymnastics

Born: January 27, 1932
Ishim, U.S.S.R. (now
Russia)

Early Life

Boris Anfiyanovich Shakhlin was born on January 27, 1932, in the town of Ishim in central Russia. He began gymnastics training at the Sverdovsk Physical Training Technical College, and went from there to the Kiev Institute of Physical Culture, where he trained under A. S. Mishanov.

Boris entered his first international competition in 1954 at the age of twenty-two. It was the World Championships in Rome, Italy, and Boris tied for fourth in the all-around event in a Soviet sweep of the first five places. He found himself on an amazingly strong team a few years after Soviet gymnasts had burst upon the international scene in the 1952 Olympics. It was anyone's guess which of the young gymnasts would ultimately challenge and inherit the supremacy of teammate and Olympic all-around champion Victor Tchoukarine.

A year after his respectable showing in Rome, in 1955 at the age of twenty-three, Boris was graduated from the Kiev Institute with the title of Honored Master of the Sport. That same year, at the European Championships in Frankfurt, West Germany, against a reduced field marked by the absence of Tchoukarine and fellow Soviet Yuri Titov, Boris was commanding. He took gold medals in the all-around competition as well as three individual events, with a silver in a fourth.

Russia's Boris Shakhlin performs on the rings during the European Artistic Gymnastic Championships in 1955.

The Road to Excellence

Boris was a gymnast characterized less by style and grace than by strength and precision. At 5 feet 7½ inches and 154 pounds, he was relatively large and solid for a male gymnast, especially when compared to the diminutive Japanese male gymnasts of the following decades. Like Tchoukarine, Boris depended on stillness and brute muscle in his routines, aiming rather for a series of stark images than for an organically flowing sequence. It is not surprising that his weakest event was the floor exercise, the only one in which he failed to gain a single medal in international competition during his entire career. A hard thinker who valued analyzing the structure and logic of moves, Boris approached his training sessions as if they were the real international competitions, and his strength and tenacity earned him the nickname "Shakhlin the Steel One."

Boris's performance at his first Olympics, the 1956 Games in Melbourne, Australia, was impressive. He was in direct competition with a strong Soviet team, Tchoukarine's dominance was clear, and the Japanese had improved tremendously since their return to international competition in Helsinki in 1952. Although Boris

placed eighth in the all-around, his solid and dexterous work on the pommel horse earned him his first Olympic gold medal, an experience he relished and was determined to repeat.

The Emerging Champion

Boris did not attend the 1957 European Championships in Paris, but he was prepared to succeed the retired Tchoukarine the following year at the World Championships in Moscow. At the age of twenty-six, he was at his peak; he had developed technical expertise but still retained the youthful energy necessary for the sport. He dominated in Moscow, taking four gold medals, including the all-around, and leading the Soviets to a team title. His five of eight possible medals set a record for World Championship competition.

By 1960, Boris was considered the world's best gymnast, and his performance at the 1960 Olympics in Rome confirmed that assessment. He took first place in the all-around, vault, parallel bars, and pommel horse and second in rings (though his all-around victory was by a slight .05-point margin over Takashi Ono of Japan). On the horizontal bar, one of Boris's leather hand guards broke, but he did not stop; dismounting with a bloody palm, he nevertheless took third in the event. Counting the team title, Boris won a total of seven medals—an Olympic record that would not be matched until the American Mark Spitz won seven swimming medals in 1972, and not broken until Soviet gymnast Alexander Dityatin won eight (of a possible eight) medals in 1980.

Boris was a member of the Soviet national team that toured the United States in early 1961, performing at meets and exhibitions in the Northeast and Midwest. As he headed toward and beyond his thirtieth birthday, though, it was inevitable that younger men would surpass him in international competition. Still, he took third in the all-around at the 1962 World Championships in

STATISTICS

Year	Competition	Event	Place	Event	Place
1954	World Championships	All-Around	4th	Pommel horse	4th
		Horizontal bar	2d	Team	1st
1955	European Championships	All-Around	1st	Pommel horse	1st
		Horizontal bar	1st	Rings	2d
		Parallel bars	1st		
1956	Olympic Games	All-Around	8th	Vault	4th
		Pommel horse	Gold	Team	Gold
1958	World Championships	All-Around	1st	Pommel horse	1st
		Horizontal bar	1st	Vault	6th
		Parallel bars	1st	Team	1st
1960	Olympic Games	All-Around	Gold	Rings	Silver
		Horizontal bar	Bronze	Vault	Gold
		Parallel bars	Gold	Team	Silver
		Pommel horse	Gold		
1962	World Championships	All-Around	3d	Rings	2d
		Parallel bars	2d	Vault	3d
		Pommel horse	2d	Team	2d
1963	European Championships	All-Around	2d	Pommel horse	3d
		Horizontal bar	1st	Rings	1st
		Parallel bars	2d	Vault	5th
1964	Olympic Games	All-Around	Silver	Vault	5th
		Horizontal bar	Gold	Team	Silver
		Rings	Bronze		
1966	World Championship	All-Around	18th	Team	2d

Prague, Czechoslovakia, placing in four events but losing the gold in the pommel horse to Yugoslav gymnast Miroslav Cerar on a contested score; and he took second all-around again at the 1963 European Championships in Belgrade, Yugoslavia, tying for gold medals in the rings and horizontal bar. At his third Olympic Games, in Tokyo, Japan, in 1964, Boris was still the man to beat, and he tied for second in the all-around, with a gold medal on the horizontal bars.

Continuing the Story

At the 1966 World Championships in Dortmund, West Germany, twelve years after his international debut, Boris's skills were clearly waning. He was eclipsed by the Japanese gymnasts—Olympic champion Yukio Endo, Akinori Nakayama, and Shuji Tsurumi—and by his teammate Mikhail Voronin. At the ripe age of thirty-four, he failed to reach the finals in any of the events. Following the tournament, he decided to end his illustrious competitive career. In February of 1967, at the Soviet National Championships, Boris retired in a ceremony marked by flowers, gifts, speeches, and a tearful farewell from the "Steel One."

Boris remained very involved in international gymnastics after his retirement. He lived in Kiev, where he served as a city councilor and was, in 1964, admitted to the Soviet Communist Party. He became an international gymnastics official shortly after his retirement, and in 1973 published a book entitled *Moia gimnastika* (my gymnastics). He was a member of the Technical Committee of the International Gymnastics Federation through the 1970's and 1980's, and was involved in the scoring controversies of the 1976 Montreal Olympics.

RECORDS
One of only two male gymnasts to win six individual gold medals in the Olympic Games (seven gold medals overall)
Set a world record for the most medals won in a single Olympiad, 7 (1960)

HONORS AND AWARDS	
1957	Decorated with the Order of Lenin
1965	Awarded the Badge of Honor

Summary

With the strength and poise of a classical gymnast, Boris Shakhlin assumed a position of supremacy for more than a decade in the enduring Soviet dynasty of world-class gymnasts. He was one of a select group of individuals to win titles in three successive Olympics, and his diligence and technical precision set a solid example for champions to come.

Barry Mann

Additional Sources:

"Boris Shakhlin (USSR)." GYMN. http://www.gymn-forum.com/bios/shakhlin_1.html. May 4, 2000.

Haycock, Kate. *Gymnastics.* New York: Crestwood House, 1991.

"Shakhlin, Boris Anfiyanovich." Britannica.com. http://www.britannica.com. 1999.

BILL SHARMAN

Sport: Basketball

Born: May 25, 1926
Abilene, Texas

Early Life

William Walton Sharman was born on May 25, 1926, in Abilene, Texas. When he was just a few years old, Bill's family moved to California, where he grew up.

It did not take Bill long to make friends in his new environment. Even at a very young age, he was a talented and versatile athlete, able to play almost any sport well.

Bill Sharman in 1956.

AP/Wide World Photos

Baseball was originally his favorite, and Bill even spent some time in the major leagues after graduating from college. When he and his father nailed a backboard up on the garage at his home, however, Bill became hooked on that game as well.

The Road to Excellence

In high school, Bill continued to do well in sports, earning varsity letters in track, tennis, football, baseball, and basketball.

He earned a scholarship to the University of Southern California (USC), where he continued to play basketball and baseball with almost equal skill. In basketball, his scoring average increased each year, and he scored more than 18 points per game in his senior year and was named All-American.

After his brief attempt at professional baseball—he could never break in to stay with the talent-rich Dodger teams in the early 1950's—Bill joined the ranks of professional basketball.

Upon joining the Boston Celtics in 1951, Bill teamed with legendary ball handler Bob Cousy to form one of the top backcourts in history. Bill realized that Cousy was the star playmaker and ball handler, so he made himself into one of the great shooters of his day.

After his first season in Boston, Bill averaged at least 16 points per game every season he played until his retirement, in 1961, from the National Basketball Association (NBA). He spent his final professional season as a player in the American Basketball League.

Bill Sharman and Cousy formed a potent pair in the Celtics' backcourt, but the team did not begin to make history and win championships until center Bill Russell came along in the fall of 1956. Before he was finished, Bill Sharman would play on four championship teams with the Celtics.

2524

STATISTICS

Season	GP	FGM	FG%	FTM	FT%	Reb.	Ast.	TP	PPG
1950-51	31	141	.391	96	.889	96	39	378	12.2
1951-52	63	244	.389	183	.859	221	151	671	10.7
1952-53	71	403	.436	341	**.850**	288	191	1,147	16.2
1953-54	72	412	.450	331	**.844**	255	229	1,155	16.0
1954-55	68	453	.427	347	**.897**	302	280	1,253	18.4
1955-56	72	538	.438	358	**.867**	259	339	1,434	19.9
1956-57	67	516	.416	381	**.905**	286	236	1,413	21.1
1957-58	63	550	.424	302	.893	295	167	1,402	22.3
1958-59	72	562	.408	342	**.932**	292	179	1,466	20.4
1959-60	71	559	.456	252	.866	262	144	1,370	19.3
1960-61	61	383	.422	210	**.921**	223	146	976	16.0
Totals	711	4,761	.426	3,143	.883	2,779	2,101	12,665	17.8

Notes: Boldface indicates statistical leader. GP = games played; FGM = field goals made; FG% = field goal percentage; FTM = free throws made; FT% = free throw percentage; Reb. = rebounds; Ast. = assists; TP = total points; PPG = points per game

The Emerging Champion

As his career progressed, Bill became the kind of shooter other players and coaches could only marvel at. His particular skill was simply a matter of dedication, concentration, and continual practice. Bill would often go out to the arena by himself, hours before the game was scheduled to start, and shoot baskets, making sure that his touch and accuracy were perfect.

Nowhere did this dedication and attention to detail show up better than at the foul line. In basketball, such shots are known as free throws, although Bill wanted to earn every point possible at the line.

Seven times he led the NBA in foul shooting, three times topping 90 percent for a season. His career percentage was 88 percent, ranking among the top ten in the game's history.

Bill was an eight-time All-Star and was selected for the team commemorating the first twenty-five years of the NBA in 1970. Five years later, he was voted into the Hall of Fame.

Continuing the Story

Even with all of his accomplishments, Bill Sharman was not finished with basketball. Whereas others might have been content with such an illustrious career, Bill kept pushing. For the 1961-1962 season, Bill served as the player-coach of the Los Angeles Jets of the American Basketball League (ABL). In nineteen games, Bill averaged 5.6 points per game. When the franchise folded, he took over as the head coach of the Cleveland

Pipers and guided them to an ABL championship. After the ABL folded, Bill moved to the collegiate level and became the head coach of California State University, Los Angeles. Compiling a 27-20 record over two seasons, Bill moved on to sports broadcasting for two years.

Bill's first NBA coaching job was with the San Francisco (now Golden State) Warriors. He guided the Warriors to the playoffs in his only two seasons with the club, taking the team all the way to the finals in his first season.

In San Francisco, Bill also helped groom future Hall of Famer Rick Barry, who was then just

NBA RECORDS

Most seasons leading in free throw percentage, 7

HONORS AND AWARDS

1949	*Sporting News* All-American
1950	Consensus All-American
1953-60	NBA All-Star Game
1953, 1955-60	All-NBA Team
1955	NBA All-Star Game most valuable player
1970	NBA 25th Anniversary All Time Team ABA Co-Coach of the Year
1972	NBA Coach of the Year
1975	Inducted into Naismith Memorial Basketball Hall of Fame
1996	NBA 50 Greatest Players of All Time Team Uniform number 21 retired by Boston Celtics

starting out his career. While playing for Bill, Barry won the only scoring title of his career.

Bill continued to make a name for himself in the American Basketball Association (ABA), which emerged in the late 1960's as a rival to the more established NBA. Bill coached the Utah Stars to the league championship in 1971.

The next season, he was even better. He moved back to Southern California and the NBA to coach the Los Angeles Lakers. As a coach, Bill used many of the same drills and theories he had developed as a player, and his judgment paid off. The Lakers won their first NBA title in the 1971-1972 season, and Bill was voted NBA Coach of the Year. Also, the Lakers finished with an amazing 69-13 regular season record, the best single-season record in NBA history. The team set a record with thirty-three consecutive victories at one point. Bill is the only coach in the history of professional basketball to win championships in three different leagues. He did it in the ABL, the ABA, and the NBA.

As a player and as a coach, Bill believed in rigorous conditioning and strict discipline. He conducted practices on a precise schedule and initiated what is termed today the "shootaround," where players go through a light morning practice prior to a game later in the day. Bill and the great UCLA coach John Wooden have similar coaching philosophies, which they express in their book titled *The Wooden-Sharman Method: A Guide to Winning Basketball* (1975).

The Lakers finished in first place the first three years that Bill coached them. After that, he moved into the team's front office and was responsible for the drafting of Earvin "Magic" Johnson and several other key players who kept the Lakers among the league's top teams through the 1980's. Bill served as the Lakers' general manager from 1976 until 1982. He then moved up to club president, retiring in 1988. He continued to serve as a special consultant with the Lakers.

In 1970, Bill was selected to the NBA's Twenty-fifth Anniversary team. In 1996, he received the prestigious honor of being named to the NBA's 50 Greatest Players of All Time Team.

Summary

Bill Sharman was one of the top players and coaches in professional basketball history. He became successful largely because of his drive and his willingness to practice as long and as hard as it took to achieve his goals. That formula has enabled him to achieve success in the NBA in four different decades.

John McNamara

Additional Sources:

Bjarkman, Peter C. *The Boston Celtics Encyclopedia.* Champaign-Urbana, Ill.: Sports Publishing, 1999.

Ryan, Bob. *The Boston Celtics—The History, Legends, and Images of America's Most Celebrated Team.* New York: Gallery Books, 1989.

Shouler, Kenneth A. *The Experts Pick Basketball's Best Fifty Players in the Last Fifty Years.* Lenexa, Kans.: Addax, 1998.

Wooden, John, Bill Sharman, and Bob Seizer. *The Wooden-Sharman Method: A Guide to Winning Basketball.* New York: Macmillan, 1975.

SHANNON SHARPE

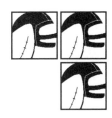

Sport: Football

Born: June 26, 1968
Chicago, Illinois

Early Life

Shannon Sharpe was born on June 26, 1968, in Chicago. His parents separated when he was a baby, and Shannon grew up in Glennville, Georgia, in a small house with his large, extended family. They were so poor that when it rained, water would pour in through the leaky tin roof and soak them while they lay in bed. When he was five, Shannon walked behind a tobacco picker, picking up the leaves that fell on the ground. In time he graduated to hanging the tobacco racks. As a kid, though, he was nicknamed "Chateau," for Chateaubriand; even then, he would talk about how he wanted the best things in life for himself and his family.

At Glennville High School, he lettered in track, basketball, and football. Because his SAT scores were too poor to allow him to play Division I football, he planned to enlist in the Air Force after graduation. His brother, Sterling, then an All-American at South Carolina, suggested that Shannon enroll at nearby Savannah State, a small, predominantly black college.

Baltimore Ravens tight end Shannon Sharpe in training in 2000.

The Road to Excellence

Once he got to college, Shannon started working out, saying he wanted to be like his brother. He began developing into a top-notch receiver, known for his deadly long pass routes. Shannon was also developing a reputation for loquaciousness, both on the field and off. Every evening he stood in front of the mirror in his dorm room, practicing colorful answers to imagined reporters' questions. By his third year, Shannon had become a three-time Division I-AA All-American, All-Conference, and All-State selection, as well as the three-time conference Offensive Player of the Year.

Although his brother, a top-ten draft selection, had begun a career with the Green Bay Packers that would make him a five-time All-Pro, Shannon was a relatively low-profile college football player. Nevertheless, he was picked in the seventh round of the 1990 National Football League (NFL) draft by the Denver Broncos. When the Denver coaches looked at Shannon they saw a wide receiver in a tight end's body. He was not only fast but also big, capable of shaking off tacklers. As Shannon's rookie season progressed, his playing time increased, and he had made 7 receptions for 99 yards by season's end.

The Emerging Champion

In 1992, Shannon began a string of 50 or more catches per season. His 53 receptions for 640 yards that year helped put him in the Pro Bowl for the first time. He and Sterling became the first brothers to lead their respective teams in catches in the same season. Midway through the following season Shannon became the full-time starting tight end. He again led the Broncos, with 81 receptions, piling up 995 receiving yards. At year's end, he was named to virtually every All-NFL team.

In 1994 Shannon's career-high 87 receptions were the most of any Bronco since Lionel Taylor had caught 100 in 1961. In eight different games, Shannon pulled down 6 or more catches. This was the third straight season in which he and Sterling led their respective teams in receptions. The next year, Shannon caught 63 passes for 756 yards and 4 touchdowns, even though he missed the final three games after suffering an orbital fracture to his left eye, for which he underwent

STATISTICS					
Season	GP	Rec.	Yds.	Avg.	TD
1990	16	7	99	14.1	1
1991	16	22	322	14.6	1
1992	16	53	640	12.1	2
1993	16	81	995	12.3	9
1994	15	87	1,010	11.6	4
1995	13	63	756	12.0	4
1996	15	80	1,062	13.3	10
1997	16	72	1,107	15.4	3
1998	16	64	768	12.0	10
1999	5	23	224	9.7	0
2000	16	67	810	12.1	5
Totals	160	619	7,793	12.6	49

Notes: GP = games played; Rec. = receptions; Yds. = yards; Avg. = average yards per reception; TD = touchdowns

surgery. He recovered sufficiently in 1996 to lead all tight ends in the NFL for receptions (80), receiving yards (1,062), and receiving touchdowns (10). Shannon was rewarded by being named All-Pro and All-Conference and being selected to his fifth consecutive Pro Bowl.

Continuing the Story

The next year, 1997, Shannon completed his second season in which he posted more than 1,000 receiving yards. He also became the first tight end to have 50 or more receptions in seven straight seasons. That year was successful for the Broncos overall; they won their division and went on to play in the Super Bowl. Shannon was his team's leading receiver in the championship game, with 5 catches for 38 yards. The Broncos went on to defeat the heavily favored Green Bay Packers to become world champions. Shannon ranked the Super Bowl victory as his most memorable in football. He presented his Super Bowl ring to Sterling as a gesture of gratitude, saying, "The biggest cause of where I am and who I am was him."

Shannon again led all NFL tight ends in receiving yards in 1998. He also posted his seventh straight season with more than 50 catches. Although Denver's first loss of the 1998 season was handed to them by Miami, the Broncos got their revenge when they beat the Dolphins in the play-offs to earn a trip back to the Super Bowl. Shannon made media headlines when he called the Dolphins' quarterback, Dan Marino, a loser on the day of the game. In the Super Bowl, a concussion knocked Shannon out of the game in the third quarter but not before he had set Denver up for their first touchdown with a reception on the Atlanta Falcons' 1-yard line. The Broncos easily defeated Atlanta for their second consecutive championship.

Although Shannon had become the Broncos' career receiving leader, he signed a four-year contract with the Baltimore Ravens in 2000. The contract was reported to be worth $12.8 million, not including a $4.5 million signing bonus. Shannon said that one of the things that attracted him to play for Baltimore was the opportunity to break the NFL record for career receptions by a tight end, held by Ozzie Newsome.

Summary

Shannon Sharpe established himself among the elite tight ends in the NFL. At 6 feet 2 inches and 240 pounds, his size combined with speed to make him an offensive juggernaut. Having set records for more receptions and more yards than any tight end in the NFL since he entered the league, the boy from Glennville, Georgia, carved a legacy as the greatest athlete to pass through that town. Always remembering where he had come from, the conditions under which he grew up, and the family who gave him so much love and support, he gave generously to Goodwill Industries as well as other charities. He also went into football's history books as the game's trash-talking king, loving every minute of it.

Elizabeth Ferry Slocum

Additional Sources:

Guss, Greg. "Tough Enough." *Sport* 89 (January, 1998): 50-53.

Latimer, Clay. "I Am a Guy Who Has to Talk." *Football Digest* 29, no. 1 (September, 1999).

Reilly, Rick. "Lip Schtick." *Sports Illustrated* 90, no. 4 (February 1, 1999): 40-41.

Torres, John Albert. *Fitness Stars of Pro Football: Featuring Profiles of Deion Sanders, Shannon Sharpe, Darrell Greene, and Wayne Chrebet.* Bear, Del.: Mitchell Lane Publishing, 2001.

PATTY SHEEHAN

Sport: Golf

Born: October 27, 1956
Middlebury, Vermont

Early Life

Patty Sheehan was born October 27, 1956, in Middlebury, Vermont, to Bobo Sheehan, a college sports coach, and Leslie Sheehan, a nurse. When Patty was ten years old, the Sheehan family moved from Vermont to Nevada.

At one year of age, Patty started skiing. By age four, she was ski racing and also playing golf. Patty learned to feel comfortable on skis by walking around with shortened skis on her feet. Her parents were avid skiers and would often ski with Patty standing between their legs. Patty's parents provided great support for her athletic efforts. Her father helped to teach her the value of top-level performance by telling her to do her very best in whatever she did.

As a child, Patty admired skiers such as Nancy Green, a Canadian who won the World Cup in 1968. She also admired some of the college athletes on her father's ski team. By age thirteen, Patty was a nationally ranked junior skier. Soon, however, her desire to excel in skiing diminished. At the same time, her interest in golf began to resurface.

The Road to Excellence

After moving from Vermont to Nevada, the Sheehan family lived on a golf course, providing Patty with many chances to practice and play. By the age of fifteen, Patty began to compete in golf tournaments.

As a young woman, Patty was winner of the Nevada State Amateur Championship from 1975 through 1978, and she won the California Amateur Championship in 1978 and 1979. Patty reached the pinnacle of her amateur career when she claimed the 1980 AIAW National Championship while attending San Jose State University. Patty was also a member of the U.S. Curtis Cup team in 1980, winning all four of her matches.

The Emerging Champion

After completing her college years at San Jose State, Patty joined the Ladies Professional Golf Association (LPGA) tour in 1980. Her talents were almost im-

Golfer Patty Sheehan scored her thirty-fifth career win at the 1996 Dinah Shore Golf Tournament.

AP/Wide World Photos

mediately obvious. She captured the attention of golf fans by winning the LPGA Rookie of the Year Award. In the following year, her second on tour, she achieved her first tour victory in the Mazda Japan Classic.

By 1983, other LPGA golfers were made even more aware that they had a serious contender at any tournament in which Patty Sheehan played. She captured four tournaments that year, including her first major title, the LPGA Championship. In addition, she collected $255,185 and won the Rolex Player of the Year Award. Patty's momentum continued into 1984, when she won four more tournaments, including another LPGA Championship, and was awarded the Vare Trophy for the low scoring average of the year at 71.40.

In 1986 and 1987, the tournament wins continued; moreover, Patty received recognition for being an outstanding person away from the golf course. In 1986, she was selected as the Samaritan Award winner. In 1987, she was among eight athletes selected by *Sports Illustrated* for the Sportsman of the Year Award, an honor given to athletes who practice the ideal of sportsmanship away from the playing arena. Patty was also recognized for her work with troubled teenagers in Santa Cruz County.

Continuing the Story

The year 1989 provided the greatest challenge of Patty's career, as she experienced two devastating setbacks within ten months. In October, the San Francisco earthquake severely damaged her house, leaving her temporarily homeless. In July, she blew an 11-stroke lead during the final round of the U.S. Women's Open. Reflecting on the year, Patty said, "I had to overcome a lot of psychological hurdles—bad memories and bad thoughts."

Patty rebounded from the obstacles of 1989 the next year by becoming the second woman to cross the $700,000 earnings mark in a season by collecting $732,618. That same year, she posted a career best scoring average of 70.62 and won five titles. She was also a member of the victorious inaugural U.S. Solheim Cup team.

The 1991 season had its ups and downs for Patty. The ups included career win number twenty-six and a total of twelve top-ten finishes. The downs came in the second half of the season,

MAJOR CHAMPIONSHIP VICTORIES	
1983-84, 1993	LPGA Championship
1992, 1994	U.S. Women's Open
1996	Nabisco Dinah Shore Championship

OTHER NOTABLE VICTORIES	
1980	AIAW National Championship
1981, 1988	Mazda Japan Classic
1982	Orlando Lady Classic
1982-83	Inamori Classic
1982, 1990	Safeco Classic
1983	Corning Classic
1983-84	Henredon Classic
1984	Elizabeth Arden Classic McDonald's Kids Classic
1985	J&B Scotch Pro-Am
1985-86, 1988	Sarasota Classic
1986	Konica San Jose Classic Kyocera Inamori Classic
1989-90, 1992	Rochester International
1990	Jamaica Classic McDonald's Championship Ping-Cellular One Golf Championship
1991	Orix Hawaiian Ladies Open
1992	Jamie Farr Toledo Classic
1993	Standard Register Ping
1995	Rochester International

when Patty suffered from tendinitis in her left index finger. Despite the physical pain, Patty recorded her second hole-in-one at the Women's Kemper Open and crossed the $3 million mark in career earnings.

Three wins in 1992 brought Patty within one win of qualifying for membership in the LPGA Hall of Fame. In her U.S. Women's Open victory, she showed nerves of steel and great determination. She birdied the final two holes of regulation to force an eighteen-hole playoff against Juli Inkster, which Patty won.

As the 1993 season began, many wondered just when the knicker-clad, energy-packed Patty Sheehan would break through the door for victory number thirty, the number of LPGA wins required for Hall of Fame admission. Patty was consumed with thoughts about the Hall of Fame.

When would she enter? How would the win come? She later recalled, "I thought about it every day, but not in a negative way. I knew it was attainable. I just had to stay out of the way and let it happen." Following her own advice, she produced an impressive five-stroke victory in the Standard Register Ping tournament.

Patty kept thinking about the importance of the thirtieth victory, even though she tried to block those thoughts from her mind. Yet the pressure also helped; Patty acknowledged that she had an enhanced "focus" during the final stretch toward the Hall of Fame. She attributed the increased concentration to the heightened level of competition on the LPGA tour. That level of competition brought out her best play, as she finished the final hole by making her fifth birdie of the round and shooting a tournament-record 17 under par. Later that season, she became the thirteenth woman inducted into the LPGA Hall of Fame. In 1994, she captured her second U.S. Women's Open title.

Patty won her sixth major tournament in 1996 at the Nabisco Dinah Shore Championship, bringing her career win total to thirty-five. She continued to play in tournaments in the following years, posting several top-ten finishes in 1998 and 1999. In 2000 Patty became interested in course design and did some consulting work for a new course in Angels Camp, California. She continued to appear in LPGA tournaments, firing a season-low 67 in the first round of the Firstar LPGA Classic.

Summary

Patty Sheehan's talent and determination brought her to the pinnacle of success in her field. Even after she attained Hall of Fame status, she remained a top competitor, as she continued to follow her father's advice to do her very best in everything.

Judy C. Peel

HONORS AND AWARDS	
1980	Curtis Cup team
1983	LPGA Player of the Year
1984	Vare Trophy
1986	Samaritan Award
1987	*Sports Illustrated* Co-Sportsman of the Year
1990	Inducted into Collegiate Hall of Fame
1993	Inducted into LPGA Hall of Fame
1994	Flo Hyman Award
	LPGA's Top 50 Players

Additional Sources:

Bamberger, Michael. "The Unseen Sheehan." *Golf Digest* 45, no. 5 (1994).

Maiorana, Sal. "Same Old Story." *Golf World* 48, no. 45 (1995).

Sheehan, Patty, with Betty Hicks. *Patty Sheehan on Golf.* Dallas, Tex.: Taylor, 1996.

Wilner, Barry. *Superstars of Women's Golf.* Philadelphia, Pa.: Chelsea House, 1997.

ART SHELL

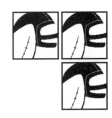

Sport: Football

Born: November 26, 1946
       Charleston, South Carolina

Early Life

Arthur Shell was born November 26, 1946, in Charleston, South Carolina. He lived with his parents, Arthur, Sr., and Gertrude Shell, and five younger siblings in a tiny red-brick dwelling in the Daniel Jenkins Project of Charleston.

The project, although situated within the stench of nearby fertilizer and sulfur plants, was friendly and safe. Devout Baptists filled the homes there and kept a protective eye on Art and the other children of the neighborhood.

Art enjoyed his childhood. Although he had to grow up quickly and look after his brothers and sister when his mother died at age thirty-five, he had fun playing basketball and football on the neighborhood playgrounds during his free time.

The Road to Excellence

A mature young man, Art attended Bonds-Wilson High School in Charleston. He applied himself to his activities and did well. As a senior, Art was named to the All-State squads in football and basketball. Soon after, he accepted a scholarship to play football at Maryland State Eastern Shore College.

At Maryland State, Art played on both the offensive and defensive lines each of his four years. In 1966 and 1967 he was named All-American by the *Pittsburgh Courier* and *Ebony* magazine. He was also named to the All-Conference team three of his four seasons with Maryland State. In addition, he was the starting center on State's basketball team, winning two letters.

By 1967, his senior year, Art had evolved into a large, strong, and agile athlete at 6 feet 5 inches and 285 pounds. He was named to the Little All-American team at offensive tackle, and had attracted the attention of the American Football League's (AFL) Oakland Raiders. They selected him in the third round of the 1968 draft.

The Emerging Champion

It was not easy for Art when he first reported to the Raiders. He had no skills in pass blocking, mainly because he had gained no such experience in college. He had a lot of learning to do.

Playing next to Gene Upshaw on the offensive

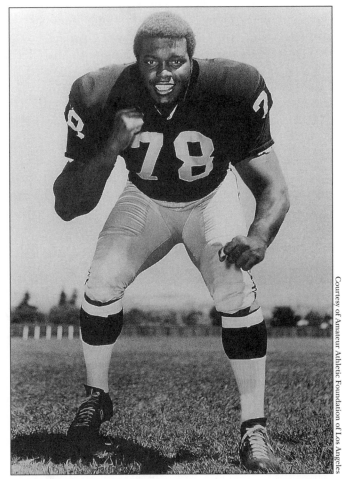

HONORS AND AWARDS

1965-67	All-Conference Team *Pittsburgh Courier* All-American *Ebony* All-American
1967	Little All-American
1973-79, 1981	NFL Pro Bowl Team
1974-75, 1977	*Sporting News* AFC All-Star Team
1989	Inducted into Pro Football Hall of Fame

line, however, was an education in itself. Art and Upshaw became quick friends, lifting weights and sharing strategies with each other. They communicated well with each other on the field, seemingly knowing what the other was going to do without a word being said. Together they became the best tackle-guard combination in the National Football League (NFL).

Because Upshaw was so outspoken, however, Art rarely got the notice he deserved. Fans and press members would approach him and ask him if he were Gene Upshaw. The lack of attention did not really bother Art. He would simply shower and dress while reporters interviewed Upshaw.

The Raiders became a dominating team during Art's tenure. Oakland played in the American Football Conference (AFC) championship games in 1970, from 1973 to 1977, and in 1980. The crowning achievement of the 1980 season was a 32-14 Super Bowl victory over the Minnesota Vikings.

Art's personal honors as a player included being named to the AFC All-Star team in 1974, 1975, and 1977, and playing in the Pro Bowl from 1973 to 1979 and in 1981. Art played in 207 games as a professional football player.

Continuing the Story

When he retired as a player in 1982, he dusted off his long-held ambition to be a football coach. In 1983 he was made the Los Angeles Raiders offensive line coach.

To his coaching Art brought a habit of close observation that he had cultivated as a player. He listened to his players' conversations; he watched endless hours of film; he observed other coaches carefully. Never saying much, he simply soaked up information and applied it to his management.

As an assistant, Art held that he learned much

from his head coaches. In a *Sports Illustrated* article by Jill Lieber, he said, "John Madden taught me about the game of people. I learned that you have to understand each individual, when to push his buttons and when not to. From Tom Flores I learned patience. He was a quiet, stoic leader. Mike Shanahan was one of the most organized people I ever met."

On October 3, 1989, Art replaced Shanahan as head coach of the Los Angeles Raiders, becoming the NFL's first African American head coach in sixty-four years. In his debut as head coach, the Raiders beat the New York Jets 14-7. Art served as the Raiders coach until he was fired at the end of the 1994 season. His record during his tenure with the Raiders was 54-38. In the late 1990's Art became the offensive line coach for the Atlanta Falcons.

Elected to the Pro Football Hall of Fame in 1989, Art joined other Raider inductees Gene Upshaw, Jim Otto, Fred Biletnikoff, and Willie Brown.

Quoted in *Sports Illustrated,* best friend Gene Upshaw reflected on Art's lifelong desire to be a coach: "There is one thing that Art and I have learned over the years: You shouldn't be afraid to dream, because you can wake up and find out it's a reality."

Summary

Rising from a little known college in Maryland to attract the attention of the Oakland Raiders, Art Shell became one of pro football's most dominating offensive linemen. Named to numerous Pro Bowl teams and playing on one Super Bowl champion team, he went on to become the first black head coach in sixty-four years of NFL history.

Rustin Larson

Additional Sources:

Attner, Paul. "NFL: Football's One Hundred Greatest Players—Better than All The Rest." *The Sporting News* 223 (November 8, 1999): 58-59, 62.

Barber, Phil. "NFL: Football's One Hundred Greatest Players—The Hit Men." *The Sporting News* 223 (November 1, 1999): 12-16.

Pro Football Hall of Fame. http://www .profootballhof.com.

BETTY SHELLENBERGER

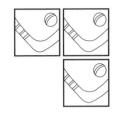

Sport: Field hockey

Born: August 8, 1921
Germantown, Pennsylvania

Early Life

Elisabeth (Betty) Shellenberger was born in Germantown, Pennsylvania, on August 8, 1921. She grew up in an area known for its excellence in field hockey, and many national and international matches were played near Betty's home.

Elisabeth Lincoln and Charles D. Shellenberger, Betty's parents, had one other child, a son, William. Betty's father was an avid sportsman and gave Betty her first squash racket when she was eight years old. At the age of nine, her parents took her to see her first field hockey game, a match between Scotland and Philadelphia. The excitement of that game convinced her she wanted to play field hockey.

The Road to Excellence

Betty attended Agnes Irwin School, a private girls' school with an excellent sports program. By the time Betty was twelve, she was playing on the school field hockey and lacrosse teams. Her coach, Agneta Powell, became an inspiration to her, encouraging her to attend a famous summer hockey camp in Mount Pocono, Pennsylvania. It was there that Betty first met camp director and coach Constance Applebee, who introduced field hockey in the United States in 1901. Applebee's coaching, along with that of other international-caliber coaches, raised Betty's playing ability to new levels. These summer camps, and her years of school competition, prepared her well for what was to come.

In 1939, at age eighteen, she competed in her first national field hockey tournament and was selected to play center forward on the United

Betty Shellenberger (left).

States' First Team. This selection identified Betty as one of the top twenty-two players in the country and established her as the best center forward. Center forward is a key position in field hockey, where most of the scoring occurs.

Betty made the first United States team again in 1940 and 1941. As the United States entered its third decade of field hockey, the country was engaged in World War II, and the executive committee of the United States Field Hockey Association (USFHA) recommended cancellation of the national tournament. Had there been United States teams from 1942 to 1945, Betty Shellenberger undoubtedly would have been on them.

The Emerging Champion

When national competition resumed in 1946, Betty was selected again as the center forward, and she continued to earn first-team recognition for the next nine years. By this time, Betty had distinguished herself as one of the best forwards ever to play the game. She also played two other offensive positions, left wing and right inner.

In addition to athletic recognition, selection to the United States team also provided opportunities for international competition and travel for those who could afford it. Because the players were amateurs, they had to pay their own travel expenses. In 1948, Betty played on the USFHA touring team competing in England.

Between 1948 and 1959, Betty toured on six occasions, competing against the top teams in Africa, Australia, Great Britain, and Holland. In 1956, Betty was elected vice captain of the team that toured Australia, and in 1959, she was elected captain of the team that traveled to Holland. On four of the tours, Betty competed in the International Federation of Women's Hockey Associations (IFWHA) tournament. The IFWHA promoted field hockey and friendship in the international community.

Field hockey was one of the few women's sports of this era to combine top-level competition with international travel. Touring teams received royal treatment wherever they went, and the players served as ambassadors for the United States and women's athletics. Only the Olympic Games provided a greater showcase for women's athletic talent, but women's field hockey would not be recognized as an Olympic sport until 1980.

HONORS AND AWARDS	
1939-41, 1946-55, 1958, 1960	USFHA All-American (first team)
1940-44, 1946-47, 1953-54, 1957-58	U.S. Women's Lacrosse Team (first team)
1948, 1955	U.S. Field Hockey Touring Team
1950, 1953, 1956, 1959	IFWHA Conference Team
1952, 1955, 1960-61	U.S. Women's Lacrosse Team (reserve team)
1956-57	USFHA All-American (reserve team)
1959	U.S. Women's Lacrosse Association Honorary Umpire Award
1961	U.S. Women's Lacrosse Association Honorary Member
1962	USFHA Honorary Member
1975	USFHA Honorary Umpire
1986	Inducted into Pennsylvania Sports Hall of Fame
1987	Distinguished Daughter of Pennsylvania Award
1988	Inducted into USFHA Hall of Fame

Continuing the Story

Because field hockey is so physically demanding, players cannot expect to be selected for the United States team indefinitely, and in 1960, Betty was chosen for the last time. She continued playing club field hockey at the master's level for several decades, however.

During her many years of competition, Betty overcame several obstacles. She received no serious injuries, survived the rigors of annual tournament competitive play—passing the close inspection of intimidating selection committees—and paid her own expenses to tournaments all over the United States and abroad. Through it all, what led to her continuing success was sheer enjoyment and love of the game, lasting friendships, and unusual athletic ability. Field hockey afforded her a unique education, with sports as her subject matter and the world as her classroom.

Betty found other avenues for her athletic talent along the way. During her years of playing competitive field hockey, she was also enjoying a dual career as an accomplished women's lacrosse player. She played three different positions, second home, third home, and goalkeeper, during her sixteen years as a United States First Team and reserve team player. (First and reserve team selections are equivalent to All-American honors.)

Betty's contributions to field hockey were not limited to the playing field. She served the

USFHA as an umpire and as treasurer, vice president, and secretary. Her exceptional service earned her an Honorary Membership in 1962, an award she also received for outstanding lacrosse service. In addition, she coached at three schools, wrote several hockey articles, and coauthored a book on field hockey for players, coaches, and umpires.

In 1986, she was inducted into the Pennsylvania Sports Hall of Fame, and in 1987, the Governor of Pennsylvania designated her a Distinguished Daughter of Pennsylvania, the highest honor conferred by the state. Perhaps Betty's greatest sports honor was her 1988 induction, as an inaugural player, into the USFHA Hall of Fame. This distinction is the most prestigious national award in the sport of field hockey. Based on a strict, objective point system, Betty qualified for the honor in every category.

Summary

Betty Shellenberger's athletic career epitomizes the life of a successful amateur sportswoman. She distinguished herself in two sports, field hockey and lacrosse, reaching the top repeatedly from 1939 until 1961. Betty's love for sports was cultivated by a supportive family, inspirational coaches, and the many friends she met all over the world. Her career is a reminder sports is more than competition; it is also making friends, learning about the world, and having fun.

Barbara J. Kelly

Additional Sources:

Lees, Josephine, and Betty Shellenberger. *Field Hockey for Players, Coaches, and Umpires.* New York: The Ronald Press, 1957.

PETER SHILTON

Sport: Soccer

Born: September 18, 1949
Leicester, England

Early Life

Peter Shilton was born on September 18, 1949, in Leicester, a large city in central England. Peter's father was a greengrocer, and the Shilton family lived in a house with a garden where Peter set up a makeshift soccer goal between two trees. When financial problems forced the Shilton family to sell the house and move, Peter took his practicing out into the street, where over and over he would toss a soccer ball high in the air and then spring up to catch it with his arms extended.

When Peter was very young, he was for some reason convinced that he would be a dwarf, so he would hang from the bannisters with his mother clutching his ankles so that he would not fall. Later, Peter confessed: "I pulled and pulled on my arms and legs everyday. Crazy, I know, but I did grow eventually, and that was all I was worried about."

By the time he was twelve, Peter would spend hours at a time organizing his soccer-playing friends so that they gave him a barrage of shots. On every occasion he checked the angle, the speed and the trajectory of the ball. He had fun, but his primary target was to become a good goalkeeper.

The Road to Excellence

Peter began his professional career in 1966 with Leicester City, a successful team that had appeared in the English League Cup Final in 1964 and 1965. Peter's position, goalkeeper, was filled on the Leicester squad by Gordon Banks, a star of the English national team and the top goalkeeper in English soccer. Peter impressed the Leicester management so strongly, though, that in 1967 the team let Banks go and installed seventeen-year-old Peter in his place. Peter played for Leicester until 1974, helping the team to an English second-division championship in 1971 and appearing in 286 games. In 1974 Peter was transferred to the Stoke City club, where he made 110 appearances in goal, and then in 1977 he moved to the Nottingham Forest team.

At Nottingham Forest Peter enjoyed his greatest professional success. In his first season there, he led the club to the English Football League championship and then on to victory in the European Cup, the most prestigious professional championship in European soccer. In the final game 0against FC Malmö of Sweden, Peter did not allow a goal, and

Peter Shilton makes a save during a match in 1977.

HONORS AND AWARDS

1971	English Second Division champion
1978	English Professional Football Association Player of the Year
1978-79	English League Cup champion
1979-80	European Cup champion
1990	English Professional Football Association Merit Award
1991	Order of the British Empire

RECORDS

Most international appearances in a lifetime, 125

Nottingham eked out a 1-0 win. In recognition of his accomplishments, Peter was chosen as Player of the Year by the English Professional Football Association.

The next year, Nottingham repeated its extraordinary success, winning the English League title again and then defending its European Cup championship. Once again, Peter's goalkeeping was a key element in the team's success, as Nottingham defeated Germany's SV Hamburg club 1-0 to retain its place as the top club in Europe.

The Emerging Champion

Although Peter's professional career was impressive, his greatest accomplishments came on another level altogether. Most European countries have dozens of professional soccer teams and hundreds of players competing on what is known as the "club" level. Only the very best of these players are selected to play for each country's national team and represent their country in international competitions such as the World Cup; selection to a national squad is an honor much like selection to an All-Star team in baseball or basketball. Peter had taken over from Gordon Banks as the English national team's goalkeeper in 1971 at the age of twenty-one. Few players are able to maintain such a level of excellence for more than a few years; even such greats as Pelé of Brazil and Johan Cruyff of Holland, who played nearly into their forties, starred in their last few seasons on the club, not the national, level. Peter, though, was still a contender for the position of England's national goalkeeper as he neared his fortieth birthday.

Peter's extraordinary longevity as a world-class player was in large part a result of a rigorous training program. In 1988, one British sportswriter observed:

No one who has watched Shilton's rigorously punishing schedule in training will be surprised by the longevity of his career. In a ceaseless pursuit of perfection he stretches himself to the point of exhaustion.

Though outstandingly talented, he has never been prepared merely to rely on his natural ability and instinctive reactions. In 1988, at the age of thirty-nine, Peter was again named as England's number-one goalkeeper, and he announced that his crowning ambition was to represent England in the 1990 World Cup competition in Italy.

Continuing the Story

In 1990, Peter's dream came true. Peter was the first player past the age of forty to compete in a World Cup since Dino Zoff had played in goal for Italy in 1982. During the competition, Peter broke the all-time record of 119 international appearances held by Pat Jennings of Northern Ireland. Although England was eliminated in a tense semifinal game with West Germany, Peter could console himself with the fact that his record-breaking total of 125 international appearances looked as though it might survive into the twenty-first century. On his return to England, Peter announced his retirement from the national team, saying "I always wanted to finish at the top."

In 1991, Peter received the Order of the British Empire (OBE) for his contributions to English sport.

Summary

Retirement is never an easy step for an elite athlete to take. Peter Shilton handled his retirement as well as he handled all the shots on goal he had faced in 125 appearances for England. Peter showed style, good sense, and excellent timing.

Scott A. G. M. Crawford

Additional Sources:

Henshaw, Richard. *The Encyclopedia of World Soccer.* Washington, D.C.: New Republic Books, 1979.

Hollander, Zander. *The American Encyclopedia of Soccer.* New York: Everett House, 1980.

WILLIE SHOEMAKER

Sport: Horse racing

Born: August 19, 1931
Fabens, Texas

Early Life

William Lee (Willie) Shoemaker was born on August 19, 1931, in a farmhouse near Fabens, Texas, a west Texas farm town. The child of Babe, a cotton mill worker, and Ruby Shoemaker, Willie was born prematurely and weighed only two and one-half pounds. The doctor told the Shoemakers that Willie would not live through the night and that he would make arrangements for the funeral. Willie's grandmother put the baby in a shoebox and placed him in the oven, leaving the door of the oven ajar so that he could breathe. Miraculously, he lived.

Willie's parents were divorced when he was four years old, and his mother took him to Winters, in central Texas, to live with her parents, who were sharecroppers. It was on his grandparents' farm that Willie rode his first horse at the age of six.

At the age of ten, Willie moved to the San Gabriel Valley in California to live with his father and stepmother. At El Monte High School, Willie failed to make the football and basketball teams but wrestled in the 95-105-pound division, finishing undefeated. He dropped out of school in the eleventh grade at the age of sixteen.

The Road to Excellence

After leaving school, Willie took a job cleaning out stalls at the Suzy Q Ranch in Puente, California, where he earned $75 a month plus room and board. Willie soon advanced to a new position at the ranch, that of exercising horses and breaking yearlings. Trainer George Reeves soon realized that Willie had potential as a jockey

and arranged for him to ride in his first race on March 19, 1949, aboard Waxahachie at Golden Gate Fields in Albany, California. At the age of seventeen, the 4-foot, 100-pound jockey finished fifth in his first race.

Willie's first victory came shortly thereafter when, on April 20, 1949, he rode Shafter V to victory. That was only the first of the 219 races that Willie won in 1949. In 1950, he tied with Joe Culmone for the national riding championship with 388 winners. Willie's mounts earned $844,040, while his great predecessor and friend, Eddie Arcaro, earned $1,410,160. Willie won

more money than any other jockey in 1951, 1953, and 1954, losing to Arcaro in 1952.

The Emerging Champion

In 1955, Willie won his first Kentucky Derby, riding Swaps to a 1½ length victory and defeating Arcaro. A year later, he became the first jockey to win more than $2 million in purse money.

Although Willie became a champion soon after his career began and experienced much success as a young jockey, his career was not without adversity. He suffered a humiliating defeat in the Kentucky Derby in 1957, riding Gallant Man. He was locked in a struggle with Iron Liege, ridden by Bill Hartack, when he mistook the sixteenth pole for the finish line and briefly stood up in the saddle; as a result, Gallant Man was passed and defeated by Iron Liege.

Willie rebounded quickly from that embarrassing defeat and won his first Belmont Stakes the next month aboard Gallant Man. The next year, Willie won his second Kentucky Derby aboard Tomy Lee and his second Belmont Stakes aboard Sword Dancer. From 1958 to 1964, he led the nation in money won and in victories.

In 1962, Willie won the Belmont Stakes riding Jaipur, and in 1963, he won the Preakness Stakes on Candy Spots. In 1965, he won the Kentucky Derby, and in 1967, he won both the Preakness and the Belmont and rode Damascus to the Horse of the Year title. That year, his mounts earned more than $3 million.

Beginning in 1968, Willie could not compete for thirteen months because he broke a leg when a horse fell on him at the Santa Anita track. His convalescence was difficult, and he had become somewhat bored with racing. His bad luck continued into the next year. He entered competition again in February of 1969, but on April 30, a horse flipped over backward on him, crushed his pelvis, tore his bladder, and damaged nerves in his legs. Willie was out for another three months, and there was doubt that he would ever ride again. In 1970, however, at the age of thirty-nine, he surpassed Johnny Longden as the jockey with the most victories in the history of horse racing, 6,033 wins.

Willie seemed to be rejuvenated, and he continued his career far beyond the age when most

MAJOR CHAMPIONSHIP VICTORIES		
Year	Race	Horse
1955	Kentucky Derby	Swaps
1957	Belmont Stakes	Gallant Man
1958	Belmont Stakes	Sword Dancer
	Kentucky Derby	Tomy Lee
1962	Belmont Stakes	Jaipur
1963	Preakness Stakes	Candy Spots
1965	Kentucky Derby	Lucky Debonair
1967	Belmont Stakes	Damascus
	Preakness Stakes	Damascus
1975	Belmont Stakes	Avatar
1986	Kentucky Derby	Ferdinand
1987	Breeders' Cup Classic	Ferdinand

jockeys retire. On March 3, 1985, he became the first jockey to earn $100 million in purse money, riding Lord at War in the Santa Anita Handicap. It was his 8,446th career win and his 917th stakes victory. In 1986, at the age of fifty-four, Willie won the Kentucky Derby, riding Ferdinand, for his fourth Derby win. With this victory, he became the oldest rider by a dozen years to win the Kentucky Derby. The next day, he won the John Henry Handicap at the Santa Anita Race Track, riding Palace Music, and later rode Ferdinand to a second-place finish in the Preakness and a third-place finish in the Belmont Stakes. In December, he brought Ferdinand from last place to win the Malibu Stakes.

In February of 1987, Willie had arthroscopic surgery to repair torn cartilage in his left knee. He recovered quickly to record a victory in the San Luis Obispo Handicap two weeks after his surgery. He finished sixth in the Kentucky Derby in 1987 and did not compete in any other Triple Crown races during that year.

Continuing the Story

In June of 1987, Willie, once again atop Ferdinand, defeated the 1987 Kentucky Derby winner, Alysheba, to win his first Breeder's Cup Classic at Hollywood Park in Inglewood, California. At the end of 1987, Willie had ridden in five different decades, had won 8,706 races, and had earned

$110 million in prize money. He had won 983 stakes victories and 245 wins in races worth more than $100,000. He had won four Kentucky Derbys, five Belmonts and Woodward Stakes, ten Santa Anita Handicaps, and eight Hollywood Gold Cups.

Willie retired from racing in 1990. His records include 8,833 career wins, 1,009 stake victories, 257 stake races with values of $100,000 or more, and more than $123 million in purses. After retiring, Willie continued his career in horse racing as a horse trainer.

In April of 1991, Willie was involved in an automobile accident that left him paralyzed from the neck down. He would never ride again but worked as a trainer until 1997.

strength and skill. He was most noted, however, for his "touch" with the horses. Willie was once known as the "Silent Shoe," but now most jockeys think that he talked exceptionally well to the horses.

Susan J. Bandy

HONORS AND AWARDS

1958	Inducted into National Horse Racing Hall of Fame
1971	National Turf Writers' Association Joe Palmer Award
1976	Eclipse Award, Special Award
1981	Eclipse Award, Outstanding Jockey Eclipse Award, Award of Merit

RECORDS AND MILESTONES

8,833 victories—the highest total of all time until broken by Laffit Pincay in 1999
Annual money leader (1951, 1953-54, 1958-64)

Summary

Willie Shoemaker is perhaps the greatest rider who ever raced, yet for many years he was always known as the jockey who misjudged the finish line in the 1957 Kentucky Derby. His victory at the 1986 Kentucky Derby at the age of fifty-four, however, erased that humiliating defeat.

He has been highly praised by his peers, who say that he did everything well, having good

Additional Sources:

Duffy, B., and R. Knight. "Adieu to Silent Shoe." *U.S. News and World Report* 108, no. 6 (1990).

Phillips, Louis. *Willie Shoemaker.* Mankato, Minn.: Crestwood House, 1988.

Shoemaker, Willie. *Shoe: Willie Shoemaker's Illustrated Book of Racing.* Chicago: Rand McNally, 1976.

FRANK SHORTER

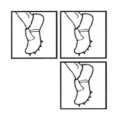

Sport: Track and field (long-distance runs and marathon)

Born: October 31, 1947
Munich, West Germany

Early Life

Frank Shorter was born on October 31, 1947, in a United States military hospital in the city of Munich in West Germany. He was the eldest of the eleven children born to Samuel and Katherine Shorter. His father was a United States Army physician stationed in Germany. After Frank's father was discharged from the Army in 1948, the Shorter family returned to the United States, where his father practiced medicine in several Eastern cities.

As a young boy, Frank was a quiet person who became very self-reliant, in part because his parents had to divide their attention among eleven children. Even as a young boy, Frank enjoyed running. When he was in junior high school, he often ran the 2 miles from his home to school. At his request, he was allowed to run laps around the football field during gym class rather than play football.

The Road to Excellence

While attending Mount Hermon, a private high school in Massachusetts, Frank displayed talent as a runner but was not so gifted that anyone could have anticipated he would become an Olympic champion. He did not even go out for the track or cross-country teams until his junior year. It was not until his senior year that Frank began to excel; he was undefeated in cross-country and at the 2-mile distance during the track season. By this time, Frank was seriously interested in distance running. When he considered which college to attend, he chose Yale University because it

had the best track coach among the Ivy League schools.

At Yale, Frank was fortunate in having Bob Giegengack, the coach of the 1964 United States Olympic track team, as his coach. Giegengack not only assigned workouts to Frank that helped him to become a bett7er runner but also explained the theory behind them so that after he

Frank Shorter won the marathon at the 1972 Munich Olympics.

left Yale, Frank was able to coach himself with considerable success. In addition to a long, steady run once a week, Giegengack's training system was based on repeated runs of a half-mile or a mile on a grassy surface with short rests between each run. The day following these hard training sessions would be limited to jogging to enable the runner's body to recover from the intense workouts.

During his first three years at Yale, Frank was a steady runner, but he rarely won first place in major meets. Because he hoped to qualify for medical school, Frank considered it important to do well as a student and he did not devote as much time to training as some distance runners did. At the end of Frank's second year at Yale, his parents moved to Taos, New Mexico. Taos was near mountains, and during the summer Frank ran in the mountains at seven thousand feet above sea level. Training in this oxygen-thin air gave Frank an advantage over other runners when he returned to Yale in the fall. In his senior year, Frank finished first in the 6-mile run and second in the 3-mile run at the National Collegiate Athletic Association championships.

The Emerging Champion

After graduating from college in 1969, Frank decided to devote himself to distance running.

He finished second in his first serious marathon race, the national championships in Eugene, Oregon, in 1971, in the respectable time of 2 hours, 17 minutes and 45 seconds (2:17:45). Later that year, he finished first in the Fukuoka Marathon in Japan in the fast time of 2:12:51, nearly 5 minutes better than his previous best.

With the 1972 Olympic Games approaching, Frank moved to Vail, Colorado, in order to train at high altitude. For two months, he ran at least 20 miles a day in the mountains. This training improved his body's ability to transport oxygen to the muscles, which gave him an advantage over runners who did not do high-altitude training. Yet all of this hard work was nearly wasted when a blister on his right foot became infected shortly before the Olympic trials. His doctor recommended that he skip the marathon trial, but fortunately the infection responded to antibiotics and Frank was able to run. He tied for first place, thus earning the right to represent the United States in the 1972 Olympic marathon.

Although ranked first in the world in the marathon in 1971, Frank was not favored to win the Olympic marathon at Munich in 1972. During the early stages of the race, Frank conserved his energy, allowing other runners to take the lead. When the leaders slowed, just beyond the 9-mile point, he accelerated and soon had a 5-second lead. He won in 2:12:19.8, only 8 seconds slower than the Olympic record.

Continuing the Story

His unexpected victory in the Olympic marathon made Frank an American national hero. His success helped make distance running popular in the United States; the number of runners in marathon races surged in the following years as millions of Americans took up jogging.

Even though a young man, Frank was not able to continue his Olympic success. He suffered a series of injuries that prevented him from performing at his best, although he did gain second place in the 1976 Olympic marathon.

STATISTICS

Year	Competition	Event	Place	Time
1969	NCAA Outdoor Championships	6 miles	1st	29:00.2
1970	National AAU Championships	10,000 meters	1st	27:24.0
		Cross-country	1st	—
1971	Pan-American Games	Marathon	1st	2:22:47
	Fukuoka Marathon	Marathon	1st	2:12:51
	National AAU Championships Indoor	3 miles	1st	13:10.6
	National AAU Championships	10,000 meters	1st	27:27.2
		Cross-country	1st	—
		Marathon	2d	2:17:45
1972	Olympic Games	10,000 meters	5th	27:51.4
		Marathon	1st	2:12:19.8
	National AAU Championships	Cross-country	1st	—
1973	National AAU Championships	Cross-country	1st	—
1974	National AAU Championships	10,000 meters	1st	28:16.0
1975	National AAU Championships	10,000 meters	1st	28:02.17
1976	Olympic Games	Marathon	Silver	2:10:45.8

MILESTONES

Ranked first in the world in the marathon in 1971
Named U.S. Athlete of the Year
Named *Track and Field News* World Athlete of the Year

HONORS AND AWARDS

1970	AAU Most Outstanding Performer, Outdoor
	Dieges Award, Indoor
1971	AAU Most Outstanding Performer, Indoor
	Dieges Award, Outdoor
1972	Long Distance Running Merit Award
	Sullivan Award
1984	Inducted into U.S. Olympic Hall of Fame

Summary

Frank Shorter was the first American since 1908 to win an Olympic marathon, and, for many American sports fans, he kindled a new interest in distance running. More than any other single individual, he was responsible for the running boom of the following years, which improved the health and fitness of millions of Americans.

Harold L. Smith

Additional Sources:

Hickok, Ralph. *A Who's Who of Sports Champions.* Boston: Houghton Mifflin, 1995.

The Lincoln Library of Sports Champions. 16 vols. Columbus, Ohio: Frontier Press, 1993.

Shorter, Frank, with Marc Bloom. *Olympic Gold: A Runner's Life and Times.* Boston: Houghton Miffin, 1984.

Wallechinsky, David. *The Complete Book of the Olympics.* Boston: Little, Brown and Company, 1991.

Watman, Mel. *Encyclopedia of Track and Field Athletics.* New York: St. Martin's Press, 1981.

JIM SHOULDERS

Sport: Rodeo

Born: May 13, 1928
Tulsa, Oklahoma

Early Life

James Arthur Shoulders was born on May 13, 1928, in Tulsa, Oklahoma. Ironically, the boy who was to become one of the all-time great rodeo stars was not raised on a ranch. His father, Jim Shoulders, was an auto mechanic who worked in the city. Jim did spend much of his early childhood on his grandfather's farm, however.

Jim first became interested in rodeo when his older brother, Marvin, began entering amateur contests. When he was thirteen, Jim was given his first chance to ride a bull at a rodeo near Collinsville, Oklahoma. Jim begged his brother to let him sit on the bull. The instant the bull made its first lunge in the chute, he clambered to safety. Marvin shoved him back on and said, "All right, kid, you want to rodeo. It's now or never." Jim accepted his brother's challenge and spurred his bull out before cheering onlookers. That day was the beginning of what was to be a long career.

The Road to Excellence

Not content to live with the thrilling memory of just one rodeo performance, Jim decided to enter the rodeo at Oilton, Oklahoma, in the summer of 1942. Even though he was only fourteen years old, he competed well enough to win eighteen dollars in prize money. This small victory convinced him that he had the talent to become a professional rodeo cowboy.

After graduating from Tulsa East Center High School, Jim became a professional rodeo cowboy. He was convinced that performing in the rodeo was the only way that a "green country boy" like him could make a lot of money. Shortly after marrying his high school sweetheart, Sharon, in 1947, he scored his first national triumph at Madison Square Garden, winning two championships and $5,000. Two years later, he earned his first World Champion All-Around Cowboy title and $21,495 in winnings.

Because there were no rodeo schools for training rodeo cowboys when Jim started out, he learned how to ride bulls and broncs by experience and observation. He had not competed long before discovering that balance is much more important than strength for a rodeo performer. Like a baseball pitcher, Jim learned to keep a book "in his head," first figuring out the bronc's style and then conditioning his reac-

tions. He also realized that, in order to stay in top shape, he had to resist the temptation to smoke and drink like the other cowboys.

The Emerging Champion

Jim was at the height of his career from 1949 through 1959. For eleven years, Jim was the best all-around cowboy on the professional circuit. During this time, he was the biggest money winner, not because he entered more rodeos than anyone else but because he always won something. Even when he did not win the big prizes, he at least walked away with first or second place. By the end of this period, Jim had collected sixteen world championships. He was seven times best in the world in bull riding, five times the all-around king, and four times bareback bronc winner.

The only year in which he was not one of the top bull riders was 1953. Jim had to sit out much of the season after a bull fell on him in Midland, Texas, and broke his collarbone. The next year, though, Jim bounced back and regained his title as champion bull rider.

Jim's success can be attributed to the fact that he was probably the toughest man in the history of rodeo competition. After breaking his collarbone in 1953, Jim participated in eight more rodeos, even though doctors had inserted a steel pin to stabilize it. In 1957, a twisting bronc snapped Jim's right collarbone again, but Jim managed to finish the ride and win the event. By 1960, his knees were in such bad shape that he had to bind them with elastic bandages before he could ride. That same year, he had to undergo plastic surgery after a spinning bull gored him in the face. Although many people would have quit after suffering only one of these injuries, Jim characteristically downplayed the severity of the pain following each mishap and then went on to put forth his best effort. Before Jim retired, he had paid a dear price for his achievements, breaking his collarbone three times, both arms twice, both knees twice, and an ankle once.

MILESTONES	
1949	World Champion All-Around Cowboy Inducted into Rodeo Hall of Fame, the National Cowboy Hall of Fame
1950	Bareback Riding Champion
1951	Bull Riding Champion
1954-59	PRCA Bull Riding Champion
1956-58	PRCA Bareback Riding Champion
1956-59	PRCA World Champion All-Around Cowboy
1959	National Finals Rodeo (NFR) Bull Riding Average Winner
1974	Inducted into Madison Square Garden Hall of Fame
1975	Inducted into Oklahoma Sports Hall of Fame
1979	Inducted into Pro Rodeo Hall of Fame

RECORDS

Captured a total of sixteen individual world championship titles on the professional circuit—the most in professional rodeo

Continuing the Story

Although Jim officially retired from Professional Rodeo Cowboys Association (PRCA) competition in the mid-1960's, he never really quit rodeo. As director of the Mesquite Shoulders corporation, Jim produced the Mesquite Championship rodeo, which he started in 1958. This rodeo, which he operated with his family, would run every weekend from April to September. He also bred rodeo stock on his 500-acre ranch near Henryetta, Oklahoma, and became one of the top professional stock contractors. Jim perhaps derived the most pleasure from his Rodeo Riding School, which was the first of its kind. He was particularly proud of the champions that he trained, including world champion George Paell and two-time World Champion All-Around Cowboy Phil Lyne.

Even though Jim retired from competition, his dominance of the sport brought him recognition. In 1974, he became the first rodeo cowboy to enter the Madison Square Garden Hall of Fame, and in 1975, he was inducted into the Oklahoma Sports Hall of Fame. In fact, Jim's name is so identifiable to sports fans that he has been featured as a Miller Lite celebrity in commercials with stars like the late Billy Martin, former New York Yankees' manager. He has also endorsed such products as Wrangler jeans.

Summary

Jim Shoulders is truly one of the legends of rodeo. His sixteen world championships are so incredible that they may never be topped. He will also be remembered as the first five-time All-Around Cowboy world champion in history. Jim's reign as champion cowboy is memorable, not only because of its duration, but also because of the tremendous endurance and determination that made it possible.

Alan Brown

Additional Sources:

Allen, Michael. *Rodeo Cowboys in the North American Imagination.* Reno: University of Nevada Press, 1998.

Coplon, Jeff. *Gold Buckle: The Grand Obsession of Rodeo Bull Riders.* New York: HarperCollins, 1995.

Fredriksson, Kristine. *American Rodeo from Buffalo Bill to Big Business.* College Station: Texas A&M, 1985.

Wooden, Wayne S., and Gavin Ehringer. *Rodeo in America: Wranglers, Roughstock, and Paydirt.* Lawrence: University Press of Kansas, 1996.

AL SIMMONS

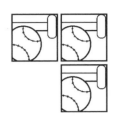

Sport: Baseball

Born: May 22, 1903
     Milwaukee, Wisconsin
Died: May 26, 1956
     Milwaukee, Wisconsin

Early Life

On May 22, 1903, one of baseball's great hitters was born of humble origins to a family of Polish immigrants in Milwaukee, Wisconsin. Although he was always proud of his Polish ancestry, Aloysius Harry Szymanski later changed his name for simplicity. He renamed himself Al Simmons after the name of a hardware company he had seen on a billboard.

While growing up, Al played baseball on the south side of Milwaukee. He practiced at it long and hard. Although he later played football briefly at Stevens Point Teachers College, baseball was his first love.

Even as a boy, Al was easily identified on the field. His light complexion never tanned, and whenever he was concentr1ating, his face would grow even whiter. As he grew older, he earned the nickname "Bucketfoot Al," because of his pe-

STATISTICS

Season	GP	AB	Hits	2B	3B	HR	Runs	RBI	BA	SA
1924	152	594	183	31	9	8	69	102	.308	.431
1925	153	658	253	43	12	24	122	129	.384	.596
1926	147	581	199	53	10	19	90	109	.343	.566
1927	106	406	159	36	11	15	86	108	.392	.645
1928	119	464	163	33	9	15	78	107	.351	.558
1929	143	581	212	41	9	34	114	**157**	.365	.642
1930	138	554	211	41	16	36	**152**	165	**.381**	.708
1931	128	513	200	37	13	22	105	128	**.390**	.641
1932	154	670	216	28	9	35	144	151	.322	.548
1933	146	605	200	29	10	14	85	119	.331	.481
1934	138	558	192	36	7	18	102	104	.344	.530
1935	128	525	140	22	7	16	68	79	.267	.427
1936	143	568	186	38	6	13	96	112	.327	.484
1937	103	419	117	21	10	8	60	84	.279	.434
1938	125	470	142	23	6	21	79	95	.302	.511
1939	102	351	96	17	5	7	39	44	.274	.410
1940	37	81	25	4	0	1	7	19	.309	.395
1941	9	24	3	1	0	0	1	1	.125	.167
1943	40	133	27	5	0	1	9	12	.203	.263
1944	4	6	3	0	0	0	1	2	.500	.500
Totals	2,215	8,761	2,927	539	149	307	1,507	1,827	.334	.535

Notes: Boldface indicates statistical leader. GP = games played; AB = at bats; 2B = doubles; 3B = triples; HR = home runs; RBI = runs batted in; BA = batting average; SA = slugging average

culiar batting stance. Although a right-hander, he stood with his left foot pointing down the third base line. This unusual position did not seem to affect the boy's balance or power at bat.

The Road to Excellence

At the start of Al's baseball career, he wrote letters to various team managers requesting tryouts on major league teams. He even wrote to his childhood hero, catcher Roger Bresnahan, then the manager of the Cleveland Indians. He also wrote to Connie Mack, owner and manager of the Philadelphia Athletics, offering to play in exchange for car fare to Philadelphia. Ignoring this request would later cost Mack dearly.

With no response from the major leagues, Simmons signed on to play semiprofessional ball. His big break came when he hit the game-winning home run to defeat the Milwaukee amateur team. This performance resulted in his signing his first professional contract with the Milwaukee Brewers in 1922, at the age of nineteen.

From the start of spring training in 1923, Al was farmed out to the Dakota League, where he hit .365 in 99 games. Then he was sent to the Texas League, where he batted .360 in 144

games. This remarkable performance caused him to be recalled to the Brewers for the last 24 games of the season, where he hit .398.

The Emerging Champion

In 1924, Connie Mack bought Al Simmons's contract for something between $40,000 and $70,000, a considerable amount of money at the time. Al played every game that season for Mack's Philadelphia Athletics, batting .308 with 102 runs batted in (RBIs) and 8 home runs.

During his second year in the major leagues, Al, with his long arms and extra-long bat, became the batting champion for the American League with 253 hits. He just missed breaking George Sisler's record of 257, set five years previously. Al's batting average that year was .384, only slightly behind that of veteran batting stars Harry Helmans and Tris Speaker. Al had at last proven himself as a major hitter.

HONORS AND AWARDS

1929	American League most valuable player
1933-35	American League All-Star Team
1953	Inducted into National Baseball Hall of Fame

In 1928, the Athletics finished second in the league. The following year, they won the pennant and the World Series, with Al opening up the most spectacular turnaround inning in World Series history. It was the seventh inning of the fourth game, with the Cubs leading. Al started the inning with a home run for Philadelphia. Nine runs later and in the same inning, he hit a single to bring in the tenth run. Philadelphia eventually won the game 10-8. The following year, Al led his team to another World Series victory, batting .381 with 165 RBIs.

In 1931, Al stayed away from spring training, holding out in contract negotiations for a $100,000 three-season salary. He signed just hours before the start of Opening Day and hit a home run his first time at bat. He ended the season with his second league batting championship in a row, and the Athletics won the pennant for the third time in succession. They lost the Series to the St. Louis Cardinals, with Al hitting .333, including 2 home runs and 8 RBIs.

In 1932, the Athletics slipped to second place, and Mack began trading away his best players because they were too expensive to keep. Even though Al led the league with 216 hits and had a batting average of .322, he was traded to the Chicago White Sox.

Continuing the Story

Al Simmons's career tapered off over the next several years. Traded from team to team, with slightly decreasing batting averages, he still was a strong player, scoring well but not spectacularly.

His glory days began to wane. Old Bucketfoot Al came within 73 hits of his lifetime goal of 3,000 base hits. For this reason, at the end of his career he regretted that earlier he had missed games and had even walked out on an occasional lopsided game. Still, after fourteen seasons, he left baseball with a career batting average of .334.

Later on, Al coached various semiprofessional teams and scouted for the majors. He was lonely, however, and he drank heavily. His wife, Doris, divorced him. On May 26, 1956, he died of a heart attack on a street in Milwaukee.

Summary

Al Simmons started his baseball career in the majors with a bang. He was selected as the American League most valuable player in 1929 and won the league batting championship twice, in 1930 and 1931. As one of baseball's finest hitters with his lifetime batting average of .334, he was inducted into the National Baseball Hall of Fame in 1953.

Nan White

Additional Sources:

Hickok, Ralph. *A Who's Who of Sports Champions.* Boston: Houghton Mifflin, 1995.

Porter, David L., ed. *Biographical Dictionary of American Sports: Baseball.* Westport, Conn.: Greenwood Press, 1987.

Shatzkin, Mike, et al. eds. *The Ballplayers: Baseball's Ultimate Biographical Reference.* New York: William Morrow, 1990.

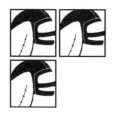

O. J. SIMPSON

Sport: Football

Born: July 9, 1947
San Francisco, California

Early Life

Orenthal James Simpson was born on July 9, 1947, in San Francisco, California. His unusual name was suggested to his mother by an aunt. During his youth, he did not take school very seriously. He was part of a gang and got into serious trouble with the police on a number of occasions.

O. J. Simpson in 1973.

His first exposure to sports began at a community center, where O. J. soon became aware of his athletic ability. Although he spent his younger years in braces due to a lack of strength in his legs, O. J. broke the 60-yard dash record at his junior high school.

The Road to Excellence

Originally, O. J. played the tackle position in high school because of his size, but when the coaches saw how he could run, he became a fullback. O. J. excelled at running the ball and was selected as an All-City player. An assistant coach advised O. J. that if he ever wanted to get anywhere he would have to work hard. O. J. never forgot that advice and developed a strong work ethic.

O. J.'s lack of interest in school, however, led to grades that were below average, so when he graduated he had to attend a two-year junior college. In his two seasons at San Francisco City College, O. J. scored 26 touchdowns and averaged 9.9 yards per carry.

O. J. went on to the University of Southern California (USC), where he became an instant sensation. In two seasons with the Trojans, O. J. ran for 3,295 yards and scored 34 touchdowns. He also led the Trojans to a national championship.

In the 1968 Rose Bowl game, O. J. was named the outstanding player. He also won the Walter Camp Award, the Maxwell Award, and *The Sporting News* College Player of the Year award. That year, O. J. set the record for the most rushing yards gained in a single season and was awarded college football's most coveted award, the Heisman Trophy.

It was not surprising when the Buffalo Bills, the lowest-ranked team in the Na-

AP/Wide World Photos

STATISTICS

		Rushing				Receiving			
Season	GP	Car.	Yds.	Avg.	TD	Rec.	Yds.	Avg.	TD
1969	13	181	697	3.9	2	30	343	11.4	3
1970	8	120	488	4.1	5	10	139	13.9	0
1971	14	183	742	4.1	5	21	162	7.7	0
1972	14	292	**1,251**	4.3	6	27	198	7.3	0
1973	14	332	**2,003**	6.0	**12**	6	70	11.7	0
1974	14	270	1,125	4.2	3	15	189	12.6	1
1975	14	329	**1,817**	5.5	**16**	28	426	15.2	7
1976	14	290	**1,503**	5.2	8	22	259	11.8	1
1977	7	126	557	4.4	0	16	138	8.6	0
1978	10	161	593	3.7	1	21	172	8.2	2
1979	13	120	460	3.8	3	7	46	6.6	0
Totals	135	2,404	11,236	4.7	61	203	2,142	10.6	14

Notes: Boldface indicates statistical leader. GP = games played; Car. = carries; Yds. = yards; Avg. = average yards per carry or average yards per reception; TD = touchdowns; Rec. = receptions

tional Football League (NFL), used their number one pick in the NFL draft to select O. J.

The Emerging Champion

O. J.'s first three years in the NFL were not as spectacular as people had imagined they would be. Part of this was due to his coaches playing him improperly. They used him as a blocking back and even tried him at wide receiver. People began to think of O. J. as another Heisman Trophy flop.

Finally, when Lou Saban took over as the head coach of the Bills, the coaching staff surrounded O. J. with a strong supporting cast of blockers, gave him the ball, and let him run. The rest is history.

O. J. eluded entire defenses that were developed specifically to stop him. On the one hand, O. J. had enough strength to run through tacklers. It was rare that one man could bring him down. In addition to his strength, O. J. had terrific speed. (At USC he had been part of a world-record 440-yard relay team.) Just when tacklers would be surrounding him on the field, he would accelerate and leave them grasping at air.

On December 16, 1973, the Bills were playing their final game of the season at New York's Shea Stadium. O. J. needed 197 yards rushing in order to gain a total of 2,000 yards for the season. On that snowy, frozen field, the Bills lost the game, but O. J. won a place in history. On his final rush

of the day, O. J. ran the left side for 6 yards, bringing his total for the year to 2,003, the most ever at that time.

On November 25, 1976, O. J. had the greatest single day an NFL running back had ever had. The Bills were playing the Detroit Lions, the top-ranked defense in the league. In 29 carries, O. J. gained 273 yards (a record that has since been broken).

Continuing the Story

At times it seemed as though O. J. had eyes in the back of his head. Just when defenders would be closing in on him from behind, he would veer away from them. When asked about this amazing ability, O. J. explained that "experience prepares you for the unexpected."

O. J. carried the ball so many times in practice and in games that he intuitively knew where the defense should be. That may be one reason why his better efforts were against the better teams. Because the defensive players were where they were supposed to be, he could anticipate their moves and adjust as necessary. In short, O. J. worked and worked, and then worked some more.

Before O. J., the standard for single-game excellence among running backs in the NFL was 100 yards rushing. O. J. would frequently have that many by half time. When the standard for excellence for a season stood at 1,000 yards, O. J.

2553

was the first to rush for 2,000. As of 2000, he still ranked third in single-season rushing yards.

In his eleven seasons, O. J. led the league in rushing four times, finishing with more than 11,000 yards rushing. He gained 200 yards in a game six times, and had 1,000-yard seasons for five consecutive years.

After his retirement from professional football, O. J. was active as a television sports commentator and an actor in such films as *The Naked Gun* series. He also became a corporate spokesperson and endorsed athletic products. In 1994 all that changed when he was charged with the murder of his former wife and another man. He was acquitted in a criminal trial but later lost in a wrongful-death suit brought against him in a civil court. Afterward he retired from public life, but his name continued to appear in the news because of the notoriety he gained during his trials.

HONORS AND AWARDS	
1967	Citizens Savings Southern California Athlete of the Year
1968	Heisman Trophy Maxwell Award Camp Award *Sporting News* College Player of the Year Citizens Savings College Football Player of the Year Rose Bowl Football Player of the Game *Sporting News* College All-American
1969	Overall first choice in the NFL draft
1970	AFL All-Star Team
1972-73, 1975	United Press International AFC Player of the Year Newspaper Enterprise Association AFC Player of the Year (1972 co-recipient)
1972-76	*Sporting News* AFC All-Star Team
1973	Associated Press NFL Player of the Year Bell Trophy Thorpe Trophy NFL Pro Bowl Player of the Game Associated Press Male Athlete of the Year *Sporting News* Sportsman of the Year Hickok Belt Seagram's Seven Crowns of Sports Award
1973-77	NFL Pro Bowl Team
1973, 1975	*Sporting News* AFC Player of the Year
1980	NFL All-Pro Team of the 1970's
1983	Inducted into College Football Hall of Fame
1985	Inducted into Pro Football Hall of Fame
1994	NFL 75th Anniversary All Time Team

Summary

As an athlete, O. J. Simpson was a "symphony on the run," with the "strength of a horse" and "the speed of a deer." Indeed, O. J. was strong, and his running was balletic and graceful. When people argue over who was the best running back ever to play in the NFL, his name always comes up. With his power and strength, his finesse and grace, and his teamwork and leadership, O. J. was a running back who combined all the attributes of athletic greatness.

Dennis M. Docheff

Additional Sources:

Aaseng, Nathan. *Football's Breakaway Backs.* Minneapolis, Minn.: Lerner Publishing, 1980.

Belsky, Dick. *The Juice: Football's Superstar.* New York: H. Z. Walck, 1977.

Hill, Raymond. *O. J. Simpson.* New York: Random House, 1975.

Jameson, Jim. *The Picture Life of O. J. Simpson.* New York: F. Watts, 1977.

Morse, Ann. *Football's Great Running Back, O. J. Simpson.* Chicago: Children's Press, 1976.

MIKE SINGLETARY

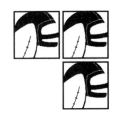

Sport: Football

Born: October 9, 1958
Houston, Texas

Early Life

Michael Singletary was born on October 9, 1958, the tenth child of a Houston Pentecostal preacher. He grew up in a tough neighborhood, where children quickly leave childhood behind. Before he was six, he had suffered through pneumonia three times. Later, his two older brothers died in accidents. His parents were divorced some time after that.

Mike grew up feeling inadequate because of his lack of height. When his mother told him to make the most of the qualities he did have, he decided to devote himself to doing all things well regardless of his size. Much of his drive came from growing up in an atmosphere of intense religious devotion. The family often spent twelve hours in church on Sundays.

Mike fell in love with football from watching it on television. He used to pretend he was too sick to go to Sunday school so he could watch National Football League (NFL) games at home. By the time he was twelve, he was so determined to play, he planned to run away. Luckily, his father gave in, and Mike joined his junior high school team as a linebacker.

The Road to Excellence

When Singletary graduated from high school, he went off to Baylor University. At first, he was so wound up in anticipation of each game that he used to start hyperventilating upon arriving at the field. He could not stop himself from endlessly running defensive plays over and over in his head. Finally he was taught relaxation techniques by his trainers. He began listen-

Chicago Bears

ing to classical music, while teammates listened to heavy metal or to soul music.

Mike became known for his preparedness before big games. He memorized all important details of the game plan weeks in advance. He

HONORS AND AWARDS

1979-80	Southwest Conference Player of the Year O'Brien Memorial Trophy
1984-85, 1988	United Press International NFC Defensive Player of the Year
1983-1991	NFL Pro Bowl Team NFL All-Pro Team United Press International All-NFC Team
1985, 1988	Associated Press Defensive Player of the Year
1989	Professional Football Writers of America All-Pro Team
1995	Inducted into College Football Hall of Fame
1998	Inducted into Pro Football Hall of Fame

studied more game film than everyone else combined.

Eventually, Mike's talents as a linebacker emerged and were given free rein. His team changed from a 5-2 defense to a 4-3 during his freshman year to take advantage of his abilities by letting him run loose in the middle. As a result, Mike averaged 15 tackles per game throughout his collegiate career. Three times, he even had 30 or more tackles in a game. He broke nine of his helmets. In 1979 and 1980, he was chosen as the Southwest Conference's Player of the Year.

The Emerging Champion

When the National Football League's (NFL) Chicago Bears drafted him in 1981, he weighed 240 pounds. He dropped his weight to 225 pounds and kept working to improve himself. From the beginning his goal was to turn himself into a complete player. He was always asking Bears coach Buddy Ryan how far he was from being the best linebacker ever and what could he do to improve. As a measure of his dedication, he constantly invited criticism.

As a rookie, he quickly acquired a reputation for being a mighty force with which to contend. They called him the "Tasmanian Devil," for the way in which he went about banging heads during games. Later, he was known as "Samurai." Yet he was never a mauler. He knew the technique of hitting in a way that was safe: with face back and head up. If he ever made a hit that was not clean, he apologized.

By 1983, Singletary had developed his skills so well that the Bears defense was on its way to the top. Although the team only finished eighth in total defense that year, in 1984 and 1985 they led the league. With Mike on their side, they were able to switch to almost all of their defensive fronts without making substitutions, which gave them a tremendous advantage. As a result, Singletary was named the United Press International NFC Defensive Player of the Year in 1984 and 1985 and again in 1988.

Mike's career was superb. He amassed an impressive 1,488 career tackles, 885 of which were solo efforts. A constant force on defense, he missed playing just two games, both in 1986. Selected to play in a team record ten Pro Bowls, Mike was All-Pro and/or All-NFL every year from 1983 until 1991.

Continuing the Story

Singletary's leadership qualities were extraordinary. Teammates could not believe his zeal and his intense drive for perfection. He became a leader by example. The Chicago Bears defense became nearly invincible, partly because of Singletary. As the defensive captain and signal caller, he also was the team's field coach. When he talked, teammates listened. No wonder—there were times when he could be heard yelling out the other team's plays even before they happened. Mike also inspired other players to stay late at practice in order to perfect a play, or to watch films on their days off. Mike's remarkable efforts on the field and his team leadership were rewarded in 1998, when he was inducted into the Pro Football Hall of Fame.

Mike's personality fooled many with its Dr. Jekyll/Mr. Hyde transformations. On the field, he seemed ferocious and driven by rage. Yet he was driven only by the desire to do his best. At home with his wife, Kim, Mike is a warm, likable fellow, and a happy one. His favorite part of a football game is the national anthem.

After his retirement from professional football, Mike became a regular on the Fortune 500 company lecture circuit. Many of his speaking topics include leadership, creation of a healthy work environment, positive response to change, and the importance of a good attitude. Mike has served as a board member of Successories, Tranzact Systems, and Focus on the Family and was a member of the NFL Advisory Council.

Summary

One of football's most dedicated players, Mike Singletary made himself into an exceptional linebacker through his will to surpass everyone else. His exceptional competitive drive also made him a superb, highly respected leader. Many considered him the ideal all-around football player.

Nan White

Additional Sources:

Barber, Phil. "NFL: Football's One Hundred Greatest Players—The Hit Men." *The Sporting News* 223 (November 1, 1999): 12-16.

Singletary, Mike. *Calling the Shots*. Chicago: Contemporary Books, 1986.

_____. *Singletary on Singletary*. Nashville, Tenn.: T. Nelson, 1991.

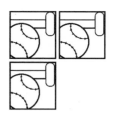

GEORGE SISLER

Sport: Baseball

Born: March 24, 1893
        Nimisila, Ohio
Died: March 26, 1973
        St. Louis, Missouri

Early Life

George Harold Sisler was born March 24, 1893, in Nimisila, Ohio, a small town near Akron. His family was relatively well-to-do for the time: Both of his parents were graduates of Hiram College, a small school in Ohio, and his father was manager of a coal mine. George's uncle was the mayor of Akron.

George was very athletic, and his baseball talents developed quickly. The town of Nimisila was too small to have a high school baseball team, so when George was fourteen, he moved to Akron to attend school there. His pitching so impressed the professional scouts that he was asked to sign a contract with the Akron team of the Ohio-Pennsylvania league.

The contract with Akron was to go into effect when George graduated from high school, but his father persuaded him to enroll at the University of Michigan instead. While at Michigan, George became known as an outstanding player,

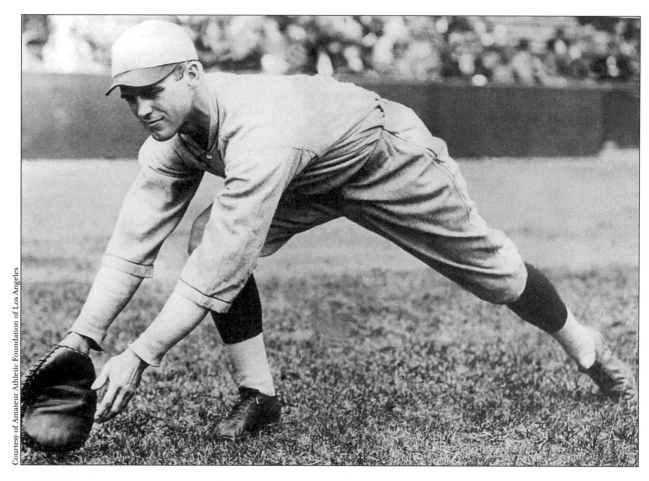

STATISTICS

Season	GP	AB	Hits	2B	3B	HR	Runs	RBI	BA	SA
1915	81	274	78	10	2	3	28	29	.285	.369
1916	151	580	177	21	11	4	83	76	.305	.400
1917	135	539	190	30	9	2	60	52	.353	.453
1918	114	452	154	21	9	2	69	41	.341	.440
1919	132	511	180	31	15	10	96	83	.352	.530
1920	154	631	**257**	49	18	19	137	122	**.407**	.632
1921	138	582	216	38	**18**	11	125	104	.371	.555
1922	142	586	**246**	42	18	8	**134**	105	**.420**	.594
1924	151	636	194	27	10	9	94	74	.305	.421
1925	150	649	224	21	15	12	100	105	.345	.479
1926	150	613	178	21	12	7	78	71	.290	.398
1927	149	614	201	32	8	5	87	97	.327	.430
1928	138	540	179	27	4	4	72	70	.331	.419
1929	154	629	205	40	9	1	67	79	.326	.423
1930	116	431	133	15	7	3	54	67	.309	.397
Totals	2,055	8,267	2,812	425	165	100	1,284	1,175	.340	.468

Notes: Boldface indicates statistical leader. GP = games played; AB = at bats; 2B = doubles; 3B = triples; HR = home runs; RBI = runs batted in; BA = batting average; SA = slugging average

perhaps the best college player in the country. The Pittsburgh Pirates purchased his contract from Akron and officially listed him as a member of their team.

It was also at Michigan that George met his future wife, Kathleen Holznagel. They eventually had one daughter and three sons, and all the boys went on to play professional baseball like their father.

The Road to Excellence

At Michigan, George was coached by Branch Rickey, who was later to become a dominant figure in modern baseball. Rickey helped George escape from the Pittsburgh contract, arguing that it had been signed while George was still a minor. The case caused considerable dispute and bitterness. After it was resolved in George's favor, he signed a contract with the St. Louis Browns, the team with which Rickey was associated. George and Rickey remained close for the rest of their lives.

George started his major league career in 1915 as a pitcher with the Browns, then managed by Rickey. When Rickey recognized George's outstanding abilities as a left-handed batter, he switched him to first base. George became an excellent fielder, leading the American League in assists six times during his career. He became

known as one of the best first basemen ever to play the game.

George batted .305 in 1916, his first full season with the Browns. He performed even better the following year, with 190 hits and a .353 average. His record was nearly as good in 1918, when he ended the season with a .341 average. His efforts, however, were obscured by the fact that he played for a weak team, the Browns, who finished far down in the standings.

George steadily developed his batting ability during this time and perfected his fielding skills as well. In the course of the 1919 season, he compiled a .352 batting average and won his first award for assists. George was ready to establish himself as one of the premier hitters in professional baseball.

The Emerging Champion

In 1920, George was the best player on the Browns' roster, and, although the team finished fourth that year, George put together the first of three consecutive outstanding seasons. He set a major league record by leading the American League in batting average (.407), games played (154), at bats (631), hits (257), and assists (140).

George, like many great hitters in baseball, had exceptional control. During his fifteen seasons in the major leagues, he struck out only 327 times. In 1920, he hit safely in almost every game he played, failing to do so in only twenty-three games. Although a relatively small man at 5 feet, 10 inches and weighing 170 pounds, George was an outstanding ballplayer.

He demonstrated his abilities again in 1921 when he had a batting average of .371 with 216 hits. Even with this performance, the Browns ended in third place. In 1922, the St. Louis team came the closest they would to winning a pennant while George played with them. The Browns battled the powerful New York Yankees throughout the season but finished behind by a single game.

During this intense battle, George was at his best. He set an American League record by hitting safely in forty-one consecutive games. This record stood until 1941, when it was broken by Joe Di-Maggio's fifty-six-game streak. George also batted .420 and led the league with 18 triples, 134 runs, 246 hits, and 125 assists. He struck out only 14 times. It was little surprise that he won the league's most valuable player award.

Continuing the Story

George missed the entire 1923 season because he was sick with a dangerous sinusitis, an inflammation of the nasal membranes. The infection caused double vision, a disaster for a major league batter. Although the condition cleared up, doubts remained about George's batting ability.

George returned in 1924 to the St. Louis Browns as a player and manager. He continued to hit over or near .300, but the Browns never finished higher than third place. In 1927, he gave up the manager's position and remained as a player.

In 1928, the Browns traded George to the Washington Senators. After only twenty games, he was traded again to the Boston Braves. He was with the Braves until 1930 and hit for an average of .300 each year.

George Sisler left major league baseball as a player in 1931, when he was sent to the minor leagues for the first time. He played and managed in Rochester, New York, and Shreveport, Louisiana, before he went into private business.

George's record in the major leagues was excellent: a .344 batting average in the American League, and a .326 average in the National League. Only a few players have done better than George's combined .340 lifetime average.

Working with his old mentor Branch Rickey, George was a scout for the Brooklyn Dodgers from 1943 through 1950. When Rickey moved to the Pittsburgh Pirate organization in 1951, George went with him and worked for Rickey and the Pirates until his death on March 26, 1973. In recognition of his achievements, George was elected to the National Baseball Hall of Fame in 1939.

Summary

George Sisler was an outstanding batter and excellent fielder who perfected his skills by practice and dedication. Although he never played on a team that reached the World Series or even won a pennant, George always performed the best he could. In doing so, he compiled one of baseball's most impressive records.

Michael Witkoski

HONORS, AWARDS, AND RECORDS

1920	Major league record for the most hits in a season (257)
1922	American League most valuable player
1939	Inducted into National Baseball Hall of Fame

Additional Sources:

Appel, Martin, and Burt Goldblatt. *Baseball's Best: The Hall of Fame Gallery*. New York: McGraw-Hill, 1977.

Porter, David L., ed. *Biographical Dictionary of American Sports: Baseball*. Westport, Conn.: Greenwood Press, 1987.

Shatzkin, Mike, et al., eds. *The Ballplayers: Baseball's Ultimate Biographical Reference*. New York: William Morrow, 1990.

SISSI

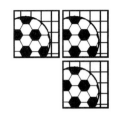

Sport: Soccer

Born: June 2, 1967
Esplanada, Bahia, Brazil

Early Life

Sisleide Lima do Amor, or Sissi (pronounced "see-SEE"), was born on June 2, 1967, in Esplanada, Bahia state, Brazil. One of seven children of a road construction worker and his wife, Sissi grew up in Salvador, in northern Brazil. She became intensely interested in soccer at a very early age, and even before she had a ball she and her playmates would practice in the streets, using oranges, rolled up socks, and other substitutes.

Soccer is very popular in Brazil, but the boys sometimes excluded Sisleide from street games on the basis of her gender. She was undaunted, however; she kept practicing, even tearing the heads from her dolls to use for soccer balls. Her parents finally bought her a ball, which was rare among the children of her neighborhood, so the boys let her play with them. Her skills as a player were noticed. By the age of fourteen, she had joined Flamengo of Feira de Santana, a professional soccer team, and moved away from her parents' home.

The Road to Excellence

In 1985, four years after her professional debut, Sisleide signed with another team and moved to Salvador. During the period from 1989 to 1996, she focused on indoor soccer and played for the Corinthians, Bordon, Marvel, Eurosport, and Sapesp. She resumed playing field soccer with Saad of Campinas and eventually transferred to Palmeiras.

In 1988 Sisleide joined the national team. As she rose in fame, her fans shortened her name to "Sissi." In many ways, Sissi's career parallels the acceptance of women's soccer, both within Brazil and internationally. Just as she was gaining national recognition, the Fédération Internationale de Football Association (FIFA), soccer's interna-

Brazilian soccer star Sissi during the women's World Cup in 1999, at which Brazil took the bronze medal.

2561

HONORS AND AWARDS

1995, 1998	South American soccer champion, with Brazilian team
1996	Bronze Medal with Brazilian Olympic Team
1999	MasterCard All-Star Team
1999	Adidas Golden Shoe, for top scorer of Women's World Cup (with Sun Wen)
1999	Silver Ball (Women's World Cup second-most valuable player)
2000	Brazilian Olympic Team

tional governing body, decided to organize a world championship series for women.

The first women's World Cup was held in 1991, hosted by China, and the second was hosted by Sweden in 1995. Although the Brazilian team finished only ninth in these two tournaments, they helped to capture the enthusiasm of the Brazilian public, which had until that time been focused largely on the male athletes, soccer being generally considered an inappropriate activity for women. In 1995 Sissi, who had been playing as a midfielder for the São Paulo women's team, was chosen for Brazil's South American championship team.

The Emerging Champion

After Brazil improved its status in women's soccer by winning the bronze medal in the 1996 Olympics, Sissi began to attract international attention. In the Games she had scored Brazil's goal in a 1-1 draw against Germany, thus allowing Brazil to advance to the semifinals and to the bronze. She played in every one of the Olympic matches. In 1998 Sissi again represented Brazil on its South American championship team and played brilliantly.

Although she missed the U. S. Women's Cup in 1998 because of a knee injury, Sissi became an international star at the 1999 women's World Cup, hosted by the United States. She began the tournament with a hat trick during a 7-1 win over Mexico. Then, she scored both of the winning goals in a game with Italy. In the quarterfinal meeting with Nigeria, the game had gone into fourteen minutes of overtime, after Brazil lost its 3-0 lead. About 25 yards away from the Nigerian goal, Sissi took a free kick with her left foot and put the ball inside the left goal post. With Sissi's dramatic kick, Brazil won 4-3 and advanced to the semifinal.

When individual players at the 1999 World Cup were compared, Sissi tied Sun Wen of China as highest scorer in the tournament, having scored a total of 7 goals and 3 assists for Brazil, which won third place. The soccer-loving Brazilians were ecstatic, and Sissi's new coach, Wilson Oliveira Rica, hailed her as "the queen of soccer."

International popularity led to speculation about her appearance. While Brazilians knew that Sissi had shaved her head in the style of Ronaldo, their male soccer star, Americans assumed that she was inspired by singer Sinead O'Connor.

Continuing the Story

On the basis of her stellar performance in the World Cup, Sissi was selected by the FIFA technical study group as one of the sixteen members of the MasterCard All-Star team of the 1999 FIFA women's World Cup. On behalf of the All-Stars, MasterCard donated $16,000 to FIFA's charity, the SOS Children's Villages, which provides homes for disadvantaged children around the world. The MasterCard All-Star team program, which was created in 1991, recognizes and honors top soccer players in this way. Sissi and Chinese star Sun Wen were awarded the Adidas Golden Shoe as the joint top scorers, and their trophies were presented at the FIFA World Player of the Year gala in Brussels, Belgium, on January 24, 2000.

On June 27, 2000, before 16,386 fans at the Foxboro Stadium in Massachussetts, Sissi played for Brazil in a game with the United States. The scoreless game was decided by a coin toss, but the fans were excited by the closely matched players, and the game helped to build interest in an important development that would result in yet another significant change for Sissi. Plans were underway for a new professional league that would combine the very best American and international players, the Women's United Soccer Association (WUSA).

Meanwhile, she continued gaining valuable experience, playing for Brazil in the 2000 Olympics in Sydney, Australia, in September. Although Germany defeated Brazil 2-0 for the bronze medal in that tournament, Sissi was recognized individually as one of the best players in the world. A month after the Olympics, she was selected for participation in the WUSA program to place foreign players in the new league. On October 30, 2000, Sissi and her Brazilian national teammate Katia, a forward, were assigned to one of the new WUSA teams, the Bay Area CyberRays, based in San Francisco.

Summary

Sissi helped to expand the Brazilian passion for soccer to include enthusiasm for women players. Through talent and determination, she be-

came one of the greatest women soccer players in the world.

Alice Myers

Additional Sources:

Rutledge, Rachel. *The Best of the Best in Soccer.* Brookfield, Conn.: Millbrook Press, 1999.

"Sun Wen and Sissi Share Adidas Top Scorer Award." *La Cancha Soccer Magazine* Online. http://www.lacancha.com/wwc72599.html.

Women's United Soccer Association On-line. http://www.wusaleague.com/.

BRUCE SMITH

Sport: Football

Born: June 18, 1963
Norfolk, Virginia

Early Life

Bruce Smith was born on June 18, 1963, to George and Annie Smith in Norfolk, Virginia. Bruce's father, a truck driver, and his mother, a plastics factory employee, worked long hours to provide for Bruce and his older brother and sister. Bruce was a chubby child who was teased and bullied by other children. Because he was too heavy to fit in any weight class, he did not play football in grammar school.

The Road to Excellence

At Booker T. Washington High School in Norfolk, he excelled at basketball, leading his team in his senior year to the 1980 Virginia AAA Championship. In addition, despite the fact that he played on an average high-school football team, he caught the eyes of numerous football recruiters and accepted a scholarship offer from Virginia Polytechnic Institute and State University in Blacksburg, Virginia.

Under coach Bill Dooley, Bruce became an outstanding player at Virginia Tech. His team, the Hokies, posted winning records each year he was there, from 1981 to 1984, and earned an invitation to the Independence Bowl his senior year. Also that year, he won the 1985 Outland Trophy, given to the best interior offensive or defensive lineman in the country.

For the Hokies, he accomplished 46 career sacks and twenty-five other tackles behind the line of scrimmage and was twice chosen the top collegiate athlete in Virginia.

The Emerging Champion

As the number one overall prospect in the country, Bruce was picked by the Buffalo Bills as the first player taken in the 1985 National Football League (NFL) draft. He was chosen over Doug Flutie, who had

AP/Wide World Photos

Bruce Smith of the Buffalo Bills in 1997. He signed with the Washington Redskins in 2000.

STATISTICS

Season	GP	Tac.	Sac.	FF	FR	Int.
1985	16	48	7.0	0	4	0
1986	16	63	15.0	3	0	0
1987	12	78	12.0	3	2	0
1988	12	56	11.0	3	0	0
1989	16	88	13.0	0	0	0
1990	16	101	19.0	4	0	0
1991	5	18	2.0	0	0	0
1992	15	89	14.0	3	0	0
1993	16	108	14.0	3	1	1
1994	15	81	10.0	5	2	1
1995	15	74	10.5	1	1	0
1996	16	90	13.5	5	1	0
1997	16	65	14.0	0	0	0
1998	15	50	10.0	2	0	0
1999	16	45	6.5	2	0	0
2000	16	57	10.0	5	0	0
Totals	**233**	**1,111**	**181.5**	**39**	**11**	**2**

Notes: GP = games played; Tac. = total tackles; Sac. = sacks; FF = forced fumbles; FR = fumble recoveries; Int. = interceptions

gotten a lot of press. In Bruce's first year as defensive end, he started in thirteen games, led the Bills in sacks, and was voted American Football Conference Defensive Rookie of the Year by the NFL Players Association.

In his second year, Bruce learned to study film of his opponents to develop strategic rushing techniques. He also began what turned into an obsession with conditioning. In 1986, Marv Levy signed on as the Bills' coach and became one of the major influences in Bruce's life. Through Levy, Bruce came to understand the necessity for discipline in developing his talent and becoming a successful professional football player. By the next year, his dedication to weight loss and conditioning paid off, giving Bruce an outstanding season. He molded his 6 foot 4 inch frame into 260 pounds and became a formidable presence on the field.

Prior to the 1988 season, Bruce tested positive for illegal drugs and was suspended for the first four games. He apologized to his family and vowed never again to make that mistake. He was selected Pro Bowl starter for the third consecutive year, despite playing only twelve games and becoming mired in team bickering over tough losses.

In 1990 Bruce was clearly one of the most dominant defensive players in football. He set another record for sacks and was named the NFL Defensive Player of the Year. He eagerly accepted his status as the player who entire offenses would try to thwart. Offensive linemen were mystified by his speed and agility.

Continuing the Story

In July, 1991, Bruce had arthroscopic surgery on his left knee and, as a result, suffered one of the most frustrating seasons of his career. He played in only five games but returned in 1992 to a full season and played in the Pro Bowl in both 1992 and 1993.

Two of his finest years were 1996 and 1997, his eleventh and twelfth years in professional football, during which he set more records. At the end of the 1999 season, Bruce, as a free agent, signed with the Washington Redskins for one year.

Bruce, an acknowledged workaholic, made a habit during football season of constantly studying, practicing, and playing. His attention to detail in planning his own strategies was surpassed only in his appraisal of his own performance after each game.

Summary

Bruce Smith's secret of success lay in his ability to develop his natural talent into a model of strength, discipline, and conditioning. Early on in Buffalo, Bruce began to change from a cocky, overweight rookie into someone who wanted to do his job extremely well. His father's failing health offered Bruce a painful lesson, challenging him to pursue longevity in health and career, rather than merely rely on natural endowments. Sustaining his performance at a high level and at an age when many other players would have retired, Bruce remained a dominant player in the NFL.

Mary Hurd

Additional Sources:

Dieffenbach, Don. "Trimming the Fat with Bruce Smith." *Sport*, January, 1996, 78-79.

Stanley, Loren. *Buffalo Bills*. Mankato, Minn.: Creative Education, 1997.

Telander, Rick. "Lean Mean Sack Machine." *Sports Illustrated* 75 (September 2, 1991): 28-32.

BUBBA SMITH

Sport: Football

Born: February 28, 1945
Beaumont, Texas

Early Life

Charles Aaron "Bubba" Smith was born on February 28, 1945, in Beaumont, Texas. He was one of three sons of Georgia and Willie Ray Smith.

Football was part of the Smith family atmosphere. Willie Ray Smith was the head football coach at Charlton Pollard High School in Beaumont, and preparing his young sons for the sport took up much of his free time.

Dinnertime conversation at the home was about football. Recreation revolved around football, whether Willie Ray and the boys were watching games on television or practicing their skills in the back yard. They ate, breathed, and slept the sport.

The Road to Excellence

Bubba and his two brothers, Willie Ray, Jr., and Tody, all played under their father at Pollard High School. Each of them won All-State football honors.

In Bubba's senior year at Pollard, he made the All-State squad, and his bruising style of play helped lead the team to an undefeated 11-0 season. At 6 feet, 8 inches and 280 pounds, it was not long before Bubba was recognized as one of the top college prospects in the nation. Many universities attempted to recruit this outstanding defensive player, but Bubba chose Michigan State University of the Big Ten Conference.

At Michigan State, Bubba honed his defensive skills. He was agile and quick. He amazed fans with his unrelenting ferocity. During a game against Pennsylvania State University his junior year, the Pittsburgh press reported that "what . . . eyewitnesses remember about Smith was the way he converted the Penn State offense into rubble

Bubba Smith of the Baltimore Colts, in 1971.

AP/Wide World Photos

by the end of the third quarter. At the start, [Rip] Engle's blockers were holding him out. Each time it was just a little harder. Near the finish, Bubba was wading right through and clamping his huge paws around the neck of the Penn State quarterback."

Fans who cheered "kill, Bubba, kill" cheered all the louder in 1965 and 1966 when Smith won All-American honors. Bubba was also named most valuable player in the Senior Bowl All-Star game in 1966.

The Emerging Champion

By then Bubba was recognized around the country as a dominating defensive end. In the

2566

combined American Football League (AFL)/
National Football League (NFL) draft in 1967,
Bubba Smith was picked in the first round by the
Baltimore Colts.

Smith played for Baltimore from 1967 to 1971,
and in that time he helped lead the Colts to the
NFL Championship game twice. Bubba was chosen for the Pro Bowl twice and made the All-
National Football Conference (NFC) team three
years in a row. In his best season, 1971, Bubba
made 9 quarterback sacks and blocked 4 field
goals.

After sitting out the 1972 season on injured reserve, Smith was traded by the Colts to the Oakland Raiders of the American Football Conference (AFC). While in Oakland, Bubba played in
two AFC Championship games, in 1973 and
1974.

While maintaining the skills and experience
of a veteran player, Smith was starting to lose his
agility and quickness. Never fully recovering
from the severe knee injury of 1972, Bubba was
released by the Raiders in 1975.

Smith was suddenly faced with the decision of
retiring from football or trying out with an NFL
team as a free agent. His love of the game won
out, however, and shortly after being released by
the Raiders, Bubba signed to play for the Houston Oilers.

Although he would never again play on a
championship team, he would play professional
football for three years before his retirement in
1977.

Continuing the Story

In retirement, Bubba sought a new line of
work. Many retired players had gone into coaching, but that was not for him. Some retired players had gone back to school for graduate degrees, but that was not for him either.

He decided to try acting. First, it was beer commercials. Next, it was television shows. There
Bubba's persona ranged from the underworld

HONORS AND AWARDS

1965	College All-American
1966	Senior Bowl All-Star Game most valuable player Chicago College All-Star Team *Sporting News* College All-American
1967	Overall first choice in the NFL draft
1970-71	NFL All-Pro Team *Sporting News* AFC All-Star Team
1971-72	NFL Pro Bowl Team
1988	Inducted into College Football Hall of Fame

bone-cruncher to the daft gentle giant. With a
steady schedule of parts to his credit, Bubba was
ready to try motion pictures.

As a movie actor, Bubba appeared as a mon-
strous police cadet in the *Police Academy* original
and sequels. These movies drew large numbers at
the box office and established Bubba Smith as a
Hollywood regular. As an extension of his *Police
Academy* work, Bubba has performed in comedy
shows to raise money for youth programs and
prevention in Los Angeles.

Summary

Raised to be a football player, Bubba Smith
emerged from All-State honors at Charlton Pollard High School to All-American honors at
Michigan State University. He was recognized as
one of the most feared defensive ends in the
NFL. His successful transition from athlete to actor has made him one of the most recognizable
and likable personalities from the world of
sports.

Rustin Larson

Additional Sources:

College Football Hall of Fame. http://college
football.org.
Reilly, Rick. "Point After: The Heavenly Hundred." *Sports Illustrated* 70, no. 20 (May 22,
1989): 104-106.

EMMITT SMITH

Sport: Football

Born: May 15, 1969
Pensacola, Florida

Early Life

Emmitt Smith III, one of five children of Emmitt Smith, Jr., and Mary Smith, was born on May 15, 1969, in Pensacola, Florida. Emmitt seemed born to play football. His father, a bus driver, was a semiprofessional player, and his mother would sometimes calm her infant son by showing him televised games. By the time Emmitt was seven, he was playing in an organized youth league, and he pursued his love of football to the exclusion of other hobbies throughout his youth. By the time he entered Escambia High School, he had developed his talent to such an extent that he earned the starting running back's job as a freshman.

Dallas Cowboys

The Road to Excellence

Young Emmitt soon showed that he was more than a match for his older competition. In his first game, he scored 2 touchdowns and ran for 115 yards. Escambia had not had a winning season in twenty-one years, but Emmitt led the team to two state titles in four seasons. At the end of his senior season, he was named the top high school player in the nation by *Parade* magazine, and his total of 8,804 yards rushing was the second-best in high school history.

Despite his success, Emmitt, according to his coaches and teammates, remained hardworking, polite, and unselfish. Many college scouts, though, remained unimpressed by his accomplishments. One scout told *Sports Illustrated* that Emmitt had been badly overrated, describing him as "a lugger, not a runner." Nevertheless, Emmitt won a full scholarship to the University of Florida and again quickly emerged as the team's top player; in his first game as a starter in his freshman season, he simply overwhelmed the powerful University of Alabama team, rushing for an incredible 224

STATISTICS

Season	GP	Rushing					Receiving			
		Car.	Yds.	Avg.	TD	Rec.	Yds.	Avg.	TD	
1990	16	241	937	3.9	11	24	228	9.5	0	
1991	16	**365**	**1,563**	4.3	12	49	258	5.3	1	
1992	16	373	**1,713**	4.6	**18**	59	335	5.7	1	
1993	14	283	**1,486**	5.3	9	57	414	7.3	1	
1994	15	368	1,484	4.0	**21**	50	341	6.8	**1**	
1995	16	377	**1,773**	4.7	**25**	62	375	6.0	0	
1996	15	327	1,204	3.7	12	47	249	5.3	3	
1997	16	261	1,074	4.1	4	40	234	5.9	0	
1998	16	319	1,332	4.2	13	27	175	6.5	2	
1999	15	329	1,397	4.2	11	27	119	4.4	2	
2000	16	294	1,203	4.1	9	11	79	7.2	0	
Totals	171	3,537	15,166	4.3	145	453	2,807	6.2	11	

Notes: Boldface indicates statistical leader. GP = games played; Car. = carries; Yds. = yards; Avg. = average yards per carry or average yards per reception; TD = touchdowns; Rec. = receptions

yards, a Florida record. He was named an All-American in each of his three college seasons, setting fifty-eight school records in the process. After a brilliant junior season, he decided to forgo his last year of college football in order to make himself eligible for the National Football League (NFL) draft.

Like their college counterparts, however, NFL scouts were not fully convinced of his ability. Several commented that he was too slow to make an effective NFL running back, while others speculated that, at 5 feet 9 inches and slightly more than 200 pounds, he would prove too small to stand up to the pounding of the professional game.

The Emerging Champion

As a result of such doubts, Emmitt was not chosen until near the end of the 1990 draft's first round, when the Dallas Cowboys selected him with the seventeenth pick. The Cowboys, who thought much more highly of Emmitt's ability than many other teams, were delighted to be able to get him with such a low pick. When club officials told reporters that Emmitt had been the team's fourth-rated choice in the entire draft, however, the young running back decided to use the leverage to strike a tough bargain in contract negotiations. As a result, he held out through his first NFL training camp and came into his rookie year virtually without preparation. Nevertheless, he earned the number-one running back job just

two games into the season. By the season's end, he had rushed for 937 yards and 11 touchdowns, and he was named the league's Offensive Rookie of the Year by the Associated Press.

The Cowboys, long one of the NFL's powers, had fallen on hard times in the late 1980's, compiling a dismal 1-15 record in the year before Emmitt's arrival. Emmitt and young quarterback Troy Aikman helped to resurrect the once-proud franchise, however, and under the coaching of Jimmy Johnson, Dallas made steady improvement. The Cowboys jumped to 7-9 in Emmitt's rookie season and to 11-5 and a playoff berth the following year; that season, he led the NFL with 1,563 yards rushing.

In 1992, both Emmitt and the Cowboys continued to improve. Emmitt repeated as the league's top rusher with 1,713 yards, and he also led the NFL with 19 touchdowns. Dallas cruised to a 13-3 record, defeating Philadelphia and San Francisco in the playoffs, and then demolished the Buffalo Bills by the score of 52-17 in Super Bowl XXVII.

Continuing the Story

After the Cowboy's triumph, however, Emmitt's contract with the team expired, and as the 1993 season neared, the two parties were far apart on a new deal. As a result, Emmitt again sat out training camp, and the holdout became a national story. The Cowboy's outspoken owner, Jerry Jones, told reporters that Emmitt was a

HONORS AND AWARDS

1987	*Parade* magazine National High School Player of the Year
1987-90	All-Southeastern Conference Team
1987-90	Consensus All-American
1990	Associated Press NFL Offensive Rookie of the Year
1991-95, 1997-99	NFL Pro Bowl
1994	Super Bowl XXVII most valuable player *Sporting News* NFL Player of the Year

"luxury, not a necessity" to the team, and the dispute dragged on into the regular season. After the Cowboys lost their first two games, however, Jones capitulated, giving his star a four-year, $13.6 million contract, and Emmitt returned to the lineup.

The Cowboys immediately caught fire, rolling to win after win, and Emmitt captured his third consecutive rushing title despite missing the two games during the holdout. Dallas was again the class of the NFL in the playoffs, and Emmitt capped off the season by running for 132 yards and 2 touchdowns in a second consecutive Super Bowl rout of the Bills. He was chosen as the game's most valuable player and also won virtually every Player of the Year honor for the regular season.

In 1994 Emmitt led the NFL with 22 touchdowns and tied for second in scoring, with 132 points. In 1995 he broke his own mark by gaining his third rushing title with 1,773 yards on 377 carries (the fourth in five years), set an NFL record for touchdowns in a single season with 25, and was a Pro Bowl Selection. Dallas fared well too. On January 28, 1996, the Dallas Cowboys won the Super Bowl 27-17 over the Pittsburgh Steelers. Emmitt scored 2 touchdowns, one of which guaranteed the Cowboys their victory. In 1996, despite numerous injuries, Emmitt was able to rush for over 1,200 yards for the sixth consecutive season, and he tied for third in the NFL with 15 touchdowns.

In the 1997-1999 seasons, he continued his assault on the record books and gained Pro Bowl honors each year. On December 11, 2000, Emmitt became only the third player in NFL history to surpass 15,000 rushing yards, joining Walter Payton and Barry Sanders. Emmitt also became only the second in league history, after Barry Sanders, to rush for 1,000 yards in ten consecutive seasons.

Summary

Few players in any sport can match Emmitt Smith's sustained record as an "impact player." At every level of competition, he overcame doubts about his ability to prove himself one of the best running backs in football history.

Brook Wilson

Additional Sources:
Bradley, John Ed. "Bottomed Out." *Sports Illustrated* 85, no. 41 (October 13, 1997): 58-61.
King, Peter. "Emmitt Unplugged." *Sports Illustrated* 84, no. 26 (July 1, 1996): 62-75.
Emmitt Smith Official Web Site. http://www.emmittsmithdirect.com.

JOHN SMITH

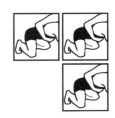

Sport: Wrestling

Born: August 9, 1965
Oklahoma City, Oklahoma

Early Life

John Smith was born on August 9, 1965, in Oklahoma City, Oklahoma, to Madalene and Lee Roy Smith. The Smiths, who lived in nearby Del City, reared ten children, four boys and six girls. Madalene worked as an obstetrics nurse, and her husband was the director of data processing for the Oklahoma Department of Transportation.

All of the Smith boys, including John, were small but very athletic and active. Wrestling, with its weight divisions, was the perfect sport for them. They were also fortunate that they lived in Oklahoma, where wrestling is extremely popular. The two oldest brothers, Lee Roy and John, started wrestling each other at an early age and gradually progressed to tournaments. They were the perfect training partners. John won the Del City championships in the fourth, fifth, and sixth grades and started drawing the attention of wrestling enthusiasts throughout the state.

The Road to Excellence

Throughout high school, John tried his hand at other sports, but his true love was always wrestling. During his high school career, he was good

American John Smith (right) won his second consecutive Olympic gold medal in wrestling in 1992.

enough to earn a scholarship to wrestling power Oklahoma State University. There he followed in the footsteps of his older brother Lee Roy, who had won the National Collegiate Athletic Association (NCAA) 142-pound title in 1980 and had taken second place in the 1983 world championships at 136.5 pounds. Lee Roy was an assistant coach at Oklahoma State during John's first three years there; however, it was not long before John started to carve a niche of his own in the 134-pound class.

Just prior to the 1985 NCAA championships in John's sophomore year at OSU, he dislocated his right shoulder. Even with this injury, John wrestled in the championships, winning four matches before he faced the University of Wisconsin's Jim Jordan in the 132-pound championship match. John pushed Jordan throughout the whole match, but he lost 7-4. John took the loss hard, and as a result, he decided to change his wrestling style.

Early in his career, John tried to outmuscle his opponents, but he also possessed amazing quickness, and he decided to develop this to his advantage. If he did not pin his opponents, he won by impressive point margins or by a technical fall, a victory awarded to a wrestler who has a 15-point lead. John usually accumulated these points by using his favorite move, a single-leg takedown.

The Emerging Champion

In 1986, John took a year off from collegiate wrestling to train and to make his debut on the international scene. For the first time in his life, he lost every match in a tournament when he competed in a tournament in Tbilisi in the Soviet Union. More committed to becoming the best wrestler in the world, John used the defeat to motivate himself to work harder on remedying his shortcomings. The extra commitment paid off when he won his weight division in the 1986 U.S. Freestyle Senior Open and the Goodwill Games. John was ready to return to the collegiate ranks in 1987 with a renewed intensity.

In John's first meet of the 1986-87 season, however, he lost to the University of Nebraska's Gil Sanchez. Inspired once again by a defeat, John then went on a 131-match, two-year winning streak. John seemed unstoppable. In 1987, he won his first NCAA national championship,

HONORS, AWARDS, AND MILESTONES

1985, 1987-88	College All-American
1986-88	Big Eight Champion
1986, 1988-91	U.S. freestyle champion
1986, 1990	U.S. Goodwill Games Gold Medalist
1987	NCAA Tournament Outstanding Wrestler
1987-88	NCAA champion
1987-92	World Championships Gold Medalist
1987, 1991	U.S. Pan-American Games Gold Medalist
1988	*Amateur Wrestling News* Man of the Year
1988, 1992	Gold Medal, Olympic Wrestling
1989	USA Wrestling Athlete of the Year Master of Technique Award
1990	U.S. Olympic Committee Sportsman of the Year Sullivan Award
1992	FILA Outstanding Wrestler of the Year
1993	Amateur Athletic Foundation World Trophy

won his weight class at the U.S. Olympic Festival, took a gold medal at the Pan-American Games, and became America's second-youngest world champion in wrestling. To cap off 1987, John was named *Amateur Wrestling News*'s Man of the Year and finished in the top ten in the balloting for the prestigious Sullivan Award, given to America's amateur athlete of the year.

Ever conscious of every facet of his sport, John had to make sure that he remained psychologically strong. His victories came easily sometimes, and he had to make sure that he did not get a false sense of security. With every victory, John worked even harder. Everything seemed ready for the 1988 Olympic Games in Seoul, Korea.

Continuing the Story

John seemed to get stronger after each of the few defeats he suffered. It thus seemed almost fortunate that his 131-match win streak was ended in the early matches of the 1988 Olympic trials, when he was defeated 7-5 by 1984 Olympic gold medalist Randy Lewis. John came back with a vengeance, winning the trials and becoming the American representative in the 136.5-pound class. Reminded of his vulnerability, John re-

2572

newed his commitment to eliminate his weaknesses before the Olympics.

John's idol was his older brother, Lee Roy; he claimed that he never would have been the wrestler that he was had it not been for his older brother's encouragement and support. Lee Roy was a member of the 1980 U.S. Olympic team that boycotted the Moscow Games. In 1984, Lee Roy was embroiled in a controversy that first had him on the U.S. Olympic team and then left him off the team. John and the whole Smith family were embittered by the decision. The fact that he would finally get the Olympic chance that Lee Roy was denied weighed heavily on John's mind.

By the time of the Olympic Games, John was the wrestler to beat in his weight class; many wrestling experts considered him the top wrestler in the world. The Soviet coaches were wary of him, since he had defeated one of their top wrestlers, Khazer Isaev, at the 1986 Goodwill Games in Moscow and then again at the 1987 World Championships. The Soviets searched republics for a wrestler to beat the 23-year-old Oklahoman. Their answer was Stepan Sarkissian, who was the 1987 European Champion in the 149.5-pound class. Sarkissian lost thirteen pounds in the hope of defeating John in the 136.5-pound division. In the final match of the Olympic competition in Seoul, however, John was not to be denied, and he defeated the Soviet 4-0 for the gold medal.

John went on to win his weight division at the U.S. National Championships in 1989, 1990, and 1991, the U.S. Olympic Festival in 1989, the 1991 World Cup championship, and the 1989 U.S. Open International Championships. He took a second consecutive Olympic gold medal in 1992. He became the only American to win six consecutive world championships. He was named the U.S. Olympic Committee Sportsman of the Year in 1990, and he capped off that year by winning the prestigious Sullivan Award, becoming the first wrestler to win the award in its sixty-year his-

tory. John returned to his alma mater, Oklahoma State, as head wrestling coach in 1992.

John led the Cowboys to a national title in 1994 and a second-place finish in 1998. Under his leadership, Oklahoma State won three Big Eight titles and a national title. John also led the U.S. freestyle team to a World Cup team title in 1997 and made history as the U.S. team won every bout in the gold-medal match against Russia. In 1998, John coached the U.S. freestyle world team to a third-place finish in the World Championships and a team title in the Goodwill Games, including three individual first-place finishes. Along with wrestling legend Dan Gable, John was selected as co-head coach of the U.S. freestyle team in the 2000 Olympics.

Summary

John Smith dedicated his life to becoming the best in his sport. John carried that dedication into his life as a collegiate and international coach, winning both national and international titles and inspiring his athletes to become champions. His success showed that it is possible to learn from defeats and become stronger than before, making him living proof that victory can grow from adversity.

Rusty Wilson

Additional Sources:

Hickok, Ralph. *A Who's Who of Sports Champions: Their Stories and Records.* Boston: Houghton Mifflin, 1995.

Levinson, David, and Karen Christenson, eds. *Encyclopedia of World Sport: From Ancient Times to Present.* Santa Barbara, Calif.: ABC-CLIO, 1996.

Mallon, Bill, and Ian Buchanan. *Quest for Gold: The Encyclopedia of American Olympians.* New York: Leisure Press, 1984.

Wallechinsky, David. *The Complete Book of the Olympics.* Boston: Little, Brown and Company, 1991.

OZZIE SMITH

Sport: Baseball

Born: December 26, 1954
Mobile, Alabama

Early Life

Osborne Earl Smith was born December 26, 1954, in Mobile, Alabama, to Clovis Smith, a laborer and truck driver, and Marvella Smith, a nursing home aide. When Ozzie was six, the Smith family moved to Los Angeles, California, and settled in the mostly black Watts area. Ozzie, his four brothers, and his one sister grew up across the street from the neighborhood recreation center, and it was there that he received his

first baseball uniform. He spent hours playing alone behind the family home, bouncing a ball off the back steps and doing his best to catch it. He would later say that this early practice helped him to develop the eye-hand coordination that would make him an outstanding fielder. He often rode city buses to Dodger Stadium, where he especially admired the play of Maury Wills, a small, quick, smooth-fielding shortstop.

The Road to Excellence

At Locke High School, Ozzie played both basketball and baseball, and many professional scouts saw him play—but they were there to watch his teammates Eddie Murray, who would go on to major league stardom as a slugging first baseman, and Marques Johnson, who would become an All-Star in the National Basketball Association.

Despite his small size—even as an adult, he would grow to only 5 feet 10 inches and less than 170 pounds—Ozzie was an impressive enough basketball player to earn scholarship offers from several colleges, but he had his heart set on a baseball career. Although he was not drafted by any professional teams, he accepted a partial academic scholarship to California Polytechnic University at San Luis Obispo, where he would get a chance to play.

Ozzie was a walk-on player at Cal Poly, but he made the varsity team after the school's starting shortstop suffered a broken arm. His college playing career was not an especially happy one; he quarreled with the team's assistant coach and on several occasions considered quitting baseball. Each time, however, his mother and his high school coach talked him into staying. Moreover, Ozzie got along well with the school's head coach, Berdy Harr, who encouraged the young shortstop to learn to switch-hit—a skill that would prove valuable in his professional career.

STATISTICS

Season	GP	AB	Hits	2B	3B	HR	Runs	RBI	BA	SA
1978	159	590	152	17	6	1	69	46	.258	.312
1979	156	587	124	18	6	0	77	27	.211	.262
1980	158	609	140	18	5	0	67	35	.230	.276
1981	110	**450**	100	11	2	0	53	21	.222	.256
1982	140	488	121	24	1	2	58	43	.248	.314
1983	159	552	134	30	6	3	69	50	.243	.335
1984	124	412	106	20	5	1	53	44	.257	.337
1985	158	537	148	22	3	6	70	54	.276	.361
1986	153	514	144	19	4	0	67	54	.280	.333
1987	158	600	182	40	4	0	104	75	.303	.383
1988	153	575	155	27	1	3	80	51	.270	.336
1989	155	593	162	30	8	2	82	50	.273	.361
1990	143	512	130	21	1	1	61	50	.254	.305
1991	150	550	157	30	3	3	96	50	.285	.367
1992	132	518	153	20	2	0	73	31	.295	.342
1993	141	545	157	22	6	1	75	53	.288	.356
1994	98	381	100	18	3	3	51	30	.262	.349
1995	44	156	31	5	1	0	16	11	.199	.244
1996	82	227	64	10	2	2	36	18	.282	.370
Totals	2,573	9,396	2,460	402	69	28	1,257	793	.262	.320

Notes: Boldface indicates statistical leader. GP = games played; AB = at bats; 2B = doubles; 3B = triples; HR = home runs; RBI = runs batted in; BA = batting average; SA = slugging average

Ozzie was drafted by the Detroit Tigers of the American League (AL) after his junior year, but he was not satisfied with the Tigers' contract offer and chose to return to school. After his senior season, he was picked by the San Diego Padres of the National League (NL) in the fourth round of the 1977 amateur draft, and he accepted a $5000 bonus to report to the Padres' Class A minor-league team in Walla Walla, Washington.

Playing for Walla Walla, Ozzie batted .303 and led the Northwest League with 30 stolen bases. Yet though his offensive skills were good, he drew far more attention for his spectacular defense. He led the league's shortstops in fielding average, assists, and double plays and was named to the Northwest League All-Star team. His impressive performance earned him an invitation to play in the winter instructional league in Arizona, a sign that he was considered a top prospect. In Arizona, his play made a strong impression on Alvin Dark, the Padres' manager, and Ozzie was told to report to the major league training camp the following spring.

The Emerging Champion

Ozzie continued to impress in spring training, and he was vaulted over the upper levels of the minor leagues. Only twenty-three years old and with just one season of professional experience, he opened the 1978 season as San Diego's starting shortstop. He soon showed that he belonged; only a few days into the season, the Padres were playing in Atlanta when Braves slugger Jeff Burroughs hit a sharp ground ball toward center field for an apparent easy hit. Ozzie made an acrobatic dive to his left to get to the ball, but just before he could glove it, the ball took a bad hop and caromed in the opposite direction. Still stretched parallel to the ground in mid-air, Ozzie managed to reach behind himself and grab the ball with his bare hand. He then landed, bounced to his feet, and threw the stunned hitter out at first. The amazing play quickly became a staple of highlight films and was acclaimed among the greatest defensive efforts of all time.

Ozzie followed up his spectacular start with a solid season, batting .258, stealing 40 bases, earning more raves for his defense, and finishing second in the voting for the NL's Rookie of the Year Award. In the next few seasons, his defense got better and better; in 1979, he led the league's shortstops in assists, and the following year he broke the all-time major league record for assists while winning the first of thirteen consecutive Gold Glove Awards.

As he progressed in the field, however, he seemed to regress as a hitter. He hit .230, .211, and .222 in consecutive seasons, earning a reputation as a classic "good-field-no-hit" player. Moreover, he became embroiled in a series of bitter contract disputes with the Padres' management. After the 1981 season, the Padres made a rare straight-up swap of shortstops with the St. Louis Cardinals, trading their young defensive wizard for the talented but inconsistent Garry Templeton.

Continuing the Story

The Padres soon came to regret the trade, as Templeton failed to live up to expectations. Ozzie, meanwhile, continued to improve, earning recognition as the top fielder of his era. He was the defensive linchpin of the Cardinals' pennant-winning teams of 1982, 1985, and 1987, setting innumerable fielding records; he soon earned the nickname "the Wizard" for his prowess with his glove. He also worked hard to improve his hitting. Though he never became a power hitter, he improved his batting average year after year. In the 1985 playoffs, he won a critical game with a home run, his first in more than three thousand at bats as a left-handed hitter. In 1987, he even broke the .300 mark, burying forever his reputation as a lightweight at the plate. He played in twelve consecutive All-Star games and often was the leading vote-getter in All-Star balloting among fans—testimony to the wide appreciation of his multiple skills. Ozzie also earned respect for his involvement in community service programs, winning the Branch

HONORS AND AWARDS	
1980-92, 1994	National League Gold Glove Award
1981-92, 1994-96	National League All-Star team Uniform number 1 retired by St. Louis Cardinals

Rickey Award in 1994 and the Roberto Clemente Award in 1995.

Ozzie finished his baseball career in St. Louis after the 1996 season. That year, he appeared in his fifteenth All-Star game, stealing the spotlight in the seventh inning when the crowd of over sixty-two thousand gave him a standing ovation. Following his career on the field, Ozzie replaced Mel Allen as host of the popular television broadcast *This Week in Baseball.*

Summary

Ozzie Smith established himself as a top-flight fielder from the moment he entered the major leagues. Not content to be known merely as a skilled one-dimensional player, however, he worked to become a potent offensive force, earning recognition as one of the best shortstops ever to play the game.

Robert McClenaghan

Additional Sources:

Eisenbath, Mike. "Cardinal Teammates Bid Fond Farewell to Ozzie Smith." *Baseball Digest* 55, no. 10 (1996).

Kennedy, Kostya, and Richard O'Brien. "The New Land of Oz." *Sports Illustrated* 86, no. 15 (1997).

Smith, Ozzie, with Rob Rains. *Wizard.* Chicago: Contemporary Books, 1988.

SINJIN SMITH

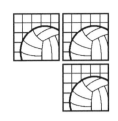

Sport: Volleyball

Born: May 7, 1957
Santa Monica, California

Early Life

Christopher St. John Smith was born on May 7, 1957, in Santa Monica, California, to Frank Smith, a college mathematics professor, and Mary Lou Smith, a former high-school coach. Sinjin (the name is a derivative of "St. John") was the most active of the Smith children. His father was the first person who taught him to appreciate volleyball. He had the opportunity to play in his backyard and at the beach with his brothers and sisters. Sinjin learned at an early age that he liked the freedom of volleyball. Other sports required the wearing of uniforms and had precise rules of play; Sinjin was drawn to volleyball because it was less restrictive and allowed him to express his personality.

The Road to Excellence

When Sinjin was growing up, volleyball was not considered a sport that boys were supposed to enjoy. In the eighth grade, he was criticized for wanting to play a "girls' sport" like volleyball. Sinjin did not let what others said about volleyball dissuade him from continuing to play. He had already seen such great volleyball players as Ron Von Hagen and Jim Menges compete, and Sinjin understood the tremendous athletic skills necessary to play at their level.

Sinjin played volleyball in high school and then decided to attend the University of California at Los Angeles (UCLA), where the men's

indoor volleyball team was highly regarded. When Sinjin was seventeen, his father died. To deal with the pain of the loss, he put more of his energy into volleyball.

The summer before Sinjin was to start at UCLA, his coach, Al Scates, got him a job at a Santa Monica beach club coaching volleyball. While working at the club, he got a chance to watch and occasionally play with Von Hagen. On one occasion, Von Hagen suggested that Sinjin

MAJOR CHAMPIONSHIP VICTORIES

1976, 1979	NCAA Championship Team
1979, 1981	World Championship of Beach Volleyball (with Karch Kiraly)
1982, 1988	World Championship of Beach Volleyball (with Randy Stoklos)
1990	U.S. Championship (with Randy Stoklos)

should start to play in beach tournaments. In Von Hagen, Sinjin had found a mentor who would instruct him on the proper way to train.

The Emerging Champion

Sinjin finally got a chance to team up with Von Hagen at a Santa Cruz beach volleyball tournament, and he also became an integral part of UCLA's volleyball team. He helped to lead the Bruins to National Collegiate Athletic Association (NCAA) championships in indoor volleyball in 1976 and 1979 and earned All-American honors in 1978 and 1979. Von Hagen had taught him how important it was to have an iron will and to play strong defense. Sinjin was graduated from UCLA with a degree in economics, but most of his focus was on perfecting his volleyball game. From 1979 to 1982, Sinjin was a distinguished member of the U.S. national volleyball team.

At the time, beach volleyball was still a fairly unrecognized sport. Sinjin won his first beach volleyball event in 1977 at the Rosecrans Open, teaming up with Mike Normand.

With the United States boycott of the 1980 Moscow Games, Sinjin lost a chance to compete in the Olympics. Because of a disagreement with the U.S. Olympic coach, Doug Beal, Sinjin was removed from the 1984 volleyball team that was to compete at the Summer Games in Los Angeles. He put his disappointment behind him and concentrated on beach volleyball. In 1981, Sinjin also began modeling part-time. He appeared in such magazines as *GQ, Playboy,* and *Vogue.* At 6 feet 3 inches and 185 pounds, Sinjin made the most of his physical stature both on the beach and in front of the camera.

In beach volleyball, there are merely two players to each team. The sport requires each player to be proficient at passing, setting, spiking, and playing defense. Over the years, Sinjin proved that he was able to play the total game. In beach volleyball circles, he earned the title "King of the Beach." Professional beach volleyball is a gruel-

ing sport, and Sinjin had to be willing to train intensely and to remain focused in order to succeed.

Sinjin also worked hard over the years to make professional beach volleyball a financially viable endeavor. He was instrumental in transforming the Association of Volleyball Professionals (AVP), which was founded in 1981, into a credible organization during a 1984 players' strike. He also helped to turn beach volleyball into a multimillion dollar business during his tenure as president of the AVP from 1987 to 1989.

Continuing the Story

Sinjin has been able to accomplish much for himself and his sport because of his competitive spirit and his willingness to stand up for what he believed was right. His success on the professional circuit is unmatched. In 1989, Sinjin became the first player to reach 100 career open wins. He reached the $1 million mark in career prize earnings in 1992. Sinjin was only the second player in the history of the sport to earn $1 million in prize money (his longtime partner, Randy Stoklos, was the first to reach that mark). Always a strong defensive player, Sinjin won the AVP Best Defensive Player Award in 1990, 1991, and 1992. For the 1994 season, Sinjin and Stoklos decided to terminate their partnership.

Sinjin, with new partner Carl Henkel, competed in the 1996 Olympic Games in the inaugural beach volleyball event, placing fifth behind the U.S. gold-medal winners Karch Kiraly and Adam Johnson. Sinjin and Carl also attempted to qualify for the 2000 Olympic Games but were unsuccessful. Until 1998 Sinjin was the all-time

HONORS AND AWARDS

1978-79	College All-American
1983-84	USVBA All-American
1990-92	AVP Best Defensive Player
1991	UCLA Sports Hall of Fame
1992	Uniform number 22 retired by UCLA

MILESTONES

Second in AVP career wins (139)

leader in career wins on the Open Beach Volley-ball circuit, at which time Kiraly surpassed him.

In addition to beach volleyball and modeling, Sinjin, who is married to model Patty Robinson, has been involved with a sportswear store, Smithers, which he owns with his family, and with Sideout Sport activewear, which he co-owns. In 1993, he opened the State Beach Cafe in Santa Monica. A tireless worker, Sinjin also found the time to put on volleyball clinics and to parti-cipate in several charities. He also served on the board of directors of the Big Brothers of America.

Summary

Sinjin Smith almost single-handedly made professional beach volleyball a thriving business. He has won three World Championships, two Tournament of Champions events, and two King of the Beach Invitationals. Second only to his ri-val and former teammate Karch Kiraly in career wins and earnings, Sinjin is one of the greatest volleyball players of all time and deserves a share in the title "King of the Beach."

Jeffry Jensen

Additional Sources:

Levinson, David, and Karen Christenson, eds. *Encyclopedia of World Sport: From Ancient Times to Present.* Santa Barbara, Calif.: ABC-CLIO, 1996.

Mallon, Bill, and Ian Buchanan. *Quest for Gold: The Encyclopedia of American Olympians.* New York: Leisure Press, 1984.

"Sinjin Smith." *Career World* 21, no. 6 (1993).

Smith, Sinjin, and Neil Feineman. *Kings of the Beach: The Story of Beach Vollyball.* Los Angeles, Calif.: Power Books, 1988.

Wallechinsky, David. *The Complete Book of the Olym-pics.* Boston: Little, Brown and Company, 1991.

STAN SMITH

Sport: Tennis

Born: December 14, 1946
Pasadena, California

Early Life

Stanley Roger Smith was born in Pasadena, California, on December 14, 1946, the son of a college athletic coach. He developed an early interest in sports, and while attending Pasadena High School excelled at both tennis and baseball.

Unlike some champions, Stan did not display extraordinary ability immediately in his chosen sport. Although he was talented, he was also chunky and ungainly. When he practiced at the Los Angeles Tennis Club, most of the outstanding teenage players shunned him.

The Road to Excellence

Stan was undaunted by the setback of encountering players who looked down on him. He resolved to make his rivals change their minds and accordingly practiced more tenaciously than anyone else. To overcome his physical awkwardness, he worked out constantly with a jump rope. His efforts soon paid off, and in 1964 he won the National Junior Singles title.

The longtime czar of Los Angeles tennis, Perry Jones, took a liking to Stan and recommended that he team up with Bob Lutz, another teenager who, like Stan, was attending the University of Southern California (USC). At USC, Stan's game continued to improve under the instruction of the university's coach, the veteran George Toley.

Several factors made Stan into a championship player. At 6 feet 4 inches in height, he was among the tallest players in the game. That gave him a considerable advantage in gaining power on his serve, which he developed into one of the fastest in tennis. Because of his strong service, he was nicknamed "the Steamer." Stan also possessed a powerful and accurate forehand. During his amateur days, at any rate, his backhand was less than outstanding; he improved this feature of his game after he turned professional in 1973.

Perhaps even more important than the quality of his shots was his rigid determination. Stan was a "straight arrow" person who concentrated single-mindedly on the task at hand. He was a leading member of the Fellowship of Christian Athletes and, in line with the ideals of that group, never allowed bad habits to interfere with his training.

Stan's personality contrasted sharply with that of his doubles partner, Bob Lutz. Bob was a

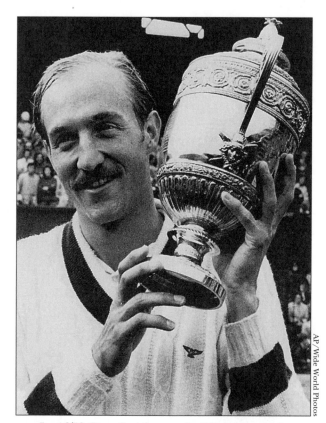

In 1972 Stan Smith won the Wimbledon title.

2580

happy-go-lucky character who often failed to devote enough time to practice. Although before Stan's rise to excellence Bob had been regarded as the better singles prospect of the two, he never fulfilled his early potential as a singles player. Nevertheless, he and Stan became one of the world's outstanding doubles teams.

The Emerging Champion

Stan's careful, almost grim preparation over a number of years paid off for him in the early 1970's. In 1971, he won the U.S. Open title at Forest Hills, New York. His opponent in the final was the Czech Jan Kodes, who lacked Stan's power but was a player of great finesse. Kodes often defeated power players by his unusual skill at returning what seemed to be sure winners. Stan's serve and all-around power proved too much for Kodes, though, and Stan won his first major title.

Stan was unable to win the Wimbledon title in 1971, although he did reach the final. Here his opponent was John Newcombe, an Australian whose power was fully a match for Stan's own. The next year, however, Newcombe was under contract with World Championship Tennis (WCT), and, under the rules then in effect, was ineligible to compete at Wimbledon.

Stan again reached the finals, and this time his opponent was the Romanian Ilie Nastase. Nastase's personality and technique were the diametric opposite of Stan's. Nastase's game stressed finesse, touch, and variety, in contrast to Stan's power and relentlessness. Stan was unemotional during play and a model of good manners. Ilie was flamboyant and temperamental; his frequent temper tantrums were notorious. In perhaps the best match of his career, Stan dispatched the fiery Romanian.

In addition to his singles titles, Stan compiled an outstanding record in Davis Cub play and in doubles matches. He and his partner, Bob Lutz,

MAJOR CHAMPIONSHIP VICTORIES AND FINALS	
1968, 1974, 1978, 1980	U.S. Open doubles (with Bob Lutz)
1969	U.S. National Championship
1970	Australian Open doubles (with Lutz)
1971	U.S. Open
1971, 1979	U.S. Open doubles finalist (with Lutz)
1971	Wimbledon finalist
1972	Wimbledon
1972, 1974, 1980-81	Wimbledon doubles finalist (with Erik van Dillen; with Lutz)
1971, 1974	French Open doubles finalist (with Tom Gorman; with Lutz)

OTHER NOTABLE VICTORIES	
1966	U.S. Hardcourt Championship doubles (with Lutz)
1966-68	U.S. Hardcourt Championship
1966, 1969, 1970	U.S. Indoor Championship doubles (with Lutz; with Arthur Ashe)
1967-68	NCAA Championship doubles (with Lutz)
1968	U.S. Indoor Championship doubles finalist (with Lutz)
	NCAA Championship
	U.S. Clay Court Championship doubles (with Lutz)
1968-72, 1978-79	On winning U.S. Davis Cup team
1969-79, 1972	U.S. Indoor Championship
1970	The Masters
1973	WCT Finals
	WCT World Doubles Championship (with Lutz)
1979	Miller Hall of Fame Championship doubles (with Lutz)
	Volvo Tennis Classic doubles (with Lutz)
	European Indoor Open doubles (with Gene Mayer)
1985-86	U.S. Open Invitational doubles (with Lutz)

became extremely adept in teamwork. Their careful strategic planning during matches refuted the charges that Stan's game was one-dimensional and that he himself was not intelligent.

Continuing the Story

In 1973, Stan turned professional. His first year proved very successful, and in it he won the WCT finals, one of the most important professional events. To do so, he had to defeat the great Australian players Rod Laver and Ken Rosewall in addition to his fellow American Arthur Ashe. His victory in this tournament was no fluke; during the year, Stan dominated Laver, one of the greatest players of all time. In both 1972 and 1973, Stan was ranked as the world's top player.

Stan's time at the pinnacle was of short duration. After 1973, his game suddenly worsened, and he plunged in the rankings. At various times in the next few years, he developed back and knee problems that sidelined him for long peri-

HONORS, AWARDS, AND MILESTONES

1968	William M. Johnston Sportsmanship Award
1968-73, 1975, 1977-79, 1981	U.S. Davis Cup team
1969	Lebair Sportsmanship Award
1969, 1971-73	Nationally ranked number one
1970-72, 1975	Nationally ranked number one in doubles
1972	Ranked number one in the world
1978	ATP-Adidas Sportsmanship Award
1979	ATF Service Award
1987	Inducted into International Tennis Hall of Fame

Summary

Stan Smith was a talented, though not extraordinary, tennis player as a teenager. His determination and constant training enabled him to surpass his erstwhile superiors and to develop into the top singles player in the United States during the early 1970's. His career peaked in the period 1971-1973. After the latter year, he was never again ranked as a great singles player, but he continued to be a topflight doubles player with his partner since college days, Bob Lutz.

Bill Delaney

ods. His injuries did not appear to be the initial cause of his decline, though; experts have never been able to agree on the cause of the slump.

Stan's determination again came to the fore. He refused to quit the game and tried time after time to return to his former excellence. Although he never again won a major singles title, his efforts once more paid off. He and Lutz continued their outstanding record as a doubles team. They were ranked as one of the best partnerships in the United States as late as 1980. After retiring from competitive tennis, Stan remained close to the game by writing articles for *Tennis Magazine*. In 2000, he served as coach of the U.S. Olympic men's tennis team at the Summer Olympics in Sydney, Australia.

Additional Sources:

Evans, Richard. *Open Tennis: 1968-1988*. Lexington, Mass.: Stephen Greene Press, 1989.

Lunde, Erik S. "Stanley Roger 'Stan' Smith." In *Biographical Dictionary of American Sports: Outdoor Sports*, edited by David L. Porter. Westport, Conn.: Greenwood Press, 1988.

"Stan Smith." In *International Who's Who in Tennis*, edited by Jane Cooke. Dallas, Tex.: World Championship Tennis, 1983.

TOMMIE SMITH

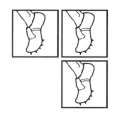

Sport: Track and field (sprints)

Born: June 5, 1944
Clarksville, Texas

Early Life

Tommie Smith was born on June 5, 1944, in Clarksville, Texas. He was the seventh of twelve children. His father, James Richard Smith, was a cotton sharecropper. His mother, Dora, was a Native American who died in 1970. As a young child, Tommie frequently accompanied his father in the cotton fields. When Tommie was six,

At the 1968 Olympics Tommie Smith (center) and John Carlos (right) raise their arms in protest against racism in the United States.

his family traveled by bus from Texas to California, where they lived and worked at a labor camp in the San Joaquin Valley. Tommie attended Stratford Grammar School and Central Union Junior High School in Lemoore.

By the time he was in the eighth grade, Tommie was over 6 feet tall and a force to contend with on the track as well as on the basketball court and the football field. In the ninth grade, he improved his time in the 100-yard dash from 10.9 to 9.9 seconds. During his senior year, Tommie ran the 100-yard dash and the 220-yard (200-meter) dash in 9.5 and 21.1 seconds, respectively, long-jumped 24 feet 6 inches, and high-jumped 6 feet 5 inches. His stellar athletic performances at Lemoore High School earned Tommie a track, football, and basketball scholarship at San Jose State College in California.

The Road to Excellence

After graduation from high school in 1963, Tommie entered San Jose State. Because of his desire to excel in academics as well as athletics, he decided to concentrate on one sport, track and field. He was fortunate to have Lloyd "Bud" Winter as his coach. Winter, who died in 1985, was considered his generation's most talented coach of sprinters. Along with Lee Evans, John Carlos, and Ronnie Ray Smith, Tommie was part of a group of sprinters who were known throughout the world as "Speed City." Wearing his trademark sunglasses, Tommie finished races with tremendous acceleration, using what was referred to as his "Tommie-jet gear."

As a sophomore in 1965, Tommie tied Frank Budd's world record of 20 seconds in the straightaway 200-meter (220-yard) dash. A year later in 1966, Tommie set a world record of 19.5 seconds for the straightaway 200 meters. Asked by Winter in the spring of 1967 to run in a race timed at both 400 meters and 440 yards (402 me-

2583

ters) against teammate Lee Evans, who was ranked first in the world in the 400 meters, Tommie set world records for both distances: 44.5 seconds in the 400 meters and 44.8 seconds in the 440 yards.

The Emerging Champion

In 1967, Tommie and other members of Speed City had their sights set on making the 1968 United States Olympic team and participating in the nineteenth Olympiad in Mexico City. Tommie was not simply a world-class sprinter; he had many other responsibilities. He had married pentathlete Denise Paschal in 1967, and in February, 1968, their son, Kevin, was born. He was working at the All-American Pontiac dealership in San Jose and finishing his college degree at San Jose State.

He was also becoming more sensitive to the civil rights issues of the 1960's. During his senior year, Tommie enrolled in a sociology class taught by Harry Edwards, a civil rights activist. Aware of complaints by African American athletes of housing discrimination and exclusion from campus social and political organizations, Edwards encouraged African American students to protest against such practices.

With similar concerns occurring throughout the country, the protests eventually included a potential Olympic boycott by African American athletes over racial injustice in the United States. In spring of 1968, a gathering in Los Angeles of African American athletes led to the development of the Olympic Project for Human Rights (OPHR). Initially not a campus radical—Tommie was in the Army Reserves Officers Training Corps (ROTC) and committed to a two-year military obligation after graduation—Tommie finally got involved in the OPHR.

\multicolumn{5}{c}{**MAJOR CHAMPIONSHIPS**}
Year	Competition	Event	Place	Time
1966	National AAU Championships	200 meters	Gold	19.5 WR
1967	NCAA Outdoor Championships	220 yards	1st	
1967	National AAU Championships	200 meters	Gold	
1967	National AAU Championships	800-meter relay	Gold	1:21.1 WR
1967	AAU sanctioned race	400 meters	1st	44.5 WR
1967	AAU sanctioned race	440 yards	1st	44.8 WR
1968	National AAU Championships	200 meters	Gold	
1968	Olympic Games	200 meters (with turn)	Gold	19.83 WR OR

Notes: WR = World Record; OR = Olympic Record

Deciding against an Olympic boycott, the athletes began a summer of intense competition at the site of the final Olympic trials near South Lake Tahoe, California. While their thoughts were turned to training in earnest, they had agreed to make statements of protest at the Olympics individually. For the final 200-meter qualifying race, Tommie finished second, guaranteeing him a spot on the Olympic team.

In his semifinal qualifying heat at the Olympics in Mexico City, Tommie won in 20.13 seconds, but he strained an adductor muscle in his left leg. Fortunately, he was able to run in the 200-meter finals, and he ran the race of his life. Starting in lane 3, with eighty thousand enthusiastic spectators watching, Tommie won the gold medal by running the first-ever sub-20-second 200-meter dash with a turn in 19.83 seconds. Peter Norman of Australia finished second, and San Jose State teammate John Carlos third.

As the three men stood on the dais to receive their medals, and as "The Star-Spangled Banner" was being played, Tommie and Carlos lowered their heads and lifted black-gloved fists in a silent protest against racism in America. Their lives were never the same after making the symbolic gesture.

Continuing the Story

Tommie and Carlos were forced to leave the Olympic village by the U.S. Olympic Committee and after returning to the United States were criticized for tarnishing America's international reputation. Tommie's track and field career was over. He lost his job at the automobile dealer-

\multicolumn{2}{c}{**HONORS**}
1978	Inducted into National Track and Field (USATF) Hall of Fame
1999	Inducted into San Jose State University Sports Hall of Fame
	Inducted into Bay Area [California] Sports Hall of Fame

ship, and when he began his final semester of college, he was not allowed to register for his remaining ROTC classes, for the Army was no longer interested in his services. The Los Angeles Rams, who had chosen him in the 1968 National Football League draft, would not have him, either. Tommie signed with the Cincinnati Bengals and spent the next three years on the team's practice squad.

Released by the Bengals in 1971 and divorced from Denise, Tommie taught fourth and fifth grade and was a track coach at Milpitas High School in California. Completing a master's degree in sociology in 1972 in Massachusetts from the Goddard-Cambridge graduate program for social change, Tommie taught sociology and coached track and field and basketball for six years at Oberlin College. In 1976, he married Oberlin graduate Denise Kyle, and they had three children. After 1978, he taught physical education and sociology and coached men's and women's track and field and cross country at Santa Monica College in California.

Summary

During his career, Tommie Smith broke or tied eleven world sprint records. His major achievement was winning a gold medal in the 200-meter dash at the 1968 Olympic Games. Throughout his adult life, Tommie defended his actions at the Olympics. What was once seen as a radical act for the Black Power movement became a symbolic gesture for human rights.

Kevin Eyster

Additional Sources:

Blair, Tim. "Memories 30 Years On: Silent Salute Continues to Be Heard." *Time International*, November 9, 1998, 28.

Moore, Kenny. "A Courageous Stand: In '68, Olympians Tommie Smith and John Carlos Raised Their Fists for Racial Justice." *Sports Illustrated* 75, no. 6 (August 5, 1991): 60-73.

_____. "The Eye of the Storm: The Lives of the U.S. Olympians Who Protested Racism in 1968 Were Changed Forever." *Sports Illustrated* 75, no. 7 (August 12, 1991): 60-71.

SAM SNEAD

Sport: Golf

Born: May 27, 1912
Ashwood, Virginia

Early Life

Samuel Jackson Snead was born on May 27, 1912, in Ashwood, Virginia. With his four older brothers and one sister, Sam grew up on a farm. Although the family was not destitute, there was little money for travel or for leisure activities. Sam enjoyed hunting and fishing, activities he continued long after leaving home. He credited squirrel hunting with developing his accurate eye, which proved to be of great value on the golf course.

His oldest brother, Harold, was Sam's mentor. They made golf clubs out of tree branches, and under Harold's tutoring, Sam showed much aptitude for the game. By age twelve he was caddying on the nearby Homestead Hotel golf course, earning some much desired pocket money. Surprisingly, he did not excel in the game while in high school.

The Road to *Excellence*

At Valley High School in nearby Hot Springs, Sam was an all-around athlete. He participated successfully in track, boxing, football, baseball, and basketball. His high school coach convinced Sam to avoid liquor and tobacco, and he abstained from both throughout his career.

In 1935, Sam became an assistant golf professional at White Sulphur Springs, West Virginia, earning $25 a week, and in 1936, he was promoted to teaching professional at Cascades Inn in Hot Springs. He turned professional in 1937, placing seventh at the Los Angeles Open and first in the Oakland Open, where he became an overnight sensation. That same year, he went on to win the Bing Crosby Invitational, the Miami Open, and the St. Paul and Nassau Opens. He was runner-up in the United States Open, phenomenal for a relative newcomer to professional golf.

Sam ended 1937 as the third-highest golfer in money won ($10,243),

Ralph W. Miller Golf Library

MAJOR CHAMPIONSHIP VICTORIES

1942, 1949, 1951	PGA Championship
1946	British Open
1949, 1952, 1954	The Masters
1964-65, 1967, 1970, 1972-73	PGA Seniors Championship

OTHER NOTABLE VICTORIES

1938	Westchester 108 Hole Open
1937-38, 1941, 1950	Bing Crosby Pro-Am
1937, 1939, 1941, 1947, 1949, 1951, 1953, 1955	Ryder Cup team
1938, 1940-41	Canadian Open
1938, 1946, 1949, 1950, 1955-56, 1960, 1965	Greater Greensboro Open
1939, 1941-42	St. Petersburg Open
1941, 1950	North and South Open
1945	Pensacola Open
1945, 1950	Los Angeles Open
1946	World Championship of Golf
1948, 1950	Texas Open
1949-50	Western Open
1950	Colonial National Invitation
1952	All-American Open Eastern Open
1956, 1960-61	World Cup Team
1961	Tournament of Champions
1964-65, 1970, 1972-73	World Seniors Championship
1969	Ryder Cup nonplaying captain
1980	*Golf Digest* Commemorative, senior tour
1982	Legends of Golf, senior tour (with Don January)

Sportswriters noted Sam's golf skills, citing his "swing of beauty" as both functional and artistic. Sam also had a grass roots appeal, his folksy manner endearing him to spectators. He was a colorful player, always friendly and a pleasure to watch. At first, the press referred to him as "the hillbilly from the backwoods of Virginia," but very soon he was affectionately nicknamed "Slammin' Sam" by both press and fans.

Although Sam served in the Navy from 1942 to 1944 and was unable to play professionally, overall, the 1940's were a successful decade for him. He won the Canadian Open in 1940 and 1941, the PGA in 1942, and the Portland and Richmond Opens in 1944. A high point was his victory in the British Open in 1946, the first time the title returned to the United States since 1933.

In spite of Sam's many tournament wins, he sometimes lost "sure" matches because of erratic putting, often losing by two, three, or four strokes. In 1949, a fine record subdued the talk that he choked in clutch situations, as he won both the PGA championship and the Masters Tournament. It was the beginning of a fantastic run of wins for Sam, who was now hitting his stride.

and in 1938, he was the number-one money winner ($19,334) as well as the most popular golfer on the circuit, drawing big crowds wherever he played. Fred Corcoran, the Professional Golfers' Association (PGA) tournament manager, recruited Sam for the professional tour, recognizing what he would be.

The Emerging Champion

Sam had a very good year in 1938. He won the Canadian Open and came in second in the United States Open and in the PGA tournament. He won the Vardon Memorial Trophy for the lowest strokes-per-round average in PGA-sponsored competition that year, the first of four such awards.

Continuing the Story

Sam's chief rival in the 1950's was another golfing great, Ben Hogan. The two monopolized the Masters Tournament, Sam winning in 1949, Ben in 1951, Sam in 1952, Ben in 1953, and Sam again in 1954. Clearly, Sam was at his peak, but he never won the big one: the United States Open. In spite of his more than one hundred tournament victories, Sam was badgered repeatedly for this failure, although he was runner-up four times. Although he wanted the victory badly, Sam was reconciled to what to him seemed fate: the victory was never to be his. He did not, however, let this failure deter him from enjoying golf and continuing to play in the manner that brought him much fame and money. He played to the best of his ability and continued his winning ways well into his sixties.

Until Arnold Palmer began dominating golf in the 1960's, Sam remained the leading money winner on the professional tour as well as the most popular figure. He also took great pride in the fact that he helped bring prestigious foreign titles to the United States. In 1946, he won the British Open and, between 1937 and 1955, he was a Ryder Cup team member eight times, playing singles and in foursomes. His record was unsurpassed: five wins and one loss in singles play and five wins and one loss in the foursomes.

Age did not slow Sam very much. He had a good year in 1955, winning four Opens. In 1956, he won the Greensboro Open. In 1965, at age fifty-two, he won the Greensboro Open again and, at age sixty-two, tied for third in the 1974 National PGA. The "swing of beauty" had not deserted him.

Summary

With Ben Hogan and Byron Nelson, Sam Snead was elected to the PGA Hall of Fame in 1953. He continued playing tournaments well into the 1970's, earning respectable scores and much adulation from fans. Fittingly, Sam won the first Legends of Golf tournament held in Austin, Texas, in 1978.

RECORDS AND MILESTONES

PGA Tour money leader (1938, 1949-50, 1955)

Credited with at least 135 wins worldwide, including a record 84 on the PGA tour

Became oldest champion at an official PGA Tour event, winning the 1965 Greater Greensboro Open at age fifty-two years and ten months

One of the founders of the Senior Tour

HONORS AND AWARDS

1938, 1949-50, 1955	PGA Vardon Trophy
1949	PGA Player of the Year
1953	Inducted into PGA Hall of Fame
1974	Inducted into PGA/World Golf Hall of Fame
1984	GWAA Richardson Award

The Golfers' Creed views the game as "a contest, calling for courage, skill, strategy, and self-control"—all of which Sam had in abundance.

S. Carol Berg

Additional Sources:

Grimsley, Will. *Golf: Its History, People, and Events.* Englewood Cliffs, N.J.: Prentice-Hall, 1966.

Snead, Sam, and George Mendoza. *Slammin' Sam.* New York: Donald I. Fine, 1986.

Snead, Sam, and Francis J. Pirozzolo. *The Game I Love: Wisdom, Insight, and Instruction from Golf's Greatest Player.* New York: Ballantine Books, 1997.

Snead, Sam, and Al Stump. *The Education of a Golfer.* New York: Simon & Schuster, 1962.

PETER SNELL

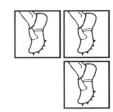

Sport: Track and field (middle-distance runs)

Born: December 17, 1938
Opunake, New Zealand

Early Life

Peter George Snell was born on December 17, 1938, in Opunake, a small coastal town in southwestern New Zealand. His father was an engineer. In 1947, Peter's family moved to Te Aroha, New Zealand, where Peter attended elementary school.

Even as a boy, Peter was extremely active. He consumed such great quantities of honey to maintain his energy that his mother would buy sixty pounds at a time to keep him supplied. When he was in secondary school, he would often play tennis all morning, play cricket all afternoon, and then run on the track in the evening.

The Road to Excellence

Although he set school records in the mile and the half-mile at Mount Albert Grammar School, his secondary school, Peter did not specialize in running. It was only one of several sports in which he competed successfully: tennis, cricket, golf, rugby, and hockey. Tennis was originally his best sport; while at Mount Albert, he reached the national quarterfinals in that sport before he was eliminated.

Despite his unwillingness to concentrate solely on middle-distance running, Peter's times steadily improved while he was at Mount Albert. In his senior year, he won the half-mile run at the Auckland Inter-Secondary Schools Athletic Championship in 1 minute 59.6 seconds. When he left school, he was initially undecided about whether

to continue in tennis or in track, but eventually decided to be a runner. Each weekend, after his job as a construction surveyor ended, he would travel to Pukekohe to help his parents build a new home for themselves. This trip became an important part of his training. He rode a bus for the first twenty miles of each trip, then ran the final ten miles.

This long-distance training helped Peter to develop the endurance base that contributed to

Peter Snell of New Zealand won the 800-meter race in the 1960 Olympics.

his success in racing. Near the end of 1957, he made a substantial improvement in his best half-mile time, lowering it to 1 minute 54.1 seconds. This attracted the attention of New Zealand's most famous track coach, Arthur Lydiard, and he became Peter's coach. Lydiard required even middle-distance runners to do marathon training, including a weekly twenty-two-mile run over a hilly course. Although Peter suffered such pain that he broke into tears the first time he ran the course, he persevered and soon began to benefit from it.

The Emerging Champion

In 1959, Peter emerged as the New Zealand national champion at both the half-mile and the mile and set a New Zealand record for the 800-meter run. Just as he was making steady improvement in his performances, he broke a bone in his leg. He was unable to train for two months, and when he returned to competition, he lost several races in relatively poor times.

From March, 1960, until the Olympic Games in August of that year, Peter did not run in any races. Instead, he concentrated on building himself up by hard training, often running one hundred miles per week. The Olympic 800-meter competition required athletes to run three heats and a final in four days, giving an advantage to the runners who had endurance as well as speed.

Peter was virtually an unknown at the 1960 Rome Olympic Games and was not expected to have a chance against the favorites in the 800-

---

RECORDS
World record at 800 meters in 1962 (1:44.3)
World record at 1 mile in 1962 (3:54.4)
World record at 1 mile in 1964 (3:54.1)
Was first man in 44 years to win the 800 meters and 1,500 meters in the same Olympic Games

HONORS AND AWARDS	
1960	World Trophy
1962	*Track and Field News* World Athlete of the Year
	Athletics Weekly World Athlete of the Year
1971	*Track and Field News* Athlete of the Decade

---

meter race. At 5 feet 10 inches and weighing 171 pounds, Peter was much heavier than most middle-distance runners, with a muscular build better suited for a sprinter than a distance runner. He ran a shrewd race, however, placing himself just behind the leader until they were only twenty-five yards from the finish line. Then he sprinted ahead, barely finishing first in the Olympic record time of 1 minute 46.3 seconds.

Continuing the Story

In 1962, Peter began to concentrate on the mile run. He was so successful that he was ranked the world's best in the mile in 1962, 1963, and 1964. He peaked in January, 1964, when he set a world record for the event in 3 minutes 54.1 seconds. In the following months, he also established world records at the mile, half-mile, 800-meter, and 1,000-meter (indoor) distances.

In 1963, however, Peter did not train consistently, and some thought he was finished as a runner. He proved them wrong at the 1964 Olympic Games. Prior to the Games, Peter ran one hundred miles a week for ten weeks. That gave him the endurance necessary to run in a short period the six races required for him to compete in both the 800 and the 1,500 meters. Despite having to run three 800-meter races in three consecutive days, he won the 800-meter final easily in an Olympic record time of 1 minute 45.1 seconds.

Peter was quite concerned about the 1,500-meter run because the final would be his sixth race in eight days and he feared his legs would be tired. He therefore concentrated on winning the race rather than running the fastest possible time. He held back until the last 200 meters of

---

STATISTICS				
Year	Competition	Event	Place	Time
1960	Olympic Games	800 meters	Gold	1:46.3 OR
1962	Commonwealth Games	880 yards	Gold	1:47.6
		Mile	Gold	4:04.6
1964	Olympic Games	800 meters	Gold	1:45.1 OR
		1,500 meters	Gold	3:38.1
Notes: OR = Olympic Record				

the race, then unleashed a powerful sprint, finishing in 3 minutes 38.1 seconds, ten yards ahead of the second-place runner.

Although he was worn out and suffering from minor injuries, after the Olympics Peter embarked on a worldwide series of races. Although he won frequently, Peter found he had to strain to defeat runners he could normally beat easily. When he began to lose races and run disappointing times despite all-out efforts, Peter accepted that he was no longer in condition to compete and retired from racing in 1965.

Summary

Peter Snell's heavy, muscular build placed him at a disadvantage when competing with lighter runners. Yet no one could exceed Peter's fierce determination to succeed, which made him the world's outstanding middle-distance runner in the early 1960's.

Harold L. Smith

Additional Sources:

Hanley, Reid M. *Who's Who in Track and Field.* New Rochelle, N.Y.: Arlington House, 1971.

The Lincoln Library of Sports Champions. 16 vols. Columbus, Ohio: Frontier Press, 1993.

Wallechinsky, David. *The Complete Book of the Olympics.* Boston: Little, Brown and Company, 1991.

Watman, Mel. *Encyclopedia of Track and Field Athletics.* New York: St. Martin's Press, 1981.

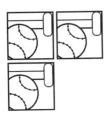

DUKE SNIDER

Sport: Baseball

Born: September 19, 1926
Los Angeles, California

Early Life

Edwin Donald "Duke" Snider (also dubbed "the Silver Fox") was born September 19, 1926, in the Boyle Heights section of Los Angeles, California. He grew up in nearby Compton. His father, Ward, worked for Goodyear Tire and Rubber and his mother, Florence, was a homemaker. Very early, Ward Snider made two lasting contributions to his son's baseball career. First, he called his son Duke. Second, he taught Duke to bat left-handed so that he would have an advantage against right-handed pitchers and also be a step closer to first base. Both of Duke's parents strongly encouraged his athletic ambitions, allowing him to do chores around the house rather than take a part-time job when he came of age so that he would have the time to play organized sports.

The Road to Excellence

The encouragement that Duke received from his parents paid off. Duke starred in baseball, basketball, and football while at Enterprise Junior High School and Compton Junior College (at that time the equivalent of the eleventh through the fourteenth grades). Among the highlights of his school sports career were a touchdown pass thrown 63 yards in the air and a no-hit game as a baseball pitcher.

Thanks in part to the publicity efforts of fellow student Pete Rozelle, who later became commissioner of the National Football League, Duke was named to a number of area All-Star teams. This recognition led to interest on the part of baseball scouts. With his father overseas because of World War II, Duke's mother helped him come to terms with the Brooklyn Dodgers in 1944.

Duke played outfield in the minor leagues for Newport News that summer. Jake Pitler, the man-ager at Newport News, saw a lot of potential in Duke. In 1945, Duke came of draft age and went into the Navy for the end of the war. In 1946, Duke had a good year at Fort Worth (AA baseball). In 1947 and 1948, he split his time between the Dodgers and their AAA affiliates in St. Paul and Montreal. While he was at spring training with the Dodgers, Branch Rickey, the club's general manager and principal owner, worked with Duke on his knowledge of the strike zone and ability to hit breaking and off-speed pitches. Duke made adjustments, learning to "wait on the ball." By 1949, he was being heralded as the Dodgers' starting center fielder and a future star.

The Emerging Champion

Getting to the major leagues had been easy for Duke. He still faced the challenges of establishing himself as a regular and fulfilling the high

2592

STATISTICS

Season	GP	AB	Hits	2B	3B	HR	Runs	RBI	BA	SA
1947	40	83	20	3	1	0	6	5	.241	.301
1948	53	160	39	6	6	5	22	21	.244	.450
1949	146	552	161	28	7	23	100	92	.292	.493
1950	152	620	**199**	31	10	31	109	107	.321	.553
1951	150	606	168	26	6	29	96	101	.277	.483
1952	144	534	162	25	7	21	80	92	.303	.494
1953	153	590	198	38	4	42	**132**	126	.336	**.627**
1954	149	584	199	39	10	40	**120**	130	.341	.647
1955	148	538	166	34	6	42	**126**	**136**	.309	.628
1956	151	542	158	33	2	43	112	101	.292	**.598**
1957	139	508	139	25	7	40	91	92	.274	.587
1958	106	327	102	12	3	15	45	58	.312	.505
1959	126	370	114	11	2	23	59	88	.308	.535
1960	101	235	57	13	5	14	38	36	.243	.519
1961	85	233	69	8	3	16	35	56	.296	.562
1962	80	158	44	11	3	5	28	30	.278	.481
1963	129	354	86	8	3	14	44	45	.243	.401
1964	91	167	35	7	0	4	16	17	.210	.323
Totals	2,143	7,161	2,116	358	85	407	1,259	1,333	.295	.540

Notes: Boldface indicates statistical leader. GP = games played; AB = at bats; 2B = doubles; 3B = triples; HR = home runs; RBI = runs batted in; BA = batting average; SA = slugging average

hopes of the Dodger brass and fans. One obstacle in the way of these goals was Duke himself: He had a tendency to put too much pressure on himself. He was particularly sensitive about striking out. On the other hand, Duke also had a tendency to let up at times rather than hustling all out.

Consequently, Duke needed encouragement as well as an occasional push. Help came from a variety of sources. Pee Wee Reese, Dodger shortstop and team captain, helped Duke to maintain his confidence and concentration. Carl Erskine, Duke's roommate on the road, inspired Duke's admiration by pitching through constant pain. Duke also gave credit to his Dodger managers, most especially Charlie Dressen, and front office figure Buzzie Bavasi. The result was Duke's emergence as an exceptional ballplayer with enough resilience to overcome low points such as his slump in the 1949 World Series.

The Dodger team gave Duke plenty of opportunities to play in other World Series, winning pennants in five of the first eight years as a regular. Duke played a key role in the team's success.Between 1949 and 1957, the Dodgers' last year in Brooklyn, Duke averaged 35 home runs and 109 runs battled in per season. His batting average for the period was a solid .305. He also played excellent defense and had a strong throwing arm.

Duke's most notable achievement during this period was his streak of five straight seasons with 40 or more home runs between 1953 and 1957, a feat still unmatched in the National League. In World Series play, Duke bounced back from a disappointing 1949 series to hit a record-tying 4 home runs in the 1952 series. He then set a record by repeating the feat in 1955, when the Dodgers won their first world championship over the Yankees. Duke hit a total of 11 World Series home runs, still a record for National Leaguers. Duke had gone from being a Series goat to being a perennial Series hero.

Continuing the Story

Duke's career declined after the 1957 season. A series of knee injuries were finally taking their toll as Duke passed the age of thirty, an important boundary line for a major league ballplayer. In addition, the Dodger team was moved to Los Angeles by new owner Walter O'Malley. Although he was from the Los Angeles area originally, the move from Brooklyn was a sad one for Duke and his family.

Sentiment aside, the move created difficulties on the field for Duke. Whereas Ebbets Field had

NATIONAL LEAGUE RECORDS	
Most consecutive seasons of at least 40 home runs, 5	
HONORS AND AWARDS	
1950-56, 1963	National League All-Star Team
1955	*Sporting News* Major League Player of the Year
1980	Inducted into National Baseball Hall of Fame
	Uniform number 4 retired by Los Angeles Dodgers

been a good hitter's park, particularly for left-handers, the Los Angeles Coliseum was a converted football field with monstrously long dimensions in right field.

In combination, these factors reduced Duke to a part-time player, but he did have a last hurrah. The Dodgers had been miserable in 1958, finishing seventh in the league. In 1959, they surprised everyone by winning the pennant and the World Series. Duke hit 23 home runs and drove in 88 runs as a part-timer while batting .308. He also hit his last World Series home run, a shot which led the Dodgers to their Series-clinching win in the sixth game.

In 1963, Duke was traded to the New York Mets, an expansion team. Despite a warm welcome by New York fans, the 1963 season was disappointing. The Mets lost 111 games and Duke was no longer able to play like an All-Star, although he did hit his 400th home run during the season. Duke asked to be traded after the season, playing one year for the Giants before calling it quits. Despite his injuries, Duke had managed to hit 407 career homers. He also had passed the 2,000-hit mark.

After his playing career, Duke managed in the minor leagues for the Dodgers and, later on, for the San Diego Padres. He then moved on to a lengthy career as a broadcaster for the Montreal Expos.

Duke became eligible for the National Baseball Hall of Fame in 1970 but was not elected immediately. The delay disappointed Duke, who later admitted that the Hall became as much of an obsession for him as his strikeouts had been. He was finally inducted into the Hall of Fame in 1980.

Summary

Duke Snider was one of the most feared left-handed sluggers in National League history as well as a top-notch defensive center fielder. A major contributor to the great Dodger teams of the 1940's and 1950's, Duke made his mark despite playing in the same town as Willie Mays, Mickey Mantle, and Joe DiMaggio. On the other hand, Duke's delayed election to the Hall of Fame indicates that he was somewhat overshadowed by these figures. He also was seen by some as an underachiever, an athlete with splendid ability who never quite reached his potential. Be that as it may, Duke did as much as anybody to immortalize Ebbets Field. Along with the men listed above, his name is synonymous with a golden era of major league baseball.

Ira Smolensky

Additional Sources:

Bjarkman, Peter C. *Duke Snider.* New York: Chelsea House, 1994.

Gelman, Steve. *The Greatest Dodgers of Them All.* New York: Putnam, 1968.

Snider, Duke, with Bill Gilbert. *The Duke of Flatbush.* New York: Kensington, 1988.

Winehouse, Irwin. *The Duke Snider Story.* New York: J. Messner, 1964.

ANNIKA SORENSTAM

Sport: Golf

Born: October 9, 1970
Stockholm, Sweden

Early Life

Born in Stockholm, Sweden, on October 9, 1970, Annika Sorenstam sought a niche in a sport not ordinarily linked with the climate of Sweden. Instead of ice skating, skiing, or tobogganing, she preferred a sport usually associated with warmer climates: golf. She began to play when she was twelve years old.

Annika had started an atheletic career in tennis, a sport that could be played indoors as well as outdoors. While she was considered a good athlete, she never reached a top-ten ranking as a junior tennis player in the city of Stockholm. So she turned to golf, a game she could practice on her own. In later life, she developed a reputation as something of a loner, and in this, golf suited her well.

The Road to Excellence

Annika was a member of the Swedish national golf team, where she came under the tutelege of head coach Pia Nilsson. Annika's training came primarily from the Swedish Golf Federation. The guidance of Nilsson, emotional support from her parents, and her own abilities and belief in her skills soon paved the way to greater opportunities. The training from the Swedish Golf Federation resulted in the award of a scholarship to the University of Arizona at Tucson.

At the university she was a two-time All-American golfer and world amateur champion in 1992. All together, while at the university, she won seven collegiate honors, including the National Collegiate Amateur Association (NCAA) championship and the College Player of the Year award. The call of the "big show" was strong, however, and in 1993, she turned professional.

The Emerging Champion

The two years of collegiate competition had helped to hone Annika's skills, and when she quit the University of Arizona in 1992 her future looked very bright. She established herself as 1993 Rookie of the Year on the Women Professional Golfers' (WPG) European Tour. That same year she joined the La-

AP/Wide World Photos

Annika Sorenstam after taking a shot in a 1996 tournament.

LPGA VICTORIES

1995	U.S. Women's Open
	GHP Heartland Classic
	Samsung World Championship of Women's Golf
1996	U.S. Women's Open
	Betsy King LPGA Classic
	Samsung World Championship of Women's Golf
1997	Chrysler-Plymouth Tournament of Champions
	Hawaiian Ladies Open
	Long's Drug's Challenge
	LPGA Skins Game
	Michelob Light Classic
	Betsy King LPGA Classic
	ITT Tour Championship
2000	Welch's Circle K Championship
	Standard Register Ping
	Nabisco Championship
	The Office Depot

dies Professional Golf Association (LPGA), competed in three events, and earned nearly $50,000.

Annika was named Rolex Rookie of the Year in 1994 on the basis of three top-ten finishes. Her native country, Sweden, honored her in 1995 when she was named Athlete of the Year, Sweden's most prestigious sports award. There seemed no end to the victories and awards bestowed on her that year. Annika competed in nineteen events, with three victories, which earned her $366,533 and made her the season's leading money winner. She won the Samsung world championship with a 45-foot chip in a sudden-death playoff, her third career victory.

Annika came into her own in 1995, winning the Heartland Classic by 10 strokes, winning the Rolex Rookie of the Year award with twelve top-ten finishes in nineteen starts. She earned nearly $700,000 and recognition as the season's top money winner.

In 1996, she won her second world championship as well as the Core States Betsy King Classic, finishing all four rounds in the 60's. She sucessfully defended her title at the U.S. Women's Open, and her career earnings topped the $1 million mark. She also earned a second Vare Trophy for achieving the lowest season scoring average. Annika's career earnings passed $2 million after winning the Longs Drugs Challenge and the J.C. Penney-LPGA Skins Game in 1997. That same year she also was victorious in the Chrysler-Plymouth Tournament of Cham-

pions, the Michelob Light Classic, and the Hawaiian Ladies Open.

There seemed to be no slowing down for Annika. Her achievements in 1998 included the Shoprite LPGA Classic, with all her rounds in the 60's, and the JAL Big Apple Classic, with four rounds in the 60's. That year she became the first player in LPGA history to finish a season with a scoring average below 70 (69.99). Annika's winning style continued through 1999, with a career total of eighteen wins. She finished the year having played twenty-one tour events and earning $837,314. Her record for the year 2000 included play in twenty LPGA tour events, and she finished first in five of them. For the year, she earned over $1 million.

In 2001, Annika began the season in spectacular fashion by winning four consecutive LPGA tournaments. In the Standard Register Ping, at Phoenix, Arizona, she became the first LPGA player in history to score under 60 in an 18-hole round by shooting a 13-under 59 in the second round. She also tied the LPGA record of 28 on nine holes.

Continuing the Story

Sportswriters following Annika's career sometimes write glowing reviews of her abilities. One writer described her as the "Swede with the heavenly swing." She has earned such praise, however. For example, she was the first foreign-born player to win the Vare Trophy for the lowest scoring average in a season.

Summary

Annika Sorenstam demonstrated skills in golf early on, a sport not usually associated with the snow and cold of Scandinavia. When she had gone as far as she could in her native country, she continued to hone her skills at the University of Arizona. After two years at the university, she left campus life and sports and turned professional.

INTERNATIONAL VICTORIES

1994	Australian Ladies Open
1995	Australian Ladies Masters
1997	Hisako Higuchi Kibun Classic

In the LPGA, she has earned many winning scores and prizes.

Albert C. Jensen

AWARDS AND HONORS	
1987-1992	Swedish National Team
1993	WPGET Rookie of the Year
1994	Solheim Cup Team LPGA Rookie of the Year
1995	Rolex Player of the Year Vare Trophy
1996	Solheim Cup Team Vare Trophy
1997	LPGA Player of the Year

Additional Sources:

Babineau, Jeff. "Annika Sorenstam." *Golf Magazine* 40, no. 7 (July, 1998): 136-137.

Burnett, Jim. "Coach Pia." *Golf Magazine* 39, no. 2 (February, 1997): 78-79.

_____. *Tee Times: On the Road with the Ladies Professional Golf Tour.* New York: Scribner, 1997.

Garrity, John. "Peer Group: Season's Top LPGA Tour Winners (A. Sorenstam and K. Webb)." *Sports Illustrated* 86, no. 19 (May 12, 1997): 68-70.

Mickey, Lisa D. "Icebreaker: Having Mended a Chilly Relationship with Sister Annika, Charlotta Sorenstam Puts the Freeze on Karrie Webb for Her First Career Victory." *Golf World* 53, no. 34 (March 24, 2000): 28-30.

SAMMY SOSA

Sport: Baseball

Born: November 12, 1968
San Pedro de Macoris, Dominican
Republic

Early Life

Samuel Peralta Sosa was born on November 12, 1968, to Juan Montero and Mireya Sosa in San Pedro de Macoris, on the western end of the Dominican Republic. His father died when Sammy was seven years old. By then the boy had begun shining shoes, washing cars, and selling oranges to help the family make ends meet.

His first love was boxing, to his mother's dismay, but his brother Jose convinced Sammy to try baseball. Since he could not afford equipment, he fashioned a glove of old milk cartons and hit a ball made of rolled up and taped socks with a tree branch. Soon he began to play for several small leagues in Santo Domingo.

The Road to Excellence

In July, 1985, a baseball scout learned about Sammy, and at the age of sixteen he signed with the Texas Rangers. Sammy made his major league debut for the Rangers on June 16, 1989. He had a tough season, though, and was sent back to the minors several times and traded to the Chicago White Sox on July 29.

The next year, his first full major league season, he was the only American League player to reach double figures in all of the following: doubles (26), triples (10), home runs (15), and steals (32). That same year he met Sonia, the woman who was to become his wife. The two had four children: Keysha; Kenia; Sammy, Jr.; and Michael. In 1991 Sammy had another bad year and spent more time with the minor leagues, and in March of 1992 he was traded to the Chicago Cubs.

The Emerging Champion

That year he was disabled twice because of injuries, but in 1993, determined to turn things around in a desire to provide for his family, Sammy began to shine as a ballplayer, hitting 33 home runs and 93 runs batted in (RBIs). In 1994 he led the Cubs in batting average, home runs, steals, and RBIs, and the following year he led

Sammy Sosa of the Chicago Cubs hits his sixty-first home run of the 1998 season.

STATISTICS

Season	GP	AB	Hits	2B	3B	HR	Runs	RBI	BA	SA
1989	58	183	47	8	0	4	27	13	.257	.366
1990	153	532	124	26	10	15	72	70	.233	.404
1991	116	316	64	10	1	10	39	33	.203	.335
1992	67	262	68	7	2	8	41	25	.260	.393
1993	159	598	156	25	5	33	92	93	.261	.485
1994	105	426	128	17	6	25	59	70	.300	.545
1995	**144**	564	151	17	3	36	89	119	.268	.500
1996	124	498	136	21	2	40	84	100	.273	.564
1997	**162**	642	161	31	4	36	90	119	.251	.480
1998	159	643	198	20	0	66	**134**	**158**	.308	.647
1999	**162**	625	180	24	2	63	114	141	.288	.635
2000	156	604	193	38	1	**50**	106	138	.320	.634
Totals	1,565	5,893	1,606	244	36	386	947	1,079	.273	.523

Notes: Boldface indicates statistical leader. GP = games played; AB = at bats; 2B = doubles; 3B = triples; HR = home runs; RBI = runs batted in; BA = batting average; SA = slugging average

in home runs and steals for the third consecutive season, setting a twentieth century Cubs record.

That same year he was chosen for his first All-Star game. Each year he piled up more records. In 1996 he became the first Cub to hit 2 home runs in one inning. Despite missing much of the season with another injury, he still hit 40 home runs for the season.

In 1997 he signed a four-year, $42.5 million contract with the Cubs, which at the time led many to believe he was overpaid. The following year he disproved that theory, however. In 1998 Sammy led the major leagues in RBIs, runs, and total bases, and his RBI total (158) was the fourth highest in National League history. He was again chosen for the All-Star team, and his thirty-third season home run gave him a career high of 249, equaling that of his boyhood hero Roberto Clemente's career total.

It was not just Sammy who was having a record-breaking season. With the St. Louis Cardinals, Mark McGwire, a good friend of Sammy's, was trying to beat the all-time record for season home runs—61—set by Roger Maris in 1961. Sammy and McGwire engaged in a good-natured race to see, first, if one or both could break that record, and second, who would come out with the most homers. McGwire broke the record first and went on to hit 70, but Sammy also broke Maris's record with 66.

It was also a big year for Sammy's charities, as he donated forty computers to schools in the Do-minican Republic for every home run he made. However, his activity in support of his people was really called for in September, when Hurricane Georges hit the Dominican Republic, destroying 90 percent of the food crops and leaving over 250 people dead and 100,000 homeless. Even before the hurricane he had donated to his hometown a baseball training center, shopping center, and water-purification equipment, but now his Sammy Sosa Charitable Foundation really went to work, arranging for tons of food, medicine, and clothing to be shipped to the Dominican Republic and raising $700,000 for hurricane relief.

That year he won numerous awards, both for his ball playing and for his humanitarian efforts, including the National League most valuable player award (MVP), the All-Star MVP award, and the Roberto Clemente Award, major league's highest honor for outstanding service to the community.

Continuing the Story

His success continued, although nothing has eclipsed the 1998 glory year. He was voted to the 1999 and 2000 All-Star teams, and in 1999 he and Cardinal slugger Mark McGwire became the first players to hit 60 home runs in two seasons.

His charity work continued, including the opening of the Sammy Sosa Children's Medical Center for Preventive Medicine in the Dominican Republic. He also attended the 1999 state of the union address and was acknowledged by

President Bill Clinton as a hero in two countries, receiving a standing ovation.

In 2000, after a feud with new manager Don Baylor, he was nearly traded to the New York Yankees. That deal and others fell through though, and Sammy went on to break new records, reaching over 50 home runs for three years in a row. The awards continued to come, including becoming the first baseball player to receive a star on the Hispanic Walk of Fame in Miami, Florida.

"Slammin' Sammy" Sosa lives in San Pedro de Macoris during the off-season, never forgetting his roots. His famous "two-finger" gesture after a hit, touching his heart, he says, is for his fans. He then blows kisses, one for his mother and one for his family back home.

Summary

Sammy Sosa proved that determination to succeed can pay off. He went from a struggling minor league player to a record-breaking sensation. His battle with Mark McGwire to surpass the 61-home-run mark brought much attention to the sport of baseball in 1998, and his charming, kind personality shone through even though McGwire broke the record first. A magnanimous star who has given back to his community, Sammy is a man who once said he wanted to be known more as a good person than as a good baseball player. He has turned out to be both.

Eleanor B. Amico

Additional Sources:

Christopher, Matt. *At the Plate with—Sammy Sosa.* Boston: Little, Brown, 1999.

Fisher, David. *Sammy Sosa.* Kansas City, Mo.: Andrews McMeel, 1999.

Noden, Merrell. *Home Run Heroes: Mark McGwire, Sammy Sosa, and a Season for the Ages.* New York: Simon and Schuster, 1998.

Sosa, Sammy, with Marcos Breton. *Sosa: An Autobiography.* New York: Warner Books, 2000.

JAVIER SOTOMAYOR

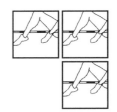

Sport: Track and field (high jump)

Born: October 13, 1967
Limonar, Matanzas, Cuba

Early Life

Javier Sotomayor was born into a working-class family in Limonar, Matanzas, Cuba, a small town east of Havana, on October 13, 1967. His parents were factory workers, and as youngsters, Javier and his older brother worked in the sugar-cane fields.

As a young boy, Javier was interested in sports, and especially in high jumping. He practiced by leaping over dried sugar cane stalks, which he would place atop large oil barrels. In Cuba, the state promotes athletic excellence by testing children at an early age for interest, agility, and coordination; children who show athletic promise are sent to special schools. At the age of nine, Javier was sent to polish his skills at a specialized school in the Ciudad Deportiva, or "city of sport."

The Road to Excellence

After being enrolled in 1976, Javier was given five sports from which to choose. The Cuban sports leaders had been grooming Javier to be a basketball player, but high jumping. As he began to progress in the sport, he caught the eye of the country's premier high jump coach, Carlos Luis Godoy, who would be the only coach Javier ever had. Shortly afterward, Javier began to make great strides and was noticed by many of the sports leaders in Cuba. Within six years, as a tall, slender fifteen-year-old, Javier was jump-

ing 6 feet 6¾ inches. By the time he was seventeen in 1984, he won the Cuban national championship with a jump of 7 feet 7¾ inches. In 1985, Javier won the Caribbean championship and placed third in World Cup competition. He was the world's best high jumper in his age group every year from age fifteen to seventeen.

Under Godoy's tutelage, Javier developed an original technique that best utilized his speed and 6-foot 4¾-inch, 181-pound frame. Most high jumpers employ the "Fosbury flop" style, in which the jumper approaches the bar parallel to the standards. Instead, Javier developed a very fast, almost head-on, approach. With this technique, and with his exceptional speed, Javier became the world's best at turning horizontal velocity into vertical lift.

Cuban Javier Sotomayor in the 2000 Olympic high jump. He won the silver medal.

By 1988, Javier was one of the top high jumpers in the world. The Pan-American Games gold medalist in 1987, he set his first world record of 7 feet 11½ inches in 1988. Javier was looking forward to the epitome of international competition, the 1988 Olympic Games in Seoul. Cuba, however, chose to boycott the Seoul Games, so Javier had to put his Olympic dreams on hold.

The Emerging Champion

Javier began 1989 in grand style by setting a new world indoor record of 7 feet 11¾ inches at the World Indoor Championships in March; the jump tied the world outdoor record he had set the previous September. The Cuban was zeroing in on what seemed to be one of the impossible barriers of sports, the 8-foot high jump. It had been thirty-three years since the first 7-foot jump by American Charley Dumas. Javier now seemed the only man capable of shattering the barrier.

On July 29, 1989, Javier was participating in the Caribbean Zone Track and Field Championships in San Juan, Puerto Rico. Late on that Saturday night, the twenty-one-year-old Cuban asked for the bar to be raised to 8 feet. After failing on his first attempt, Javier gradually started to pace the infield to prepare himself for the next attempt. Gradually, the crowd began to systematically clap in support of Javier's next try. Javier slightly grazed the bar as he cleared the standards. The bar wobbled but stayed in place. The mythical 8-foot barrier was finally broken.

Less than two months later, in September, 1989, Javier sprained his ankle at the World Cup and finished in third place. The month did end well, however, when he married the Cuban women's high jump champion Maria del Carmen Garcia.

Whereas 1989 was a highlight year in Javier's career, 1990 was one of tragedy for the Cuban jumper. In that year, his only coach, Carlos Godoy, died at the age of sixty-four. Moved by the loss of his mentor, Javier refused to take another coach, and he dedicated all of his future victories to Godoy's memory.

Continuing the Story

The Pan-American Games were scheduled for Havana in 1991. For a country in dire economic straits, the task of building world-class athletic facilities and housing for the best athletes from the Western Hemisphere was monumental. In order to arouse support from the Cuban population, many athletes joined work crews, volunteering for manual labor to help build facilities. One of the most visible workers was Javier, and his dedication to his country and sport was not lost on his fellow Cubans. He became one of the most popular idols for Cuba's youth. Even Cuban track legend Alberto Juantorena had to take a back seat in his own son's eyes; the boy wanted to grow up to be like the high jumper.

After a twelve-year absence, Cuba was to reappear on the Olympic stage once again at the 1992 Barcelona Games, and Javier's goal of participating in the Olympics seemed within reach. Just as the 1992 Games approached, however, he aggravated an irritating Achilles tendon injury that threatened to dampen his first Olympic appearance. Adding to Javier's concern was the strain of being chosen as the favorite in the high jump. The Olympic competition was not of the highest quality, but Javier won his first Olympic gold medal with a jump of 7 feet 8 inches, the lowest winning height in sixteen years.

MAJOR HIGH JUMP COMPETITIONS

Year	Competition	Place
1985	World Cup	3d
	IAAF World Indoor Championships	2d
1987	Pan-American Games	1st
	World Championships	9th
1989	World Cup	3d
	IAAF Indoor Championships	1st
1990	Central-American Games	1st
1991	Pan-American Games	1st
	World Championship	2d
	IAAF World Indoor Championships	3d
1992	Olympic Games	Gold
	World Cup	2d
1993	World Championships	1st
	IAAF World Indoor Championships	1st
1995	IAAF World Indoor Championships	1st
1997	World Championships	1st
1998	Goodwill Games	1st
1999	IAAF World Indoor Championships	1st
2000	Olympic Games	Silver

The increasing economic burden placed on Cuba by the collapse of the Soviet Union forced government sports officials to find new ways to support Cuban sports. Many avenues were explored. It was finally announced in October, 1993, that many top Cuban athletes, led by Javier, would be allowed to compete as professionals for a Spanish athletic club. Many observers both in and out of Cuba believed that this landmark decision was a direct result of Javier's accomplishments and his devotion to Cuba.

Though he did not surpass his mark of 8 feet ½ inch, Javier continued to dominate the high jump event, winning the World Championships in 1993 and 1997 and taking the gold medal in the 1998 Goodwill Games. At the 1999 Pan-American Games, however, Javier tested positive for cocaine use and was stripped of the gold medal that he had just won.

The International Amateur Athletic Federation imposed a mandatory two-year ban that would have prevented Javier's appearance in the 2000 Olympics in Sydney. He disputed the charge of cocaine use and successfully lobbied for his reinstatement in time for the 2000 Olympics. His presence in Sydney met with mixed reactions, but despite the controversy Javier took home the silver medal.

RECORDS AND MILESTONES

Set world record in high jump, 8' ½"
First high jumper to clear 8 feet
Set world age group records each year from ages fifteen to nineteen

Summary

As of 2001 no one had surpassed Javier Sotomayor's incredible world-record mark in the high jump. His persistence and dedication have reaped rewards not only for himself but also for his country, and his achievements have ranked him as the greatest high jumper of all time.

Rusty Wilson

Additional Sources:

Wallechinsky, David. *The Complete Book of the Olympics.* Boston: Little, Brown and Company, 1991.

WARREN SPAHN

Sport: Baseball

Born: April 23, 1921
Buffalo, New York

Early Life

Warren Edward Spahn was born on April 23, 1921, in Buffalo, New York, the oldest son of six children of the Edward Spahns. Ed, a wallpaper salesperson, played third base for the semi-professional Lake City Athletic Club baseball team and wanted Warren to play major league baseball. When Warren was a small boy, Ed taught him how to throw and catch. They often attended Buffalo Bisons minor league home games, where Warren learned about pitching.

Courtesy of Amateur Athletic Foundation of Los Angeles

The Road to Excellence

A left-hander, Warren played first base for the Lake City Athletic Club midget team as a nine-year-old and later joined the senior team. He graduated from South Park High School in Buffalo, pitching four years for his baseball team. Boston Red Sox scout Billy Meyer wanted to sign Warren, but Ed insisted that his son finish high school first.

In 1940, the Boston Braves signed Warren and sent him to the Bradford, Pennsylvania, team in the low minor leagues. At Bradford, Warren tore tendons in his left shoulder and was struck on the nose with a thrown ball. He still struck out nearly one batter per inning with his fastball. Warren continued to pitch well for Evansville, Indiana, of the Class B Three-I League in 1941, and for Hartford, Connecticut, of the Class A Eastern League in 1942. The Braves, managed by Casey Stengel, called Warren up in September, 1942. Warren made four major league appearances and struggled in both starts.

The U.S. Army drafted Warren in 1942 for World War II service. He fought as a combat engineer in Europe and was wounded by shrapnel at the Battle of the Bulge. No other major leaguer won a battlefield commission for bravery in action.

The Emerging Champion

Warren was discharged from the Army on April 23, 1946, and rejoined the Boston Braves. He starred several times in relief before manager Billy Southworth started him against the Brooklyn Dodgers. The twenty-five-year-old did not pitch well in his first two starts but then won five straight games. Warren was not happy, however, because his fiancée, Lorene Southard, was living sixteen hundred miles away in Tulsa, Oklahoma. Warren and Lorene were married in August, 1946, and later had one son, Gregory. Warren

STATISTICS

Season	GP	GS	CG	IP	HA	BB	SO	W	L	S	ShO	ERA
1942	4	2	1	15.2	25	11	7	0	0	0	0	5.74
1946	24	16	8	125.2	107	36	67	8	5	1	0	2.94
1947	40	35	22	289.2	245	84	123	21	10	3	7	2.33
1948	36	35	16	257.0	237	77	114	15	12	1	3	3.71
1949	38	38	25	302.1	283	86	151	21	14	0	4	3.07
1950	41	39	25	293.0	248	111	191	21	17	1	1	3.16
1951	39	36	26	310.2	278	109	164	22	14	0	7	2.98
1952	40	35	19	290.0	263	73	183	14	19	3	5	2.98
1953	35	32	24	265.2	211	70	148	23	7	3	5	2.10
1954	39	34	23	283.1	262	86	136	21	12	3	1	3.14
1955	39	32	16	245.2	249	65	110	17	14	1	1	3.26
1956	39	35	20	281.1	249	52	128	20	11	3	3	2.78
1957	39	35	18	271.0	241	78	111	21	11	3	4	2.69
1958	38	36	23	290.0	257	76	150	22	11	1	2	3.07
1959	40	36	21	292.0	282	70	143	21	15	0	4	2.96
1960	40	33	18	267.2	254	74	154	21	10	2	4	3.50
1961	38	34	21	262.2	236	64	115	21	13	0	4	3.02
1962	34	34	22	269.1	248	55	118	18	14	0	0	3.04
1963	33	33	22	259.2	241	49	102	23	7	0	7	2.60
1964	38	25	4	173.2	204	52	78	6	13	4	1	5.29
1965	36	30	8	197.2	210	56	90	7	16	0	0	4.01
Totals	750	665	382	5,237.6	4,830	1,434	2,583	363	245	29	63	3.09

Notes: Boldface indicates statistical leader. GP = games played; GS = games started; CG = complete games; IP = innings pitched; HA = hits allowed; BB = bases on balls (walks); SO = strikeouts; W = wins; L = losses; S = saves; ShO = shutouts; ERA = earned run average

finished the 1946 season with eight wins and five losses.

At spring training in 1947, Warren improved his pitching delivery and developed curveball and change-up pitches. He recorded twenty-one victories and kept six opponents scoreless, hurling four consecutive shutouts in September. His emergence sparked the Braves' resurgence. In 1948, Warren helped the Boston Braves capture their first National League pennant in thirty-five years. The Braves lacked pitching depth, sparking the jingle, "Spahn and Sain and pray for rain." Warren's 2-1, 14-inning masterpiece against the Brooklyn Dodgers put the Boston Braves in first place. In the Series, Warren hurled nearly 6 innings of one-hit relief, winning the fifth game against the Cleveland Indians.

Continuing the Story

Warren was the most dominant major league left-hander from 1949 to 1963. He pitched for the Braves in Boston through 1952 and in Milwaukee from 1953 to 1964. His blazing fastball and curveball helped him lead the National League in strikeouts from 1949 through 1952. He developed superb control and a deceptive

pickoff move and added a wicked screwball and slider, giving him four quality pitches. Batters remained off-stride because crafty Warren changed locations and speeds.

No major league left-hander won more games (363) or won at least twenty games for more seasons (thirteen) than Warren. He led the National League in victories for eight seasons, including from 1957 through 1961, and lost 245 decisions. Nearly 2,600 batters struck out against Warren. He held opponents scoreless 63 times, the most by any National League left-hander. Opponents scored around 3 earned runs per game against Warren, but the Braves often gave him limited support. Warren once struck out 18 Chicago Cubs and hit a home run in a 15-inning 2-1 loss.

With Warren's help, the Milwaukee Braves captured the 1957 and 1958 National League pennants. Warren won twenty-one games in 1957, earning the Cy Young Award as the best major league pitcher. The Braves took their first World Series title since 1914, with Warren winning game 4 against the New York Yankees. Warren recorded twenty-two victories in 1958 and triumphed in two World Series contests, including his brilliant 2-hit shutout in game 4. The New

HONORS AND AWARDS

1947, 1949-54, 1956-59, 1961-63	National League All-Star Team
1953, 1957-58, 1960	*Sporting News* Major League All-Star Team
1953, 1957-58, 1961	*Sporting News* Outstanding National League Pitcher
1957	National League Cy Young Award
1961	*Sporting News* National League All-Star Team
1973	Inducted into National Baseball Hall of Fame Uniform number 21 retired by Atlanta Braves

York Yankees, however, regained the World Series crown.

On September 16, 1960, Warren hurled the first no-hitter of his career against the Philadelphia Phillies. The 4-0 victory gave Warren his twentieth for that season. Five days after his fortieth birthday, he pitched the only no-hitter of the 1961 major league season. That 1-0 masterpiece came against the San Francisco Giants. A packed Milwaukee County Stadium, on August 11, 1961, witnessed Warren earn his 300th career major league triumph against the Chicago Cubs. Warren surpassed Eddie Plank for wins by a left-handed pitcher by defeating the Pittsburgh Pirates on September 28, 1962. Sandy Koufax overtook him as the National League's best left-hander after the 1963 season.

Warren closed his major league career with the New York Mets and San Francisco Giants in 1965. He remained in baseball as a major league scout and coach and as a minor league manager and pitching instructor through 1981. The raw-boned, 6-foot, 175-pounder with a hawklike nose, receding hairline, and long, narrow jaw retired to his eight-hundred-acre cattle ranch in Hartshorne, Oklahoma.

In 1973, the National Baseball Hall of Fame inducted Warren in his first year of eligibility. Warren hit more home runs (35) than any other National League pitcher. Managers seldom pinch-hit for Warren, who led the National League nine consecutive seasons in complete games and pitched more than five thousand career innings.

Summary

Warren Spahn set new records of achievement by mastering the art of pitching as few others have. Warren impressed others as humble, genial, witty, reliable, consistent, and intelligent and demonstrated strength of character, competitive zeal, and physical stamina. He ranks among the most popular and respected players to perform in the major leagues.

David L. Porter

Additional Sources:

Bjarkman, Peter C. *Warren Spahn.* New York: Chelsea House, 1994.

Shapiro, Milton J. *The Warren Spahn Story.* New York: Julian Messner, 1960.

Silverman, Al. *Warren Spahn: Immortal Southpaw.* New York: Bartholomew House, 1961.

TRIS SPEAKER

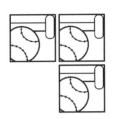

Sport: Baseball

Born: April 4, 1888
     Hubbard, Texas
Died: December 8, 1958
     Lake Whitney, Texas

AP/Wide World Photos

Tris Speaker of the Red Sox in 1912.

Early Life

Tristram E. Speaker spent his youth around Hubbard, Texas, where he was born on April 4, 1888. As a boy Tris enjoyed both riding horses and playing baseball. Tris was right-handed but broke his right arm in a fall from his horse while in his teens. For the rest of his life, he batted and threw left-handed. After high school, where he was an all-around athlete, he worked as a cow-puncher and as a telegraph linesman. The death of his father left his mother to rear seven children. Tris was to be devoted to her his whole life. He was her youngest child and only son.

The Road to Excellence

Tris broke into baseball in 1906 at age seventeen as a pitcher and outfielder for Cleburne in the North Texas League. His average reached .314 next season for Houston in the Texas League and gained him a Boston Red Sox contract. He hit only .158 for seven games, however. The next year, 1908, had to be humbling for Tris. He paid his own way to the Red Sox training camp at Little Rock, Arkansas, and was left there as payment of the field rental fee.

It was not enough to break the great self-confidence of Tris Speaker. He proceeded to win the American Association batting title with an average of .350. That catapulted him into the majors for good. Self-confidence and studious knowledge of the game of baseball were Tris's strongest traits.

The Emerging Champion

Tris became more renowned for his fielding than for his hitting. In this area, he always gave credit to pitcher Cy Young, who "hit fungos to me by the hour. I got to . . . studying his fungo swing and . . . could start after the ball before he actually hit it." That was not the whole story, however; those who saw both play say Tris was faster and more graceful than Joe DiMaggio.

From 1910 until he left the Red Sox in 1915, Tris was center fielder between Harry Hooper and "Duffy" Lewis. Many experts claim that this was the greatest defensive outfield in the history of baseball. Tris's speed in the field and his prematurely gray hair produced his nickname, "the Gray Eagle."

It was in the outfield that Tris Speaker created his own legend. He "had to be seen to be believed." Tris played a dangerously shallow center field, a few yards behind second base. He was thus able to cover second base in bunt situations, to turn grounders through the middle into outs and even double plays, and to catch line drives that would normally be hits, often converting them into double plays as well. His speed and instincts (as well as the "dead" ball in use until the early 1920's) allowed him to play shallow and still race backward to catch long balls. He always felt he saved more games by catching would-be singles than he lost by missing an occasional double or triple. His 448 assists and 139 double plays (including some unassisted) are major league records for outfielders; his 6,791 putouts constitute a record second only to that of Willie Mays.

In terms of individual glory at the plate, Tris Speaker was unlucky to be playing at the same time as Ty Cobb and Babe Ruth, who joined Boston in the 1914 season. Tris was modest and businesslike, whereas Cobb and Ruth were flamboyant personalities both on and off the field.

In any other period, Tris's five seasons over .380 would have won the headlines, but Cobb did it nine times, including three seasons over .400, and Ruth's 50 to 60 home runs were already a leg-

end after the era of the dead ball, when hitting even 15 homers was rare. In nineteen full seasons, mainly from 1909 to 1915 with Boston and from 1916 to 1926 with the Cleveland Indians, Tris batted over .300 eighteen times. His remarkable lifetime average of .344, seventh highest among all hitters, was overshadowed by Cobb's .367. In more than 10,200 times at bat, Tris struck out only 220 times. His 3,515 hits rank fifth.

A contract dispute was the reason for Tris's trade to Cleveland in 1916. The threat of players jumping to the new Federal League had caused inflated salaries. When that league folded in 1915, there was a glut of players seeking jobs with established major league teams. Boston owner Joe Lannin wanted to cut Tris's salary from $15,000 plus a $5,000 bonus to $9,000 dollars. As a result, Tris was traded to Cleveland for two players and $50,000, the most ever paid for one player up to that time.

Continuing the Story

Tris Speaker's teams were quite successful. The Red Sox won the pennant and World Series in 1912 and 1915, as did the Indians in 1920 with

STATISTICS

Season	GP	AB	Hits	2B	3B	HR	Runs	RBI	BA	SA
1907	7	19	3	0	0	0	0	1	.158	.158
1908	31	118	26	2	3	0	12	9	.220	.288
1909	143	544	168	26	13	7	73	77	.309	.443
1910	141	538	183	20	14	7	92	65	.340	.468
1911	141	510	167	34	13	8	88	80	.327	.492
1912	153	580	222	**53**	12	**10**	136	98	.383	.567
1913	141	520	190	35	22	3	94	81	.365	.535
1914	158	571	**193**	**46**	18	4	100	90	.338	.503
1915	150	547	176	25	12	0	108	69	.322	.411
1916	151	546	**211**	**41**	8	2	102	83	**.386**	**.502**
1917	142	523	184	42	11	2	90	60	.352	.486
1918	127	471	150	**33**	11	0	73	61	.318	.435
1919	134	494	146	38	12	2	83	63	.296	.433
1920	150	552	214	**50**	11	8	137	107	.388	.562
1921	132	506	183	**52**	14	3	107	74	.362	.538
1922	131	426	161	**48**	8	11	85	71	.378	.606
1923	150	574	218	**59**	11	17	133	**130**	.380	.610
1924	135	486	167	36	9	9	94	65	.344	.510
1925	117	429	167	35	5	12	79	87	.389	.578
1926	150	540	164	52	8	7	96	86	.304	.469
1927	141	523	171	43	6	2	71	73	.327	.444
1928	64	191	51	22	2	3	28	29	.267	.450
Totals	2,789	10,208	3,515	**792**	223	117	1,881	1,559	.344	.500

Notes: Boldface indicates statistical leader. GP = games played; AB = at bats; 2B = doubles; 3B = triples; HR = home runs; RBI = runs batted in; BA = batting average; SA = slugging average

MAJOR LEAGUE RECORDS
Most doubles, 792
Most World Series triples, 4 (record shared)

HONORS AND AWARDS
1912   American League most valuable player
1937   Inducted into National Baseball Hall of Fame

Tris as player-manager. In 1920, Tris, now thirty-two years old, rushed in from the outfield after the final out, collected the game ball, and climbed into the stands to hug his mother. In all, Tris managed the Indians from 1919 to 1926 with a record of 616 wins and 520 losses for a .542 winning percentage.

Tris resigned after the 1926 season in the face of charges that he, Ty Cobb, and others had fixed a game in 1919. In that game, Cleveland lost to Detroit. In fact, on the day in question, Tris hit a single and two triples for Cleveland. It did not seem that he was "throwing" the game. He and Cobb were exonerated by Commissioner Kenesaw Mountain Landis and both returned to baseball, but from then on, they lived in the shadow of that scandal. Both ended their major league careers in 1928 in the Philadelphia Athletics outfield.

Tris married Mary Frances Cudahy in 1925. After two years as player-manager of Newark of the International League (1929 and 1930), he became for a time a radio broadcaster. He died December 8, 1958, in Lake Whitney, Texas.

Summary

Tris Speaker was perhaps the greatest center fielder to play the game of baseball. Joe DiMaggio, his chief rival for this title, held Tris as his model. Tris revolutionized the position by playing it more shallow than anyone else before him. Although DiMaggio hit more home runs, Tris surpassed him in every other category of batting and fielding.

Daniel C. Scavone

Additional Sources:

Appel, Martin, and Burt Goldblatt. *Baseball's Best: The Hall of Fame Gallery.* New York: McGraw-Hill, 1977.

Porter, David L., ed. *Biographical Dictionary of American Sports: Baseball.* Westport, Conn.: Greenwood Press, 1987.

Shatzkin, Mike, et al., eds. *The Ballplayers: Baseball's Ultimate Biographical Reference.* New York: William Morrow, 1990.

MARK SPITZ

Sport: Swimming

Born: February 10, 1950
Modesto, California

Early Life

Mark Andrew Spitz was born on February 10, 1950, in Modesto, California. He was the first of three children born to Arnold, a scrap-metal dealer, and Lenore Spitz.

When Mark was about six years old, the family went out in their small boat to the nearby Stockton Channels, which empty into the San Francisco Bay. Following his father's instructions, Mark learned to swim that day.

Arnold Spitz, especially in his son's early life, proved to be highly influential. A firm believer that parents should devote themselves to their children, he went to extraordinary lengths to promote his only son's athletic career.

It was in 1958 that Mark began to show his extraordinary talent at the local YMCA. The eight-year-old's performance was noticed, especially by his father.

The Road to Excellence

With nine-year-old Mark's swimming talent becoming even more apparent, the entire family moved so Mark could receive the best training available. Mark began swimming at the Arden Hills Swim Club in Sacramento, California, under the guidance of Sherman Chavoor, the same man who would later coach Mark at the Munich Olympics. At the age of ten, Mark set the first of many records, this one in his age group for the butterfly stroke.

Between the ages of twelve and fourteen, Mark continued his training with the Aqua Bears in Oakland, California, and then at the Pleasant Hill Swim Club. Trained as a distance swimmer when he was young, Mark has remarked that the early endurance and stamina training benefited him in the sprinting events for which he later became famous.

When Mark was fourteen, his parents made a second decision that would influence their son's career. Once again, the entire Spitz household moved, this time to Walnut Creek, California, so that Mark could be coached by Olympic trainer George Haines and be teammate to a former Olympic gold medalist at the Santa Clara Swim Club.

At the age of sixteen, Mark won his first national championship in the 100-meter butterfly.

At the 1972 Olympics, swimmer Mark Spitz won seven gold medals.

Although the Santa Clara High School student emulated the older swimmers, he never managed to gain their acceptance. With so much public attention focused on the young swimmer, Mark had developed quite an ego and was thought conceited by his teammates. Mark, though, has always ignored his critics, simply letting his performance in the water do the talking.

The Emerging Champion

Mark was always an individual who pursued every task with concentrated effort and a dedicated will to succeed. He was also lucky to have been born with two physical traits that have helped him. First, he has extraordinarily large scoop-shaped palms that can push tremendous amounts of water. Second, Mark has the unusual gift of knees that flex forward so as to give him a thrust that goes six to twelve inches deeper in the water than that of his competitors.

Mark used these advantages to set six world records before the 1968 Olympics in Mexico City. Haines and Mark both felt that he should be able to capture an equal number of gold medals competing in those same events at the Olympics. This prediction received much attention because no single athlete in Olympic history had ever won so many events.

No one was more disappointed than Mark when he managed to win only two gold medals (what would have been momentous for most athletes), and both of those were in relay, not individual events.

Mark returned, somewhat humbled, and enrolled as a predental student at Indiana University, where coach James E. "Doc" Counsilman helped Mark to mature. At last, Mark became respected, as well as liked, by his fellow collegiate teammates.

Mark did not give up after Mexico City. Instead, he poured extra energy into preparation for the next Olympics, to be held in Munich, Ger-

STATISTICS				
Year	Competition	Event	Place	Time
1967	Pan-American Games	100-meter butterfly	1st	56.20
		200-meter butterfly	1st	2:06.42
		4×100-meter freestyle relay	1st	3:34.08
		4×200-meter freestyle relay	1st	8:00.46
		4×100-meter medley relay	1st	3:59.31
1968	Olympic Games	100-meter freestyle	Bronze	53.0
		100-meter butterfly	Silver	56.4
		4×100-meter freestyle relay	Gold	3:31.7
		4×200-meter freestyle relay	Gold	7:52.33
1969	NCAA Championships	200-yard freestyle	1st	1:39.53
		500-yard freestyle	1st	4:33.48
		100-yard butterfly	1st	49.69
1970	NCAA Championships	100-yard butterfly	1st	49.82
1971	NCAA Championships	100-yard butterfly	1st	49.42
		200-yard butterfly	1st	1:50.10
1972	Olympic Games	100-meter freestyle	Gold	51.22 WR, OR
		200-meter freestyle	Gold	1:52.78 WR, OR
		100-meter butterfly	Gold	54.27 WR, OR
		200-meter butterfly	Gold	2:00.70 WR, OR
		4×100-meter freestyle relay	Gold	3:26.42 WR, OR
		4×200-meter freestyle relay	Gold	7:35.78 WR, OR
		4×100-meter medley relay	Gold	3:48.16 WR, OR
	NCAA Championships	500-yard freestyle	3d	—
		100-yard butterfly	1st	
		200-yard butterfly	1st	1:46.898

Notes: WR = World Record; OR = Olympic Record

many. In 1972, Mark was fiercely competitive and more confident than ever. He arrived announcing that he would win a gold medal in each event in which he competed, for a total of seven. This time, Mark swam as he never had before. He set world records in each event, making modern Olympic history as he won a perfect seven out of seven competitions, bringing home more gold medals than any Olympian in history.

Continuing the Story

As Mark slept in the Olympic Village the night after receiving his history-making seventh gold medal, Palestinian terrorists invaded the Olympic Village, where they killed two Israeli athletes and took nine more hostage. Mark, being Jewish, was feared to be another possible target and was rushed home.

After twelve years of strenuous, continuous training, Mark retired, truly at the top of his sport. The Olympic hero possessed the handsome looks necessary to capitalize on his success. He entered the businesses of commercial endorsements and sportscasting. Close to breaking another record, Mark, wearing only his famous mustache, Olympic swim trunks, and seven gold medals, became the second best-selling pinup ever, outsold only by actress Betty Grable. Dental school became a distant memory as Mark acquired wealth, fame, and a $65,000 racing yacht. Mark married Susan Weiner; their son's name is Matthew.

Almost twenty years later, in early 1990, the forty-year-old Mark set out to make a comeback in the sport of competitive swimming, in hopes of eventually competing for the U.S. swimming team at the 1992 Summer Olympics in Barcelona, Spain. Back-to-back losses against superstar swimmers Tom Jager and Matt Biondi did not exactly jump-start Mark's comeback bid, although to his credit he did not give up right away. Through the first half of 1991, he remained determined to complete his full schedule of races, with a view toward the summer of 1992. His comeback was short-lived. He was unable to qualify in the Olympic trials, finishing more than two seconds over the required time limit.

Summary

A graceful athlete who has always held himself up to the highest criteria for success, Mark Spitz achieved greatness in the 1972 Olympics. His notorious temperament and often indelicate comments did not keep him from being a public hero. Mark earned millions as a poster boy and

RECORDS
Set 26 world records and 25 national records
Won 24 National AAU Championships
Held 8 NCAA titles and was a 4-time NCAA champion in the 100-yard butterfly
First man to win 7 gold medals in one Olympic Games—all in world record time

HONORS AND AWARDS	
1967, 1971-72	World Swimmer of the Year
1968, 1971	Robert J. H. Kiphuth Award, Long Course
1971	Sullivan Award
1972	Robert J. H. Kiphuth Award, Short Course
	AAU Swimming Award
	Associated Press Male Athlete of the Year
	World Athlete of the Year
1977	Inducted into International Swimming Hall of Fame
1983	Inducted into U.S. Olympic Hall of Fame

product endorser as the image of the mustached young man with his seven gold medals pervaded the American media.

Leslie A. Pearl

Additional Sources:

Besford, Pat. *Encyclopedia of Swimming.* New York: St. Martin's Press, 1976.

Edelson, Paula. *Superstars of Men's Swimming and Diving.* Philadelphia: Chelsea House, 1999.

Hickok, Ralph. *A Who's Who of Sports Champions.* Boston: Houghton Mifflin, 1995.

Schapp, Dick. *An Illustrated History of the Olympics.* New York: Alfred A. Knopf, 1975.

Whitten, Phillip. "Mark Spitz Back in the Swim." *Swim Magazine* 11, no. 5 (1995).

KEN STABLER

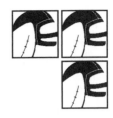

Sport: Football

Born: December 25, 1945
Foley, Alabama

Early Life

Kenneth Michael Stabler was born on December 25, 1945, in Foley, Alabama, to Leroy and Sally Stabler. Leroy, nicknamed "Slim," was a crackerjack auto mechanic from whom Ken inherited a love of sports, fast cars, and music. Young Stabler was very close to his father, and from an early age was his constant companion on hunting and fishing trips.

At Foley High School, Ken became an avid baseball and basketball player, but Slim urged him to concentrate on football. He started out as a defensive back and kick returner, earning the nickname "Snake" because he made serpentine cuts across the field. He also found ways to get into trouble with both his coach, Ivan Jones, and the law, but his renegade high jinks did not stop him from earning the quarterback spot in his junior year. As a senior in 1963, he gained berths on two All-American teams. Although Ken was heavily recruited as a baseball player, he opted to go to the University of Alabama to play football under the school's legendary coach, Bear Bryant.

The Road to Excellence

At Alabama, Ken had to follow in the footsteps of Joe Namath, one of the game's great quarterbacks. In 1964, Ken's freshman

year, Namath was in his last year at the school, and his slot in 1965 was filled by his backup, Steve Sloan, who led Alabama to a national championship in an Orange Bowl victory over Nebraska. Stabler earned the starting quarterback slot the next year, and although Alabama compiled an 11-0 record, the Crimson Tide finished third in the postseason voting for the national championship. Ken was chosen as most valuable player in

Oakland Raiders

the Sugar Bowl, but he always regretted that his team was not given top collegiate honors. He was a tough, die-hard competitor who did not like to come in second best.

The next year, Ken had to start all over again as the last quarterback on Alabama's depth chart. He had torn a knee ligament in spring practice and began missing both his classes and practice. Familial problems with Slim's excessive drinking also took their toll, and Bryant finally had to suspend Ken when he lost his academic eligibility. He made up course work in summer school and fought his way back to reclaim the starting assignment. The knee injury continued to plague him and deprived him of some mobility; however, it did not stop him from winning that year's game against arch-rival Auburn with a 47-yard run and leading Alabama to an 8-1-1 record and a Cotton Bowl bid.

The Emerging Champion

Ken signed a professional contract with the Oakland Raiders of the American Football League (AFL) in March of 1968. In his first training camp with Oakland, he found that he could not throw the ball with the power the Raider style of play required, so he returned to Alabama and began working with weights to strengthen his throwing arm. After Ken underwent a knee operation, Oakland sent him to the Spokane Shock-ers of the Continental League to see how well his knee would hold up. It did not fare well, and Ken, relegated to the Raider injured-reserved list, began to lose his confidence. He walked out of camp, and eventually he had to talk the new Raider coach, John Madden, into giving him another career chance.

Snake quickly showed Madden that although his troublesome knee limited his movement, he could read defenses like few other quarterbacks. Moreover, he had a great "touch"—a quick release and an ability to lay the ball into a barely open receiver's arms even while being hit. His was not a pretty style, but in combination with such great receivers as the Raiders' Fred Biletnikoff and Dave Casper, it would prove a deadly accurate one.

Ken was with the Raiders for nearly five years before becoming the starting quarterback. By then he was twenty-seven, and the AFL had merged with the National Football League (NFL). For the next six years with Oakland, he played like a man bent on making up for lost time. The Raiders, noted for taking on misfits from other teams, were dreaded for their tough, aggressive, wide-open play, and Snake loved both the style and its chief genius, Coach Madden. It was a team that played mean right up to the last tick of the game clock, and Ken soon earned a reputation for bringing the team from be-

STATISTICS

Season	GP	PA	PC	Pct.	Yds.	Avg.	TD	Int.
1970	3	7	2	28.6	52	7.43	0	1
1971	14	48	24	50.0	268	5.58	1	4
1972	14	74	44	59.5	524	7.08	4	3
1973	14	260	163	**62.7**	1,997	7.68	14	10
1974	14	310	178	57.4	2,469	7.96	**26**	12
1975	14	293	171	58.4	2,296	7.84	16	24
1976	12	291	194	**66.7**	2,737	**9.41**	27	17
1977	13	294	169	57.5	2,176	7.40	20	20
1978	16	406	237	58.4	2,944	7.25	16	30
1979	16	498	304	61.0	3,615	7.26	26	22
1980	16	457	293	64.1	3,202	7.01	13	28
1981	13	285	165	57.9	1,988	6.98	14	18
1982	8	189	117	61.9	1,343	7.11	6	10
1983	14	311	176	56.6	1,988	6.39	9	18
1984	3	70	33	47.1	339	4.84	2	5
Totals	184	3,793	2,270	59.8	27,938	7.37	194	222

Notes: Boldface indicates statistical leader. GP = games played; PA = passes attempted; PC = passes completed; Pct. = percent completed; Yds. = yards; Avg. = average yards per attempt; TD = touchdowns; Int. = interceptions

hind and winning games with seconds to spare.

Between 1973 and 1980, when he was traded to Houston, many considered him the most dangerous quarterback in the NFL. He directed Oakland's dynamic offense in each American Football Conference (AFC) championship game from 1973 to 1977 and led the Raiders to a 32-14 rout of the Minnesota Vikings in Super Bowl XI in 1977. In the 1976 season, he led the league with a 66.7 percent pass completion record and averaged almost 10 yards per completion. He also threw for 27 touchdowns and only 17 interceptions in 291 attempts, a fine performance for a man noted for throwing the ball to receivers in a crowd.

Continuing the Story

At Houston, Ken encountered a more conservative style of play under the team's defense-minded coach, Bum Phillips. Ken complained that his chief role was to hand the ball to the Oilers' great running back, Earl Campbell, and that the game philosophy of Phillips, whom he personally liked, was to play so as not to lose rather than to go all out for a win. He faced the same problem after he moved to the New Orleans Saints, a team that featured another great running back, George Rogers. Although he had some brilliant moments reminiscent of his great years with Oakland, Snake never fully adjusted to the ball-control style. The years, too, punished Ken, and he retired at the end of the 1984 season at the age of thirty-nine, regretting only that he had not been able to play his entire career with the freewheeling Raiders.

In the 1990's Ken became a corporate motivational speaker, talking to people about teamwork and leadership, especially from the viewpoint of

HONORS AND AWARDS	
1973-74, 1977	NFL Pro Bowl Team
1974	Associated Press NFL Player of the Year United Press International Player of the Year
1974-76	*Sporting News* AFC Player of the Year
1976	Bert Bell Trophy

sports. He has also had considerable involvement in the support of charities. He has lent his support and name to such events as the FloraBama Toyota Ken Stabler Celebrity Golf Classic. In 1996 and 1997 the Golf Classic directed its efforts toward the building of a Ronald McDonald House in the area of Point Clear, Alabama.

Summary

Ken Stabler's relatively late career start and impaired movement have always inspired moot speculation about what he might have accomplished under different circumstances. He was certainly one of the great drop-back quarterbacks in the NFL and an inspiring presence on the field. Few others have commanded the team loyalty that he earned from his fellow players at Oakland.

John W. Fiero

Additional Sources:

Aaseng, Nathan. *Football's Winning Quarterbacks.* Minneapolis, Minn.: Lerner Publishing, 1980.

Feinberg, William H. *Ken Stabler.* Mankato, Minn.: Creative Education, 1978.

Libby, Bill. *Ken Stabler: Southpaw Passer.* New York: Putnam, 1977.

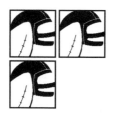

JOHN STALLWORTH

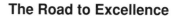

Sport: Football

Born: July 15, 1952
Tuscaloosa, Alabama

Early Life

Johnny Lee Stallworth was born on July 15, 1952, in Tuscaloosa, Alabama, not far from the University of Alabama. John's parents, David and Mary Stallworth, remember their son as being a bit clumsy and accident-prone as a youngster. He once lost a part of his tongue in a fall from a chair. On another occasion, John nearly hanged himself while playing in a tree. His most serious accident occurred, however, when his brother, David Jr., nearly severed John's thumb with an axe while splitting logs. Fortunately, doctors were able to repair the thumb, and John's hand healed completely.

As a youngster, John demonstrated a talent for catching the football. In neighborhood pickup games he always played end. The game's rules were such that three completed passes made a first down. John would often catch all three for his team.

The Road to Excellence

John did not attempt to play organized football until his junior year at the predominantly white Tuscaloosa High School. His first coach was not very encouraging. He told John that he was too skinny to play end and even suggested that he might never play college football because of his slight build. Though he never caught a pass that first season, John was determined to prove his coach wrong.

The following year, a new coach took over and immediately recognized John's potential. He also realized that the team lacked a quarterback capable of throwing the football, so he switched John to the running back position to take better advantage of John's speed. John earned All-State honors at this new position even though his team won only one game. As a result of the team's poor record, college recruiters did not spend much time looking at players from Tuscaloosa High School.

STATISTICS

Season	GP	Rec.	Yds.	Avg.	TD
1974	13	16	269	16.8	1
1975	11	20	423	21.2	4
1976	8	9	111	12.3	2
1977	14	44	784	17.8	7
1978	16	41	798	19.5	9
1979	16	**70**	1,183	16.9	8
1980	3	9	197	21.9	1
1981	16	63	1,098	17.4	5
1982	9	27	441	16.3	7
1983	4	8	100	12.5	0
1984	16	80	1,395	17.4	11
1985	16	75	937	12.5	5
1986	11	34	466	13.7	1
1987	12	41	521	12.7	2
Totals	165	537	8,723	16.2	63

Notes: Boldface indicates statistical leader. GP = games played; Rec. = receptions; Yds. = yards; Avg. = average yards per reception; TD = touchdowns

Fortunately, Alabama A&M, a small African American college in Normal, Alabama, offered John a scholarship. At A&M John finally got his chance to develop his pass-catching skills and by his sophomore year was the football team's starting wide receiver.

Even though Alabama A&M did not receive much national recognition, in John's senior year he was selected to play in the 1974 Senior Bowl. Although he played just half the game and caught only one pass, it was enough for the Pittsburgh Steelers. A few months later they selected him in the fourth round of the 1974 National Football League (NFL) draft and signed him to his first professional contract.

The Emerging Champion

Although he performed brilliantly at times, injuries kept John from being a full-time starter for the Steelers until his fourth season. After catching 16 passes for 269 yards as a rookie (1974), John started nine games in 1975. During that stretch, he tied for the league lead in average yards per catch with a 21.2-yard average.

Finally, in 1977, after an injury-free preseason, he assumed a permanent starter's role. From 1977 until 1979, John started every game for the Steelers and was thought by most to be one of the NFL's best wide receivers. In 1979, he led the league in receptions and won numerous post-

season awards, including being voted the team's most valuable player by his teammates.

Many observers felt that John played his best in the really important games. For instance, in Super Bowl XIII against the Dallas Cowboys, John caught 3 passes for 115 yards and 2 touchdowns in just the first half. Unfortunately, an injury sidelined him the rest of the game. The following year, in Super Bowl XIV against the Los Angeles Rams, John proved to be the difference in the game. Trailing the Rams 19-17 in the final quarter, Steelers quarterback Terry Bradshaw connected with John on a 73-yard touchdown pass to take the lead. Later in the game, his remarkable 45-yard over-the-shoulder catch between a crowd of defenders set up a touchdown run by teammate Franco Harris to seal the victory.

Seemingly cursed by an injury jinx, John spent much of the 1980 and 1983 seasons on the Steelers' injured reserve list. Steelers fans and the media began to question whether the aging wide receiver could again triumph over injury and return to top form for the 1984 season.

Continuing the Story

While others may have had their doubts, John was confident that he still had the ability to compete in the NFL. Even after a rigorous off-season rehabilitation program, John reported to the 1984 Steelers training camp as a question mark. He wasted little time, however, answering his doubters.

At the age of thirty-two, John not only returned to the starting lineup but had his finest season ever. His hard work and determination paid off, as he set single-season team records for catches (80) and yards (1,395), and career marks for catches (387), yards (6,799), touchdown receptions (55), most 1,000-yard seasons (3), and most 100-yard games (27). John's record-setting performance earned him his fourth selection to the NFL Pro Bowl. He was also named the Steelers' most valuable player for the second time and the NFL Comeback Player of the Year.

The following season proved John's amazing 1984 comeback season was no fluke. With 75 catches, he again led his team in receptions and added to his all-time team-leading numbers. After a promising 14-catch start in the first three

HONORS, AWARDS, AND RECORDS

1974	Senior Bowl All-Star Team
1979	Alabama Professional Athlete of the Year *Sporting News* AFC All-Star Team
1980, 1983-85	NFL Pro Bowl Team
1980	Set NFL record for the highest average yards per catch in a Super Bowl game (40.3)
1985	NFL Comeback Player of the Year
1989	Inducted into Alabama Sports Hall of Fame
2000	Inducted into Division II Football Hall of Fame

games of the 1986 season, however, John was sidelined with a serious knee injury.

Finally, following the 1987 season, though he once again led his team in receptions, John announced his retirement, leaving the game as the fifteenth-leading receiver in NFL history. He became the chief executive officer of an aerospace engineering company, Madison Research Corporation, in Huntsville, Alabama. He has been honored with a U.S. Postal Service commemorative postal cancellation on February 2, 2000, at the John Stallworth Postal Station in Normal, Alabama. He was inducted into the Division II Football Hall of Fame in 2000.

Summary

John Stallworth's fourteen seasons in the NFL were the fulfillment of boyhood dreams. His determination to overcome size limitations, playing on unrecognized high school and college teams, and injury are examples of his desire to be the best. While others may have quit, John's perseverance made him one of the game's greatest performers.

Joseph Horrigan

Additional Sources:

Aaseng, Nathan. *Football's Sure-Handed Receivers.* Minneapolis, Minn.: Lerner Publishing, 1980.
Wiley, Ralph. "You Have to Be a Fool at Times." *Sports Illustrated* 64, no. 11 (August 25, 1986): 36-40.

WILLIE STARGELL

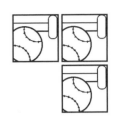

Sport: Baseball

Born: March 6, 1941
      Earlsboro, Oklahoma
Died: April 9, 2001
      Wilmington, North Carolina

Early Life

Wilver Dornell Stargell was born on March 6, 1941, in the small town of Earlsboro, Oklahoma. He was the son of William and Verlene Stargell. When Willie was quite young, his family moved to Oakland, California, where he spent his childhood and adolescence. Willie grew up in an eco-nomically depressed neighborhood in Oakland, but this difficult childhood instilled in him a so-cial conscience and a deep sense of personal re-sponsibility. He never forgot the poverty of his youth. He remained proud of his parents, who taught him to recognize the dignity of each per-son. He attended public schools in Oakland.

The Road to Excellence

As a teenager, Willie excelled in baseball, bas-ketball, and track at Oakland's Encinal High School. He then went to Santa Rosa Junior Col-lege in California, where he played on the baseball team until he signed with the Pittsburgh Pirates in 1958. He played for almost four full sea-sons on various minor league teams in the Pittsburgh Pirates' organiza-tion as he perfected his skills as an outfielder and as a power hitter. He began with the Roswell, New Mex-ico, team in 1959. He then played on minor league teams in North Da-kota, North Carolina, and Illinois. Late in the 1962 season, he was called up by the Pittsburgh Pirates at the relatively young age of twenty-one. Although he was originally signed as an outfielder, he was very flexible. Beginning with his rookie season of 1963, Willie often played first base as well. He was definitely a team player.

The Emerging Champion

Willie spent his entire twenty-one-year career in the major leagues with the Pittsburgh Pirates. He and his wife, Dolores, reared their three children in Pittsburgh. Throughout the 1960's and the 1970's, Willie was

National Baseball Library, Cooperstown, New York

2619

a very productive home-run hitter. He hit 475 homers and twice led the National League in homers: first in 1971, with 48 homers, and then in 1973, with 44 homers. Some of his homers were extremely long. For thirty years, Willie was the only batter to have hit a home run out of Dodger Stadium, and he did this twice. He is generally considered to be the leading left-handed slugger of his generation. Despite his very real accomplishments as a power hitter, Willie Stargell is remembered above all for his performance in 1979 during the National League Championship Series and in the World Series and for his service to the community.

Continuing the Story

In 1971, the legendary Roberto Clemente was the acknowledged leader of the Pirates. Sparkling fielding and hitting by Clemente helped the Pirates to defeat the Baltimore Orioles in a seven-game series. Clemente's death in December, 1972, in an airplane crash left a void in the Pittsburgh team that Willie filled. Willie was not a leader for the Pirates only. He also became involved in social causes. He helped to raise money

for research on sickle-cell anemia (a serious illness that often strikes African Americans), and he also assisted with Pittsburgh's Job Corps and Neighborhood Youth Corps. He became an admired member of the Pittsburgh community.

By 1979, however, Willie's career seemed to be coming to an end. In 1979, "Pops," as the younger Pittsburgh players called him, had an extraordinary year. He helped the Pirates to win their first Eastern Division Championship in the National League since 1975. He and Keith Hernandez tied in the voting for the most valuable player award in the National League. Willie was then thirty-eight years old, making him the oldest player ever selected as a most valuable player.

His performances in the 1979 National League Championship Series and in the 1979 World Series were even more impressive. In the Championship Series, his batting average was .455, and he won the first game with a 3-run homer in the eleventh inning. In the World Series against the Baltimore Orioles, Willie drove in 7 runs with 3 homers. His batting average was .400. In the seventh game, the Orioles were lead-

STATISTICS

Season	GP	AB	Hits	2B	3B	HR	Runs	RBI	BA	SA
1962	10	31	9	3	1	0	1	4	.290	.452
1963	108	304	74	11	6	11	34	47	.243	.428
1964	117	421	115	19	7	21	53	78	.273	.501
1965	144	533	145	25	8	27	68	107	.272	.501
1966	140	485	153	30	0	33	84	102	.315	.581
1967	134	462	125	18	6	20	54	73	.271	.465
1968	128	435	103	15	1	24	57	67	.237	.441
1969	145	522	160	31	6	29	89	92	.307	.556
1970	136	474	125	18	3	31	70	85	.264	.511
1971	141	511	151	26	0	**48**	104	125	.295	.628
1972	138	495	145	28	2	33	75	112	.293	.558
1973	148	522	156	**43**	3	**44**	106	**119**	.299	**.646**
1974	140	508	153	37	4	25	90	96	.301	.537
1975	124	461	136	32	2	22	71	90	.295	.516
1976	117	428	110	20	3	20	54	65	.257	.458
1977	63	186	51	12	0	13	29	35	.274	.548
1978	122	390	115	18	2	28	60	97	.295	.567
1979	126	424	119	19	0	32	60	82	.281	.552
1980	67	202	53	10	1	11	28	38	.262	.485
1981	38	60	17	4	0	0	2	9	.283	.350
1982	74	73	17	4	0	3	6	17	.233	.411
Totals	2,360	7,927	2,232	423	55	475	1,195	1,540	.282	.529

Notes: Boldface indicates statistical leader. GP = games played; AB = at bats; 2B = doubles; 3B = triples; HR = home runs; RBI = runs batted in; BA = batting average; SA = slugging average

HONORS AND AWARDS

1964-66, 1971-72, 1978	National League All-Star Team
1979	National League most valuable player, co-recipient
	Sporting News Major League Player of the Year
	World Series most valuable player
	National League Championship Series most valuable player
	Associated Press Male Athlete of the Year
	Sports Illustrated Sportsman of the Year, co-recipient
	Sporting News Man of the Year
1988	Inducted into National Baseball Hall of Fame
	Uniform number 8 retired by Pittsburgh Pirates

ing 1-0 in the sixth inning when Willie hit a 2-run homer, giving Pittsburgh a lead that it never relinquished. Willie was named the most valuable player in the 1979 World Series. He played with the Pirates until 1982. In 1988 (his first year of eligibility), he was elected to the National Baseball Hall of Fame in Cooperstown, New York.

Willie joined the Pirates staff as first-base coach in 1985 but moved to the Atlanta Braves organization the following year. He returned to Pittsburgh in 1997 as a special assistant to general manager Cam Bonifay.

After his retirement, Willie struggled with a kidney disorder that required weekly dialysis. In the fall of 1999, he suffered a near-fatal infection that began from a small cut on his finger and spread throughout his body. After almost two months of hospitalization, he returned to his duties with the Pirates in early 2000, but ailing health resulting from his kidney disorder led to his death in April, 2001.

Summary

Willie Stargell has been called the "Pride of Pittsburgh" not only because of his impressive accomplishments as a power hitter but especially because of his service to the community. He strove to improve the quality of life for the under-privileged members of the Pittsburgh community.

Edmund J. Campion

Additional Sources:

Shannon, Mike. *Willie Stargell.* New York: Chelsea House, 1992.

Stargell, Willie. *Out of Left Field: Willie Stargell and the Pittsburgh Pirates.* New York: Two Continents, 1976.

Stargell, Willie, and Tom Bird. *Willie Stargell: An Autobiography.* New York: Harper & Row, 1984.

BART STARR

Sport: Football

Born: January 9, 1934
Montgomery, Alabama

Early Life

Bryan Bartlett Starr was born on January 9, 1934, in Montgomery, Alabama, the elder of two boys of a military family. Bart's father, Ben Starr, a master sergeant in the U.S. Army Air Corps, was an athlete himself and often took to the field with his boys and other children for pickup football games.

Ben Starr was a good coach, and both sons caught on quickly to the basics of passing and tackling. When Bart's younger brother Hilton died from an infected cut, twelve-year-old Bart and his father tried to fill the painful gap with sports.

Bart was a quiet boy and was so small that his junior high school football uniform drooped all over. His father told him not to worry; he would grow.

The Road to Excellence

Bart made the Lanier High School football team but seemed to lack the size to play much. He decided to quit but changed his mind—a lucky decision, as it turned out.

Bart became starting quarterback in his junior year when the first-string quarterback broke his leg, and by the end of the next season his clutch play and cool head attracted big-time college scouts. He chose the University of Alabama to stay near his sweetheart, the future Cherry Starr.

A star quarterback and punter in his first two seasons for the Crimson Tide, Bart suffered a back injury that took him out of action late in his junior season. Then, in Bart's senior year, a new head coach decided to field a team of younger players. After being compared with the best passers in the school's history, Bart spent most of his last college season on the bench. Meanwhile, he

Bart Starr of the Green Bay Packers in 1966.

continued to get top grades in the classroom.

The Green Bay Packers, suffering a string of bad seasons, picked Bart in the seventeenth round of the National Football League (NFL) draft in 1956. His confidence shaky, Bart felt that he had only a remote chance of making the team, but he turned down an offer to play professional football in Canada.

All summer he practiced throwing a football through a suspended tire; his wife Cherry retrieved the ball. He narrowly made the Packers' roster as a backup.

The Emerging Champion

Bart spent most of his first three seasons as a backup quarterback, playing well at times for a losing team. In those early years, Bart's leading competitors for the starting job helped him the most in sharpening his quarterbacking skills.

The big college setback still haunted Bart. Though he played brilliantly at times, he lacked confidence, brooding over every bad throw or interception. His big chance to gain it back came when the hard-nosed Vince Lombardi took over as the coach of the struggling but talented team in 1959.

Bart finally won the starting job by impressing Lombardi with a combination of accurate passing and shrewd play-calling. The Packers started winning.

In 1960, Bart piloted the team to its first divisional title in sixteen seasons, completing 57 percent of his 172 passes. He convinced a lot of people that being soft-spoken did not mean he lacked toughness. The team again captured the title, and the National Football League Championship, in 1961.

Not everyone was a believer, though. Over the next few years, his more illustrious teammates, Jim Taylor and Paul Hornung, stole the media spotlight. Some said Bart's talent lay simply in the machine-like way he carried out Lombardi's cautious strategy.

Bart was not bothered by such talk, especially after winning the NFL crown again in 1962 as the

league's best passer, an honor he regained in 1964, with a 60 percent completion rate and 15 touchdown passes. In 1965, Bart took the Packers to yet another NFL Championship with an offense that depended almost completely on his 56 percent completion rate and 16 touchdown passes.

Continuing the Story

Bart had to wait until late in his career to get full credit. Rather than demand praise off the field, however, he convinced people with his consistent, winning ways.

The polite country boy had the football world cheering in 1966 and 1967 with his cool, heroic performances in some of the most exciting games ever played.

His off-the-field involvement in a host of community groups won him still more respect. After his playing days, he would be asked to run for the U.S. Senate.

When the Packers faced injuries, advancing age, and a divisional race with the Baltimore Colts in 1966, Bart answered with pinpoint passing (he led the league again) and a record low interception rate.

In the thrilling championship game against the Dallas Cowboys he slipped tackles to pass for 4 touchdowns and 304 yards. The Packers then

				STATISTICS				
Season	GP	PA	PC	Pct.	Yds.	Avg.	TD	Int.
1956	9	44	24	.545	325	7.4	2	3
1957	12	215	117	.544	1,489	6.9	8	10
1958	12	157	78	.497	875	5.6	3	12
1959	12	134	70	.522	972	7.3	6	7
1960	12	172	98	.569	1,358	7.9	4	8
1961	14	295	172	.583	2,418	8.2	16	16
1962	14	285	178	.624	2,438	8.6	12	9
1963	13	244	132	.540	1,855	7.6	15	10
1964	14	272	163	.599	2,144	7.9	15	4
1965	14	251	140	.557	2,055	8.2	16	9
1966	14	251	156	.621	2,257	**9.0**	14	3
1967	14	210	115	.547	1,823	**8.7**	9	17
1968	12	171	109	.637	1,617	**9.5**	15	8
1969	12	148	92	.621	1,161	7.8	9	6
1970	14	255	140	.549	1,645	6.5	8	13
1971	4	45	24	.533	286	6.4	0	3
Totals	196	3,149	1,808	.574	24,718	7.8	152	138

Notes: Boldface indicates statistical leader. GP = games played; PA = passes attempted; PC = passes completed; Pct. = percent completed; Yds. = yards; Avg. = average yards per attempt; TD = touchdowns; Int. = interceptions

won the first Super Bowl against the American Football League's Kansas City Chiefs on January 15, 1967. Bart was named the Super Bowl most valuable player and the NFL Player of the Year.

The next year, in the now-famous NFL championship "Ice Bowl" game against the Dallas Cowboys, with below-zero weather and a whipping wind, Bart took the ball over the frozen goal line for the winning score with just seconds left on the clock. The Packers then beat the Oakland Raiders in Super Bowl II.

Bart's place in history as the leader of one of football's greatest dynasties was secure.

He led the league in passing two more seasons before retiring in 1972. Bart spent ten years as a coach and an executive for the Packers, and then entered business. He was elected to the Pro Football Hall of Fame in 1977.

Bart became president of his own firm, has been a member of the President's Commission on Physical Fitness, and has been a member of the boards of directors of major public companies. Bart is also a dynamic speaker who inspires and motivates audiences with his stories and lessons from the world of sports.

Summary

The name Bart Starr is identified with one of the greatest football teams ever. On a squad of stars, Bart was a calm and careful leader who relied on consistency and pluck rather than flash.

NFL RECORDS
Highest passing efficiency rating in postseason games, 104.8

HONORS AND AWARDS	
1961-63, 1967	NFL Pro Bowl Team
1966	Associated Press NFL Player of the Year
	United Press International NFL Player of the Year
	Thorpe Trophy
	Newspaper Enterprise Association NFL Player of the Year
1967-68	NFL Super Bowl most valuable player
1970	NFL All-Pro Team of the 1960's
1977	Inducted into Pro Football Hall of Fame
	Uniform number 15 retired by Green Bay Packers

In his playing days he was often compared with Johnny Unitas, one of the greatest quarterbacks of the same era. As a Hall of Fame member, Bart is recognized as one of the best in any era, especially under pressure. Though not gifted with dazzling talent, Bart found a way to win the big game.

Kenneth Ellingwood

Additional Sources:

Maule, Tex. *Bart Starr, Professional Quarterback.* New York: F. Watts, 1973.

Schorr, Gene. *Bart Starr: A Biography.* Garden City, N.Y.: Doubleday, 1977.

Starr, Bart. *Starr: My Life in Football.* New York: Morrow, 1987.

ROGER STAUBACH

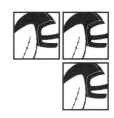

Sport: Football

Born: February 5, 1942
Silverton, Ohio

Early Life

The only child of hardworking and devout Roman Catholic parents, Roger Thomas Staubach was born on February 5, 1942, in Silverton, a small Ohio town outside Cincinnati. His father, a salesman in the shoe and leather business, was a large man of German ancestry. His mother was a tall, stately Irish woman. Roger acquired from his parents a strong physical build, a vibrant Christian faith, and a fiercely competitive spirit.

Young Roger began playing organized sports at age six. A gifted athlete, he excelled in all sports. As a preteen, he starred as a catcher in baseball, a guard in basketball, and a halfback and an end in football. It was during his sophomore year at Purcell High School that his coach told him to switch to quarterback. Roger protested this change, but his coach's order prevailed. When Roger graduated in 1960, he was considered one of the best high school quarterbacks in the country.

The Road to Excellence

Deciding what college to attend troubled Staubach. Although he was recruited by some forty schools, the college he liked most, the University of Notre Dame, expressed little interest in

Quarterback for the Dallas Cowboys Roger Staubach in the 1978 Super Bowl against the Broncos.

him. He seriously considered Purdue University, but then finally decided on the U.S. Naval Academy. His verbal Scholastic Aptitude Test scores were below Annapolis standards, and so before he could attend the Naval Academy he would first have to complete a year at a college prep school. During the summer following his graduation, Roger played in a final high school football game, the Ohio All-Star game. After the game, Notre Dame offered him a full scholarship. Having already given his word to the Navy coaches, Staubach rejected the belated offer. The ensuing fall he attended the New Mexico Military Institute, his way station to a fabulous collegiate career at the Naval Academy.

At Navy, Roger distinguished himself as a center fielder in baseball and as a quarterback in football. An excellent runner with a strong, precise arm, Staubach was a lethal threat whenever he touched the ball. As a junior, he led the 1963 Midshipmen to nine victories (including wins over the Universities of Michigan, Pittsburgh, and Notre Dame, as well as arch-rival Army) and a second-place national ranking. His spectacular season earned him the Heisman Trophy, an honor rarely bestowed upon a junior athlete.

The Emerging Champion

In the spring of 1964, Roger was drafted in the tenth round by the Dallas Cowboys of the National Football League (NFL). Though he had won the Heisman, his selection was somewhat of

a surprise. After all, he still had one year remaining in college, and then a four-year commitment to the Navy to fulfill. No matter how talented, few athletes are able to compete in the NFL after such a prolonged layoff.

Staubach was no ordinary athlete. After fulfilling his commitment in the Navy (which included a tour of duty in Vietnam), in 1969 he reported to training camp as a twenty-seven-year-old rookie. A determined competitor, Roger worked extra hard to regain his playing form and to learn the complex Cowboy offensive system. Success did not come quickly. Roger played backup to Craig Morton for two and a half years before Coach Tom Landry named him the Cowboys' number-one quarterback. He responded to the opportunity by leading the Cowboys to ten straight wins and their first Super Bowl victory in 1972. At the end of his first year as a starter, Roger was the NFL's leading passer, a dangerous opportunity runner who averaged 8.4 yards per carry, and an inspirational leader of a team that was destined for greatness.

Continuing the Story

Throughout the 1970's, "Roger the Dodger" personified the Dallas Cowboys, "America's Team." A master of the two-minute offense operating out of the shotgun formation, Staubach performed best in pressure situations. Twenty-four times he guided the Cowboys to come-from-behind fourth-quarter victories. On fourteen of

STATISTICS

Season	GP	PA	PC	Pct.	Yds.	Avg.	TD	Int.
1969	6	47	23	.489	421	9.0	1	2
1970	8	82	44	.537	542	6.6	2	8
1971	13	211	126	.597	1,882	8.9	15	4
1972	4	20	9	.450	98	4.9	0	2
1973	14	286	179	.626	2,428	8.5	**23**	15
1974	14	360	190	.528	2,552	7.1	11	15
1975	13	348	198	.569	2,666	7.7	17	16
1976	14	369	208	.564	2,715	7.4	14	11
1977	14	361	**210**	.582	**2,620**	7.3	**18**	9
1978	15	413	231	.559	3,190	7.7	25	16
1979	16	461	267	.579	3,586	7.8	27	11
Totals	131	2,958	1,685	.570	22,700	7.7	153	109

Notes: Boldface indicates statistical leader. GP = games played; PA = passes attempted; PC = passes completed; Pct. = percent completed; Yds. = yards; Avg. = average yards per attempt; TD = touchdowns; Int. = interceptions

these occasions, the go-ahead scores took place inside the final two minutes of regulation or in overtime. Five times Roger was rated the NFL's top passer. His greatness, however, is best measured in team success rather than in individual statistics. During his extraordinary career, the Cowboys made eleven consecutive playoff appearances, won eight division titles, and brought home two Super Bowl championships.

After twenty concussions and seventeen shoulder separations, Roger announced his retirement after the 1979 season. Leaving the playing field for the business world, he founded a firm to buy and sell land and to represent clients in the market for office space. By 1990, the Staubach Company, with offices in six cities across the country, was generating revenues estimated at $19 million a year. Roger has also worked a great deal as a corporate representative.

In 1985, the first year of his eligibility, Roger was inducted into the Pro Football Hall of Fame. At this time, he invited his former coach, Tom Landry, to introduce him during the induction ceremonies. Five years later, Roger returned to Canton, Ohio, this time at Landry's request, to help induct his former coach into that distinguished hall of honor.

Summary

At the time of his retirement, Roger Staubach ranked as the leading passer in NFL history. His

HONORS AND AWARDS	
1963	Heisman Trophy
	Maxwell Award
	Camp Award
	Sporting News College Football Player of the Year
	Citizens Savings College Football Player of the Year
	Sporting News College All-American
1971	*Sporting News* NFC Player of the Year
	Bell Trophy
1971, 1976-79	*Sporting News* NFC All-Star Team
1972	NFL Super Bowl most valuable player
1972, 1976-80	NFL Pro Bowl Team
1980	NFL All-Pro Team of the 1970's
1981	College Football Hall of Fame
1985	Inducted into Pro Football Hall of Fame
1990	NCAA Silver Anniversary Award

storybook career affirms that perseverance pays, even as it rebuts the often-stated assumption that good guys always finish last.

Terry D. Bilhartz

Additional Sources:

Aaseng, Nathan. *Football's Winning Quarterbacks.* Minneapolis, Minn.: Lerner Publishing, 1980.

Burchard, Marshall, and Sue Burchard. *Sports Hero Roger Staubach.* New York: Putnam, 1973.

Staubach, Roger. *Time Enough to Win.* Waco, Tex.: Word Books, 1980.

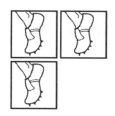

RENATE STECHER

Sport: Track and field (sprints)

Born: May 12, 1950
Suptitz, East Germany

Early Life

Renate Meisner was born on May 12, 1950, in Suptitz, East Germany, a small town in southeast Germany, in what was East Germany until 1990.

She was an athletic girl who participated in many different sports while growing up. At thir-

teen, she started to run in cross-country races, but soon discovered that she liked the sprint events better. Although she had a better build for the sprints, they did not come easily for her. She had to work extremely hard to learn the finer points of the events.

The Road to Excellence

Renate became good enough at the sprints to join the Chemie Sports Club in Torgau, an industrial town of approximately 18,500 citizens, on the Elbe River. After a short time, she moved on to the larger Sports Club Motor in Jena. It was here that she would settle and start to bloom as an athlete.

Her first successes came at the age of sixteen, when she took first place in the 100 meters at the 1966 Spartakiad of Children and Young People, a national sports festival conducted in East Germany. Later, during the 1966 European Junior Games, she was a member of the winning East German 4×100-meter relay team. Noted for her extremely strong build (she was 5 feet 6 inches tall and weighed 152 pounds), she started to draw the attention of the national sports administrators and some international track officials.

During the 1968 European Junior Games, Renate showed her growing durability by taking silver medals in the 100 meters, the 200 meters, and the 4×100-meter relay. She also began to explore other events, such as the long jump, where she has recorded a jump of 18 feet 6 inches, and the five-event pentathlon, where she totaled 4,297 points.

In 1970, Renate exploded into the international track world when she set her first world record by running the 100 meters in 11.0 seconds. The next year she won both the 100 and 200 meters at the European Track and Field championships. She quickly became noted for her strength and consistency. At the same time,

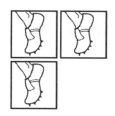
Renate Stecher of the German Democratic Republic leads the field in the 200-meter dash en route to a gold medal during the 1972 Olympic Games in Munich.

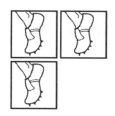Tony Duffy/Allsport

2628

STATISTICS

Year	Competition	Event	Place	Time
1969	European Outdoor Championships	4×100-meter relay	1st	43.6
1970	European Indoor Championships	60 meters	1st	7.4
1971	European Outdoor Championships	100 meters	1st	11.4
		200 meters	1st	22.7
	European Indoor Championships	60 meters	1st	7.3
1972	Olympic Games	100 meters	Gold	11.07
		200 meters	Gold	22.40 WR
		4×100-meter relay	Silver	42.95
	European Indoor Championships	50 meters	1st	6.25
1974	European Outdoor Championships	100 meters	2d	—
		200 meters	2d	—
		4×100-meter relay	1st	42.51
	European Indoor Championships	60 meters	1st	7.16
1976	Olympic Games	100 meters	Silver	11.13
		200 meters	Bronze	22.47
		4×100-meter relay	Gold	42.56 OR

Notes: WR = World Record; OR = Olympic Record

Renate began her studies in physical education in hopes of becoming a coach of young athletes.

The Emerging Champion

The year 1971 is also remarkable in Renate's life for a more personal reason. It was that year that she married her Sports Club Motor Jena teammate, Gert Stecher, a 400-meter hurdles champion. Before December, 1971, Renate competed under her maiden name of Meisner, but after that time the name Renate Stecher would grace the record books. Gert quickly joined Renate's long-time coach, Horst-Dieter Hille, in Renate's training. It was largely the trio's ability to work together that ensured Renate's continued presence on the top pedestal of the winner's podium.

In 1972, the German Democratic Republic (East Germany) competed in the Olympic Games for the first time as an independent team. Before, the East German athletes had competed as members of a united German team composed of athletes from both east and west. In the 1972 Games, Renate came to world prominence by taking the gold medal in the 100 meters and the 200 meters. She lost out on the gold in the 4×100-meter relay by .14 second.

Continuing the Story

In Ostrava, Czechoslovakia, on a rainy June 3, 1973, Renate became the first woman in history to break the 11-second barrier in the 100 meters with a time of 10.9 seconds. From August, 1970, to June, 1974, Renate won an unprecedented ninety straight individual outdoor races.

As the time approached for the 1976 Montreal Olympic Games, Renate's record-setting performances became fewer. Her last of fifteen personal records came on July 21, 1973. In the 1974 European Championships, she took second in both the 100 and the 200 to Irena Szewinska from Poland. It became apparent to her that she could not continue the strenuous regimen needed to continue as the world's fastest woman too much longer. Montreal would be her last Olympic Games.

Reflecting on her string of victories until 1974, Renate gave a clue about the philosophy that kept her on top. "Whoever believes himself unbeatable, has already half lost," she said.

In Montreal, Renate faced strong competition from younger sprinters. The finals of the 100 meters were on July 26, 1976. With less than three feet separating the first three finishers, Renate took the silver medal behind West Germany's Annegret Richter (11.08 seconds) and ahead of

RECORDS

Five world records at 100 meters: 1970, 1971, 1972 (11.0), 1973 (10.9), 1973 (10.8)
Two world records at 200 meters: 1972 (22.4), 1973 (22.1)
Four world records at 4×100-meter relay: 1972 (42.9), 1973 (42.6), 1974 (42.6), 1974 (42.5)
American indoor record at 50 meters in 1971 (6.0)
First woman to break the eleven seconds barrier in the 100 meters in 1973 (10.9)

HONORS AND AWARDS

1971, 1973	Athletics Weekly World Athlete of the Year
1973	Women's Track and Field World Athlete of the Year

West Germany's Inge Helten (11.17). Renate's time was 11.13 seconds. In the 200 meters, Renate finished third with a time of 22.47 seconds. On July 31, Renate won her final Olympic medal, a gold for the 4×100-meter relay. The race ended her Olympic career.

Less than a month later, on a rainy Saturday afternoon in Warsaw, Poland, Renate Stecher ran her last race. She won the 200 meters in 22.65 seconds, defeating her teammate, Barbel Eckert, who had won the event in Montreal. After the race, the thousands of spectators in the stadium gave her a standing ovation. Her long-time rival Irena Szewinska presented Renate with a red crystal cup in remembrance of their many confrontations.

Summary

Renate Stecher was a quiet champion who let her actions on the track speak for her. She became a living example to many of what can be done with dedication, a positive attitude, and hard work. As a physical education teacher and track coach, she is passing along those same lessons to German youngsters who wish to follow in her footsteps.

Rusty Wilson

Additional Sources:

Wallechinsky, David. *The Complete Book of the Olympics.* Boston: Little, Brown and Company, 1991.

Watman, Mel. *Encyclopedia of Track and Field Athletics.* New York: St. Martin's Press, 1981.

ALFREDO DI STEFANO

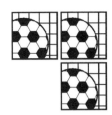

Sport: Soccer

Born: July 4, 1926
　　　　Buenos Aires, Argentina

Early Life

Alfredo di Stefano was born on July 4, 1926, in Buenos Aires, Argentina. His parents were both of Italian descent, and his father had played professional soccer.

Alfredo was born and raised in a working-class section of Buenos Aires. Like most Argentinean boys he loved playing soccer, and he spent hours with a ball at his feet, practicing and perfecting his skills.

In addition to soccer, Alfredo enjoyed running in cross-country races as a youngster. These

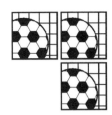

Alfredo Di Stefano in 1964.

trials of strength and endurance greatly enhanced Alfredo's stamina, which was always a trademark of his soccer game.

The Road to Excellence

As Alfredo entered his teens, it became increasingly obvious that he was going to be an outstanding soccer player. Not only did he possess the intricate skills necessary for good ball control and distribution, but also he had great strength, which meant he was able to use his talent even in the most physically demanding games.

Much to the delight of his family, in 1942 Alfredo was signed by River Plate, a famous club from Buenos Aires. After a two-year apprenticeship in which he further developed his all-around skills, Alfredo made his debut for the River Plate First Team in 1944.

At the time, Alfredo could not establish himself on the River Plate team, although he was recognized as a tremendous prospect. In order for Alfredo to gain regular first-team experience, he was loaned to the Huracan club for a year in 1945. With Huracan his career really took off. Alfredo scored 50 goals in sixty-six games and returned to River Plate with even greater feats expected of him.

Alfredo more than lived up to his billing. He displaced the legendary center-forward Adolfo Pedernera on the River Plate team and established himself as the most consistent goal-scorer in Argentinean soccer. Alfredo's performances were so outstanding that it was just a matter of time before he was selected for the Argentinean national team. Consequently, in 1947 he played the first of his seven games for the blue-and-white of Argentina.

The Emerging Champion

By his early twenties, Alfredo had established himself as one of the brightest young stars of

Hulton Getty/Archive Photos

HONORS AND AWARDS

1956-60	European Cup champion
1957, 1959	European Player of the Year
1960	Intercontinental Cup champion

MILESTONES

European Cup all-time leading scorer (49 goals)
42 international appearances for Argentina, Colombia, and Spain

South American soccer. However, he was soon tempted to leave his native country. The Colombian soccer league had broken away from the international governing body of soccer and was offering huge salaries. In 1949, Alfredo joined the mass exodus of Argentinean soccer stars when he joined the Colombian club Millonarios de Bogota.

With Millonarios Alfredo played on a team almost exclusively made up of fellow Argentineans. In Colombia he matured into a superlative player and dominated the league. In his four years at Millonarios he made 292 appearances and scored a staggering 259 goals. Alfredo led the team to two league titles and was even chosen on four occasions for the Colombian national team.

Alfredo was the most influential player in all of South America. His incredible exploits soon came to the envious attention of Santiago Bernabeu, the owner of the Spanish giants Real Madrid. When Alfredo eventually signed with Real in 1953, Bernabeu stated that the "White Arrow" had transformed the face of European soccer with one stroke of his pen.

As the Real Madrid captain, Alfredo helped the club achieve successes that even their most loyal supporter would have thought impossible. With Alfredo playing as a deep-lying center-forward, Real Madrid won the European Cup five consecutive times beginning in 1956. Alfredo was at the heart of these triumphs, which established Real Madrid as one of the greatest soccer teams of all time. He was a dominant captain who led by example; he could dribble, tackle, head, and pass the ball. His tactical awareness was superb, and he had a tenacious attitude on the field. All in all, Alfredo was a complete player.

Alfredo's greatest triumph came in the 1960 European Cup Final. Playing in Glasgow in front of 135,000 fans, Alfredo inspired Real to a 7-3 victory over the West German club Eintracht Frankfurt. In one of the most breathtaking displays ever, Alfredo scored a hat trick (three goals in one game) and mesmerized the crowd with his never-ending stamina and superb skills.

Continuing the Story

Between 1953 and 1964 Alfredo played 624 times for Real and scored 405 goals. He was even selected for the Spanish national team after he became a Spanish citizen. He went on to play thirty-one games for his adopted country and scored 23 goals.

Despite Alfredo's great ability, there was a price to pay for such single-minded commitment to winning. Alfredo was never hesitant about criticizing mistakes made by inferior teammates. On the soccer field Alfredo had to be the leader, and everyone else had to follow him. Inevitably, this caused conflict with some of the other great players on the Real team. Didí, the brilliant Brazilian, and Raymond Kopa, the French superstar, were even forced to leave Real in order to escape Alfredo's domineering personality.

Having led Real Madrid for over a decade, in 1964 Alfredo moved to Español, where he spent the last two seasons of his illustrious career. After scoring 19 goals in eighty-one games for Español, Alfredo, nearing forty, retired as a player in 1966.

Alfredo moved into soccer coaching and management. He enjoyed relatively successful spells in Argentina, Spain, and Portugal. At one time he was even in charge of his beloved Real Madrid. However, Alfredo's managerial career never approached the kind of success he had achieved as a player. His uncompromising attitude, as well as a tendency to expect too much from those less gifted than himself, often made Alfredo unpopular with his playing staff. It was frequently difficult for him to motivate players as a manager as he had done when he was orchestrating the team as a player.

Summary

Alfredo di Stefano was one of the greats of soccer. His technical brilliance and endless stamina distanced him from all but the very best. What made Alfredo different from many gifted players was his single-minded attitude toward winning. He was determined to succeed, and this total commitment was communicated to his teammates. Not only was Alfredo one of the best players ever to play the game, he also inspired his Real Madrid players to become one of the best club teams of all time.

David L. Andrews

Additional Sources:

Cantor, Andrés, and Daniel Arcucci. *Goooal!: A Celebration of Soccer.* New York: Simon & Schuster, 1996.

Galeano, Eduardo. *Soccer in Sun and Shadow.* New York: Verso, 1998.

Gardner, Paul. *The Simplest Game: The Intelligent Fan's Guide to the World of Soccer.* 3d ed. New York: Macmillan, 1996.

_____. *Soccer Talk: Life Under the Spell of the Roundball.* Chicago: Masters Press, 1996.

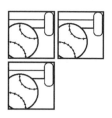

CASEY STENGEL

Sport: Baseball

Born: July 30, 1890
      Kansas City, Missouri
Died: September 29, 1975
      Glendale, California

Early Life

Charles Dillon Stengel was born on July 30, 1890, in Kansas City, Missouri. His nickname "Casey" came from the city of his birth, which is often referred to as "K.C." He was the third and last child of Jennie and Louis Stengel. His mother was of Irish descent and his father was of German ancestry. Louis Stengel was an insurance agent, and his family enjoyed a reasonably comfortable lifestyle. Casey spent his childhood and adolescence in Kansas City. At Central High School, he played on the basketball, football, and baseball teams, but baseball was always his preferred sport.

The Road to Excellence

In 1909, Central High in Kansas City won the Missouri baseball tournament, and Casey was the winning pitcher in the championship game. The following year, he began his minor league career in Kankakee, Illinois. After the 1910 season, he began attending Western Dental School in Kansas City, but he withdrew from dental school in order to resume his baseball career. Although he would later become famous for his many practical jokes and for his convoluted but witty manner of speaking, called "Stengelese," Casey Stengel was a very intelligent person.

After only two years in the minors, he was called up by the Brooklyn Dodgers and batted four for four in his very first game in September, 1912. He played in the outfield, his major league career lasting fourteen seasons. He had a respectable career batting average of .284. His most successful seasons were 1922 and 1923, when he batted .368 and .339, respectively, for the New York Giants, who played in the World Series in both years.

Casey had moments of greatness as a player. The high point of his career as a player took place during the first game of the 1923 World Series. In the ninth inning of this game against the Yankees, Casey broke a tie with a dramatic inside-the-park homer. In 1923, Casey met Edna Lawson, whom he married the following year. Casey and Edna had no children. Edna died in 1978, three years after Casey's death.

The Emerging Champion

Although Casey Stengel played in the major leagues for fourteen seasons, his forty years as a manager constituted a much more significant contribution to the history of baseball. In 1925,

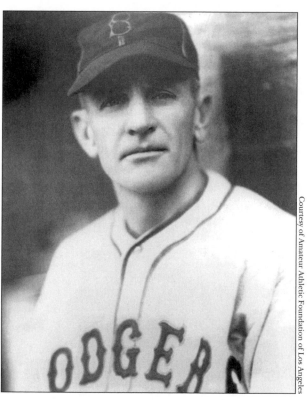

Courtesy of Amateur Athletic Foundation of Los Angeles

2634

STATISTICS

Season	GP	AB	Hits	2B	3B	HR	Runs	RBI	BA	SA
1912	17	57	18	1	0	1	9	13	.316	.386
1913	124	438	119	16	8	7	60	43	.272	.393
1914	126	412	130	13	10	4	55	60	.316	.425
1915	132	459	109	20	12	3	52	50	.237	.353
1916	127	462	129	27	8	8	66	53	.279	.424
1917	150	549	141	23	12	6	69	73	.257	.375
1918	39	122	30	4	1	1	18	12	.246	.320
1919	89	321	94	10	10	4	38	43	.293	.424
1920	129	445	130	25	6	9	53	50	.292	.436
1921	42	81	23	4	1	0	11	6	.284	.358
1922	84	250	92	8	10	7	48	48	.368	.564
1923	75	218	74	11	5	5	39	43	.339	.505
1924	131	461	129	20	6	5	57	39	.280	.382
1925	12	13	1	0	0	0	0	2	.077	.077
Totals	1,277	4,288	1,219	182	89	60	575	535	.284	.410

Notes: GP = games played; AB = at bats; 2B = doubles; 3B = triples; HR = home runs; RBI = runs batted in; BA = batting average; SA = slugging average

Casey was thirty-five years old; he realized that his career as a player would soon end, but he wanted to remain in baseball. In 1925, he became the player-manager for the Eastern League team in Worcester, Massachusetts. He earned his reputation as a skilled manager who knew how to develop the talents of young players. Between 1925 and 1948, Casey rarely had the opportunity to manage a truly competitive team in either the major or the minor leagues. From 1934 to 1936, he managed the lowly Brooklyn Dodgers, and then he managed the equally weak Boston Braves from 1938 until 1943. Despite his best efforts, his Brooklyn and Boston teams never finished above fifth place.

In 1948, however, George Weiss, the general manager of the New York Yankees, hired Casey to manage the Yankees, who had fallen to third place in 1948. Hiring Casey struck many baseball reporters as an odd decision because Casey was then fifty-eight years old and had never enjoyed great success as a manager. George Weiss's decision turned out to be brilliant. Casey managed the Yankees for twelve seasons, from 1949 until 1960. During these years with the Yankees, his team won ten American League pennants and seven World Series championships. The Yankees won the World Series five years in a row between 1949 and 1953, a record never matched before or since. In 1960, however, the Yankees lost the World Series to the Pittsburgh Pirates when Bill Mazeroski hit a ninth-inning homer in the seventh game to give Pittsburgh a dramatic victory. Just five days later, the owners of the Yankees fired Casey Stengel. His baseball career appeared to be finished.

Continuing the Story

Casey was then seventy years old, and no one would have imagined that the best was still to come for him. Just one year later, George Weiss, the first general manager of the newly created New York Mets, persuaded the Mets' owner, Joan Payson, to hire Casey to manage her team. For three and a half seasons, Casey managed the Mets, who were clearly the worst baseball team then in the major leagues. Casey's fine sense of humor and his sincere enthusiasm for his "Amazing Mets" created an extraordinary amount of good will for this expansion team, which would win the World Series in 1969, four years after a broken hip forced Casey to retire permanently from baseball in the summer of 1965.

The next year, the baseball writers decided to waive the requirement that a player wait five years before becoming eligible for election to the National Baseball Hall of Fame so that Casey could be elected while he was still alive. A secret vote was taken, and he was inducted into the Hall of Fame in Cooperstown, New York, on July 25, 1966, with Ted Williams. Casey was justly proud of his election to the Hall of Fame. He even signed his letters "Casey Stengel, Hall of Famer." Casey Stengel died from cancer on September

29, 1975, at the age of eighty-five, in Glendale, California.

Summary

Even many years after his death, Casey Stengel is remembered fondly by baseball fans as a creative manager who combined a fiercely competitive spirit with a wonderful sense of humor. He was magnanimous both in his years of triumph with the Yankees and during his losing seasons with the Mets. At Casey's funeral, his former player Richie Ashburn said of Casey: "He was the happiest man I've ever seen." This is an accurate assessment of Casey's greatness.

Edmund J. Campion

Additional Sources:

Allen, Maury. *You Could Look It Up: The Life of Casey Stengel.* New York: Times Books, 1979.

Bak, Richard. *Casey Stengel: A Splendid Baseball Life.* Dallas: Taylor, 1997.

Creamer, Robert W. *Casey: The Life and Legend of Charles Dillon Stengel.* Englewood Cliffs, N.J.: Prentice-Hall, 1967.

_____. *Stengel: His Life and Times.* New York: Simon & Schuster, 1984.

Durso, Joseph. *Casey and Mr. McGraw.* St. Louis: The Sporting News, 1989.

Stengel, Casey, and Harry T. Paxton. *Casey at the Bat: The Story of My Life in Baseball.* New York: Random House, 1962.

MAJOR LEAGUE RECORDS
Most World Series championships as manager, 7 Most consecutive World Series championships as manager, 5 Most league championships as manager, 10

HONORS AND AWARDS	
1949, 1953, 1958	*Sporting News* Manager of the Year
1966	Inducted into National Baseball Hall of Fame Uniform number 37 retired by New York Yankees and the New York Mets

INGEMAR STENMARK

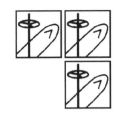

Sport: Skiing

Born: March 18, 1956
Josejoe, Lapland, Sweden

Early Life

Ingemar Stenmark was born on March 18, 1956, in Josejoe, Lapland, Sweden. He grew up in Tärnaby, Sweden, a village of about seven hundred people near the Norwegian border, only about fifty miles south of the Arctic Circle.

Ingemar began skiing at age five. His father, Erik, in addition to owning and operating a bulldozer, owned three ski lifts on a small ski mountain called Laxiallet, which means "Salmon Mountain." Ingemar used to ski to school sometimes.

His father was his first coach. The elder Stenmark had once skied competitively, and he once had placed fifth in the Swedish slalom championships. Ingemar won his first race at age seven, and his exceptional talent was obvious by the time he was thirteen. By that time, he had a new coach, who, after seeing Ingemar ski, predicted he would one day be a champion.

The Road to Excellence

When Ingemar was sixteen, he quit school in order to ski full-time. Ingemar felt that he could not develop his skiing talent to its fullest and be a good student at the same time. He decided he would do one thing well, as well as he could. Later in life, Ingemar would say that the fun and challenge of his sport was that on every run he had the chance of making it a perfect run. Ingemar set out chasing perfection, and if he did not achieve it, he came very close.

Ingemar joined the World Cup circuit at seventeen, in the 1973-1974 season. At age eighteen, the following season, he won his first World Cup race. He did even better through the rest of the season. He stayed in contention for the overall World Cup title, in which skiers earn points

Skiier Ingemar Stenmark after a 1983 race.

for their performances over the whole season.

On the last day of the season, Ingemar still had a chance to win the title. He was second to Italy's Gustavo Thoeni, and the title came down to a final slalom. Thoeni beat Ingemar and took the World Cup, but it was still an outstanding season for the young Swede, who placed second in the overall World Cup.

Ingemar's style was smooth, graceful, and effortless. People said he looked as unhurried as a recreational skier. The effortless appearance of his skiing, however, was the result of his tremendous strength. Doctors in Sweden once tested Ingemar and declared that he was one of the strongest men in the country. He was not, however, exceptionally big, at 6 feet and 175 pounds. His strength may have been hereditary—legend has it that his grandfather once strangled a bear.

The Emerging Champion

Ingemar continued his pursuit of perfection the following season as he came closer. In the 1975-1976 season, Ingemar won the overall

World Cup title, becoming the first Scandinavian ever to do so. He also raced in the Olympic Games in Innsbruck and took a bronze medal in the slalom.

Ingemar, however, would only get better. He won the overall World Cup title again the next year, 1976-1977, and again the year after that, 1977-1978. In 1978, he had compiled so many points by January, that he had clinched the title, and the races in February and March did not even matter.

Of the three events in the World Cup competition, the slalom, the giant slalom, and the downhill, Ingemar only raced in two of them. He had never raced in downhills. Ingemar felt that the slalom and the giant slalom were the more technical events requiring agility, strength, and great skill, while the downhill was more a matter of brute speed.

Ingemar rarely even trained for the downhill. He felt it would take time from his training for the other two events—time he felt he could not afford to lose as he chased after the perfect run. Following Ingemar's three consecutive World Cup wins, however, the scoring system was changed. The system used to compute the overall winner would award more points to those skiers who competed in all three events.

It was the next year that Ingemar took a bad fall training for the downhill. He sustained a concussion and was out for several weeks. If he had been considering racing the donwhill, perhaps the fall convinced him the downhill was not for him. He skipped all the downhills that year, but he came closer still to perfection in the other two events.

In the 1978-1979 season, Ingemar won fourteen World Cup races, a record, surpassing the mark of twelve set by Jean-Claude Killy in 1967. The following year, Ingemar dominated at the Olympics in Lake Placid, taking two gold medals—one in the slalom and one in the giant slalom. American skier Phil Mahre called Ingemar's style letter-perfect, as Ingemar continued to master these two events.

Continuing the Story

Following the Lake Placid Games in 1980, Ingemar turned semiprofessional and continued to race in professional circles. Off the moun-

MAJOR CHAMPIONSHIPS

Year	Competition	Event	Place
1974	World Championships	Giant slalom	9th
	World Cup	Overall	12th
1975	World Cup	Overall	2d
		Giant slalom	1st
		Slalom	1st
1976	Olympic Games	Slalom	Bronze
	World Cup	Overall	1st
		Giant slalom	1st
		Slalom	1st
1977	World Cup	Overall	1st
		Giant slalom	2d
		Slalom	1st
1978	World Championships	Giant slalom	1st
		Slalom	1st
	World Cup	Overall	1st
		Giant slalom	1st
		Slalom	1st
1979	World Cup	Overall	5th
		Giant slalom	1st
		Slalom	1st
1980	Olympic Games	Giant slalom	Gold
		Slalom	Gold
	World Cup	Overall	2d
		Giant slalom	1st
		Slalom	1st
1981	World Cup	Overall	2d
		Giant slalom	1st
		Slalom	1st
1982	World Championships	Giant slalom	2d
		Slalom	1st
	World Cup	Overall	2d
		Giant slalom	2d
		Slalom	2d
1983	World Cup	Overall	2d
		Giant slalom	2d
		Slalom	1st
1988	Olympic Games	Slalom	5th
1989	World Championships	Overall	6th

HONORS, AWARDS, AND RECORDS

1976	First Scandinavian to win the World Cup
1976-80	World Cup Competitor of the Year
1977	*Ski Racing* magazine Competitor of the Year

tain, however, Ingemar had been shy and very quiet. He earned the nickname "the Silent Swede," and while his teammates and others on the World Cup tour would go out to socialize or dance, Ingemar would usually be found in the basement of his hotel, working on his skis.

He turned down many offers from ski companies during his amateur career, skiing loyally on his Elan skis. Other companies offered him up to twenty times what Elan paid him in endorsement fees, but Ingemar felt it right to continue with Elan, since the company had helped the Swedish team in Ingemar's first years when it was poor and unsuccessful.

Several years after turning pro, Ingemar was allowed to return to the amateur World Cup when some rules concerning payments to ath-letes were changed. In 1989, Ingemar's sixteenth season, Ingemar finished a respectable sixth in the World Alpine Ski Championships. He was thirty-two years old. Ingemar retired at the end of that season.

Summary

Ingemar Stenmark amassed eighty-five World Cup victories during his career, far more than any other skier. While he shunned the fame and fortune that came with his success, he sought perfection in his skiing. He specialized in only two events, but in those two he was the master.

Robert Passaro

Additional Sources:

Levinson, David, and Karen Christenson, eds. *Encyclopedia of World Sport: From Ancient to Present.* Santa Barbara, Calif.: ABC-CLIO, 1996.

Masia, Seth. "Six Ways to Get It." *Ski* 60, no. 6 (1996).

Wallechinsky, David. *The Complete Book of the Olympics.* Boston: Little, Brown and Company, 1991.

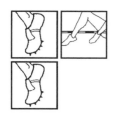

HELEN STEPHENS

Sport: Track and field

Born: February 3, 1918
Fulton, Missouri

Early Life

Helen Stephens was born on February 3, 1918, in Fulton, Missouri, and reared in the rural farm country of Calloway County. She loved to run, and by mid-adolescence she was a well-built near-six-footer. At Fulton High School, one of the standard physical education tests was a timed

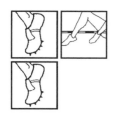

Helen Stephens is congratulated by fellow American Alice Arden after winning the gold medal in the 100-meter dash during the 1936 Olympic Games in Berlin.

run of 50 yards. Helen sprinted the distance and recorded a time of 5.8 seconds. A startled but excited Burton Moore, the track and field coach at Fulton High School, pointed out to Helen that this time, although unofficial, tied the then-world record.

The Road to Excellence

Natural athletes are a rarity in top-level track and field. Most often it is gifted and talented athletes with high levels of natural ability who become the best as a result of sustained training. Helen was no exception. She ran with rare form and excellent acceleration and trained hard. Barry Hugman and Peter Arnold, in *The Olympic Games* (1988), quote Helen's reply to a question about how and why she ran as well as she did: "I guess it came from chasing jackrabbits on dad's farm."

In the history of American women's track and field, much attention has been paid to the exploits of Babe Didrikson, who took the 80-meter hurdles and javelin gold medals at the 1932 Los Angeles Olympics. In fact, despite having a short career, Helen's athletic achievements were just as impressive as Didrikson's.

America has been described as a wonderful melting pot where various immigrant groups settle and then intermingle. Lewis Carlson and John Fogarty, two American sport historians, in their wonderful *Tales of Gold* (1987), interview a series of great American athletes. One of their interviews was with Helen Stephens. She told them that her father's name was Anglo-German and her mother's name was Pennsylvania Dutch, and that on her grandfather's side of the family there was a Cherokee Indian.

The Emerging Champion

In *Tales of Gold*, Helen describes how she learned to put the shot on her father's farm: "I

STATISTICS

Year	Competition	Event	Place	Time/Distance
1935	National AAU Outdoor Championships	100 meters	1st	11.6 WR
		200 meters	1st	24.6
	National AAU Indoor Championships	50 yards	1st	6.6
		Long jump	1st	8′ 8¼″
		Shot put	1st	39′ 7¼″
1936	Olympic Games	100 meters	Gold	11.5
		4×100-meter relay	Gold	39.8
		Javelin	10th	—
	National AAU Outdoor Championships	100 meters	1st	11.7
		8-lb. shot put	1st	41′ 8½″
	National AAU Indoor Championships	50 yards	1st	6.6
		Long jump	1st	8′ 8″
		Shot put	1st	41′ 7″
1937	National AAU Indoor Championships	50 yards	1st	6.5
		220 yards	1st	28.5
		Shot put	1st	44′ 11½″.

Note: WR = World Record

couldn't afford $2.50 for a shot put, but my dad had broken a 16-pound anvil pounding something or other on it. So I started throwing one of the pieces. My brother and I spent a couple of years readying me for my shot-put debut. He always says that he should get some credit for this because he was my retriever."

In the 1930's, opportunities for female athletes were virtually nonexistent. In March of 1935, Helen's coach, Burton Moore, who had been guiding and directing her training in running and throwing, found out about an American Athletic Union (AAU) meet in St. Louis. They traveled to the competition in the face of the superintendent of schools, who hoped that they would get "this foolishness out of [their] systems." At this meet, Helen won AAU titles in the 50-meter dash, the standing broad jump, and the shot put. The most sensational victory was her gold medal in the 50-meter dash, for she defeated Stella Walsh, the 1932 Olympic champion in the 100 meters.

It should be emphasized that Helen was a virtually unknown seventeen-year-old high school senior who defeated the American and Olympic champion. Not only did Helen take the AAU title, but she also equaled the official world record. In *Tales of Gold,* Helen laughingly recalls that a *Post Dispatch* profile of her, following the AAU successes, had a photograph of her looking rustic (shotgun in hand and hunting dog at her heels) with the caption, "From farm to fame in 6.6 seconds."

One year later, Helen and Stella Walsh resumed their rivalry. In 1935 and 1936, Helen continued to train enthusiastically. Training partners were frequently male college athletes, and she often ran repetition runs at 400 and 800 meters. Helen's ability to hold her form and run through and beyond the finishing line was developed as a result of these stamina-building activities.

At the Berlin Olympics, Helen won her first-round heat and the semifinals of the 100-meter dash. In the finals, she beat Stella Walsh by 2 yards and set an unofficial world record (because of the following wind) of 11.5 seconds. A second gold medal followed in the 4×100-meter relay, but here Helen was indeed lucky. The German women had a lead of 8 meters, but on their final lap, the baton was dropped.

Helen achieved fame of another sort when she met leading Nazi Hermann Goering. She recalled him as being flirtatious and as saying "Auf Wiedersehen, Fraulein Stephens."

Continuing the Story

Helen was much more than the world's best 100-meter runner. She won AAU titles in events as varied as the 200 meters and the shot put. At the 1936 Olympics, she finished in tenth place in the women's javelin.

During her amateur career—two and a half years—Helen was never beaten in a sprint race.

Following her amateur track and field career, Helen toured the country with a women's basketball team known as the All-American Redheads.

HONORS AND AWARDS

1936	Associated Press Female Athlete of the Year
1950	Associated Press Tenth Greatest Female Athlete in the World from 1900 to 1950
1975	Inducted into National Track and Field Hall of Fame

After that, she formed another women's basketball team called the Helen Stephens Olympic Co-Eds.

With Babe Didrikson, she became one of the first female athletes who found a degree of recognition in the world of professional sport and entertainment. She endorsed Quaker Oats, ran handicap professional races against Jesse Owens, and, she reports in *Tales of Gold,* in 1952, when she weighed 195 pounds, she tossed the shot nearly 55 feet when the women's world record was about 50 feet.

Summary

Known as the "Fulton Flash," Helen Stephens is remembered for her startling feats as a schoolgirl and for her victory and world record at the 1936 Olympics in the 100 meters. To read her own words in *Tales of Gold* is a delight, because what comes across is a larger-than-life character who lived life to the fullest. During the 1930's, a period of little opportunity for women in sports, she hit the headlines and showed that women could succeed in international sport. She served as a marine in World War II and would continue to stay active in the Senior Olympics. She worked for many years for the Defense Mapping Agency Aerospace Center in St. Louis.

Scott A. G. M. Crawford

Additional Sources:

Carlson, Lewis H., and John J. Fogarty, eds. *Tales of Gold: An Oral History of the Summer Olympic Games Told by American Gold Medal Winners.* Chicago: Contemporary Books, 1987.

Collins, Douglas. *Olympic Dreams: One Hundred Years of Excellence.* New York: Universe, 1996.

Tricard, Louise M. *American Women's Track and Field: A History, 1895 Through 1980.* Jefferson, N.C.: McFarland, 1996

JILL STERKEL

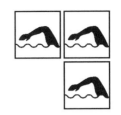

Sport: Swimming

Born: May 27, 1961
Hollywood, California

Early Life

Jill Ann Sterkel was born on May 27, 1961, in Hollywood, California. She moved to nearby Hacienda Heights three years later. Hers was an athletic family. Her father, James Leroy, had played basketball for the University of Southern California, and her mother, Joanne Karen Johnson Sterkel, was a fine swimmer. Jill, her brother Jon Michael, and her sister Jodi all attended college on swimming scholarships.

Jill and her brother first took swimming lessons with other neighborhood children when Jill was about five years old. At the end of the last lesson, the teacher threw pennies into the pool.

The children rushed to pick them from the bottom. Jill and Jon got the most pennies, just as they would win many prizes at swimming meets to come.

The Road to Excellence

When Jill was only six years old, coach Don Garman asked her to join the Hacienda Heights Aquatic Club. He taught her the skills that would someday make her a champion. He also encouraged her to aim for the top. While attending elementary school, she worked with Coach Garman and competed at local meets.

Jill did so well that, by age ten, she was asked to join the El Monte Aquatics Club, which competed at national meets. At her new club, Jill practiced longer and harder than ever, sometimes as many as twelve hours a week. In 1974, she entered her first big meet, the United States Indoor Championships at Dallas, Texas. Although she did not finish in the top three at that meet, it was the first of many nationals in which she would compete during the next fifteen years.

When she was only fourteen, Jill competed in her first important international contest, the 1975 Pan-American Games. There she won a gold medal in the 4×100-meter freestyle relay and a silver in the 100-meter freestyle race.

Even though she spent much time swimming, Jill loved all sports. She took part in many activities at Orange Grove Junior High School. Outside of school, she played on a softball team that competed in tournaments and regional games.

The Emerging Champion

While Jill was becoming a world-class swimmer, American women were very successful in Olympic swimming. They expected to keep on winning at the 1976 Games in Montreal, Canada. Fifteen-year-old Jill was the youngest person on the Olympic swim team that year. She was se-

2643

lected for both the 100-meter freestyle and the 4×100-meter freestyle relay.

Her team had a hard time at Montreal. The tiny country of East Germany, which had not won a single gold medal in women's swimming in 1972, won eleven golds in 1976. The Soviets took another. Jill finished seventh in the 100-meter freestyle, and her teammates earned four silver and two bronze medals, but no gold.

Their last hope was the 4×100-meter freestyle relay. The East German women held the world record of 3 minutes 44.82 seconds. They were favored to win that last gold medal. Jill and her teammates rose to the challenge. They won the gold medal and broke East Germany's world record.

As soon as the United States team won, the crowd was on their feet. Coaches, swimmers, fans, and television commentators all rejoiced at the victory. The celebration lasted a long time. It was the biggest moment in Jill's young life, and one she has never forgotten.

Two years later, at the 1978 World Championships, Jill and the American team won the 4×100-meter freestyle relay again and set a new world record. At the 1979 Pan-American Games, Jill had one of her biggest meets ever, winning three gold medals and one silver.

Continuing the Story

By that time, Jill was one of the best female swimmers in America. She was named California Athlete of the Year in 1978 and 1979. She was also Athlete of the Year at Glen A. Wilson High School for four years as a member of the swimming, water polo, and volleyball teams. The swimming team won the state championship her senior year, when she also made All-State in volleyball.

Swimming had brought Jill excitement and world travel and

now gave her another reward. She had scholarship offers from colleges all over the country. She decided to swim for Coach Paul Bergen's Lady Longhorns at the University of Texas at Austin. Coach Bergen became another important person in her career. Under his guidance, Jill led the University of Texas to two Association for Intercollegiate Athletics for Women (AIAW) national championships in 1981 and 1982, while winning many individual titles. In 1981, she won the Honda Broderick Cup as the top female college athlete in America.

Her biggest disappointment came in 1980, when the United States team boycotted the Moscow Olympics. Yet she did not give up. Instead,

STATISTICS

Year	Competition	Event	Place	Time
1975	Pan-American Games	100-meter freestyle	2d	58.57
		4×100-meter freestyle relay	1st	3:53.31
1976	Olympic Games	4×100-meter freestyle relay	Gold	3:44.82 WR, OR
1978	World Championships	4×100-meter freestyle relay	1st	3:43.43 WR
1979	Pan-American Games	100-meter freestyle	2d	56.24
		100-meter butterfly	1st	—
		4×100-meter freestyle relay	1st	3:45.82
		4×100-meter medley relay	1st	4:13.24
1981	World University Games	100-meter freestyle	1st	—
		200-meter freestyle	1st	—
		100-meter butterfly	1st	—
		4×100-meter freestyle relay	1st	—
		4×100-meter medley relay	1st	—
	U.S. Nationals	50-meter freestyle	1st	—
		100-meter freestyle	1st	—
1982	World Championships	100-meter freestyle	3d	56.27
		4×100-meter freestyle relay	2d	3:45.76
		4×100-meter medley relay	2d	4:08.12
	NCAA Championships	50-yard freestyle	2d	—
		100-yard freestyle	2d	—
		50-yard butterfly	1st	—
		100-yard butterfly	1st	—
	U.S. Nationals	50-yard freestyle	2d	—
		100-yard freestyle	1st	—
		200-yard freestyle	2d	—
		100-yard butterfly	1st	—
1983	Pan-American Games	4×100 freestyle relay	1st	3:46.46
	NCAA Championships	50-yard butterfly	—	24.26
		100-yard butterfly	1st	53.54
		400-yard freestyle relay	1st	3:21.34
1984	Olympic Games	4×100-meter freestyle relay	Gold	3:43.43
1988	Olympic Games	50-meter freestyle	Bronze	—
		4×100-meter freestyle relay	Bronze	—

Notes: WR = World Record; OR = Olympic Record

Jill worked even harder toward the 1984 Games, where she won another gold medal.

Although she practiced between twenty-one and twenty-five hours a week, Jill also graduated from the University of Texas in 1984. The next year, she became assistant coach of the women's team there. She also kept swimming, and was on the United States water polo team that won a bronze medal at the 1986 World Championships. She loved racing most of all, however, and began training seriously again in 1987. Her efforts paid off. Although she was the oldest member of the women's swim team, Jill won two bronze medals at the 1988 Olympics. In 1991, she completed her master's degree and retired from competition to become the head coach of the women's swimming team at Indiana University.

Jill returned to her alma mater, the University of Texas, in 1995 as the swim team's head coach. She led the Longhorns to two Big Eight championships and finished in the top three of the NCAA Championships three times.

Summary

Jill Sterkel grew up in California, the home state of many of America's greatest swimming and diving champions. Her very athletic family supported her efforts wholeheartedly. She learned to swim before she started school and won an Olympic gold medal at age fifteen. All through

---

RECORDS

First woman in history to be on four Olympic teams (1976, 1980, 1984, 1988)
Fifteen times AAU/U.S. Swimming champion

HONORS AND AWARDS

1978-79	California Athlete of the Year
1980-81	Honda Broderick Cup (the first swimmer to win this award)
1981	College Female Athlete of the year

---

high school and college, Jill was one of the top female swimmers in America.

Even though she practiced long hours and traveled the world, Jill was a fine student. Soon after graduation, she became an assistant college coach and began graduate school. A high school, college, Olympic, and world champion and a head coach, Jill is one of the most outstanding women in the history of American swimming.

Mary Lou LeCompte

Additional Sources:

Besford, Pat. *Encyclopedia of Swimming.* New York: St. Martin's Press, 1976.

Levinson, David, and Karen Christenson, eds. *Encyclopedia of World Sport: From Ancient Times to Present.* Santa Barbara, Calif.: ABC-CLIO, 1996.

Mallon, Bill, and Ian Buchanan. *Quest for Gold: The Encyclopedia of American Olympians.* New York: Leisure Press, 1984.

Wallechinsky, David. *The Complete Book of the Olympics.* Boston: Little, Brown and Company, 1991.

TEÓFILO STEVENSON

Sport: Boxing

Born: March 29, 1952
Camagüey, Cuba

Early Life

The life of Teófilo Stevenson is not well known by the world outside of his native Cuba. He was born March 29, 1952, in Camagüey, Cuba, an island only ninety miles from the United States, but much more distant in way of life. When he was born on March 29, 1952, Cuba was a place where people from the United States went for their va-

Cuban boxer Teófilo Stevenson won his third Olympic gold in 1980.

cations. Life in Cuba would change seven years later, when Fidel Castro overthrew the government and a communist way of life would change the way of thinking for the young school boy.

Under a different political system, life did not become any easier. Teófilo and his family continued to live the simple peasant life. They were, however, forced to obey a ruling by the government that involved getting the youth of the nation physically fit by participation in sports. The nation had a long history of success in boxing. Two former world champions were national heroes in the years before Castro. Kid Chocolate was champion in the 1930's and Kid Gavilan was world-famous twenty years later.

The Road to Excellence

When Teófilo was still in high school, his body was filling out. He weighed nearly 200 pounds by the time he was seventeen. He had the opportunity to become part of baseball, the national sport, or the one-on-one competition of boxing. History was to prove that he made a wise choice.

The communist government established schools to teach the sport of boxing. By 1970, the growing Teófilo was learning his trade and winning three-round bouts against opponents throughout Cuba.

Even though amateur bouts only last for three three-minute rounds, Teófilo learned how difficult training was. As he trained, he had to box at full speed for three rounds, moving every second of the three minutes.

The Cuban government wanted the sports champions to meet and defeat the best in the rest of the world. Every four years, the Pan-American Games are held. They are similar to the Olympics, with all the nations in North and South America taking part.

It was at these games that the nearly 6-foot 6-inch future champion would meet different op-

RECORDS

One of only two boxers to capture three Olympic gold medals
One of only two boxers to capture three Amateur World Championships

HONORS, AWARDS, AND MILESTONES

1972	World Trophy
1972, 1976, 1980	Olympic super heavyweight Gold Medalist
1974, 1978, 1986	Amateur World heavyweight champion
1975, 1979	Pan-American Games heavyweight Gold Medalist

ponents who would test his ability. In 1971, Teófilo progressed all the way to the championship bout before losing to the American Duane Bobick.

The Emerging Champion

Defeat discourages some people, but Teófilo learned from this loss. Amateur boxers under the communist system fought with a style of standing tall and jabbing straight with the left hand. Teófilo had long arms and could land his jab easily. What he now developed was a right hand that was thrown straight and with power.

The world was soon to learn how powerful he had become as a puncher. One year after losing to Duane Bobick, he was in Munich, Germany, representing Cuba in the Olympic super heavyweight division. In the quarterfinals, Teófilo once again met Duane Bobick. In round three, a series of hard blows closed Bobick's left eye, and he was put down for the full count. Teófilo went on to win the gold medal.

Cuba had its third world champion, and heavyweights are popular all over the world. In any country outside a communist nation like Cuba, an Olympic champion would become a professional. After he won the Olympic title, many promoters and managers from outside of Cuba offered the champion almost $2 million to become a professional.

Teófilo's reply to that was, "I believe in the revolution. I don't believe in professionalism." His ambition was to win three Olympic gold medals.

For two years after the 1972 Olympics, Teófilo fought throughout the world. In 1974, he fought and won the second most important amateur honor, the Amateur World Heavyweight Championship. More pressure was put on him to be-

come a professional, but he had more amateur championships that he wanted to win. In 1975, he won the Pan-American Games title that he failed to win in 1971.

The stage was set for the 1976 Olympics in Montreal. One of his opponents on the way to the finals was John Tate from the United States. Tate was knocked out in less than two minutes. Only two years after being knocked out by Teófilo, Tate was to win the professional world heavyweight championship.

New contenders kept coming along to challenge the aging Teófilo. In 1978, he retained his Amateur World Championship, and the following year, he won a second Pan-American Games Championship.

Continuing the Story

The 1970's were over, and Teófilo had achieved all of his goals except for winning his third straight Olympic gold medal. That had been his stated goal since Munich in 1972.

Controversy surrounded the 1980 games held in Moscow. Many of the free-world nations refused to take part because of the Soviet invasion of Afghanistan. In the final bout, Teófilo won a unanimous decision over the Soviet champion, Pyotr Zaev.

This Olympic title put him in a class with only one other three-time Olympic boxing champion, the legendary Hungarian, Laszló Papp. He, like Teófilo, came from a communist country and never was allowed to become a professional until he was more than thirty. Teófilo continued to compete in international bouts but was now losing to young boxers he would have defeated a few years before.

There was a chance he could try for a fourth Olympic title in 1984. Once again, politics took control of sports. This time, Cuba refused to take part in the 1984 Games in Los Angeles.

A near-fatal accident at about this time closed out the active boxing career of Teófilo. A stove in his home exploded and he suffered serious burns over much of his body. Reports out of Cuba about his condition were limited because of the government's control of the press. Eventually, he recovered from his burns.

He would go on to teach and train the future amateur champions of his country. Much has changed in the world since he was champion. He, however, lives in one of the most controlled nations in the world. By Cuban standards, he lives a comfortable life. What he has that no government can either give or take away is the love and respect of his fellow Cubans.

Summary

As a boxer, Teófilo Stevenson was feared for his accurate left jab, his overall hand speed, and the powerful right hand that helped him win his first gold medal. As a citizen of Cuba, he was always loyal to the ideals of his nation.

The boxing career of Teófilo was a case of both what was and what might have been. In the world of amateur boxing, his name stands at the very top. He was successful in world competition for a full decade. What might have been had he turned professional is something that will never be known. What is known is that he met and de-feated many boxers who were later to become successful professionals.

Bruce Gordon

Additional Sources:

Goldman, Herbert G., ed. *The Ring 1985 Record Book and Boxing Encyclopedia.* New York: Ring Publishing, 1985.

Levinson, David, and Karen Christenson, eds. *Encyclopedia of World Sport: From Ancient Times to Present.* Santa Barbara, Calif.: ABC-CLIO, 1996.

Mullan, Harry. *The Ultimate Encyclopedia of Boxing: The Definitive Illustrated Guide to World Boxing.* Edison, N.J.: Chartwell Books, 1996.

Odd, Gilbert E. *Encyclopedia of Boxing.* New York: Crescent Books, 1983.

Schulman, Arlene. *The Prize Fighters: An Intimate Look at Champions and Contenders.* New York: Lyons and Burford, 1994.

DAVE STEWART

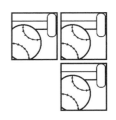

Sport: Baseball

Born: February 19, 1957
Oakland, California

Early Life

David Keith Stewart was born on February 19, 1957, in Oakland, California. Son of David and Nathalie Stewart, he had a brother and five sisters. His father worked long hours as a longshoreman and died in 1972, when Dave was fifteen years old. His mother worked in a cannery until 1973.

Dave grew up in a tough neighborhood within walking distance of the Oakland Coliseum. His home was near one of the poorest communities

Dave Stewart in 1994.

in Oakland. He experienced all the temptations that poor city neighborhoods contain, including drugs and gang activity. He was able to stay out of trouble not only by applying the values that he learned from his parents but also by spending his free time playing sports at the Boys Club.

The Road to Excellence

Dave loved baseball from a very early age. His father took him to San Francisco Giants baseball games. After his father's death, he became a fan of the Oakland Athletics and a member of Reggie's Regiment, a group devoted to the great Athletics baseball player, Reggie Jackson. On occasion, he received money to wash one of Reggie's vintage cars.

Dave learned to play sports from his older brother, Gregory. His Little League coach, Howard Bess, helped shape his character and baseball skills. He played baseball at St. Elizabeth High School in Oakland. Rickey Henderson, a fellow Oakland Athletic, played ball with Dave on an American Legion team in Oakland. Until he became a professional baseball player in 1975, Dave came nearly every day to play sports at the Ossian Carr Clubhouse, a branch of the Oakland Boys Club.

Dave's father did not want him to become a ballplayer, because he was afraid Dave would not be able to make a living. In high school, however, Dave shared one dream with his lifelong friend, Wornel Simpson: to make a lot of money when he grew up in order to help others in his disadvantaged community. Contrary to what his father thought possible, he earned the money to fulfill his high school dream by playing baseball.

The Emerging Champion

Dave's first six years as a major league player were discouraging. Although he was a promising pitcher for the Los Angeles Dodgers, he did not prove to be a big winner and was traded to the Texas Rangers in 1983. He did not succeed as a starting pitcher for the Rangers. He had a record of no wins and six losses with the Rangers in 1985, when he was traded to the Philadelphia Phillies. While he pitched for the Phillies, an arm injury required surgery. The Phillies released Dave in 1986. It was the low point of his professional baseball career.

Two weeks after the Phillies released him, he was hired by the Oakland Athletics. In Tony La Russa's first game as Athletics manager on July 2, 1986, he gave Dave his first assignment as starting pitcher for Oakland. Dave beat Cy Young Award winner Roger Clemens of the Boston Red Sox. In his first season with the Athletics, he won nine and lost five games. It was only the beginning of his accomplishments. In the 1987 season, he won twenty games. He went on to become the only pitcher in the 1980's to win twenty or more games three seasons in a row. In 1990, Dave won twenty-two games.

Dave's sudden success as a pitcher is credited to his mastery of the forkball, a pitch he learned from Sandy Koufax in 1982. His return to his hometown motivated him to succeed for himself and his neighborhood. Playing ball in Oakland meant that he was among friends who loved him whether he was a success or not.

Dave had an especially good opportunity to contribute to his hometown in the 1989 World Series, when the Oakland A's battled the San Francisco Giants. A strong earthquake hit the Oakland and San Francisco area on October 17, 1989, during a World Series game. A considerable amount of damage occurred in San Francisco and Oakland. Dave spent the first night at the collapsed Nimitz Freeway, helping the rescuers save the lives of people trapped in their cars. Dave pitched two of the four games that won the World Series for Oakland and was named the Series' most valuable player. Oakland's win boosted the morale of the entire community, enabling it to better deal with the tragedy of the earthquake. Dave donated a large part of his World Series earnings to earthquake relief projects in Oakland.

Continuing the Story

Once Dave established himself as an outstanding pitcher, he turned to the needs of his community. He realized that he was able to become a success in life even though he grew up in a neighborhood filled with drugs, gangs, and crime, because the activities at the Boys Club kept him off the streets. He began to fulfill his dream of contributing time and money to his old neighborhood. He sponsored many community pro-

STATISTICS

Season	GP	GS	CG	IP	HA	BB	SO	W	L	S	ShO	ERA
1978	1	0	0	2.0	1	0	1	0	0	0	0	0.00
1981	32	0	0	43.0	40	14	29	4	3	6	0	2.51
1982	45	14	0	146.1	137	49	80	9	8	1	0	3.81
1983	54	9	2	135.0	117	50	78	10	4	8	0	2.60
1984	32	27	3	192.1	193	87	119	7	14	0	0	4.73
1985	46	5	0	85.2	91	41	66	0	6	4	0	5.46
1986	37	17	4	161.2	152	69	111	9	5	0	1	3.95
1987	37	37	8	261.1	224	105	205	**20**	13	0	1	3.68
1988	37	37	14	275.2	240	110	192	21	12	0	2	3.23
1989	36	36	8	257.2	260	69	155	21	9	0	0	3.32
1990	36	36	11	267.0	226	83	166	22	11	0	**4**	2.56
1991	35	35	2	226.0	245	105	144	11	11	0	1	5.18
1992	31	31	2	199.3	175	79	130	12	10	0	0	3.66
1993	26	26	0	162.0	146	72	96	12	8	0	0	4.44
1994	22	22	1	133.3	151	62	111	7	8	0	0	5.87
1995	16	16	0	81.0	101	39	58	3	7	0	0	6.89
Totals	523	348	55	2,626.7	2,499	1,034	1,741	168	129	19	9	3.95

Notes: Boldface indicates statistical leader. GP = games played; GS = games started; CG = complete games; IP = innings pitched; HA = hits allowed; BB = bases on balls (walks); SO = strikeouts; W = wins; L = losses; S = saves; ShO = shutouts; ERA = earned run average

HONORS AND AWARDS

1989	American League All-Star Team
	World Series most valuable player
1990	Roberto Clemente Award
1990, 1993	American League Championship Series most valuable player

grams, such as sports activities for children, drug education programs, and programs for teenage mothers and children with learning problems. With his childhood friend, Wornel Simpson, he started Stewart's Corporations for Kids to involve businesses in rebuilding poor neighborhoods. Because of his extraordinary spirit of giving, he received the twentieth Roberto Clemente Award in 1990.

Dave finished the 1992 season for Oakland with a 12-10 record and pitched a complete game victory in a losing effort against the Toronto Blue Jays in the American League Championship Series (ALCS). The following year he joined Toronto, earning two victories in the ALCS and appearing in his fifth World Series.

In 1995 Dave returned to Oakland for his final season, where he started sixteen games but earned only three victories against seven losses. In July, he announced his retirement and later that year he joined the A's front office. After spending time in the Padres organization as a pitching coach in 1997-1998, Dave became assistant general manager for Toronto in 1999. It was widely believed that it was only a matter of time before he became a general manager in the major leagues himself.

Summary

Dave Stewart's pitching was crucial to Oakland's victories. He pitched two of the four games that gave Oakland the 1989 World Series Championship. He was the only pitcher in the 1980's to win twenty games three years in a row. He provides an example of someone who does not forget the needs of the people where he grew up just because he has become a success.

Evelyn Toft

Additional Sources:

Axthelm, Pete, and Pamela Abramson. "Winning for the Neighborhood." *Newsweek* 111, no. 22 (1988).

Kroichick, Ron. "From the Scrap Heap to the Penthouse . . . Dave Stewart." *Sport* 82, no. 7 (1991).

Wulf, Steve. "Dave Stewart." *Sports Illustrated* 79, no. 26 (1993).

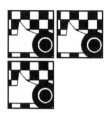

JACKIE STEWART

Sport: Auto racing

Born: June 11, 1939
Milton, Dumbartonshire, Scotland

Early Life

John Young Stewart was born on June 11, 1939, at Milton in Dumbartonshire, Scotland. His parents were able to afford to send their youngest son to a good school.

Living in the Scottish countryside, Jackie spent much time shooting and fishing, but it was motor sport that caught his imagination. It was as if driving were in his blood.

The Stewarts were a family dominated by motoring. Jackie's father had been a motorcycle racer before he set up a successful car dealership and garage. Even more of an inspiration to Jackie was his elder brother, Jimmy, who raced in the early 1950's.

The Road to Excellence

Jackie yearned to drive racing cars. Unfortunately, as a result of Jimmy's numerous crashes, his parents were set against his emulating his brother. In 1961, unknown to his parents, Jackie started racing for a local sponsor named Barry Filer.

Jackie's driving remained hidden from his parents until 1962, when he decided to get married. His marriage to Helen MacGregor was covered by the local press, which revealed his secret career. By this time Jackie could not be stopped.

Jackie's racing career took off quickly. Some fine performances in local races encouraged David Murray to invite him to join the Ecurie Ecosse racing team. Jackie jumped at the chance. Joining this team gave Jackie exposure to the whole of the racing industry. In 1963, he won fourteen out of twenty-three starts, and in 1964, twenty-eight out of fifty-three starts.

After the impressive beginning of his career, Jackie moved up the motor racing ladder when he signed, with Ken Tyrrell, to race in Formula Three. In March, 1964, Jackie made his debut in Formula Three racing at Snetterton in England. It was also the first time he had ever driven a single-seater.

In his first outing, Jackie greatly impressed Ken Tyrrell, who two days later offered him a ride in Formula One. As young as he was, Jackie was extremely shrewd and knew his own limitations. He turned down Tyrrell's offer, preferring to work his way slowly through Formula Three, then Formula Two. This meant that, by the time

Auto racer Jackie Stewart in 1973.

he got to Formula One, he would be a more experienced, knowledgeable, and, he hoped, more successful driver.

Jackie soon dominated Formula Three and Formula Two racing, and by the end of 1964 he was testing Formula One cars for the Lotus team. He had completed his driving apprenticeship and now was ready for the big-time.

The Emerging Champion

Jackie's first Formula One season was 1965. He signed for the BRM team as second driver to the legendary Graham Hill. Jackie's learning process began all over again. As always, he did not take long to adjust to the higher level of competition. In his first Grand Prix, in South Africa, he finished sixth. Following three second-place finishes, Jackie astounded the racing world by winning the Italian Grand Prix at Monza. In his first season, Jackie could already compete with the best in the sport.

Winning the Monaco Grand Prix in 1966 was a significant landmark in Jackie's career. Victory on the demanding Monte Carlo circuit confirmed his technical excellence as a driver. Everything was going according to plan for Jackie until the Belgian Grand Prix.

On a treacherously wet circuit, Jackie left the track at 150 miles per hour and plowed into a tree. He was trapped in the car with leaking fuel burning his skin. Jackie remained there for more than half an hour until he was finally freed from the wreckage. He had always been concerned with the safety aspect of racing. This incident made him determined that, however fast he would race, safety was of the utmost importance.

Jackie began the 1967 season as BRM's premier driver, Graham Hill having moved to Lotus. Unfortunately, the season proved to be disappointing; because of a succession of mechanical failures, he failed to win a single Grand Prix.

When, in 1968, Ken Tyrrell offered him a job, Jackie accepted. Not only was he glad to join a team with a reliable car, he also relished the opportunity of working again with the man who had given him his big break in racing.

Continuing the Story

With Tyrrell, Jackie was transformed from a promising driver into a legitimate challenger for

GRAND PRIX AND OTHER VICTORIES	
1965, 1969	Italian Grand Prix
1966	Tasman Cup Series Championship
1966, 1971, 1973	Monaco Grand Prix
1968-69, 1973	Netherlands Grand Prix Dutch Grand Prix
1968, 1971, 1973	German Grand Prix
1968, 1972	United States Grand Prix
1969-70	Race of Champions
1969-71	Spanish Grand Prix
1969, 1971	British Grand Prix
1969, 1971-72	French Grand Prix
1969, 1971, 1973	World Championship of Drivers
1969, 1973	South African Grand Prix
1971	Can-Am Challenge Cup Race (Mid-Ohio) Can-Am Challenge Cup Race (Mont-Treblant Circuit)
1971-72	Canadian Grand Prix
1972	Argentine Grand Prix
1973	Belgian Grand Prix

the world title. The 1968 season brought victories at the Dutch, German, and United States Grand Prix, and a respectable second-place finish in the driver's championship behind Graham Hill.

Jackie's year was 1969. He won six Grand Prix and skated to the World Championship of Drivers. Ironically, it was his victory at Monza, where he had won his first Grand Prix, that confirmed the winning of his first world crown.

In 1970, the Tyrrell team had severe car trouble. With only a win in Spain, Jackie had no chance of regaining his title. He remained loyal to Tyrrell, and by the start of the 1971 season, he had a competitive car again. That was all he needed, and he won his second World Championship.

A stomach ulcer hampered the defense of his title in 1972, and the time he missed in midseason cost him dearly in his struggle to catch the young Emerson Fittipaldi. In 1973, however, in a new Tyrrell, Jackie was fit for the whole season and won his third World Championship. In the course of the season, he exceeded twenty-five Grand Prix wins, the record number of victories set by the late, great Jim Clark, a fellow Scot. The German Grand Prix at Nurburgring saw Jackie set a new record mark with twenty-seven.

Jackie retired after the 1973 season. He had shown the world that he was one of the greatest drivers ever, and he had nothing else to prove in motor racing. Retirement did not mean inactivity for the likable Scotsman. He immersed himself in his business interests and still found plenty of time to indulge in his numerous hobbies, especially shooting, fishing, and golf.

Summary

Although Jackie Stewart was almost destined to become a racing driver, he was not necessarily destined to become a great one. Jackie possessed a single-minded attitude toward his driving career. He was clinically efficient on the track, combining great technique with a fervent concern for safety. These qualities made him one of the best drivers ever.

David L. Andrews

HONORS AND AWARDS	
1966	Indianapolis 500 Rookie of the Year
1971	Order of the British Empire
1973	*Sports Illustrated* Sportsman of the Year British Broadcasting Corporation Sports Personality of the Year
1990	Inducted into International Motor Sports Hall of Fame

Additional Sources:

Corson, Richard. *Champions at Speed.* New York: Dodd, Mead, 1979.

Cutter, Robert, and Bob Fendell. *The Encyclopedia of Auto Racing Greats.* Englewood Cliffs, N.J.: Prentice-Hall, 1973.

Engel, Lyle Kenyon, and the editors of Auto Racing Magazine. *Jackie Stewart: World Driving Champion.* New York: Arco, 1970.

Henry, Alan. *Grand Prix Champions: From Jackie Stewart to Michael Schumacher.* Osceola, Wis.: Motorbooks International, 1995.

Stewart, Jackie, and Peter Manso. *Faster! A Racer's Diary.* New York: Farrar, Strauss, and Giroux, 1972.

PAYNE STEWART

Sport: Golf

Born: January 30, 1957
   Springfield, Missouri
Died: October 25, 1999
   Mina, South Dakota

Early Life

William Payne Stewart was born on January 30, 1957, to William Louis Stewart and Bee Payne Stewart in Springfield, Missouri. The youngest of three children, Payne showed more interest than his sisters in following his father's footsteps on the golf course. He received his first set of golf clubs, when he was four, from his father, Bill Stewart, who was an accomplished amateur golfer himself.

The Road to Excellence

Payne was an all-around athlete while growing up. He played Little League baseball, basketball, and football. His main interest, however, remained golf. By junior high he had won several local tournaments.

In his freshman year of high school, Payne joined the golf team. It was evident early on that golf was Payne's best sport. He had a natural, fluid motion in his swing. By the end of his freshman year, Payne and his father had established a plan. He was going to play golf professionally.

During breaks from school, Payne and his father often played at Hickory Hills Country Club. They also matched Payne's extraordinary golfing ability against other players. It was at this time that Payne honed his competitive edge. He learned that if you play well, you get paid. If you do not, you go home with nothing

Payne was offered a golf scholarship to Southern Methodist University (SMU) in

Texas, and he majored in business. During his senior year, Payne won three tournaments. After graduation, he won the Missouri state amateur title.

The Emerging Champion

After graduating from SMU in 1979, Payne played in the PGA Tour Qualifying School, at-

Payne Stewart putts in the 1999 MCI Classic.

2655

PGA TOUR VICTORIES

1982	Quad Cities Open
1983	Walt Disney World Classic
1987	Bay Hill Classic
1989	MCI Classic
	PGA Championship
1990	MCI Classic
	Byron Nelson Classic
1991	U.S. Open
1995	Houston Open
1999	Pebble Beach Pro-Am
	U.S. Open

tempting to earn his PGA tour card, which would allow him to compete with professionals. Unfortunately, Payne did not make the cut. Realizing that he had to do something to earn money while he waited for his next chance at the school, Payne got a job at a local department store. This type of work was not for him, so Payne took the advice of a friend and joined the eleven-event Asian Golf Tour, playing throughout Southeast Asia, Indonesia, and India. His father and five other men formed a partnership to sponsor Payne on the tour.

During the tour, Payne sharpened his skills, made lasting friendships, and developed a reputation as a prankster. He also learned that the game was not about being perfect, it was about getting the job done.

Payne tried for this PGA tour card a second time in 1980 but again missed the cut. Undaunted, he continued playing abroad. Finally, in 1981, Payne earned his tour card. Having won the Indian Open and the Indonesian Open, Payne was invited to play in the British Open that same year. He finished last.

Continuing the Story

During the 1980's, the PGA Tour had a qualifying system in which members had to qualify on Monday in order to play each week. Payne did not pass a Monday qualifier until March of 1982. He won his first PGA tournament at the Magnolia Classic in April of 1982 in Mississippi. Unfortunately, since the match was being played at the same time as the Masters in Georgia, this did not

count as a win for Payne.

It was about this time that Payne developed his unique style of dress on the links. He often wore knickers, knee socks, and a tam-o'-shanter while playing. He received a lot of ribbing from his fellow golfers, but positive response from the fans and media. Even his game benefited. "When I put my work clothes on," he once said, "I get all fired up." It may have been a coincidence, but that year Payne won his first official PGA tournament, at the Quad Cities Open in Illinois, wearing his trademark outfit.

Payne played well over the next several years, finishing second in six PGA tournament events in 1984. In 1986 he earned sixteen top-ten finishes, a PGA Tour record at the time. Although Payne was playing well, he was not winning. In 1984 and 1986 he set records for the most money ever won without winning a tournament. He came back in 1987, winning the Hertz Bay Hill Classic in Orlando, his hometown.

He continued to play well in 1988 but still was not winning. On the advice of a good friend, he visited a sports psychologist. The doctor noticed that Payne was having difficulty focusing on anything for too long. It was at this time that Payne was diagnosed with attention deficit disorder. He tried taking prescription drugs, but they did not work for him. Instead, he and his coaches developed a routine to help him focus on the easier, mundane shots.

By 1989 Payne was affectionately known as "the best player never to have won a major." Determined to shake this unofficial title, Payne won the PGA Championship that year. It was his first major. He then went on to win the U.S. Open at Hazeltine in 1991.

The highlight of Payne's career came in 1999,

INTERNATIONAL VICTORIES

1981	Indian Open (Asia)
	Indonesian Open (Asia)
1982	Coolangatta-Tweed Head Classic (Australia)
1990	World Cup (Individual)
1991	Heineken Dutch Open (Europe)
1993	Hassan II Trophy (Morocco)

HONORS AND AWARDS

1979	All-American
1979	Missouri Amateur Champion
1987, 1989, 1991, 1993, 1999	Ryder Cup team
1988	All-Around category winner Nabisco Statistics
1989	Nabisco Statistics scoring leader
1991-1993	Skins Game winner

when he once again won the U.S. Open. Also important to Payne were his five chances to play in the Ryder's Cup, the biannual tournament pitting the best golfers in the United States against those from Europe.

At the request of a longtime friend, Payne became involved in planning golf courses. It was during a trip to Dallas to visit a new course that the plane Payne was on crashed in Mina, South Dakota, on October 25, 1999.

Summary

Payne Stewart was spontaneous, outspoken, charitable, and extremely confident, and he always wore his emotions on his sleeve. He was never afraid to shed a tear of joy, or sadness, in front of others. He was also a devoted son, husband, and father. Payne always considered his ability to play golf a God-given talent and was not ashamed to proclaim his faith in public. His strong family life, along with his faith in God, were what kept him going through the ups and downs of life as a professional golfer.

Maryanne Barsotti

Additional Sources:

Arkush, Michael. *I Remember Payne Stewart*. Nashville, Tenn.: Cumberland House, 2000.

Guest, Larry. *The Payne Stewart Story*. Emeryville, Calif.: Woodford Press, 2000.

Steel, Donald. *Records, Facts, and Champions*. Middlesex, England: Guiness Superlatives, 1987.

Stewart, Tracey. *Payne Stewart: The Authorized Biography*. Nashville, Tenn.: Broadman and Holman, 2000.

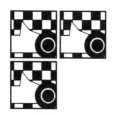

TONY STEWART

Sport: Auto racing

Born: May 20, 1971
Columbus, Indiana

Early Life

Tony Stewart was born on May 20, 1971, in Columbus, Indiana. At the age of eight he raced go-karts in his backyard. In 1983, before he was even a teenager, Tony won the International Karting Federation national championship. Four years later, in 1987, he was victorious in the World Karting Association national championship.

The Road to Excellence

In 1989 Tony graduated to three-quarter midget cars and then quickly moved on to extend his driving apprenticeship by taking the wheel of United States Automobile Club midgets, silver-crown racers, and sprint cars. In 1995 he made automobile history by becoming the first driver to win the USAC Triple Crown, meaning he was the champion of the top three divisions in the same year.

In 1996 Tony felt he had the experience and competitive focus to join the Indy Racing League (IRL). It was obviously the right decision for him as he took the award for Rookie of the Year in the IRL's inaugural year. The following year he added to his 1996 successes by securing one victory, four pole positions, and the IRL championship. At this stage in his career Tony had to decide whether he wanted to stay with the IRL; try lucrative Formula One Grand Prix racing, which would have required signing up with a European auto maker; or switch to National Association for Stock Car Auto Racing (NASCAR).

The Emerging Champion

A key catalyst in Tony's exploring racing opportunities with NASCAR was Joe Gibbs, who was head coach of the Washington Redskins football organization from 1981 to 1993 and led his team to three Super Bowl championships. In his post-football life Gibbs enthusiastically embraced motor sports and became the owner of the Home Depot

Racer Tony Stewart prepares for the 1996 Indianapolis 500.

2658

NASCAR AND OTHER VICTORIES

1983	International Karting Federation National Championship
1987	World Karting Association National Championship
1995	USAC Triple Crown
1999	Exide NASCAR Select Batteries 400
	Dura Lube 500K
	Pennzoil 400
2000	MBNA Platinum 400
	Kmart 400
	Jiffy Lube 300
	MBNA Gold 400
	NAPA 500
	Pennzoil 400

Team. Gibbs linked up with Tony, and for two years, 1997 and 1998, Tony challenged himself by combining two racing roles. He took part in the IRL circuit and the NASCAR Busch Series Grand National Division. Very few drivers are able to successfully compete in different racing categories. Not surprisingly, in 1999 Tony committed to full-time Winston Cup racing as a member of the Home Depot Team under the tutelage of Gibbs.

In 1999 Tony won three Winston Cup races. He may be best remembered for his extraordinary performance in July of that year, when he took part in two races, the Indianapolis 500 and the Coca-Cola 600, and completed a total of 1,090 racing miles. He finished ninth and fourth, respectively, and displayed uncommon resilience and stamina. He racked up NASCAR victories at Richmond, Virgina, Phoenix, Arizona, and Homestead, Florida. He was also named Rookie of the Year by NASCAR.

Continuing the Story

While 1999 was a very satisfying year for Tony in the Winston Cup series—thirty-four races, three wins, thirteen top-five positions, twenty-

one top-ten finishes, two pole positions, and $3 million in prize money. In 2000, Tony doubled his number of Winston Cup victories, achieving six, the most wins of any driver. His six wins broke the record for most wins by a sophomore driver, beating Dale Earnhart's 1980 record of four wins.

The points-scoring system used in the Winston Cup series and the parity achieved by the fiercely competitive nature of the racing teams create Cup standings in which a host of drivers occupy the top ten places and are separated by relatively small point margins. At the end of the 2000 season, Tony finished sixth; he had earned 4,570 points and $3.1 million.

Summary

Tony Stewart became known in his field as one of the brightest prospects in NASCAR racing. After only a few years of professional racing he had achieved many honors, including the Indianapolis 500 Rookie of the Year award and the NASCAR Rookie of the Year award.

Scott A. G. M. Crawford

HONORS, AWARDS, AND MILESTONES

1995	U.S. Auto Club Triple Crown winner; first driver to ever win the National Midget, Sprint, and Silver Crown championships in one year
1996	Indy Racing League Rookie of the Year
	Indianapolis 500 Rookie of the Year
	Indy 500 pole sitter
1997	Indy Racing League Champion
1999	NASCAR Rookie of the Year
	Set fast lap record at Indianapolis for the IRL

Additional Sources:

Mello, Tara Baukus. *Tony Stewart.* Philadelphia: Chelsea House, 2000.

Pillsbury, Richard. "Stock Car Racing." In *The Theater of Sport*, edited by Karl B. Raitz. Baltimore: Johns Hopkins University Press, 1995.

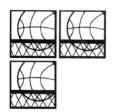

JOHN STOCKTON

Sport: Basketball

Born: March 26, 1962
Spokane, Washington

Early Life

John Houston Stockton was born on March 26, 1962, to Jack and Clementine Stockton. His father owned and operated a neighborhood tavern that stood next door to the Stockton house.

Stockton began playing basketball as a youth on the court behind his house; his first competition came from his older brothers. He was often the smallest player in those early games, but he compensated by playing harder and smarter than anyone else. He would retreat to that backyard basketball court in all kinds of weather, rain or shine, sometimes playing until late at night, in order to make himself a better player. "The only person in the world who thought John would play in the NBA was John," his father later recalled.

The Road to Excellence

John did not have far to go to continue his basketball career. He played his high school basketball at Gonzaga Prep in Spokane and later attended Gonzaga University, the local college in Spokane. His coaches at both schools began to notice that John was an uncommon player. While most other players looked to shoot the ball whenever they got it, John was more eager to pass, an ability that made him an extremely valuable player.

John never did grow very big. At 6 feet 1 inch and 170 pounds, he was no bigger than many of the fans who would come to watch his high school and college games. He played smarter and with more determination than anyone around him, and he was blessed with an uncanny ability to see all the players on the court at once, which contributed to his amazing passing ability.

John's college career started slowly at first, and he averaged just 3 points per game in his freshman season at Gonzaga. As time went on, however, he adjusted to the level of competition, and he averaged 20 points per game in

Courtesy NBA

STATISTICS

Season	GP	FGM	FG%	FTM	FT%	Reb.	Ast.	TP	PPG
1984-85	82	157	.471	142	.736	105	415	458	5.6
1985-86	82	228	.489	172	.839	179	610	630	7.7
1986-87	82	231	.499	179	.782	151	670	648	7.9
1987-88	82	454	.574	272	.840	237	**1,128**	1,204	14.7
1988-89	82	497	.538	390	.863	248	**1,118**	1,400	17.1
1989-90	78	472	.514	354	.819	206	**1,134**	1,345	17.2
1990-91	82	496	.507	363	.836	237	**1,164**	1,413	17.2
1991-92	82	453	.482	308	.842	270	**1,126**	1,297	15.8
1992-93	82	437	.486	293	.798	237	**987**	1,239	15.1
1993-94	82	458	.528	272	.805	258	**1,031**	1,236	15.1
1994-95	82	429	.542	246	.804	251	1,011	1,206	14.7
1995-96	82	440	.538	234	.830	226	916	1,209	14.7
1996-97	82	416	.548	275	.846	228	860	1,183	14.4
1997-98	64	270	.528	191	.827	166	543	770	12.0
1998-99	50	200	.488	137	.811	146	374	553	11.1
1999-00	82	363	.501	221	.860	215	703	990	12.1
2000-01	82	328	.504	227	.817	277	713	944	11.5
Totals	1,340	6,329	.517	4,276	.824	3,637	14,503	17,725	13.0

Notes: Boldface indicates statistical leader. GP = games played; FGM = field goals made; FG% = field goal percentage; FTM = free throws made; FT% = free throw percentage; Reb. = rebounds; Ast. = assists; TP = total points; PPG = points per game

his senior season. Moreover, he was always a marvelous passer.

The Emerging Champion

Small Gonzaga University is not a hotbed of professional basketball prospects, but John's talents were so obvious to National Basketball Association (NBA) scouts that several teams were interested in drafting him out of college. The Utah Jazz chose John with the sixteenth pick overall in the 1984 NBA draft.

Again, John struggled at first adjusting to a new level of competition. He did not start regularly in his first three seasons in the league. Instead, he backed up solid veteran Ricky Green at point guard. In his first three seasons, John did not average more than 8 points per game.

Yet things were changing in Utah. The year after the Jazz drafted John, the team selected a burly forward named Karl Malone out of another little-known college. Together, Malone and John would make Utah one of the best teams in the league during the late 1980's and early 1990's.

In the 1987-1988 season, John almost doubled his scoring, raising his average to 14.7 points per game. He also led the NBA in assists. That would be only the beginning; John went on to become the league's annual leader in assists,

dishing out more than 1,000 assists in five consecutive seasons.

Continuing the Story

During the late 1980's, John became known as the best passer in the game, and he and Malone became one of the best combinations in professional basketball. Malone would get open underneath the basket or on the fast break, and John would get the ball to him for another 2 points for Utah. It was a combination that was hard to beat. John and Malone even shared most valuable player honors in the 1993 NBA All-Star game, which was played on their home floor in Utah.

As John continued to play well, players, coaches, and sportswriters from all over the league began to notice him. He made the All-Star team four years in a row, and he became a more dangerous shooter during those years as well, averaging as many as 17.2 points per game. John did not rest on the defensive end of the court either, earning a reputation as a tenacious defender and twice leading the league in steals. Although he was among the smallest players in the league, John clearly showed that he belonged in professional basketball and that he deserved to be mentioned as among the best players of his time.

The ultimate accolade came following the 1991-1992 NBA season. For the first time ever,

HONORS AND AWARDS

1988-90,1992-93,1996	All-NBA Second Team
1988-96	Led NBA in assists per game
1989,1991-92	NBA All-Defensive Second Team
1991,1997,1999	All-NBA Third Team
1989-97, 2000	NBA All-Star Team
1992,1996	Gold Medal, Olympic Basketball
1993	NBA All-Star Game most valuable player
1994-95	All-NBA First Team
1996	NBA 50 Greatest Players of All Time Team

NBA players would be allowed to play on the U.S. Olympic team. The biggest stars in basketball were picked for the squad, including Michael Jordan, Magic Johnson, and Larry Bird. Basketball experts knew the team would need good passers and picked John for the team, which easily captured the gold medal for the United States. John earned another gold medal playing for the United States on "Dream Team II" in the 1996 Olympics in Atlanta. As part of the celebration of the golden anniversary of the NBA during the 1996-1997 season, John was named to the NBA's 50 Greatest Players of All Time Team.

John owns almost every passing record in the NBA, including the most career assists (13,790), the most assists in a single season (1,126), the most seasons with over 1,000 assists (7), the most times leading the league in assists (9), the most consecutive years leading the NBA in assists (9), and the highest career assist average (11.0). He also holds the career record for the most steals (2,844). John has been selected to the All-NBA First Team twice (1994, 1995), the All-NBA Second Team six times (1988, 1989, 1990, 1992, 1993, 1996), and the All-NBA Third Team three times (1991, 1997, 1999). He has been named an NBA All-Star on nine occasions.

Former Utah Jazz coach Frank Layden thinks that John is the best pure point guard to ever play in the NBA. John has a keen sense of where everyone is on the court and makes precision passes. He is extremely intense and focused on the basketball court and always gives everything he has to win. John and Karl Malone have performed the pick and roll more effectively and consistently than any other duo in the history of the NBA. After leading the NBA in assists every year from 1988 to 1996, John's average dropped to 7.5 in 1999 but increased to 8.6 in 2000. On November 26, 2000, John established the NBA record for the most games played for one team, 1,271 games with the Utah Jazz, which broke the previous record of 1,270 games played by John Havlicek for the Boston Celtics.

Summary

Although he might not have looked like a basketball player, John Stockton proved that he could succeed in the NBA thanks to his determination and court awareness. His ball handling and passing skills and his consistent play made him one of the best point guards in basketball history.

John McNamara

Additional Sources:

Bjarkman, Peter C. *The Biographical History of Basketball.* Chicago: Masters Press, 1998.

Deseret News Firm. *The Jazz: Utah's Dream Team.* Salt Lake City, Utah: Deseret News, 1997.

Lewis, Michael C. *To the Brink: Stockton, Malone, and the Utah Jazz's Climb to the Edge of Glory.* New York: Simon & Schuster, 1998.

Shouler, Kenneth A. *The Experts Pick Basketball's Best Fifty Players in the Last Fifty Years.* Lenexa, Kans.: Addax, 1998.

DWIGHT STONES

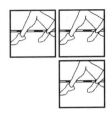

Sport: Track and field (high jump)

Born: December 6, 1953
Los Angeles, California

Early Life

Dwight Stones was born on December 6, 1953, in Los Angeles, California, to Richard and Sandy Stones. The Stoneses were barely more than teenagers when Dwight was born and they went through a great deal of marital strife in Dwight's early years. Their second child, Tammy, came when Dwight was five and brought family tensions to a climax.

Instead of a regular kindergarten experience, Dwight was sent to a military academy where he boarded all week. He disliked the brutality of the school and wanted to be home. When Dwight's parents divorced, he returned home and became very close to his mother, promising her that one day he would be a great baseball star and buy her a sable coat.

On July 21, 1963, at the age of nine, Dwight discovered the high jump event while watching the Soviet high jumper, Valery Brumel, compete and set a world record. Brumel became his idol that day, almost ten years to the day that Dwight himself would set a world record in the event. Dwight said goodbye to baseball and constructed a crossbar and jumping pit in his back yard.

High jumper Dwight Stones at the 1976 Olympics.

AP/Wide World Photos

2663

The Road to Excellence

Dwight had spent part of his adolescence in a private church school, but as he moved into his teen years, he entered Glendale High School. Outside the public school system that his mother had regarded as too liberal, Dwight had become fiercely independent, and he brought this spirit with him to the highly structured teenage world of the public high school.

He disliked team sports and found in the world of track and field and the high jump event a way to express his individuality and to seek personal achievement.

At first, the tall and lanky Dwight (6 feet 5 inches by the time he was a senior) entered track and field sports because he thought it might make him popular, especially with young ladies. When he found that, in fact, he was good at what he was doing, he began to concentrate on the discipline he needed to be the best he could be.

He adopted the jumping style of former Olympian Dick Fosbury, whose "Fosbury flop" featured a leap over the crossbar backward, head first instead of the traditional feet-first style.

Dwight's brash and often egotistical behavior alienated him from his teammates, however. His high school coach, John Barnes, a former 1952 Olympian, steadied the conceited young man and helped him to see that his potential was tied to self-control.

As a high school senior in 1971, Dwight cleared 7 feet for the first of many times in his career, and was offered a scholarship at the University of California at Los Angeles (UCLA).

The Emerging Champion

Dwight's career at UCLA was off to a remarkable start when he made the United States Olympic team as an eighteen-year-old college freshman and headed for Munich. There he jumped 7 feet 3 inches and earned a bronze medal. It seemed clear to track and field experts that Dwight was destined to be the greatest high jumper of all time, even better than his idol, Valery Brumel.

After this great success, Dwight became bored and impatient with his coaching and the overall situation at UCLA and eventually dropped out. He aligned himself with the Pacific Coast Club, an independent, amateur track and field organization, and participated in meets both nationally and internationally under their auspices.

Dwight was bringing attention to a somewhat obscure event and doing so in grand style. He became famous for his outspokenness and for his outlandish Mickey Mouse T-shirts that he would discard only minutes before his competitions. To a public accustomed to silent, and virtually interchangeable, track athletes, Dwight stood out. He became known as "the mouth with legs."

Dwight made predictions about how high he would jump in order to draw fans to the major track and field events. In so doing, he became in a sense the kind of athlete that sports fans love to hate. In 1973, he set the world indoor record at 7 feet 6½ inches. Between 1973 and 1976, Dwight would break and then extend his own world indoor and outdoor records in the high jump several times.

Continuing the Story

Dwight hoped that the Olympics in Montreal would be the shining, climactic moment that would make his controversial public image worth all the pain it had brought him. He could not

STATISTICS

Year	Competition	Event	Place	Height
1972	Olympic Games	High jump	Bronze	7′ 3″ (2.21 meters)
	NCAA Championships	High jump	3d	7′ 2″
1973	National AAU Outdoor Championships	High jump	1st	7′ 5″
	National AAU Indoor Championships	High jump	1st	7′ 0″
1974	National AAU Outdoor Championships	High jump	1st	7′ 3¼″
1975	National AAU Indoor Championships	High jump	1st	7′ 3″
1976	Olympic Games	High jump	Bronze	7′ 3″ (2.21 meters)
	NCAA Outdoor Championships	High jump	1st	7′ 7″
	NCAA Indoor Championships	High jump	1st	7′ 3″
	National AAU Outdoor Championships	High jump	1st	7′ 4¼″
1978	National AAU Indoor Championships	High jump	1st	7′ 4½″
1982	National AAU Indoor Championships	High jump	1st	7′ 4½″
1984	Olympic Games	High jump	4th	—

imagine another third place finish, and in fact anticipated that he would dominate the event—perhaps by as much as four inches.

Unfortunately, the weather in Montreal and the overall conditions in Olympic Stadium did not cooperate. On the day of the final round, a downpour made the footing on the approach slippery, and Dwight hydroplaned, unable to match the height of the eventual winner. He reluctantly accepted the bronze medal. Four days later, Dwight would set a world outdoor record with a jump of 7 feet 7¼ inches.

In 1978, Dwight competed in the World Superstars competition sponsored by the ABC television network and earned more than $30,000. This participation embroiled him in a bitter dispute with the Amateur Athletic Union that resulted in his being stripped of his amateur status and kept him from participating in sanctioned national and international events.

Dwight eventually regained his amateur status, but not his form. He made the 1980 Olympic team but did not compete because of the United States Olympic boycott against the Moscow site. His talents faltering, Dwight made one last attempt, at the age of thirty-five, to compete at his former level, but found he could cross the bar at a level no higher than 7 feet at the 1988 Olympic trials in Indianapolis. He then became a sought-after television commentator for track and field events.

Summary

Dwight Stones remains one of the most colorful characters in American track and field leg-

HONORS, AWARDS, AND RECORDS	
1972	Won Pacific-Eight Conference title
1973	Set a world indoor record in the high jump (7′ 6½″) Set a world record in the high jump (7′ 6⅝″)
1975-76	*Track and Field* News Indoor Athlete of the Year
1976	Set world records in the high jump twice (7′ 7″ and 7′ 7¼″) Set a world outdoor record in the high jump (7′ 7¼″)

end. His fiery and sometimes outlandish behavior brightened up a sport often beset by dull sameness. Despite his heartbreaking third-place finishes at the Olympic games and his controversies with amateur athletic officials, Dwight brought to track and field competition a verve and an independence that has rarely been seen before or since.

Bruce L. Edwards

Additional Sources:

Bateman, Hal. *United States Track and Field Olympians, 1896-1980*. Indianapolis, Ind.: The Athletics Congress of the United States, 1984.

Hickok, Ralph. *A Who's Who of Sports Champions*. Boston: Houghton Mifflin, 1995.

The Lincoln Library of Sports Champions. 16 vols. Columbus, Ohio: Frontier Press, 1993.

Wallechinsky, David. *The Complete Book of the Olympics*. Boston: Little, Brown and Company, 1991.

Watman, Mel. *Encyclopedia of Track and Field Athletics*. New York: St. Martin's Press, 1981.

CURTIS STRANGE

Sport: Golf

Born: January 30, 1955
Norfolk, Virginia

Early Life

Curtis Northrup Strange was born on January 30, 1955, in Norfolk, Virginia. His father was a golf professional. Curtis spent part of his boyhood doing chores around the professional shop for his dad. When he was seven, he began to play golf. By eight years of age, he was playing at the White Sands Country Club in Virginia Beach every day. At age fourteen, Curtis lost his thirty-nine-year-old father to cancer. This tragedy left him determined to succeed at the game of golf.

The Road to Excellence

In college at Wake Forest University in Winston-Salem, North Carolina, Curtis was nicknamed "Brutus" by his fraternity brothers. His golf game was formidable. He won the 1973 South-eastern Amateur at age eighteen. He was National Collegiate Athletic Association (NCAA) champion and Western Amateur champion in 1974. In the NCAA Championship, coming to the last hole, he needed to make an eagle 3 on a water-guarded par 5 to win the individual title and carry his team to victory. Curtis used a 1-iron to bring the ball to within ten feet of the hole and sank the putt. He won the Eastern Amateur in 1975, which his father had won in 1957. In 1975, he was also North and South Amateur champion. That same year, he was on the Walker Cup team, taking 3½ points of a possible 4. In addition, he was 1974 College Player of the Year and 1975 and 1976 Virginia State Amateur champion. In 1976, he again won the North and South Amateur Championship and decided to turn professional after a short but brilliant amateur career.

It was during this period of time that he met his wife, Sarah. They were married and later had two sons, Thomas Wright III and David Clark.

The Emerging Champion

In the spring of 1977, Curtis attended golf qualifying school and turned professional. His first two years as a professional resulted in Curtis's lowest rankings and money winnings as a professional golfer. He ranked eighty-seventh and eighty-ninth in 1977 and 1978, respectively. He won useful, although not large, sums of

Golfer Curtis Strange putts at the Masters in 1995.

money before breaking into the top sixty. His third year as a professional saw Curtis jump to twenty-first in the rankings, and in his fourth year, he was up to number three. It was in 1979 and after that he became a big money winner and a highly consistent player. He won his first tournament in 1979, the Pensacola Open, with a 62 in the third round. He won the Houston Open and the Westchester Classic the following year when, with $271,888, he was third in winnings and third in stroke average. At age twenty-seven in 1983, he was destined to become a major championship winner and a frequent tournament winner.

Curtis did not win a tournament in 1981 or 1982, but topped $200,000 in winnings both years. He lost in a playoff for the 1981 Tournament Players Championship. In 1982, he set a new income high for a nonwinner, with winnings of $263,378, and was third in stroke average. In 1983, Curtis won the Sammy Davis, Jr.-Greater Hartford Open. In 1984, he won the LaJet Classic. Curtis had another big year in 1985, winning the Honda Classic, Panasonic-Las Vegas Invitational, and Canadian Open. That year at the Masters, everything was going right. He said, "I had blinders on and I was making a lot of birdies starting Friday morning and continuing on until the very end Sunday." He did not finish with a win, one of the rare occasions on which Curtis did not come through in the clutch.

Continuing the Story

In 1986, Curtis won the Houston Open, and in 1987, he won the Canadian Open, the Federal Express-St. Jude Classic, and the NEC World Series of Golf.

Curtis's strength has been control. He does not make long drives, although he can on occasion, but he can drive straight, especially under pressure. He was ranked fifth, third, and eleventh in driving accuracy on the tour during 1988, 1989, and 1990. He has been a very good iron player, making many holes from the fairway. He ranked as high as twelfth in greens hit in regulation in 1987. He proved to be a deadly putter. He was among the top twenty in the tour's putting statistics in 1989.

In 1988, Curtis was on the Independent Insurance Agent Open, the Memorial Tournament, and the Nabisco Championship at Pebble Beach,

MAJOR CHAMPIONSHIP VICTORIES	
1988-89	U.S. Open

OTHER NOTABLE VICTORIES	
1974	NCAA Championship World Amateur Cup
1975-76	North and South Amateur
1979	Pensacola Open
1980	Manufacturers Hanover Westchester Classic Michelob-Houston Open
1983	Sammy Davis, Jr. Greater Hartford Open
1983, 1985, 1987, 1989	Ryder Cup team
1985	Panasonic-Las Vegas Invitational
1985, 1987	Canadian Open
1986	Houston Open
1988	Memorial Tournament Nabisco Championships
1993	Greg Norman's Holden Classic

his biggest money day. There he birdied the second extra hole to defeat Tom Kite. It was worth $360,000 plus the season-long bonus money of $175,000. The most important victory of the year was the United States Open. In 1988, he was obvious choice for Player of the Year. His victory in 1988 at the Country Club in Brookline, Massachusetts, was in a playoff over Nick Faldo, 71 to 75. In 1989, he played brilliantly through the final holes at Oak Hill in Rochester, New York, to win again. He became the first since Ben Hogan (1950-1951) to win the title in back-to-back years.

When Curtis Strange teed off at Medinah in 1990, he was attempting something few golfers have had an opportunity to accomplish: winning three consecutive United States Open titles. The last man to make the attempt was Ben Hogan in 1952. Curtis's bid for the third consecutive was not successful, as he shot an opening 73 followed by a second round of 70. He came close again in 1994 when he missed the playoff by one stroke.

In 1999, Curtis was selected to captain the 2000 U.S. Ryder Cup team. That year he also had three top twenty-five finishes. His best finish in 2000 was a tie for fifteenth at the MCI Classic. Curtis began a career in broadcasting in 1997 when he joined ABC Sports as lead golf analyst

RECORDS AND MILESTONES

PGA Tour leading money winner (1985, 1987-88)

Set a record on the PGA Tour in 1987, winning $925,941

First player in Tour history to exceed $1 million in official earnings in a single season (1989). He won four times that year and collected $1,147,644

HONORS AND AWARDS

1974	College Player of the Year
1980	*Golf Digest* Most Improved Player
1985, 1987	*Golf* magazine Player of the Year
1985, 1987-88	Arnold Palmer Award as leading money winner Golf Writers Player of the Year *Golf Digest* Byron Nelson Award
1988	PGA Player of the Year

and continued to cover tournaments for ABC in 2000.

Summary

Since joining the tour, Curtis Strange has won seventeen tournaments. Curtis can be counted as one of the all-time greats in the game of golf. He won twelve times on the PGA tour in six years. He was three-time winner of the Arnold Palmer Award as leading money winner. In 1989, he became the first player in tour history to exceed the $1 million mark in official earnings in a single season. He won four times that year and collected $1,147,644.

From childhood to adulthood, Curtis has worked on mastering the skills of the sport, competing and sharing his knowledge with others. His outstanding professional career has been highlighted with back-to-back United States Open wins.

Judy C. Peel

Additional Sources:
Hawkins, John. "A Man for All Seasons." *Golf World* 49, no. 14 (1995).
_____. "What a Strange Trip It's Been." *Golf World* 52, no. 16 (1998).
Kiersh, Ed. "Curtis Strange." *Sport* 88, no. 4 (1997).
Moriarity, Jim. "Q and A with Curtis Strange." *Golf World* 49, no. 20 (1995).
Strange, Curtis, with Kenneth Van Kampen. *Win and Win Again: Techniques for Playing Consistently Great Golf*. Chicago: Contemporary Books, 1990.

DARRYL STRAWBERRY

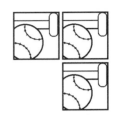

Sport: Baseball

Born: March 12, 1962
Los Angeles, California

Early Life

Darryl Eugene Strawberry was born on March 12, 1962, in Los Angeles, California. Darryl was graduated from Crenshaw High School. Other famous graduates of Crenshaw include former National Basketball Association star Marques Johnson, former National Football League star Wendell Tyler, and Detroit Tigers infielder Chris Brown. At Crenshaw High School, Darryl hit .371 with 4 home runs as a junior and .400 with 5 home runs as a senior. Darryl was clearly a gifted young athlete. When not playing baseball, Darryl helped his high school basketball team win the city championship. Darryl came from a sports-minded family: Brother Michael played minor league ball with the Dodgers, and brother Ronnie played college ball in Los Angeles.

The Road to Excellence

Darryl Strawberry was the first player in the nation to be selected in the 1980 draft. Drafted by the New York Mets and assigned to Kingsport in the Appalachian League, Darryl responded by getting a hit in his very first professional at bat. In 1982, Darryl led the Texas league in home runs (34), walks (100), and slugging percentage (.604), and he was named the league's most valuable player. He was elevated to Tidewater of the International League in 1983 and helped the Tides capture the International League post-season Championship. The next stop for Darryl was the major leagues.

Big things were expected from Darryl right from the beginning. As a number-one draft choice in a city that placed high demands on its athletes, Darryl Strawberry became a household name even before he set his eyes on Shea Stadium. Darryl was frequently compared to the likes of Hank Aaron, Willie Mays, and Ted Williams. A long way from his Los

New York Yankee Darryl Strawberry during a spring training game in March, 1997.

AP/Wide World Photos

STATISTICS

Season	GP	AB	Hits	2B	3B	HR	Runs	RBI	BA	SA
1983	122	420	108	15	7	26	63	74	.257	.512
1984	147	522	131	27	4	26	75	97	.251	.467
1985	111	393	109	15	4	29	78	79	.277	.557
1986	136	475	123	27	5	27	76	93	.259	.507
1987	154	532	151	32	5	**39**	108	104	.284	.583
1988	153	543	146	27	3	39	101	101	.269	**.545**
1989	134	476	107	26	1	29	69	77	.225	.466
1990	152	542	150	18	1	37	92	108	.277	.518
1991	139	505	134	22	4	28	86	99	.265	.491
1992	43	156	37	8	0	5	20	25	.237	.385
1993	32	100	14	2	0	5	12	12	.140	.310
1994	29	92	22	3	1	4	13	17	.239	.424
1995	32	87	24	4	1	3	15	13	.276	.448
1996	63	202	53	13	0	11	35	36	.262	.490
1997	11	29	3	1	0	0	1	2	.103	.138
1998	101	295	73	11	2	24	44	57	.247	.542
1999	24	49	16	5	0	3	10	6	.327	.612
Totals	1,583	5,418	1,401	256	38	335	898	1,000	.259	.505

Notes: Boldface indicates statistical leader. GP = games played; AB = at bats; 2B = doubles; 3B = triples; HR = home runs; RBI = runs batted in; BA = batting average; SA = slugging average

Angeles home and under such pressure to perform well, Darryl put together an excellent first season. Voted the National League Rookie of the Year, Darryl set several Mets club records, including most home runs by a left-handed batter (26), most home runs by a rookie (26), and most runs batted in by a rookie (74).

The Emerging Champion

Darryl hit 81 home runs during his first three years in the major leagues. Baseball experts were amazed at his home-run power. Although his swing looked effortless, Darryl hit some of the longest home runs recorded in baseball history. During a home-run hitting contest at the 1986 All-Star game in Houston, for example, Darryl showed his awesome power by striking a speaker hanging from the roof in center field.

The 1986 baseball campaign was a year neither Darryl nor any baseball fan will likely forget. The top vote-getter in the major league All-Star balloting with a record number of 1,619,516 votes, Daryl led the Mets in home runs and runs batted in (RBIs). In 1986, Daryl led all players in the League Championship Series against Houston with 2 home runs and 5 RBIs and inspired his team not to give up. The Mets rallied from behind on several occasions, including a 2-out, 3-run rally in the sixth game of

the World Series against the Boston Red Sox. Many will never forget the chanting of "Darryl, Darryl" by the Boston Red Sox fans, a custom that has now become a baseball ritual in many ballparks.

As he clearly emerged as one of the New York Mets' all-time best power hitters and reached superstar status after only a few seasons, life in New York, both on and off the playing field, was not easy for Darryl. He was often criticized by coaches, fans, and even some of his own teammates. No matter how well he performed, the New York fans and media never seemed satisfied and wanted more and more from the tall, lean right fielder.

Continuing the Story

Difficulties in his personal life did not help the young superstar. On February 3, 1990, Darryl, after admitting an alcohol problem, entered a rehabilitation center for alcohol abuse in New York. Having taken the courageous step to admit his problem, Darryl rejoined the team in time for spring training. After starting the season slowly, Darryl put together an eighteen-game hitting streak, hit 18 home runs in the month of June, and never looked back. Often credited with single-handedly carrying the team, Darryl kept the Mets in the pennant race until the last week of the season and ended the year with one of his best home-run productions (37) and drove in 101 RBIs.

At the end of the 1990 season, Darryl realized a lifelong dream by signing a five-year contract worth $20.5 million to play with the Los Angeles Dodgers. The pressures of playing in New York were behind him. Beginning in the spring of 1991, Darryl would play every day in front of his family, his childhood friends, and the enthusiastic Dodger fans, all waiting for big things from their hometown hero. He also began to talk openly about his recent conversion to Christianity—the source, he said, of a newfound sense of peace that now influenced him both as an athlete and as a person.

During the 1991 season, Darryl got off to a slow start. By mid-season, he was still hitting poorly, and his well-publicized conversion came under some criticism by those who claimed that he had lost his competitive, aggressive nature. Near the end of summer, however, Darryl somehow found it in time to kindle the Dodgers' play-off hopes. His teammates rallied around the rejuvenating presence of this bona fide superstar, and the resulting esprit de corps carried them through the last days of a close divisional race. They eventually lost the National League West division championship to a fired-up Atlanta Braves team by a single game. For the season, Darryl contributed a splendid 28 home runs and 99 RBIs.

For the next six seasons, Darryl struggled on and off the field. He spent two more seasons with the Dodgers and one with the Giants, then landed on the Yankee roster in 1995. During that time, he was convicted of tax evasion and assault. In 1995, he tested positive for cocaine use and was suspended from baseball for sixty days.

Having entered a drug rehabilitation center and submitted to regular drug testing, Darryl seemed to have turned things around for himself in New York. He had one of his strongest seasons

in 1998, playing in 101 games and hitting 24 homers. In October, as the Yankees were preparing to win their twenty-fourth world championship, Darryl underwent surgery to remove a cancerous tumor from his intestines. Even cancer did not stop him for long.

In the off-season following his surgery, Darryl joined the Yankees' AAA team in Columbus to get back into shape. He returned to the Yankee lineup in 1999, playing only twenty-four games but hitting homers in both the American League Division and Championship Series as the Yankees went on to win their second consecutive world championship.

Darryl tested positive again for cocaine in January, 2000, and received a one-year suspension. He also began chemotherapy treatment for his cancer, which came out of remission and was believed to have spread. At the age of thirty-eight, with his health deteriorating and once again in trouble with drugs, Darryl was not expected to return to baseball. He was fighting for much more than a return to the field. He was fighting for his life.

Summary

During his turbulent baseball career, Darryl Strawberry's natural talent on the field was equaled by his recklessness in his personal life. During his eight seasons with the Mets, he averaged 30 home runs each season and led them to two National League pennants and a World Championship, adding a second in 1999 with the Yankees. Though drug and health problems interrupted what could have been a Hall of Fame career, Darryl's accomplishments in the game of baseball have been considerable, and in the end he must be remembered for what he achieved and not what might have been.

Mary McElroy

Additional Sources:

Klapisch, Bob. *High and Tight: The Rise and Fall of Dwight Gooden and Darryl Strawberry.* New York: Villard, 1996.

Strawberry, Charisse, and Darryl Strawberry. *Recovering Life.* Farmington, Pa.: Plough, 1999.

Strawberry, Darryl, with Don Gold. *Hard Learnin'.* New York: Berkley Books, 1990.

HONORS AND AWARDS

1980	Overall first choice in the Major League Baseball draft
1983	National League Rookie of the Year
1984-91	National League All-Star Team

PICABO STREET

Sport: Skiing

Born: April 3, 1971
Triumph, Idaho

Early Life

Picabo Street was born on April 3, 1971, in Triumph, Idaho, to Roland Street II, a stonemason, and Dee Street, a music teacher. Picabo has an older brother, Roland III. The town of Triumph is located near the ski area of Sun Valley. Until she was three years old, her counterculture parents referred to Picabo as "Baby Girl." She was given the name Picabo because she liked to play the children's game of peek-a-boo. When the family decided to travel to Mexico and Central America, her parents had to put specific names on the children's passport applications. Her parents were free-thinking and believed that their children could give themselves their own names when they felt like it.

Until Picabo was fourteen, there was no television in the Street home. She was very active as a child and enjoyed playing with the local boys. There were only eight children in the entire town of Triumph, and Picabo was the only girl. Blessed with fearlessness as a child, she began skiing at her elementary school after it had begun a weekly ski program. Although her parents could not afford to dress Picabo in the latest ski clothes and accessories, she regularly beat children who were much older and who could afford to wear expensive ski apparel.

The Road to Excellence

In 1986 at the age of fifteen, Picabo was chosen for the United States junior ski team. She showed so much promise on the junior team that she was moved up to the United States ski team in 1987. Always a free spirit and a fiery competitor, she had trouble doing what the coaches told her to do. Although the coaches recognized that Picabo had the potential to be one of the best competitors on the ski team, they found her independent attitude difficult to handle. In 1990, she was suspended from the team because of her rebellious nature. Picabo visited her father, who was working in Hawaii, and he encouraged her to become more disciplined.

By the time she returned to the ski team in 1991, she was in excellent shape. At 5 feet 7 inches and weighing around 160 pounds, Picabo had molded herself into a powerful physical specimen. In 1991 and 1992, she was the North American Championship Series overall cham-

Skiier Picabo Street won a gold medal at the 1998 Winter Games.

AP/Wide World Photos

MAJOR CHAMPIONSHIPS

Year	Competition	Event	Place
1993	World Championships	Combined downhill/slalom	2d
		Downhill	10th
1994	Olympic Games	Super giant slalom (Super-G)	10th
		Downhill	Silver
1995	World Cup	Downhill standings (6 wins)	1st
1996	World Championships	Super-G	3d
1996	World Cup	Downhill standings (3 wins)	1st
1996	World Championships	Downhill	1st
1998	Olympic Games	Downhill	6th
		Super-G	Gold

pion. Picabo continued to improve, and she competed on her first World Cup circuit in 1992. She became the top United States female racer by improving her world ranking from forty-first to eighth place on the World Cup circuit. While there were still some experts who believed that Picabo was too undisciplined to succeed, she surprised both fans and critics alike at the 1993 World Alpine Ski Championships in Morioka, Japan, by capturing the silver medal in the combined downhill and slalom.

The Emerging Champion

In addition to winning the silver medal at Morioka, Japan, in 1993, Picabo won the gold medal at the United States Alpine Championships and the United States Super-Giant Slalom (Super-G) title. She was becoming popular with the media not only for her talent on the slopes but also for her all-American good looks and her willingness to speak her mind. While her coaches remained nervous with Picabo's impetuous nature, the media and the public fell in love with her zest for life.

Her next challenge would be at the 1994 Winter Olympics in Lillehammer, Norway. It was her dream to win an Olympic medal. In dramatic fashion Picabo's dream came true, when she won the silver medal in the downhill. She may have been edged out for the gold medal by Germany's Katja Seizinger, but Picabo was extremely satisfied with her results.

Building upon her silver medal at Lillehammer, Picabo had a marvelous 1994-1995 season

on the World Cup circuit. She won six out of the nine downhill races on the circuit that season and, therefore, captured the World Cup women's downhill title for 1995. Picabo was the first American—male or female—to win a World Cup downhill season championship. In 1996, she captured her second World Cup women's downhill title and won a gold medal in the downhill at the World Championships held in Sierra Nevada, Spain.

Picabo was at the top of the skiing world and had become a media celebrity, but on December 4, 1996, she suffered a debilitating knee injury while training in Vail, Colorado. She had torn the anterior cruciate and medial collateral ligaments in her left knee and needed many months of physical therapy before she could get back to skiing competitively.

Continuing the Story

Picabo persevered through six months of physical therapy and finally was able to resume skiing in July, 1997. She competed in several World Cup events toward the end of the year. Her confidence was on the rise when she had another accident on January 31, 1998, at a World Cup event in Are, Sweden. The accident took place merely six days before the 1998 Winter Olympics were to start. She suffered a minor concussion, a neck injury, and an assortment of bruises.

Not to be deterred, Picabo competed in the Winter Olympics at Nagano, Japan. Although her head and neck were still sore, she dramatically won the gold medal in the Super-G. She did not get to savor this victory for very long before tragedy struck once again. On March 13, 1998, she broke her left leg in nine places and tore ligaments in her right knee while competing in the final race of the World Cup season at Crans Montana, Switzerland. Always pushing herself, she would need to take more than a year off from skiing in order to properly recuperate from such a horrific accident.

As a world-renowned athlete and celebrity, Picabo appeared in commercials for various

2673

products. She also served as director of skiing at the Park City Mountain Resort located in Utah. Picabo was determined to be ready to compete again at the 2002 Winter Olympics in Salt Lake City, Utah.

Summary

Picabo Street established herself as one of the premier skiers of the 1990's. She was a fiery competitor who was not afraid to take risks in order to succeed on the slopes. Always outspoken and independent, she became a spokesperson for young girls who believed that they could also succeed if they worked hard enough and had nerves of steel. Picabo's love of skiing and love of competition made her one of the best skiers that the United States ever produced.

Jeffry Jensen

Additional Sources:

Cooper, Christin. "Picabo Rules." *Skiing* 48 (September, 1995): 102-107.

Dippold, Joel. *Picabo Street: Downhill Dynamo.* Rev. ed. Minneapolis: Lerner Publishing, 1998.

Layden, Tim. "Street Fighting." *Sports Illustrated* 88 (February 23, 1998): 40-45.

Reece, Gabrielle. "Picabo." *Women's Sports and Fitness,* November/December, 1998, p. 70-73.

Reibstein, Larry. "The Golden Girl." *Newsweek* 131 (February 23, 1998): 46-48.

SHIRLEY STRICKLAND-DE LA HUNTY

Sport: Track and field (sprints and hurdles)

Born: July 18, 1925
  Guildford, Western Australia, Australia

Early Life

In 1912, Fanny Durack became Australia's first woman to win an Olympic gold medal with a swimming victory in Stockholm. Australian sports historians Reet and Max Howell, in their *Foundations of Physical Education* (1984), quote from a 1912 interview with Miss Durack in an issue of the *Bulletin:* "I can spend hours in the water, and feel just as fresh coming out as I did going in. . . . I'm a good advertisement for swimming as exercise for girls."

Shirley Strickland was very much in the mold of Fanny Durack. She was born on July 18, 1925,

Shirley Strickland-de la Hunty competes in the 100-meter dash during the 1952 Olympic Games in Helsinki, where she won the bronze medal.

in Guildford, Western Australia, Australia. She loved running in the outdoors, and Western Australia is a state known for its wonderful beaches and warm climate. There was little warning, however, that Shirley was to go on to win an incredible total of seven Olympic medals.

The Road to Excellence

In many respects, Shirley began her climb to prominence in the shadow of the great Fanny Blankers-Koen of the Netherlands. It was Blankers-Koen who dominated the 1948 London Olympics with victories in the 100 meters, 200 meters, 80-meter hurdles, and the 4×100-meter relay. Nevertheless, in several of these contests, Shirley's presence sharpened the level of competition.

In the 100 meters, Shirley came in to win a bronze medal for Australia in a time of 12.2 seconds. She nearly repeated this performance in the 200 meters, where she placed fourth. Barry Hugman and Peter Arnold, in their *The Olympic Games* (1988), mention that several years later, an expert scrutinizing the photo-finish of this race declared that Strickland should have been awarded the bronze.

In the relay, Shirley showed her mettle by taking Australia into the lead on her leg, the third one. On the final leg, however, the thirty-year-old Blankers-Koen came through to take the gold. There was only .1 second between first and second—The Netherlands, 47.5 seconds, Australia, 47.6 seconds. Shirley went home without a gold medal but had a silver and two bronzes as a consolation. The other bronze medal was in the 80-meter hurdles, which was to become Shirley's premier event.

The Emerging Champion

Nothing stokes the competitive fire more effectively than near success, or silver and bronze med-

2675

als rather than gold. Shirley found that her teaching career allowed her to continue training year round and, four years later at the 1952 Helsinki Olympics, she hit top form. Female sprinters/hurdlers tend to mature in their early and mid-twenties, but, at twenty-seven years old, Shirley was in her prime. In the 100 meters, she took a bronze medal, the gold medalist being teammate Marjorie Jackson.

In the 80-meter hurdles, Shirley had revenge over Fanny Blankers-Koen, who hit the first two hurdles and stopped running. Shirley raced to the finishing line to win the elusive gold medal, setting Olympic and world records.

The relay was an upset of sorts. Australia, with Shirley showing great acceleration, set a world record of 46.1 seconds in the first heat. In the finals, however, a last changeover of the baton was mishandled and both the United States and West Germany set a world record of 45.9 seconds.

Continuing the Story

By 1956, Shirley, as many female athletes do, had integrated her name with that of her husband, becoming Shirley Strickland-de la Hunty. Not only had Shirley a new name, but she was thirty-one years of age, a mother, and an assistant lecturer in physics and mathematics at a Western Australian polytechnic, not far away from the University of Western Australia, where she had graduated in 1948.

There are many reasons to account for Shirley's longevity in track and field. Obviously, she trained intelligently and did the correct amount of stretching and flexibility exercises. Another point is that the 80-meter hurdles were primarily made for sprinters. The hurdles were less than three feet in height, and the event was ideal for Shirley's blazing speed. A final point is that the early 1950's saw a cluster of world-ranked Australian female track runners, including Shirley, Betty Cuthbert, Majorie Jackson-Nelson, and Marlen Matthews-Willard. Their exploits and successes created a sort of group sense of identity and permanence.

Another key factor in maintaining Shirley's concentration on track and keeping morale high was the role of her father. He had been an outstanding sprinter/hurdler, and his enthusiasm for what she did and his coaching role gave her the secure support that every good athlete relies upon.

At the 1956 Olympics, the world record holder, Zenta Gastl of Germany, was eliminated in the semifinals. In the finals, the athletes ran into the wind, but Shirley, after a good start, raced away to win in 10.7 seconds, an Olympic record.

In the first heat of the 4×100-meter relay, the Australians set a world record of 44.9 seconds. They had done the same thing four years earlier and had then finished as an "also ran" in fifth place.

STATISTICS

Year	Competition	Event	Place	Time
1948	Olympic Games	100 meters	Bronze	12.2
		200 meters	4th	—
		80-meter hurdles	Bronze	11.4
		4×100-meter relay	Silver	47.6
1950	Commonwealth Games	80-meter hurdles	Gold	11.6
		110-yard×220-yard×110-yard relay	Gold	47.9
		660-yard relay	Gold	1:13.4
1952	Olympic Games	100 meters	Bronze	11.5
		80-meter hurdles	Gold	10.9 WR, OR
		4×100-meter relay	5th	46.6
1956	Olympic Games	80-meter hurdles	Gold	10.7 WR
		4×100-meter relay	Gold	44.5 WR, OR

Notes: WR = World Record; OR = Olympic Record

RECORDS

First woman to break 11 seconds for the 80-meter hurdles
First Australian female track runner to win an Olympic gold medal
Shares record 7 Olympic medals with Irena Szewinska (née Kirszenstein)
Set world record at 100 meters in 1955 (11.3)
Set Australian records in 80-meter hurdles (10.7), 100 yards (11.0), and 400 meters, 440 yards (57.4)

HONORS AND AWARDS

1955	World Trophy

This time, however, there was no disaster. Shirley Strickland ran the first leg for the Australians and they took the gold medal in an Olympic and world record time of 44.5 seconds.

Summary

Shirley Strickland-de la Hunty was not only a highly successful athlete but also a versatile human being who succeeded in a variety of areas. At three successive Olympics she collected seven Olympic medals, three gold, one silver, and three bronze. She graduated from a good university, married, raised a family, and taught successfully. Shirley is generally considered one of the greatest woman sprinter/hurdlers of all time. English journalist and track administrator Jack Crump spoke of Shirley as "that grand athlete." He never uttered a truer word.

Scott A. G. M. Crawford

Additional Sources:

Drummond, Siobhan, and Elizabeth Rathburn, eds. *Grace and Glory: A Century of Women in the Olympics.* Chicago: Triumph Books, 1996.

Layden, Joe. *Women in Sports.* Santa Monica, Calif.: General Publishing, 1997.

Markel, Robert, Susan Waggoner, and Marcella Smith, eds. *The Women's Sports Encyclopedia.* New York: Henry Holt, 1997.

Wise, Michael T., Christina Bankes, and Jane Laing, eds. *Chronicle of the Olympics, 1896-1996.* New York: DK Publishing, 1996.

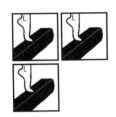

KERRI STRUG

Sport: Gymnastics

Born: November 19, 1977
Tucson, Arizona

Early Life

Kerri Allison Strug was born on November 19, 1977, in Tucson, Arizona, and is the daughter of a heart surgeon. She began gymnastic classes when she was three years old, following in the footsteps of her older brother, Kevin, and older sister, Lisa, who were aspiring gymnasts. A young daredevil, Kerri would often walk around the house on her hands. When Kerri was seven, her older sister attended gymnastic coach Bela Karolyi's summer camp in Houston. The coaches at the camp saw Kerri doing back flips and predicted she could become an Olympic champion.

The Road to Excellence

Kerri began competing in the gymnastics Class III division at age eight and won so many events that the next year she went on to the advanced optionals and state competitions and later the junior elite level. In 1989 at age twelve she captured the Junior B National Championship. The next year Kerri left home to train with Bela and Martha Karolyi in their gym in Houston, Texas.

Although her early gymnastics career forced her to live in several different places, her parents made a point of having Kerri attend regular schools rather than using a tutor to teach her at the gym. They felt it was important that she be around other children who were not involved in gymnastics. Kerri would work out in the gym from 7:30 to 10:30 A.M., then attend school from 11 A.M. to 3:30 P.M. She would return to the gym for practice from 5 to 8:30 P.M., and then do her homework in the evening. Even with this busy schedule, she finished high school a year early, earning all A's.

The Emerging Champion

In 1991 Kerri took first place in the vault competition of the U.S. Gymnastics Championships, becoming the youngest female ever to win an event title. That same year she joined the team that won the 1991 World Championships silver

An injured Kerry Strug at the 1996 Olympics, after her final vault clinched the U.S. team's gold medal.

medal. Kerri went to the 1992 Olympics in Barcelona, Spain, with high hopes but missed qualifying for the all-around finals by .014 of a point. She took home a team bronze medal but was disappointed to not make the all-around and vowed to make a comeback in 1996. Karolyi also seemed disappointed and retired from coaching soon after the competition.

Kerri's comeback bid was difficult. She bounced from coach to coach, and in 1993 she tore a stomach muscle. The following summer she fell from the uneven parallel bars, resulting in a severe back sprain that required intensive physical therapy.

By 1994, however, she was back in action, helping Team USA take second place in the Team World Championships. The next year she captured first place in the U.S. Olympic Festival's all-around competition. Meanwhile, Karolyi had come out of retirement and in 1995 began coaching Kerri once more. That year Kerri helped the U.S. women's gymnastics team take the bronze medal in the 1995 World Championships team competition. In 1996 she won the gold medal in the all-around competition of the McDonald's American Cup.

Kerri attracted worldwide attention during the 1996 Summer Olympics in Atlanta. Coming into the last team event, the vault, the American women's team led the Russian team by a slim margin. Kerri was the last to vault. On her first vault she suffered a fall, resulting in two torn ligaments and a serious ankle sprain, and scoring only a 9.162. Unaware that a poor performance by the Russian team on the balance beam had clinched the U.S. team's first-place spot, Kerri believed that without a strong second vault, the Americans could not take home the gold medal. The wildly cheering, pro-U.S. crowd quieted as Kerri clinched her teeth and limped down the runway in severe pain to earn a score of 9.712.

Following her final vault, Kerri was placed on a stretcher to be taken to the hospital for X-rays, but her teammates refused to proceed to the medal stand without her. Karolyi lifted the 4-foot 9-inch eighteen-year-old off her stretcher. In an emotional moment, the U.S. team marched out to accept their gold medals as a group, with Kerri in Karolyi's arms. Unfortunately, the injury prevented Kerri from competing in any individual

MAJOR CHAMPIONSHIPS			
Year	Competition	Event	Place
1991	World Gymnastics Championships	Women's team	2d
1992	Olympic Games	Women's team	3d
1994	Team World Gymnastic Championships	Women's team	2d
1995	World Gymnastics Championships	Women's team	3d

events leading to the all-around championships two days later, a goal she had held onto for the past four years.

Continuing the Story

Kerri received numerous awards as a result of her courage during the 1996 Olympic Games, including the Olympic Spirit Award, the ESPY Award for Performance Under Pressure, the Arete Award for Most Courageous Moment, the Hugh O'Brian Award for Most Inspirational Performance, and the Cedars-Sinai 1996 Courageous Athlete of the Year Award. Kerri and her Olympic teammates were featured on a Wheaties cereal box and on many television talk shows. She also appeared on the covers of *Time* and *People* magazines and on episodes of *Beverly Hills 90210*, *Saturday Night Live*, and *Touched by an Angel*.

She became a spokesperson for the Children's Miracle Network and Special Olympics and was featured on the 1996 Barbara Walters's "Ten Most Fascinating People" special. She was also involved with DARE, Pediatric AIDS, and the Make-A-Wish Foundation and received a Reebok/Lady Foot Locker Giving Back Award, presented by the Women's Sports Foundation. Kerri participated in the MGM/Ice Capades and the 1996 world gymnastics tour, then attended the University of California, Los Angeles, and Stanford University.

Summary

Kerri Strug demonstrated a unique courage that resulted in one of the most dramatic moments of the modern Olympic Games. By making a second vault on her injured ankle, eliminating herself from the later individual competitions, Kerri sacrificed her chance at an all-around medal for the good of her team.

Cheryl Pawlowski

2679

Additional Sources:

Hoffer, Richard. "Day 5: A Most Unlikely Hero." *Sports Illustrated*, August, 1996, 40.

Starr, Mark. "Leap of Faith: Gymnastics with One Inspirational Vault, the U.S. Women's Team Won a Gold Medal—and an Honored Place in Olympic History." *Newsweek* 5 (August 5, 1996): 40.

Strug, Kerri, Greg Brown, and Doug Keith. *Heart of Gold*. Dallas, Tex.: Taylor Publishing, 1996.

Strug, Kerri, and John P. Lopez. *Landing on My Feet: A Diary of Dreams*. Kansas City, Mo.: Andrews McMeel, 1998.

Wulf, Steve. "Faster, Higher, Braver: The U.S. Women Gymnasts Were the Saving Graces During the First Week of the Ill-Fated Centennial Games." *Time* 8 (August 5, 1996): 32.

NAIM SULEYMANOGLU

Sport: Weightlifting

Born: January 23, 1967
Ptichar, Bulgaria

Early Life

Naim Suleymanoglu was born Naim Suleimanov on January 23, 1967, in Ptichar, Bulgaria, a mountain village near the border of Bulgaria and Turkey. Naim's father, a miner and farmer, was barely 5 feet tall, and his mother stood only 4 feet 7½ inches, so it was no surprise that Naim,

too, was very small. Despite his size, young Naim enjoyed lifting rocks, branches, and other heavy objects, and at the age of ten, though he was less than 3 feet 9 inches tall, he impressed the adults at a local weightlifting center with his ability to carry the heavy plates used by the lifters.

The Road to Excellence

Because of his obvious talent, Naim was enrolled in one of Bulgaria's special sports schools when he was twelve in order to develop his lifting ability. His progress was almost unbelievably rapid. At the age of fourteen, he competed at the World Junior Championships in Brazil, and even though he was competing against lifters as much as five years older, he won the world nineteen-and-under title. Even more incredibly, his performances were within 5½ pounds of the world record for the combined lift. At the age of fifteen, he set his first world record. It would not be his last.

In the 1984 European Championships, at the age of sixteen, Naim became only the second man in history to lift three times his body weight overhead by hoisting 370 pounds. Though he stood only 5 feet tall and weighed less than 124 pounds, he was soon proclaimed the strongest man, pound-for-pound, in the world, and he was given the nickname "Pocket Hercules" by the press. He was an overwhelming favorite to take three gold medals in his weight class in the 1984 Olympic Games in Los Angeles.

Naim Suleymanoglu of Turkey is the first weightlifter to earn three Olympic gold medals.

2681

CHAMPIONSHIP TITLES

1982	World Junior bantamweight champion
1983	World Championships Silver Medalist (bantamweight division)
1984-86, 1988	European featherweight champion
1985-86	World featherweight champion
1988	Olympic gold Medalist (featherweight division)
1992	Olympic gold Medalist (featherweight division)
1996	Olympic gold Medalist (featherweight division)

The Emerging Champion

Bulgaria, though, joined the Soviet Union in its boycott of the 1984 Olympics in retaliation for the United States-led boycott of the 1980 Moscow Games, so Naim's Olympic plans were put on hold. Moreover, it was not long before Naim decided he did not want to be known as an international representative of Bulgaria.

Naim's family was part of a large minority of Bulgarians of Turkish descent living near the Bulgarian-Turkish border. In 1985, the Bulgarian government attempted to "Bulgarize" the Turkish minority, closing the mosques where the ethnic Turks practiced their Islamic faith and requiring that all Turkish names be changed to Slavic ones. Many Bulgarian Turks were killed and hundreds arrested in protests of the name-changing campaign. When Naim returned to Bulgaria from a training camp in Australia, he discovered that his name had been changed without his consent. The Bulgarian government had ordered him to use the name Naum Shalamanov.

The name change angered Naim, and though he continued to compete for the Bulgarian team and even set records under his new name, secretly he had decided to defect from Bulgaria at the first opportunity. At the World Cup competition in Melbourne, Australia, in December, 1986, Naim got his chance. Although the Bulgarian team had reportedly grown suspicious of Naim and assigned security guards to watch him, at the competition's closing banquet Naim managed to excuse himself, ostensibly to visit the men's room. Instead, Naim met another Bulgarian defector, and the two drove away into hiding.

At first, the president of the Bulgarian Weightlifting Federation claimed that Naim had been kidnapped by Turkish terrorists. Naim, though, assured police that he had left the team on his own, and he asked the Turkish government to grant him political asylum. He announced, too, that he was changing his name again—to its most-Turkish variation, Naim Suleymanoglu, which in Turkish means "Naim, the son of Suleyman."

Naim's request for Turkish asylum was granted almost immediately. He flew to London, and there the private jet of Turkey's prime minister, Turgat Ozal, picked Naim up and flew him to a hero's welcome in Ankara, Turkey. When he got off the plane in his new country, Naim kissed the airport runway.

The Turkish Weightlifting Federation supplied Naim with his own apartment and automobile and began paying him a monthly salary of $1,000, about three times as much as the average Turk made. Naim, though, was not able to repay his adopted country for its generosity immediately. Under the rules of the International Weightlifting Federation, Naim's citizenship change meant that he was required to wait twelve months before he was eligible to represent his new country in international competition.

When Naim did return to competition after a sixteen-month layoff, he did so in dramatic fashion. At the 1988 European Championships in Cardiff, Wales, Naim began the competition by setting a world record in the snatch, hoisting 150 kilograms—more than 330 pounds—over his head. In the process, he became the first man in history to snatch two and one-half times his body weight. Naim took the meet's gold medals for his weight class in the snatch, the clean and jerk, and the combined lift. More impressive still, his combined lift total was more than 5 pounds higher than the total of the winning lifter in the next-

RECORDS

Most combined lift weight lifted by a bantamweight, 661¼ pounds (1984)
Most weight snatched by a featherweight, 336 pounds (1988)
Most weight jerked by a featherweight, 418¾ pounds (1988)
Most combined lift weight lifted by a featherweight, 755 pounds (1988)
Youngest world record holder ever, 15 years 123 days (1982)
First man to snatch 2½ times own bodyweight

higher weight division. Naim's popularity in Turkey was so great that the entire meet was shown on Turkish television.

Continuing the Story

Naim's domination of the European Championships again made him a clear favorite for the Olympic Games. At the 1988 Olympics in Seoul, South Korea, Naim had to compete against his former Bulgarian teammates, who had claimed that they would erase all Naim's marks from the record books within a few years.

Naim responded in typical style, setting new world records in every event and sweeping the Olympic gold medals for his weight class. Naim's combined-lift total of 755 pounds was more than 60 pounds higher than the total lifted by the silver medalist, Stefan Topurov, a former teammate of Naim's from the Bulgarian squad. Naim was Turkey's first gold medalist in twenty years, and he gave credit to his new countrymen for his Olympic triumph. "I owe my success to the fifty-six million Turkish people who support me and love me," he said. "My strength comes from them." Naim returned to a hero's welcome in Turkey, where he is treated like a movie star.

Naim won the gold medal again in 1992 for the 60-kilogram (132-pound) division, lifting a combined total of 705 pounds. In 1996 Naim moved up to the 64-kilogram (141-pound) division and won his third gold medal, with a world record combined lift total of 738.5 pounds. With his third Olympic gold in hand, and widely considered one of the greatest weightlifting champions of all time, Naim retired.

Prior to the 2000 Olympics in Sydney, Naim announced that he would try for an unprecedented fourth gold medal. With just more than six months to prepare, Naim easily qualified. His performance at the Games, however, was disappointing. He missed on all three of his lifts and saw his record of three gold medals tied by Pyrros Dimas and Akakios Kakiasvilis of Greece.

Summary

Naim Suleymanoglu overcame both opposing weightlifters and a hostile government on his way to his record-breaking Olympic victory. Under any name, he has proven himself a champion. His seven world titles, six European championship medals, and three Olympic gold medals rank him among the century's greatest athletes.

Brook Wilson

Additional Sources:

Chidley, Joe, and James Deacon. "Getting It All Together." *Maclean's* 109, no. 32 (1996).

Hoffer, Richard. "An Uplifting Experience." *Sports Illustrated* 85, no. 7 (1996).

Levinson, David and Karen Christenson, eds. *Encyclopedia of World Sport: From Ancient Times to Present.* Santa Barbara, Calif.: ABC-CLIO, 1996.

Smith, Gary. "The Weight of the World." *Sports Illustrated* 77, no. 3 (1992).

Wallechinsky, David. *The Complete Book of the Olympics.* Boston: Little, Brown and Company, 1991.

SUN WEN

Sport: Soccer

Born: April 6, 1973
Shanghai, China

Early Life

Sun Wen (pronounced "soon when") was born on April 6, 1973, in Shanghai, China. When she was a child, it was not culturally popular or acceptable for a girl to play soccer or any sports. However, her father, Sun Zhong Gao, encouraged her to start playing the sport when she was ten years old. An avid soccer fan amd recreational player himself, Wen's father took her to try out for a local soccer team at a children's sports center in Shanghai. At age thirteen, Wen began standard training.

The Road to Excellence

While involved in regular soccer training, Wen continued her studies and earned a degree in languages, specializing in Mandarin. She made her first international appearance in 1990 and quickly earned a reputation as a gifted forward who could create scoring opportunities, both for herself and for her teammates.

The Emerging Champion

Wen scored twice in China's semifinal game at the 1995 Fédération Internationale de Football Association (FIFA) women's World Cup. In the 1996 Olympics, Wen helped China earn the silver medal. She scored her team's only goal in the 2-1 loss to the Americans, who were hosting the tournament. In the first half of that game, she received a pass from Zhou Hua and sent the ball over the U.S. goalie Briana Scurry.

Continuing the Story

Wen scored two goals in the first six minutes of the game against Taipei in the semifinals of the tenth Asian games, the tournament that qualified China to play in the 1999 FIFA women's World Cup. During this World Cup, held in the United States from June 19 through July 10, 1999, Wen emerged as the individual most highly rated by 150 accredited journalists. She won the Adidas Golden Ball Award for being the best player and shared the Adidas Golden Shoe as the joint top scorer with Brazilian Sissi.

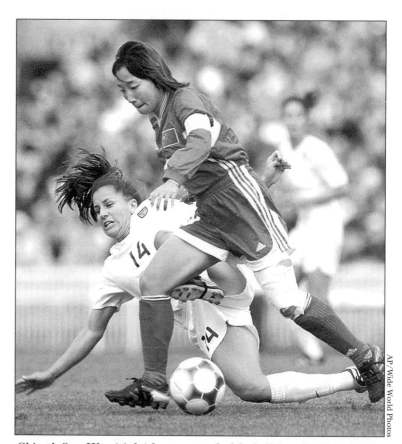

China's Sun Wen (right) keeps control of the ball from Joy Fawcett in a September, 2000, game against the United States.

2684

In interviews with the press in 1999, Wen spoke of her poetry, some of which has been published in newspapers, and her plans to earn a master's degree, perhaps in the United States. She was also featured in advertisements on U.S. television.

In February, 2000, major U.S. media companies, women soccer stars, and individual investors formed the Women's United Soccer Association (WUSA), the top women's professional soccer league in the world. With franchises in Atlanta, Boston, Carolina, New York, Philadelphia, San Diego, the San Francisco Bay Area, and Washington, the league's inaugural season was planned to begin in April, 2001.

In the meantime, Wen continued to distiguish herself in the 2000 Pacific Cup, in which she was injured during a game with Canada, and in the 2000 Olympics. On November 29, 2000, Wen and four other World Cup Chinese socccer players (midfielder Liu Ailing, goalkeeper Gao Hong, and defenders Wen Lirong and Fan Yunjie) signed with the WUSA.

Summary

With her excellence in the field of soccer, Sun Wen has contributed to increasing national popular support for the sport in China. Through her interest in popular culture and her awe-inspiring athletic skill, she has made substanial contributions to international goodwill.

Alice Myers

MAJOR CHAMPIONSHIPS

Year	Competition	Place
1991	Women's World Cup	5th
1992	Olympic Games	Gold
1993	World Championships	1st
1994	World Goodwill Games	1st
1995	Women's World Cup	4th
1996	Olympic Games	Silver
1998	Goodwill Games	2d
1998	Asian Games	1st
1999	Women's World Cup	2d
1999	Chinese Women's Super Cup with Shanghai team	1st

Additional Sources:

"Chinese Team, Led by High-Scoring Forward, Has Traveled the Long Road to Success." *Los Angeles Times,* July 9, 1999, p. D1.

Springer, Shira. "China's Winning Ways: National Women's Soccer Team Follows an Unforgiving Daily Schedule in Pursuit of First World Cup Title." *Boston Globe,* July 4, 1999.

Xueqin, Jiang. "Olympics: China, Ahead of the Field." *Asiaweek,* September 6, 2000, 1.

DON SUTTON

Sport: Baseball

Born: April 2, 1945
Clio, Alabama

Early Life

Donald Howard Sutton was the eldest of three children born to tenant farmers in Clio, Alabama, on April 2, 1945. He was born in a tar-paper shack, grew up in the little coal town, and credits his hardworking father, Howard, with giving him his work ethic. Don began playing baseball with a bat that was full of nails and listening to games on the radio late at night. He began throwing curveballs in the sixth grade under the

Pitcher for the Angels, Don Sutton in 1986.

guidance of his teacher, Henry Roper, who had pitched in the Giants organization. As an eleven-year-old, Don's pitching record was 9-0. His idol was the great Phillies pitcher Robin Roberts.

The Sutton family eventually moved to the Pensacola area of Florida, where Don also played high school football and basketball, was an A student, and was runner-up in the Florida Boy of the Year contest. He briefly attended Mississippi College before being signed to a professional contract with the Los Angeles Dodgers by Leon Hamilton, the Dodgers' legendary scout in the South. Don married and in time became the father of his first two children, Daron and Staci. Daron would grow up to become a college and minor league pitcher and, like his father, a baseball telecast analyst.

The Road to Excellence

Don pitched only one year in the minor leagues. He began 1965 with Santa Barbara in the California League but was soon promoted to Albuquerque. He won twenty-three games in thirty starts for the two teams and never saw the minor leagues again.

Barely twenty-one years of age, Don came to the Los Angeles Dodgers in 1966 and appeared in thirty-seven games, thirty-five as a starting pitcher. He was the fourth starter in a pitching rotation that also featured Sandy Koufax, Don Drysdale, and Claude Osteen. His 12-12 record that year, along with a 2.99 earned run average (ERA) and only 192 hits allowed in 225⅔ innings, earned him *The Sporting News* Rookie Pitcher of the Year award. His 209 strikeouts in 1966 were the most by a National League (NL) rookie since Grover Cleveland Alexander's 227 in 1911. He had the perfect build for a major league pitcher, at 6 feet 1 inch tall and 185 pounds.

Don's rookie year served as a harbinger of things to come. Only twice during the next

STATISTICS

Season	GP	GS	CG	IP	HA	BB	SO	W	L	S	ShO	ERA
1966	37	35	6	225.2	192	52	209	12	12	0	2	2.99
1967	37	34	11	232.2	223	57	169	11	15	1	3	3.95
1968	35	27	7	207.2	179	59	162	11	15	1	2	2.60
1969	41	41	11	293.1	269	91	217	17	18	0	4	3.47
1970	38	38	10	260.1	251	78	201	15	13	0	4	4.08
1971	38	37	12	265.1	231	55	194	17	12	1	4	2.54
1972	33	33	18	272.2	186	63	207	19	9	0	**9**	2.08
1973	33	33	14	256.1	196	56	200	18	10	0	3	2.42
1974	40	40	10	276.0	241	80	179	19	9	0	5	3.23
1975	35	35	11	254.1	202	62	175	16	13	0	4	2.87
1976	35	34	15	267.2	231	82	161	21	10	0	4	3.06
1977	33	33	9	240.1	207	69	150	14	8	0	3	3.18
1978	34	34	12	238.1	228	54	154	15	11	0	2	3.55
1979	33	32	6	226.0	201	61	146	12	15	1	1	3.82
1980	32	31	4	212.1	163	47	128	13	5	1	2	**2.20**
1981	23	23	6	158.2	132	29	104	11	9	0	3	2.61
1982	34	34	6	249.2	224	64	175	17	9	0	1	3.06
1983	31	31	4	220.1	209	54	134	8	13	0	0	4.08
1984	33	33	1	212.2	224	51	143	14	12	0	0	3.77
1985	34	34	1	226.0	221	59	107	15	10	0	1	3.86
1986	34	34	3	207.0	192	49	116	15	11	0	1	3.74
1987	35	34	1	191.2	199	41	99	11	11	0	0	4.70
1988	16	16	0	87.1	91	30	44	3	6	0	0	3.92
Totals	774	756	178	5,275.8	4,692	1,343	3,574	324	256	5	58	3.26

Note: Boldface indicates statistical leader. GP = games played; GS = games started; CG = complete games; IP = innings pitched; HA = hits allowed; BB = bases on balls (walks); SO = strikeouts; W = wins; L = losses; S = saves; ShO = shutouts; ERA = earned run average

twenty-two seasons would he win fewer than eleven games. When the articulate young pitcher soon found work in the off-season as a disc jockey at California radio stations, it was yet another sign of things to come.

The Emerging Champion

The pitching rotation of Koufax, Drysdale, Osteen, and Sutton proved to be the only four-some in baseball history in which every member pitched 40 or more shutouts during his career. Perhaps Don suffered by comparison with these great Dodger pitchers who were closing out their careers as he was beginning his. Still, in his first five seasons in the majors (1966-1970), he averaged thirteen wins per year. By the end of his career, Don would win 128 games more than Osteen, 115 games more than Drysdale, and 159 games more than Koufax—the latter two of whom were Hall of Fame pitchers.

Continuing the Story

By the 1970's, Don had become the ace of the Dodger pitching staff. During the decade, he never won fewer than twelve games annually. His best season was 1976 (21-10 with a 3.06 ERA). Apart from 1976, Don's most wins in any year were nineteen, but by the time he left the Dodgers, following the 1980 season, he had won 230 games. He was the team leader in wins, losses, games pitched, games started, strikeouts, innings pitched, hits allowed, shutouts, and opening-day starts (seven). He never struck out fewer than 128 batters in a season and struck out 200 or more five times. During his best year (1969), he struck out 217.

Don pitched for the Dodgers in three League Championship Series—1974, 1977, and 1978—and in three World Series—1974, 1977, and 1978. His record was 3-1 in the League Championship Series and 2-2 in the World Series. He was not an overpowering pitcher, as were Koufax and Drysdale. However, because of his excellent physical condition, he could be relied upon to pitch well over 200 innings every year. He gained a reputation as a "money player," the pitcher a manager wanted on the mound during a crucial game. Don's best pitch was an impressive curveball—so impressive, in fact, that he was often accused of "doctoring" the baseball with

2687

sandpaper. In 1978, he was ejected from a game for defacing the ball, but, when he threatened a lawsuit, the league let him off with a warning.

After fifteen seasons in Los Angeles, Don spent 1981-1987 pitching for Houston and for Milwaukee, California, and Oakland in the American League (AL). He pitched for Milwaukee in the 1982 AL League Championship Series and for California in the 1986 League Championship Series. While in Milwaukee, he also appeared in his fourth World Series in 1982. He returned to Los Angeles for an abbreviated 1988 season, collecting the last 3 of his 324 career victories. Don struck out 100 or more batters for twenty-one consecutive seasons and struck out 99 in his last full season, 1987. He pitched five one-hitters and nine two-hitters. His lifetime winning percentage was .559, and his ERA was 3.26. By the time of his retirement, Don had defeated every team in the major leagues.

Several factors may account for Don's greatness being insufficiently appreciated both during and after his career. He won twenty or more games only once, and he never won the Cy Young award. He never pitched a no-hitter. He was a member of excellent pitching staffs—seven times his staff led the National League in ERA—so he often shared the spotlight with other fine pitchers. Sophisticated, forthright, and outspoken, Don was not a person to curry favor. Once he even had a highly publicized altercation with a teammate, the popular Steve Garvey. The fact remains that only a tiny minority of all the pitchers who have ever played have won 300 games or more, and Don is a member of that elite minority.

Summary

A crowning achievement of Don Sutton's career was starting, winning, and being named

HONORS AND AWARDS

1966	*Sporting News* Rookie of the Year
1972, 1973, 1975, 1977	National League All-Star
1997	All-Star Game most valuable player
1998	Inducted into National Baseball Hall of Fame

most valuable player of the 1977 All-Star game. Overall, he allowed no runs in 8 All-Star innings. He used his speaking ability in announcing postseason games when his team was not involved. After retirement from baseball, he became a full-time member of the Atlanta Braves radio and television crew.

He was inducted into the Baseball Hall of Fame in Cooperstown, New York, on July 26, 1998, after having been passed over on four previous ballots. Don settled in Roswell, Georgia, with his wife, Mary, and his third child, daughter Jacqueline. Born sixteen weeks premature, Jacqueline (Jackie) had been given about a 100-1 chance to live. In his emotional induction speech into the Hall of Fame, Don expressed his gratitude for Jackie's being there to share the moment with him.

Patrick Adcock

Additional Sources:

Anderson, Bruce. "Little D Has His Biggest Day." *Sports Illustrated* 64 (June 30, 1986): 78.

Bell, Marty. "Don Sutton Does Not Bleed Dodger Blue." *Sport* 66 (June, 1978): 80-82.

Fimrite, Ron. "Blood on the Dodger Blue." *Sports Illustrated* 49 (September 4, 1978): 24-25.

Gay, Phillip Timothy. "Peach Brandy Man." *Sports Illustrated* 51 (August 13, 1979): 140-42.

Shatzkin, Mike, et al., eds. *The Ballplayers: Baseball's Ultimate Biographical Reference.* New York: Arbor House-William Morrow, 1990.

GUNDE SVAN

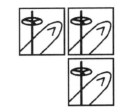

Sport: Skiing

Born: January 12, 1962
Dala-Jaerna, Sweden

Early Life

Gunde Svan was born on January 12, 1962, in Dala-Jaerna, Sweden. Cross-country skiing is an important sport in Sweden, and the best racers are major sports stars there.

Gunde's mother, who was forty-four when he was born, encouraged him to begin skiing at an early age. Gunde competed in his first ski race at age three. He remained standing at the starting line when all of the other racers began skiing; his mother got him to begin skiing by running alongside him. She continued to run with him all the way to the finish line.

The Road to Excellence

Early in his career, Gunde received instruction from his Uncle Ernst, a former skier who had competed in the Swedish national championships. As Gunde grew older, however, he began to rely more heavily on his own training methods. Even as a young skier, Gunde drove himself hard. He was unusually disciplined in his training. He claims that he never missed a single day of training after the age of eleven, except for when he was sick or injured.

Unlike many other skiers, Gunde never took time off following the end of the ski season. He trained about eight hundred hours a year and kept a diary of each day's workout. Gunde designed his own training routine, which included some unusual workouts such as running through swamps in heavy boots. He never shared all of the details of his training methods because he felt that keeping them a secret gave him an advantage over his opponents.

The Emerging Champion

Although Gunde did not rely heavily on coaches to develop his ability, he was inspired by other skiers. Three men were particularly influential. The first was Sixten Jernberg, a Swedish cross-country skier who won nine Olympic medals between 1956 and 1964. He was an idol to many young Swedish skiers.

Another influential skier was an American, Bill Koch. When he was fourteen, Gunde saw Koch on television competing at the 1976 Winter Olym-

pic Games in Innsbruck, Austria. Koch scored a major upset when he placed second in the 30-kilometer race and became the first American to win an Olympic cross-country medal. Gunde was impressed by what he saw and became even more determined to become a world-class skier.

The third athlete who influenced Gunde was a fellow Swede, Thomas Wassberg, who was almost six years older than Gunde. While Gunde was still a teenager, Wassberg won the World Cup title as the best cross-country skier in the world. As Gunde began to gain national and international prominence, he viewed Wassberg as his mentor. In the years that followed, Gunde and Wassberg won several world championship and Olympic medals skiing together on the Swedish relay team.

Gunde first emerged as an important competitor with a thirteenth-place finish in the 15-kilo-

meter race at the 1982 World Championships. At the end of the 1982 season, however, he ranked only fifty-seventh in the World Cup standings, which reflect a skier's performance during the entire year.

His intense training schedule and strong competitive spirit resulted in a dramatic improvement the following year. He jumped to second place in the World Cup standings and won major races in Alaska and Canada. In fact, 1983 marked the beginning of a remarkable nine-year string of successes matched only by the performance of Gunde's idol, Sixten Jernberg.

Perhaps Gunde's most impressive performance came in the 1984 Winter Olympic Games in Sarajevo, Yugoslavia. Gunde won a medal in every men's event, including a gold in the 15-kilometer, a bronze in the 30-kilometer, a silver in the 50-kilometer events, and another gold in the team relay.

Continuing the Story

Gunde's 1984 Olympic success made him a major sports star in Sweden and other Scandinavian countries. He had agreements with more than twenty companies to endorse their products. His financial success made it possible for him to continue to train and to compete full time.

As Gunde's fame grew, his mother developed a Gunde Svan museum in her house. Thousands of fans have visited the house to view his medals and other skiing memorabilia.

In the years following the 1984 Olympic Games, Gunde won the 1985 and 1986 World Cup titles, and several World Championship medals. If the 1984 Olympic Games were Gunde's most spectacular performance, the 1988 Games in Calgary, Alberta, Canada, may have been his most satisfying. He was troubled by injuries and illness throughout the 1987 season.

Going into the Calgary Olympics, experts predicted that his best chances for a medal were in the 15- and 30-kilometer races. In the opening days of Olympic competition, however, Gunde and his Swedish teammates failed to win a single medal in the 15- and 30-kilometer races.

Finally, in the men's 4×10-kilometer team relay, Gunde's Swedish team won a gold medal, edging out the Soviet Union in a close race.

MAJOR CHAMPIONSHIPS

Year	Competition	Event	Place
1982	World Championships	15 kilometers	13th
	World Cup	Overall	57th
1983	World Cup	Overall	2d
1984	Olympic Games	15 kilometers	Gold
		30 kilometers	Bronze
		50 kilometers	Silver
		Team relay	Gold
	World Cup	Overall	1st
1985	World Championships	30 kilometers	1st
		50 kilometers	1st
		Team relay	3d
	World Cup	Overall	1st
1986	World Cup	Overall	1st
1987	World Championships	15 kilometers	23d
		30 kilometers	7th
		Team relay	1st
	World Cup	Overall	3d
1988	Olympic Games	15 kilometers	13th
		30 kilometers	10th
		50 kilometers	Gold
		Team relay	Gold
	World Cup	Overall	1st
1989	World Championships	15-kilometer classic	6th
		15-kilometer freestyle	1st
		50-kilometer freestyle	1st
		Team relay	1st
	World Cup	Overall	1st
1990	World Cup	Overall	2d
1991	World Championships	15-kilometer freestyle	2d
		30-kilometer classic	1st
		50-kilometer freestyle	2d

HONORS AND AWARDS

1984	*Ski Racing* magazine Skier of the Year
1984-86, 1988	International Nordic Skier of the Year

Then, five days later, Gunde defeated the defending world champion, Maurilio De Zolt of Italy, to win the premier event of cross-country skiing, the 50-kilometer race, with a time of slightly more than two hours.

Gunde followed his Olympic success with consecutive overall first-place finishes in the 1988 and 1989 World Cup competitions, and he placed second overall in the 1990 World Cup. In the 1989 World Championships he had four first-place finishes, including the 50-kilometer freestyle and the team relay events.

Following his first-place finish in the 30-kilometer classic at the 1991 World Championships, where he also placed second in both the 15-kilometer and 50-kilometer freestyle events, Gunde decided to retire.

Summary

Gunde Svan was clearly the best cross-country skier of the 1980's, succeeding at distances ranging from 15 kilometers to 50 kilometers and always skiing well when the pressure was the greatest. His success is based on a dedication to hard training and a strong desire to win. He is an example of an athlete who relied on his own judgment and self-motivation to develop his skills and stay on top of his sport for several years.

Wayne Wilson

Additional Sources:

Levinson, David, and Karen Christenson, eds. *Encyclopedia of World Sport: From Ancient to Present.* Santa Barbara, Calif.: ABC-CLIO, 1996.
Wallechinsky, David. *The Complete Book of the Olympics.* Boston: Little, Brown and Company, 1991.

LYNN SWANN

Sport: Football

Born: March 7, 1952
　　　Alcoa, Tennessee

Early Life

Lynn Curtis Swann was born on March 7, 1952, in Alcoa, Tennessee, to Willie Swann, an airplane maintenance worker, and Mildred (McGarity) Swann, a dental assistant. When Lynn was two years old, the Swann family moved to the San Francisco Bay area and settled in Foster City, California.

At Serra High School in Foster City, Lynn attracted considerable attention with his athletic prowess. He was named a high school All-American as a football player, and he also excelled at track and field, winning the California high school long jump championship. Lynn was heavily recruited by colleges eager to have such a talented and versatile athlete on their teams; from among the many offers he chose to attend the University of Southern California (USC), a school with a long history of excellence in both track and field and football.

The Road to Excellence

At USC, Lynn's success continued. The rules of the time did not permit freshmen to play varsity sports, but at the beginning of Lynn's sophomore year he was moved into the Trojans' starting varsity team as a wide receiver. Lynn held his starting spot for the rest of his college career and earned selection as an All-American wide receiver as a senior in 1973. That season, Lynn was the Pacific Eight Conference's leading receiver, and he capped off his college career with five catches in USC's Rose Bowl loss to Ohio State on New Year's Day, 1974. By then, he had set USC's all-time record with 95 career receptions and had gained 1,562 yards, the second-best mark in the school's history.

As he had in high school, Lynn showed himself to be a versatile performer, becoming USC's

third-leading all-time punt returner and lettering in track and field. As a sophomore, Lynn posted a 24-foot 10-inch long jump, and he was once timed at 9.8 seconds in the 100-yard dash. Though he stood only 5 feet 11 inches tall and weighed just 180 pounds, his speed and leaping ability made him a nightmare for opposing defensive backs; few could match his speed, and he could out-jump even the tallest to catch high passes. USC's coach, John McKay, paid tribute to Lynn's multiple talents. "He is as important to us as Johnny Rodgers was to Nebraska," McKay noted, referring to the great Cornhusker flanker.

Lynn Swann in 1975.

STATISTICS

Season	GP	Rec.	Yds.	Avg.	TD
1974	12	11	208	18.0	2
1975	14	49	781	13.0	**11**
1976	12	28	516	18.4	3
1977	14	50	789	15.8	7
1978	16	61	880	14.4	11
1979	13	41	808	10.7	5
1980	13	44	710	10.1	7
1981	13	34	505	14.9	5
1982	9	18	265	14.7	0
Totals	116	336	5,462	16.3	51

Notes: Boldface indicates statistical leader. GP = games played; Rec. = receptions; Yds. = yards; Avg. = average yards per reception; TD = touchdowns

"In our offense, Swann is called on to run, block, and catch passes, and he is excellent at all three."

The Emerging Champion

Lynn's stellar college performances attracted the attention of professional football scouts, and Lynn was chosen by the Pittsburgh Steelers in the first round of the 1974 National Football League (NFL) draft. After receiving a bachelor's degree in public relations from USC in 1974, Lynn joined the Steelers, an up-and-coming team that was amassing one of the greatest collections of young talent the NFL had ever seen. In addition to Lynn, the Steelers in the early 1970's acquired quarterback Terry Bradshaw, running back Franco Harris, and defensive stars Joe Greene and Jack Lambert, each a future Hall of Famer. Pittsburgh's young stars blended their talents to form a team that would dominate the NFL in the latter half of the decade.

In Lynn's rookie season, 1974, he was used by the Steelers primarily as a kick returner. Though he compiled a 14.1-yard average as a punt returner, the fourth-best mark in Steelers history, and led the league with 577 punt-return yards, his 18.9-yard average as a pass receiver was even more impressive, and the Steelers made him a starting wide receiver in time for the playoffs.

Lynn's promotion paid the Steelers immediate dividends. In the American Football Conference (AFC) championship game that season against the Oakland Raiders, Lynn caught a touchdown pass to win the game and send the Steelers to their first-ever Super Bowl. The Steelers downed the Minnesota Vikings 16-6 in Super Bowl IX, and Pittsburgh's reign as the NFL's biggest power had begun.

The Steelers bulldozed their way through the NFL in the 1975 season, posting a 12-2 regular-season record and brushing aside Baltimore and Oakland in the playoffs to reach their second consecutive Super Bowl. Lynn had a splendid season, catching 49 passes for 781 yards and scoring 11 touchdowns, but his best performance that year was still to come.

In the AFC title game against Oakland, Lynn had gone up to catch a pass and had received a smashing forearm blow to the head from the Raiders' George Atkinson. The impact knocked Lynn out, and after he had been revived he could not keep his balance well enough even to sit up straight on the team bench. He was rushed to a hospital, where doctors diagnosed a concussion. Their prescription was for Lynn to rest, but the Steelers' victory meant that the team was to play the Dallas Cowboys in Super Bowl X in just two weeks.

Though Lynn had been warned that another such hit could cause him more damage, he chose to play against Dallas. Lynn was motivated in part by remarks made in a newspaper article by Dallas defender Cliff Harris, who said he thought that Lynn, perhaps fearful of another injury, might be easily intimidated. Angered by such comments, Lynn set out to prove that he still had the courage to take the pounding of pro football.

Lynn answered Harris on the field. Super Bowl X belonged to him; he caught 4 passes for 161 yards, a Super Bowl record, and scored the game's winning touchdown on a 64-yard fourth-quarter bomb from Bradshaw. Pittsburgh stopped the Cowboys 21-17, and Lynn was an easy choice as the game's most valuable player.

Continuing the Story

Perhaps the most dangerous play in pro football is the pass to a receiver over the middle of the opposing line of scrimmage. To catch such passes, a receiver must jump high in the air, leaving himself exposed to vicious hits from defenders on all sides, and must concentrate only on the ball. Many receivers have suffered career-ending injuries going over the middle, and many more cannot learn to ignore the danger involved well

HONORS AND AWARDS

1973	College All-American
1975, 1977-78	AFC All-Star Team
1976	Super Bowl most valuable player
1977-79	NFL Pro Bowl Team
1979	National Association for the Advancement of Colored People Image Award
1980	Multiple Sclerosis Man of the Year
1981	NFL Man of the Year
1985	AFL-NFL 1960-84 All-Star Second Team

enough to execute the play. So when Lynn received another concussion, again from the Raiders' Atkinson, in the opening game of the 1976 season, there was good reason to wonder if he would have the confidence to regain his old form.

Lynn proved such speculation groundless, though. He came back from that injury to earn selection to the Pro Bowl for the third time, and though the Steelers did not reach the Super Bowl that year or the next, Lynn remained one of the league's best and guttiest receivers. In 1979 Pittsburgh returned to the Super Bowl, beating the Cowboys again, 35-31, and the next year the Steelers cemented their place among pro football's all-time greatest teams by dumping the Los Angeles Rams 30-19 in Super Bowl XIV.

Though Lynn was a valuable performer throughout the Steelers' championship era, he continued to absorb a tremendous pounding, and after the 1982 season he elected to retire as a player. Calling on his education in public relations and his experience as an athlete, he went to work for ABC Television as a football analyst. In 1985, the Pro Football Hall of Fame named Lynn to its AFL-NFL 1960-1984 All-Star Second Team.

Lynn continued full-time with ABC Sports and settled in Pittsburgh. He became the national spokesperson for Big Brothers/Big Sisters of America and served on its national board of directors. Lynn has created a youth scholarship fund for the Pittsburgh Ballet Theatre School, which has benefited hundreds of talented students.

Summary

Lynn Swann combined his considerable athletic talent with the courage and single-mindedness essential to a top receiver. As a key performer on the NFL's best team of the 1970's, Lynn left football fans with unforgettable memories of spectacular catches and grace under pressure.

Brook Wilson

Additional Sources:

Aaseng, Nathan. *Football's Sure-Handed Receivers.* Minneapolis, Minn.: Lerner Publishing, 1980.
"Black History Month—Football Great Lynn Swann." *Time* Online. http://www.time.com/time/community/transcripts/1999/021799 swann .html.

LIEM SWIE-KING

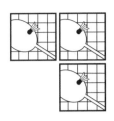

Sport: Badminton

Born: 1955
　　　Kudus, Indonesia

Early Life

Liem Swie-King was born in 1955 in Kudus, Indonesia, a small city in the central region of Java, the major island of Indonesia. Liem grew up in an athletic family of two brothers and two sisters. One of his older sisters was good enough to make the national Uber Cup team (the women's international badminton team championships, played every three years).

Liem began playing badminton when he was in elementary school. In Indonesia, badminton is as popular as baseball is in the United States. Liem, like many schoolchildren in the United States, practiced his favorite sport every day after school at the local badminton club. Liem was a strong

boy and developed an outstanding smash, the most powerful offensive stroke in badminton.

The Road to Excellence

Liem quickly became one of the best junior players in the country. When he was eighteen years old and had graduated from high school, Liem was selected to train with the top players in the country at the Indonesian National Badminton Center. At the National Center, Liem was able to watch and play against the great Rudy Hartono, then the top player in the world and considered by many to be the best player in the history of badminton.

Liem was a shy, quiet eighteen-year-old. It was intimidating to be the youngest player, living and training year-round with the best in the world. With the help of national coaches, Liem continued to improve. He quickly became known as "the next Rudy Hartono." It was unfair to expect Liem to measure up against Hartono's achievements; his position was comparable to replacing Michael Jordan on a basketball team or following Babe Ruth in baseball.

Not possessing great footwork, Liem did not move around the court as smoothly or as easily as other players. Liem was much more powerful than most, however; he made up for his footwork by being extremely quick. When many opponents thought they had him beaten, Liem could make a quick jump across the court and powerfully smash the shot for a winner. Because of this quickness, it was hard to hit a shot by him. Likewise, when an oppo-

MAJOR CHAMPIONSHIP VICTORIES

| 1976, 1979, 1982 | Thomas Cup championship team |
| 1978-79, 1981 | All-England Badminton Championships |

nent gave him a chance, he was powerful enough to hit a winning offensive shot. Liem made his first Thomas Cup team (the men's international badminton team championships, played every three years) in 1975-1976 and helped the other great Indonesian players like Hartono win the world team championship.

The Emerging Champion

With Hartono moving closer to thirty years old, typically over-the-hill for international badminton players, Liem was seen as the next great champion. He did not disappoint his country. In the 1978 All-England Badminton Championships (the unofficial world championships), Liem won the prestigious men's singles title. He was the best badminton player in the world and the Indonesians celebrated with their new champion. Liem followed the 1978 championship by winning the 1979 and 1981 All-England Badminton Singles Championships as well.

Following Hartono was not easy for Liem. Many people expected him to win as often and as easily as Hartono, who was considered the best player in history.

Continuing the Story

Although Liem never achieved the legendary status of Hartono in his native Indonesia, he was still a national hero and a role model for Indonesian youth. His three All-England Singles Championships were won with great pride by him and his country.

Liem remained at the top of international badminton for several more years. He never won another singles world championship, but he helped lead Indonesia to several Thomas Cup team titles. He retired in 1986 at thirty-one years old, quite old by badminton standards. The physical demands of training were too much for him to continue.

Liem did not stay close to badminton after he retired. He became a very successful businessman, owning several hotels, theaters, and apartment complexes. He married and had two children.

Summary

Although certainly one of Indonesia's greatest sports champions, Liem Swie-King will unfortunately be remembered as the player who followed in the footsteps of Rudy Hartono. In that sense, life was not fair for Liem, but he could not control the comparisons that many fans made; he could only train to be the best player he could be. His three world championships are evidence that he did quite well for himself.

Jon R. Poole

Additional Sources:

Bloss, Margaret Varner, and R. Stanton Hales. *Badminton.* Boston: McGraw-Hill, 2001.

Davis, Pat. *Guinness Book of Badminton.* New York: Sterling, 1984.

International Badminton Federation. *Sixty Years: 1936-1996, Sixtieth Jubilee Factbook.* Colorado Springs, Colo.: United States Badminton Association, 1996.

Levinson, David, and Karen Christenson, eds. *Encyclopedia of World Sport: From Ancient Times to Present.* Santa Barbara, Calif.: ABC-CLIO, 1996.

SHERYL SWOOPES

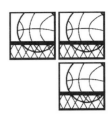

Sport: Basketball

Born: March 25, 1971
Brownfield, Texas

Early Life

Sheryl Swoopes was born on March 25, 1971, and grew up in Brownfield, Texas, a small town near Lubbock, Texas. She learned her basketball skills early playing with her three brothers and their friends. Getting the opportunity to play regularly with boys helped Sheryl develop a more physical game and work harder on her ball-handling skills. Her mother, Louise, watched all her children as they starred in school.

The Road to Excellence

Sheryl played basketball for Brownfield High School, being named Texas Player of the Year as a junior. When she graduated in 1989 she won a scholarship to the University of Texas. After attending for a few days Sheryl left the school and returned home. She had trouble with the immense size of the school and decided to start her career at a junior college in Texas. Sheryl was also named to the U.S. Olympic Festivals South team in 1989, though she was unable to play because of injuries.

The Emerging Champion

Sheryl started her basketball career at Southern Plains Junior College in Texas, where she was named Junior College Player of the Year in 1991. She averaged 21.5 points with 11.9 rebounds to lead her squad. In 1991 and 1992 she was selected as a junior college All-American.

Sheryl finished her career at Texas Tech, playing for the Lady Raiders. By 1993 she had become the National College Player of the Year for the school. Texas Tech compiled a 58-8 record during Sheryl's two years with the club. She was selected Southwestern Conference Player of the Year in 1992 and 1993. The Lady Red Raiders won the NCAA Championship in 1993, with Sheryl being named the most valuable player of the Final Four. Sheryl scored a record 47 points in the championship game.

WNBA star Sheryl Swoopes moves the ball in the 1999 All-Star game.

STATISTICS

Season	GP	FGA	FGM	FG%	FTA	FTM	FT%	Reb.	Ast	TP	PPG
1997	9	53	25	.472	14	10	.714	15	7	64	7.1
1998	29	405	173	.427	86	71	.826	149	62	453	15.6
1999	32	489	226	.462	122	100	.820	202	127	585	18.3
2000	31	484	245	.506	145	119	.821	195	119	643	20.7
Totals	101	1,431	669	.468	367	300	.817	561	315	1,745	17.3

Notes: GP = games played; FGA = field goals attempted; FGM = field goals made; FG% = field goal percentage; FTA = free throws attempted; FTM = free throws made; FT% = free throw percentage; Reb. = rebounds; Ast. = assists; TP = total points; PPG = points per game

Also in 1993 Sheryl was named the Babe Zaharias Female Athlete of the Year, which brought with it a $10,000 scholarship for her to finish her degree in exercise and sports science. All together, Sheryl was named Player of the Year by nine different sporting magazines and organizations, based on her performance in 1993. Her number, 22, was retired by the school in February, 1994.

Continuing the Story

After leaving college Sheryl went to play in Bari, Italy, for a year before returning to the states to participate in the 1994 World Championships and Goodwill Games. In 1996 she played for the Olympic team in Atlanta and again in 2000 in Sydney, Australia.

Sheryl's basketball playing took her to the Women's National Basketball Association (WNBA) in 1997, when she joined the Houston Comets. She quickly established herself as a force to be reckoned with, being named to the All-WNBA First Team from 1998 to 2000. One of her greatest joys, however, comes not from the court but from being a mom. Her son Jordan Eric Jackson was born on June 25, 1997. Within six weeks of giving birth to her son Sheryl was back on the court playing at almost full strength. She was named a starter for the Western Conference All-Stars in 1999 and again in 2000. In 2000 Sheryl was recognized as the most valuable player in the league and the Defensive Player of the Year. Nike created a shoe in her honor called Air Swoopes.

Sheryl missed the 2001 season after tearing a knee ligament during a workout. However, she remained with the Comets as an assistant coach.

Summary

Sheryl Swoopes has established herself as one of the premier female basketball players of all time. She has brought to the game a new image as she and fellow basketball stars Lisa Leslie and Rebecca Lobo have become the spokespeople for the WNBA. The threesome have signed many endorsements and modeling contracts, which have brought increased exposure to the league and to the sport of women's basketball.

Leslie Heaphy

Additional Sources:
Burgan, Michael. *Sheryl Swoopes*. Philadelphia: Chelsea House, 2001.
"Hooping History." *Jet* 96 (August 16, 1999): 44.
Luscombe, Belinda. "Swoopes, There She Is." *Time* 150 (August 18, 1997): 79.
Wallner, Rosemary. *Sheryl Swoopes*. Mankato, Minn.: Capstone High-Interest Books, 2001.

HONORS AND AWARDS

1991	Junior College Player of the Year
1993	NCAA Final Four most valuable player
	NCAA championship team
	National Player of the Year
1994	Uniform number 22 retired by Texas Tech
1996, 2000	Gold Medal with U.S. Women's National Team, Olympic Games
1998-2000	All-WNBA First Team
1999-2000	NBA All-Star Team, league's leading vote-getter
2000	WNBA most valuable player
	WNBA Defensive Player of the Year

IRENA SZEWINSKA

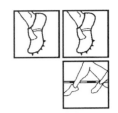

Sport: Track and field (sprints and long jump)

Born: May 24, 1946
Leningrad, U.S.S.R. (now St.
Petersburg, Russia)

Early Life

Born Irena Kirzenstein in a Leningrad refugee camp to Jewish parents from Poland, she discovered running at an early age. In 1960 she watched U.S. Olympic track star Wilma Rudolph run. Fascinated, Irena hoped to emulate her. Several months later she won her first track competition and began training seriously. She set her sights on breaking world records like her idol, Rudolph, and becoming an Olympic champion.

Irena Szewinska of Poland won the 200 meters at a 1974 meet.

In 1961 she won her first competition. The press recognized her potential and began writing about her. She continued the hard work of training and, little by little, improved her performance.

The Road to Excellence

Her first major competition was the European Junior Championships in Warsaw, Poland, in 1964. She won several races, including her favorite, the 200 meters. This win helped her to qualify for the 1964 team Poland sent to the Olympic Games in Tokyo. She was scheduled to compete in three events: the long jump, the 200 meters, and the 4×100-meter relay.

When she looked at her competition, she felt inadequate and under a great deal of pressure. As she waited for her event, however, the eighteen-year-old athlete began to realize that she was at the Olympics as part of an elite group of competitors and a long, prestigious tradition. She set her sights on first making the finals in the long jump. After making the finals, her goal was to improve upon her own personal best. This strategy led to her winning the silver medal in the long jump.

Her next event was the 200 meters. The race consisted of two qualifying rounds leading to the final event. In each stage of this race she again was intent on improving her personal bests. Again the strategy paid off, and again she won the silver medal.

Her final event was the 4×100-meter relay. The Americans were considered the surefire winners; however, the Polish team was ambitious. They won the gold and set a world record in the process. Irena left Tokyo with three Olympic medals and was a star in Poland.

One year later, still working to improve her personal bests, Irena set a world record in the 200 meters, toppling Wilma Rudolph's record.

2699

MAJOR CHAMPIONSHIPS

Year	Competition	Event	Place
1964	European Junior Championships	200 meters	1st
	Olympic Games	200 meters	Silver
		Long jump	Silver
		400-meter relay	Gold
1968	Olympic Games	100 meters	Bronze
		200 meters	Gold
1972	Olympic Games	200 meters	Bronze
1976	Olympic Games	400 meters	Gold

won the 200 meters a number of times and had established world records, she would turn her full attention to another event. Now thirty years old, Irena faced stiff competition from eighteen-year-old Christina Brehmer of East Germany. The race was neck-and-neck for the first 300 meters. After that, however, Irena pulled away, finishing in the world record time of 49.28 seconds.

In addition to Irina's sports career, she found time to earn a master's degree in economics and marry her fiancé, Janusz Szewinska.

The Emerging Champion

In 1968 Irena competed in her second Olympics, this time in Mexico City. She competed in four events and medaled in two. She brought home a bronze medal in the 100-meter sprint and a gold in her favorite event, the 200 meters. While winning the gold she also set a world record.

After Mexico City, she continued training and competing, entering events around the world. By 1970 she was exhausted. That year she gave birth to her first son, Andreas, and went on a brief hiatus from training. By the end of the year, however, she was again competing. Unfortunately, she had not trained enough and was not yet back to form—the results of those races were not among her best.

In 1971 Irena's life was further complicated when she broke her ankle and was unable to train for almost a year. Despite the setbacks, she decided to compete in her third Olympics, this time in Munich, Germany. Her extended break in training had its effect on her performance. She left Munich with one lone medal, a bronze in the 200 meters.

Ever the competitor, she was already planning for the 1976 Olympics in Montreal. She was, however, beginning to realize that competing in so many events was taking its toll on her. As difficult as the decision was, she decided to limit herself to the 400-meter race. She felt since she had already

Continuing the Story

The 1980 Olympic Games in Moscow were her last Olympics and the end of her track career. During the semifinals of the 400 meters she pulled a muscle and was eliminated from the competition.

In 1983 she attended the World Championships in Stuttgart, Germany. There she experienced a thrill to rival many of her wins: She met Wilma Rudolph. Irena shook the American track star's hand and told her how happy she was to finally meet her idol.

Summary

Known by her compatriots as "Queen of the Track," Irena Szewinska was one of the most successful female track stars in history. She competed at five Olympics, competed in five different events, and won seven gold medals. She often said sport was her passion and she never grew tired of competing. Her greatest gift was her desire to improve her performance. Rather than worry about her competition, she always chose to concentrate on beating herself and improving on her own personal bests. In this manner she established her own place in the record books.

Deborah Service

Additional Sources:

Hanley, Reid M. *Who's Who in Track and Field.* New Rochelle, N.Y.: Arlington House, 1973.
"Irena Szewinska." International Amateur Athletic Federation Online. http://www.iaaf.org/athletes/legends/Szewinska.html.

JUNKO TABEI

Sport: Mountaineering

Born: September 22, 1939
Miharu Machi, Japan

Early Life

Junko Ishibashi was born September 22, 1939, in Miharu Machi, a market town in northern Japan. The fifth of seven children, her first taste of the adventure of mountain climbing came at the age of ten. On a school field trip, her teacher guided Junko and some of her classmates to the top of a 6,000-foot mountain. This experience led to a fascination with mountains and moun-

taineering that would become her passion in the years to come.

The Road to Excellence

After graduating from Tokyo's Showa Women's University in 1962, Junko took a job as a middle school teacher. She also joined a men's climbing club. Barely 5 feet tall and weighing 93 pounds, this bespectacled woman found that she was nonetheless the equal of many of the male climbers. Subsequently, she climbed several of Japan's best-known peaks, including its

The southern face of Mount Everest, where Junko Tabei made her landmark climb to the 29,035-foot peak in 1975.

AP/Wide World Photos

highest mountain, the 12,388-foot Mount Fuji. As her confidence and mountaineering skills grew, her goal became to climb what she termed the "white mountains" throughout the world.

In 1965 she met Masanobu Tabei, a fellow mountaineer. Despite Junko's mother's objection—Tabei was not a college graduate—the two were married three years later. In the years to come, they would raise two children: a daughter, Noriko, and a son, Shinya.

In 1969 Junko established a women's mountaineering club, and in 1970 her club decided to climb 24,787-foot Annapurna III in the Himalayas. The expedition would include 8 climbers, 14 sherpas, 114 porters, a doctor, and a reporter. The climbers arrived in Kathmandu in March of that year.

The traditional approach to climbing in the Himalayas is to lay siege to the mountain. That is, over a period of time, climbers—and especially sherpas—set up and stock a series of camps at higher and higher levels. This gradual movement up the mountain allows time for the human body to acclimatize to increasing elevation. Camp 1 was established at 14,370 feet. This was followed by other camps, culminating with camp 5 at 22,300 feet. Junko, Hiroko Hirakawa, and two sherpas were selected by Eiko Miyazuki, the expedition leader, to make the final assault on the summit from Camp 5. After a determined effort, the four reached the top on May 19, 1970.

The Emerging Champion

Following their success on Annapurna III, Miyazuki and Junko decided to attempt Mount Everest in the Himalayas with an all-woman team. In 1971 they received a permit to climb Everest in 1975. Thus began a long period of extensive planning and fund-raising. The expedition was sponsored by the mountaineering club, andfunds were secured from sources including *Yomiuri Shimbun*, the Tokyo newspaper, as well as Nikon Television. Also, Junko resigned from her teaching job in 1973 and used her retirement benefits to help pay for the expedition.

At 29,035 feet, Mount Everest is the highest point on Earth and has long been a target for world-class mountaineers. Despite determined British efforts in the 1920's to climb the mountain, the first confirmed ascent was not made un-

TABEI'S CONQUEST OF THE SEVEN SUMMITS			
Year	Mountain	Elevation in feet	Location
1975	Everest	29,035	Nepal
1980	Kilimanjaro	19,340	Tanzania
1987	Aconcagua	22,834	Argentina
1988	McKinley	20,320	United States
1989	Elbrus	18,510	Russia
1991	Vinson Massif	16,066	Antarctica
1992	Carstensz Pyramid	16,023	Indonesia

til 1953 by Edmund Hillary, a beekeeper from New Zealand, and by Tenzing Norgay, a Nepalese sherpa. In the intervening years, a number of men had climbed the mountain—but no woman had done so.

The all-woman Japanese Everest expedition involved 14 women, 500 porters, 23 sherpas, and a doctor. On March 16, 1975, base camp was established at the foot of the Khumbu glacier. It then took nearly two weeks to rig a route of aluminum ladders and fixed lines through the treacherous Khumbu ice fall. By April 3 they had established Camp 1 at the top of the ice fall and over the following weeks established a series of camps higher up the mountain. On May 4, disaster struck. An avalanche rolled over seven climbers and six sherpas asleep in their tents. Two of the sherpas were seriously injured, as was Junko. It took several days for her to recover.

As a result of the lost time and equipment, only one summit attempt by two climbers could be supported. On May 13 Junko and sherpa Ang Tshering established Camp 6 at 27,887 feet. On May 15 the two left for the summit, only to be turned back by bad weather. On May 16 they tried again, leaving camp at 5:00 A.M. Junko's 31-pound load included cameras, drinks, flags, and oxygen cylinders. While the mountain has been climbed without using bottled oxygen, most climbers sleep wearing an oxygen mask at high camp and breathe a steady flow of the gas on summit day. At 8:30 A.M. the two reached the South Summit and, with Tshering breaking trail through deep snow, the pair finally reached the summit of Mount Everest at 12:30 P.M. At thirty-five years of age, and with a two-year-old daughter at home, Junko became the first woman to stand on the highest point on the earth.

Continuing the Story

Junko continued to climb. In 1992 she became the first woman to complete the "Seven Summits." The Seven Summits represent the highest points on each of the earth's seven continents. Over the years, Junko has climbed more than seventy major peaks all over the world and has received numerous awards. Deeply concerned about the natural environment, Junko has been directly involved in "cleanup" climbs in both Japan and the Himalayas and became director of the Japanese chapter of the Himalayan Adventure Trust, an organization whose goal is to preserve the mountain environment.

Summary

As a successful Japanese woman in the male-dominated sport of mountaineering, Junko Tabei has been an inspirational role model for women—and all mountaineers—in Japan and around the world. She followed a dream that took her to the tops of the "white mountains" and to the top of her sport.

Russell N. Carney

Additional Sources:

Ahluwalia, H. P. S. *Faces of Everest.* New Delhi: Vikas Publishing House, 1978.

Birkett, Bill, and Bill Peascod. *Women Climbing: 200 Years of Achievement.* London: A & C Black, 1989.

Horn, Robert. "No Mountain Too High for Her." *Sports Illustrated* 84, no. 17 (April 29, 1996).

McLoone, Margo, and Kathryn Besio. *Women Explorers of the Mountains: Nina Mazuchelli, Fanny Bullock Workman, Mary Vaux Walcott, Gertrude Benham, Junko Tabei.* Mankato, Minn.: Capstone Press, 2000.

Seghers, Carroll, II. *The Peak Experience: Hiking and Climbing for Women.* Indianapolis, Ind.: Bobbs-Merrill, 1979.

RYOKO TAMURA

Sport: Judo

Born: September 6, 1975
Fukuoka, Japan

Early Life

Ryoko Tamura was born in Fukuoka, Japan, on September 6, 1975. At the age of eight she became interested in judo, which her brother, who was three years older than Ryoko, often practiced. Ryoko insisted that her brother teach her judo techniques. At first all the members of the Tamura family were opposed to Ryoko's interest in judo, but they relented eventually and let her practice. As Ryoko began to win tournaments and travel extensively, her mother accompanied her.

The Road to Excellence

During her high school, college, and graduate school years Ryoko trained for judo while attending classes and, eventually, working for Toyota. During all these years she would rise early, jog, go to school or work, and then spend three hours every day practicing judo.

Her hard work paid off. The 4-foot 9-inch, 106 pound judoka won the All-Japan women's extra lightweight title in 1991. Ryoko won the title for ten consecutive years, including a win in April, 2000, when she had a sprained ring finger on one hand and fractured cartilage and a severed tendon on the other.

The Emerging Champion

In addition to being the Japanese extra lightweight women's champion for ten years, Ryoko was also the extra lightweight champion of the Fukuoka International Women's Competition for eleven years. She first won the championship in 1990, at which time she was the youngest woman ever to win it. In December, 1999, she defeated her rival, Cuban Amarilo Savon, to take the title, but in so doing she hurt her hand, fracturing cartilage and severing a tendon. As Ryoko did not want to have her hand cut, she decided to let it heal with surgery. The healing process took several months, and,

Ryoko Tamura (top) pins Russian Lioubov Brouletova in the 2000 Olympics judo match. Tamura won the gold medal.

2704

thus, she was still injured at the time of the All-Japan competitions in 2000. Some thought that, because of her injuries, she would not be able to participate in the 2000 Olympics, but upon winning the All-Japan title, she became a member of the Japanese Olympic team.

Besides winning both the Japanese championships ten times and the Fukuoka International Women's championships eleven times before 2001, she had also won four world championship gold medals: in 1993, 1995, 1997, and 1999. In 1992 she had represented Japan at the Olympic Games in Barcelona, Spain. At those games she demonstrated her signature maneuver, the *seoi-nage*, which is a shoulder throw. At Barcelona Ryoko won a silver medal when she was able to defeat her hero, Karen Briggs of Britain, who Ryoko said inspired her to practice judo when she watched Briggs compete at the Fukuoka Women's Championships before Ryoko herself became a serious contender for titles. However, at Barcelona, Ryoko lost in the finals to France's Cecile Nowak, who took the gold.

In 1996 Ryoko represented Japan in the Olympic Games in Atlanta, Georgia. It was a foregone conclusion that Ryoko would win a gold here. Between the 1992 Barcelona Games and the 1996 Atlanta Games Ryoko had won every match in which she had competed. She easily moved into the championship match in Atlanta, and all bets were on her to take home a gold. However, it was not to be. Ryoko dislocated her finger and was beaten by North Korea's only judo entrant at the Games, Kye Sun Hui. Hui walked away with the gold; Ryoko had to settle for a silver. Ryoko's upset was considered by many to be one of the most notable events at the Atlanta Games.

Continuing the Story

Frustrated in Atlanta, Ryoko looked ahead to Sydney, where she planned to let nothing prevent her from winning a gold medal. Her plan came to fruition. In the finals of the extra lightweight women's championship Ryoko took less than 40 seconds to score a victory over her oppo-

MAJOR JUDO CHAMPIONSHIPS, EXTRA LIGHTWEIGHT CLASS

Year	Competition	Place
1990-2000	Fukuoka International Women's Competition	1st
1991-2000	All-Japan Women's Judo Competition	1st
1992	Olympic Games	Silver
1993,1995,1997,1999	Women's World Judo Competition	1st
1996	Olympic Games	Silver
2000	Olympic Games	Gold

nent, Russian Lioubov Brouletova. Ryoko threw Brouletova on her back, using *uchi-mata* (the inner thigh throw) to score *ippon*, the ultimate 10-point score awarded to players who throw opponents flat on their backs. The *ippon* score wins the match for the player who scores it. The brilliant final play came after Ryoko's lackluster first match at Sydney, which remained scoreless until the last 2 seconds of play, when Ryoko managed to score *yuko* against her opponent, Chinese player Zhao Shunxin.

Summary

Ryoko Tamura perfected her judo techniques for fifteen years before she won an Olympic gold medal at the age of twenty-three. She continued to play judo all the way through high school, college, and graduate school. By the time she won the gold she was an employee of Toyota and a doctoral student at the Tokyo Sports University. When she first competed in the Olympics at Barcelona, she was a mere fifteen, agile and fast. By the time she competed at Sydney her movement was slower; she had to substitute strategy for the agility and speed that she had displayed as a teenager.

Ryoko, the darling of both the Japanese public and the Japanese media, was given the nickname "Yuwara-chan," which recognizes her resemblance in both appearance and attitude to the perky Yuwara, a Japanese animated character. She is loved and respected because she exhibits many of the qualities admired by Japanese society. She insists that judo has given her much, teaching her the true meaning of the Japanese idea of *rei*, respect for others, and showing her that she must always do her best.

Annita Marie Ward

Additional Sources:

Bhattacharji, Alex, et al. "Tough Judo Player in Pink." *Sports Illustrated for Kids* 9 (July, 1996): 56.

Wallechinsky, David. *The Complete Book of the Summer Olympics 2000.* Woodstock, N.Y.: Overlook Press, 2000.

Warden, Steve. "Ryoko Tamura's Loyal Fans Follow Her to Atlanta." *Knight-Ridder/Tribune News Service,* July 26, 1996, p. 726K7384.

FRAN TARKENTON

Sport: Football

Born: February 3, 1940
Richmond, Virginia

Early Life

Francis Asbury Tarkenton was born on February 3, 1940, in Richmond, Virginia, where his father, Dallas, was a minister in the Pentecostal Church. The family moved to Washington, D.C., in 1945, then returned south and settled in Athens, Georgia, in 1951.

Minnesota Viking Fran Tarkenton in a 1978 game.

AP/Wide World Photos

The Tarkentons were not rich—as late as 1950, his father earned $50 weekly—but Francis and his brothers, Dallas, Jr., and Wendell, lacked no necessities. Fran idolized his father, his major inspiration. Dallas, Sr., was a big-hearted man, always willing to see the good in others while not diluting his own beliefs and practices. He was a strict disciplinarian, yet a sensitive, kind father who instilled self-control in his children. Fran grew up neither smoking nor drinking, a pattern he continued throughout his career. Dallas, Sr., died in December, 1975, watching his son lead the Vikings in a division playoff game.

The Road to Excellence

In high school, playing for the Athens Trojans, Fran decided to become a professional athlete. Coach Weyman Sellers toughened his players with frequent and long scrimmages. Fran has credited him with teaching the fundamentals and techniques of playing quarterback that contributed much to his success throughout his career. Fran graduated from high school as an All-State quarterback.

At the University of Georgia, Fran's skills were further developed by head coach Wally Butts, and especially by freshman coach Quinton Lumpkin. Fran expected to be the number-one quarterback, but Coach Butts had other plans, using Fran rarely and only for short plays. The coach's tongue-lashings were hurtful, too, and a frustrated Fran and two teammates decided to quit the University of Georgia and enroll at Florida State University. Lumpkin talked them into remaining.

With Lumpkin's encouragement, Fran's self-confidence blossomed, as did the skills that attracted National Football League (NFL) scouts in his junior and senior years. In 1959, his most successful year, Fran led the Bulldogs to a 9-1 season and a 14-0 victory over the University of Mis-

2707

souri in the Orange Bowl. In 1960 he was drafted in the third round of the NFL draft by the Minnesota Vikings, an expansion team.

The Emerging Champion

The Vikings and Fran began life in the NFL in 1961. They surprised everyone with a season-opening 37-13 victory over the Chicago Bears. Fran completed 17 of 23 passes for 4 touchdowns and ran for another. Yet the Vikings won only three games that year and two in 1962. The most wins, eight, came in 1964. Fans still found the Vikings an exciting team, led by an imaginative and unpredictable quarterback.

Supporters and critics alike noted Fran's "scrambling" style, his ability to leave the pocket and run wildly while looking for a receiver. Traditional thinking held that quarterbacks should stay safely in the pocket, but Fran parlayed his scrambling style into many touchdown drives.

Consistent disagreement with the head coach, Norm Van Brocklin, along with the team's disappointing showing, fed his desire to play elsewhere, and in 1967 Fran signed with the New York Giants. This team had a losing record, and things did not improve much during Fran's stay from 1967 through 1971, although the Giants

rose to third place in 1967 after finishing last in 1966. While the Giants never won a championship during these years, Fran continued to prove himself one of the most self-reliant and fearless quarterbacks in the game.

In New York, as in Minnesota, Fran was affable, articulate, and willing to talk with the press and the fans. He hosted a weekly television show. A contract dispute occurred in 1971, however, and caused bad feelings between Fran and Giants owner Wellington Mara. Although an agreement was reached in time for the 1971 season, the two men agreed that a trade would be best and, by the season's end, Fran was back with the Minnesota Vikings.

Continuing the Story

When Fran returned to the Vikings in 1972, he was approaching the peak of his career. In eleven seasons he had completed almost 55 percent of his passes for 28,484 yards and 216 touchdowns. Head coach Bud Grant had high praise for Fran, citing his hard work, dedication, and leadership abilities.

His tenacity and quickness helped lead the Vikings to six Central Division championships (1973-1978) and three Super Bowls (1973, 1974,

STATISTICS

Season	GP	PA	PC	Pct.	Yds.	Avg.	TD	Int.
1961	14	280	157	.561	1,997	7.1	18	17
1962	14	329	163	.495	2,595	7.9	22	25
1963	14	297	170	.572	2,311	7.8	15	15
1964	14	306	171	.559	2,506	8.2	22	11
1965	14	329	171	.520	2,609	7.9	19	11
1966	14	358	192	.536	2,561	7.2	17	16
1967	14	377	204	.541	3,088	8.2	29	19
1968	14	337	182	.540	2,555	7.6	21	12
1969	14	409	220	.538	2,918	7.1	23	8
1970	14	389	219	.563	2,777	7.1	19	12
1971	13	386	226	.585	2,567	6.7	11	21
1972	14	378	215	.569	2,651	7.0	18	13
1973	14	274	169	.617	2,113	7.7	15	7
1974	13	351	199	.567	2,598	7.4	17	12
1975	14	425	**273**	.642	2,994	7.0	25	13
1976	13	412	**255**	.619	2,961	7.2	17	8
1977	9	258	155	**.601**	1,734	6.7	9	14
1978	16	572	**345**	.603	3,468	6.1	**25**	32
Totals	246	6,467	**3,686**	.570	**47,003**	7.3	**342**	266

Notes: Boldface indicates statistical leader. GP = games played; PA = passes attempted; PC = passes completed; Pct. = percent completed; Yds. = yards; Avg. = average yards per attempt; TD = touchdowns; Int. = interceptions

and 1976). It remained one of the greatest disappointments to Fran that his team never won the Super Bowl during his tenure. He was still an achiever, though, and the 1975 season was a personal and NFL high: Fran completed 273 of 425 passes and threw 25 touchdowns. The Associated Press voted him the NFL's Offensive Player of the Year.

Near the end of his career, Fran increased his business contacts and interests. Even in his early years, Fran had prepared for retirement. He bought real estate in Minnesota and Georgia, endorsed products, owned stock in several companies, and started companies of his own. Fran was determined not to end up like so many other retired athletes, lacking business acumen and financial security. By the late 1960's, he was already a millionaire.

In May, 1996, Fran had total shoulder replacement surgery to replace his right shoulder, which had plagued him since his high school days and shortened the passes he had been able to throw. Fran's pain-free shoulder enabled him to work eighteen-hour days and pursue entrepreneurial interests. He has launched eight small businesses, including the Fran Tarkenton Small Business NETwork, a membership group for small business owners. Fran has been seen on television with five different infomercials.

Summary

When he retired after the 1978 season, Fran Tarkenton held a number of NFL records: most touchdown passes, most completed passes, and most yardage. Through eighteen seasons, his drive, self-discipline, and durability earned him much respect. Coach Bud Grant, speaking in the midst of the 1975 season, summed up his admiration by stating: "He's got a gift. Maybe the word is instinct. What a coach admires as much as his physical ability and his mental sharpness is his maturity." Others agreed, and in 1986, Fran was elected to the Pro Football Hall of Fame.

S. Carol Berg

Additional Sources:

Burchard, Marshall. *Sports Hero, Fran Tarkenton.* New York: Putnam, 1977.

Hahn, James, and Lynn Hahn. *Tark!: The Sports Career of Francis Tarkenton.* Mankato, Minn.: Crestwood House, 1981.

Klobuchor, Jim, and Fran Tarkenton. *Tarkenton.* New York: Harper & Row, 1976.

NFL RECORDS

Most touchdown passes, 342
Most passing yards, 47,003
Most completions, 3,686

HONORS AND AWARDS

1965	NFL Pro Bowl Co-Player of the Game
1965-66, 1975-77, 1968-71	NFL Pro Bowl Team
1975	Associated Press Offensive Player of the Year United Press International NFC Player of the Year *Sporting News* NFC Player of the Year Bell Trophy Thorpe Trophy Newspaper Enterprise Association NFC Player of the Year
1980	NFL All-Pro Team of the 1970's
1986	Inducted into Pro Football Hall of Fame
1987	Inducted into College Football Hall of Fame Uniform number 10 retired by Minnesota Vikings

GOOSE TATUM

Sport: Basketball

Born: ca. May 3, 1921
  probably Clarion, Arkansas
Died: January 18, 1967
  El Paso, Texas

Early Life

As for so many African American athletes born in the first decades of the twentieth century, the early life of Reece "Goose" Tatum is hidden in obscurity. Even the date of his birth is in dispute, with most commentators claiming it probably occurred several years before the given date of 1921. The son of an itinerant Methodist minister, Goose attended segregated schools in small-town Arkansas. While playing football, some one said he looked like a goose, and the nickname stuck.

By the late 1930's, after several years of sandlot and semiprofessional baseball, Goose was playing professional baseball for the Birmingham Barons and later the Indianapolis or Cincinnati Clowns in the popular but segregated Negro League. Generally a first baseman or pitcher, Goose, with his 84-inch reach, was an imposing threat out on the pitching mound. He was a gifted natural athlete who also excelled at football and, eventually, basketball.

The Road to Excellence

In 1942, Abe Saperstein signed Goose to play for his legendary Harlem Globetrotters exhibition basketball team. Saperstein had created the Globetrotters in Chicago in 1927—the team at its inception had nothing to do with the real Harlem—and by the end of the 1930's the team had achieved considerable popularity at a time when professional sports were still segregated and African Americans were barred from competing with white athletes. Goose was an instant star with the Globetrotters, where his physical abilities were combined with a madcap sense of basketball humor. Soon Goose would become

famous as "the Clown Prince of Basketball."

After serving in the Army Air Corps in World War II, where he refined his basketball skills, Goose returned to the Globetrotters. By the end of the 1940's the Globetrotters had become one of America's most recognizable athletic attractions. Some, however, doubted that the Globetrotters really were as excellent as their on-court record indicated, inasmuch as their victories were inevitably won against their all-white traveling opponents, also owned by Saperstein, who were cast as the stooges and foils for the talented Globetrotters.

APA/Archive Photos

The Emerging Champion

The Globetrotters were more than mere entertainment and Goose was much more than just a famous clown, though he was noted for stunts like hiding the basketball under his jersey while the opposing players wandered confusedly around the court, or falling down, apparently seriously injured, only to vault upright with a smile, his eyes flashing. He would borrow eyeglasses from a spectator and place them on the referee's nose or attach a long rubber band to the basketball, then shoot it toward the basket, only to have it return to his enormous hands. In 1948 and again in 1949, the Globetrotters defeated one of the premier professional basketball teams, the Minneapolis Lakers. The Globetrotters engaged in a series against the best college and university players in 1950, with the Globetrotters winning eleven of the eighteen games in the so-called World Series of Basketball. The following year the Globetrotters won fourteen of eighteen games against the college all-stars, and Goose was selected as the series' most valuable player. In 1952 the Globetrotters were again victorious against the collegians, eleven games to five, and again Goose was the most valuable player.

The Globetrotters also traveled widely, touring Alaska in 1949 and Central and South America in 1950, where they played before 50,000 fans in Rio de Janeiro, Brazil. In 1951, 75,000 people saw them perform in Berlin, fifteen years after the 1936 Olympics made a star of Jesse Owens, whose accomplishments disproved the pernicious racial theories of Adolf Hitler. The Globetrotters toured the world in 1952. Wherever they played, Goose was always one of the featured players. During his basketball career he set scoring records in the Chicago Stadium (55 points) and the Cow Palace in San Francisco (64 points). The clown had a very accurate hook shot. It was not all just for laughs.

Continuing the Story

The Globetrotters and Goose were featured in two films during the 1950's: *Harlem Globetrotters* and *Go, Man, Go.* Goose was very well paid by Saperstein, making more than $40,000 per year, which at the time was much more than most white professional basketball players. However, he was always chronically out of funds, frequently having to borrow from Saperstein. Though a clown on the court, like many professional comedians—and "the Goose" was that as well as a talented basketball player—he was a loner, often restless and melancholy when off the court. He frequently refused to travel with the rest of the team, preferring to fly or take the train by himself.

In 1955 Goose left Saperstein and the Globetrotters and founded his own basketball team, the Harlem Road Kings, later known as the Stars and the Magicians, and he played with his team until his death. Money was one incentive: His income rose to approximately $65,000 per year after leaving the Globetrotters. Still, his financial problems continued and he served a short prison sentence in 1961 after being convicted of not paying $186,000 in income taxes. Returning to his first sport, he also purchased an interest in a Negro League baseball team, the Detroit Clowns, occasionally playing first base and center field. By the mid-1960's Goose's health had begun to fail. He died in El Paso, Texas, in 1967. He was supposedly forty-five at the time of his death, but many believed he was several years older.

Summary

Goose Tatum's life was both a triumph and a tragedy. He achieved fame and financial success during his lifetime. His tragedy was that much of his athletic career took place in a United States that was largely segregated, even within the professional sporting arena. Goose was by all accounts an excellent basketball player, but how great he might have become in a later era is impossible to know. Still, for most Americans of the mid-twentieth century, black and white, there was only one "Goose," and he was a superstar.

Eugene Larson

Additional Sources:

Menville, Chuck. *The Harlem Globetrotters: Fifty Years of Fun and Games.* New York: McKay, 1978.

Nack, William. "On the Road Again and Again." *Sports Illustrated* 62 (April 22, 1985): 78-92.

Smith, Marshall. "Basketball's Court Jester." *Life,* March 9, 1953, 91-94.

"A Trio of Goose Tatums." *Ebony,* April, 1962, 65-70.

Wilker, Josh. *The Harlem Globetrotters.* Philadelphia: Chelsea House, 1997.

CHARLEY TAYLOR

Sport: Football

Born: September 28, 1942
Grand Prairie, Texas

Early Life

Charles Robert Taylor was born on September 28, 1942, in Grand Prairie, Texas. He was one of seven children of Myrtle and Tyree Taylor. Charley's father worked at various jobs, including bank employee, porter, and mechanic. Charley's

mother remarried by the time he was a student at Grand Prairie's Dalworth High School, and Charley enjoyed a good relationship with his stepfather.

In high school, Charley went out for football. Although other players got to pick their positions on the field, by the time it was Charley's turn, all positions but tackle were taken. As a sophomore, however, he got to play end, and in his last two years, he starred as a fullback.

The Road to Excellence

Charley's stepfather played an important role in his stepson's developing career. When the boy injured his ribs in his first year, his mother demanded he stop playing for good. Charley's stepfather convinced her that football might be a good thing for him. Eventually, he led his team to the semifinals of his high school playoffs. Charley graduated with All-State recognition in football, basketball, and track.

When Charley decided to enlist in the United States Air Force after graduating, again his stepfather persuaded him that college was an opportunity not to be missed. As a result, he enrolled at Arizona State University the following autumn. Charley started out playing end again, but when his coach needed a halfback because all his runners were injured, Charley enthusiastically volunteered for the position. Soon after, he broke his neck and for six months had to wear a body cast and then a brace. Somehow, by the following year, he was back on the football field as a half-back. By his junior year, Taylor was excelling as a running back.

STATISTICS

Season	GP	Rec.	Yds.	Avg.	TD
1964	14	53	814	15.4	5
1965	13	40	577	14.4	3
1966	14	**72**	1,119	15.5	12
1967	12	**70**	990	14.1	9
1968	14	48	650	13.5	5
1969	14	71	883	12.4	8
1970	10	42	593	14.1	8
1971	6	24	370	15.4	4
1972	14	49	673	13.7	7
1973	14	59	801	13.6	7
1974	14	54	738	13.7	5
1975	14	53	744	14.6	6
1977	12	14	158	11.3	0
Totals	165	649	9,140	14.1	79

Notes: Boldface indicates statistical leader. GP = games played; Rec. = receptions; Yds. = yards; Avg. = average yards per reception; TD = touchdowns

He earned honorable-mention All-American that year and the following, having rushed for 1,162 career yards on 194 carries. In 1963, Arizona honored him as Athlete of the Year. To top off his achievements with still more recognition, at the College All-Star game, Taylor was voted most valuable player.

The Emerging Champion

Charley was selected in the first round of the 1964 National Football League (NFL) draft by the Washington Redskins. His first year, he played halfback and was sensational. He rushed for 755 yards, caught 53 passes for 814 yards, and set an NFL record for receptions by a running back. He was chosen the Rookie of the Year and was the first rookie to finish in the top ten in both rushing and pass receiving in twenty-one years. In addition, a poll of coaches ranked Taylor among the NFL's top running backs. Yet those same coaches also indicated that Charley exhibited too much anxiousness as a runner. He needed to cultivate the habit of giving his blockers time to set up. As a rookie, Charley had lost one hundred yards on end sweeps because he was so speedy that he left his blockers behind.

In 1966, the Redskins switched Taylor from running back to wide receiver. Charley was furious. It reminded him of his high school days, when he had had no say in what position he played. It all turned out for the best, though, because that same year and the following one as well he led the NFL with receptions (72 and 70). As a result, he was named to the All-NFL First Team.

Continuing the Story

Although he had initially resisted switching to wide receiver, Charley realized that it gave him the chance to do what he did best—catching the ball and running with it. Before long, he had become well known as one of the most consistent pass receivers in the NFL.

By 1970, Charley began missing games due to injuries, though he still played enough to average a formidable number of catches each season. By 1975, he had barely surpassed the established career record for passes caught, with 635 receptions. Then, after more injuries and 14 more receptions to add to his grand total, Taylor retired in 1977.

For someone who was not happy about being a wide receiver, Taylor adapted well to the change and made the best of it. It brought out his greatest strength: his consistency. Out of thirteen seasons played, he caught 649 receptions, picked up 9,140 yards receiving, and caught 79 touchdown passes. He also rushed for 1,488 yards. As one of the NFL's leading career receivers, he earned

HONORS AND AWARDS

1963	Hula Bowl All-Star Team Shrine College All-Star Team Arizona Athlete of the Year
1964	United Press International NFL Rookie of the Year Bell Trophy Sporting News NFL Rookie of the Year Chicago College All-Star Game most valuable player
1964, 1966	Sporting News NFL Eastern Conference All-Star Team
1964-69, 1974-75	All-NFL Team
1965-68, 1973-76	NFL Pro Bowl Team
1970	NFL All-Pro Team of the 1960's
1974	Sporting News NFC All-Star Team
1984	Inducted into Pro Football Hall of Fame

All-NFL First Team honors six times, played in eight Pro Bowls and one Super Bowl, and set ten Redskins records.

After retiring, Charley continued with the Redskins, serving as a personnel scout for three seasons. Then he became the team's receivers coach in 1981. Charley belongs to the Arizona State University Sports Hall of Fame and the Texas Sports Hall of Fame. Finally, in 1984, he was honored with induction into the Pro Football Hall of Fame. In the late 1990's Charley concentrated on charities for children. In 2000 he was the organizer of the Second Annual Charley Taylor/Les Brown Charity Golf Tournament. The purpose of the tournament is to raise money for foster children.

Summary

Charley Taylor started his football career in various positions, with various degrees of success. He played well enough to become the first NFL rookie in twenty-one years to finish in the top ten in both rushing and pass receiving. When he was switched to wide receiver, he found his niche at last.

Nicholas White

Additional Sources:

"From the Gridirons to the Greens." *ESPN* Online. http://espn.go.com/community/s/2000/0628/608756.html.

Pro Football Hall of Fame. http://www.pro footballhof.com.

JIM TAYLOR

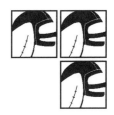

Sport: Football

Born: September 20, 1935
Baton Rouge, Louisiana

Early Life

Born on September 20, 1935, in Baton Rouge, Louisiana, to an invalid father who died an early death and a mother who toiled for low wages in the damp and steam of a laundry, James Charles Taylor spent most of his early years overcoming the obstacles that severe poverty placed in his way.

"We were real poor," Jim remembered. "I must have pedaled my bike [delivering newspapers] a million miles." As a young man, Jim worked as a "roughneck" for local oil companies, swinging a sledgehammer and stacking heavy pipes. All the hard work and intense conditioning paid off because it gave Jim the will to succeed and a body built to absorb punishment.

The Road to Excellence

At first, young Jim's body did not seem fit for any sport, much less for football, which he avoided until his junior year in high school. At 5 feet 9 inches tall and 155 pounds, he did not feel he was big enough to play the sport. One year later and fifteen pounds heavier, Jim changed his mind. He also played basketball and became the first player from his school to make All-American teams in both sports.

In the fall of 1954, Jim enrolled at Louisiana State University, where he played for Pop Strange, who called him "the finest freshman athlete I've ever seen." Unfortunately, the freshman's performances in the classroom did not match his gridiron achievements, because Jim flunked out of LSU in 1955.

Not one to quit under adversity, Jim transferred to Hinds Junior College, where he met his future wife, Dixie Grant, and raised his grades so that Paul Dietzel, whom he called "the Great White Father," could welcome him back to LSU. In 1956, Dietzel allowed Taylor to languish on the bench for five games before starting him at fullback. Jim immediately rewarded his coach by leading the Southern Conference in scoring that season with 59 points.

During his senior year, Jim finished third in the nation in scoring with 86 points and made most All-American teams as the top fullback in the country. By this time, professional scouts were knocking at the young man's door.

Green Bay Packer Jim Taylor in a 1967 game.

AP/Wide World Photos

2715

The man the Green Bay Packers selected as their second draft choice in 1958 stood 5 feet 11 inches tall and weighed about 215 pounds. Although not particularly impressive by National Football League (NFL) standards, years of lifting weights and performing isometric exercises gave Jim the strength of a young bull. He had a 19-inch neck and bulging, rock-hard thighs. Potential tacklers not impressed with Jim's size before the game changed their minds during the contest.

The Emerging Champion

At first, Jim's professional career showed little promise. Coach Ray McLean kept him mostly on the bench. When he did play, it was on the "suicide teams" where players incurred more injuries. Like Dietzel, however, McLean saw Jim's potential toward the end of his first season. Too valuable to waste on the bench or risk during kickoffs, Jim became the Packers' starting fullback during the final two games, gaining 246 yards.

When Vince Lombardi became Green Bay's coach in 1959, he needed a fullback to power the legendary Packer sweeps that would carry the team to glory in the 1960's. All of Jim's years of hard work paid off. Pedaling his bike a "million miles," swinging the heavy hammer, lifting oil pipe, and forcing himself to study hard served him well on his way to becoming a Hall of Fame, All-Pro fullback.

The 1960's were glory years for Jim as well as the Packers. After finishing fifteenth in rushing with 452 yards in 1959, he led Green Bay to a Western Division title in 1960. Millions of fans watched Jim stamp his imprint on professional football during the 1960 NFL Championship Game, which the Packers lost to Philadelphia, 17-13. The game ended with Jim plowing hard toward the goal, dragging Eagles with him, before being brought to the turf by Chuck Bednarik's game-saving tackle as time elapsed. Eight yards from the goal line a new era had dawned.

The next season, 1961, Jim led the Packers to an NFL Championship and finished second to Jim Brown in rushing with 1,307 yards. He enjoyed his best season in 1962, leading the league in three categories: 19 touchdowns (setting an NFL record), 114 points, and 1,474 yards rushing. Jim also supplied the needed power, grinding out 85 yards when freezing weather dictated a ground game in the Packers' 16-7 championship victory over the New York Giants.

Continuing the Story

In 1963 and 1964, Jim achieved his fourth and fifth consecutive 1,000-yard seasons (setting an NFL record). The Packers failed to win any titles, and some analysts thought he had lost some of the toughness that characterized his earlier performances. Seven years of absorbing punishment by some of the NFL's largest and meanest defenses had taken its toll, and even Jim admit-

STATISTICS

| Season | GP | Rushing | | | | | Receiving | | | |
		Car.	Yds.	Avg.	TD	Rec.	Yds.	Avg.	TD
1958	12	52	247	4.8	1	4	72	18.0	1
1959	12	120	452	3.8	6	9	71	7.9	2
1960	12	230	1,101	4.8	11	15	121	8.1	0
1961	14	243	1,307	5.4	15	25	175	7.0	1
1962	14	272	**1,474**	5.4	**19**	22	106	4.8	0
1963	14	248	1,018	4.1	9	13	68	5.2	1
1964	13	235	1,169	5.0	12	38	354	9.3	3
1965	13	207	734	3.5	4	20	207	10.4	0
1966	14	204	705	3.5	4	41	331	8.1	2
1967	14	130	390	3.0	2	38	251	6.6	0
Totals	132	1,941	8,597	4.4	83	225	1,756	7.8	10

Notes: Boldface indicates statistical leader. GP = games played; Car. = carries; Yds. = yards; Avg. = average yards per carry or average yards per reception; TD = touchdowns; Rec. = receptions

HONORS AND AWARDS

1958	College All-American
1961-65	NFL Pro Bowl Team
1962	Associated Press NFL Player of the Year Thorpe Trophy
1965	National Football Association Championship Game most valuable player
1970	NFL All-Pro Team of the 1960's
1976	Inducted into Pro Football Hall of Fame Uniform number 31 retired by New Orleans Saints

ted that he no longer consistently "tried to run over the defenders."

While Jim's rushing and scoring totals declined in his final two years, he still contributed stellar single-game performances as a clutch player. Sportswriters named him the most valuable player in Green Bay's 23-12 championship victory over the Cleveland Browns in 1965. He led all rushers in the Packers' 35-10 thrashing of the Kansas City Chiefs in Super Bowl I.

Jim's last year in Green Bay brought him little happiness. The Packers signed two new running backs, Jim Grabowski and Donnie Anderson, for a million dollars in bonus money. When Jim asked Lombardi (also the general manager) for a comparable raise, the answer was a resounding "No!" The two Packer greats parted company, and Jim finished his career in New Orleans in 1967. While Louisiana gave Jim a rousing welcome, he must have known that, to millions of fans, his real home would always be Green Bay.

Living in retirement, Jim made personal appearances from his home in Baton Rouge, Louisiana, where it all started in 1935.

Summary

Very few players who participate in the violent world of professional football have ever loved the contact more than Jim Taylor. Vince Lombardi called Jim "the most determined runner I've ever seen." The man with the strength of a bull and the fearlessness of a Bengal tiger became one of history's greatest fullbacks.

J. Christopher Schnell

Additional Source:

Pro Football Hall of Fame. http://www.pro footballhof.com.

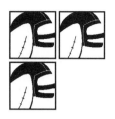

LAWRENCE TAYLOR

Sport: Football

Born: February 4, 1959
Williamsburg, Virginia

Early Life

Lawrence Taylor was born on February 4, 1959, in Williamsburg, Virginia. He grew up on the outskirts of the restored colonial village in a middle-class environment. His father worked at the shipyards in Newport News, and his mother was a schoolteacher.

Although bright, Lawrence was not a good student. The middle of three boys, he spent his early youth hustling candy on the playgrounds, thus earning himself the nickname "Candy Man." While his mother encouraged his studies, his father, a baseball fan, stressed sports.

Lawrence's first sport was baseball. Short and stocky, he did not begin football until he was fifteen. His early games were with the Williamsburg Jaycees. He played linebacker, who is, as he says, "the quarterback on defense because you controlled the game from there."

The Road to Excellence

In his sophomore year at Lafayette, the only high school in town, Lawrence was still playing for the Jaycees. Melvin Jones, an assistant at the high school who would become head coach, took him aside for a little talk. According to Lawrence, the gist of the speech was that "if you were black and from the rural South, you thought about football the way other kids thought about careers in law or medicine."

Convinced that Jaycee football was "Little League," Lawrence in his ju-

nior year went out for the team at Lafayette. At first he was just a second-string defensive lineman who stood 5 feet 7 inches tall and weighted 180 pounds, and who ran the 40-yard dash in 4.9 seconds.

All of Lawrence's hard work paid off in the fifth game of the season, a turning point in his career. Inserted into the game at defensive and against arch-rival Bethel, Lawrence played well. With a minute to go the score was tied 0-0. Lawrence rushed their punter and blocked the kick, and Lafayette recovered the ball for a game-winning touchdown.

Courtesy of the New York Football Giants, Inc.

Lawrence Taylor during his early playing days with the Giants.

By his senior year, he had grown to 6 feet 1 inch and 205 pounds. He won honors as an outside linebacker/defensive end. Because he had been a late bloomer, he was not heavily recruited by colleges. Despite attempts by Coach Jones to compare Lawrence to former National Football League (NFL) great Dick Butkus, Lawrence received offers from only two of the schools he was seriously considering. He chose the University of North Carolina.

The Emerging Champion

At Chapel Hill, Lawrence spent his first two years drinking and fighting in bars, doing more damage off the field then on it. As mostly a special teams player, his kamikaze tactics earned him nicknames like "The Monster" and "Filthy McNasty." Moreover, after his freshman year, Billy Dooley, the coach who had recruited him, left.

Coincidence struck his junior year. As in high school, he played well against his team's fifth opponent, North Carolina State University. A nose guard his first two years, he was moved to outside linebacker, where in his last two seasons he started every game.

At this point he met and fell in love with Linda Cooley, whom he married in 1981. Rearranging his priorities, he started devoting more of his life to football and Linda and less to his off-the-field shenanigans. "I played for Linda on Saturday afternoons," he says. "And I played for myself. . . . The type of respect I had been looking for all along came from playing good, hard football week after week."

By his senior year Lawrence was 6 feet 3 inches and 230 pounds and had gotten even faster. His team went 11-1 and won the Bluebonnet Bowl. That year, 1981, he had 69 solo tackles, was named Atlantic Coast Conference Player of the Year, and earned consensus All-American honors.

In 1981 the New York Giants made Lawrence the second pick overall in the NFL draft, selecting him over better-known linebackers. Lawrence

HONORS AND AWARDS	
1981	East-West Shrine All-Star Team Japan Bowl All-Star Team Consensus All-American Atlantic Coast Conference Player of the Year
1982	NFL Player Association NFC Linebacker of the Year Associated Press NFL Defensive Rookie of the Year Bell Trophy (the season's top rookie)
1982-83, 1986	Associated Press NFL Defensive Player of the Year
1982-84, 1986	Seagram's Seven Crowns of Sports Award
1982-91	NFL Pro Bowl Team
1983, 1985-86	NFL All-Pro Team
1983, 1986	United Press International NFC Defensive Player of the Year
1986	Professional Football Writers of America NFL Player of the Year
1989	Associated Press All-Pro Team United Press International All-NFC Team Professional Football Writers of America All-Pro Team All-NFL team
1994	NFL 75th Anniversary All Time Team
1999	Inducted into Pro Football Hall of Fame

had an immediate impact on the Giants, whose strong defensive tradition had lapsed during the past two decades. In his rookie year, Lawrence, now called L. T., recorded 133 tackles and 9.5 quarterback sacks. He was voted NFL Rookie of the Year and led the Big Blue to the playoffs with a 9-7 record.

Continuing the Story

Not many athletes could match L. T.'s first season. L. T. kept getting better. In his first nine years in the league, he made the Pro Bowl each year. He has been All-NFL, NFL Player of the Year, and NFL Defensive Player of the Year.

The high point in L. T.'s career came in 1986. He recorded 20.5 quarterback sacks, only 1.5 off the NFL record. As a result, the Giants went 14-2, made the playoffs, and beat the Denver Broncos 39-20 to win Super Bowl XXI. Head coach Bill Parcells said that "Lawrence was the start. He was the start of everything." He helped to redefine the position of outside linebacker and set the standard by which others are judged.

Why was L. T. such a success? According to Lawrence himself, there were two reasons: First, he saw the whole field quickly. "You get this speed flash . . . so you automatically know that a ball is going to a certain place." Second, L. T. had a tendency to free-lance. No matter what his role was supposed to be on a certain play, he relied less on technique and more on instinct. As he once said, "I believe the strength of my game absolutely depends on instinct."

Third, L. T. had determination. Twice, once in 1985 and again in 1988, L. T. admitted to substance abuse problems. Both times he successfully fought to overcome them.

Summary

Lawrence Taylor was the dominant defensive player in the NFL during the 1980's. By creating

a new position, the linebacker-lineman who rushes the quarterback, he set the standard by which all pass rushers are evaluated. Many agree that he is among the game's premier players at any position, anytime.

Charles A. Sweet, Jr.

Additional Sources:

"From the Gridirons to the Greens." *ESPN* Online. http://espn.go.com/community/s/2000/0628/608756.html.
Pro Football Hall of Fame. http://www.pro footballhof.com.

MAJOR TAYLOR

Sport: Cycling

Born: November 26, 1878
      Indianapolis, Indiana
Died: June 21, 1932
      Chicago, Illinois

Early Life

Marshall Walter Taylor was born on a dirt farm just outside Indianapolis, Indiana, on November 26, 1878. His African American parents, Gilbert and Saphronia Taylor, were children of Kentucky slaves.

Marshall was among the youngest of the Taylors' eight children. To make ends meet, his father supplemented the meager farming income by becoming a coachman for a wealthy white family; the family practically adopted young Marshall. Marshall lived with this family for the next four to five years, experiencing the privileges of the white upper class, including expensive clothes and toys and even private tutoring.

From his parents Marshall learned the value of hard work. From his semiadoptive family he learned self-confidence and the possibility of expanding his own horizons.

Marshall took to athletics naturally. He earned the respect of his playmates by holding his own in tennis, baseball, football, roller skating, and running. He could also ride a bicycle like the wind.

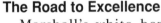

The Road to Excellence

Marshall's white benefactors moved to Chicago when the youngster was about thirteen, and Marshall went home to his family's farm. In his spare time, he taught himself all kinds of bicycle stunts and tricks. Eventually, the owner of a local bicycle shop was so impressed with Marshall that he offered him the job of shop boy. Part of his duties, as a publicity stunt, was to dress up in a full soldier's uniform and entertain passersby with his nifty stunt riding. From then on Marshall's nickname became "Major."

Major began racing bicycles at the age of fifteen. He won his first race, a 10-mile event against amateur male cyclists. He also entered and usually won various boys' races in Indiana and Illinois. Because of his African American heritage, however, he could not belong to any of the exclusively white bicycling clubs.

HONORS, AWARDS, AND MILESTONES

1898-1900	U.S. Professional Sprint Champion
1899	World Professional Sprint Champion 1-Mile World Champion
1989	Inducted into U.S. Bicycling Hall of Fame

Racial prejudice increased in Indianapolis in the late 1890's. Louis "Birdie" Munger, a white ex-racer and an Indianapolis bicycle manufacturer who saw potential greatness in Major, took the young cyclist under his wing. Munger invited Major to accompany him when he relocated his bicycle factory to the East, in Worcester, Massachusetts, a city more tolerant of African Americans.

Before Major had turned eighteen, he had gained a wonderful reputation as a graceful yet powerful sprint rider. In his professional debut at Madison Square Garden in New York, he created a sensation by defeating the reigning American sprint champion, Eddie Bald. The "Dusky Wheelman," as Major was sometimes called, was already on his way to cycling immortality.

The Emerging Champion

At the end of his second year as a professional, Major established his international reputation when he beat the star Welsh cyclist Jimmy Michael. In the process, he broke the world record twice. Major's spunky and never-say-die riding style set him apart from his competitors. His popularity with Northern racing fans and promoters soared with each successive victory.

Yet however popular Major was with the racing supporters, he was openly disliked by his fellow professional circuit riders, mostly because he was black—and talented. Fearing that Major's successes threatened their assumed physical superiority, they conspired to prevent him from winning the national championship by riding against him in combinations. As a group, they could pocket him in, elbow and bump him, and otherwise frustrate any normal racing strategy Major might have used. Major decided to use his famous "gunpowder start," figuring that if they could not catch him from the start they could not prevent him from winning. It worked.

Major's natural gifts, combined with his poise, intelligence, and self-control, helped him to overcome the harassment. In 1899, at the age of twenty-one, he won the World Championship 1-Mile; later in the year (and again in 1900) he won the coveted American sprint championship. No American rider before him had attained such a convincing level of excellence.

Continuing the Story

In the early years of the twentieth century, cycling was big in America, but even bigger in Europe. Major was lured to France to race against the world sprint champion, Edmond Jacquelin, and also to compete against other national champions throughout Europe.

Major was warmly received by the Europeans. In a short four months he achieved heroic stature, as the press celebrated his splendidly muscled body, his high character, his modesty and courtesy—and his winning ways. He rode in nearly every European capital and soundly beat all the European champions; he also met Jacquelin, losing the first match but winning the second.

Major continued racing for the rest of the decade. Eventually, physical fatigue and the stress of continued racial harassment in America on and off the racing track forced his retirement in 1910.

With his wife, Daisy, and his daughter, Rita Sydney Taylor, Major, then quite wealthy, continued to live in Worcester for the next twenty years. Ex-athletes then, however, could not capitalize much on their fame; it was doubly hard for African American athletes, as social discrimination severely limited their opportunities.

Major drifted into poverty as one business venture after another failed. Following his gradual financial collapse, his marriage also failed. He moved to Chicago in 1930, practically penniless. Without bitterness or self-pity, he died two years later in the Cook County Hospital charity ward at the age of fifty-three.

Summary

In his day, the golden age of bicycle racing, Major Taylor was known as the fastest bicycle rider in the world. He was also the only professional African American in an otherwise white sport. The racial harassment he faced on and off the track demanded heroic personal qualities. In spite of these hardships, he became the first African American world champion rider and the second African American world champion in any sport. Major Taylor, the gentleman athlete, stands as an example of what it means to pursue and achieve athletic excellence against all odds.

William Harper

Additional Sources:

Ashe, Arthur R., Jr. *A Hard Road to Glory: A History of the African American Athlete, 1619-1918.* Vol. 1. New York: Amistad Press, 1993.

Nye, Peter. *Hearts of Lions: The History of American Bicycle Racing.* New York: W. W. Norton, 1988.

Ritchie, Andrew. *Major Taylor: The Extraordinary Career of a Champion Bicycle Racer.* San Francisco: Bicycle Books, 1988. Reprint. Baltimore: Johns Hopkins University Press, 1996.

Taylor, Major. *The Fastest Bicycle Rider in the World: The Autobiography of Major Taylor.* Reprint. Brattleboro, Vt.: S. Greene Press, 1972.

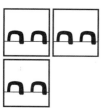

VICTOR TCHOUKARINE

Sport: Gymnastics

Born: November 9, 1921
Krasnoarmeyskoye, U.S.S.R. (now
Ukraine)
Died: August, 1984
Moscow, U.S.S.R. (now Russia)

Early Life

Victor Ivanovich Tchoukarine was born on November 9, 1921, in the village of Krasnoarmeyskoye, near the Dnieper River in the Ukrainian Soviet Republic. He began his involvement in gymnastics as a child and made his competitive debut in 1938.

However, World War II interrupted Victor's early career. He fought on the front in the Soviet army, was injured and captured, and spent four years as a prisoner of war in Germany. Upon his return home after the war, he was so weak and physically deteriorated that his mother could not positively recognize him except by a childhood scar. Doctors told Victor that he would never do gymnastics again. However, enduring injuries and captivity during the war had strengthened him, and he had developed the characteristics of will and perseverance that later helped him as an international gymnastics competitor.

The Road to Excellence

Unlike most male gymnasts in later decades, who begin training and competing internation-

Russia's Victor Tchoukarine in action on the pommel horse during the World Gymnastic Championships in Rome in 1954.

AP/Wide World Photos

ally in their late teens, Victor truly began his career in his late twenties. He studied and trained at the Lvov Institute of Physical Culture, graduating in 1950, earning the title of Honored Master of the Sport in 1951, and competing as a member of the Burevestnik Sports Society. In that same year, he won his third successive title as Soviet Gymnastics Champion and became a member of the Soviet Communist Party.

At the time of Victor's emergence, the world of international gymnastics was undergoing immense change. Prior to the 1952 Olympics in Helsinki, Finland, Soviet athletes did not participate, and international men's gymnastics competition had been dominated by Finnish, Swiss, and German competitors. In 1952, the modern age of gymnastics began with the entry onto the mats and apparatus of the strong Soviet and Japanese men, who would immediately attain long-lasting domination over the sport.

Victor was a classically trained gymnast whose style was marked by restraint, precision, and strength. Rather than incorporating dramatic moves or clever tricks into his routines, he utilized a static technique, especially on the rings, where his upper-body strength allowed him to move slowly and surely into traditional positions. His strength also helped him on the parallel bars and the pommel horse, two of his stronger events. He was a focused performer, calm and shy in public, who did exercises to train his mind as well as his body.

The Emerging Champion

The 1952 Olympics were Victor's first taste of international competition. Already established over teammates Grant Chaguinyan and Valentin Mouratov as the Soviet champion, Victor made an authoritative display in Helsinki, taking gold medals in the all-around, pommel horse, and vault competitions and a silver medal in the rings and parallel bars. In addition, the Soviets took the team title with an impressive margin over the Swiss.

With the explosion of the Soviets onto the international scene, the gymnastics world came

MAJOR CHAMPIONSHIPS					
Year	Competition	Event	Place	Event	Place
1952	Olympic Games	All-Around	Gold	Rings	Silver
		Horizontal bar	5th	Vault	Gold
		Parallel bars	Silver	Team	Gold
		Pommel horse	Gold		
1954	World Championships	All-Around	1st	Pommel horse	3d
		Floor exercise	4th	Rings	4th
		Parallel bars	1st	Team	1st
1956	Olympic Games	All-Around	Gold	Parallel bars	Gold
		Floor exercise	Silver	Pommel horse	Bronze
		Horizontal bar	4th	Team	Gold

alive. After the Helsinki Olympics, Victor faced a great deal of competition from both his own team and others, an array of gymnasts prepared to challenge the world superiority he established in Helsinki.

On the national level, he repeated his Soviet championships in 1953 and 1955. His experiences and views led in 1955 to a book, *Put'k vershinam* (the road to the peaks), which gained him further fame among the Soviet peoples.

Internationally, Victor tied with teammate Mouratov for the all-around title at the 1954 World Championships in Rome, Italy, leading a Soviet sweep of the first five places. He also took a gold medal in the parallel bars and placed among the top four competitors in every event but the horizontal bar, consistently his weakest.

At the 1956 Olympics in Melbourne, Australia, Victor faced new challenges, including Yuri Titov and Boris Shakhlin on his own team and a vastly improved Japanese squad led by Takashi Ono and Masao Takemoto. During a warm-up, Victor injured his thumb, but rather than dropping out of particular events or withdrawing from the Games completely, he proceeded according to plan with his rehearsed routines. Not only did he make it through the competition, but he walked away with three gold medals, including his second successive Olympic gold medal as all-around champion. In the face of adversity, Victor's supremacy was confirmed.

Continuing the Story

Victor retired from competition after the 1956 Olympics, still a champion at the age of thirty-five, but he continued his work in gymnastics as a trainer and coach. For his accomplishments in international contests, he was honored by the Soviet government with the Order of Lenin.

In 1961, Victor became coach of the gymnastics team of the Armenian Republic. Two years later he became an assistant professor at his alma mater, the Lvov Institute of Physical Culture, and in 1971 he was appointed the institute's Head of Gymnastics. The following year he was given the title of Honored Coach of the Ukrainian Republic.

Victor Tchoukarine died of stomach cancer in Moscow in the summer of 1984 at the age of sixty-two.

Summary

At a time when men's gymnastics was coming of age and entering a new era in its competitive energy, technical demands, and audience ap-

---

HONORS AND AWARDS

1956	Decorated with the Order of Lenin

---

peal, Victor Tchoukarine led the Soviet team to lasting domination and set the standard against which his eventual successors—Boris Shakhlin, Yukio Endo, Nikolai Andrianov—were forced to strive.

Barry Mann

Additional Sources:

Brokhin, Yuri, and Glenn Garelik, trans. *The Big Red Machine: The Rise and Fall of Soviet Olympic Champions.* New York: Random House, 1978.

Wise, Michael T., Christina Bankes, and Jane Laing, eds. *Chronicle of the Olympics, 1896-1996.* New York: DK Publishing, 1996.

BILL TERRY

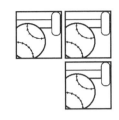

Sport: Baseball

Born: October 30, 1898
      Atlanta, Georgia
Died: January 9, 1989
      Jacksonville, Florida

Early Life

William Harold Terry was born on October 30, 1898, in Atlanta, Georgia, but spent most of his childhood as well as many of his later years in Memphis, Tennessee. Details about his early years are scanty, but he seems to have had as a boy the qualities of shrewdness, self-confidence, and leadership that he displayed later.

The Road to Excellence

Bill began to pitch professionally at the age of sixteen, playing in the Georgia-Alabama League and, for two years thereafter, at Shreveport in the Texas League. Then, despite an overall record of 27-14, he dropped out of professional baseball for the next four years.

These years were far from time lost, however. He operated a filling station and foresaw opportunities in the oil and automobile industries that he would later put to good use. Meanwhile, he played semiprofessional baseball and attracted the interest of the New York Giants.

In 1922, the Giants sent the now twenty-three-year-old prospect to Toledo of the American Association, where he continued to pitch and often played first base. As a pitcher, he proved only mediocre, winning 9 and losing 9 with a rather high earned run average of 4.26, but he began to show the hitting and fielding ability that later made him a champion.

Beginning in 1923, he stuck exclusively to first base and batted an awesome .377; he also led the league in fielding at his position with only 7 errors in 109 games. Manager John McGraw of the Giants decided that Bill was ready to help the parent club.

He played in three games for the Giants at the end of that season and played part-time in 1924 but found National League pitching much tougher. His .239 average was hardly adequate for a first baseman, but McGraw saw ability in him and decided to install him as a regular in 1925.

The Emerging Champion

In 1925, two future baseball greats began playing first base regularly for New York teams: Lou

National Baseball Library, Cooperstown, New York

2727

Gehrig with the Yankees and Bill Terry with the Giants. Gehrig had more power, but Bill hit with as much consistency and displayed more fielding grace and range. In that first season as a regular, Bill batted .319.

Bill was an assertive young man, a natural leader, but he was playing for a manager who did not intend to share any of his authority with his young first baseman. John McGraw had been managing almost continuously in the major leagues from the time Bill was born, and he had earned the nickname "Little Napoleon."

There were frequent clashes between the two. Bill defied McGraw whenever possible. Each spring, he held out for more money and issued ultimatums from his Memphis home: "Pay me or trade me." Players had very little bargaining strength in the 1920's, however, and McGraw had no intention of trading his young star.

Bill capped a half-dozen excellent seasons in 1930 when he batted .401 with an astonishing 254 hits and 129 runs batted in. There had been other .400 hitters, but in the next sixty years, no National Leaguer and only one major leaguer—Ted Williams—would accomplish the feat.

Continuing the Story

In 1932, the Giants, who had won ten pennants under McGraw but had not won since 1924, Bill's first year with the club, slipped badly. The team, usually in contention, was mired in the second division in June when McGraw, now nearly sixty years old, decided to quit.

More than a few eyebrows were raised when Little Napoleon picked as his successor his old nemesis, Bill Terry. Now Bill faced the difficult challenge of combining the duties of player and manager. He insisted on, and received, even more authority than McGraw had enjoyed. With Bill having the final word on all player personnel matters, the Giants reigned as world champions in 1933.

In 1934, he committed his biggest baseball blunder when, asked for his assessment of the struggling Brooklyn Dodgers by a reporter, he responded, "Is Brooklyn still in the league?" The infuriated Dodgers won their final two games from the Giants and knocked them out of the pennant race. Since that time, managers have shown much more caution in evaluating weaker opponents.

In 1936 and 1937, the Giants again won pennants under Bill, although losing to their New York rivals, the Yankees, both years in the World Series. After the 1936 season, Bill retired as a player with a .341 lifetime batting average and a well-deserved reputation as the best-fielding first baseman of his era. He managed the Giants through 1941, then turned to oil and cotton speculation and then to an automobile distributorship in Florida. He also served as president of the South Atlantic League from 1954 to 1958.

STATISTICS

Season	GP	AB	Hits	2B	3B	HR	Runs	RBI	BA	SA
1923	3	7	1	0	0	0	1	0	.143	.143
1924	77	163	39	7	2	5	26	24	.239	.399
1925	133	489	156	31	6	11	75	70	.319	.474
1926	98	225	65	12	5	5	26	43	.289	.453
1927	150	580	189	32	13	20	101	121	.326	.529
1928	149	568	185	36	11	17	100	101	.326	.518
1929	150	607	226	39	5	14	103	117	.372	.522
1930	154	633	**254**	39	15	23	139	129	**.401**	.619
1931	153	611	213	43	**20**	9	**121**	112	.349	.529
1932	154	643	225	42	11	28	124	117	.350	.580
1933	123	475	153	20	5	6	68	58	.322	.423
1934	153	602	213	30	6	8	109	83	.354	.463
1935	145	596	203	32	8	6	91	64	.341	.451
1936	79	229	71	10	5	2	36	39	.310	.424
Totals	1,721	6,428	2,193	373	112	154	1,120	1,078	.341	.506

Notes: Boldface indicates statistical leader. GP = games played; AB = at bats; 2B = doubles; 3B = triples; HR = home runs; RBI = runs batted in; BA = batting average; SA = slugging average

HONORS AND AWARDS

1933-35	National League All-Star Team
1954	Inducted into National Baseball Hall of Fame
	Uniform number 3 retired by San Francisco Giants

Perhaps because of his abrasiveness with sportswriters, Bill Terry was not elected to the National Baseball Hall of Fame until 1954. Still in good shape, he cracked a home run in an old-timers' game that summer in Yankee Stadium.

Bill remained active throughout a long life and died a wealthy man at the age of ninety in Jacksonville, Florida, on January 9, 1989.

Summary

Asked for the secret of hitting, Bill Terry replied, "Confidence." He seems always to have had confidence in himself, in his ability, and in his judgment. Although he could be harsh in his treatment of subordinates, his players, recognizing his commitment to their best interests and those of the team, respected and liked him as a manager.

Few men have attained similar success at both playing and managing. A longtime observer of baseball explained Bill's success by pointing to his knowledge—of the game, of players, of business, and of people generally.

Robert P. Ellis

Additional Sources:

Shatzkin, Mike, et al., eds. *The Ballplayers: Baseball's Ultimate Biographical Reference.* New York: William Morrow, 1990.

Stein, Fred. *Under Coogan's Bluff: A Fan's Recollections of the New York Giants Under Terry and Ott.* Glenshaw, Pa.: Chapter and Cask, 1981.

Williams, Peter. *When the Giants Were Giants: Bill Terry and the Golden Age of New York Baseball.* Chapel Hill, N.C.: Algonquin Books of Chapel Hill, 1994.

VINNY TESTAVERDE

Sport: Football

Born: November 13, 1963
Brooklyn, New York

Early Life

Vinny Testaverde was born on November 13, 1963, in Brooklyn, New York. He grew up in Elmont, Long Island, with his parents and sister. Because of his football prowess in high school as a quarterback, Vinny was offered a full scholarship to the University of Miami, where he became one of the best college quarterbacks of all time. He set a Miami Hurricanes' record in passing yardage with 6,058 yards—6,580 including bowl games—and also became the Hurricanes'

New York Jet Vinny Testaverde after winning the AFC divisional playoff in January, 1999.

leader with 48 touchdown passes, a record later tied by Steve Walsh. Vinny compiled a nation-high 165.8 passer rating as a senior in 1986 while leading Miami to an 11-0 regular season record as he connected on 414 of 628 passes (65.9 percent) for 5,795 yards, 47 touchdowns, and 24 interceptions. Before he ever played for the National Football League (NFL), he won numerous awards including college football's 1986 Heisman Trophy for the best college football player. He was named the 1986 Italian American Athlete of the Year and was a unanimous All-America selection. He was also a finalist for the Sullivan Award, given to the nation's top amateur athlete.

The Road to Excellence

Vinny began a strong career in the NFL after being the first-round draft choice of the Tampa Bay Buccaneers in 1987. He earned an All-Rookie selection from *Football Weekly* and *Football Digest* in his first campaign. In 1988 he passed for 3,240 yards to rank fifth in the National Football Conference (NFC) and ninth in the NFL. Vinny's yardage total was then a career best and became the fourth-highest season mark for the Buccaneers. He also set a league record of 35 interceptions that year. In 1989 he twice won the NFC Offensive Player of the Week award as he threw for a total of 20 touchdown passes, tying the team single-season record set by Doug Williams in 1980.

In 1993 Vinny was traded to the Cleveland Browns, where he threw for 2,575 yards and had a quarterback rating of 85.7. He also set an NFL record against the St. Louis Rams by completing 91.3 percent of his passes, (21 out of 23) for 216 yards and 2 touchdowns.

The Emerging Champion

In the Browns' 1995 season, Vinny tied for third in the American Football Conference (AFC)

STATISTICS

Season	GP	PA	PC	Pct.	Yds.	Avg.	TD	Int.
1987	6	165	71	.430	1,081	6.55	5	6
1988	15	466	222	.476	3,240	6.95	13	35
1989	14	480	258	.538	3,133	6.53	20	22
1990	14	365	203	.556	2,818	7.72	17	18
1991	13	326	166	.509	1,994	6.12	8	15
1992	14	358	206	.575	2,554	7.13	14	16
1993	10	230	130	.565	1,797	7.81	14	9
1994	14	376	207	.551	2,575	6.85	16	18
1995	13	392	241	.615	2,883	7.35	17	10
1996	16	549	325	.592	4,177	7.61	33	19
1997	13	470	271	.577	2,971	6.32	18	15
1998	15	421	259	.615	3,256	7.73	29	7
1999	1	15	10	.667	96	6.40	1	1
2000	16	590	328	.556	3,732	6.33	21	25
Totals	174	5,203	2,897	.557	36,307	6.98	226	216

Notes: GP = games played; PA = passes attempted; PC = passes completed; Pct. = percent completed; Yds. = yards; Avg. = average yards per attempt; TD = touchdowns; Int. = interceptions

with a then-career-high 87.8 quarterback rating. He threw for 17 touchdowns and 10 interceptions that season while completing 241 of 392 passes for a career-high 61.5 percent; he also threw for 2,883 yards.

In 1996 Vinny joined the Baltimore Ravens, where he hoped to continue his success. That year he was named to the AFC Pro Bowl as the third quarterback, the first time in his career he was selected for the Pro Bowl. He also won the Ravens' most valuable player award. Statistically, 1996 was one of Vinny's most successful years as he completed 325 of 549 passes for 4,177 yards—second in the NFL—with 33 touchdowns and 19 interceptions, for an 88.7 quarterback rating. In 1997 Vinny suffered a knee injury, which caused him to miss the last three games of the season.

Continuing the Story

Vinny became a New York Jet in 1998 and enjoyed even greater success as a pro football player. After the Jets' starter, Glenn Foley, suffered a knee injury, Vinny became the full-time starting quarterback, leading the Jets to a 12-4 record and coming within one game of going to the Super Bowl. Even though he did not play the full season, he threw for 3,256 yards, 29 touchdowns, and 7 interceptions in 1998, again being selected for the Pro Bowl.

The Jets came into the 1999 season as favorites to win the Super Bowl, but it was not to be. In the first game of 1999, against the New England Patriots, Vinny suffered a season-ending tendon injury, which ruined his hopes for the championship. Then his father, Al, succumbed to a heart attack during that season, a painful loss for Vinny.

In the 2000 season, however, Vinny came back strong with career highs in both pass attempts and completions.

Summary

Vinny Testaverde has had a solid career as an NFL quarterback, despite injuries, the loss of his father, and his habit of throwing interceptions. A family man who comes from Italian roots and enjoys visiting with his friends and family in Elmont, New York, Vinny has set more than his share of records in the NFL.

Richard Slapsys

Additional Sources:

Hersch, Hank. "Trials of Testaverde." *Sports Illustrated* 69, no. 27 (December 19, 1988): 44.

King, Peter. "Vinny Testaverde." *Sports Illustrated* 73, no. 20 (November 12, 1990): 64.

_____. "Vinny, Vidi, Vici." *Sports Illustrated* 90, no. 2 (January 18, 1999): 32.

Zimmermann, Paul. "Vinny's Vindication." *Sports Illustrated* 82, no. 1 (January 9, 1995): 51.

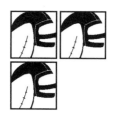

DERRICK THOMAS

Sport: Football

Born: January 1, 1967
Miami, Florida
Died: February 8, 2000
Miami, Florida

Early Life

Derrick Vincent Thomas was born on New Year's Day, 1967, in Miami, Florida, the son of Edith Morgan and U.S. Air Force captain Robert Thomas. At age five Derrick lost his father when he was shot down over North Vietnam during a 1972 bombing mission designated Operation: Linebacker Two. Initially declared missing in action, Captain Thomas was pronounced dead in 1980.

Raised primarily by his mother, Edith, Derrick led a troubled life as a youngster. He began committing petty crimes and at age fifteen was sent to Dade Marine Institute, a school for juvenile offenders, following his arrest for burglary, vandalism, and theft. The school provided Derrick with an opportunity to turn his life around, and he took advantage of it, scoring well on his tests while at the same time developing an interest in such activities as scuba diving and boating. He completed the six-month program in a record four months.

The Road to Excellence

In 1985 Derrick graduated from South Miami High School, where he excelled as a running back and tight end. Pursued by dozens of colleges, he accepted a football scholarship to the University of Alabama. During his junior and senior years, Derrick was recognized as the nation's leading pass rusher and in 1988 won the Butkus Award as the top collegiate linebacker. Derrick set Alabama school records with 52 sacks and 74 tackles behind the line of scrimmage. He also recorded 204 tackles, 12 forced fumbles, 4 fumble recoveries, 5 blocked kicks, 1 safety, and 1 touch-

down. As a senior he finished tenth in the Heisman Trophy balloting and was a unanimous All-American First Team selection.

Derrick was selected by the Kansas City Chiefs in the first round of the 1989 National Football League (NFL) draft and was the fourth pick overall, following Troy Aikman, Tony Mandarich, and Barry Sanders. He was the first linebacker ever drafted by the Chiefs in the first round.

Linebacker for the Kansas City Chiefs Derrick Thomas waves to fans in 1991.

The Emerging Champion

Derrick immediately became a dominating force on the Chiefs' defense. In his first NFL season, he recorded 55 quarterback pressures and 10 quarterback sacks. He was named Defensive Rookie of the Year by the Associated Press, *Pro Football Weekly, College and Pro Football Newsweekly,* and the NFL's Players' Association. He was also an All-NFL selection by *Sports Illustrated* and a Second Team All-Pro pick by *College and Pro Football Newsweekly.* His impressive rookie season was capped when he was named as a Pro Bowl starter for the American Conference team.

Continuing the Story

In only his second full season in the NFL, Derrick achieved perhaps his most impressive single-game performance. In a November 11, 1990, contest against the Seattle Seahawks, he sacked opposing quarterback Dave Krieg 7 times, establishing a new NFL record, and forced 2 fumbles. He nearly registered his eighth sack on the final play of the game, but Krieg escaped his grasp to throw a game-winning touchdown pass.

Derrick was a mainstay of a defensive team that spurred the Chiefs to over one hundred victories in the 1990's, one of only three NFL teams to reach that milestone. His brand of football was the big play, a style adopted by the entire defensive team. Its aim was simply to make a sack, block a punt, force a fumble or an interception, and return the football for a touchdown.

In 1993 Derrick was selected as the NFL Man of the Year, an award that recognizes both on-field performance and community service. His charitable works on behalf of disadvantaged children began soon after his entry into the NFL. In 1990 he founded the Third and Long Foundation, which promoted literacy among academically challenged students. In addition, he made frequent visits to sick children across the country. Through his generosity thousands of inner-city youth were able to attend Chiefs home games. For his efforts he was awarded the Byron White Humanitarian Award in 1995.

By 1997 there were signs that Derrick's career was beginning to wane. An injury to his left tricep tendon and the use of a bulky arm brace slowed his movements considerably, and he ended up missing 4 games. The following year he started

STATISTICS

Season	GP	Tac.	Sac.	FR	Int.
1989	16	N/A	10.0	1	0
1990	15	N/A	**20.0**	2	0
1991	16	N/A	13.5	4	0
1992	16	N/A	14.5	3	0
1993	16	N/A	8.0	1	0
1994	16	N/A	11.0	3	0
1995	15	N/A	8.0	1	0
1996	16	N/A	13.0	1	0
1997	12	N/A	9.5	0	0
1998	15	N/A	12.0	2	0
1999	16	60	7.0	1	1
Totals	169	N/A	126.5	19	1

Notes: Boldface indicates statistical leader. GP = games played; Tac. = total tackles; Sac. = sacks; FR = fumble recoveries; Int. = interceptions

only 10 games, the lowest total of his career. In 1999 a mediocre season for both him and the Chiefs raised questions about how much longer his career would last.

On January 23, 2000, Derrick was driving to the airport with two friends when his vehicle skidded out of control and crashed on an icy road, throwing him from the car and killing one of the passengers. The third passenger suffered only minor injuries. Derrick, however, was left with two fractured vertebrae and was paralyzed from the chest down. On January 24 he was transported to Jackson Memorial Hospital in Miami, where he underwent spinal cord surgery. On February 8, following two weeks of medical treatment, Derrick died suddenly after suffering cardiorespiratory arrest caused by a massive blood clot that had formed in his pulmonary artery.

Summary

Derrick Thomas's legacy as a professional football player is an impressive one. During his eleven-year career he was named to the Pro Bowl nine times, and in terms of sacks he was ranked ninth on the league's career list. Though he was recognized as one of the NFL's premier linebackers, Derrick's style did not always fit the profile of the position. At one stage the Chiefs invented a new position for him, called the Falcon, which called for a combination of linebacker-lineman skills. The move was a testimony to the unique blend of talents Derrick brought to the football field.

William H. Hoffman

2733

Additional Sources:

Chavez, Luciana. "Gimme Three Steps." *The Sporting News* 22, no. 51 (December 22, 1997): 36-37.

Posnanski, Joe, and Dave Sloan. "Thrown for a Loss: Thomas." *The Sporting News* 8, no. 224 (February 21, 2000): 32-34.

Silver, Michael. "The Beat Goes On." *Sports Illustrated* 85 (September 16, 1996): 38-41.

FRANK THOMAS

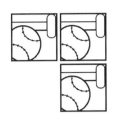

Sport: Baseball

Born: May 27, 1968
Columbus, Georgia

Early Life

Born in Columbus, Georgia, on May 27, 1968, Frank Edward Thomas, Jr,. was the youngest of five children raised by his mother, Charlie Mae, a textile worker, and her husband, Frank, Sr., a Baptist deacon and bail bondsman. Frank performed extremely well in all sports, and his prowess as a budding baseball star showed at an early age, when he was a hitter feared by opposing Little League hurlers. A natural and versatile African American athlete who grew to 6 feet 5 inches and wore size fourteen shoes, Frank starred in three high school sports–basketball, baseball, and football. Auburn University awarded Frank a football scholarship in 1986, but after one season he switched to baseball.

The Road to Excellence

During his three seasons of college baseball, Frank walloped 49 homers for a school record and was the Southeastern Conference's most valuable player (MVP) in 1989. In that same year, the Chicago White Sox organization picked him as its seventh choice in the free-agent draft. Frank began his minor league stint in the A Division with Sarasota, then moved up to the AA Birmingham. The promising youngster led the Southern League with a .581 slugging percentage and .487 on-base percentage while batting .323 with 18 home runs and 71 runs batted in (RBIs) in 109 games. Baseball America named him the 1990 Minor League Player of the Year.

The Emerging Champion

Frank made his major league debut in Chicago during the final two months of the 1990 season. Appearing in sixty games, he responded by hitting .330, with 7 home runs and 31 RBIs. Frank soon emerged as a regular fixture in the White Sox lineup, playing first base or serving as designated hitter. His first two full seasons demonstrated superstar potential as he consistently posted spectacular offensive stats, hitting over .300, launching more than 20 or 30 home runs and topping 100 RBIs. The baseball world began to notice that an impressive new star had arrived on the scene.

As Frank's career progressed, so did his already impressive prowess in all facets of hitting

Frank Thomas of the White Sox slams a double in a 1999 game.

STATISTICS

Season	GP	AB	Hits	2B	3B	HR	Runs	RBI	BA	SA
1990	60	191	63	11	3	7	39	31	.330	.529
1991	158	559	178	31	2	32	104	109	.318	.553
1992	160	573	185	**46**	2	24	108	115	.323	.536
1993	153	549	174	36	0	41	106	128	.317	.607
1994	113	399	141	34	1	38	**106**	101	.353	**.729**
1995	**145**	493	152	27	0	40	102	111	.308	.606
1996	141	527	184	26	0	40	110	134	.349	.626
1997	146	530	184	35	0	35	110	125	**.347**	.611
1998	160	585	155	35	2	29	109	109	.265	.480
1999	135	486	148	36	0	15	74	77	.305	.471
2000	159	582	191	44	0	43	115	143	.328	.625
Totals	1,530	5,474	1,755	361	10	344	1,083	1,183	.321	.579

Notes: Boldface indicates statistical leader. GP = games played; AB = at bats; 2B = doubles; 3B = triples; HR = home runs; RBI = runs batted in; BA = batting average; SA = slugging average

and offense. Frank's first seven seasons represent a record for offensive consistency. From 1991 through 1997, his combined statistical yearly averages came to .323 in batting percentage, over 33 home runs, 117 RBIs, and 119 bases on ball. As a result, this White Sox slugger rates very high on the list of all-time great hitters in many offensive categories. Frank led the American League in walks four times, and the 29 intentional passes he received in 1995 are a league record.

Recognition for such excellence was forthcoming. In 1993, after blasting 41 home runs, along with his usual awesome stats in other categories, he received the American League's MVP award by unanimous vote. Only nine other past MVP recipients had earned this honor. In 1994, his batting average reached a high of .353, and he became the eleventh American League player to receive multiple MVP awards. Sportswriters began calling Frank "Big Hurt," a nickname representing the damage this towering 275-pound slugger inflicted on opposing pitchers. The "Big Hurt" was a five-time American League All-Star choice between 1993 and 1997. In the latter year, he also won the American League batting title, hitting .347.

Continuing the Story

After 1997, Frank's stellar career encountered a temporary bump in the road. Although his other offensive stats remained high, his 1998 batting average plummeted below .300 for the first time. In the following season, he managed to hit .315, but his power stats dropped off to a career

low. Although these offensive figures would more than satisfy many fellow major leaguers, some sportswriters and critics began to suggest that the slugger's former magic touch was gone, his career on a downward spiral, his earlier motivation and drive sagging, and his future with the White Sox uncertain.

The 2000 baseball season silenced these premature judgements. The "Big Hurt" rebounded with a vengeance to put on another spectacular offensive display for awed baseball fans. Moreover, Frank barely fell short of earning his third MVP award after leading the talent-loaded White Sox team to a division title.

On the personal side, Frank's character and demeanor contradict his "Big Hurt" nickname. This gentle giant's modesty, kindness, and mild-mannered disposition did not change in the face of fame and success. Those who know him well suggest that "Big Teddy Bear" is a more fitting description of his nature. Concerned with helping others battle disease and misfortune, he established the Frank Thomas Charitable Foundation in 1993. This combination of stardom and admirable personal qualities may have attracted his wife, Elise Silver, whom he met in 1992. They became the parents of several children.

Summary

Frank Thomas's baseball career is distinguished by year upon year of great offensive power and productivity, placing him among the all-time great players of the game. In his heyday,

Frank rated first among active players in on-base percentage and was among the leaders in other categories, such as walks, total bases, home runs, RBIs, and batting average. When Frank's career on-base and slugging percentages were combined, he ranked first among all active players. Clearly, the "Big Hurt" contributed to making the White Sox a frequent contender or leader in the American League Central Division during the 1990's.

David A. Crain

Additional Sources:

Deane, Bill. *Sports Great Frank Thomas.* Berkeley Heights, N.J.: Enslow, 2000.

Reilly, Rick. "The Big Hurt." *Sports Illustrated* 81 (August 8, 1994): 16-22.

Rushin, Steve. "No Doubting Thomas." *Sports Illustrated* 70 (September 16, 1991): 30-32, 35.

Thornley, Stew. *Frank Thomas: Baseball's Big Hurt.* Minneapolis, Minn.: Lerner Publishing, 1997.

Wulf, Steve. "Big Hurt." *Sports Illustrated* 79 (September 13, 1993): 40-43.

ISIAH THOMAS

Sport: Basketball

Born: April 30, 1961
Chicago, Illinois

Early Life

In the poverty-stricken West Side Chicago neighborhood known as K-Town (because so many street names began with the letter K), Isiah Lord Thomas III was born on April 30, 1961, the youngest of nine children.

Isiah Thomas of the Pistons goes to the hoop in the 1994 game.

Although life in the gang-infested K-Town was at best dangerous and difficult, Isiah's mother and father did the best they could to bring up their large family. Isiah's father was a foreman at International Harvester for a time, but when the plant closed, leaving Isiah Thomas II jobless, frustration and anger set in. Eventually he left home, leaving Mary Thomas in charge of the nine children, seven of whom were boys.

Mary Thomas was determined not to have her boys pulled into the West Side's gang life. She encouraged them to pursue athletics instead of getting involved in crime. In spite of her efforts, however, several of her sons were seduced by drugs and gangs. Only the youngest, Isiah, remained the family's hope for a better life beyond the grip of poverty.

The Road to Excellence

The journey to the promised land of wealth and safety was to be led by the young Isiah Thomas. The three-year-old Isiah would often be the halftime entertainment at the local Catholic Youth Organization basketball games. Wearing an oversized jersey and shoes, he would toss up shots with a high arc. "Isiah was amazing," recalled his brother Alexis.

Isiah continued to hone his skills throughout childhood at Gladys Park, just two blocks from his home. When he was in eighth grade, he tried for a basketball scholarship with Weber High School of the city's Catholic basketball league. The coach of that school, however, rejected Isiah because he thought he was too small. The coach at St. Joseph High, Gene Pingatore, secured a scholarship for Isiah. Pingatore said Isiah was "a winner" who "had that special aura." Isiah became an honors student at St. Joseph, and he led its basketball team to a second-place trophy in the state championship tournament in his junior year. The next year, he was one of the

STATISTICS

Season	GP	FGM	FG%	FTM	FT%	Reb.	Ast.	TP	PPG
1981-82	72	453	.424	302	.704	209	565	1,225	17.0
1982-83	81	725	.472	368	.710	328	634	1,854	22.9
1983-84	82	669	.462	388	.733	327	914	1,748	21.3
1984-85	81	646	.458	399	.809	361	1,123	1,720	21.2
1985-86	77	609	.488	365	.790	277	830	1,609	20.9
1986-87	81	626	.463	400	.768	319	813	1,671	20.6
1987-88	81	621	.463	305	.774	278	678	1,577	19.5
1988-89	80	569	.464	287	.818	273	663	1,458	18.2
1989-90	81	579	.438	292	.775	308	765	1,492	18.4
1990-91	48	289	.435	179	.782	160	446	776	16.2
1991-92	78	564	.446	292	.772	247	560	1,445	18.5
1992-93	79	526	.418	278	.737	232	671	1,391	17.6
1993-94	58	318	.417	181	.702	159	399	856	14.8
Totals	979	7,194	.452	4,036	.759	3,478	9,061	18,822	19.2

Notes: GP = games played; FGM = field goals made; FG% = field goal percentage; FTM = free throws made; FT% = free throw percentage; Reb. = rebounds; Ast. = assists; TP = total points; PPG = points per game

nation's most sought-after basketball players, being recruited by more than one hundred colleges.

Indiana University was Isiah's ultimate choice. Under coach Bob Knight, Isiah made the All-Big Ten team in his first season. In his second season, Isiah was named All-American and led his Hoosiers to the Final Four of the National Collegiate Athletic Association (NCAA) Tournament. Indiana won the 1981 national championship, defeating Louisiana State University in the semifinal round and the University of North Carolina in the final round. Isiah was named the tournament's most outstanding player. The next season, because of difficulties with Indiana's coach, Isiah decided to leave Indiana *and* turn professional.

The Emerging Champion

Isiah was picked second overall in the June 5, 1981, National Basketball Association (NBA) draft. He signed a $1.6-million contract with the Detroit Pistons, whose record in the 1980-1981 season was the second worst in the league. Isiah now had enough money to help his family out of poverty and soon bought his mother a house in the Chicago suburb of Clarendon Hills.

Isiah's fortunes were only beginning, however. As a point guard, he proved himself a team leader in his rookie year with the Pistons.

In the 1983-1984 season, the Pistons had their first winning record in seven years: forty-nine wins, thirty-three losses. That season, averaging 21.3 points and 11 assists, Isiah signed a new ten-year contract worth more than twelve million dollars. He was also named most valuable player in the All-Star game that year, posting 21 points and 15 assists. The next season, Isiah set an NBA record for assists: 1,123. In 1986, he was once again MVP of the All-Star game, leading the Eastern Conference to a win with 30 points, 10 assists, and 5 steals.

In 1987, the Pistons had emerged from being among the worst in the conference to legitimate playoff contenders. Throughout the playoffs, Isiah averaged 20.6 points per game. In the Eastern Conference championship series, the Pistons stretched the defending world champion Boston Celtics to the full seven games but lost the last, bitterly contested game. That season, however, through Isiah's leadership, the Pistons proved they were championship caliber.

Continuing the Story

In 1988, the Pistons beat the Celtics for the Eastern Conference championship and went on to the league championship series against the Los Angeles Lakers, the defending world champions. In game 6 of that series, Isiah gave one of his all-time best performances.

As good as his performance was in the 1988 series with the Lakers, Isiah would have to wait until 1989 to wear the world championship ring. In 1989, the Pistons again played the Lakers and swept the two-time champions in four games. In 1990, the Pistons repeated as world champions, led by the dynamic play of the great guard, Isiah Thomas. He was named the NBA finals MVP. Isiah was once quoted as saying that he wanted "to establish in Detroit (what) they've done in Boston since the 1950's and 1960's, in terms of tradition, in terms of pride, in terms of style of play."

Isiah is only the fourth player in NBA history to collect more than 9,000 assists. He was an excellent passer and a smooth, clever playmaker. Despite his constant friendly smile, Isiah was a tough, fierce competitor. A dangerous shooter from anywhere on the floor, Isiah was a very unselfish, team-oriented player. He served as the president of the NBA Players Association from the late 1980's into the early 1990's. Because of a series of injuries during the 1993-1994 season, Isiah slowed down considerably. A torn Achilles tendon in April, 1994, brought an end to his illustrious career. He had been an NBA All-Star twelve times (1982-1993) and a member of the All-NBA First Team on three occasions (1984, 1985, 1986).

Following his retirement, Isiah became part owner and executive vice president of the Toronto Raptors. As part of the celebration of the golden anniversary of the NBA during the 1996-1997 season, Isiah was named to the NBA's 50 Greatest Players of All Time Team. He left the Raptors during the 1997-1998 season and became a color analyst for the National Broadcasting Corporation (NBC) on its NBA telecasts.

In August 1999, Isiah purchased the Continental Basketball Association (CBA) for $10 million, with the goal to create a minor league basketball system for the NBA. In 2000, Isiah was inducted into the Naismith Memorial Basketball Hall of Fame. Later in the year, he was named the head coach of the Indiana Pacers. Off the court, Isiah is very active as a charity worker and is involved in educational, anticrime, and antipoverty programs for young people.

HONORS, AWARDS, AND RECORDS

1980	Men's U.S. Olympic Basketball Team All-Big Ten Team
1981	NCAA Tournament Most Outstanding Player NCAA All-Tournament Team Consensus All-American
1982	NBA All-Rookie Team
1982-93	NBA All-Star Team
1984-86	All-NBA First Team NBA All-Star Game most valuable player
1987	Kennedy Citizenship Award
1988	NBA record for the most points in one quarter of a Finals game (25)
1990	NBA Finals most valuable player
1996	NBA Greatest 50 Players of All Time Team
1999	Named one of the twenty best NBA players of all time
2000	Inducted into Naismith Memorial Basketball Hall of Fame Uniform number 11 retired by Detroit Pistons

Summary

Although considered small in size for the NBA, Isiah Thomas has always been big in character. It is a quality he possessed when he led the Indiana Hoosiers to the NCAA crown and a quality he maintained as he led the Detroit Pistons to their world championships of 1989 and 1990.

Rustin Larson

Additional Sources:

Bjarkman, Peter C. *The Biographical History of Basketball.* Chicago: Masters Press, 1998.

Dolin, Nick, Chris Dolin, and David Check. *Basketball Stars: The Greatest Players in the History of the Game.* New York: Black Dog and Leventhal, 1997.

Mallozzi, Vincent M. *Basketball: The Legends and the Game.* Willowdale, Ont.: Firefly Books, 1998.

Rosenthal, Bert. *Isiah Thomas, Pocket Magic.* Chicago: Children's Press, 1983.

Shouler, Kenneth A. *The Experts Pick Basketball's Best Fifty Players in the Last Fifty Years.* Lenexa, Kans.: Addax, 1998.

KURT THOMAS

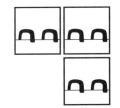

Sport: Gymnastics

Born: March 29, 1956
Miami, Florida

Early Life

Kurt Thomas was born on March 29, 1956, in Miami, Florida. A child small for his age, he grew up in a rough urban neighborhood and developed street sense quickly. When Kurt was seven, his father, Robert, a manager at a meat company, was killed in an automobile accident, leaving Eleanore Thomas, a secretary, to raise her three sons and daughter alone.

By that time, 1963, Kurt was already doing handstands as the tumbler in the neighborhood circus. When he was nine, doctors informed Kurt's mother that his small size was due to heart murmurs—a blessing in disguise (his stature) for the future gymnast. At fourteen, as a 4-foot 9-inch, 77-pound sophomore at Miami Central High School, he wandered into a local college gymnasium and was thrilled by a gymnast's daring moves on a horizontal bar. By a stroke of luck, a man named Don Gutzier had just come to begin a gymnastics program at Miami Central. The young gymnast enrolled and was on his way.

The Road to Excellence

During the early 1970's, Kurt began competing at high school and amateur competitions. It was at the 1972 Amateur Athletic Union Junior Olympics that he first faced Bart Conner, who would prove a constant rival in coming years. In 1974, Roger Counsil, gymnastics coach at Indiana State University, scouted Kurt and was impressed with his positive attitude, ambition, and toughness.

At Indiana State, Kurt was allowed to take a reduced course load to allow for international competition. He trained hard, with three two-hour sessions daily. As a freshman, he placed ninth in National Collegiate Athletic Association

(NCAA) competition. He had grown to 5 feet 5 inches; with his long arms, short legs, and good strength-to-weight ratio, he managed with ease on the pommel horse and rings. Given his independent personality, he brought original, often balletic elements to his floor exercise routines. He also incorporated tricks—quick, daring attention-getting moves, such as a triple flyaway dismount from the horizontal bar—that further personalized his style.

In 1991 Kurt Thomas became the oldest man, at thirty-six, to make the national gymnastics team.

2741

It was at the 1975 Criterion Cup in Barcelona, Spain, that Kurt introduced a move that caught the attention of the gymnastics world and eventually took his name: the "Thomas Flair," a flashy series of swinging leg moves first used on the pommel horse and later incorporated into floor exercises. The move has become a standard element of the gymnastics repertoire.

The Emerging Champion

Kurt was bringing to men's gymnastics the attention that performers like Olga Korbut and Cathy Rigby were bringing to women's. The combination of his handsome, boy-next-door looks and his confident, even defiant attitude held great audience appeal.

Meanwhile, Kurt continued to develop his technical expertise. *Sports Illustrated* magazine picked him to win the gold medal on the pommel horse at the 1976 Olympics in Montreal, but he hurt his finger just before the Games and competed without distinction.

Following Montreal, Kurt underwent a spiritual transformation and adopted a Christian way of life. On December 31, 1977, he married Beth Osting, a farm girl from Rushville, Indiana, he had met at an Indiana State sorority party. His friend and mentor Counsil was his best man.

Kurt won three successive United States Gymnastics Federation titles from 1976 to 1978 and took second place to Japanese gymnast Mitsuo Tsukahara in the 1977 American Cup in New York, where he scored 9.6 or higher in all six individual events. In 1977, he was placed ninth in international rankings.

His greatest triumphs were soon to come. At the 1978 World Cup in São Paulo, Brazil, and the 1979 World Cup in Tokyo, Japan, Kurt placed second and fourth, respectively. At the 1978 World Championships in Strasbourg, France, his gold medal in the floor exercise was the first gold medal won by an American in Olympic or World Championship competition since 1932. The following year, at the World Championships in Fort Worth, Texas, he placed second in the all-around behind the Soviet Alexander Dityatin and earned two individual golds, two more individual silvers, and a team bronze, for a total of six medals.

With his success in Fort Worth, Kurt was eager to compete at the 1980 Olympics and was picked by many as favorite on the pommel horse and floor exercise. Unfortunately, political difficulties led to a United States boycott of the Moscow Olympics: a lifetime dream became a lifetime disappointment. Instead, Kurt had to settle for an impressive showing at the 1980 American Cup, where he was first all-around and earned a perfect score of 10 on the horizontal bar.

Continuing the Story

By 1980 Kurt was quite a media star. He had appeared on numerous television talk shows and kept a busy schedule of interviews, exhibitions, and press appearances.

STATISTICS

Year	Competition	Event	Place	Event	Place
1975	Pan-American Games	All-Around	3d	Pommel horse	2d
		Floor exercise	6th	Vault	2d
		Horizontal bar	3d	Team	1st
1976	NCAA Championships	All-Around	1st		
	Olympic Games	All-Around	21st		
1977	NCAA Championships	All-Around	1st		
	American Cup	All-Around	2d		
1978	Champions All	All-Around	1st		
	American Cup	All-Around	1st		
	World Cup	All-Around	2d	Pommel horse	3d
		Floor exercise	2d	Rings	5th
		Horizontal bar	2d	Vault	7th
		Parallel bars	4th		
	World Championships	All-Around	6th	Team	4th
		Floor exercise	1st		
1979	American Cup	All-Around	1st		
	World Cup	All-Around	4th	Parallel bars	8th
		Floor exercise	6th	Pommel horse	3d
		Horizontal bar	5th		
	American Cup	All-Around	1st	Pommel horse	2d
		Floor exercise	1st	Rings	1st
		Horizontal bar	1st	Vault	2d
		Parallel bars	1st		
	World Championships	All-Around	2d	Parallel bars	2d
		Floor exercise	1st	Pommel horse	2d
		Horizontal bar	1st	Team	3d
1980	American Cup	All-Around	1st		
	Pacific Gymnastics Championships	All-Around	1st	Team	1st

RECORDS AND MILESTONES
First U.S. gymnast to win a gold medal in world-class competition in thirty-six years (the 1978 World Championships)
Has won the most gold medals in Dial-American Cup competition (37)
First U.S. gymnast to make a significant impact in world gymnastics
Introduced the "Thomas Flair" in international pommel horse competition; a similar maneuver performed on the floor is also called a "Thomas"

HONORS AND AWARDS	
1977	U.S. Gymnastics Federation Gymnast of the Year
1979	Nissen Award
	CBS Athlete of the Year
	Laurel Wreath Athlete of the Year
	Dunlop Amateur Athlete of the Year
	Sullivan Award (first gymnast to receive this honor)
1979-80	Amateur Athlete of the Year
1990	Inducted into U.S. Gymnastics Hall of Fame

thirty-four, Kurt began training seriously. He attended several meets in the winter of 1990-1991, competing well enough to aim at a berth on the U.S. team at the 1992 Barcelona Olympics. At age thirty-six, in 1992, Kurt was the oldest gymnast to ever make the national team. He did not, however, make the 1992 Olympic team.

During the 1990's, Kurt opened the Kurt Thomas School of Gymnastics in Plano, Texas. In addition to coaching, he continued to do tours and exhibitions—never tiring of the work needed to maintain his skill set or of performing for an audience.

With the disappointment of the Olympic boycott, Kurt retired from amateur competition and turned "professional," developing and touring gymnastics road shows. In 1980, he teamed with writer Kent Hannon on a book, *Kurt Thomas on Gymnastics* (1980), in which he reflected on his career, gave advice to young gymnasts, and offered candid opinions on such topics as coaching, judging, and his rivalry with Conner. He also began writing an ongoing column in *International Gymnast* magazine, addressing his large following among aspiring gymnasts (including the Friends of Kurt Thomas Club), and opened his own summer training center, the Gymnastics Camp with a Flair.

Through the 1980's, Kurt considered a return to competition, and the issue of his amateur or professional status—a distinction not clearly defined in the sport—received much attention. Rather than compete at the 1984 Olympics in Los Angeles, as he had hoped to do, he served as a television commentator, a role he repeated four years later at the Seoul Olympics. In 1986, he appeared in a film, *Gymkata*, which capitalized on his popularity and gymnastics skills.

His hopes for a comeback continued through the 1980's, and in the spring of 1990, at the age of

Summary

Through perseverance and hard work, Kurt Thomas developed from a boy on the streets of Miami into a world-class gymnast. Though he did not win at the Olympics, his consistently excellent performances in national and international competition were exemplary. His innovation is marked by the fact that three moves used in international competition are named for him. In addition, his personality and originality helped to transform and popularize men's gymnastics.

Barry Mann

Additional Sources:

Hickok, Ralph. "Thomas, Kurt." *A Who's Who of Sports Champions: Their Stories and Records.* New York: Houghton Mifflin, 1995.

Klein, Frederick C. "Thirtysomething Gymnast Tries Again." *The Wall Street Journal*, September 21, 1990, p. A12.

Randle, Kathy, and Marty Newsom. "1990 USGF Men's Winter Nationals." *International Gymnast*, February, 1991, 20.

Robison, Nancy. *Kurt Thomas: International Winner.* Chicago: Children's Press, 1980.

Thomas, Kurt, and Kent Hannon. *Kurt Thomas on Gymnastics.* New York: Simon and Schuster, 1980.

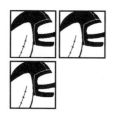

THURMAN THOMAS

Sport: Football

Born: May 16, 1966
Houston, Texas

Early Life

Thurman Lee Thomas was born on May 16, 1966, in Houston, Texas. He was reared by his mother, Terlisha, and her second husband, Gilbert Cockrell, after his natural parents divorced when he was very young. As an only child, Thurman had a lonely childhood, especially during the period between his parents' divorce and his mother's remarriage.

As a boy, Thurman dreamed of playing professional baseball; however, his childhood hero was professional football player Walter Payton, the star running back for the Chicago Bears. Thur-

Buffalo Bills

man admired Payton, who excelled despite his relatively small size. Thurman would later wear number 34 on his jersey, the same number Payton wore with the Bears. Thurman, too, was not big. He was invariably the smallest boy on the block, and he often had to prove himself to others who doubted his abilities.

The Road to Excellence

Thurman chose to concentrate on football in high school, and he made the varsity team at Willowridge High School in Missouri City, Texas, a suburb of Houston, for three years. Although he was a standout player and was chosen All-State and Player of the Year by the Houston Touchdown Club, he always felt slighted, as many people often rated him behind other high-school players in the Houston area.

After high school, Thurman enrolled at Oklahoma State University (OSU), where he became an instant star as a running back. His freshman year was highlighted by his Gator Bowl performance; he ran for 155 yards and was selected most valuable player of the game.

Thurman continued to excel throughout his college career, gaining nearly 4,600 yards during his four years at OSU, second best in Big Eight Conference history. In a game against Iowa State, he rushed for 293 yards, an OSU single-game record.

Had he not been hampered during his junior year by a knee injury that required surgery, he would likely have become the conference's all-time leading rusher. The knee injury also cost him an opportunity to win the Heisman Trophy, an annual award given to the outstanding college football player in the United States. Interestingly, Barry Sanders, a future Heisman Trophy winner, had to settle for being a substitute for Thurman when they were both attending OSU.

STATISTICS

Season	GP	Rushing					Receiving			
		Car.	Yds.	Avg.	TD	Rec.	Yds.	Avg.	TD	
1988	15	207	881	4.3	2	18	208	11.6	0
1989	16	298	1,244	4.2	6	60	669	11.2	6
1990	16	271	1,297	4.8	11	49	532	10.9	2
1991	15	288	1,407	**4.9**	7	62	631	10.2	5
1992	16	312	1,487	4.8	9	58	626	10.8	3
1993	16	**355**	1,315	3.7	6	48	387	8.1	0
1994	15	287	1,093	3.8	7	50	349	7.0	2
1995	14	267	1,005	3.8	6	26	220	8.5	2
1996	15	281	1,033	3.7	8	26	254	9.8	0
1997	16	154	643	4.2	1	30	208	6.9	0
1998	14	93	381	4.1	2	26	220	8.5	1
1999	5	36	152	4.2	0	3	37	12.3	1
2000	9	28	136	4.9	0	16	117	7.3	1
Totals	182	2,877	12,074	4.2	65	472	4,458	9.4	23

Notes: Boldface indicates statistical leader. GP = games played; Car. = carries; Yds. = yards; Avg. = average yards per carry *or* average yards per reception; TD = touchdowns; Rec. = receptions

The Emerging Champion

Professional football owners are hesitant to draft college players who have had knee injuries. For this reason, six other running backs had already been selected in the 1988 National Football League (NFL) draft when the Buffalo Bills' general manager, Bill Polian, convinced Bills' owner Ralph Wilson to gamble a second-round pick on Thurman. The gamble would pay enormous dividends for the Bills.

Thurman, called "squatty" by his teammates because of his short and compact build, wanted to prove that his stature would not keep him from being an outstanding player. He proved that immediately, as he had an impressive rookie season, finishing third in the NFL in rushing in spite of missing almost two games with injuries. In his second year, he was selected to the Pro Bowl after he tied for the American Football Conference (AFC) lead in touchdowns and tied an NFL record for most catches in a playoff game.

In 1990, Thurman had another stellar season, leading the NFL in total yards from scrimmage with 1,829 and leading the AFC in rushing with 1,297 yards. In addition, the Bills made their first Super Bowl appearance in Super Bowl XXV, with Thurman rushing for 135 yards in a losing cause against the Giants. Had the Bills won the game, many believe, Thurman would have been voted the game's most valuable player, an honor that went instead to the Giants' Ottis Anderson.

In 1991, Thurman received the ultimate recognition of his talents: He was selected as the NFL's Player of the Year by both the Associated Press and the Professional Football Writers Association. That year also marked the third consecutive season in which he rushed for more than 1,000 yards.

Continuing the Story

Thurman continued to be one of the premier running backs in the NFL, and he was often referred to as the best all-purpose running back in the league. In 1992, he led the NFL in total yards from scrimmage for the fourth consecutive sea-

HONORS AND AWARDS

1984	Gator Bowl most valuable player
1985, 1987	College All-American
1987	Big Eight Offensive Player of the Year
1989-93	NFL Pro Bowl Team
1991	Associated Press NFL Player of the Year Professional Football Writers Association NFL Player of the Year *Sporting News* NFL Player of the Year United Press International AFC Offensive Player of the Year

son, breaking a record held by the great Jim Brown.

Thurman made his mark off of the field as well. He did not forget those who helped him in the past and those who needed help. He donated more than $125,000 to Oklahoma State to thank the school for providing him with the opportunity to play football, and he also made contributions to the United Negro College Fund and set up a scholarship at a Buffalo college to pay tuition for needy students.

In 1994 Thurman attained the 1,000-yard rushing mark for the sixth straight season, with 1,093 yards and 7 touchdowns on 287 carries. In 1995 and 1996 he tallied his seventh and eighth consecutive 1,000-yard seasons. In 1996 he became only the fourth player in NFL history to have made 60 rushing touchdowns and 20 receiving touchdowns. In 1997 Thurman became only the third NFL player ever to gain 10,000 rushing yards and total 400 receptions.

After 1997, Thurman's productivity and playing time diminished. In 2000 he signed with his former AFC East rivals, the Miami Dophins. Injuries again curtailed his playing time, and he retired in early 2001.

Summary

Always conscious of his small stature, Thurman Thomas wanted to prove that he could be the best running back in professional football. His determination to excel and to be recognized as a great football player, and his willingness to help others in need, made Thurman one of the greatest athletes both on the football field and off.

Stephen Schwartz

Additional Sources:

Savage, Jeff. *Thurman Thomas: Star Running Back.* Hillside, N.J.: Enslow Publishers, 1994.
Thurman Thomas Official Web Site. http://www.thurmanthomas34.com.

DALEY THOMPSON

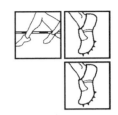

Sport: Track and field (decathlon)

Born: July 30, 1958
London, England

Early Life

Francis Morgan (Daley) Thompson is only the second athlete in Olympic history to win back-to-back decathlons (Moscow, 1980; Los Angeles, 1984) and is probably unique in competing as a serious contender in four Olympic decathlons. Born in London, England, on July 30, 1958,

Daley Thompson won his second Olympic decathlon in 1984.

to a Scottish mother and a Nigerian father, Daley grew up as a tough competitor in life and in sport. His gregarious, cocky, cheerful, and irreverent public personality hides a shy, highly disciplined private individual whose early dedication to athletics won him the Sussex Schools 200-meter title in 1974. It was apparent from his size, speed, and high level of skill in a number of events that he could be a successful decathlete. Also, his ability to perform at his best under pressure gave him a competitive edge in the grueling decathlon.

The Road to Excellence

In June of 1975, when he was still only sixteen, Daley entered his first decathlon at the Welsh Open Championship. He scored an impressive 6,685 points in his debut. Daley soon demonstrated that he would be a serious contender for the title of "World's Greatest Athlete." Before he had even won a major championship, he made the British Olympic team and finished eighteenth in the decathlon at the 1976 Montreal Games. He had just turned eighteen. Bruce Jenner, the gold medal winner, was impressed by his performance and predicted a great future for Daley. Four years later, Daley would succeed Jenner as Olympic decathlon champion at the Moscow Games. In the meantime, he continued to compile an impressive list of victories. He was European Junior Decathlon Champion in 1977 and European Decathlon Silver Medalist and Commonwealth Decathlon Gold Medalist in 1978.

The Emerging Champion

Because of the boycott of the 1980 Moscow Olympics, Daley's most serious rival for the gold medal, Guido Kratschmer of West Germany, was not going to be at the Games. Daley, however, competed with him in May and set a world record of 8,622 points. Kratschmer regained the title in June with 8,649 points, and, when Daley went to Moscow later that summer, he hoped to get it back.

There was no one who really challenged Daley at Moscow except the Soviet decathletes, and the one who promised to give him the most competition withdrew after being injured. Daley was on a world-record pace before it rained on the second day. He won his first Olympic gold medal with a total of 8,495 points but was far short of Kratschmer's 8,649.

For the next few years, Daley and another West German, Jürgen Hingsen, traded world records in the decathlon. On September 7 and 8, 1982, Daley beat Hingsen, the world-record holder, in Athens at the European Championships and set a new world record of 8,743 points. Hingsen soon reclaimed the title, but when the two met face-to-face at the World Championships at Helsinki in 1983, Daley beat him with a world-record performance. By the time of the 1984 Los Angeles Olympics, however, Daley's best of 8,743 points had once more been surpassed by

Hingsen at 8,798. Even though Hingsen had twice broken Daley's world record, he had lost to him the five times they had met, and Daley had been undefeated in competition since 1978. Everyone wondered whether Hingsen could beat Daley at the Los Angeles Olympic Games.

Continuing the Story

The Los Angeles decathlon was held on Wednesday and Thursday, August 8 and 9. Daley and Hingsen were both twenty-six; both had broken the world record three times. Coached by Bruce Longden and encouraged by his American training partner, John Crist, and his English roommate, discus thrower Richard Slaney, Daley started strong. He took first place in the 100 meters (10.44 seconds) and the long jump, leaping 26 feet 3½ inches. Only four men in history had jumped farther. Although he placed behind Hingsen in the shot put, he still achieved a personal best of 51 feet 7 inches. Daley was relaxed and in high spirits. Hingsen was not. Daley managed 6 feet 8 inches in the high jump and 46.97 seconds in the 400 meters. At the end of the first day of competition, he led with 4,633 points. No one had ever before broken the 4,600 mark on the first day of competition.

On the second day, Daley finished behind Hingsen in the 110-meter hurdles with a time of 14.34 seconds. The pressure began to mount for Daley when his first two throws in the discus were dismal. It looked as if Hingsen would take the lead. Knowing that his last throw had to be his best, Daley threw the discus 152 feet 9 inches, a personal best, and preserved his lead. During the pole vault, Hingsen became ill, and Daley sailed over the bar at 16 feet 4¾ inches. His lead widened when he tossed the javelin 214 feet. It was all over before the final event, the 1,500 meters, and Hingsen congratulated Daley at the start of the race.

Daley had set a goal for himself of 9,000 points, and even though he had performed brilliantly, that point total was out of reach. Breaking Hingsen's world

STATISTICS

Year	Competition	Event	Place	Points/Time
1976	Olympic Games	Decathlon	18th	7,434
1978	Commonwealth Games	Decathlon	1st	8,467
	European Championships	Decathlon	2d	8,289
1980	Olympic Games	Decathlon	Gold	8,495
1982	Commonwealth Games	Decathlon	1st	8,424
	European Championships	Decathlon	1st	8,743 WR
1983	World Championships	Decathlon	1st	8,774 WR
1984	Olympic Games	Decathlon	Gold	8,847 WR, OR
		4×100-meter relay	7th	39.13
1986	Commonwealth Games	Decathlon	1st	8,663
	European Championships	Decathlon	1st	8,811
1987	World Championships	Decathlon	9th	8,124

Notes: OR = Olympic Record; WR = World Record

RECORDS AND MILESTONES

European Junior Decathlon champion in 1977
Set a world record in the decathlon in 1980 (8,622 points)
By 1984, had broken the world decathlon record three times

record of 8,797 points, however, was still possible. The 1,500 meters was Daley's weakest event. He had never matched his personal best of 4 minutes 20.8 seconds, set when he was eighteen, but all he had to do was run 4 minutes 34.8 seconds. His time was 4 minutes 35 seconds. He won the gold but he missed the record by 2 points. In 1986, however, a review of his decathlon performance by the International Amateur Athletic Federation added a point to his total, and he was, belatedly, given a share of the world's record.

In the 1988 Seoul Olympics, Daley, at age thirty, tried for an unprecedented third gold medal in the decathlon. He was in third place behind Christian Schenk and Torsten Voss of East Germany, the world champion at the time, when he was injured in the pole vault. The 1,500 meters ended what was the longest day of decathlon competition in Olympic history. At 9:15 P.M., Daley was simply worn out. He completed the race in 4 minutes 45.11 seconds but did not finish in the top three.

Summary

Daley Thompson is one of the greatest athletes of the twentieth century. His Olympic career spanned more than a decade: He competed in the Montreal (1976), Moscow (1980), Los Angeles (1984), and Seoul (1988) Games. He is one of only two athletes who won back-to-back Olympic decathlons. An intense competitor who was totally devoted to his athletic training, Daley always strived to be the best. Humorous yet serious, from an early age he set goals for himself and overcame obstacles by facing them straight on. Unlike many athletes, he thrived on competition and pressure and was at his best when things looked worst.

Robert B. Kebric

Additional Sources:

Thompson, Daley, with Neil Wilson. *Daley: The Last Ten Years.* London: Collins, 1986.

Wallechinsky, David. *The Complete Book of the Olympics.* Boston: Little, Brown and Company, 1991.

Watman, Mel. *Encyclopedia of Track and Field Athletics.* New York: St. Martin's Press, 1981.

JENNY THOMPSON

Sport: Swimming

Born: February 26, 1973
Dover, New Hampshire

Early Life

Born in Dover, New Hampshire, on February 26, 1973, Jenny Thompson was the youngest of four children of Phil and Margrid Thompson. When Jenny was two, her parents divorced, and Margrid became a single mother to four children. She worked hard to provide her children with active childhoods, making made sure they all played sports, encouraging them to take music lessons, and driving them to all sorts of activities.

The Road to Excellence

Jenny took flute lessons, piano lessons, toe and tap dancing lessons, and tennis lessons. She enjoyed her swimming lessons the most. Jenny soon began to win regional swim meets. To make it easier for the thirteen-year-old to swim with the Seacoast Swimming Association, Margrid moved the family north from Georgetown, Massachusetts, to Dover, New Hampshire, in 1986. The move was a sacrifice for Margrid, who now had a two-hour round-trip commute to work.

Jenny quickly moved up in the junior national rankings while training with Seacoast. As a New England swimmer in a sport dominated by girls from warmer climates, she attracted the attention of many college swimming powerhouses because of her speed, strength, and competitiveness. She was recruited by Stanford University coach Richard Quick and enrolled at the California school in the fall of 1991 on a swim-

Swimmer Jenny Thompson, the most decorated American female athlete in Olympic history, in 1997.

2750

ming scholarship. During her four years at Stanford, Jenny led her team to National Collegiate Athletic Association (NCAA) team championships each year.

The Emerging Champion

In 1992 Jenny broke the world record at the United States Olympic trials, swimming the 100-meter freestyle in 54.48 seconds. She was the first American woman in sixty-one years to set the world record in this event. At the 1992 Olympics in Barcelona, Spain, Jenny had to settle for a disappointing silver medal in the 100-meter freestyle, losing to Chinese swimmer Zhuang Yong. However, Jenny did win gold in the 4×100-meter freestyle relay and the 4×100-meter medley relay.

At the 1994 World Championships in Rome, Jenny was recovering from a broken arm. This limited her effectiveness, and she did not set any world records at the meet. Her relay teams placed second in the 4×100-meter freestyle and in the 4×100-meter medley, and third in the 4×200-meter freestyle.

In 1995 Jenny graduated from Stanford and continued training for the 1996 Olympics in Atlanta. She was a strong favorite at the Olympic trials in Indianapolis in March, 1996. The pressure of being in the spotlight got the best of her, and she finished third in the 100-meter freestyle, her strongest event. She also finished third in the 50-meter freestyle. According to Jenny, her coach Richard Quick, and her mother, the 1996 Olympic trials were a turning point in her swimming career. She regained her focus and had a great Olympics. Jenny's team won gold in the 4×100-meter freestyle relay and the 4×200-meter relay. She won a third gold medal in the 4×100-meter medley relay.

\multicolumn{4}{c}{**MAJOR CHAMPIONSHIPS**}			
Year	Competition	Event	Place
1987	Pan-American Games	50-meter freestyle	1st
		100-meter freestyle	3d
		4×100-meter freestyle relay	1st
1989	Pan-Pacific Championships	50-meter freestyle	1st
		100-meter freestyle	2d
		4×100-meter freestyle relay	1st
1991	World Championships	4×100-meter freestyle relay	1st
	Pan-Pacific Championships	50-meter freestyle	1st
		4×100-meter freestyle relay	1st
1992	Olympic Games	100-meter freestyle	Silver
		4×100-meter freestyle relay	Gold
		4×100-meter medley relay	Gold
1993	Pan-Pacific Championships	50-meter freestyle	1st
		100-meter freestyle	1st
		100-meter butterfly	1st
		4×100-meter freestyle relay	1st
		4×200-meter freestyle relay	1st
		4×100-meter medley relay	1st
1994	Long Course World Championships	4×100-meter freestyle relay	2d
		4×200-meter freestyle relay	3d
		4×100-meter medley relay	2d
1995	Pan-Pacific Championships	50-meter freestyle	2d
		100-meter freestyle	1st
		100-meter butterfly	2d
		4×100-meter freestyle relay	1st
		4×200-meter freestyle relay	1st
		4×100-meter medley relay	2d
1996	Olympic Games	4×100-meter freestyle relay	Gold
		4×200-meter freestyle relay	Gold
		4×100-meter medley relay	Gold
1997	Short Course World Championships	50-meter freestyle	2d
		100-meter freestyle	1st
		100-meter butterfly	1st
		4×100-meter medley relay	2d
	Pan-Pacific Championships	50-meter freestyle	2d
		100-meter freestyle	1st
		100-meter butterfly	1st
		4×100-meter freestyle relay	1st
		4×200-meter freestyle relay	1st
		4×100-meter medley relay	1st
1998	Long Course World Championships	100-meter freestyle	1st
		100-meter butterfly	1st
		4×100-meter freestyle relay	1st
		4×200-meter freestyle relay	2d
		4×100-meter medley relay	1st

Continuing the Story

Despite not medaling in an individual event, Jenny received endorsement contracts with Speedo and the vitamin company Envion. Combined with prizes from the 1997, 1998, and 1999 World Championships, the endorsements allowed Jenny to focus on training without having to take a full-time job. She prepared for the 2000 Olympics in Sydney, Australia. In 1999 at the Pan-

MAJOR CHAMPIONSHIPS

Year	Competition	Event	Place
1999	Short Course World Championships	50-meter freestyle	2d
		100-meter freestyle	1st
		50-meter butterfly	1st
		100-meter butterfly	1st
	Pan-Pacific Championships	50-meter freestyle	1st
		100-meter freestyle	1st
		100-meter butterfly (WR: 57.88)	1st
		4×100-meter freestyle relay	1st
		4×200-meter freestyle relay	1st
		4×100-meter medley relay	1st
2000	Olympic Games	100-meter freestyle	Bronze
		100-meter butterfly	5th
		4×100-meter freestyle relay (WR: 3:36.61)	Gold
		4×200-meter freestyle relay	Gold
		4×100-meter medley relay (WR: 3:58.30)	Gold
	Short Course World Championships	50-meter butterfly	1st
		100-meter butterfly	1st
		100-meter freestyle	2d
		4×200-meter freestyle relay	2d
		4×100-meter medley relay	3d
		4×100-meter freestyle relay	4th

Note: WR = World Record

Pacific Championships, Jenny set a world record in the 100-meter butterfly, breaking the record set by American Mary T. Meagher in 1981.

At the age of twenty-seven, Jenny qualified for the United States Olympic team by winning the 100-meter freestyle at the Olympic trials in Indianapolis, Indiana, in August, 2000. She set a national record in the event. She also won the 100-meter butterfly and earned spots on the 4×100-meter freestyle relay, 4×200-meter freestyle relay, and 4×100-meter medley relay teams.

Before the Sydney Olympics, Jenny caused some controversy in women's sports by posing topless in *Sports Illustrated* with her hands covering her breasts. Despite the potentially distracting criticism, she won four medals in Sydney, including three gold medals in the relay events. She won a bronze medal in the 100-meter freestyle in a tie with American teammate Dara Torres.

Jenny became the most decorated female American athlete in Olympic history when she won her tenth medal in Sydney. Her medal to-tal included eight gold medals from three Olympics. According to Jenny, the 2000 Olympics were her last as a competitive swimmer. Her future plans included attending Columbia University Medical School.

In October, 2000, Jenny was named the Women's Sports Foundation Sportswoman of the Year. Some observers noted a paradox: an athlete who won her gold medals as a member of a team being recognized for individual achievement. The awards committee explained that Jenny was recognized for her achievements from August, 1999, through July, 2000, without considering her Olympic medals.

Summary

Throughout her long swimming career, Jenny Thompson exhibited perseverance and a competitive spirit. She rebounded from a dismal performance at the 1996 Olympic trials to win gold at the 1996 Olympics. In addition to her Olympic medals, she won twenty-three national titles and twenty-six NCAA championships. Even after reaching the age when most swimmers retire, Jenny continued training and breaking world records to reach a level of excellence of truly Olympic proportions.

John David Rausch, Jr.

Additional Sources:

Brant, Martha. "Grannies of the Games." *Newsweek* 136, no. 7 (August 14, 2000): 40-42.
Donnelly, Sally B. "A Solitary Pursuit." *Time* 156, no. 6 (August 7, 2000): 90.
Greenburg, Doreen, and Michael Greenberg. *Fast Lane to Victory: The Story of Jenny Thompson.* Terre Haute, Ind.: Wish Publishing, 2001.
McCallum, Jack. "Unflagging." *Sports Illustrated* 93, no. 6 (August 14, 2000): 52-57.

IAN THORPE

Sport: Swimming

Born: October 13, 1982
      Paddington, Australia

Early Life

Ian Thorpe was born on October 13, 1982, in Paddington, Australia, a suburb of Sydney. His father, Ken, had been pressured by his own father to play cricket; therefore Ken and Margaret, Ian's mother, resolved not to push their children where sports were concerned. Ian nonetheless started swimming at the age of eight after having become tired of watching his older sister, Christina, compete at swim meets. Ian was diagnosed with an allergy to chlorine; undaunted, he swam wearing a nose guard, and eventually his allergy cleared up by itself.

One disputed explanation for Ian's swimming success began to make itself known at an early age: The boy had exceptionally big feet. Physiologists and other experts commenting on his later accomplishments were divided on the issue of whether large, flipperlike feet provide any real advantage in competitive swimming. Ian's appendages would not stop growing until they had reached shoe size 17.

The Road to Excellence

Ian made his international swimming debut in March, 1997, at the Pan-Pacific Championships in Fukuoka, Japan. At fourteen, he was the youngest swimmer selected to the Australian national team since the fourteen-year-old John Konrads swam in 1956. At the Pan-Pacifics, Ian improved on his personal best times in all events he entered, ultimately winning a silver medal behind his teammate Grant Hackett in the 400-meter freestyle.

The following January, Ian and Hackett were on the 4×200-meter freestyle relay team at the World Swimming Championships. The team set a Commonwealth record as they won the event.

In Ian's other race, the 400-meter freestyle, he narrowly beat Hackett, by 0.15 of a second. Ian expressed astonishment at the outcome. He had become the youngest male world champion in history.

The Australian Swimming Championships followed, where Ian set another Commonwealth record with his time of 1:47.24 in the 200-meter freestyle. Victories that followed in 1998 included the Commonwealth Games, where he won four gold medals, the FINA World Cups, and the World Short Course Championships in Hong Kong. In November, 1998, Ian was named *Swimming World* magazine's Male Swimmer of the Year.

Australia's Ian Thorpe won the 400-meter freestyle swim and set a new world record at the 2000 Sydney Olympics.

2753

MAJOR SWIMMING CHAMPIONSHIPS

Year	Competition	Event	Place
1997	Pan-Pacific Championships	400-meter freestyle	2d
1998	World Short Course Championships	200-meter freestyle	1st
		400-meter freestyle	2d
		4×100-meter freestyle relay	1st
	World Championships	400-meter freestyle	1st
		4×200-meter freestyle relay	1st
	Commonwealth Games	200-meter freestyle	1st
		400-meter freestyle	1st
		4×100-meter freestyle relay	1st
		4×200-meter freestyle relay	1st
1999	Pan-Pacific Championships	200-meter freestyle	1st WR
		400-meter freestyle	1st WR
		4×100-meter relay	1st
		4×200-meter freestyle relay	1st WR
2000	Olympic Games	400-meter freestyle	Gold WR
		4×100-meter freestyle relay	Gold WR
		4×200-meter freestyle relay	Gold WR
		200-meter freestyle	Silver
	Australian Swimming Championships and Olympic Trials	200-meter freestyle	1st
		400-meter freestyle	1st
		100-meter freestyle	4th
2001	World Championships	200-meter freestyle	1st WR
		400-meter freestyle	1st WR
		800-meter freestyle	1st WR
		4×100-meter freestyle relay	1st
		4×100-meter freestyle relay	1st WR
		4×100-meter medley relay	1st CR

Note: WR = World Record; CR = Championships Record

The Emerging Champion

The following year, at the 1999 Pan-Pacific Championships, Ian's rise to the upper echelons of the swimming world continued. He set world records with his times in the 200- and 400-meter freestyle events and helped his team set another world record in the 4×200-meter relay. He won a fourth gold medal with the 4×100-meter freestyle relay team. In the aftermath of the games, Ian was featured prominently in reports by the media, which had dubbed him "Thorpedo." The media storm had begun.

Shortly afterward, at the Australian Short Course Championships, he won two more gold medals. He was named Australian Swimmer of the Year and *Swimming World*'s World Swimmer of the Year. Additional accolades included his being named Young Australian of the Year, honoring him as one of Australia's highest achievers, and winning the Young Australian Sports Award. He had broken ten world records in just two years' time.

His rise to the top was so fast that some eyed it with suspicion, though rumors of drug use could not be proven. Living at home with his parents and eating, as he said, 99 percent of his meals there, helped him focus totally on his goals. In fact, swimming was hardly mentioned in the Thorpe household, although Ian credited his family's support in allowing him to excel in feats he could not have otherwise accomplished.

The media's attention was so thoroughly focused on Ian at the 2000 Olympic trials that the head Australian swimming coach was driven to remind people that Ian was only seventeen years old. At the trials, Ian did not disappoint. He lowered the world-record time he had set for the 400 meters, then bettered the time he had established for the world's fastest 200-meter race. At a press conference after the trials, he repeatedly said how proud he was to have qualified for the Australian Olympic team. His humility was also in evidence when, in a television-studio waiting room, he met Shane Gould, Australia's darling of the 1972 Olympics. As she showed him her collection of swimming medals, she said, "You'll have a bunch of your own soon." Ian replied, "I'd be happy with one."

Continuing the Story

As the 2000 Olympics drew closer, every move Ian made was reported by the media, and his fans recognized him everywhere he went. He moved his Olympic training base out of Australia—to Colorado Springs, Colorado—to minimize local distractions. Upon his return to Sydney in the weeks leading up to the Games, Ian saw his face plastered on billboards around his hometown.

Despite the pressure heaped on Sydney's hometown boy, Ian won three gold medals, each in world record time, at the Olympic Games. He swam 3:40.59 in the 400-meter freestyle event. Of the two relays he won with his team, records were set of 3:13.67 for the 4×100-meter freestyle relay and 7:07.05 for the 4×200-meter freestyle relay. In addition, Ian won a silver medal in the 200-meter freestyle race.

After the Olympics ended, Ian dove into a tank full of sharks for a sponsor's publicity stunt at his first public appearance in Sydney. He made the talk-show circuit in both Australia and the United States and also wrote a book, *Ian Thorpe: The Journey* (2000).

At the Ninth World Swimming Championships in Fukoda, Japan, in July, 2001, Ian turned in a performance reminiscent of Mark Spitz's legendary feat at the 1972 Olympics. Although his six gold medals fell one shy of Spitz's seven, his performance was in many ways more impressive because of the high-quality of his competition. He set world records in six individual events—the 100-, 400-, and 800-meter freestyles—and anchored Australia to wins in the 4×100-meter medley relay and 4×100- and 4×200-meter freestyle relays—the last of these in a world-record time.

Along the way, Ian's 4×100-meter freestyle relay team dealt the United States its first-ever loss in that event, and Australia collected thirteen gold medals overall to beat a U.S. swimming team for the first time ever in a major competition. Ian himself set a record for world records by raising his personal total to 17 (12 individual, 5 relay), to move ahead of fellow Australian Dawn Fraser's long-standing record of 14. Not surprisingly, he was named the male swimmer of the meet.

Summary

More than just an outstanding swimmer, Ian Thorpe has been compared to golf phenomenon Tiger Woods for the scope of his influence on youth in sports. "He's become a similar type of hope, a role model," said 1988 Olympic 200-meter champion Duncan Armstrong.

Although swimming was his stated priority, demands on his free time increased even more after his Olympic victory. As a Young Australian of the Year honoree, he was a role model for all Australians, noted for his humility, intelligence, and strength of character.

Elizabeth Ferry Slocum

Additional Sources:

Dusevic, Tom. "The Stuff of Heroes." *Time International* 156 (September 25, 2000): 64.

"Ian Thorpe." *Time* 156 (September 11, 2000): 76.

Smith, Gary. "A Kid Who Is Pure Gold." *Reader's Digest* 156 (June, 2000): 74-81.

JIM THORPE

Sport: Track and field, Football, and Baseball

Born: May 22, 1888
  Indian Territory
  Near Prague, Oklahoma
Died: March 28, 1953
  Lomita, California

Early Life

James Francis Thorpe was born on May 22, 1888, in the United States Indian Territory near

Jim Thorpe in 1909.

National Archives

the present-day town of Prague, Oklahoma. Jim was more than one-half Native American. His Indian name, Wa-Tho-Huck, means Bright Path. His father, Hiram Thorpe, was part Irish and part Sac and Fox Indian. Jim's mother, Charlotte Vieux Thorpe, was part French and part Potawatomie Indian. Jim was the great-grandson of Black Hawk, the great war chief of the Chippewa who also led the Sac and Fox. This colorful heritage was a source of pride for Jim and may also have been the source of his physical prowess.

Jim had eighteen full or half brothers and sisters, including a twin brother who died at the age of eight. Both of Jim's parents died by the time he was sixteen. These tragedies left Jim alone in the world because he had never been close to his other relatives. Jim's early education was at the Sac and Fox Reservation School and at Haskell Institute for Indians in Lawrence, Kansas.

The Road to Excellence

In 1904, shortly before his father's death, Jim was sent to Carlisle Institute in Pennsylvania, a trade school for Native Americans. Jim received training in agriculture and in tailoring, but his major interest was athletics.

Jim's start in organized football came in 1907 at the age of nineteen. Playing in an intramural league, he attracted the attention of the coaching staff, headed by Glenn "Pop" Warner, who became one of the leading coaches in the history of college football. Jim was soon on the Carlisle varsity team. This promotion was made after Pop Warner watched Jim twice run the entire length of the field during practice, eluding a horde of potential tacklers each time. Early in a game against Pennsylvania, Carlisle's star halfback was helped off the field with a knee injury, and Pop Warner signaled Jim into the game. On his first play, Jim lost 5 yards. On his second play, he ran 75 yards for a touchdown. The Pennsylvania

BASEBALL STATISTICS

Season	GP	AB	Hits	2B	3B	HR	Runs	RBI	BA	SA
1913	19	35	5	0	0	1	6	2	.143	.229
1914	30	31	6	1	0	0	5	2	.194	.226
1915	17	52	12	3	1	0	8	1	.231	.327
1917	103	308	73	5	10	4	41	40	.237	.357
1918	58	113	28	4	4	1	15	11	.248	.381
1919	62	159	52	7	3	1	16	26	.327	.428
Totals	289	698	176	20	18	7	91	82	.252	.377

Notes: GP = games played; AB = at bats; 2B = doubles; 3B = triples; HR = home runs; RBI = runs batted in; BA = batting average; SA = slugging average

team included four All-Americans, but they lost that game 26-6.

The 1908 football season at Carlisle opened with Jim as a starting halfback. It was another successful year for Jim and for Carlisle. Against Pennsylvania, Jim made two long touchdown runs in a tie game. At the end of the season, Jim was named a third-team halfback on the Walter Camp All-American team. In spite of his honor, a restless Jim left Carlisle at the end of the 1908-1909 school year. For the next two years, he played professional baseball in Rocky Mount, North Carolina.

The Emerging Champion

In 1911, Jim Thorpe received a letter from Pop Warner urging him to return to Carlisle. Having become bored with baseball, Jim returned in time for the 1911 football season. This turn of events set the stage for his greatest two years in football and perhaps the happiest two years of his life after the death of his parents.

Jim was now twenty-three years old, standing almost 6 feet tall and weighing 185 pounds. He was at his physical peak. In his first 1911 game, he played seventeen minutes and scored 17 points as a runner and as a kicker. Later, in an 18-15 victory over a talented Harvard team, Jim scored all the Carlisle points with a 75-yard touchdown run and 4 field goals, one from almost 50 yards. Against a tough schedule, Jim led Carlisle to a 11-1 record that year, and he was named by Walter Camp as a first-team All-American halfback.

The 1912 season was more of the same for Jim. Against a pow-

erful Army team, Jim was ripping holes in the West Point defense. On the Army bench was the future general and president, Dwight Eisenhower, a potential All-American. "Ike" was sent into the game determined to stop "that Indian." When the game was over, Carlisle had won 27-6, and "that Indian" had played the entire 60 minutes and had performed one of the most amazing feats in football history. After a 90-yard kickoff return by Jim was nullified by an offside penalty, Jim ran the next kickoff 95 yards for a touchdown. Eisenhower left the game with a knee injury that eventually ended his football career. In 1912, Jim set a new college scoring record with 198 points and was again a Walter Camp All-American.

Continuing the Story

A major characteristic in Jim's athletic career was versatility. Early in his Carlisle days, he began competing in track events. Pop Warner was again his coach. Jim proved to be as outstanding in track as he was in football.

In the summer of 1912, between his two greatest football seasons, Jim went to Stockholm, Sweden, as a member of the United States team for the fifth modern Olympic Games. These games included the pentathlon, a five-event competi-

TRACK AND FIELD STATISTICS

Year	Competition	Event	Place	Points/Height/Distance
1912	Olympic Games	Decathlon	Gold	8,412
	Olympic Games	Pentathlon	Gold	7,000
	Olympic Games	High jump	4th	6′ 1½″ (1.87 meters)
	Olympic Games	Broad jump	7th	22′ 71¼″ (6.89 meters)

HONORS AND AWARDS

1908, 1911-12	Walter Camp All-American
1912	U.S. Olympic Pentathlon Gold Medalist
	U.S. Olympic Decathlon Gold Medalist
	Proclaimed the greatest athlete in the world by King Gustav V of Sweden
	World Trophy
	Citizens Savings College Football Player of the Year
1950	Voted the outstanding male athlete and the greatest football player of the first half of the twentieth century (Associated Press poll of sportswriters and broadcasters across the country)
1951	Inducted into College Football Hall of Fame
1963	Named to NFL All-Pro Team of the 1920's
	Inducted into Pro Football Hall of Fame
1975	Inducted into National Track and Field Hall of Fame
1983	Inducted into U.S. Olympic Hall of Fame

tion, and the decathlon, consisting of ten events. The gold medals for both were awarded to Jim. King Gustav V of Sweden proclaimed Jim the greatest athlete in the world.

Soon after the end of the 1912 football season, Jim's world began to crumble. It was revealed that he had played professional baseball in 1909 and 1910. Jim had not realized that, according to the rules of the Amateur Athletic Union, this disqualified him for the Olympics. The Olympic committee demanded the return of the medals Jim had won in Stockholm. Jim was shocked and humbled.

Jim left Carlisle and spent the next six years in major league baseball. He returned to football in 1920 in what became the National Football League (NFL), which he helped to establish and of which he was honorary president. He retired as a player in 1929 from the New York Giants.

Jim's later years demonstrate that being a success in athletics does not guarantee being a success in life. A failure in marriage and usually broke, he acted in Hollywood films, lectured on his life, and became involved in Native American politics. He died of a heart attack in his mobile home in Lomita, California, on March 28, 1953.

Summary

A hero can be defined as someone who performs deeds that others admire but cannot themselves perform. Jim Thorpe qualifies as this type of hero. His greatest honor came to his family in 1982, when the International Olympic Committee returned his medals from the 1912 Olympics.

Glenn L. Swygart

Additional Sources:

Lipsyte, Robert. *Jim Thorpe.* New York: Harper-Collins, 1993.

Newcombe, Jack. *The Best of the Athletic Boys: The White Man's Impact on Jim Thorpe.* Garden City, N.Y.: Doubleday, 1975.

Sanford, William R. *Jim Thorpe.* New York: Crestwood House, 1992.

Schoor, Gene. *The Jim Thorpe Story: America's Greatest Athlete.* New York: Archway, 1969.

Wheeler, Robert W. *Jim Thorpe: World's Greatest Athlete.* Rev. ed. Norman: University of Oklahoma Press, 1979.

NATE THURMOND

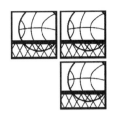

Sport: Basketball

Born: July 25, 1941
Akron, Ohio

Early Life

Nathaniel Thurmond was born in Akron, Ohio, on July 25, 1941. While a young boy, he was given the nickname of "Nate." During his career as a professional basketball player, he would be called "Nate the Great."

Nate had an older brother, Ben. Their father made a good living while working in the Firestone rubber plant in Akron, while their mother was a beautician. The Thurmond family never had a lot of money, but there was much love in the house along with the material necessities. Mr. and Mrs. Thurmond taught their sons not to be arrogant and to treat others well.

Shortly after Nate retired from professional basketball, he made it a point to sit down with both of his parents and thank them for everything.

The Road to Excellence

Nate was encouraged by his father and brother to try sports, so he played basketball at Spicer Elementary School. There Nate played against a team coached by his future high school coach, Joe Siegferth. Joe remembers young Nate as a "tall and skinny kid with sort of a pot belly." He did not realize that he would see Nate again on a basketball court.

Siegferth was named basketball coach at Akron Central High, and the freshman class included Nate Thurmond. Nate was a nice boy and coachable, but he was average as a player. Every season, however, he got better and grew larger.

As a 6-foot 9-inch senior, Nate played forward because he was not considered strong and aggressive enough to play the center position. He averaged 12.9 points per game and was emerging as a good defensive player and rebounder. Nate was named to the All-City and honorable mention All-State teams. Yet no one could imagine his professional basketball future. In the school yearbook, Nate wrote, "I would like to return to Central High as a basketball coach."

In 1959, Nate enrolled at Bowling Green State University in his home state of Ohio. Nate's high school coach had also played there and was still friends with coach Harold Anderson. Anderson was glad to have Nate but was more interested in his Central High teammate, Elijah Chatman.

Nate refined his skills and became Bowling Green's varsity center as a sophomore. He led the team in both scoring and rebounding and would dominate rebounding in the Mid-American Conference (MAC) for three seasons. Bowling Green won the MAC title in 1962 and 1963, and Nate was named to the All-American team both seasons.

The Emerging Champion

Nate was now fully grown, very strong, and 6 feet 11 inches tall. Because of his impressive defensive and rebounding skills, he was already being compared with the center of the Boston Celtics, Bill Russell. The San Francisco Warriors picked Nate in the first round of the 1963 National Basketball Association (NBA) draft.

In Nate's first NBA season, he was the backup center to the great Wilt Chamberlain. He was named to the NBA All-Rookie team despite his limited role. The following year, however, Nate was to get his chance. Near the All-Star break in 1965, the Warriors traded Chamberlain to the Philadelphia 76ers. Nate responded and even won a spot on the West All-Star team. He finished that 1964-1965 season with a surprising 16.5-points-per-game scoring average. Never known as a scorer, Nate raised his average to almost 22 points per game in the following seasons.

Nate was to become a fixture at the center position for the Warriors for eleven seasons. Despite his rapid rise among the NBA's "big men," Nate did not reach superstar status quickly. He suffered a series of injuries throughout his career. In the 1967-1968 season, a broken hand kept him out of the playoffs, and in 1969-1970, he missed most of the season with a knee injury. Nate was even considering an early retirement. He remembered the little agreement he and his mother had years ago when he quit his piano lessons: Do what you want and we'll back you up—as long as you do your best. Nate's best was yet to come.

Continuing the Story

In his comeback season of 1970-1971, Nate scored 43 points in one game against the Detroit Pistons. In 1971-1972, he passed the 10,000-point mark while averaging more than 20 points per game for the fifth season in a row. It was his development of an all-around game that landed Nate in seven NBA All-Star games. It will be primarily for rebounding and defense, however, for which Nate will be remembered. He was named to five NBA All-Defensive teams, and the great Kareem Abdul-Jabbar would call Nate "the toughest defender I ever faced."

Nate was traded to the Chicago Bulls in 1974 and played there until traded again in November of 1975 to the Cleveland Cavaliers. Nate was now thirty-four years old and two knee operations had

STATISTICS

Season	GP	FGM	FG%	FTM	FT%	Reb.	Ast.	TP	PPG
1963-64	76	219	.395	95	.549	790	86	533	7.0
1964-65	77	519	.419	235	.658	1,395	157	1,273	16.5
1965-66	73	454	.406	280	.654	1,312	111	1,188	16.3
1966-67	65	467	.437	280	.629	1,382	166	1,214	18.7
1967-68	51	382	.411	282	.644	1,121	215	1,046	20.5
1968-69	71	571	.410	382	.615	1,402	253	1,524	21.5
1969-70	43	341	.414	261	.754	762	150	943	21.9
1970-71	82	623	.445	395	.730	1,128	257	1,641	20.0
1971-72	78	628	.432	417	.743	1,252	230	1,673	21.4
1972-73	79	517	.446	315	.718	1,349	280	1,349	17.1
1973-74	62	308	.444	191	.666	878	165	807	13.0
1974-75	80	250	.364	132	.589	904	328	632	7.9
1975-76	78	142	.421	62	.504	415	94	346	4.4
1976-77	49	100	.407	68	.642	374	83	268	5.5
Totals	**964**	**5,521**	**.421**	**3,395**	**.667**	**14,464**	**2,575**	**14,437**	**15.0**

Notes: GP = games played; FGM = field goals made; FG% = field goal percentage; FTM = free throws made; FT% = free throw percentage; Reb. = rebounds; Ast. = assists; TP = total points; PPG = points per game

slowed him, but his experience and fiery spirit inspired the Cavaliers. He led a team of ordinary players on a relatively new expansion team into the NBA playoffs. The 1975-1976 Cavalier season was called the "Miracle of Richfield" (for the Richfield Coliseum).

The grateful Cavaliers retired Nate's number 42 jersey in 1977 after his fourteenth, and last, season. The Golden State Warriors (formerly the San Francisco Warriors) then made Nate the first NBA player to have his number retired by two teams.

On July 1, 1984, Nate Thurmond was inducted into the Naismith Memorial Basketball Hall of Fame in Springfield, Massachusetts, with six others, including his college coach, Harold Anderson. Nate was a very quick big man, a tenacious rebounder, great shot blocker, and smooth shooter. He was a total team-oriented player who cared more about winning than statistics. Some basketball critics labeled Nate as the best balanced package for an NBA center, providing just the right mix of offense and defense. He was the first player in NBA history to record a quadruple double. It happened in 1974 when he scored 22 points, collected 14 rebounds, had 13 assists, and blocked 12 shots in a game against the Atlanta Hawks.

He still holds the NBA record for most rebounds in one quarter of play, with 18 against the Baltimore Bullets on February 28, 1965. As part of the celebration of the golden anniversary of the NBA during the 1996-1997 season, Nate was selected as a member of the NBA's 50 Greatest Players of All Time Team.

After retirement, Nate worked briefly as a sports broadcaster prior to becoming involved in public relations with the Warriors. He continued to make a number of appearances each year on behalf of charities and youth camps in the San Francisco area. Nate also began operating Big Nate's Barbecue, a rib and chicken restaurant in San Francisco. In 2000, plans were being made to

name the basketball courts in the Golden Gate Park Panhandle after Nate.

HONORS, AWARDS, AND RECORDS

1961-63	All-Mid-American Conference Team
1962-63	Consensus All-American
1963	Record for the most rebounds in an NCAA Tournament game (31)
1964	NBA All-Rookie Team
1965	NBA record for the most rebounds in a quarter (18)
1965-68, 1970, 1973-74	NBA All-Star Team
1969, 1971-74	NBA All-Defensive Team
1977	Uniform number 42 retired by Golden State Warriors and the Cleveland Cavaliers
1984	Inducted into Naismith Memorial Basketball Hall of Fame
1996	NBA 50 Greatest Players of All Time Team

Summary

"There are other centers in the league who do some things better than Nate," Warriors coach Al Attles said one year. "But who can do as many things as well as Thurmond can?" Nate went on to collect more than 14,000 points and 14,000 rebounds in the NBA.

Beyond those attributes, Nate was described in one Warrior media guide as being "solid as Gibraltar, honest as a day in June, dependable as a '41 Chevy, and the bronze from which statues are created." After Nate's playing career ended, the Warriors made him their director of community relations.

Ronald L. Ammons

Additional Sources:

Bjarkman, Peter C. *The Biographical History of Basketball.* Chicago: Masters Press, 1998.
Dolin, Nick, Chris Dolin, and David Check. *Basketball Stars: The Greatest Players in the History of the Game.* New York: Black Dog and Leventhal, 1997.
Mallozzi, Vincent M. *Basketball: The Legends and the Game.* Willowdale, Ont.: Firefly Books, 1998.
Shouler, Kenneth A. *The Experts Pick Basketball's Best Fifty Players in the Last Fifty Years.* Lenexa, Kans.: Addax, 1998.

Sport: Rodeo

Born: March 5, 1929
 Mission Ridge, South Dakota
Died: January 28, 1990
 Ramona, California

Early Life

Casey Tibbs was born March 5, 1929, in Mission Ridge, South Dakota, to John and Florence Tibbs. Casey was the youngest of ten children (five brothers and four sisters).

John Tibbs raised horses, and Casey took to the saddle almost immediately. He was breaking horses for six to ten dollars a head by the time he was thirteen. Casey soon decided to compete in rodeo full-time. He entered an amateur contest and won four first prizes.

This good beginning was soon followed by a broken ankle. Also, Casey's father saw no reason for any of his children to leave the ranch. He was opposed to life on the rodeo circuit. Still, Casey persevered and persuaded his mother to sign a letter of consent so he could enter professional competitions.

The Road to Excellence

When he was fifteen, Casey won his first day money (any rodeo prize money) riding a bucking horse at McLaughlin, South Dakota. It was only eighty-seven dollars, but Casey was hooked.

Rodeo competitions differ from most sports in that the contestants' entry fees become the prize money to be won or lost. Casey found it necessary to work part-time as a ranch hand to supplement his income. He

was in fifth place in the saddle bronc competition by the time he was seventeen. He was in third place the next year, and number one by age nineteen.

In rodeo competition, there are two kinds of bronc rides, bareback and saddle. A bareback rider must stay on the horse for 8 seconds, whereas a saddle bronc rider must ride for 10 seconds. Needless to say, although the prize money is extremely generous in terms of the length of actual competition, the horse seldom cooperates with the rider. The rider is judged not only on his form but also on the ferocity of the horse's reaction. The judges award half the points for one and half for the other.

Rodeo is a highly contested sport; even a modest competition may draw a hundred riders in the saddle and bareback categories. Moreover, big rodeos occur throughout the year, and riders have very little time between contests.

Prorodeo Hall of Fame and Museum of the American Cowboy, Colorado Springs, Colorado

A rider must enter as many competitions as possible, because championships are assessed on the basis of prize money won in a year. Finally, while contestants may compete in a single event, most try to capture the All-Around title awarded by the Professional Rodeo Cowboys Association (PRCA). In order to qualify for the All-Around title, a rider must compete in at least three events.

The Emerging Champion

Casey chose to concentrate on saddle bronc, bareback bronc, and bull riding. All three events are dangerous and injuries are common, but Casey was extremely successful as a rodeo performer. He won seven professional circuit saddle bronc and bareback riding championships and was the World Champion All-Around Cowboy on two occasions.

Admittedly, Casey paid for his triumphs with numerous broken bones and assorted fractures, but he obviously loved his work. The monetary rewards were substantial (he earned a record $42,065 in 1955), but the excitement and the ever-present danger were intoxicating as well.

Casey lived his life on the rodeo circuit at a rapid pace. Moreover, he stood out from the crowd with his flashy purple outfits and his Cadillac convertibles in the same color. For all his antics, Casey was an exceptional performer.

He developed an exemplary feeling for what could and could not be done with a horse. Indeed, Casey was often able to persuade even "bad" mounts to give him a winning ride. Riders are assigned mounts on the basis of a lottery system in which the luck of the draw dramatically affects chances for success.

Casey was not physically heavy in his active years, so he developed a riding style that involved "floating" a horse rather than "anchoring" himself to the saddle in the fashion of heavier, brawnier riders. This trademark rocking-chair style was often imitated, but none succeeded in matching the skill with which Casey forked a bronc coming out of the chute. In 1951, he won the professional titles in saddle bronc riding, bareback rid-

MILESTONES	
1949	Professional Saddle Bronc Riding Champion
1951	PRCA Bareback Riding Champion Inducted into Rodeo Hall of Fame, the National Cowboy Hall of Fame
1951-54, 1959	PRCA Saddle Bronc Riding Champion
1951, 1955	PRCA World Champion All-Around Cowboy
1979	Inducted into ProRodeo Hall of Fame

RECORDS
Won six professional circuit saddle bronc riding championships—the most in professional rodeo
At age twenty, the youngest professional rodeo cowboy ever to win a world championship title in any event (record shared with Ty Murray)

ing, and the All-Around Cowboy division. This unprecedented display of skill and stamina is yet to be equaled.

Continuing the Story

The time a bronc rider spends at work is short—Casey once remarked, "I'm on and off a bronc before I can take a deep breath"—but the working conditions are physically demanding. After thirty-nine breaks and fractures, several more than once, Casey decided it was time to pursue a less demanding regimen. Unfortunately, Casey adhered to the cowboy lifestyle indicated by Willie Nelson's revealing lyric "Mamas don't let your sons grow up to be cowboys." As a star on the rodeo circuit, he earned a great deal of money, but his expenses were equally high.

The entry fees, hospital bills, transportation from contest to contest, and living expenses while competing make up a considerable investment for a rodeo performer. Casey'e exotic outfits, his addiction to flashy automobiles, and his inclination to gamble with his life and his prize money left him rich in awards but short on cash. Furthermore, his reputation as a practical joker cost him a career as a film star.

Still, the toughness that sustained him on the circuit remained and the ex-All-Around Cowboy survived. He undertook a career as a stuntman, raised horses on ranches in California and South Dakota, organized rodeos around the world, served as a representative for numerous corporations, and produced an award-winning film *Born to Buck* (1967). He died of cancer in 1990 at the age of sixty.

Summary

Casey Tibbs was founder of the Professional Rodeo Cowboys Association and a charter member of the ProRodeo Hall of Fame. He is credited with bringing professional rodeo to national attention. He was for more than a decade America's best-loved cowboy.

J. K. Sweeney

Additional Sources:

Allen, Michael. *Rodeo Cowboys in the North American Imagination.* Reno: University of Nevada Press, 1998.

Fredriksson, Kristine. *American Rodeo from Buffalo Bill to Big Business.* College Station: Texas A&M, 1985.

Wooden, Wayne S., and Gavin Ehringer. *Rodeo in America: Wranglers, Roughstock, and Paydirt.* Lawrence: University Press of Kansas, 1996.

BERTHA TICKEY

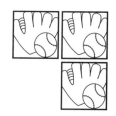

Sport: Softball

Born: March 13, 1924
Orosi, California

Early Life

Bertha Petinak was born on March 13, 1924, in the town of Orosi, California, in the midst of the hot San Joaquin Valley. One of seven children, Bertha was the only daughter born to her parents, John and Ann Petinak, who came to America in 1910 from Yugoslavia.

Like most of the families of European descent, the Petinak family had a strong work ethic and, because of their Old World customs, wanted their only daughter to learn cooking and sewing and other household duties expected of a lady and future housewife.

Although Bertha loved sports, she followed her parents' wishes. She would sit with them and do her homework and even taught her mother to speak and read English.

At thirteen, however, Bertha found herself head of the household when both of her parents died within a year of each other. Bertha looked after her brothers until they were on their own. She had learned to play softball from her brothers, including the skills of pitching and the overall game.

The Road to Excellence

In high school, Bertha was allowed to play on the boys' baseball team. When she was fifteen, she learned about a girls' team in Dinuba, California, and tried out. She made the team as a shortstop and played her first game for Alta Chevrolet in 1939.

The team's pitcher was Ruth Hanson, who, while driving home from school

one day, was involved in an automobile accident. She died shortly thereafter. Bertha took over as the team's pitcher and started a career that would be unequaled in the history of softball.

While she was playing for Alta Chevrolet, the San Jose team invited Bertha to the Amateur Softball Association (ASA) tournament in Chicago. Bertha played three innings in the tournament. It was not the fun she expected it to be because she was too nervous to enjoy it. She returned home and practiced her pitching skills.

Bertha Tickey (right) and Joan Joyce in 1968.

STATISTICS

Season	GP	IP	HA	BB	SO	W	L	ERA
1956	22	167.0	40	35	258	19	3	0.71
1957	26	176.0	46	21	302	22	3	0.28
1958	27	191.0	48	22	297	24	0	0.37
1959	30	206.0	52	27	298	21	3	0.27
1960	24	157.0	41	21	253	18	2	0.49
1961	23	140.0	47	26	196	16	2	0.70
1962	35	211.0	68	36	303	24	1	0.40
1963	28	192.0	59	24	310	25	2	0.44
1964	45	306.0	102	36	447	32	5	0.32
1965	19	118.0	42	36	124	16	1	0.53
1966	33	187.0	59	39	260	26	2	0.22
1967	22	132.2	35	30	188	17	1	0.21
1968	34	219.0	74	42	293	25	1	0.29
Totals	368	2,402.2	713	395	3,529	285	26	0.38

Notes: GP = games played; IP = innings pitched; HA = hits allowed; BB = bases on balls (walks); SO = strikeouts; W = wins; L = losses; ERA = earned run average

In 1940, Bertha joined the Orange, California, Lionettes. The Lionettes were formed in 1937, and their manager, Elwood Case, had heard about the youngster from Dinuba who had the ability and desire to excel as a pitcher.

In 1942, Bertha married Jim Ragan. They had one child, a daughter, Janice, who was born in Orange in 1943. Jim and Bertha eventually divorced.

The war years were quiet years for softball because the blackouts, alerts, gas rationing, and the need for defense workers halted the progress of athletics.

The Emerging Champion

In 1950, Bertha pitched the Lionettes to the first of four ASA National Championships. She also hurled the team to national titles in 1951, 1952, and 1955.

The 1950 national title was especially memorable for Bertha because she hurled five victories in six tournament games against the best the nation had to offer. Her only loss was a heartbreaker, 1-0 in 11 innings to the defending champion Phoenix Ramblers.

With only a twenty-minute rest between games, Bertha came back in the second and deciding game to beat the same Phoenix Ramblers, 3-1, in 15 long, grueling innings.

The championship capped a remarkable season for Bertha in which she won sixty-five games, lost only eight, fanned 795 batters in 513 innings, pitched 54 shutouts, hurled 9 no-hitters, and

yielded only 143 hits, or less than two per game. During that season, she hurled a remarkable 143 consecutive scoreless innings.

From that point on, the past became prologue as Bertha led her team to three more national championships before she announced in 1955 that she was leaving the Lionettes to play for the Raybestos Brakettes of Stratford, Connecticut.

Although the first three years with the Brakettes were good ones, the team still had not won an ASA National Championship. In 1958, however, the Brakettes won what would be their first of twenty-one ASA National Championships. Bertha was a member of seven of those teams, in 1958, 1959, 1960, 1963, 1966, 1967, and 1968.

Continuing the Story

Another turning point of Bertha's career came in 1963, when she married Ed Tickey, who had played for the Raybestos men's teams and was their starting catcher from 1955 to 1960. He also had played for two major league baseball organizations, the New York Giants and the Brooklyn Dodgers.

Bertha knew that eventually, like any other athlete, she would have to retire. That announce-

HONORS AND AWARDS

ASA All-American eighteen seasons
Inducted into National Softball Hall of Fame (1972)

ment came after the 1967 season.

Bertha, who had hurled many dramatic and inspiring games during her career, saved the best for last as she hurled a no-hit shutout game against Redwood City, California, 10-0.

In 1968, Ralph Raymond took over the team's management and had assembled an outstanding team, but the pitching staff was depleted because Donna Lopiano was attending graduate school and Donna Hebert underwent shoulder surgery.

Bertha came out of her brief retirement and showed she still had the skills that had made her a living legend in the annals of women's fast-pitch softball. She compiled a record of twenty-five wins and only one loss, and in her last national tournament, she hurled a perfect game against Houston, Texas, and a 13-inning no-hitter against Fresno, California. She was again named an All-American, the eighteenth time she had been so honored. This time her retirement was permanent.

Summary

Four years later, Bertha Tickey was inducted into the National Softball Hall of Fame, an honor that is reserved for only the sport's greatest players. Through her hard work, dedication, commitment, and perseverance, Bertha showed that she belonged in that exclusive group in a career that may not be equaled in the annals of women's softball.

Bill Plummer III

Additional Sources:

Bealle, Morris A. *The Softball Story: A Complete, Concise, and Entertaining History.* Washington, D.C.: Columbia, 1957.

Dickson, Paul. *The Worth Book of Softball: A Celebration of America's True National Pastime.* New York: Facts on File, 1994.

Markel, Robert, Susan Waggoner, and Marcella Smith, eds. *The Women's Sports Encyclopedia.* New York: Henry Holt, 1997.

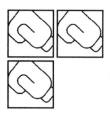

DICK TIGER
Richard Ihetu

Sport: Boxing

Born: August 14, 1929
Amaigbo, Orlu, Nigeria
Died: December 14, 1971
Aba, Nigeria

Early Life

Richard Ihetu, later to gain fame as Dick Tiger, was born on August 14, 1929, in Amaigbo, Orlu, Nigeria. With his four brothers and two sisters, he helped his parents work the farmland that gave them their meager existence.

The family moved to the capital city of Lagos when Dick was a teenager. As a young boy, he was taught to be polite and respectful. He always avoided fighting of any kind, but the English soldiers stationed in Lagos promoted the sport of boxing. Soon they were teaching the strong, growing boy the basic skills of the sport. By the time he was eighteen, he had reached the physical size and weight he would be for the rest of his life. He stood 5 feet 8 inches and weighed a solid 160 pounds. He became a professional boxer in his early twenties and fought sixteen times in nearly four years in his homeland. Dick earned only two hundred dollars for all these bouts.

The Road to Excellence

In 1955, he was already mature as a fighter. At twenty-six years of age, he went to London, England, for a chance at gaining world recognition and to earn a better living. He had to work a ten-hour-a-day factory job to pay for his lodging and training expenses. Success was not immediate, as he lost four straight bouts in England. He was seriously considering giving up and going back home to Nigeria when, at last, he won a fight with a dramatic one-round knockout and his spirits were lifted. Up until this time he had no manager who could help guide his career. A fellow Nigerian and world featherweight champion, Hogan Kid Bassey, introduced him to Jersey Jones and Jimmy August. They wanted to manage a champion as much as Dick wanted to be one.

It took just twenty-one months after his first victory in England for him to become a champion the first time. He scored a nine-round knockout over Pat McAtee to win the British Empire middleweight title. This victory encouraged

Dick Tiger in 1953.

Archive Photos

RECOGNIZED WORLD MIDDLEWEIGHT CHAMPIONSHIP BOUTS

Date	Location	Loser	Result
Oct. 23, 1962	San Francisco, Calif.	Gene Fullmer	15th-round decision
Feb. 23, 1963	Las Vegas, Nev.	(Gene Fullmer, opponent)	15th-round draw
Aug. 10, 1963	Ibadan, Nigeria	Gene Fullmer	7th-round technical knockout
Dec. 7, 1963	Atlantic City, N.J.	Dick Tiger (Joey Giardello, winner)	15th-round decision
Oct. 21, 1965	New York City, N.Y.	Joey Giardello	15th-round decision
Apr. 25, 1966	New York City, N.Y.	Dick Tiger (Emile Griffith, winner)	15th-round decision

RECOGNIZED WORLD LIGHT HEAVYWEIGHT CHAMPIONSHIPS

Date	Location	Opponent	Result
Dec. 16, 1966	New York City, N.Y.	José Torres	15th-round decision
May 16, 1967	New York City, N.Y.	José Torres	15th-round decision
Nov. 17, 1967	Las Vegas, Nev.	Roger Rouse	12th-round technical knockout
May 24, 1968	New York City, N.Y.	Dick Tiger (Bob Foster, winner)	4th-round knockout

his managers to take him to the United States in the summer of 1959. Dick's managers had a policy of never selecting easy opponents. Over a period of nine months, he fought eight times and won five times. He made his first visit to Canada in June, 1959, and surprisingly, lost his Empire title. Less than six months later, however, he returned to win back the title.

The Emerging Champion

There was now a chance to gain the biggest prize of all, a world championship. To achieve that meant fighting one of the most rugged champions of the past fifty years, Gene Fullmer. Fighting the best people available and avoiding no one was not common boxing practice, but Dick Tiger always believed in giving his best against the best.

On October 23, 1962, in San Francisco, California, the thirty-three-year-old Nigerian became world middleweight champion after fifteen hard-fought rounds. A crowning point in his career came ten months later, when Dick returned to his native Nigeria to defend his title against the same Gene Fullmer. Before his home folks, he won by stopping the American in seven rounds.

His winning and losing habit started again when the fancy boxing Philadelphian, Joey Giardello, took the title with a decision in fifteen rounds. Dick was now thirty-four years of age, which is considered old for a fighter. Dick, however, was always well-conditioned, having led a life free from drinking and smoking. He sur-

prised many people by winning the championship back from Giardello nearly two years later.

Just before turning thirty-seven, he lost his title for the last time by a decision to the legendary Emile Griffith. This seemed like a logical time to retire, but Dick had a wife and four children to support, and still needed to earn more money for the present as well as for after his fighting ended.

Continuing the Story

A year after losing his middleweight championship, Dick added some extra weight to fight at the 175-pound light heavyweight level. Champion José Torres thought he would have an easy defense of his title against the aging Nigerian. The fight was held in the famed Madison Square Garden in New York City on December 16, 1966. The amazing Dick Tiger surprised both Torres and the world by winning a fifteen-round decision. To prove the win was not just a stroke of luck, he fought Torres a second time and won again.

Following a knockout victory over Roger Rouse in Las Vegas, Nevada, Dick defended his title against one of the hardest punchers of any weight division, Bob Foster. The champion was now thirty-eight years old and long past the time when boxers have retired. In round four, a big left hook put Dick down and out.

The proud ex-champion continued to fight for two more years. His last professional bout was against his old foe, Emile Griffith, when Dick was forty-one. When his ring battles were over, Dick

STATISTICS

Bouts, 81
Knockouts, 26
Bouts won by decision, 35
Knockouts by opponents, 2
Bouts lost by decision, 15
Draws, 3

HONORS AND AWARDS

1962, 1965	*Ring* magazine Merit Award
1962, 1966	Neil Trophy
1974	Inducted into *Ring* magazine Boxing Hall of Fame
1991	Inducted into International Boxing Hall of Fame

returned to live in his native land, where, in the Nigerian-Biafra War, he lost much of the wealth earned by his feats in the ring.

Fate was to deal Dick one last blow: He was diagnosed as having pancreatic cancer. The beloved hero of Nigeria died when he was only forty-two years of age.

Summary

Fans today may not remember the man who held two universally recognized championships. Dick Tiger was not a flamboyant athlete like many featured in the media today, but a quiet, unassuming man who was always gentle in manner. When he died, American writer and artist Ted Carroll summed him up in one simple sentence: "He was that rare individual whose abilities in his chosen profession matched his qualities as a man."

Bruce Gordon

Additional Sources:

Mee, Bob. *Boxing: Heroes and Champions.* Edison, N.J.: Chartwell Books, 1997.

Toperoff, Sam. "Dick Tiger Was a Champion in Both the Ring and His African Homeland." *Sports Illustrated* 65 (October 13, 1986): 6-13.

Walsh, Peter. *Men of Steel: The Lives and Times of Boxing's Middleweight Champions.* London: Robson, 1993.

BILL TILDEN

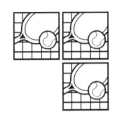

Sport: Tennis

Born: February 10, 1893
     Philadelphia, Pennsylvania
Died: June 5, 1953
     Hollywood, California

Early Life

William Tatem Tilden II was born on February 10, 1893, in Philadelphia, Pennsylvania, the second youngest of five children. Three of the children died during a diphtheria epidemic in 1884; only Bill and his older brother, Herbert,

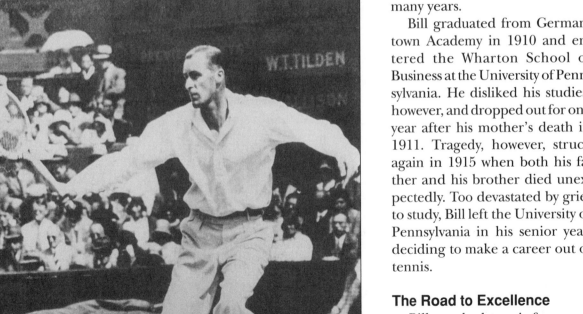

survived. Herbert introduced Bill to tennis, but the boy showed little skill in the early years.

William Tilden, Sr., a wealthy businessman, was often away from home, so Bill became very close to his mother, Linie, who, fearing for his health, had Bill educated at home by private tutors. In 1908, however, Linie contracted Bright's disease, and, with Herbert finishing school and preparing to marry, Bill was sent to Germantown Academy. While attending school there, he lived with a maiden aunt and her niece, his cousin. Since he never married, these two women remained his "family" for many years.

Bill graduated from Germantown Academy in 1910 and entered the Wharton School of Business at the University of Pennsylvania. He disliked his studies, however, and dropped out for one year after his mother's death in 1911. Tragedy, however, struck again in 1915 when both his father and his brother died unexpectedly. Too devastated by grief to study, Bill left the University of Pennsylvania in his senior year, deciding to make a career out of tennis.

The Road to Excellence

Bill coached tennis for a year at Germantown Academy and at the University of Pennsylvania before entering competition. He was given a national ranking of seventy and entered the U.S. National Championship matches in 1916, but he lost in the first round. In 1918 and 1919, however, he did reach the final round of com-

Courtesy of the International Tennis Hall of Fame

petition but lost again. Bill worked hard at building his game, spending many hours on the courts. He mastered a variety of strokes, learning the chops, half volleys, and short lobs that would supplement his already strong forehand and serve.

In 1920 Bill played the reigning Wimbledon titleholder, Gerald L. Patterson of Australia, winning the match with a combination of strokes and an awesome serve, to become the first American to win the men's Wimbledon singles title. That same summer, he won the U.S. National Championship at Forest Hills, defeating the number-one ranked U.S. player, Bill Johnston. He was now a giant of the game, bringing a virile athletic image to the sport.

Like his contemporaries Babe Ruth in baseball and Jack Dempsey in boxing, Bill caught the public's imagination at home and abroad. Not only was he proficient, but he also had a powerful personality, dominating any place he was as he dominated the court. He had a natural grace, aided by his physique—tall, broad-shouldered, lean—and nimble footwork. Even in his rare defeats, he was the center of attraction.

The Emerging Champion

Combining intelligence with hard work, Bill mastered the game completely, and it brought him great fame and wealth. He spent money lavishly, traveling widely and entertaining generously. He was often in the company of other celebrities such as movie stars and politicians. In spite of these distractions, Bill continued to play great tennis. He won the U.S. Clay Court Championship singles six consecutive years (1922-1927), the U.S. National Championship doubles five times, the mixed doubles four times, and the U.S. Indoor Championship doubles four times. He took the Wimbledon singles title three times:

MAJOR CHAMPIONSHIP VICTORIES AND FINALS

1913-14, 1922-23	U.S. National Championship mixed doubles (with Mary K. Browne; with Molla B. Mallory)
1916-17, 1919, 1924	U.S. National Championship mixed doubles finalist (with F. A. Ballin; with Mallory)
1918-1919, 1927	U.S. National Championship finalist
1918, 1921-22, 1923, 1927	U.S. National Championship doubles (with Vincent Richards; with Brian Norton; with Francis T. Hunter)
1919, 1926	U.S. National Championship doubles finalist (with Richards; with Alfred Chapin)
1920-25, 1929	U.S. National Championship
1920-21, 1930	Wimbledon
1927	Wimbledon doubles (with Hunter) French Championship mixed doubles finalist (with L. de Alvarez)
1927, 1930	French Championship finalist
1930	French Championship mixed doubles (with Cilly Aussem)

OTHER NOTABLE VICTORIES

1918, 1922-27	U.S. Clay Court Championship
1919-20, 1926, 1929	U.S. Indoor Championship doubles (with Richards; with Frank Anderson; with Hunter)
1920	U.S. Indoor Championship
1920-26	On winning U.S. Davis Cup team
1921-22, 1924	U.S. Indoor Championship mixed doubles (with Mallory; with Hazel Wightman)
1930	Italian Championship Italian Championship doubles (with Wilbur Coen)
1931, 1935	U.S. Pro Championship
1932	U.S. Pro Championship doubles (with Bruce Barnes)
1934-36, 1938, 1937	Professional World Doubles Tournament (with Ellsworth Vines; with Henri Cochet)

1920, 1921, and 1930 (the latter at age thirty-seven). Between 1920 and 1930, Bill played on the U.S. Davis Cup team, leading the United States to victory in seven consecutive years.

In 1926 Bill severely injured his knee, and victories became much harder to come by. He and the great French player René Lacoste traded wins between 1926 and 1930. One of the most thrilling matches between them occurred in 1928 in France. The United States Lawn Tennis Association (USLTA) banned Bill only days before the match for violating the player-writer rule, which specified that no amateur player could receive money in connection with the sport. Bill, however, was being paid at the time to write tennis columns. Upon protest by France and by the U.S. ambassador to France, Bill was reinstated. An underdog, since Lacoste had won their previous four meetings, Bill electrified the spectators with his brilliant play, confusing Lacoste's game plan with versatile shots. Bill was at his peak.

Continuing the Story

In 1931 Bill turned professional, forming the Tilden Tennis Tours, Inc., with his former doubles partner, Frank Hunter. They made their first appearance at Madison Square Garden in February, pioneering the way for players who preferred "cash to cups." Bill went on to win the U.S. Pro Championship singles title in 1931 and 1935 as well as the doubles in 1932. Although a big draw on tours, he was a poor businessman, running into financial problems through bad investments and careless spending habits. By the end of the 1930's, Bill was almost broke. Still, to most fans, he remained the personification of tennis. His instinctive showmanship was as sharp as ever: He knew the moves and gestures calculated to win over any audience.

After World War II, Bill helped organize the Professional Tennis Players Association and still played well enough to draw crowds, often reaching the quarterfinals in pro tournaments. In the following years, however, Bill openly came out as a homosexual, and by the 1940's, he was openly

---

HONORS, AWARDS, AND MILESTONES

1920-25	Ranked number one in the world
1920-29	Nationally ranked number one
1920-30	U.S. Davis Cup team
1931	Turned professional
1949	Named the tennis athlete of the first half-century (Associated Press poll)
1959	Inducted into National Lawn Tennis Hall of Fame

---

defending homosexuality. In November, 1946, he was arrested by the Beverly Hills police on a morals charge. Taken to court, he was found guilty and was sentenced to several months in prison. When Bill came out, he was broken in health and in spirit.

Living in Hollywood from the 1940's until his death, Bill gave lessons on friends' private courts, earning much-needed money. Still enthusiastic about the game, Bill was planning to play in the U.S. Pro Championship that was to be held in Cleveland in June of 1953. He died, however, of an apparent heart attack alone in his apartment the night before his scheduled departure.

Summary

Although Bill Tilden died in relative obscurity, his career was illustrious. His virtuosity, concentration, and "cannonball" serve earned him the admiration of all. In 1949, an Associated Press poll cited him as the tennis athlete of the first half-century, giving him 310 votes out of a possible 391; the runner-up received 32 votes. In 1969, a panel of international writers put him at the head of their collective all-time ranking. Few would dispute Bill's title as one of the greatest tennis players who ever lived.

S. Carol Berg

Additional Sources:

Deford, Frank. *Big Bill Tilden: The Triumphs and the Tragedy.* New York: Simon & Schuster, 1976.

Tilden, Bill. *Match Play and the Spin of the Ball.* Edited by Stephen Wallis Merrihew. 2d ed. New York: American Lawn Tennis, 1925.

_____. *My Story: A Champion's Memoirs.* 2d ed. New York: Hellman, Williams & Company, 1948.

Voss, Arthur. *Tilden and Tennis in the Twenties.* Troy, N.Y.: Whitston, 1985.

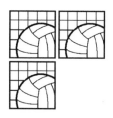

STEVE TIMMONS

Sport: Volleyball

Born: November 29, 1958
Newport Beach, California

Early Life

Steve Timmons was born on November 29, 1958, in Newport Beach, California. He started playing competitive volleyball at the age of fourteen, but his main interest was basketball. As he was growing up, his goal was to make it to the National Basketball Association (NBA) and play professional basketball like his heroes Wilt Chamberlain, Jerry West, and Julius Erving.

Steve was a 1978 graduate of Newport Harbor High School, where he starred in both volleyball and basketball. He did not start playing high-school volleyball until his junior year. After high school, he attended Orange Coast College in Costa Mesa, California. At Orange Coast, he was the starting center for the basketball team, which won the 1979 California junior college championship.

Steve began to favor volleyball over basketball, and he transferred to the University of Southern California (USC) on a volleyball scholarship. While at USC, he earned a bachelor's degree in communication.

The Road to Excellence

Steve played volleyball and basketball for the USC Trojans from 1980 to 1982. During that time, the volleyball team reached the National Collegiate Athletic Association (NCAA) Final Four all three years and won the NCAA championship in 1980. Steve was named to the 1981 and 1982 All-Conference team as well as to the 1981 Second Team All-American and the 1982 First Team All-American squads.

In May of 1981, Steve was selected to play for the U.S. volleyball team. At 6 feet 5 inches in height and weighing 205 pounds, Steve played the position of outside hitter. Opponents came

to fear the player wearing number 6 in later years because of Steve's incredible talent for spiking the ball.

In 1982, the U.S. national team went to Argentina to play in the world championships. Steve was left behind because the coaches thought he was too inconsistent and inexperienced. In 1983, he missed the cut for the Pre-Olympic tournament in Long Beach, California. Instead, the coaches of the U.S. team sent him to play with the Pan-American Games squad.

The Emerging Champion

In November of 1983, the U.S. national team was scheduled for an important competitive se-

Steve Timmons in 1993.

ries against the Cuban national team. The series was four months away, and Steve was determined to be a standout in the series and to make the 1984 U.S. Olympic team. He began to lift weights to strengthen his body.

During the six-match series with Cuba, he had 120 kills (unreturned spikes) and 28 stuff blocks. After he learned that he had clinched a spot on the U.S. Olympic team, he sat in the locker room by himself and wept.

Steve was at his best during the 1984 Olympics, when the U.S. team beat Brazil in the final match to earn the first U.S. gold medal in men's volleyball. He accomplished 106 kills in the tournament and was named the most valuable player of the Olympic tournament.

After the 1984 Olympics, Steve suffered a career-threatening knee injury during a tournament in South Korea. Doctors told him he would not be able to compete for a year or more, but Steve was determined to get healthy. He began competing again within seven months. During the next few years, he helped lead the U.S. team in accomplishing the "triple crown" of international volleyball: winning the 1984 Olympics in Los Angeles, California, the 1985 World Cup in Tokyo, Japan, and the 1986 World Championships in Paris, France.

After his injury in 1984, Steve spent his time away from volleyball designing a new type of fluorescent yellow volleyball, which became a hit with beach-goers. He began his own sporting-goods company, "Redsand," in San Diego, California. The company produced Steve's own line of beachwear designed for players of sand volleyball.

In 1988, Steve joined three other former Olympians from the 1984 U.S. team to compete in the Olympics in Seoul, Korea. Steve set the mood for the American team with his passion, determination, and intensity. The U.S. team met the Soviets in the final match of the Seoul Olympics. The Americans won the match in four games. After the match, the Soviet coach said that Steve had shown flair, fire, and incredible poise during the entire match.

Continuing the Story

In 1989, Steve left the U.S. national team to play beach volleyball and to get married. Later, he joined the Italian professional volleyball

MAJOR CHAMPIONSHIP VICTORIES

1984, 1988	Gold Medal, Olympic Volleyball
1985	Gold Medal, World Cup
1986	Silver Medal, Goodwill Games Gold Medal, World Championships
1987	Gold Medal, Pan-American Games
1991	World Club Championship team
1992	Bronze Medal, Olympic Volleyball Bronze Medal, World League Championship

league. In 1990, he played for the Il Messaggero team of Ravena, Italy. His salary was $1 million per year. He led the Italian team to a 24-0 record and the division title in 1990. Steve and his Italian team won the 1991 Club World Championships, and the team was the runner-up in the Italian League in 1992.

At the age of thirty-three, Steve rejoined the U.S. national team to represent the United States at the Barcelona Olympics in 1992, along with former teammates Jeff Stork (setter) and Bob Ctvrtlik (outside hitter).The team earned a bronze medal. Later that year, in the 1992 World League Tournament against Japan, Steve was picked as the most valuable player on the U.S. team. The Japanese most valuable player was Masafumi Ohura, and both players were given new tennis rackets along with their awards. Steve convinced Ohura to play imaginary tennis with him on the volleyball court after the ceremony. The crowd cheered loudly as the two players darted across the court, pretending to lob and smash. The display showed that although he was a serious competitor, Steve remained a child at heart.

Between 1989 and 1994 Steve also competed on the beach volleyball circuit, winning the FIVB Japan Open with partner Karch Kiraly in 1989. After only moderate success on the AVP tour in 1994, Steve decided to retire from competition.

HONORS AND AWARDS

1980	NCAA All-Tournament Team
1981-82	College All-American
1998	Inducted into Volleyball Hall of Fame

He was married in 1997 to actress and model Debbe Dunning, with whom he has a daughter, Spencer Schae.

Summary

Steve Timmons will be remembered around the world as one of volleyball's great players. As a key performer for three U.S. Olympic teams, he left volleyball fans with many memories of his spectacular kills.

Steve was inducted into the volleyball Hall of Fame in 1998.

Kathy Davis

Additional Sources:

Anderson, B. "Their Final Shots." *Sports Illustrated,* July 10, 1989.

Lidz, F. "The Guy Has a License to Kill." *Sports Illustrated,* September 14, 1988.

Mallon, Bill, and Ian Buchanan. *Quest for Gold: The Encyclopedia of American Olympians.* New York: Leisure Press, 1984.

Noden, M. "A Rare Old Bird." *Sports Illustrated* 76, no. 20 (1992).

Wallechinsky, David. *The Complete Book of the Olympics.* Boston: Little, Brown and Company, 1991.

Y. A. TITTLE

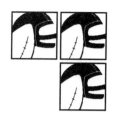

Sport: Football

Born: October 24, 1926
Marshall, Texas

Early Life

Yelberton Abraham Tittle, Jr., better known as Y. A., was born on October 24, 1926, in Marshall, Texas, a small lumber town near the Louisiana border. Y. A.'s father was a rural postman named Yelberton Abraham, Sr. Y. A. was the second of three sons reared by Alma and Yelberton Tittle. Both parents taught their children to work hard in every task.

Y. A. was a big-eared, bony-faced boy who did not look the part of the great athlete that he would become. He also had asthma, but this did

not stop him from playing football. Football was the sport to play in that part of Texas, and Y. A. began throwing a football as soon as he could get his hand around it. Y. A.'s boyhood idol was the great Washington Redskins quarterback Sammy Baugh.

The Road to Excellence

Y. A. was a 6-foot 185-pound star tailback for the Marshall High School football team. He also led the team to the state finals. In 1943, he was named to the All-State team.

Many colleges sought Y. A. not only for his football skills but also because he was ineligible for the military draft due to his asthma. He chose

New York Giant Y. A. Tittle recovers from a hit in a 1964 game.

Louisiana State University and was given a scholarship. With the team short of players as a result of the war, Y. A. made the starting lineup as a seventeen-year-old freshman in 1944. In the final game of that year, Y. A. completed 15 of 17 passes for 300 yards and three touchdowns to lead LSU to a crushing 25-6 defeat of arch-rival Tulane University.

LSU quarterback coach Carl Brumbaugh had a significant impact on Y. A.'s career in his sophomore season. Brumbaugh introduced him to the T-formation that was currently revolutionizing the game. When LSU switched over to the T-formation, Y. A. turned into a great quarterback because that formation enabled him to use his greatest skill—his passing ability. Y. A. became one of the finest collegiate quarterbacks of his time, along with Bobby Layne of the University of Texas, Charley Conerly of the University of Mississippi, and Harry Gilmer of the University of Alabama. He gained All-Southeastern Conference honors in his junior and senior seasons and led LSU to the 1946 Cotton Bowl.

The Emerging Champion

Y. A. graduated from LSU in 1948 but was overlooked by National Football League (NFL) teams. The Cleveland Browns of the old All-America Football Conference (AAFC) selected him. The Browns quickly traded Y. A. to the Baltimore Colts, and Y. A. became the Colts' starting quarterback. In his first professional game, he set four AAFC records as he led the Colts to a 45-28 victory over the New York Giants. Then the AAFC folded after the 1949 season and Y. A. joined the San Francisco 49ers of the NFL.

Frankie Albert was the 49ers quarterback at the time, so Y. A. sat on the bench until Albert retired in 1952. Y. A. then took over as starting quarterback and kept the job for the next eight years. His best year with the 49ers was 1957, when he led the team to a first-place tie with the Detroit Lions for the Western Conference title. Y. A. combined with receiver R. C. Owens to produce the famous alley-oop pass that helped the 49ers win several games. Y. A. was also chosen for the All-NFL team that year.

In 1961, the 49ers began looking for a younger quarterback. When they found one, they traded the thirty-five-year-old Y. A. to the New York Giants. It was a trade they would regret. In New York, Y. A. emerged as a late-blooming star at an age when most quarterbacks are retired. He led the Giants to three straight Eastern Conference Championships from 1961 to 1963. He passed for an incredible 86 touchdown passes

STATISTICS

Season	GP	PA	PC	Pct.	Yds.	Avg.	TD	Int.
1948	14	289	161	.557	2,522	8.7	16	9
1949	11	289	148	.512	2,209	7.6	14	18
1950	12	315	161	.511	1,884	6.0	8	19
1951	12	114	63	.552	808	7.1	8	9
1952	12	208	106	.510	1,407	6.8	11	12
1953	9	259	149	.575	2,121	8.2	20	16
1954	12	295	170	.576	2,205	7.5	9	9
1955	12	287	147	.512	2,185	7.6	**17**	28
1956	10	218	124	.569	1,641	7.5	7	12
1957	12	279	176	.631	2,157	7.7	13	15
1958	11	208	120	.577	1,467	7.1	9	15
1959	11	199	102	.513	1,331	6.7	10	15
1960	9	127	69	.543	694	5.5	4	3
1961	13	285	163	.572	2,272	8.0	17	12
1962	14	375	200	.533	3,224	8.6	**33**	20
1963	13	367	221	.602	3,145	8.6	**36**	14
1964	14	281	147	.523	1,798	6.4	10	22
Totals	201	4,395	2,427	.552	33,070	7.5	242	248

Notes: Boldface indicates statistical leader. GP = games played; PA = passes attempted; PC = passes completed; Pct. = percent completed; Yds. = yards; Avg. = average yards per attempt; TD = touchdowns; Int. = interceptions

HONORS, AWARDS, AND RECORDS

1946-47	All-Southeastern Conference Team
1954-55, 1958, 1960, 1962-63	NFL Pro Bowl Team
1957, 1961-63	All-NFL Team
1957, 1962	United Press International NFL Player of the Year
1957, 1962	Newspaper Enterprise Association NFL Player of the Year
1961, 1963	Thorpe Trophy (1963 co-recipient)
1962	NFL record for the most touchdown passes in a game (7) (record shared)
1963	Associated Press NFL Player of the Year
1971	Inducted into Pro Football Hall of Fame Uniform number 14 retired by New York Giants

during those seasons and was chosen as the NFL Player of the Year in 1962 and 1963. The only goal that eluded him was the NFL championship.

Continuing the Story

Y. A. was a tremendous competitor who fired up the Giants and led them to three of their greatest years. His courage inspired fans and teammates alike. While opposing linemen rushed after him, Y. A. would calmly hold on to the ball and throw when he felt ready. The oncoming linemen never hurried or scared Y. A. In the 1963 NFL Championship Game against the Chicago Bears, Y. A. hurt his left knee so badly that by halftime he could not bend it. Yet he played the whole game, and his teammates said that they would always remember Y. A.'s courage that day.

Y. A. was first and foremost a great passer. He had a strong right wrist that helped him delay his passes as long as possible. He was adept at throwing long or short passes and could throw them sidearm or overhand. Giants coach Allie Sherman called Y. A. the best quarterback he had

ever seen. Former teammate Ed Henke said that there was not a finer person in professional football. Y. A., embarrassed by such praise, said that he was a professional who worked hard to do his best week after week.

Y. A. retired after the 1964 season after completing 2,427 passes for 33,070 yards and 242 touchdowns in his seventeen-year career. He was selected to the Pro Football Hall of Fame in 1971 and is also a member of the Texas Sports Hall of Fame.

After retiring from football, Y. A. continued working hard. He purchased an ownership in an insurance company in Palo Alto, California.

Summary

Y. A. Tittle is known as the greatest quarterback in New York Giants history. He will be best remembered for having achieved great success at an age when most football players are finished. His career is an inspiration for anyone in any profession who is discouraged. When the 49ers gave up on Y. A., he did not give up. He proved that success can come at any age by working hard and remaining dedicated to the goal.

Nan White

Additional Sources:

De Laet, Dianne Tittle. *Giants and Heroes: A Daughter's Memoir of Y. A. Tittle.* South Royalton, Vt.: Steerforth Press, 1995.

LaBlanc, Michael L., and Mary K. Ruby, eds. *Professional Sports Team Histories: Football.* Detroit: Gale, 1994.

Tittle, Y. A., and Don Smith. *I Pass! My Story.* New York: Franklin Watts, 1964.

EDDIE TOLAN

Sport: Track and field (sprints)

Born: September 29, 1908
        Denver, Colorado
Died: January 31, 1967
        Detroit, Michigan

Early Life

Thomas Edward (Eddie) Tolan was born on September 29, 1908, in Denver, Colorado. Shortly after his birth, his parents moved the family to

Winner of the 100-meter dash Eddie Tolan is congratulated by Olympic official William May Garland in 1932.

AP/Wide World Photos

Detroit, Michigan. Experiencing difficult times in Detroit, Eddie's parents separated, and he and his two sisters were raised by his mother, Alice.

Alice Tolan encouraged her children to get a good education. Eddie attended Cass Technical High School in Detroit and distinguished himself as an excellent student. He was also a standout in both football and track. His extraordinary athletic ability enabled Eddie to develop into one of Michigan's best high school quarterbacks. Though weighing only 132 pounds, Eddie once scored six touchdowns in a single game, a feat he considered his greatest athletic thrill.

During the spring, Eddie ran track, and in his senior year he won both the Detroit city championship and Michigan state championship in the 100- and 220-yard sprints.

The Road to Excellence

His high school athletic exploits earned Eddie a scholarship to the University of Michigan at Ann Arbor. At 5 feet 7 inches and 140 pounds, Eddie had a difficult time achieving the same football success he had enjoyed in high school. Although football was his favorite sport, Eddie took the advice of his football coach and, after his freshman year, decided to *devote* all of his time and energy to track.

Eddie attempted to qualify for the 1928 Olympic team in his specialties, the 100 and 220, but failed to place in the top three in either event. Disappointed, but benefiting from the world-class experience, the speedster returned to the University of Michigan track team and promptly set the school and conference record in both the 100- and 220-yard sprints.

In 1929, Eddie was ranked as one of the best American sprinters. He bettered the world record in the 100 yards twice and became the first runner in track history to be clocked officially at 9.5 seconds in the 100-yard distance.

STATISTICS

Year	Competition	Event	Place	Time
1929	National AAU Championships	100 meters	1st	10.0
		200 meters	1st	21.9
1930	National AAU Championships	100 meters	1st	9.7
1931	National AAU Championships	200 meters	1st	21.0
	NCAA Championships	220 yards	1st	21.5
1932	Olympic Games	100 meters	Gold	10.3 WR, OR
		200 meters	Gold	21.2 OR

Notes: OR = Olympic Record; WR = World Record

During the next two years, Eddie won almost every major track title. In addition to winning races, Eddie was making excellent grades and graduated from the University of Michigan with a B.S. degree in education. He hoped to continue his education the following year and pursue his lifelong dream of becoming a medical physician.

The Emerging Champion

Events of 1932, however, delayed his plans for a medical career. In that summer, he qualified for the United States Olympic team that would participate in the Los Angeles Games a month later. Despite his tremendous collegiate record, Eddie entered the Games as an underdog to Ralph Metcalfe of Marquette University and George Simpson of Ohio State University, because both had beaten him in the Olympic trials.

At the Los Angeles Games, the nearsighted Michigan sprinter, with his glasses taped to his head, withstood a strong finish from Ralph Metcalfe and won the 100 meters in a photo finish. Two judges timed Eddie in 10.3 seconds and a third in 10.4 seconds, while three judges timed Metcalfe in 10.3 seconds. The photograph, however, showed that Eddie was the winner by a margin of one inch. The 10.3 was both an Olympic and a world record.

His second gold medal was won in the 200 meters. Eddie ran a 21.2, setting another Olympic record and once again beating Metcalfe and Simpson. Despite two gold medals and a world record in the 100, Eddie was not selected by the Olympic coaches to run on the 4×100-meter relay team, which won a gold medal and set a new world record.

Eddie, nicknamed the "Midnight Express," was the first black athlete to win two gold medals at the Olympics and to be called the "fastest man alive." His accomplishments encouraged African Americans to believe that they could do the same. Eddie's sprint victories in 1932 paved the way for other African American sprinters such as Jesse Owens, a 100- and 200-meter gold medal winner in 1936, and Harrison Dillard, a double sprint winner in 1948. It is ironic that both of these men shared the Olympic record of 10.3 with Eddie until it was finally broken in 1960 by Germany's Armin Hary, who lowered the Olympic mark to 10.2.

Continuing the Story

Eddie's mother was also proud of her son's Olympic victories, but she was prouder of his determination to be a physician. After the Olympics, however, Eddie was not able to return to college to pursue his dream of a medical career. The United States was in the midst of a great economic depression and jobs were extremely hard to find.

Two Olympic gold medal victories in Los Angeles, however, enabled Eddie to land a job as a vaudeville actor and tour the United States with Bill "Bojangles" Robinson, the famous dancer. He appeared on stage as the "world's fastest human" and told the audience stories about his experiences at the Olympic Games. The money he earned did not go to finance his study of medicine but rather for the support of his mother and two sisters in Detroit.

As the months went by, the 1932 Olympic Games were forgotten, and Eddie's vaudeville career ended. In 1933, at the age of twenty-six, Eddie got a job as a filing clerk in the Detroit County Record Office. Two years later, Eddie used his education degree and taught physical education to children in a Detroit elementary school. Eddie held that post until he died of a heart attack at the age of fifty-eight in 1967. He had never married.

RECORDS

World record at 200 meters in 1929 (21.1)
World record at 100 meters twice in 1929 (10.4)
World record at 100 yards twice in 1929
Broke 100 meters world record eight times from 1929 to 1932
First runner officially clocked at 9.5 in 100 yards (1929)
First African American to win two gold medals at the Olympic Games

HONORS AND AWARDS

1982   Inducted into National Track and Field Hall of Fame

Summary

Three years before he died, Eddie Tolan was asked by a reporter what he considered to be the biggest change in the sport since he had competed. Eddie remarked, "The attitude toward Negroes. Back in my day, if you saw a Negro in sports, you knew he had to be head and shoulders above the rest." Eddie played a major role in that change of attitude and the stereotypical perception of the black athlete in sport. He was recognized for his track achievements in 1982 when he was elected to the National Track and Field Hall of Fame.

William G. Durick

Additional Sources:

Findling, John E., and Kimberly D. Pelle, eds. *Historical Dictionary of the Modern Olympic Movement.* Westport, Conn.: Greenwood Press, 1996.

Hickok, Ralph. *A Who's Who of Sports Champions.* Boston: Houghton Mifflin, 1995.

Knapp, Ron. *Top Ten American Men Sprinters.* Springfield, N.J.: Enslow, *1999.*

ALBERTO TOMBA

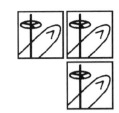

Sport: Skiing

Born: December 19, 1966
San Lazzaro di Savenna, Italy

Early Life

Alberto Tomba was born on December 19, 1966, in San Lazzaro di Savenna, near Bologna, Italy, to Franco Tomba, a wealthy clothier, and Maria (Grazia) Tomba. He was the younger of two brothers. The family lived in a sixteenth century villa on the outskirts of Bologna, close to the Apennines mountains.

In his youth, Alberto's father had been a competitive skier, and he encouraged both of his sons to do well at skiing and any other sport they tried. When they were growing up, it seemed that Alberto's older brother, Marco, was the better skier. Alberto's father encouraged his younger son to play soccer and to forget about being a competitive skier. Alberto was outraged by his father's comments, and he decided that he would show his father that he was the superior skier in the family.

The Road to Excellence

Alberto had started taking skiing lessons when he was only six. By the time he was a teenager, his enthusiasm and raw talent impressed his instructors. When Alberto was eighteen, he was selected to the Italian World Cup team for the 1985-1986 season. Although he was still considered too immature and somewhat overweight, Alberto skied well enough to be ranked fifteenth overall in the world in Alpine skiing.

At 6 feet and 200 pounds, Alberto was an aggressive slalom skier. Possessing good upper-body strength, he would power his way through gate poles as he made a straight line down a course. Alberto chose to specialize in two of the five Alpine events, the slalom and the giant slalom. Because of his crushing style, Alberto was the first competitive skier to wear a helmet while skiing the giant slalom. Unfortunately, he lacked self-discipline during his first season of World Cup competition. At this stage of his career, Alberto was more interested in visiting his girlfriend than in training.

Although he was earning a reputation more for being a fun-loving and eccentric personality than for being a top Alpine skier, Alberto won a

Italian skiing sensation Alberto Tomba races in the 1998 World Cup.

bronze medal in the giant slalom at the 1987 World Cup Games in Switzerland; he was the only Italian to win a medal at the games. Historically, the Italian World Cup team had consisted of mostly Italians from the far north of the country. When Alberto became the first lowland skier to crack the top ranks of the Italian team, he became a hero among southern Italians.

The Emerging Champion

For the 1987-1988 World Cup season, Alberto reduced his total body fat from 17 percent to only 10 percent by hard training and dieting. With the guidance of his coaches, the more fit and more powerful Alberto won a total of nine World Cup races during the season. For his efforts, he finished the season second overall in the World Cup standings. With characteristic flair, Alberto made outrageous remarks concerning his prowess as a skier that caught the skiing world off guard. By the time of the 1988 Winter Olympics in Calgary, Alberta, Canada, Alberto had already won seven of his nine World Cup races, and he was ready to show the world that he was the best Alpine skier alive.

At twenty-one, Alberto was on the verge of becoming one of Alpine skiing's great heroes. Although the experts were not convinced that he could beat such skiing legends as Ingemar Stenmark and Pirmin Zurbriggen, he amazed even himself by capturing the gold medal in both the slalom and giant slalom.

Alberto was now a superstar in his native Italy. Through commercial endorsements, he began earning more than $1 million a year. Although he finished second overall for the World Cup season, Alberto did win the slalom and giant slalom World Cup titles. He became somewhat complacent during the next season, however, and finished only third overall.

During the early part of the 1989-1990 season, Alberto broke his collarbone in a super-giant slalom race at Val d'Isère, France. He was forced to take three months off to recuperate. Alberto's father made sure that his famous son had everything he needed to recapture top form, including the hiring of 1972 Olympic gold medalist Gustavo Thoeni as his personal ski coach. The new regime began paying dividends during the 1990-1991 World Cup season, when Alberto won six World Cup races.

MAJOR CHAMPIONSHIPS

Year	Competition	Event	Place
1987	World Cup	Giant Slalom	3d
1988	World Championships	Giant Slalom	1st
		Slalom	1st
	Olympic Games	Giant Slalom	Gold
		Slalom	Gold
1992	World Championships	Giant Slalom	1st
	Olympic Games	Giant Slalom	Gold
		Slalom	Silver
1994	Olympic Games	Slalom	Silver
1995	World Cup	Overall	1st
		Slalom	1st
		Giant Slalom	1st
1996	World Championships	Slalom	1st
		Giant Slalom	1st
	World Cup	Slalom	1st
1997	World Championships	Slalom	3d
1998	World Cup	Slalom	1st

Continuing the Story

In addition to winning six World Cup races during the 1990-1991 season, Alberto won the World Cup giant slalom title and finished second overall behind Luxembourg's Marc Girardelli. He regained his dominance of Alpine skiing during the 1991-1992 World Cup season. By the end of January, 1992, Alberto had an insurmountable point lead in the slalom, and the World Cup title was once again his.

Alberto was confident going into the 1992 Winter Olympics in Albertville, France. More than twenty thousand Italian fans made the trip to Albertville to cheer their countryman to victory, and Alberto did not disappoint them. He became the first skier to win an Alpine gold medal in the same event in consecutive Olympics. With his gold medal in the giant slalom, Alberto had won three Olympic Alpine gold medals in his career, tying the record for Olympic Alpine events.

Finn Christian Jagge from Norway beat Alberto in the slalom, so Alberto had to settle for the silver medal in that event. After the 1992 Winter Olympics, Alberto had trouble staying motivated for the World Cup races. During the 1992-1993 World Cup season, various nagging illnesses kept him from being a dominant force. Always a flamboyant personality, "La Bomba," as he came to be known, became a larger-than-life public figure who thrived on being in the spotlight. Although Alberto did not do as well as he had hoped at the 1994 Winter Olympics in Lillehammer, Norway—merely winning the silver medal in the slalom—he did capture his third World Cup slalom title in the 1993-1994 season.

In 1995, at the age of twenty-eight, Alberto swept the World Cup with an overall win and first-place finishes in the slalom and giant slalom events. He won the slalom event in the 1996 World Cup, and he added the slalom and giant slalom titles at that year's World Championships as well.

With a disappointing third-place finish at the 1997 World Championships, Alberto seemed to lose his edge. In 1998 he did not finish the slalom and giant slalom events, leaving the Olympics with no medals. He bounced back at the 1998 World Cup competitions, however, finishing first in the slalom event. This last win brought his World Cup victory total to fifty, and Alberto decided to retire prior to the 1999 World Cup season.

After his retirement, Alberto appeared in the annual Lexus Tomba Tour, begun in 1999, to raise money for junior ski racing programs and children's charities in the United States.

Summary

Alberto Tomba combined grace and strength to become the greatest Alpine skier of his day. In addition to his prowess on skis, Alberto displayed a magnetic personality and a love for being the center of attention. He may have been brash, but he brought excitement to Alpine skiing as few other skiers had done before him.

Jeffry Jensen

Additional Sources:

"Alberto Tomba." *Current Biography* 54, no. 5 (1993).

Kerig, Bill. "On the Spot." *Skiing* 49, no. 2 (1996).

Levinson, David, and Karen Christenson, eds. *Encyclopedia of World Sport: From Ancient to Present*. Santa Barbara, Calif.: ABC-CLIO, 1996.

Wallechinsky, David. *The Complete Book of the Olympics*. Boston: Little, Brown and Company, 1991.

Courtesy of Amateur Athletic Foundation of Los Angeles

BILL TOOMEY

Sport: Track and field (decathlon)

Born: January 10, 1939
Philadelphia, Pennsylvania

Early Life

William Anthony Toomey was born on January 10, 1939, in Philadelphia, Pennsylvania. His father was a wealthy wine company executive who provided young Bill with lots of opportunities to participate in sports. While Bill was still a young boy, his family moved to California.

Bill's first love was basketball, but he was overweight and slow on his feet. He was so clumsy that his classmates often laughed at him when he participated in sports.

When he was thirteen years old, he had an accident that appeared to end any hopes he had of becoming an athlete. A friend tossed a glass plate at him that cut a nerve in his wrist so badly that Bill needed six operations to restore his right arm to 75 percent of its normal use.

The Road to Excellence

Through hard work, Bill was able to make the baseball, basketball, and football teams at the high school he attended in California. Because the injury to his wrist had cut off his ability to feel anything in the fingers of his throwing hand, he eventually decided to concentrate on track instead, where he participated in the long jump and the quarter-mile run.

Upon graduation from high school, Bill attended the University of Colorado, where he competed in the quarter-mile run and the long jump for two years, but he never won

a major championship. He then decided to switch to the pentathlon, an event consisting of five different track and field events. That seemed to be a good move, for Bill won the national Amateur Athletic Union (AAU) pentathlon championship in 1960, 1961, 1963, and 1964.

In 1963, Bill decided to begin competing in the decathlon. The decathlon is made up of ten events and is like a miniature track meet. Each competitor must participate in all ten events: the

100-meter dash, the 400-meter dash, the 1,500-meter run, the high hurdles, the long jump, the high jump, the pole vault, the discus throw, the shot put, and the javelin throw. Points for each event are scored according to a set of established tables. The winner is the competitor with the most total points from the ten events. This grueling competition is undoubtedly the toughest individual test of speed, strength, stamina, and spirit ever devised. That is why the winner of the Olympic decathlon is often given the title "the world's greatest athlete."

STATISTICS

Year	Competition	Event	Place	Points/Time
1960	National AAU Outdoor Championships	Pentathlon	1st	3,010
1961	National AAU Outdoor Championships	Pentathlon	1st	3,482
1963	National AAU Outdoor Championships	Pentathlon	1st	3,365
1964	National AAU Outdoor Championships	Pentathlon	1st	3,687
1965	National AAU Outdoor Championships	Decathlon	1st	7,764
1966	National AAU Outdoor Championships	Decathlon	1st	8,234
1967	Pan-American Games	Decathlon	1st	8,044
	National AAU Outdoor Championships	Decathlon	1st	7,880
	National AAU Indoor Championships	Sprint medley relay	1st	1:51.6
1968	Olympic Games	Decathlon	Gold	8,193 OR
	National AAU Outdoor Championships	Decathlon	1st	8,037
1969	National AAU Outdoor Championships	Decathlon	1st	7,818

Note: OR = Olympic Record

The Emerging Champion

Bill was twenty-four years of age when he participated in his first major decathlon competition. Many people were skeptical, because this is somewhat old to begin competing in an event as demanding as the decathlon. After having some success in his first decathlon competition, he was convinced that this was his sport. He then began touring the United States for every decathlon meet he could find in an effort to improve his skills.

In 1964, he tried out for the United States Olympic team and narrowly missed making the team. Over the next several years, Bill used all his free time for practice and spent his summer vacations from his teaching job to travel abroad to compete in decathlon meets.

His dedication soon began to pay off. In 1965, Bill won his first major victory when he won the first of his record five AAU decathlon titles. In 1967, he won the decathlon at the Pan-American Games. This victory set the stage for the competition he wanted to win most of all: the Olympic decathlon at Mexico City in 1968.

Bill's preparation for this event had been long and difficult. During the six years that he had been training and competing in the decathlon, he not only had to overcome the handicap from his childhood accident but also had to overcome a shattered kneecap, hepatitis, and mononucleosis.

After the first day of the two-day competition at Mexico City, Bill was in first place with a record first-day score of 4,499 points. On the second day, however, he experienced a near catastrophe when he missed in his first two tries at the warm-up height in the pole vault. Bill used all his courage and willpower to clear the bar on his third and final attempt, keeping him in contention for the gold medal.

Bill was still ahead of his thirty rivals going into the final event, the grueling 1,500-meter run. Running on sheer determination, Bill won the race and clinched the gold medal for the decathlon. Thus, at the age of twenty-nine, Bill had become the oldest person to ever win the decathlon. In the process, he had set an Olympic record with 8,193 points.

Continuing the Story

The following year, Bill exceeded his Olympic performance when he set a world record of 8,417 points in the decathlon. As a result of that achievement, he was named World Athlete of the Year by *Track and Field News* magazine, an incredible accomplishment for someone who was then thirty years of age and who had not started competing in the decathlon until he was twenty-four years old. When he retired at the age of thirty-one, he had recorded eight of the twelve highest decathlon scores (total points) ever made.

HONORS, AWARDS, AND RECORDS

1969	*Track and Field News* World Athlete of the Year
	Athletics Weekly World Athlete of the Year
	Sullivan Award
	Hall of the Athlete Foundation Athlete of the Year
	World Trophy
	Set a world decathlon record (8,417 points)
1975	Inducted into National Track and Field Hall of Fame
1984	Inducted into U.S. Olympic Hall of Fame

Summary

Perhaps a real key to Bill Toomey's success was his attitude toward his sport. He said that he truly enjoyed the decathlon, whereas too many athletes do not really enjoy their sport. He was not concerned with receiving recognition for being successful in the decathlon. It was simply enough to know that he had done his best and had accomplished his goals.

William R. Swanson

Additional Sources:

Bateman, Hal. *United States Track and Field Olympians, 1896-1980.* Indianapolis, Ind.: The Athletics Congress of the United States, 1984.

Hickok, Ralph. *A Who's Who of Sports Champions.* Boston: Houghton Mifflin, 1995.

Toomey, Bill, and Barry King. *The Olympic Challenge, 1988.* Costa Mesa, Calif.: HDL, 1988.

Wallechinsky, David. *The Complete Book of the Olympics.* Boston: Little, Brown and Company, 1991.

Watman, Mel. *Encyclopedia of Track and Field Athletics.* New York: St. Martin's Press, 1981.

JOE TORRE

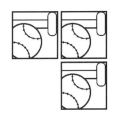

Sport: Baseball

Born: July 18, 1940
Brooklyn, New York

Early Life

Joe "The Godfather" Torre was born to Joseph and Margaret Torre in Brooklyn, New York, on July 18, 1940. Growing up in a baseball-loving family and in an era (1940's-1950's) when the three New York teams were dominating baseball, it was natural that Joe would take an interest in playing the game. He was further inspired in his baseball pursuits by his older brother Frank, who established a successful career as a first baseman for the great Milwaukee Braves teams of the 1950's. Joe's first extensive experience with the game was playing with a sandlot club called the Brooklyn Cadets, who played about a hundred games a year. Joe continued playing baseball in high school at St. Francis Preparatory in Williamsburg, New York.

Joe Torre (left) with Warren Spahn after a win in 1963.

The Road to Excellence

Joe's success in baseball encouraged him to follow in his brother's footsteps by trying for a career in professional baseball. None other than Frank's team, the Braves, gave him his first opportunity to play professional baseball by signing him to a minor league contract. Joe's advancement through the minors was rapid. At the age of eighteen he began the year with Eau Claire in the lower minors, was promoted to Louisville, and was then brought up to the major league Braves at the end of the 1960 season. Joe, only nineteen at the time, hit a pinch-hit single in his first at bat off of Harvey Haddix.

The Emerging Champion

Joe won a spot on the Milwaukee Braves roster in 1961 and quickly established himself as a solid baseball player. He batted .278 his rookie year and finished second in the Rookie of the Year voting to Hall of Famer Billy Williams. Joe was a semi-regular his first two seasons but became an everyday player in 1963 with a breakout season. That year Joe hit .293, with 14 home runs, and made the All-Star team for the first time. During that season, Joe proved to the baseball world that he was one of the finest catchers in the major leagues.

Continuing the Story

Joe improved on the All-Star performance of the 1963 season with an even better year in 1964. That season he batted over .300 for the first time (.321), had over 100 runs batted in (RBIs) for the first time (109), finished first in fielding percentage among Na-

2789

STATISTICS

Season	GP	AB	Hits	2B	3B	HR	Runs	RBI	BA	SA
1960	2	2	1	0	0	0	0	0	.500	.500
1961	113	406	113	21	4	10	40	42	.278	.424
1962	80	220	62	8	1	5	23	26	.282	.395
1963	142	501	147	19	4	14	57	71	.293	.431
1964	154	601	193	36	5	20	87	109	.321	.498
1965	148	523	152	21	1	27	68	80	.291	.489
1966	148	546	172	20	3	36	83	101	.315	.560
1967	135	477	132	18	1	20	67	68	.277	.444
1968	115	424	115	11	2	10	45	55	.271	.377
1969	159	602	174	29	6	18	72	101	.289	.447
1970	161	624	203	27	9	21	89	100	.325	.498
1971	161	634	**230**	34	8	24	97	**137**	**.363**	.555
1972	149	544	157	26	6	11	71	81	.289	.419
1973	141	519	149	17	2	13	67	69	.287	.403
1974	147	529	149	28	1	11	59	70	.282	.401
1975	114	361	89	16	3	6	33	35	.247	.357
1976	114	310	95	10	3	5	36	31	.306	.406
1977	26	51	9	3	0	1	2	9	.176	.294
Totals	2,209	7,874	2,342	344	59	252	996	1,185	.297	.452

Notes: Boldface indicates statistical leader. GP = games played; AB = at bats; 2B = doubles; 3B = triples; HR = home runs; RBI = runs batted in; BA = batting average; SA = slugging average

tional League catchers (.995), and came in fifth in the most valuable player (MVP) voting.

His performance slipped a bit in 1965, but he rebounded strongly in 1966–the Braves' first in Atlanta—with one of his finest seasons. Joe again hit over .300, had over 100 RBIs, and set a career high in home runs, with 36. The rigors of catching and injuries appeared to have caught up with Joe the next two seasons as he experienced significant drops in all three major hitting categories (batting average, home runs, and RBIs). The Braves, perhaps thinking that Joe's career was headed in a downward spiral, traded him for former MVP Orlando Cepeda after the 1968 season.

The Cardinals made Joe their everyday first baseman in 1969 and, relieved of the rigors of catching, Joe responded with a comeback season and drove in over 100 runs. The next year, alternating between catcher, first base, and third base, he finished in the top ten in several hitting categories, including second in hitting at .325.

In 1971, as the Cardinals' regular third baseman, Joe led the National League in batting average (.363), hits (230), RBIs (137), and total bases (352) and finished in the top three in several other hitting categories. He was named the Na-

tional League's MVP for his accomplishments. Joe continued to post solid numbers with the Cardinals over the next three years.

Following the 1974 season, the Cardinals traded Joe to the New York Mets. Joe's skills had declined noticeably, and he was unable to duplicate his past successes. On July 21, 1975, he set a dubious major league record by grounding into four straight double plays. Joe was popular with Mets fans, however, and when the Mets fired manager Joe Frazier on May 31, 1977, they named Joe their player-manager. He retired as a player eighteen days later.

Joe was fired in 1981 after five losing seasons but was quickly hired as manager by the Atlanta Braves for the 1982 season. His 1982 team won the division title, but second-place finishes the next two years led to Joe's dismissal after the 1984 season. Joe took a broadcasting job with the California Angels and remained with them for several years before accepting a managerial position with the Cardinals in 1990. His teams had modest success, but a poor start in 1995 doomed him to his third managerial firing partway through that season. Thus, when the Yankees surprisingly picked Joe to manage their team on November 2, 1995, skeptics had a field day decrying the hiring of a "three-time loser."

Joe silenced the skeptics by not only leading the Yankees to the playoffs his first five years as manager but also winning each of the four World Series the Yanks appeared in during that span. Along the way Joe's teams set a record by winning fourteen consecutive Series games, and his 1998 team set the all-time record for wins, with an amazing 125-50 record. Joe was named Manager of the Year in 1996 and 1998.

Summary

In an era dominated by pitching, Joe Torre, a nine-time All-Star, produced solid career numbers of 252 home runs, 1,185 RBIs, and a .297 batting average. He eventually managed every team he played for, a testimony to his popularity. His deft handling of Yankee players and the founding of yet another Yankee dynasty have elevated Joe to the position of one of the great managers in baseball history.

Paul J. Chara, Jr.

Additional Sources:

King, George. *Unbeatable! The Historic Season of the 1998 World Champion New York Yankees.* New York: Harper Mass Market Paperbacks, 1998.

Torre, Joe, and Henry Dreyer. *Joe Torre's Ground Rules for Winners: Twelve Keys to Managing Team Players, Tough Bosses, Setbacks, and Success.* New York: Hyperion, 1999.

Torre, Joe, and Tom Verducci. *Chasing the Dream: My Lifelong Journey to the World Series.* New York: Bantam Books, 1998.

DARA TORRES

Sport: Swimming

Born: April 15, 1967
Beverly Hills, California

Early Life

Dara Torres, the first American to swim in four Olympics, was born on April 15, 1967, in Beverly Hills, California. In 1985 she graduated from Westlake School for Girls, where many classmates were daughters of Hollywood celebrities. In 1983, while still in high school, Dara swam the world's best time in the 50-meter freestyle (25.62 seconds), although a world record in this event was not recognized.

The Road to Excellence

In 1984 Dara qualified for the Olympics in Los Angeles. As a member of the 4×100-meter freestyle relay team, she won a gold medal. She enrolled at the University of Florida, where she earned twenty-eight All-American honors in swimming. At the 1987 Pan-Pacific Championships, Dara won three gold medals, for the 100-meter freestyle, 4×100-meter freestyle relay, and the 4×100-meter medley relay. When her swimming eligibility ended, she played outside hitter on the Florida Gators volleyball team. During her tenure at Florida, she interned with CNN and NBC sports and graduated with a degree in broadcasting.

In 1988 Dara set the American 100-meter freestyle record (55.30 seconds). At the 1988 Seoul Olympics she won a bronze medal as part of the 4×100-meter freestyle relay team and a silver medal for the 4×100-meter medley relay. Following these Olympics she left competition and became a sports commentator for NBC sports, but her retirement was short-lived. The breaking of her 100-meter freestyle record, combined with her viewing the tape of her seventh-place finish in this event in the 1988 Olympics, motivated her to return to the pool.

The Emerging Champion

Dara put her television career on hold and began to train for the 1992 Olympics with the aim of winning an individual medal. She made the

Dara Torres reacts after winning the 50-meter freestyle at the 2000 Olympic trials. She then won five medals in Sydney.

AP/Wide World Photos

team and won a gold medal as part of the world-record-setting 4×100-meter freestyle relay team. This medal earned Dara the distinction of being the only American woman to win a swimming medal at three consecutive Olympics.

Following these Olympics she retired for a second time and moved to New York City to pursue a career in television. She signed with a modeling agency and became the first female athlete to appear in the *Sports Illustrated* swimsuit issue. Her work on television included sports commentary for ESPN, TNT, Fox News, and Fox Sports. She also hosted a science and technology show on the Discovery Channel and was a spokesperson for a Tae-Bo video.

Continuing the Story

In 1999 friends urged Dara to try a second comeback. She moved to Palo Alto, California, to begin training to earn a spot on the 2000 Olympic team. Among the obstacles she had to overcome were asthma, a finger held together by screws and a titanium plate, the fact that she had not swum even one lap in seven years, and her age of thirty-two. At the U.S. Open Championships in December, 1999, Dara reestablished herself as a world-class swimmer by finishing the 50-meter freestyle with a time of 25.29 seconds, the fourth-fastest ever by an American woman.

At a Santa Clara, California, meet in June, 2000, she set a new American record in the event (24.73 seconds). At the Olympic trials Dara broke the old American record in the 100-meter butterfly with a time of 57.58 seconds and qualified for three individual events.

STATISTICS

Year	Competition	Event	Place
1984	Olympic Games	4×100-meter freestyle relay	Gold
1987	Pan-Pacific Championships	100-meter freestyle	1st
		4×100-meter freestyle relay	1st
		4×100-meter medley relay	1st
1988	Olympic Games	4×100-meter freestyle relay	Bronze
		4×100-meter medley relay	Silver
1992	Olympic Games	4×100-meter freestyle relay	Gold
2000	Olympic Games	4×100-meter freestyle relay	Gold
		100-meter butterfly	Bronze
		100-meter freestyle	Bronze
		50-meter freestyle	Bronze
		4×100-meter medley relay	Gold

In Sydney, her fourth Olympics, Dara won five medals: a gold in the 4×100-meter freestyle relay, a bronze in the 100-meter butterfly, a bronze in the 100-meter freestyle, a bronze in the 50-meter freestyle, and a gold in the 4×100-meter medley relay. She swam the anchor (freestyle) leg for the medley team that set a world record (3:58.30). After the Olympics, she retired from swimming and returned to New York City.

Summary

Dara Torres is one of America's most decorated female swimmers. She won nine medals in four different Olympics (1984, 1988, 1992, and 2000) and set several American records in sprint events during her career. Perhaps her greatest contribution was one reason she gave for returning to swimming in 1999—to show people they should not let age limit their dreams.

Marlene Bradford

Additional Sources:

Brant, Martha. "Grannies of the Games: Olympic Women Swimmers over or Approaching Thirty." *Newsweek* 136, no. 7 (August 14, 2000): 40-42.

Levin, Dan. "She's Set Her Sights on L.A." *Sports Illustrated* 60 (June 18, 1984): 40.

"Olympics 2000—Happily Retired for Seven Years, Model-Swimmer Dara Torres Returns for a Record Fourth Trip to the Games." *People*, September 18, 2000, 201-204.

Torres, Dara. "Dara to Dream." *Women's Sports and Fitness* 3, no. 4 (April, 2000): 39-42.

INDIVIDUAL RECORDS SET

Year	Record	Event	Time
1988	American	100-meter freestyle	55.30
2000	American	50-meter freestyle	24.73
	American	100-meter butterfly	57.58

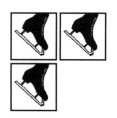

JAYNE TORVILL and CHRISTOPHER DEAN

Sport: Figure skating

Born: Jayne Torvill
October 7, 1957
Nottingham, England

Born: Christopher Dean
July 27, 1958
Nottingham, England

Early Life

Jayne Torvill and Christopher Colin Dean were born in Nottingham, England, the city famous as the home of the legendary Robin Hood. Jayne was born on October 7, 1957, and Christopher was born on July 27, 1958.

Both Jayne and Christopher came from middle-class backgrounds. Jayne's parents, George and Betty Torvill, ran a news agents' shop. Christopher's father, Colin Dean, was an electrician.

Neither family had any particular skating background. Jayne was about nine years old when she went to the ice rink with a school group. Christopher began skating at age ten at the encouragement of his mother after he received a pair of skates as a Christmas present.

They knew little of each other as skaters during their early years of development, but both showed seriousness and dedication to skating. Jayne followed a traditional path of advancement through junior figure skating in compulsory figures and pairs competition. In 1970, when she was twelve, she won the British junior pairs championship with her partner, Michael Hutchinson. The following year, she and Michael won the British senior pairs title. After 1972, when her partner moved to London, she continued as a solo skater in the ladies' event.

Christopher began as an ice dancer. He and his partner, Sandra Elson, were the British junior dance champions in 1974, and they placed well in senior ice dancing competition also.

The Road to Excellence

In 1975 Christopher and his first partner were no longer skating together, and he was looking for another partner. Janet Sawbridge, a professional skater and former British ice dancing

Jayne Torvill and Christopher Dean made an Olympic comeback ten years after their gold-medal-winning skate in 1984. They took the bronze in 1994.

champion, suggested that Jayne and Christopher should try skating together. The difference in their heights—Jayne is about 5 feet 1 inch and Christopher is 5 feet 9 inches—posed a minor obstacle. The two began to enjoy working together as a team. Sawbridge served as their coach and trainer.

Jayne and Christopher began to progress well in their development as an ice dancing couple. During their first full season of competition in 1976, they placed first in a summer European circuit at St. Gervais, France, and second at the West German skating center at Oberstdorf. They were fourth in the British championships. The next year, 1977, they improved to a first at Oberstdorf in the summer. By placing third at the British championship, they earned their first chance to compete at the European and world championships, which were held in the late winter of 1978.

Following the world championships in Ottawa, Canada, their first trainer, Janet Sawbridge, resigned. Soon thereafter, Betty Callaway, who had coached a championship Hungarian ice dancing pair, became their new coach. The talents of Jayne, Christopher, and Betty complemented one another well. Jayne and Christopher continued to add technical skill and polish to their presentation. During the fall of 1978, they became the British ice dancing champions. They retained this position from 1978 through 1983-1984, when they turned professional.

They constantly moved up in major international competition. By 1980, their fourth-place finish at the European and World Championships, and a fifth place at the Winter Olympics in Lake Placid, New York, showed that they were about to break through into the top ranks of ice dancing.

The Emerging Champion

The major problem that Jayne and Christopher faced during the early years of their partnership was finding adequate time for training. They both worked full-time, Jayne as a clerk at the Norwich Union insurance firm and Christopher as a police officer in Nottingham. Their different schedules meant grueling early-morning or late-night workouts.

After their strong showing in 1980, they left their jobs to devote their efforts to training.

MAJOR CHAMPIONSHIPS

Year	Competition	Place
1978	European Championship	9th
	World Championship	11th
1979	European Championship	6th
	World Championship	8th
1980	European Championship	4th
	Olympic Games	5th
	World Championship	4th
1981	European Championship	1st
	World Championship	1st
1982	European Championship	1st
	World Championship	1st
1983	World Championship	1st
1984	European Championship	1st
	Olympic Games	Gold
	World Championship	1st
1994	Olympic Games	Bronze

Grants from several sources, including the Sports Aid Foundation and especially the Nottingham City Council, helped support them through the several years leading to the Olympics in 1984.

The wisdom of their decision and the generosity of their supporters were soon rewarded. Jayne and Christopher placed first in all competitions in 1981, making them British, European, and world champions in ice dancing. For their achievements, Queen Elizabeth II awarded them honors as Members of the Order of the British Empire.

At this point in their career, Jayne and Christopher began to use their creativity to lift the sport of ice dancing to an entirely new level. The original competition programs that they developed for the winter 1982 season reflected their unique approach. Both the original short program and the free dance were conceived as a unified presentation of a particular theme. The short program was a slow, moving interpretation of "Summertime," and the free dance was set to music from *Mack and Mabel*, a Broadway show about Mack Senett, a producer of silent film comedies, and his leading lady, Mabel Norman. Again, they captured the British, European, and world championships with their innovative performances.

They continued to move forward with their ice dancing along these interpretive lines. For the 1983 competition, they conceived their famous "Barnum on Ice," depicting the circus, complete with jugglers and tightrope walkers, set to music from the stage show *Barnum.* An injury to Jayne's shoulder forced them to withdraw from the European Championships, but they won the world championship again.

The winter of 1984 was the pinnacle of their amateur career. They brought together their technical skating ability, inventive choreography, and personal rapport to create two pieces unparalleled in the history of this sport. Their original short program interpreted the Spanish dance the *paso doble* as a unified theme. Jayne became the cape while Christopher portrayed the matador. During the course of the dance, he twirled her around him, dragged her along behind him, and ended by flinging Jayne, as the cape, onto the ice.

Their free dance to Maurice Ravel's *Boléro* (1928) depicted a love story in which the passion of the couple builds dramatically with the progressive intensity of the music. Their masterful original performances earned them the European and world championship titles. They also won the gold medal at the 1984 Olympics in Sarajevo, Yugoslavia, receiving perfect 6.0 scores from all judges for artistic impression—a first in Olympic figure skating judging.

Continuing the Story

With their 1984 Olympic gold medal, Jayne and Christopher had accomplished all their goals in amateur skating. To continue their artistic development of ice dancing, they turned professional in 1984. They promptly won the world professional championships in that year.

During 1985 and 1986, Jayne and Christopher formed their own professional skating company and toured throughout the world. Unfortunately, the company had to disband after Christopher broke his wrist in 1986. In 1987, they appeared as special guest artists with the Ice Capades. In 1988, they combined their talents with ice skaters from the Soviet Union. This all-star group gave performances on tour for two

RECORDS
Most perfect marks received by any athletes in figure skating history (136 career total)
Only skating team to be awarded nine perfect (6.0) marks from all judges in world competition

HONORS AND AWARDS	
1981	Both named as Members of the Order of the British Empire Sportswriters' Sportswoman of the Year (Torvill)
1981-82	Named Team of the Year by the British Sportswriters Association
1984	BBC Sports Personality of the Year (Torvill)
1989	Inducted into World Figure Skating Hall of Fame

years. In 1990, they returned to professional competition and won the world professional championships in ice dancing.

Free from the restrictive rules that govern amateur skating, Jayne and Christopher have been able to enhance the creative interpretation that they bring to ice dancing. They can explore a greater variety of musical forms and new possibilities for expression through the technical aspects of ice dancing. For example, in "Winter Dreams," set to music by the Russian composer Nikolay Rimsky-Korsakov, they translate the balletic jeté into rapid movements on the ice.

The perfection of their ability has been the result of hard work and intense dedication to their sport. Throughout their career, this concentration has left little time for outside pursuits. In the early 1990's they began to expand their interests. Christopher acquired a house in the English countryside, where he enjoyed gardening. He has done commentary on ice skating for the British Broadcasting Corporation.

He is also a sought-after choreographer. In 1991, he married the French Canadian world champion ice dancer Isabelle Duchesnay. He had been her and her brother-partner's choreographer for several years. The two were divorced in 1993. Christopher met his next wife—American national and world champion singles skater Jill Trenary—while on tour. They were married in 1994, and Jill gave birth to their son, Jack Robert, in November, 1998. In 1999, in addition to his other commitments, Christopher was named director of the dance program, choreographer, and dance coach at the World Arena in Colorado Springs, Colorado.

2796

Meanwhile, Jayne married American sound engineer Philip Christensen in 1990. She and Christopher continued to skate in tours, shows, exhibitions, and professional competitions, winning most. In 1994, they returned to competitive skating and the Olympic Games in Lillehammer, Norway. They took the bronze medal, which was a disappointment to them and to the audience in attendance. They then returned to their professional pursuits. They announced at the end of 1998 that they would no longer be touring together.

Summary

Jayne Torvill and Christopher Dean have the distinction not only of being champions at every level of competitive ice dancing but also of rais-

ing the character of their sport to new heights. Their technical perfection, creative artistry, and unified expressiveness are unmatched in the history of ice dancing.

Karen Gould

Additional Sources:

Torvill, Jayne, and Christopher Dean, with John Hennessy. *Torvill and Dean*. North Pomfret, Vt.: David & Charles, 1983.

Torvill, Jayne, with John Man. *Torvill and Dean: The Autobiography of Ice Dancing's Gold Medal Winners*. Secaucus, N.J.: Carol, 1998.

Shuker-Haines, Frances. *Jayne Torvill and Christopher Dean: Ice Dancing's Perfect Pair*. Woodbridge, Conn.: Blackbirch Press, 1995.

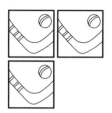

ANNE BARTON TOWNSEND

Sport: Field hockey

Born: March 8, 1900
Philadelphia, Pennsylvania
Died: February 3, 1984
Merion, Pennsylvania

Early Life

Anne Barton Townsend was born on March 8, 1900, in Philadelphia, Pennsylvania, the daughter of Mr. and Mrs. J. Barton Townsend of Philadelphia. Her father was a wealthy banker, and Anne enjoyed a privileged childhood. The family belonged to private clubs like the Merion Cricket Club, where Anne learned many sports, including tennis and swimming, that she enjoyed all her life.

Anne was educated at Agnes Irwin, a private boarding school. There she had the opportunity to learn and compete in team sports such as lacrosse, basketball, and her first love, field hockey.

When Anne enrolled at the University of Pennsylvania following her graduation from Irwin, few American women attended college. The National Collegiate Athletic Association (NCAA) did not yet govern women's college athletics. The few women's college teams seldom played beyond their local area and rarely received any publicity. Anne was captain of both the basketball and field hockey teams at Pennsylvania. Although unknown nationally, she was the best woman athlete at the university when she graduated in 1921.

The Road to Excellence

By that time, Anne was certain that sports would always be an important part of her life. She was independently wealthy and not in need of work. Nevertheless, she took a job as field hockey coach at her alma mater, Agnes Irwin. She later coached at another private school, Shady Hill.

While passing on her love of hockey to countless young players, Anne continued to compete on the field hockey team at the Merion Cricket Club. At that time, the best hockey teams in America came from clubs, not colleges. Many of the top players came from Pennsylvania, which had more than twenty women's teams.

Betty Shellenberger

HONORS, AWARDS, AND MILESTONES

1923-38, 1947	USFHA All-American
1923-38	USFHA National Team Captain
1928-32	USFHA President
1932-33	USFHA Secretary
1933	USFHA Honorary Member
1933-34, 1936, 1938	U.S. Lacrosse Association First Team
1933-48	President, International Federation of Women's Hockey Associations
1965	Inducted into Pennsylvania Sports Hall of Fame

To help promote the sport, Anne helped organize the United States Field Hockey Association (USFHA) in 1922. Thanks in part to her leadership, the organization grew strong. It still governs women's Olympic field hockey today.

In 1924, Anne was chosen for the first USFHA All-American team to travel abroad. She played the key position of center halfback on the team that played in England that fall. Although it included America's best players, Anne's team soon learned that the United States was far behind the English in field hockey. They lost by scores like 11-0 and 9-0. Anne and her teammates came home determined to improve their sport.

Anne became well known as an outstanding woman athlete of the 1920's and 1930's. Because of her outstanding manners, attractiveness, and love of sport, several women's magazines wrote about her as an outstanding role model for young women. She was also engaged for a while to an architect named Livingston Smith, but she never married. Sports became her first love, and her teammates and the young players she coached, her family.

The Emerging Champion

Anne was a regular on the All-American hockey teams, being named a total of seventeen times at four different positions. She was also captain of fourteen of those All-American teams, beginning in 1923.

From 1928 through 1932, she was president of the USFHA, and she was its secretary in 1932 and 1933. She also earned a national umpire's rating in field hockey and helped promote the sport through her writing.

From 1924 to 1929, Anne was Field Hockey Contributing Editor to the *Sportswoman*, America's first magazine for women athletes. After her term ended in 1929, she continued to write hockey articles for the magazine.

When the International Federation of Women's Hockey Associations (IFWHA) was formed in 1933, Anne was elected president. She remained in that post through 1948.

During her long years serving the IFWHA, Anne was captain of two All-American teams that competed in international tournaments. The first was in Denmark in 1933, the second in her hometown of Philadelphia in 1936.

During the 1930's, Anne continued her interest in other sports. She was four times named All-American in lacrosse. She was nationally ranked in tennis and won Pennsylvania state championships in both tennis and squash. Nevertheless, she dedicated most of her efforts to hockey. She felt it was the best team sport for girls and women because it brought out the best in sportsmanship and comradeship.

Continuing the Story

In 1946, Anne and a longtime friend and fellow teacher, May P. Fogg, formed the Merstead Hockey and Lacrosse Camps at Camden, Maine. There they hoped to help teach the next generation of young women players. The next year, forty-seven-year-old Anne was named All-American in field hockey for the last time.

Although her hockey-playing days were over, Anne remained active. She played tennis and golf, swam, and won the United States Senior Women's Doubles Squash championship at age fifty-seven. The next year, she began learning to bowl.

Her interest in writing also continued. She wrote book reviews for the *Philadelphia Inquire* and was the author of two books: *Field Hockey* (1936) and *Chapel Talks for School and Camp* (1961).

For the remainder of her life, Anne retained an active interest in the sports she loved. She was an avid follower of her old team, the Merion Cricket Club, until she died in 1984 at age eighty-three.

Summary

Anne Barton Townsend was the most outstanding player and leader in the early years of

American field hockey. She played because she loved to play, not for glory or for money, which was not available to American women athletes of her time. Anne played on her last national field hockey team at age forty-seven. She remained active in sports all her life.

Anne was instrumental in founding both the USFHA and the IFWHA. She served more than twenty years as an officer of these organizations. As a writer, teacher, coach, and camp director, she helped to promote women's field hockey and to train thousands of new players. Independently wealthy, she spent much time and money serving the sport worldwide. Thanks in no small part to Anne Townsend's tireless and pioneering efforts, field hockey is today an Olympic sport for women.

Mary Lou LeCompte

Additional Sources:

Hickok, Ralph. *A Who's Who of Sports Champions.* Boston: Houghton Mifflin, 1995.

Porter, David L., ed. *Biographical Dictionary of American Sports: Outdoor Sports.* Westport, Conn.: Greenwood Press, 1988.

Townsend, Anne B. *Field Hockey.* New York: Charles Scribner's Sons, 1936.

TONY TRABERT

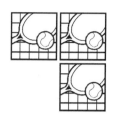

Sport: Tennis

Born: August 16, 1939
Cincinnati, Ohio

Early Life

Marion Anthony Trabert was born August 16, 1930, in Cincinnati, Ohio. His father, Archibald Taylor, was a sales engineer for the General Electric Company. Tony was the youngest of three brothers. Like many famous athletes, Tony became interested in sports at an early age, starting to play tennis when he was only six years old.

He continued to play tennis in high school and college, but tennis was not his only sport. He also played on his high school and college basketball teams. He attended Walnut Hills High School and the University of Cincinnati.

The Road to Excellence

There was never any doubt that tennis was Tony's major sport, and in 1951, he won the National Collegiate Athletic Association Singles title. An outstanding college player, however, is very different from a world-class tennis champion. How did Tony make the transition?

Several qualities in his game enabled him to stand out from his competitors. He was strong and had a powerful serve. His ground strokes were impressive: He hit the ball with unusual force and accuracy. If he was having a good day, few players could stay on the court with him. Interestingly, many American tennis champions have had powerful ground strokes in their play: Don Budge and Ellsworth Vines are the most famous of these. Tony also could hit remarkable recovery shots. He was often able to return shots that seemed

sure winners for his opponent, who would be surprised to see the ball come back and would flub the next shot and lose the point.

Tony had another strong point that many aggressive, attacking players lack. A fierce attacking game is difficult to sustain for a long time. Often, attacking players will become tired and lose to opponents who can keep the ball in play. This slowdown is especially common in the last rounds of men's tournaments, which usually last five sets. Tony found the answer to this problem. He was superbly conditioned and spent hours on exercise each day of preparation for a tournament. He would play five sets

with ease, and opponents who waited for the rapid pace of his attack to falter were disappointed.

The Emerging Champion

Tony's attacking game and physical fitness were enough to give him championship potential. To play at the highest level, however, talent is not enough: Skill and knowledge are also required. Tony was fortunate in winning the friendship of Bill Talbert, an experienced champion and a master of tennis technique. He worked on building all phases of Tony's game, and with Talbert's help, Tony began to win major championships while he was still in college.

In 1950, Tony won the French Championship doubles title with Talbert, a feat he repeated in 1954 and 1955 with Vic Seixas. Tony became an expert on the strategy of doubles and later wrote a book on the subject.

He also became a mainstay of the American Davis Cup team, compiling an excellent record in his five years on the team. Probably his most famous Davis Cup match, however, was a loss. In Melbourne, Australia, in 1953, his opponent was the young Australian Lew Hoad, whose game was an exaggerated version of Tony's own. When Hoad was in form, even Tony could not stop him, and he lost a close five-set match.

In spite of the loss, Tony's rise to the top continued unabated in the succeeding two years. In 1953, he won the United States National Championship singles title at Forest Hills without losing a set in the entire tournament. In 1954, he won the French Championship, a feat few Americans have matched. Most players from the United States perform badly on the hard clay surfaces of the French courts.

Continuing the Story

Tony established himself as the best amateur singles player in the world in 1955. In that year, he again won the French Championship. He also won the United States National Championship and Wimbledon, the latter without the loss of a set. These three tournaments were three legs of tennis's Grand Slam. The final part of the Grand Slam, the Australian Championship, eluded him; Ken Rosewall defeated him in the semifinals.

Tony thus failed to achieve tennis's supreme feat, a Grand Slam; it has been won by only two male players, Don Budge and Rod Laver. Nevertheless, Tony stood at the top of amateur tennis. He decided to turn professional the following year, 1956.

Jack Kramer, the main promoter of professional tennis, signed Tony to a series of matches against the professional champion, Pancho Gonzales. The more experienced Gonzales, who had the fastest service in tennis and an extraordinary will to win, overpowered his challenger. Gonzales won the series of matches, 74-27.

As a professional, Tony did well but was never a real standout. He was runner-up to Alex Olmedo in 1960 for the United States Pro Championship singles title. After he retired from active

MAJOR CHAMPIONSHIP VICTORIES AND FINALS	
1950, 1954-55	French Championship doubles (with Bill Talbert; with Vic Seixas)
1953, 1955	U.S. National Championship
1954	U.S. National Championship doubles (with Seixas) Wimbledon doubles finalist (with Seixas)
1954-55	French Championship
1955	Wimbledon Australian Championship doubles (with Seixas)
OTHER NOTABLE VICTORIES	
1950	Italian Championship doubles (with Talbert) Pacific Southwest Championship doubles (with Fred Schroeder)
1951	NCAA Championship
1951, 1955	U.S. Clay Court Championship
1951, 1954, 1955	U.S. Clay Court Championship doubles (with Hamilton Richardson; with Seixas)
1954	On winning U.S. Davis Cup team
1954, 1955	U.S. Indoor Championship doubles (with Talbert; with Seixas)
1955	U.S. Indoor Championship
1956	U.S. Pro Championship doubles (with Rex Hartwig)

HONORS, AWARDS, AND RECORDS

1951-55	U.S. Davis Cup team
1953, 1955	Nationally ranked number one
1956	Turned professional
1970	Inducted into National Lawn Tennis Hall of Fame
1976-80	U.S. Davis Cup team captain

play, he became a teaching professional and television commentator. He also served as captain of the United States Davis Cup team in the late 1970's.

Summary

Tennis was a popular sport in the United States in the ten years after World War II, and many young athletes tried their hand at the game. Most of them featured an aggressive game, and Tony Trabert was one of the best, if not the best, of the lot. His powerful ground stroke and superb conditioning enabled him to take the giant step from good player to great player. He was the best amateur in the world in 1955, the year he won three major singles championships.

Bill Delaney

Additional Sources:

Collins, Bud. "Tony Trabert." In *Bud Collins' Tennis Encyclopedia*, edited by Bud Collins and Zander Hollander. 3d ed. Detroit: Visible Ink Press, 1997.

Lunde, Erik S. "Marion Anthony 'Tony' Trabert." In *Biographical Dictionary of American Sports: Outdoor Sports*, edited by David L. Porter. New York: Greenwood Press, 1988.

Nicholson, Chris. "In the Age of Innocence." *Tennis* 32 (September, 1996): 129-131.

"Tony Trabert." In *International Who's Who in Tennis*, edited by Jane Cooke. Dallas, Tex.: World Championship Tennis, 1983.

PIE TRAYNOR

Sport: Baseball

Born: November 11, 1899
      Framingham, Massachusetts
Died: March 16, 1972
      Pittsburgh, Pennsylvania

Early Life

Harold Joseph "Pie" Traynor was born on November 11, 1899, in the town of Framingham, Massachusetts. One in a family of seven children, Harold noted the struggle of his father, James, a printer, to earn a living. Once remarking that his son, exhausted, came in from play as dirty as "pied type," James inadvertently created a nickname that would always be associated with the youth.

Pie Traynor grew up in a low-income neighborhood in Somerville, Massachusetts, and developed an interest in sports even though his hardworking father had little time to encourage him. Pie played football and hockey well but developed a special interest in baseball, even though he once had two front teeth knocked out when he played catcher without a mask.

By the time he was twelve, Pie was an enthusiastic fan of the Boston Braves and the Boston Red Sox. He walked three miles to Boston to work as an office boy and kept the admirable habit all of his life, frequently walking from his team's hotel to the ballpark and back. Pie began to play sandlot baseball seriously, and, though the local townsfolk began to recognize his superior talent, when he showed up one day at the Braves' practice field for a tryout, he was chased away. He continued playing the sandlots, hoping for a professional career.

The Road to Excellence

Pie's abilities could not remain hidden long, and in 1920 he was offered a contract by Portsmouth of the Virginia League. Pie happily accepted, feeling that a solid performance would encourage the Red Sox to bring him home to the major leagues. Working hard to polish his developing skills, Pie sparkled in the field and hit a respectable .270 in 104 games. The Red Sox thought about this hometown prospect and then made an offer, but they were too late. Pie's contract had been purchased for ten thousand dollars by the Pittsburgh Pirates. With high hopes, Pie arrived in time for the 1920 season. For a time, however, his career seemed in jeopardy.

Pie was not an immediate standout with the Pirates, who were looking for someone to replace

Pie Traynor, manager of the Pittsburgh Pirates, in 1938.

STATISTICS

Season	GP	AB	Hits	2B	3B	HR	Runs	RBI	BA	SA
1920	17	52	11	3	1	0	6	2	.212	.308
1921	7	19	5	0	0	0	0	2	.263	.263
1922	142	571	161	17	12	4	89	81	.282	.375
1923	153	616	208	19	**19**	12	108	101	.338	.489
1924	142	545	160	26	13	5	86	82	.294	.417
1925	150	591	189	39	14	6	114	106	.320	.464
1926	152	574	182	25	17	3	83	92	.317	.436
1927	149	573	196	32	9	5	93	106	.342	.455
1928	144	569	192	38	12	3	91	124	.337	.462
1929	130	540	192	27	12	4	94	108	.356	.472
1930	130	497	182	22	11	9	90	119	.366	.509
1931	155	615	183	37	15	2	81	103	.298	.416
1932	135	513	169	27	10	2	74	68	.329	.433
1933	154	624	190	27	6	1	85	82	.304	.372
1934	119	444	137	22	10	1	62	61	.309	.410
1935	57	204	57	10	3	1	24	36	.279	.373
1937	5	12	2	0	0	0	3	0	.167	.167
Totals	1,941	7,559	2,416	371	164	58	1,183	1,273	.320	.435

Notes: Boldface indicates statistical leader. GP = games played; AB = at bats; 2B = doubles; 3B = triples; HR = home runs; RBI = runs batted in; BA = batting average; SA = slugging average

the recently retired, legendary Honus Wagner. Pie was not impressive at shortstop; his hitting suffered. Disappointed but not discouraged, he was sent down to Birmingham of the Southern Association for more practice and experience. He returned to the big league club briefly at the end of the season.

The turning point in Pie's career, however, came at the beginning of the 1922 season, when manager George Gibson moved him to third base. Immediately, Pie began to shine brilliantly beyond anyone's expectations. His expert, often acrobatic fielding bordered constantly on the sensational. He covered the foul line so well and controlled so wide a range that rarely would a ball elude him; he displayed a whiplash arm and fielded bunts with intense anticipation. Pie began to develop a style that would be unmatched by any third baseman of his day.

The Emerging Champion

Pie's skill as a much-respected placement hitter became a concern among opponents. The sharply toned instincts behind his remarkable fielding prowess enabled him to exercise acute bat control. He seldom struck out. In his second year as a regular, Pie batted .338, made 208 hits, drove in 101 runs, and scored 108 runs. In the 1925 World Series, facing the Hall of Fame

fastball pitcher of the Washington Senators, Walter (Big Train) Johnson, Pie hit a home run his first time at bat. In 1930, Pie hit for a high of .366. For ten seasons, Pie hit over .300 and continued to field his position with outstanding skill, leading his team to two pennants and one World Series triumph. Seven times in his career, Pie surpassed 100 runs batted in; his 2,228 putouts for many years constituted the all-time record for third basemen. He amassed a total of 3,556 assists.

More important than Pie's impressive statistics was his being regarded by peers as the essential team player. His qualities of leadership were inspirational to the Pirates during his playing days. When, in 1934, the team got off to a slow start, Pie was named player-manager. Always a determined competitor, Pie was injured in a collision at home plate and his playing career was virtually ended.

Continuing the Story

By 1936, Pie had become a bench manager, but he would never bring another pennant to Pittsburgh. His post as manager lasted until 1939. He remained with the Pirate organization as scout for the team, and at every Pittsburgh tryout and training camp, Pie could be seen teaching the rookies, looking to pass on the techniques that had contributed to his success. He

HONORS AND AWARDS

1933-34	National League All-Star Team
1948	Inducted into National Baseball Hall of Fame
	Uniform number 20 retired by Pittsburgh Pirates

would try to instill in his pupils a special pride in unselfish team play and in adhering to a rigorous work ethic.

For a while, Pie went into radio broadcasting, and in 1944, he was named sports director for a Pittsburgh station. He had by then become a prominent part of Pittsburgh Pirate history and lore. In national baseball circles, the name Pie Traynor had become synonymous with third base. In 1948, Pie was named to the National Baseball Hall of Fame in Cooperstown, New York, and during the centennial season of baseball, 1969, a poll of sportswriters selected him as the game's greatest third baseman. He died in Pittsburgh on March 16, 1972.

Summary

While Pie Traynor rose to the highest levels of achievement as the consummate third baseman, his quiet role as cooperative team player and inspirational team leader contributes to his sterling reputation as well. His example was worth emulation. He worked tirelessly to improve himself. Although he paid his dues in the minor league, his start in the majors was not at all promising. Undaunted, he worked harder to enhance his skills and maintain a positive mental attitude. With this strength of mind and spirit, Pie Traynor not only achieved greatness in his athletic career but also set the standard for playing his position. Thus, his energetic blend of inspiration, leadership, and performance augments significantly his impressive Hall of Fame achievements.

Abe C. Ravitz

Additional Sources:

Appel, Martin, and Burt Goldblatt. *Baseball's Best: The Hall of Fame Gallery.* New York: McGraw-Hill, 1977.

Murray, Tom. *Sport Magazine's All-Time All Stars.* New York: Signet, 1977.

Shatzkin, Mike, et al., eds. *The Ballplayers: Baseball's Ultimate Biographical Reference.* New York: William Morrow, 1990.

VLADISLAV TRETIAK

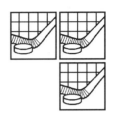

Sport: Ice hockey

Born: April 25, 1952
       Moscow, U.S.S.R. (now Russia)

Early Life

Vladislav Tretiak was born in Moscow, the capital of the Soviet Union, on April 25, 1952. His father was an air force pilot, his mother, a physical education teacher.

The whole Tretiak family was athletic. In the Soviet Union, branches of the government, places of employment, labor unions, or other organizations sponsor sports clubs. Vladislav's mother was a swimming instructor at one of these clubs, the Central Army Club in Moscow. His older brother was a swimmer for Dynamo, the club sponsored by the Soviet security police.

Vladislav was active in several sports. At first, he went to his brother's club and tried swimming, then diving, gymnastics, and finally soccer. Then, when he was ten, Vladislav asked his mother if he could go to work with her. As they were passing the ice rink on the way to the swimming pool, he noticed young boys playing ice hockey.

He fell in love with the sport but was more in love with the uniforms. Soon afterward he tried out for the team. The only position open in which a uniform was available was goalie. Thus the career of, in many experts' minds, the greatest goalie to play the game was born.

The Road to Excellence

In 1967, four years after young Vladislav became a goalie to have a uniform, he moved up to the senior team of the famous Central Army Club. At fifteen, Vladislav became the team's youngest player. He imitated his idols and learned the finer points of the game. Still, his age held him back. In July, when the team moved to another city to train, he was left behind to join the club's junior team.

That year, his team won the national junior title and Vladislav was named the best junior goalie in the Soviet Union. In 1969, with Vladislav in goal, the juniors won the World Championship. When he returned to his country he moved, at the age of sixteen, to the senior team.

The Emerging Champion

Vladislav seized the opportunity of his promotion to the senior team and dedicated himself to becoming the greatest goalie he could. Under the tutelage of the legendary coach Anatoli Tarasov, the young goalie suffered grueling exercises devised for him. As Vladislav's reputation grew, Tarasov reminded him, "Don't listen to compliments. When they praise you, they steal from you."

Vladislav Tretiak in 1983.

AP/Wide World Photos

2807

HONORS AND AWARDS

1970-71, 1973-75, 1977-79, 1981-84	World Championship Team Member
1972, 1976, 1984	Olympic Gold Medal
1980	Olympic Silver Medal
1981	Canada Cup MVP
1981-82	Golden Stick Award
1989	Inducted into Hockey Hall of Fame Order of Lenin

Dedication was one of Vladislav's strongest characteristics. The coaching staff ordered extra work that lasted long after all the other players and coaches went home. Vladislav stayed alone until he completed every exercise. By the end of the season, he was the Central Army Sports Club goalie. Vladislav led Central Army to the national championships, and later that year, 1970, he took the national team to the World Championship. He also would lead them in defense of their World Championship in 1971.

In February, 1972, in Sapporo, Japan, Vladislav became the youngest Olympic gold medalist in Soviet hockey history. The nineteen-year-old led the powerful Soviet team to a 4-0-1 series record, including a 5-2 gold medal championship victory over Czechoslovakia. The Soviets scored 33 goals while allowing only 13. Yet, later that same year, they lost the World Championship to Czechoslovakia, only to regain the title in 1973, 1974, and 1975.

In 1976, at Innsbruck, Austria, Vladislav again led the Soviets to an Olympic gold medal. This time they had a perfect 5-0 record while scoring 40 goals to 11 for the opposition. Vladislav was rapidly becoming a living legend in hockey.

Continuing the Story

Beginning in 1972, the Soviets played a biannual series against All-Star teams from professional teams in the West. In 1972, the Soviets played a team from the National Hockey League (NHL). The teams played eight times in twenty-six days. Vladislav was in goal for every game. Although the Soviets lost the series 4-3-1, Vladislav drew much attention by taking on some of hockey's greatest players. In the games, both teams scored a total of 32 goals, proving that

Vladislav was as good as the best in the NHL.

In 1974, the Soviet team faced an All-Star team from the now-defunct World Hockey Association (WHA). The Soviets won 4-1-3, with Vladislav allowing only 25 goals while playing in seven of the eight games. Many teams in the professional NHL and WHA showed interest in the young Soviet goalie. Still, his interest was with the Soviet team.

After losing the World Championship to the Czechs again in 1976 after the Olympics, the Soviets won the title again in 1977, 1978, and 1979. Then came the Olympic Games in Lake Placid and the United States' "Miracle Team." Just days before the start of the Games, the Soviets, who had beaten the NHL All-Star team, destroyed the United States 10-3. The Soviets were the top team in the Olympic tournament, while the Americans were seventh seed. Now the two teams would meet to see who would play in the title game against Finland.

On February 22, 1980, the Soviets and Americans faced off. By the end of the first period, the Americans were losing 2-1, but with one second left, Mark Johnson slipped a goal past Vladislav to tie the score at 2-2. As the second period began, Vladislav was mysteriously not in goal and did not return for the rest of the game. The Americans went on to win 4-3 and finally won the gold medal with the Soviets taking the silver. Vladislav never got over the defeat. "In the most difficult moments, I will always help the team, and the team believes in me," he said four years after the defeat. "I will remember this the rest of my life."

The Soviets, with Vladislav in goal, went on to win the World Championship in 1981, 1982, and 1983. In 1984, at Sarajevo, Yugoslavia, Vladislav led the Soviets in regaining the Olympic gold medal. Afterward, he retired from hockey at the age of thirty-one.

In 1994, Vladislav attended Living Legends Night at Moscow's Ice Palace hockey rink, where he saw his jersey number 20 retired, an honor never before given in the former Soviet Union. After that time, Vladislav consulted as a part-time coach to the Chicago Blackhawks and continued to run goal-tending training programs in the United States and Canada.

2808

Summary

Hockey fans will always compare goalies to Vladislav Tretiak. There will always be a legendary quality to the man. In 1989, he was elected to the Hockey Hall of Fame. He attained this stature through hard work and dedication to his sport and his country.

Rusty Wilson

Additional Sources:

Lilley, Jeffrey. "Russian Revolution." *Sports Illustrated* 80, no. 1 (1994).

MacGregor, Scott, and Larry Wigge. "A Safety Nyet." *The Sporting News* 20, no. 53 (1996).

Orr, Frank. *Great Goalies of Pro Hockey.* New York: Random House, 1973.

LEE TREVINO

Sport: Golf

Born: December 1, 1939
Dallas, Texas

Early Life

Lee Trevino was born on December 1, 1939, into a fatherless home on the outskirts of Dallas, Texas. Lee and his two sisters were raised by his mother, Juanita, and their maternal grandfather, Joe Trevino, who worked as a gravedigger. As a young man, Joe Trevino immigrated from Mexico. The family lived in a four-room shack without electricity or plumbing, which was located next to the Glen Lakes Country Club.

When Lee was six years old, he began to look through the fence separating his frame house from the Country Club to watch the men playing golf. He found an old golf club, cut it down to his

size, and played a two-hole course he designed in his front yard.

After completing the seventh grade, Lee quit school and worked as a caddy at Glen Lakes Country Club. At the end of the day, Lee would play a few holes. At the age of fifteen, Lee played his first complete 18 holes of golf and shot a 77.

The Road to Excellence

Lee Trevino was only seventeen when he lied about his age to join the United States Marines. He served four years with the Marines. While playing on the Third Marine Division golf team, Lee began taking the game of golf seriously.

After Lee was discharged from the Marines in 1961, he worked at Hardy's Driving Ranch and Pitch 'n' Putt course, operated by Hardy Greenwood. Lee needed additional income to survive, so he would "hustle" golfers by offering to play them by using a Dr. Pepper bottle as a club. He would wrap tape around the neck of the Dr. Pepper bottle so it would not slip. Lee would hit the golf ball with a baseball swing and putt croquet style. In three years, Trevino claimed, he never lost a bet playing golf with a Dr. Pepper bottle.

Martin Lettunick, a millionaire, heard about Lee and convinced him to move to El Paso. Lee arrived at El Paso with fifty dollars in his pocket. Lettunick helped him get a job as assistant professional at Horizon Hills Country Club. Lee's salary was thirty dollars a week. During Lee's off hours at Horizon Hills, he would practice and practice. Most days, he would hit a minimum of five hundred balls.

The Emerging Champion

In 1966, Lee earned his Class A card, which enabled him to play in professional golf tournaments. Lee's first professional tournament was the United States Open in 1966 at the Olympic Country Club in San Francisco. He tied for fifty-fourth place and won six hundred dollars. Lee's wife sent in the registration fee for the 1967 United States Open. Golfers must qualify for this tournament by playing two rounds of golf. Lee qualified with the lowest score in the United States by shooting a 69 and a 67 for a total of 136. He finished in fifth place in the 1967 Open, played at Baltusrol Country Club, and won six thousand dollars. Trevino won a total of twenty-eight thousand dollars that year and was named Rookie of the Year by the Metropolitan Golf Writers' Association.

In 1968, Lee had his first great year on the Professional Golfers' Association (PGA) tour. By United States Open time in June, he had pocketed fifty-four thousand dollars. Lee won the United States Open, played at Oak Hill Country Club in Rochester, New York, and was the first person to shoot all four rounds in the 60's. He also tied Jack Nicklaus's Open record of 5 under par 275. Lee was only the third person to make the United States Open his first major tournament win. The win in the 1968 Open pushed him over the hill to golf stardom.

Lee won the Hawaiian Open in 1968, which was worth twenty-five thousand dollars in prize money. For the 1968 year, Lee won a total of $132,127, which placed him sixth on the money list. Several people in 1968 thought Lee was merely a very lucky person with little golfing ability, but he would prove them all wrong by demonstrating his ability as one of the greatest golfers in history. In 1970, Trevino won more prize money than any other professional golfer ($157,037). That would be the only year he would lead the PGA in money won. He finished second on the money list three times.

MAJOR CHAMPIONSHIP VICTORIES

1968, 1971	U.S. Open
1971-72	British Open
1974, 1984	PGA Championship
1990	U.S. Senior Open

OTHER NOTABLE VICTORIES

1968	Hawaiian Open
1968-71, 1974	World Cup Team
1969, 1971, 1973, 1975, 1979, 1981	Ryder Cup Team
1971-72, 1980	Danny Thomas-Memphis Classic
1971, 1977, 1979	Canadian Open
1972	Greater Hartford Open
1973	Doral-Eastern Open Jackie Gleason-Inverarry Classic
1975	Florida Citrus Open
1976, 1978	Colonial National Invitation
1978	Lancome Trophy
1980	Tournament Players Championship San Antonio, Texas, Open
1981	MONY Tournament of Champions
1985	Ryder Cup team captain
1990, 1995	Transamerica Senior Golf Championship
1991	Aetna Challenge
1991-93	Vantage of the Dominion
1992	The Tradition Las Vegas Senior Classic
1992, 1994	PGA Seniors Championship
1993	Nationwide Championship
1993, 2000	Cadillac NFL Golf Classic
1994	Royal Caribbean Classic Paine Webber Invitational Bell Atlantic Classic Bell Southern Senior Classic
1994-95	Northville Long Island Classic
1996	Emerald Coast Classic Australian PGA Seniors Championship
1998	Southwestern Bell Dominion

Lee was known as "the Merry Mex" or "Super Mex" for his ability to talk and joke on the golf course. Lee would relieve stress by telling a joke or making light of a golf shot.

In 1975, Lee was struck by lightning while playing at the Western Open near Chicago. The lightning struck a nearby lake, traveling through the ground to where Lee was leaning on his golf

RECORDS AND MILESTONES
Twenty-seven wins on the regular tour
First golfer to win at least $1 million on the Senior Tour
PGA Tour leading money winner (1970)
Finished second on the earnings list three times

HONORS AND AWARDS	
1967	*Golf Digest* Rookie of the Year
1970-72, 1974, 1980	PGA Vardon Trophy
1971	Hickok Belt
	Sporting News Man of the Year
	Golf Digest Byron Nelson Award for Tournament Victories
	PGA Player of the Year
	Associated Press Male Athlete of the Year
	Sports Illustrated Sportsman of the Year
	GWAA Player of the Year
1972	GWAA Charlie Bartlett Award
1980	GWAA Ben Hogan Award
1981	Inducted into PGA/World Golf Hall of Fame
1985	GWAA Richardson Award
1990	Senior PGA Tour Player of the Year
	Senior PGA Tour Rookie of the Year

defeated Gary Player and Lanny Wadkins at Shoal Creek by shooting all four rounds in the 60's.

Lee joined the Senior Tour in 1989, and in 1990 he earned both the tour's Rookie of the Year and Player of the Year awards. In his first year as a senior, he won the U.S. Senior Open and the Transamerica Senior Golf Championship.

By 2000, Lee had accumulated twenty-nine Senior Tour victories, including two victories at the PGA Seniors Championship in 1992 and 1994. He also ranked tied for thirtieth in Greens in Regulation Percentage in 2000.

Summary

Lee Trevino's humble beginnings had a lasting effect on his entire life. He never forgot that he was a fatherless Mexican American with a seventh-grade education who was raised on bare floors with too little food and even less money. Lee believed in working hard to accomplish one's goal.

Lee has a true love of golf. He is perhaps one of the few senior tour players who would play for the love of the game even if no prize money were available.

Peter W. Shoun

club. Lee almost died from the electrical shock. The shock also caused a problem in Lee's back. In 1976, he had an operation to correct a herniated disk in his back. Lee's back has been a constant problem since that time. He jogs and stretches every day to maintain flexibility and strength.

Continuing the Story

In 1980, at the age of forty and with his back problem, Lee had a great year. He won three tournaments and $385,814. For the fifth time, he won the Vardon Trophy, the award given for the lowest stroke average per round; his stroke average of 69.73 was the best on the PGA circuit in thirty years. Lee did not miss a cut in twenty-one tournaments and finished in the top five eleven times.

By 1984, Lee had gone three and one-half years without a tour victory. He turned this situation around by winning his second PGA Championship. It was one of the outstanding sports stories of the year. At the age of forty-four, Lee

Additional Sources:

Gilbert, Thomas W. *Lee Trevino.* New York: Chelsea House, 1992.

Kramer, Jon. *Lee Trevino.* Austin, Tex.: Raintree Steck-Vaughn, 1996.

Trevino, Lee, and Sam Blair. *The Snake in the Sandtrap (and other Misadventures on the Golf Course).* New York: Holt, Rinehart, and Winston, 1985.

_____. *They Call Me Super Mex.* New York: Random House, 1982.

Wheelock, Warren, and J. O. "Rocky" Maines, Jr.. *Hispanic Heroes of the U.S.A.* St. Paul, Minn.: EMC Corp., 1976.

FELIX TRINIDAD

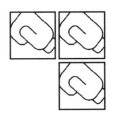

Sport: Boxing

Born: January 10, 1973
Cupey Alto, Puerto Rico

Early Life

Felix (Tito) Trinidad was born in Puerto Rico on January 10, 1973. At age twelve the future champion was introduced to boxing by his father, Felix, Sr., who was, in 1979, featherweight champion. Young Felix's talents were immediately recognized. With the guidance of his father, he had, in a short time, won five Puerto Rican national amateur championships and had an ama-

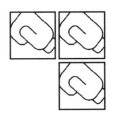

Puerto Rican boxer Felix Trinidad (left) after reclaiming the 2000 WBA super welterweight title.

teur career record of 51-6, twelve of which wins were by knockout. In all his efforts he was supported by his three sisters and two brothers; the family was always supportive and close.

While Felix's amateur victories were impressive, his father was concerned that he had not developed the punching power needed for him to compete as a professional. The young athlete grew in strength and size until, in 1990, his punching power was equal to his boxing prowess, and he entered the professional arena.

The Road to Excellence

The first ten bouts of Felix's professional career left no doubt that he had mastered the skill of a slugger. He defeated nine of the ten opponents by knockout. In thirty-six outings he achieved thirty victories by knockout, earning him the highest knockout percentage of any boxer in history.

Determination and the ability to overcome adversity are key elements in Felix's success. In a 1991 bout with Jake Rodriquez he injured his left hand in the fourth round. In spite of excruciating pain, he continued to fight for six rounds, winning the fight by unanimous decision. The following year he fought Argentina's Alberto Cortez in Paris. Cortez was a formidable opponent and knocked Felix down in the second round, the first knockdown of his professional career. Thinking he would end the bout in the third round, Cortez was surprised when Felix unleashed a barrage of punches that prompted the referee to stop the fight, declaring Felix the winner.

The Emerging Champion

In June of 1993 Felix fought two-time world champion Maurice Blocker for the International Boxing Federation welterweight title. The match was short as Felix defeated his opponent in the

2813

BOXING RECORD

Date	Opponent	Result
Mar. 10, 1990	Angel Romero	Knockout
Apr. 7, 1990	Israel Ponce	Knockout
June 21, 1990	William Lopez	Knockout
July 27, 1990	Omar Alegre	Knockout
Sept. 6, 1990	Jose Vilarino	Knockout
Oct. 3, 1990	Valentin Ocasio	Win
Nov. 13, 1990	Luis Perez	Knockout
Mar. 13, 1991	Noe Rivera	Knockout
May 1, 1991	Felix Vasquez	Knockout
June 21, 1991	Manuel Soles	Knockout
July 10, 1991	Darren McGrew	Win
Oct. 25, 1991	Lorenzo Bouie	Knockout
Dec. 6, 1991	Jake Rodriguez	Win
May 3, 1992	Raul Gonzalez	Knockout
July 18, 1992	Joe Alexander	Knockout
Dec. 3, 1992	Alberto Cortez	Knockout
Feb. 13, 1993	Henry Hughes	Knockout
Feb. 20, 1993	Pedro Aguirre	Knockout
May 8, 1993	Colin Tomlinson	Knockout
June 19, 1993	Maurice Blocker	Knockout
Aug. 6, 1993	Luis Garcia	Knockout
Oct. 23, 1993	Anthony Stephens	Knockout
Jan. 29, 1994	Hector Camacho	Win
Sept. 17, 1994	Luis Ramon Campas	Knockout
Dec. 10, 1994	Oba Carr	Knockout
Apr. 8, 1995	Roger Turner	Knockout
Nov. 18, 1995	Larry Barnes	Knockout
Feb. 10, 1996	Rodney Moore	Knockout
May 18, 1996	Freddie Pendleton	Knockout
Sept. 7, 1996	Ray Lovato	Knockout
Jan. 11, 1997	Kevin Lueshing	Knockout
Aug. 23, 1997	Troy Waters	Knockout
Apr. 3, 1998	Mahenge Zulu	Knockout
Feb. 20, 1999	Pernell Whitaker	Win
May 29, 1999	Hugo Pineda	Knockout
Sept. 18, 1999	Oscar De La Hoya	Win
Mar. 3, 2000	David Reid	Win
July 22, 2000	Mamadou Thiam	Knockout
Dec. 2, 2000	Fernando Vargas	Technical knockout
May 12, 2001	William Joppy	Technical knockout

second round, establishing his reputation as a champion who had both the prowess of a skillful boxer and a powerful knockout punch. In the same year he successfully defended his title against the number-one contenders Luis Garcia and Anthony Stephens.

It was 1994, however, that established Felix as one of the best. On January 29 of that year he fought and defeated Hector "Macho" Camacho, an international favorite. After an eight-month break from boxing, Felix returned to the ring to fight Luis Ramon "Yory Boy" Campas, who delighted the crowd and stunned Felix with a second-round knockdown. Campas's moment of glory was short-lived, however, as Felix returned in the fourth round to score a deci-

sive victory over his opponent. A second-round knockdown was repeated in December when Felix faced Oba "Motor-City" Carr. Again, Felix rallied to score an eighth-round technical knockout.

In 1995 Felix faced Roger "Stingray" Turner, the number-nine contender for the title. This time the second round proved to be the undoing of Turner as Felix delivered a left hook that ended the fight by technical knockout (TKO). By 1996 Felix was definitely a headliner, attracting large crowds and defeating both Rodney Moore and Freddie Pendleton.

The match against Kevin Lueshing was Felix's first victory of 1997. Once again, however, the second round proved unlucky for Felix, and Lueshing knocked Felix to the canvas. As in the past, Felix asserted his control in the third round and scored a TKO, making the fight his thirty-first win. Felix moved up to the super welterweight division to defeat Troy Waters at Madison Square Garden in the summer of 1997.

Continuing the Story

More than twelve thousand fans filled the stands at the Coliseo de Ruben Rodriguez when, on April 3, 1998, Felix returned to Puerto Rico to defend his welterweight title against Zaire's Mahenge Zulu. The fight lasted four rounds before Mahenge was defeated by TKO. Felix returned to Madison Square Garden in 1999 to defend his title against six-time world champion Pernell "Sweet Pea" Whitaker. After twelve rounds of fighting, the judges declared Felix the victor.

The attention was then on a bout with Oscar de la Hoya, but Columbia's Hugo Pineda first had to be defeated. Felix defended his title at the Roberto Clemente Coliseo before a crowd of eight thousand. The victory was accomplished by the fourth round, and Felix and his trainer father then looked ahead to the de la Hoya fight.

The much-anticipated bout with de la Hoya took place on September 18, 1999. The two fighters, in spite of their physical similarities—Felix is 5 feet 10 inches, de la Hoya 5 feet 11 inches—were very different. While de la Hoya was something of a matinee idol, having a large following and endorsements, which made him a familiar face on television and magazines, Felix was an island favorite who could boast of a large and enthusiastic following from the Puerto Rican community. Both fighters had earned reputations as hard hitters and knowledgeable boxers.

The fight lasted for twelve rounds, ending in a close but unchallenged victory for Felix and making him both International Boxing Federation and the World Boxing Council welterweight champion. The double champion, Felix, continued to astound boxing fans on March 3, 2000, in a bout with David Reid, which resulted in another victory and added the World Boxing Association super welterweight championship to his list of achievements. A bout with Fernando Vargas on December 2, 2000, made him the International Boxing Federation titleholder and the undisputed king of the 154-pound division.

Summary

Felix Trinidad is a champion who mastered the skill of boxing and defeated the best opponents the sport has to offer. His many titles are testament to his hard work and natural talent.

Don Evans

Additional Sources:

Hoffer, Richard. "Class Dismissed." *Sports Illustrated*, September 27, 1999, 56.

Nack, William. "Star Power." *Sports Illustrated*, February 19, 1996, 30.

"Oscar vs. Felix." *Sports Illustrated*, September 20, 1999, 29.

"The Upper Hand." *Sports Illustrated*, March 13, 2000, 52.

CHARLEY TRIPPI

Sport: Football

Born: December 14, 1922
Pittston, Pennsylvania

Early Life

Charles Louis Trippi was born on December 14, 1922, in Pittston, Pennsylvania, in the heart of the state's coal region. The son of Italian coal miner Joseph Trippi and his wife Jennie, Charley was one of five children. He had a brother, Sam, and three sisters, Angelina, Mary, and Jennie.

In Pittston, football was as important as coal mining. All the boys played, and young Charley was no exception. At Pittston High School, Charley wanted to play tackle, but at 160 pounds he lacked the size. He played center for a while, but his high school coach was impressed by his running ability and soon made him a running back. While in high school, Charley began developing not only his running but his passing and kicking skills. After graduation, when he did not receive any college offers, he spent a year at LaSalle Academy on Long Island, New York.

The Road to Excellence

Trippi enrolled at the University of Georgia in 1941 and soon became a football star. By now he was 6 feet and 185 pounds. Georgia Bulldogs coach Wally Butts was also impressed with Charley's running ability—so much so that he moved the team's All-American tailback, Frank Sinkwich, to fullback and made Charley the starting tailback. In his sophomore year, Charley's all-around talent as a runner, passer, and punter began to emerge. Led by Trippi, the Bulldogs went to the 1943 Rose Bowl and defeated the University of California at Los Angeles 9-0. Charley was selected as the game's most valuable player after he ran and passed for over 200 yards.

At this point in his career as a college football star, Charley answered the call of duty and entered the U.S. Army Air Force in 1943. He served

for two years and continued to play football on the All-Service team.

After being discharged from the service, Trippi returned to the University of Georgia in 1945. He led the Bulldogs to an undefeated season in 1946 and a 20-10 victory over the University of North Carolina in the Sugar Bowl. He was a unanimous selection to the All-American team

STATISTICS

Season	GP	Car.	Rushing Yds.	Avg.	TD	Rec.	Receiving Yds.	Avg.	TD
1947	11	83	401	4.8	2	23	240	10.4	0
1948	12	128	690	**5.4**	6	22	228	10.4	2
1949	12	112	553	4.9	2	34	412	12.1	6
1950	12	99	426	4.3	3	32	270	8.4	1
1951	12	78	501	6.4	4	0	0	0.0	0
1952	12	72	350	4.9	4	5	66	13.2	0
1953	12	97	433	4.5	0	11	87	7.9	2
1954	12	18	152	**8.4**	1	3	18	6.0	0
1955	5	0	0	0.0	0	0	0	0.0	0
Totals	100	687	3,506	5.1	22	130	1,321	10.2	11

Notes: Boldface indicates statistical leader. GP = games played; Car. = carries; Yds. = yards; Avg. = average yards per carry *or* average yards per reception; TD = touchdowns; Rec. = receptions

and also won the Maxwell Award as the nation's best college player. A true winner, Trippi played in only three losing games during his three years with Georgia.

The Emerging Champion

Charley became known as "Triple-threat" Trippi because of his superb running, accurate passing, and strong punting. He also played defensive safety. Butts had called him the best tackler he had ever seen. His versatility extended to other sports as well. A great baseball player, Charley was selected to the baseball All-America team in 1946. He was the Bo Jackson of his era and could have chosen either professional football or baseball. In 1947, after graduating from Georgia, he actually did play a season of professional baseball with a minor league team. Football, though, remained his first love.

The year 1947 was a good time for Charley to enter professional football. The All-America Football Conference (AAFC) was competing with the National Football League (NFL) for players, so versatile players like Charley were a valuable commodity. Charley wisely chose to play for the NFL's Chicago (now Phoenix) Cardinals. He signed a four-year $100,000 contract—the most paid to any player up to that time. Charley immediately proved his worth. In his rookie season, he became a star halfback and led the Cardinals to the NFL Championship. In the 1947 NFL Championship Game against the Philadelphia Eagles, he gained more than 300 yards and scored 2 touchdowns to lead the Cardinals to a 28-21 victory. This great first season was only the beginning of Charley's great football career. In his nine seasons with the Cardinals, he set team records in rushing, punt return yardage, touchdowns, and best season punting average.

Continuing the Story

Charley's greatest skill was his running ability. He was a fast, creative runner who always seemed able to elude tacklers to gain yardage. He had a knack for gaining big yardage whenever he carried the ball. He led the league in average yards per carry in 1954 and established a Cardinal record in the same category.

Yet the key to Charley's greatness was his all-around talent. As a punter, Charley averaged almost 50 yards per punt, which ranked him among the sport's best. He was an accurate passer and a sure-handed receiver as well. In his professional career, he accumulated more than 7,000 yards. Cardinals coach Jimmy Conzelman called Charley the greatest player he had coached in two decades.

Trippi's career as a football player ended in 1955 after he was badly injured in a game against the San Francisco 49ers. He was hit from the blind side and knocked unconscious. He recovered and returned to play a few games later in the season, but finally, at age thirty-two, he decided to retire.

Charley remained with the Cardinals as a coach for two years. Then he returned to coach at his alma mater, the University of Georgia. In 1968, Charley Trippi's football greatness was recognized with his selection to the Pro Football Hall of Fame.

Subsequently, Charley became involved in real estate in Athens, Georgia, where he made his home. His first wife, Virginia, died in 1971. He later married Peggy McNiven in 1977. He has two daughters, Joanne and Brenda, and a son, Charles, Jr.

Summary

Charley Trippi was one of the last triple-threat players; he was also one of the best. Versatile players like Charley were rare back then and are virtually nonexistent in the modern era of the specialist. Charley rose from humble roots in Pennsylvania's coal mining country and went on to achieve football fame with the University of Georgia Bulldogs and later with the Chicago Cardinals. A true champion, he was one of those rare players who could do it all on the football field.

Nan White

HONORS, AWARDS, AND RECORDS

1943	Rose Bowl Game most valuable player
1945	Chicago College All-Star Game most valuable player Overall first choice in the NFL Draft
1946	Maxwell Award Camp Award Consensus All-American (football) All-American (baseball)
1947	NFL record for the most touchdowns on punt returns, one game (1) (record shared)
1948	*Sporting News* NFL All-Star Team
1953-54	NFL Pro Bowl Team
1959	Inducted into College Football Hall of Fame
1963	NFL All-Pro Team of the 1940's
1968	Inducted into Pro Football Hall of Fame
1991	Inducted into Rose Bowl Hall of Fame

Additional Sources:

Hickok, Ralph. *A Who's Who of Sports Champions.* Boston: Houghton Mifflin, 1995.

LaBlanc, Michael L., and Mary K. Ruby, eds. *Professional Sports Team Histories: Football.* Detroit: Gale, 1994.

Porter, David L., ed. *Biographical Dictionary of American Sports: Football.* Westport, Conn.: Greenwood Press, 1987.

BRYAN TROTTIER

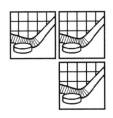

Sport: Ice hockey

Born: July 18, 1956
Val Marie, Saskatchewan, Canada

Early Life

Bryan John Trottier, a native of the prairie province of Saskatchewan in western Canada, was born on July 18, 1956, in Val Marie, a whistle-stop town of about 250 people. This semiarid, high plains region just north of Montana is wheat, cattle, and cowboy country.

Bryan was the oldest of four children. From his mother he inherited Irish ancestry. His paternal grandfather, a rancher, was a mixture of French and Cree Indian background. The grandmother was pure Chippewa. Bryan's father, Eldon "Buzz" Trottier, worked as a cowhand, rodeo rider, and road construction crewman at sites across western Canada and the western United States. In 1962, he took over the Trottier cattle ranch, a 960-acre spread in a long, flat valley flanked by rolling, yellow-green hills.

Most of young Bryan's after-school hours and weekends were taken up tending horses, cows, and hay. As he grew older, he rode herd, checked fences, and learned to rope.

The Road to Excellence

Bryan began skating at age six on the nearby Frenchman River, which is frozen from October through February. Because of his ranch chores, Bryan took up hockey later than many Canadian youths, at age nine. Making up for lost time, he was playing five games a week by age fifteen in Val Marie, Climax, and Swift Current. Bryan credits his father with being his best hockey coach. "Buzz," who knew the game well, put a high priority on body checking and playing a hard offensive game all over the ice rather than simply trying to score goals. Buzz also taught the boy to play the guitar. Around 1970, Bryan, his sister, and his father formed a professional singing combo; they performed country western and country rock routines at weddings and local entertainment spots for a number of years thereafter.

In 1972, Bryan started playing junior hockey with the Swift Current Broncos. In his second and third seasons, he came on strong with 112 and 144 points, respectively. After the second season, scouts recommended Bryan to the New York Islanders, a struggling National Hockey League (NHL) expansion club that needed a good center. None was presently available in the league. Although coach Al Arbour had never

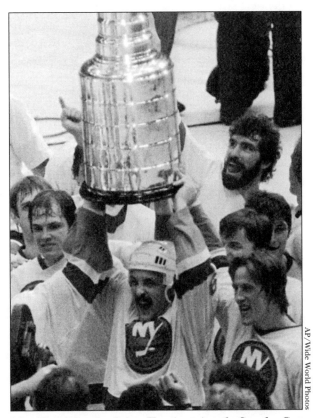

New York Islander Brian Trottier raises the Stanley Cup as teammates celebrate the Islanders' second consecutive championship in 1981.

2819

heard of this new prospect, the Islanders looked to the future; they picked Bryan in the second round of the 1974 draft, two years before an amateur would normally be eligible at age twenty. Needing more experience, Bryan played his third season in Lethbridge, Alberta, where the Broncos relocated. In the fall of 1975, Bryan arrived in New York.

The Emerging Champion

The nineteen-year-old cowboy from Saskatchewan who sang country ballads in his natural western drawl became a hit with teammates, management, and coaching staff. The Islanders presently had two fine goalies plus star defenseman and scoring threat Dennis Potvin. Bryan's addition created the first strong offensive line in the team's four-year history. Bryan's 63 assists and 95 total points were new NHL first-season records. This fine performance won Trottier the Calder Memorial Trophy as the league's best rookie.

Bryan's greatest hockey talent was his ability to do everything well—skating, shooting, stick-handling, passing, checking, and defense. He was a two-way threat who played hard and effectively on both offense and defense. Bryan was a

smart, deceptive skater who kept his upper body straight to avoid giving away his moves and was always alert for openings. If the Islanders needed to respond to a fast-skating, wide-open attack, or when a hard-hitting game was called for, Bryan adapted well to either style of play. He intercepted passes, outmaneuvered defensemen to pick up rebounds, and back-checked well to hinder other players from getting into scoring position. At 5 feet 10 inches and 195 pounds, he could jolt opponents with furious but clean checks. Moreover, Bryan had a marvelous ability to stay on his feet when hit hard; he seemed to be immune to pain or fatigue. An unselfish player, the Islanders' center preferred to set up his wings for scoring rather than to take the shot himself. Yet, he scored his share of goals. "He Skates, He Sings, He Scores," proclaimed the heading on a *New York Times* feature story about this do-it-all center.

Continuing the Story

In 1980, the once lowly Islanders dethroned Montreal as professional hockey's dominant team and won the first of four successive Stanley Cup championships. Bryan's regular and postseason play was an important ingredient in this success. With the addition of rookie Mike Bossy in 1977, the Islanders were loaded with talent. The high-scoring front line of Bryan, Bossy, and Clark Gillies was nicknamed "The Trio Grande." Bryan and his right wing, Bossy, a prolific scorer, meshed perfectly on and off the ice. It was easy for Bryan, who shoots left-handed, to hit the right-handed Bossy's extended stick. When Bossy accumulated 69 goals in 1978-1979, Bryan assisted on 43.

Bryan's impressive career achievements include the league scoring title and most valuable player (MVP) award in 1979 and the 1980 Stanley Cup MVP award. Bryan was consistently among the league's best in plus-minus ratio (the difference between goals scored for and against the team when he was on the ice) and in points-per-game average.

STATISTICS					
Season	GP	G	Ast.	Pts.	PIM
1975-76	80	32	63	95	21
1976-77	76	30	42	72	34
1977-78	77	46	**77**	123	46
1978-79	76	47	**87**	**134**	50
1979-80	78	42	62	104	68
1980-81	73	31	72	103	74
1981-82	80	50	79	129	88
1982-83	80	34	55	89	68
1983-84	68	40	71	111	59
1984-85	68	28	31	59	47
1985-86	78	37	59	96	72
1986-87	80	23	64	87	50
1987-88	77	30	52	82	48
1988-89	73	17	28	45	44
1989-90	59	13	11	24	29
1990-91	52	9	19	28	24
1991-92	63	11	18	29	54
1993-94	41	4	11	15	36
Totals	**1,279**	**524**	**901**	**1,425**	**912**

Notes: Boldface indicates statistical leader. GP = games played; G = goals; Ast. = assists; Pts. = points; PIM = penalties in minutes

HONORS, AWARDS, AND RECORDS

1976	Calder Memorial Trophy
1978-79	NHL First Team All-Star
1982, 1984	NHL Second Team All-Star
1979	Art Ross Trophy Hart Memorial Trophy Challenge Cup All-Star Team member
1980	Conn Smythe Trophy
1982	NHL record for the most goals in a period (4) (record shared)
1988	Budweiser NHL Man of the Year
1989	Clancy Memorial Trophy
1997	Inducted into Hockey Hall of Fame

Constant physical punishment and injury finally began to take a toll. After an off season in 1984-1985, Bryan fought off pain to enjoy three good years in succession. After the 1989-1990 season, when physical problems again reduced his playing time and effectiveness, the Pittsburgh Penguins picked up Bryan as a free agent.

After his retirement, Bryan held coaching positions with the Pittsburgh Penguins, minor league hockey's Portland Pirates, and the Colorado Avalanche as an assistant under Bob Hartley in 1998. In 1997, Bryan was inducted into the Hockey Hall of Fame.

Bryan and his wife Nickie, whom he met at the Islanders' training camp in September, 1976, have two children, Bryan, Jr., and Lindsay. During the off-season periods, Bryan helps out at the family ranch, which he hopes to run after his father retires. Bryan's two brothers, Monty and Rocky, also play hockey and aspire to professional careers.

Summary

After fifteen professional seasons in New York, Bryan Trottier departed as the Islanders' career leader in assists and total points. He also ranks very high among NHL career scoring leaders. Although Bryan probably did not dominate in any one facet or skill of the game, his impressive versatility caused many to rate him as hockey's best all-around, all-purpose player in his prime years.

David A. Crain

Additional Sources:

Aaseng, Nathan. *Hockey's Greatest Scorers*. Minneapolis, Minn.: Lerner Publishing, 1984.

Fischler, Stan, and Shirley Walter Fischler. *The Hockey Encyclopedia*. New York: Macmillan, 1983.

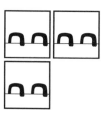

MITSUO TSUKAHARA

Sport: Gymnastics

Born: December 22, 1947
Tokyo, Japan

Early Life

Mitsuo Tsukahara was born on December 22, 1947, in Tokyo, Japan. He began his study of gymnastics at the age of twelve, after watching the 1960 Rome Olympics on his television at home and finding himself drawn by the beauty of the sport. As he developed his abilities, his favorite apparatus was the horizontal bar; he found he had great trouble with the vault. He trained hard—five hours a day through his teen years—to confront his weaknesses and achieve the versatility and consistency of an all-around competitor.

Mitsuo began competing for the team at Nippon Taiso Daigaku (Japan Physical Education College). It was on the entrance examination day at the university that he met Chieko Oda, a fellow gymnast who competed in the 1968 Olympics and who was later to become Mitsuo's wife.

The Road to Excellence

Mitsuo's second major international competition was at the 1970 World Championships in Ljubljana, Yugoslavia, where he took a silver medal in the all-around competition. More impressive, however, was his gold medal in the vault, where he debuted a daring combination that was soon to bear his name and become a standard element in the gymnastics repertoire. The "Tsukahara Vault" consisted of a half-turn of the body during the approach and a one-and-one-half back somersault to land. It was a vault that looked easy but was difficult to execute well. As always, Mitsuo earned high points for risk and originality.

His career, however, had only begun. He was a handsome and charismatic young man who loved to travel and enjoyed interacting with his audiences. At a meet in Pennsylvania during a tour of the United States in 1972, when the Japanese were given brass buckets full of apples, they warmly tossed the apples back to the joyful crowds. Later, after Mitsuo and his teammates earned especially high scores, the American fans spilled out onto the floor in a burst of enthusiasm and support.

In 1972, Mitsuo competed again in the Olympics. He went to Mu-

STATISTICS

Year	Competition	Event	Place	Event	Place
1968	Olympic Games	Floor exercise	4th	Team	Gold
		Rings	4th		
1970	World Championships	All-Around	2d	Vault	1st
		Floor exercise	5th	Team	1st
		Rings	2d		
1972	Olympic Games	All-Around	8th	Rings	Bronze
		Horizontal bar	Gold	Team	Gold
1974	Riga International	All-Around	2d		
	Moscow News Meet	All-Around	4th		
	World Championships	All-Around	5th	Rings	4th
		Horizontal bar	6th	Team	1st
1975	World Cup	All-Around	5th	Rings	1st
		Horizontal bar	1st	Vault	4th
		Parallel bars	2d	Team	1st
	Pre-Olympics Meet, Montreal, Canada	All-Around	1st	Parallel bars	1st
		Floor exercise	1st	Pommel horse	6th
		Horizontal bar	1st	Rings	1st
1976	American Cup	All-Around	4th		
	Olympic Games	All-Around	Bronze	Vault	Silver
		Horizontal bars	Gold	Team	Gold
		Parallel bars	Bronze		

nich with a knee injury but nevertheless earned his first Olympic gold medal on the horizontal bar and finished eighth in the all-around, with the championship going to his teammate Sawao Kato. Again, he impressed the gymnastics world with his knack for innovation by introducing his somersault dismount from the horizontal bar.

The Emerging Champion

In the four years before the next Olympics, Mitsuo was extremely active. He and Oda were married in late 1972 and soon became parents to a son. Mitsuo worked for the Kawai Corporation, a manufacturer of musical instruments, and trained in the company's gymnastics club, coached by former Olympic gymnast Masao Takemoto. Meanwhile, he competed regularly at meets, including the 1974 Riga International, the 1974 Moscow News Meet, the 1974 World Championships in Varna, Bulgaria, the 1975 Chunichi Cup, a 1975 tour of the Western United States, the 1975 World Cup in London, and the 1976 American Cup in New York City. In all these competitions he showed well, consistently placing in the top five and taking occasional gold in the horizontal bar or rings competitions.

Perhaps his most impressive showing was at the 1975 Pre-Olympics in Montreal, where he dominated many of the same competitors he would face the following year at the Olympics. At the Pre-Olympics, he took an astounding five gold medals in the all-around, floor exercise, rings, parallel bars, and horizontal bar, thereby proving himself to be a versatile champion.

Mitsuo's performance at the Olympics itself was almost as strong. He took a total of five medals there, including a bronze in the all-around behind the Soviet champion Nikolai Andrianov and his own teammate Kato, and another gold on the horizontal bar, still his favorite apparatus. He also earned a gold medal as a member of the Japanese team, his fourth as a participant in the so-called "V-10" dynasty, a series of ten Japanese men's team titles in Olympic and World Championship competitions stretching from the 1960 Olympics in Rome—Mitsuo's original inspiration—to the 1978 World Championships in Strasbourg, France.

Continuing the Story

By the 1976 Games in Montreal, Mitsuo was twenty-eight years of age, much older than many of his competitors. Though still ranked ninth in-

MILESTONES

1970	"Tsukahara Vault" gymnastics maneuver is named after him

ternationally in 1977 and performing well at that year's American Cup, his ability to compete against younger men was waning. He continued training and competing, but his hopes to participate at the 1980 Olympics in Moscow were ended with the Japanese decision to boycott the Games, and Mitsuo's twelfth-place finish in the Japanese team trials failed to qualify him for the 1981 World Championships in Moscow. By then he was thirty-three years old and ready to retire.

Though no longer competing, Mitsuo remained quite active in gymnastics. In 1982, he published a book, *Endless Challenge,* on his career and experiences. That same year, he became Master of the Asahi Gymnastics School in Tokyo, where his wife also coached. With his modest charm and friendly disposition, Mitsuo had become well known in Japan and was often delighted upon being recognized by appreciative fans in the street. Through the 1980's, he served as a coach to the Japanese national women's gymnastics team and as a sports commentator for Japanese television. Mitsuo continued coaching

through the 1990's and was proud to see his son, Naoya, on the Japanese national team. Naoya qualified for the horizontal bar event finals at the 2000 Olympic Games in Sydney, Australia.

Summary

Throughout his career, Mitsuo Tsukahara embodied many of the finest qualities of a champion gymnast: versatility, team spirit, positive attitude, and hard work. Through his decades of involvement in all aspects of gymnastics as well as through the popular vault that bears his name, he earned his place as an innovative champion of the sport.

Barry Mann

Additional Sources:

Fink, H. "Tsukahara, Mitsuo (JPN)." Worldsport Networks. http://gymnastics.worldsport .com/profiles/tsuk.html.

Haycock, Kate. *Gymnastics.* New York: Crestwood House, 1991.

"Mitsuo Tsukahara." Yahoo! Sport: Olympic Games 2000. http://uk.sports.yahoo.com/ oly/oldgames/bio/14190.html. November 9, 2000.

Storm, Stephanie. "For a Japanese Gymnast, Honor Thy Father." *The New York Times,* September 5, 2000, p. D1.

EMLEN TUNNELL

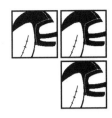

Sport: Football

Born: March 29, 1925
    Bryn Mawr, Pennsylvania
Died: July 23, 1975
    Pleasantville, New York

Early Life

The man who became the first black player to be elected to the Pro Football Hall of Fame was born on March 29, 1925, in Bryn Mawr, Pennsylvania, a suburb of Philadelphia. Emlen Tunnell enjoyed playing football at an early age. By the time he was old enough to attend Radnor High School, he was good enough to make the football team as a freshman. Although he was slow to develop as a player, he worked hard at improving his skills, and by his junior year, his running and passing attracted the attention of several collegiate coaches.

After graduating from Radnor, Emlen attended the University of Toledo on a scholarship. In his freshman year, he suffered a major setback when he broke his neck during a scrimmage. He was told that he would never be able to play football again. Amazingly, he returned and played the next season with a neck brace. In spite of his injury, Emlen played football with a vengeance and earned a reputation for being a vicious tackler. He also played basketball and led his team to the National Invitational Tournament championship game in 1943.

The Road to Excellence

Like many athletes of his time, Emlen left college and joined the armed services during World War II. He was rejected by the Army because of his neck injury, so he joined the Coast Guard. During his shore leaves, Emlen played football for the Fleet City Bluejackets of New London, Connecticut. His outstanding play against other great players from college and professional ranks again earned him scholarship offers from many colleges.

After being discharged from the Coast Guard, Emlen accepted a scholarship from the University of Iowa and resumed his education. He also returned to his football career and again showed tremendous talent. He developed into an all-around player at Iowa: a swift runner, a sure-handed receiver, and a bruising defensive player.

During his senior year, an eye injury sidelined Emlen. He graduated from Iowa in 1948 and decided to pursue a professional football career. When he was not chosen in the National Football League (NFL) draft, Emlen went to the office of the New York Giants seeking a tryout. Giants

New York Giant Emlen Tunnell in 1951.

owner Tim Mara was impressed by Emlen and decided to invite him to the Giants' preseason training camp. It was a decision Mara would never regret.

The Emerging Champion

Emlen became the first black player ever to play for the Giants. At 6 feet 1 inch and 210 pounds, Emlen played in the backfield on both offense and defense. Since he did not get much playing time on offense, he concentrated on defense. There he emerged as a star. In his rookie season, Emlen intercepted four passes in one game. After that achievement, he was given a permanent spot as a defensive safety. Emlen became a key man in the Giants' famous "umbrella defense" of the early 1950's, along with Tom Landry, Otto Schnellbacher, and Harmon Rowe. He became a feared defensive player and was known for his great ability to thwart opposing pass receivers and to intercept passes.

Although he did not play on offense, Emlen got a chance to run with the ball as a punt and kick returner. He soon excelled at this. In 1951, he ran back four returns for touchdowns, an NFL record. In 1952, he gained an incredible 924 yards on interceptions, punt returns, and kick returns, and outgained the leading offensive running back in the league, Dan Towler of the Los Angeles Rams, in total season yardage. In 1953, he gained 819 total yards—again, more than most running backs in the league.

Continuing the Story

Emlen played eleven seasons for the Giants and led them to three Eastern Conference championships and one league championship. He later played three seasons for the powerful Green Bay Packers under the legendary Vince Lombardi. In 1961, he once again played on a championship team when the Packers crushed his former team, the Giants, 37-0. He was chosen to the All-NFL team four times and established league records for interceptions, interception yardage, punt returns, and punt return yardage.

By 1961, at the age of thirty-six, Emlen no longer had as much speed as he once had, but he continued to inspire his younger teammates with his experience and courageous play. He retired

NFL RECORDS
Most interception return yards, 1,282

HONORS AND AWARDS	
1951-58, 1960	NFL Pro Bowl Team
1963	NFL All-Pro Team of the 1950's
1967	Inducted into Pro Football Hall of Fame
1969	Named best all-time NFL defensive safety

following the Packers' championship victory over the Giants.

Emlen was the first great defensive player in professional football. He was the main part of the Giants' great "umbrella defense" that revolutionized defensive play. Great quarterbacks such as Otto Graham, Bob Waterfield, Norm Van Brocklin, and Johnny Unitas dominated the game in the 1950's. Yet the Giants' innovative pass defense, led by Emlen, gave these quarterbacks plenty of trouble. Emlen was also the first defensive player to become a scoring threat as a punt and kickoff returner. In his fourteen seasons, Emlen played 158 games in a row, which is high on the all-time list. He was inducted into the Pro Football Hall of Fame in 1967 and was named the NFL's best all-time defensive safety in 1969.

Emlen married Patricia Dawkins in 1962. He returned to the Giants as a scout the same year, helping to discover and to develop young players. A few years later, he became the first African American coach in pro football. He served as a Giants defensive coach until the 1973 season, when he became the Giants' assistant director of player personnel. Emlen died of a heart attack on July 23, 1975, while attending a Giants team meeting.

Summary

Emlen Tunnell had to overcome many difficult situations to play professional football: breaking his neck in college, serving in the military, being ignored in the NFL draft, and being a black athlete at a time when blacks were not readily accepted. He overcame these obstacles to become one of the game's greatest defensive players and kick returners. In so doing he displayed not only awesome physical ability but also the courage to accept any challenge.

Nan White

Additional Sources:

Hand, Jack. *Heroes of the NFL.* New York: Random House, 1965.

LaBlanc, Michael L., and Mary K. Ruby, eds. *Professional Sports Team Histories: Football.* Detroit: Gale, 1994.

Tunnell, Emlen. *Footsteps of a Giant.* Garden City, N.Y.: Doubleday, 1966.

GENE TUNNEY

Sport: Boxing

Born: May 25, 1898
New York, New York
Died: November 7, 1978
Greenwich, Connecticut

Early Life

Gene Tunney's background was unusual for a boxer. Born on May 25, 1898, in Greenwich Village in New York City, James Joseph Tunney was of Irish descent. He graduated from parochial school in 1911 and from La Salle Academy in 1915. His educational level exceeded that of many other boxers, and his interest in learning never left him. After his schooling ended, he worked for the Ocean Steamship Company of New York as a clerk.

When America entered World War I in 1917, Gene enlisted in the Marine Corps and went to France with the American Expeditionary Force (AEF). In 1919, he won the light heavyweight championship of the AEF.

The Road to Excellence

After Gene's discharge from the Marines, he decided to become a professional boxer. The choice was unusual for someone of his educational background, but he had proved his talent in the Marines and believed that he had a chance to become a success.

Gene had to overcome a major obstacle. He was not an extremely powerful puncher like his greatest rival, Jack Dempsey. Fighting skill did not come naturally to Gene, and his achievements were the result of hard work and study. His style emphasized correct technique rather than slugging away at the opponent. He rarely made a mistake in the ring and, although through experience he developed a strong knockout punch, he often won his matches by outscoring his opponents.

Gene's methodical approach went even further. He carefully studied other boxers, learning their strengths and weaknesses and continually adding to his store of techniques. He also scouted his opponents and was thoroughly familiar with the styles of the men he fought.

Gene's careful preparation paid off, and he became a successful light heavyweight. He won the United States light heavyweight championship in 1922 and lost only one match in his career in that division.

The Emerging Champion

Gene's one loss was to Harry Greb, one of the toughest light heavyweights of all time and prob-

RECOGNIZED WORLD HEAVYWEIGHT CHAMPIONSHIPS

Date	Location	Opponent	Result
Sept. 23, 1926	Philadelphia, Pa.	Jack Dempsey	10th-round unanimous decision
Sept. 22, 1927	Chicago, Ill.	Jack Dempsey	10th-round unanimous decision
July 26, 1928	New York City, N.Y.	Tom Heeney	11th-round technical knockout

ably the dirtiest of all major fighters. Greb had amazing endurance and was able to withstand Gene's punches while dishing out a continual assortment of low blows and punches to the back of the neck. One of Greb's favorite techniques was a head butt, delivered when the fighters were clinched. He never let up and gave Gene a severe beating.

Gene took the loss in stride and continued with his program of boxing study and rigorous training. He refused to let the setback interfere with his career and defeated Greb in 1923 to regain the light heavyweight title. In 1924, he defeated Georges Carpentier, the most popular fighter in France.

Gene then entered the heavyweight division, where he faced his supreme challenge. The world heavyweight champion was Jack Dempsey, considered by most boxing authorities as one of the greatest fighters of all time. He was also one of the hardest punchers in the history of boxing, and few opponents remained standing after Dempsey had rushed at them with a rain of blows. Gene followed his usual plan. He made a careful study of Dempsey and decided to try to outbox the fierce champion. Gene's plan proved a success in the match, held in Philadelphia on September 23, 1926. His steady jabs wore Dempsey out, and he did not succumb to the temptation to abandon science and become involved in a slugfest. To do so with Dempsey would have been fatal. At the end of the tenth round, Dempsey was out on his feet and Gene Tunney won a unanimous decision. He had won the title by defeating a boxing legend.

Continuing the Story

Many boxing fans dismissed Gene's victory as a fluke. Dempsey had not trained very much for the bout and had been upset and distracted because of legal disputes with his former manager,

Jack Kearns. Like Gene, Dempsey was a man of great fortitude, and he was determined to regain his title.

Gene had to face another problem. His scientific style and refusal to slug toe-to-toe with opponents were not popular with the fans. Even worse for his popularity, Jack Dempsey was extremely well-liked, and Gene's victory won him few new friends.

Gene was undaunted and once more followed his characteristic methods of careful training and preparation for the return match with Dempsey. The bout, this time held in Chicago, took place on September 22, 1927, one year after Gene had won the title.

Gene's methods at first proved highly successful. Even against a much better trained Dempsey, Gene's boxing skill put him well ahead until the seventh round, when Dempsey sprang at Tunney with one of his famed charges, backed him into a corner, and knocked him down.

Instead of retreating to a neutral corner, as the rules of the match required, Dempsey stood over his opponent for several seconds. Exactly how long he did this has been much disputed, but it was at least 4 seconds before the referee began his count. Gene was able to get up before the count reached ten. By the next round, he was ready to resume his former tactics, and he continued to outscore Dempsey until the end of the match. He was awarded a unanimous decision. The "long count" has made this match the most

STATISTICS

Bouts, 77
Knockouts, 43
Bouts won by decision, 21
Bouts won by fouls, 1
Bouts lost by decision, 2
Draws, 1
No decisions, 8
No contests, 1

HONORS AND AWARDS

1928	*Ring* magazine Merit Award
1941	Walker Memorial Award
1954	Inducted into *Ring* magazine Boxing Hall of Fame
1990	Inducted into International Boxing Hall of Fame

controversial bout in the history of heavyweight fighting.

After defeating Tom Heeney in 1928, Gene retired from boxing. He served as a corporate director for a number of businesses and banks and was Chairman of the Board of the American Distilling Company. His business career was interrupted by World War II, in which he served as director of physical fitness for the United States Navy. He died in 1978.

Summary

Gene Tunney illustrates the virtue of careful preparation. Although not the most naturally gifted heavyweight boxer of his era, he was one of the most intelligent. He made boxing into a genuine science and planned his bouts with the skill of a general going into battle. His technique enabled him to conquer one of the most powerful of all heavyweight boxers.

Bill Delaney

Additional Sources:

Evensen, Bruce J. *When Dempsey Fought Tunney: Heroes, Hokum, and Storytelling in the Jazz Age.* Knoxville: University of Tennessee Press, 1996.

Heimer, Mel. *The Long Count.* New York: Atheneum, 1969.

Mee, Bob. *Boxing: Heroes and Champions.* Edison, N.J.: Chartwell Books, 1997.

Van Every, Edward. *The Life of Gene Tunney: The Fighting Marine.* New York: Dell, 1926.

LUDMILA TURISHCHEVA

Sport: Gymnastics

Born: October 7, 1952
Grozny, U.S.S.R. (now Russia)

Early Life

Ludmila Turishcheva was born in Grozny, in the then Soviet Union, on October 7, 1952. At the age of ten, she began her training as a gymnast. She distinguished herself as a talented athlete quickly and was discovered by Coach Vyacheslav Rastaratsky.

Ludmila worked very hard, practicing five hours a day. She was successful in all four individual events for women: the balance beam, the vault, the floor exercise, and the uneven parallel bars. Although Ludmila competed well in all events, she excelled in the balance beam and the floor exercise.

The Road to Excellence

In 1966, at the age of thirteen, Ludmila won the gymnastics competition of the Dynamo Sports Club, one of the largest sports clubs in the Soviet Union. She continued to improve, quickly passed through the ranks of the Soviet gymnastics system, and in 1967 became a member of the Soviet national gymnastics team. As a member of the national team, Ludmila worked hard to improve her skills and was an unexpected winner of the U.S.S.R. Gymnastics Cup. In 1968, she went to the Olympic Games in Mexico City, where she earned her first gold medal as a member of the Soviet team, which won the team competition.

By 1970, Ludmila was considered a world-class gymnast, and during that year she captured her first international individual title at the World Championships, where she was awarded gold medals in the floor exercises and the all-around event. A year later, she won the all-around event in the European Championships and was considered by many to be the world's best gymnast. As the all-around European champion, she was prepared to win a medal at the Olympic Games in Munich, West Germany.

The Emerging Champion

The Soviet Union had previously dominated the team competition in gymnastics, win-

Ludmila Turishcheva competes in the women's gymnastic competition at the 1972 Olympic Games in Munich.

2831

ning gold medals in the Olympic Games of 1960, 1964, and 1968, and Larisa Latynina, Ludmila's predecessor, had won gold medals in the floor exercises in the 1956, 1960, and 1964 Olympic Games and gold medals in the all-around event in 1956 and 1960. However, the competition in gymnastics was better than ever in the 1972 Olympic Games. Ludmila's toughest competitors in the individual events proved to be Karen Janz of East Germany and Olga Korbut, Ludmila's teammate.

Janz won the vault, while Ludmila earned a bronze medal in the event. In the parallel bars, Ludmila failed to capture a bronze medal by a fraction of a point, with Janz earning a gold medal.

Ludmila was overshadowed in the floor exercise and the balance beam by Olga Korbut, who immediately captured the hearts of the press and fans around the world, winning gold medals in these events and a silver in the uneven bars. Ludmila placed fifth in the balance beam but

gave a stunning performance in the floor exercise. She scored 19.550 points to Korbut's 19.575 to earn a silver medal.

Ludmila captured her second Olympic gold medal in the team competition with a Soviet victory over Czechoslovakia, which earned the silver medal, and East Germany, which won the bronze medal. She overcame marginal defeats with fine performances in all four events of the all-around competition. She established herself as the best all-around gymnast with a nearly perfect score of 9.90 (a perfect score is 10.0) in the floor exercises, earning her second gold medal of the Games.

After the Olympic Games, Ludmila continued her dominance in international competition. She claimed all five gold medals in the 1973 European Championships at Wembley, England. At the World Championships in Varna, Bulgaria, in 1974, she won the floor exercise and balance beam, her best two events, and again earned the title as best all-around. Although 1973 may have

STATISTICS

Year	Competition	Event	Place	Event	Place
1968	Olympic Games	Team	Gold		
1969	European Championships	All-Around	3d	Uneven parallel bars	3d
		Floor exercise	3d		
1970	World Championships	All-Around	1st	Vault	3d
		Floor exercise	1st	Team	1st
		Uneven parallel bars	2d		
1971	European Championships	All-Around	1st	Balance beam	2d
		Floor exercise	1st	Vault	1st
		Uneven parallel bars	2d		
1972	Olympic Games	All-Around	Gold	Balance beam	5th
		Floor exercise	Silver	Vault	Bronze
		Uneven parallel bars	4th	Team	Gold
1973	European Championships	All-Around	1st	Balance beam	1st
		Floor exercise	1st	Vault	1st
		Uneven parallel bars	1st		
1974	World Championships	All-Around	1st	Balance beam	1st
		Floor exercise	1st	Vault	2d
		Uneven parallel bars	3d	Team	1st
1975	European Championships	Floor exercise	3d		
	World Cup	All-Around	1st	Balance beam	1st
		Floor exercise	1st	Vault	1st
		Uneven parallel bars	1st		
1976	Olympic Games	All-Around	Bronze	Vault	Silver
		Floor exercise	Silver	Team	Gold
		Balance beam	4th		

HONORS, AWARDS, AND RECORDS

1973	Won all five individual events at the 1973 European Championships
1975	Won all five individual events at the 1975 World Cup
1987	Inducted into Sudafed International Women's Sports Hall of Fame
1998	Inducted into International Gymnastics Hall of Fame

been Ludmila's best year, in 1975 she swept all five individual events at the World Cup Meet.

The level of gymnastics competition continued to improve and, once again, Ludmila faced formidable competitors in the 1976 Olympic Games in Montreal, Canada. Nelli Kim, her teammate, and Nadia Comaneci of Romania provided a challenge for the twenty-three-year-old veteran. Kim and Comaneci won all the individual gold medals, but Ludmila gave impressive performances, winning a bronze in the all-around and silver medals in the vault and the floor exercise. She earned a gold medal as the Soviet Union claimed its fifth team event victory.

Continuing the Story

Many athletes are successful because they are dedicated to their sport and are physically gifted. Often success and notoriety in sports are due to innovative changes that athletes make in their sport or, in more recent times, because of personal characteristics that are idealized and popularized by the media. Ludmila Turishcheva was dedicated and gifted, yet she retained a classic, traditional style of performance and was an older, physically larger gymnast than the more popular Olga Korbut and Nadia Comăneci. During Ludmila's years as a competitor, fans and journalists were more attracted to the young and delicate gymnasts, and Ludmila was largely ignored. For years she was considered the world's best gymnast, yet she was overshadowed first by Korbut and later by Comaneci. She has often been referred to as the most underrated and least appreciated champion in the world.

Ludmila retired after the Montreal Games and married a fellow Olympian from the Soviet Union, runner Valery Borzov, who had won gold medals in the 100- and 200-meter dashes in 1972 and the bronze in the 100 meters in 1976. Her love for and dedication to gymnastics prompted her to study sports psychology at the Rostov Phys-

ical Culture Institute to begin her career as a gymnastics coach.

Ludmila gave birth to a daughter in 1978 and established herself as an outstanding coach. She and her husband moved to Kiev, Ukraine, where she became head coach of the national team and served, for a time, as president of the Ukrainian Gymnastics Federation. While there, she guided the career of Lilia Podkopayeva, a gymnast who became, in 1996, the first woman since Ludmila herself to simultaneously hold the European, World, and Olympic all-around titles. Ludmila also served as a member of the International Gymnastics Federation Women's Technical Committee and became a top-rated judge, working at world and Olympic competitions.

Summary

Ludmila Turischeva's career as a gymnast began when she was ten years of age and continued until she was twenty-three. Her career is regarded as unusually long and successful; her greatest rivals were much younger and had begun their careers at a much younger age. She dominated international competition for many years, excelling in the all-around events when specialization in individual events was more highly regarded. She also continued as a champion when she was physically larger than many of the champions and retained a more traditional style of performance than was popular at the time. Ludmila was the last great female gymnast before the sport became dominated by "pixies."

Susan J. Bandy

Additional Sources:

"Class of 98: Lyudmila Turishcheva." *International Gymnast* Online. http://www.intlgymnast.com/week/ighof98/turi.html.

Golubev, Vladimir. *Lyudmila Turishcheva.* Translated from the Russian by Christopher English. Moscow: Progress Publishers, 1979.

_____. *Soviet Gymnastics Stars.* Moscow: Progress Publishers, 1979.

Simons, Minot. *Women's Gymnastics, a History: Volume 1, 1966-1974.* Carmel, Calif.: Welwyn, 1995.

"Where Are They Now: Lyudmila Turishcheva." *International Gymnast* Online. http://www.intlgymnast.com/paststars/psoct99/psoct99.html. October, 1999.

2833

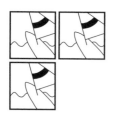

TED TURNER

Sport: Yachting

Born: November 19, 1938
Cincinnati, Ohio

Early Life

Robert Edward Turner III, better known as Ted, was born on November 19, 1938, in Cincinnati, Ohio. The future yachtsman and businessman was the son of Ed Turner, a cotton farmer turned salesman, and his wife Florence, whose grandfather had the first chain grocery store in Cincinnati. Ted's childhood was rather turbulent, marked by a move to Georgia and frequent separations from his family starting at the age of six.

In what was perhaps a misguided effort to prepare Ted for the competitive world of big business, his father could be unduly harsh in one moment, yet exceedingly generous in another. The volatility of the father-son relationship began to show early in Ted's personality. Always a bit mischievous, he earned the nickname "Terrible Ted" at the McCallie School in Chattanooga, Tennessee, one of several boarding schools he attended in his youth. Still, Ted was an outstanding student, particularly interested in history and the classics. He proved early to be an outstanding orator, becoming the Tennessee state high school debating champion when he was seventeen.

Ted Turner (center) with wife Jane Fonda and others on his yacht in a 1997 regatta.

The Road to Excellence

As a college student at Brown University in Providence, Rhode Island, Ted wanted to major in the classics, but at his father's insistence, he switched to accounting. At Brown University, Ted also had the opportunity to hone the sailing skills he had developed as a child. He loved sailing and proved it by winning his first nine regattas as a member of the school's sailing team.

His abilities were not lost on the members of the Noroton Yacht Club in nearby Connecticut, who offered him a chance to race lightning boats for them during the summer. It seemed like the perfect summer for Ted, but his father, who had become the owner of an expanding outdoor advertising company, wanted him at home. Ted expressed his disappointment through such rowdy behavior that he was suspended from Brown University. The suspension led to a stint in the Coast Guard, at the behest of his father.

When Ted was twenty-five his father committed suicide, and Ted took over the family business. At the time, it was in serious trouble, but through a series of brilliant strategies, Ted was able to turn it into not one but several thriving enterprises that included a cable television station, the Atlanta Braves baseball team, and the Atlanta Hawks basketball team. His management style was so enthusiastic, creative, and high-profile that he gained a reputation among his peers as being somewhat outrageous.

The Emerging Champion

The adjectives "courageous" and "tenacious" (both used by Ted as names for his yachts) more aptly explain his unusual success in his sailing endeavors. In the years when Ted was developing his business skills, he was working equally hard to develop his sailing skills. He worked tirelessly to know all that he could about sailing and about the boats in which he would be racing, and he would accept nothing less than perfection from these boats and their crews.

Among his many sailing victories were three United States 5.5-meter championships (5.5-meter boats are about eighteen feet long, with a jib, which is a small sail forward of the mast, and a mainsail). Ted is best known, however, for his 1977 America's Cup victory over Australia in his 12-meter yacht *Courageous*.

MAJOR CHAMPIONSHIP VICTORIES

1963	U.S. Y-Flyer Championship
1965	North American Flying Dutchman Champion
1966	Southern Ocean Racing Conference Champion
1971	World Championship (5.5-meter)
1977	America's Cup (as skipper)
1979	Fastnet Rock Championship (as skipper)

The America's Cup race began in 1851, when the New York Yacht Club sent the schooner *America* to compete against a British schooner for the Hundred Guinea Cup. The *America* won the race, and the trophy was renamed the America's Cup. This race is the most venerable of all international yacht racing events. One must first defeat one's compatriots in trial races to earn the right to represent one's country in competition for the coveted cup.

Ted lost those trials in his 1974 attempt to defend the cup, yet even though he had expended immense time, effort, and money only to lose, he took the defeat as the true competitor he was, and he vowed to return for the next trials. His competitive spirit drove him to prepare excellently for the 1977 trials, which he won handily, as he did the America's cup race against Australia later that year. For his fine performance in the 1977 race and his many previous victories, he won his third Yachtsman of the Year award.

Continuing the Story

Ted continued to sail with exceptional intelligence and fearless enthusiasm. He also enjoyed a fair amount of good fortune, as in 1979 when he won the Fastnet Rock race off the coast of Ireland. In that race, a severe storm took the lives of fifteen of his fellow sailors.

His thriving business enterprises included CNN, the cable television news network. His oratorical skills have not diminished, and he is a highly regarded speaker, particularly at business conventions. He has used his influence and wealth to establish the Goodwill Games, an international athletic event based on the spirit of friendly competition. Ted's efforts in this area were aimed at improving relations between the United States and the Soviet Union through sports events.

2835

Widely known throughout the business and sports worlds as a mercurial and formidable competitor of legendary tenacity and versatility, he became the owner of a plantation near Atlanta, Georgia, the home base of his many enterprises. Twice divorced, once from actress Jane Fonda, he is the father of two daughters and three sons.

Summary

Ted Turner was one of the most versatile competitors in the yachting world. He has excelled in many different racing categories including the prestigious 12-meter class, in which he and his crew defended the America's Cup for the United States in 1977. This same versatility and excellence have characterized his business career. He has become one of the most influential names in cable television. He also owns the Atlanta Braves and the Atlanta Hawks and has instituted the Goodwill Games, which promote international athletic competition.

A brilliant, sensitive youngster, given to mischievous activities, Ted channeled his childhood insecurities into highly constructive accomplishments. Capable of accurately perceiving the

HONORS AND AWARDS

1970, 1973, 1977, 1979	U.S. Yachtsman of the Year

smallest details or the broadest general concepts, Ted can be characterized as a man who thrives on adversity. That he has successfully mingled his diverse interests and abilities into a rich and purposeful life is a fitting testament to his ability to put dreams fearlessly into action.

Rebecca J. Sankner

Additional Sources:

Conner, Dennis, and Michael Levitt. *The America's Cup: The History of Sailing's Greatest Competition in the Twentieth Century.* New York: St. Martin's Press, 1998.

Hickok, Ralph. *A Who's Who of Sports Champions.* Boston: Houghton Mifflin, 1995.

Turner, Ted, and Gary Jobson. *The Racing Edge.* New York: Simon & Schuster, 1979.

Van Atta, Dale. "Meet Ted Turner." *Reader's Digest* 153, no. 917 (1998).

Vaughn, Roger. *Ted Turner, Mariner, and the America's Cup.* Boston: Little, Brown, 1975.

JACK TWYMAN

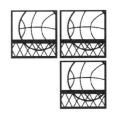

Sport: Basketball

Born: May 11, 1934
Pittsburgh, Pennsylvania

Early Life

Jack Twyman was born on May 11, 1934, in Pittsburgh, Pennsylvania. Pittsburgh has always been a rugged, sports-minded city, a steel-mill town that fueled the dreams of many young men who hoped to be football players.

Jack's dreams were different. He grew up hoping to be a professional basketball player, even though Pittsburgh itself had no professional team.

In fact, in the early 1950's, when Jack was growing up, there were only eight teams in the National Basketball Association (NBA). That meant there were fewer than one hundred potential spots on player rosters.

Jack was not discouraged by the odds, however, and worked hard every day to improve his basketball skills. By the time he reached high school, he was tall and lanky and destined to be a high-scoring forward at Central Catholic High School.

The Road to Excellence

After his sterling high school career, he attracted the attention of the University of Cincinnati and earned a full basketball scholarship. At college, Jack took nothing for granted and worked hard to start in his freshman year, an unusual feat at the time.

He preserved his edge in what was becoming in many ways a sport for bigger, faster men by a rugged off-season conditioning program. During the summers, he practiced 100 foul shots per day, as well as 200 jump shots and 150 set shots. It was this routine that he would take with him into the professional ranks and that would earn the admiration and respect of veteran players.

As a four-year starter on the University of Cincinnati team, Jack was a standout leader and was chosen an All-American in 1954-1955. At the time of his graduation, Jack was the second all-time leading rebounder in University of Cincinnati history.

Jack's college success earned him the status of a second-round draft pick of the Rochester Royals in 1955, and he entered the National Basketball Association as a highly touted 6-foot 6-inch forward.

Jack Twyman of the Cincinnati Royals drives to the basket in a game against the St. Louis Hawks in 1960.

The Emerging Champion

When Jack entered the NBA, he endured the trials that most rookies in any sport face. He handled well the new pressures of nearly daily travel and the skepticism of his teammates and his opponents, as well as the referees who are sometimes thought to give the benefit of the doubt to veteran players over inexperienced rookies.

Jack steadily increased his playing time in his first year as a Royal until he was a starter. Very quickly, Jack became one of the best pure-shooting forwards in the first two decades of the NBA. Jack was especially deadly from the corners, sinking jump shots that, under contemporary rules, would be worth three points instead of two.

Jack made the NBA All-Star team for the first time in 1957 in just his second year in the league and went on to be named to the All-Star squad six more times in his career. His scoring average in the 1959-1960 season, his best year, was 31.2 points per game. Jack's average was second only to that of the high-scoring center Wilt Chamberlain, quite an achievement for a forward well-known for his unselfishness and acute passing skills.

Jack and Oscar Robertson led the Royals to the Eastern Division finals in 1963, where they lost to the Boston Celtics in seven games. At one stretch during his career, Jack played in 609 consecutive games. During the 1963-1964 season, Jack suffered a broken hand, causing him to sit out for twelve games, and his scoring average dipped to 15.9 points per game. The Royals again made it to the Eastern Division finals before losing to the Celtics once more.

Jack was outstanding in the 1964 playoffs, averaging 20.5 points and 8.7 rebounds per game. After serving as a reserve rather than a starter during the 1965-1966 season, Jack retired as only the sixth player to garner over 15,000 points in a NBA career. He was one of the best pure-shooting forwards during his tenure in the NBA.

Continuing the Story

Most champion athletes have a defining moment in their career that demonstrates their special talent. Jack's moment came not on the court as much as it did off the court. During Jack's career, the Rochester/Cincinnati Royals never won a championship. While Jack's dreams of becoming a successful and well-regarded professional basketball player were fulfilled early in his life, his basketball achievements probably will always be overshadowed by the humanitarian care he expressed for a teammate of his on the Royals.

In a time when racial relations were much less open between whites and blacks, Jack befriended a young African American player named Maurice Stokes, who himself was from Pittsburgh. The two of them roomed together on the road. On the court, they anticipated each other's moves and made a scoring tandem feared throughout the league.

In their third year together on the Royals, the team moved from Rochester to Cincinnati. In March of 1958, Stokes was stricken with paralysis,

STATISTICS

Season	GP	FGM	FG%	FTM	FT%	Reb.	Ast.	TP	PPG
1955-56	72	417	.422	204	.685	466	171	1,038	14.4
1956-57	72	449	.439	276	.760	354	123	1,174	16.3
1957-58	72	465	**.452**	307	.775	464	110	1,237	17.2
1958-59	72	710	.420	437	.783	653	209	1,857	25.8
1959-60	75	870	.422	598	.785	664	260	2,338	31.2
1960-61	79	796	.488	405	.731	669	225	1,997	25.3
1961-62	80	739	.479	353	.815	638	323	1,831	22.9
1962-63	80	641	.480	304	.811	598	214	1,586	19.8
1963-64	68	447	.450	189	.829	364	137	1,083	15.9
1964-65	80	479	.443	198	.828	383	137	1,156	14.5
1965-66	73	224	.450	95	.812	168	60	543	7.4
Totals	823	6,237	.450	3,366	.778	5,421	1,969	15,840	19.2

Notes: Boldface indicates statistical leader. GP = games played; FGM = field goals made; FG% = field goal percentage; FTM = free throws made; FT% = free throw percentage; Reb. = rebounds; Ast. = assists; TP = total points; PPG = points per game

HONORS AND AWARDS

1955	College All-American
1957-63	NBA All-Star Team
1960, 1962	All-NBA Team
1975	Inducted into Black Athletes Hall of Fame
1980	NCAA Silver Anniversary Award
1982	Inducted into Naismith Memorial Basketball Hall of Fame
1996	Ohio Professional and Amateur Athlete Lifetime Achievement Award
	Uniform number 27 retired by Sacramento Kings

a delayed reaction resulting from a fall on the court several days before that had caused severe brain damage. Stokes was in a coma for four months.

After Stokes had awakened, Jack visited him consistently and assumed all responsibility for his care and rehabilitation, becoming Stokes's legal guardian. Jack's special friendship with Stokes continued until Stokes's eventual death and was chronicled many times during and since Jack's playing days. In 1973, a movie titled *Maurie* portrayed the special relationship between Stokes and Jack.

For more than thirty years, Jack has annually organized the Maurice Stokes Memorial Benefit Basketball Game, an event that during Stokes's lifetime drew star NBA players annually to raise money for his care and rehabilitation.

Later, the basketball event was refocused to provide funds for needy retired professional players from the game's earlier days, when paychecks and retirement funds were not as lucrative as they are today.

After leaving professional basketball, Jack went on to a successful career as an insurance executive, serving as a vice president of A. W. Shell Insurance Company in Cincinnati, and a sports broadcaster for the American Broadcasting Corporation (ABC). Being one of the first retired athletes to become a sports broadcaster, Jack helped establish a trend for future sports retirees. After five years of broadcasting, Jack became the top executive of Super Food Services, a major Midwest food distributor. In 1996, he received the Ohio Professional and Amateur Athlete Lifetime Achievement Award.

Summary

Jack Twyman was inducted into the Naismith Memorial Basketball Hall of Fame in 1982. This was an honor that his basketball career alone could have earned him, but it was also a recognition of his love and commitment to his fallen teammate, Maurice Stokes.

Jack has lived his life by the biblical motto, "Greater love hath no man than this, that a man lay down his life for his friends." Truly, he was a champion in the sport of basketball, but more importantly, in the spirit of kindness and compassion.

Bruce L. Edwards

Additional Sources:

Bjarkman, Peter C. *The Biographical History of Basketball.* Chicago: Masters Press, 1998.

Isaacs, Neil D. *Vintage NBA: The Pioneer Era, 1946-1956.* Indianapolis, Ind.: Masters Press, 1996.

Pluto, Terry. *Tall Tales: The Glory Years of the NBA.* Lincoln: University of Nebraska Press, 2000.

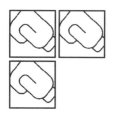

MIKE TYSON

Sport: Boxing

Born: June 30, 1966
   Brooklyn, New York

Early Life

Michael Gerald Tyson was born on June 30, 1966, in a ghetto section of Brooklyn, New York. He was the youngest of three children and never knew his father. Growing up in the Brownsville slums, he seemed destined to live a life of poverty and crime.

Mike spent much of his boyhood in a gang, vandalizing his neighborhood. On the verge of becoming a serious criminal, Tyson was sent to a reformatory school in upstate New York. Even that school could not handle Mike's violent temperament, and he was sent to another school reserved for the most difficult students.

A counselor saw Mike's athletic potential and began to teach him boxing fundamentals. The discipline of the sport helped to reform Mike, and his school performance improved. Mike began to attract attention, but now for good reasons.

The Road to Excellence

The counselor introduced Mike to Cus D'Amato, a famous fight trainer and manager. Although D'Amato was seventy years old, and Mike only thirteen, the sage trainer befriended Mike, eventually becoming his legal guardian. As Mike grew, D'Amato taught the younger fighter the

Mike Tyson (left) celebrates a victory with promoter Don King in 1995.

RECOGNIZED WORLD HEAVYWEIGHT CHAMPIONSHIPS

Date	Location	Loser	Result
Nov. 22, 1986	Las Vegas, Nev.	Trevor Berbick	2d-round technical knockout
Mar. 7, 1987	Las Vegas, Nev.	James Smith	12th-round unanimous decision
May 30, 1987	Las Vegas, Nev.	Pinklon Thomas	6th-round technical knockout
Aug. 1, 1987	Las Vegas, Nev.	Tony Tucker	12th-round unanimous decision
Oct. 16, 1987	Atlantic City, N.J.	Tyrell Biggs	7th-round technical knockout
Jan. 22, 1988	Atlantic City, N.J.	Larry Holmes	4th-round technical knockout
Mar. 20, 1988	Tokyo, Japan	Tony Tubbs	2d-round knockout
June 27, 1988	Atlantic City, N.J.	Michael Spinks	1st-round knockout
Feb. 25, 1989	Las Vegas, Nev.	Frank Bruno	5th-round technical knockout
July 21, 1989	Atlantic City, N.J.	Carl Williams	1st-round technical knockout
Feb. 10, 1990	Tokyo, Japan	Mike Tyson (Buster Douglas, winner)	10th-round knockout
Mar. 16, 1996	Las Vegas, Nev.	Frank Bruno	3d-round knockout
Sept. 7, 1996	Las Vegas, Nev.	Bruce Seldon	1st-round knockout
Nov. 9, 1996	Las Vegas, Nev.	Mike Tyson (Evander Holyfield, winner)	11th-round technical knockout
June 28, 1997	Las Vegas, Nev.	Mike Tyson (Evander Holyfield, winner)	3d-round disqualification

skills and philosophies that would take him to the top of the heavyweight world.

In 1981 and 1982, Mike won the boxing Junior Olympiad championship. His success continued in 1983 and 1984, when he won several tournaments, including the United States Junior Championships. Mike also won the National Golden Gloves heavyweight championship in 1984. He won the silver medal in the Olympic trials, losing to Henry Tillman, a boxer whom Mike would later defeat as a professional.

In March, 1985, Mike turned professional, winning his first bout by a knockout. His amazing succession of victories quickly gained the attention of the entire sporting world. Within twenty months, he won twenty-five fights, twenty-three by knockout.

A master of intimidation, Mike had most of his opponents convinced they would lose before they stepped into the ring. At 5 feet 11 inches and 215 pounds, Mike's compact build gave him an aura of explosiveness. Often wearing black trunks and shoes with no socks, Mike forsook showmanship for serious business in the ring.

As his opponents fell, Mike's stature rose. He gained nicknames like "Kid Dynamite" and "Iron Mike." Many experts saw the brash young fighter as the savior to a dull and listless division. Not since the days of Muhammad Ali had a heavyweight generated such interest.

The Emerging Champion

As Mike Tyson came onto the boxing scene, the heavyweight division was in disarray. The three boxing commissions, the International Boxing Federation (IBF), the World Boxing Association (WBA), and the World Boxing Council (WBC), each had a different champion. Many experts saw Mike as the boxer most likely to unify the three titles.

Mike began his unification quest by challenging Trevor Berbick for the WBC title. Entering the fight a three-and-one-half to one favorite, Mike beat Berbick by a knockout in the second round. On that day, November 22, 1986, Mike Tyson became the WBC champion and the youngest heavyweight champion ever, at twenty years, five months.

Four months later, on March 7, 1987, Mike challenged James Smith for the WBA crown. Mike scored a twelfth-round unanimous decision over Smith to become the WBA champion. Mike was on course in his unification quest.

The IBF champion, Tony Tucker, was the last person standing between Tyson and the undisputed heavyweight title. Tucker also proved to be Mike's toughest opponent. On August 1, 1987, the two fighters went the full twelve rounds in a close contest, which Mike won by unanimous decision.

Mike became the toast of the sports scene. The fighter's youth, charisma, and seeming invincibility vaulted him to worldwide popularity. He was also one of the world's richest athletes, having earned more than sixty million dollars by 1989.

Continuing the Story

As Mike's fame spread, so did the reports on his background and personal life. Mike fueled a

STATISTICS

Bouts, 52
Knockouts, 42
Bouts won by decision, 7
Knockouts by opponents, 3

flood of stories with his whirlwind romance and sudden marriage to actress Robin Givens on February 7, 1988. The following eight months were among the most turbulent in Mike's life, finally resulting in a filing for divorce on October 8, 1988.

In spite of a trying personal life, Mike continued his dominance in the ring. He reigned as the heavyweight champion for three years, with ten title defenses. Indeed, Mike brought back the excitement that had been missing since the days of Muhammad Ali.

Then, on February 10, 1990, Mike met lightly regarded James "Buster" Douglas, in Tokyo, Japan. Oddsmakers had refused to make odds on the fight because few people expected Douglas to last past the first round. Douglas, however, shocked the sports world with one of the most stunning sports upsets in history.

Douglas controlled the fight until Mike knocked him down late in the eighth round, but Douglas came back strong, knocking out Mike in the tenth round. The fight was surrounded by controversy resulting from inconsistencies in the referee's count. The result stood, however, and Douglas became the champion.

Undaunted, Mike was determined to regain his crown. Within one year of his defeat, Mike fought twice more, winning both bouts by knockouts. Before Mike could get a rematch with Douglas, Douglas lost the title in a bout with Evander Holyfield in October, 1990.

In the months that followed, many people in the boxing world predicted that Mike would soon regain the heavyweight crown. The fearsome power and aggressive attitude that took him to the top, they said, would restore him as a top contender. As an indication that he was perhaps already on his way back up, Mike won a twelfth-round unanimous decision over opponent Donovan "Razor" Ruddock on June 28, 1990.

Then, Mike was accused of raping a contestant in the Miss Black America Pageant in an Indianapolis hotel room sometime on the morn-ing of July 19, 1991. For the previous three days, July 17-19, he had been in the city as an honorary guest of the 21st Indiana Black Expo, a festival of African American culture. In the aftermath, he also became the target of two civil lawsuits alleging sexual harassment and asking for more than $100 million in damages. Mike was formally indicted by a Marion County, Indiana, grand jury on October 10, 1991, and charged with rape.

In the interim, a world championship match with heavyweight titlist Holyfield scheduled for November 8 was postponed after Mike injured his ribs during a training session. On February 10, 1992, Mike was convicted and spent the next three years in prison. He was released on March 25, 1995, and was fighting again five months later. In 1996, he won the WBA heavyweight title after knocking out Frank Bruno in the third round. He added the WBC title in September of the same year when he destroyed Bruce Seldon with a knockout in under two minutes of the first round.

Mike faced his first real challenge since returning to boxing when he faced Evander Holyfield on November 9, 1996. Mike's considerable punching power and the intimidation that he inspired in his opponents was not enough to get him past Holyfield, who won by technical knockout (TKO) in the eleventh round of one of the most exciting heavyweight title fights in boxing history. Soon after, talk began circulating about a rematch as commentators and fans alike anticipated another exiting bout.

The rematch took place on June 28, 1997. In one of the most bizzare fights in boxing history,

RECORDS

Captured his first world heavyweight title at 20 years 145 days of age—the youngest world heavyweight champion in professional boxing history

HONORS AND AWARDS

1981-82	Junior Olympiad Champion
1983-84	U.S. Junior Champion
1983	National Golden Gloves silver medalist
1983	U.S. Champion (versus the Federal Republic of Germany)
1984	U.S. Olympic Trials silver medalist
1984	National Golden Gloves heavyweight champion
1986, 1988	*Ring* magazine Merit Award
1988	WBC Boxer of the Year

an outmatched Mike Tyson was disqualified in the third round for biting Holyfield's ears, even removing a portion of the right ear and spitting it onto the mat. Two days later, the Nevada State Athletic Commission revoked Mike's boxing license.

After a year of numerous legal problems outside of boxing, Mike's license was reinstated in 1999, but his legal troubles continued when he was charged with assault on two motorists following a traffic accident. Mike's agitated behavior during news conferences and a no contest ruling following a late hit in his bout with Orlin Norris on October 24 made it apparent that he had lost his focus on boxing.

Mike fought three times in 2000, winning each bout by knockout and continuing his effort to regain a heavyweight title. Though he continued to win, he had Holyfield and Lennox Lewis standing between him and a heavyweight championship, and his future in the sport still fascinated boxing fans. In mid-2001, however, new charges of sexual assault were raised against him, again clouding his future.

Summary

Mike Tyson may well become a legend. Raised in the worst slums of New York, he emerged from his harsh environment with the determination to succeed. With the aid of his supportive trainer, Cus D'Amato, Mike stormed to the top of the heavyweight world, becoming the most exciting champion since his idol, Muhammad Ali.

As Mike's career has progressed, each bout has added an intriguing chapter to the story. Although his ultimate stature as a boxing legend still lies in the future, and though fans and critics alike deplore so much of his behavior in and outside the ring, few would deny the great success of his impressive early years as champion.

William B. Roy

Additional Sources:
Berger, Phil. *Blood Season: Mike Tyson and the World of Boxing.* New York: Morrow, 1989.
Heller, Peter. *Bad Intentions: The Mike Tyson Story.* New York: Da Capo Press, 1995.
Hoffer, Richard. *A Savage Business: The Comeback and Comedown of Mike Tyson.* New York: Simon & Schuster, 1998.
Mullan, Harry. *The Ultimate Encyclopedia of Boxing: The Definitive Illustrated Guide to World Boxing.* Edison, N.J.: Chartwell Books, 1996.
Torres, Jose. *Fire and Fear: The Inside Story of Mike Tyson.* New York: Times Books, 1989.

WYOMIA TYUS

Sport: Track and field (sprints)

Born: August 29, 1945
Griffin, Georgia

Early Life

Wyomia Tyus was born on August 29, 1945, in the small community of Griffin, Georgia. The town of Griffin is located approximately thirty miles south of Atlanta.

The youngest of four children, Wyomia had three older brothers. Wyomia's father, Willie Tyus, was a dairy worker. Marie Tyus, Wyomia's mother, worked in a laundry. When Wyomia was fifteen years old, her father died.

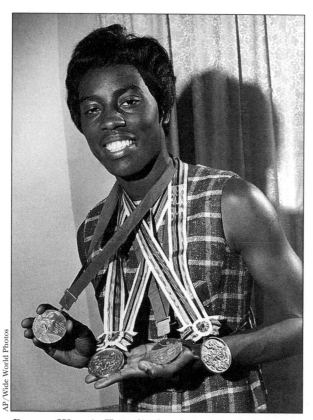

Runner Wyomia Tyus displays her gold and silver medals from the 1964 Olympics and her two golds from the 1968 Games.

Although one of Wyomia's brothers played on the high school football team, her other two brothers were not athletes. Wyomia, on the other hand, very much enjoyed sports. Her favorite sport in high school was basketball. When the basketball season ended, Wyomia missed competing in sports, so she decided to participate in track and field during the spring. Originally, Wyomia directed her efforts to the high jump, but she struggled to clear the bar at 4 feet. Realizing that the high jump was not for her, she switched to the running events.

The Road to Excellence

Wyomia's decision to concentrate on running was one that would change her life. Specializing in the short-distance races (including the 50-, 75-, 100-, and 200-yard dashes, as well as the 400-yard relay), Wyomia experienced much success as a sprinter.

Wyomia's track success can partially be attributed to the well-known Tennessee State University track coach, Ed Temple. Coach Temple would frequently attend high school track competitions in hopes of identifying potential athletes for his nationally known women's track team at Tennessee State University. While on a recruiting trip at the Georgia high school championships during the summer of 1961, Coach Temple spotted gangling fifteen-year-old Wyomia Tyus. Although Coach Temple knew Wyomia was not the fastest runner at the meet, he was impressed with her determination.

During the summer of 1961, Wyomia entered Coach Temple's month-long summer training program. Wyomia was thrilled that Coach Temple was impressed enough with her abilities to put her in his program. After a month of training, Wyomia competed in the Amateur Athletic Union (AAU) girls' national championships in Gary, Indiana. Although she did not win, Wyomia gained valuable experience and knowledge.

This experience and knowledge was evident a year later when she successfully competed in the girls' national championships in Los Angeles. Wyomia not only won the 50-, 75-, and 100-yard races, but she also broke two American records.

Wyomia continued her success in 1963, winning the 75- and 100-yard dashes in the girls' AAU national championships in Dayton, Ohio. The very next month, Wyomia competed in the AAU women's meet, where she finished second in the 100-yard run. The second-place finish enabled Wyomia to compete in a United States-Soviet Union meet held in Moscow. Although Wyomia was disappointed with her fourth-place finish, Coach Temple knew Wyomia was gaining additional valuable experience.

The Emerging Champion

Wyomia entered Tennessee State University on a track scholarship during the fall of 1963. Under the direction of Coach Temple, Wyomia became one of the famous "Tigerbelles." A lean but powerful runner, Wyomia thrived in an environment that produced a total of twenty-nine Olympic athletes from 1956 to 1972.

The year 1964 was a busy one for Wyomia. She was clearly becoming one of the top sprinters in the United States as she won the 100-meter dash at the AAU women's national championships. Two weeks after this, she returned to the Soviet Union, wanting desperately to improve upon her disappointing performance the year before. Wyomia finished second to Edith McGuire, her close friend in college.

Upon her return to the United States, Wyomia participated in the United States Olympic trials in New York. Wyomia wanted to go to Tokyo, the site of the 1964 Olympic Games, very badly. She was extremely nervous and tried

STATISTICS

Year	Competition	Event	Place	Time
1963	National AAU Championships Outdoor	4×100-meter relay	1st	46.7
1964	Olympic Games	100 meters	Gold	11.4 WR
		4×100-meter relay	Silver	43.9
	National AAU Championships Outdoor	100 meters	1st	11.5
1965	National AAU Championships Indoor	60 yards	1st	6.8
	National AAU Championships Outdoor	100 meters	1st	10.5
		4×100-meter relay	1st	46.5
	National AAU Championships Indoor	50 yards	1st	6.8
1966	National AAU Championships Indoor	60 yards	1st	6.5
	National AAU Championships Outdoor	100 meters	1st	10.5
		200 meters	1st	23.8
		4×100-meter relay	1st	45.7
	National AAU Championships Indoor	50 yards	1st	6.5
1967	Pan-American Games	200 meters	1st	23.7
	National AAU Championships Indoor	60 yards	1st	6.7
		50 yards	1st	6.7
1968	Olympic Games	100 meters	Gold	11.0 WR
		200 meters	6th	23.0
		4×100-meter relay	Gold	42.8 WR
	National AAU Championships Outdoor	200 meters	1st	23.5
	National AAU Championships Indoor	640-yard relay	1st	1:10.8

Note: WR = World Record

hard to gain a spot on the team. Wyomia managed a third-place finish in the 100-meter dash and thus qualified for membership on the Olympic team.

Although Coach Temple originally viewed the 1964 Olympic Games as Wyomia's preparation for the 1968 Olympic Games, Wyomia had other ideas. At the age of nineteen, a relaxed Wyomia Tyus not only won the 100-meter dash by two yards but also equaled the world's record of 11.4 seconds held by Wilma Rudolph. Wyomia also won a silver medal as part of the 4×100-meter women's relay team. Now the fastest woman in the world and an Olympic champion, Wyomia was four years ahead of Temple's projections.

Between 1964 and 1968, Wyomia continued to run. One of the highlights of this period was her return to the Soviet Union in 1965. Making up for her disappointing performance in 1963, Wyomia won the 100-meter dash, placed second in the 200-meter dash (a new event for her), and turned a 4-yard deficit into a 5-yard advantage as she anchored the 400-meter relay team to victory. Wyomia's performance, as well as the performance of the United States women's track team, was viewed by millions of Americans on television and helped to elevate women's track from obscurity. There was little doubt that Wyomia was the fastest woman in the world.

Continuing the Story

Wyomia's Olympic success did not end with the 1964 Olympic Games in Tokyo. At the age of twenty-three, a mature Wyomia in 1968 once again qualified for the women's Olympic track team. Wyomia was to accomplish a feat at the 1968 Olympic Games in Mexico City that no person, male or female, had ever achieved. Wyomia was the first athlete ever to win the gold medal in the 100-meter event in two successive Olympiads. Wyomia turned in a record-breaking performance in the 100-meter dash, reducing the world's record to 11.0 seconds. She won a second gold medal as the women's 400-meter relay team set another world record.

Notwithstanding the excellent performances of many American athletes, the 1968 Olympic Games have often been remembered for the Black Power issue. Although a threatened boycott of the Olympic Games by African American athletes did not materialize, two male sprinters, John Carlos and Tommie Smith, engaged in an act of protest during the playing of the "Star-Spangled Banner" at the medal presentation ceremony. Both Carlos and Smith were suspended from the United States team and ordered to leave the Olympic Village. The Black Power issue stirred Wyomia as well. During a news conference, Wyomia indicated that the winning 400-

---

RECORDS
Set world records in the 100 meters 3 times: 1964 (11.4), 1965 (11.1), 1968 (11.0)
Only one of two athletes to win the gold medal in the 100 meters event in two successive Olympiads

HONORS AND AWARDS
1965 Saettel Award
1968 *Athletics Weekly* World Athlete of the Year
1981 Inducted into Sudafed International Women's Sports Hall of Fame
1985 Inducted into U.S. Olympic Hall of Fame

meter relay team was dedicating their win to John Carlos and Tommie Smith.

Summary

Although Wyomia Tyus was quiet and somewhat shy, her superb record speaks for itself. In a span of eight years, Wyomia accumulated an impressive list of track accomplishments as she became the world's fastest woman sprinter. Wyomia Tyus is a twentieth century sports champion in every sense of the term.

Elaine M. Blinde

Additional Sources:

Bateman, Hal. *United States Track and Field Olympians, 1896-1980*. Indianapolis, Ind.: The Athletics Congress of the United States, 1984.

Hickok, Ralph. *A Who's Who of Sports Champions*. Boston: Houghton Mifflin, 1995.

Tyus, Wyomia. *Inside Jogging for Women*. Chicago: Contemporary Books, 1978.

Wallechinsky, David. *The Complete Book of the Olympics*. Boston: Little, Brown and Company, 1991.

Watman, Mel. *Encyclopedia of Track and Field Athletics*. New York: St. Martin's Press, 1981.

JOHNNY UNITAS

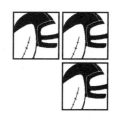

Sport: Football

Born: May 7, 1933
Pittsburgh, Pennsylvania

Early Life

John Constantine Unitas was born May 7, 1933, in Pittsburgh, Pennsylvania. He was the third of four children and was born into a poor family.

His father, Leon, died in 1938. He had operated a small coal delivery business, which his wife, Helen, took over after his death. She also worked at an office-cleaning job to support the family and eventually became a bookkeeper after going to night school to learn accounting.

Legend has it that Johnny, at age twelve, vowed that he would become a professional football player. His determined, often cocky attitude saw him through a childhood that was anything but easy.

The Road to Excellence

Johnny played high school football at St. Justin's High School and in his senior year was named as the quarterback on Pittsburgh's All-Catholic High School team.

Johnny's high school coach saw potential in the young quarterback and contacted various colleges in hopes of persuading them to recruit Johnny.

He was not yet the ideal size for college football. In his last year in high school he was 5 feet 11 inches tall and weighed 140 pounds. The universities of Notre Dame, Indiana, and Pittsburgh all showed some interest in Johnny, but eventually decided he was too small and not good enough. Finally, the University of Louisville gave him a scholarship. He enrolled in 1951. Louisville was not the place for big-time college football. Johnny has recalled that

the team was not even in a league. When he graduated in 1955, he had grown to 6 feet 1 inch and nearly 200 pounds.

He was drafted in the ninth round of the National Football League (NFL) draft by the Pittsburgh Steelers, even though the Steelers had three other quarterbacks at the time. Unitas was cut from the team. A still-determined Johnny tried to persuade the Cleveland Browns to give him a tryout, but they turned him away. Johnny ended up playing on a semiprofessional sandlot team called the Bloomfield Rams, in Pittsburgh.

Quarterback Johnny Unitas in 1960.

2847

STATISTICS

Season	GP	PA	PC	Pct.	Yds.	Avg.	TD	Int.
1956	12	198	110	.556	1,498	7.6	9	10
1957	12	301	172	.571	**2,550**	8.5	**24**	17
1958	10	263	136	.517	2,007	7.6	**19**	7
1959	12	367	**193**	.526	**2,899**	7.9	**32**	14
1960	12	378	**190**	.503	**3,099**	8.2	**25**	24
1961	14	420	229	.545	2,990	7.1	16	24
1962	14	389	222	.571	2,967	7.6	23	23
1963	14	410	**237**	.578	**3,481**	8.5	20	12
1964	14	305	158	.518	2,824	9.3	19	6
1965	11	282	164	.582	2,530	9.0	23	12
1966	14	348	195	.560	2,748	7.9	22	24
1967	14	436	255	**.585**	3,428	7.9	20	16
1968	5	32	11	.344	139	4.3	2	4
1969	13	327	178	.544	2,342	7.2	12	20
1970	14	321	166	.517	2,213	6.9	14	18
1971	13	176	92	.523	942	5.4	3	9
1972	8	157	88	.561	1,111	7.1	4	6
1973	5	76	34	.447	471	6.2	3	7
Totals	211	5,186	2,830	.546	40,239	7.8	290	253

Notes: Boldface indicates statistical leader. GP = games played; PA = passes attempted; PC = passes completed; Pct. = percent completed; Yds. = yards; Avg. = average yards per attempt; TD = touchdowns; Int. = interceptions

He was making six dollars per game when the general manager of the Baltimore Colts, Don Kellett, began hearing reports indicating how good Johnny was. Kellett made a now-famous eighty-five-cent phone call to Pittsburgh and offered Johnny a seven-thousand-dollar contract with the Colts as a backup to quarterback George Shaw.

The Emerging Champion

Johnny did not play much with the Colts until the fourth game of the 1956 season, against the Chicago Bears. George Shaw had been injured and had to be carried off the field. Johnny came in and on his first pass attempt threw an interception.

The slow start did not discourage Johnny. He eventually earned the starting quarterback job and in the last game of the season threw a 53-yard scoring pass to beat the Washington Redskins.

The following year Johnny led the NFL in passing yardage with 2,550 yards and in touchdown passes with 24. The Colts had an up-and-down year and eventually finished in third place.

The next season, 1958, Johnny led the Colts to the NFL Championship in a sudden death victory over the New York Giants. Sportswriters have called it the greatest game ever played. The Colts

had jumped out to a 14-3 lead by halftime. On the Colts' first drive of the second half, Johnny came out passing. The Colts marched all the way to the Giants' 1-yard line but were stopped there. The Giants took over and charged down the field for a touchdown. The Colts could not score on their next possession, and when the Giants got the ball back, they again found the end zone and took a 17-14 lead.

When the Colts got the ball back deep in their own territory with only two minutes to play, Johnny came onto the field and did what would make him famous. Keeping his poise under pressure, he led the Colts down the field to set up a 20-yard Steve Myhra field goal to tie the game. The game went into overtime. Johnny brought the Colts 80 yards to score a touchdown and a 23-17 victory.

The following year the Colts again won the NFL Championship, beating the Giants again, 31-16. Johnny passed for 265 yards and 2 touchdowns in the game.

Continuing the Story

Johnny continued to set records as a quarterback. From 1956 to 1960, he set a record by throwing at least one touchdown pass in forty-seven consecutive games.

In the 1960 season, Johnny suffered a fractured vertebra, and it kept him from running with the ball. Opposing teams could now contain him more easily. He suffered numerous injuries throughout his career, including broken ribs, punctured lungs, and torn knee cartilage. Johnny played through the pain, but it looked like his career was winding down. He had to sit out much of the 1968 season with injuries, but he came back and led the Colts to victory in Super Bowl V over the Dallas Cowboys in 1970.

In 1973, Johnny was traded to the San Diego Chargers, and he played there for one season. He was nearing the end of his eighteen-year career, and his playing time in San Diego was limited. By the time he retired at the end of the season he held the NFL records for the most pass attempts, most completions, most yardage, most 300-yard games, and most touchdown passes.

Johnny won the NFL's most valuable player award in 1959, 1964, and 1967. He won the Jim Thorpe Award, as the most valuable player as voted by NFL players, in 1957 and 1967. He was named All-Pro in 1957, 1958, 1964, 1965, 1966, and 1967. In 1970, the Associated Press named him the NFL Player of the Decade for the 1960's, and in 1979 he was named to the Pro Football Hall of Fame. In 1994 Johnny was selected to the NFL's 75th Anniversary All Time Team.

Aside from the awards, the records, and the statistics, Johnny was known for his ability to keep cool under pressure. He led last-minute drives, calling about 70 percent of the plays himself, to set up game-winning opportunities.

In the late twentieth century, Johnny became active as a corporate representative. He has also been an important supporter of civic and charitable organizations. He has founded the Johnny Unitas Golden Arm Educational Foundation, which, along with the Unitas Management Corporation in Riderwood, Maryland, is headed by Johnny's son, John C. Unitas, Jr. In 1987 the founda-

tion began awarding the Johnny Unitas Golden Arm Award to each year's best senior college quarterback in the country. The foundation promotes football on all levels and gives financial assistance to underprivileged and deserving young scholar-athletes.

Summary

Johnny Unitas never gave up even when it seemed no team wanted him. Always determined and rarely losing his composure, he proved himself to be one of the greatest quarterbacks of all time.

Robert Passaro

Additional Sources:

Hoffer, Richard. "The Twentieth Century/Our Favorite Games." *Sports Illustrated* 91, no. 16 (October 25, 1999): 118-123.

Rothschild, Richard. "A Great Unsurpassable Mark." *Chicago Tribune*, November 25, 2000, pp. 1, 8.

Zimmerman, Paul. "NFL Preview 1998/The Quarterback: Revolutionaries." *Sports Illustrated* 89, no. 7 (August 17, 1998): 78-85.

NFL RECORDS

Most consecutive games with at least one touchdown pass, 47

HONORS AND AWARDS

1957-58, 1964-67	NFL All-Pro Team
1957, 1967	Thorpe Award
1958-59	National Football Association Championship Game most valuable player
1958-60, 1964, 1967	*Sporting News* Western Conference All-Star Team
1958-65, 1967-68	NFL Pro Bowl Team
1959, 1964, 1967	United Press International NFL Player of the Year *Sporting News* NFL Player of the Year Bell Trophy Newspaper enterprise Association NFL Player of the Year
1960-61, 1964	NFL Pro Bowl Co-Player of the Game
1964, 1967	Associated Press NFL Player of the Year
1970	Associated Press NFL Player of the 1960's NFL Man of the Year NFL All-Pro Team of the 1960's
1979	Inducted into Pro Football Hall of Fame Uniform number 19 retired by Indianapolis Colts
1994	NFL 75th Anniversary All Time Team

WES UNSELD

Sport: Basketball

Born: March 14, 1946
Louisville, Kentucky

Early Life

Westley Sissel Unseld was born on March 14, 1946, in Louisville, Kentucky. His mother, Cornelia, worked in the cafeteria at Newburg Elementary School in Louisville, and his father, Charles D. Unseld, worked as an oiler for International Harvester.

Wes, as he was called, grew up in an environment infused with great basketball. The rivalry between the University of Louisville and the University of Kentucky was a yearly event that enthralled the population.

As a young boy, Wes honed his basketball skills on the playgrounds of Louisville, dreaming that someday he would be involved in big-time basketball, perhaps even playing for one of the universities in the state.

The Road to Excellence

Wes emerged as a high-caliber basketball player at Louisville's Seneca High School. In the 1962-1963 season, and again in 1963-1964, Wes led his high school team to the Kentucky state championship.

His abilities as a player did not go unnoticed by the universities in the state. In 1964, Wes was the first African American player recruited by the University of Kentucky. Although this was a great opportunity, Wes chose to attend the University of Louisville because it was close to home and his father could watch him play.

During his freshman season at Louisville, Wes immediately assumed a leadership role, scoring 501 points for a remarkable 35.8 points-per-game average, with 331 rebounds. The scoring and rebounds did not diminish in the next three years of Wes's college career. For the 1965-1966 season, Wes scored 518 points and took 505 rebounds; in 1966-

Courtesy of Amateur Athletic Foundation of Los Angeles

2850

STATISTICS

Season	GP	FGM	FG%	FTM	FT%	Reb.	Ast.	TP	PPG
1968-69	82	427	.476	277	.605	1,491	213	1,131	13.8
1969-70	82	526	.518	273	.638	1,370	291	1,325	16.2
1970-71	74	424	.501	199	.657	1,253	293	1,047	14.1
1971-72	76	409	.498	171	.629	1,336	278	989	13.0
1972-73	79	421	.493	149	.703	1,260	347	991	12.5
1973-74	56	146	.437	36	.655	517	159	328	5.9
1974-75	73	273	.502	126	.685	1,077	297	672	9.2
1975-76	78	318	**.561**	114	.585	1,036	404	750	9.6
1976-77	82	270	.490	100	.602	877	363	640	7.8
1977-78	80	257	.523	93	.538	955	326	607	7.6
1978-79	77	346	.577	151	.643	830	315	843	10.9
1979-80	82	327	.513	139	.665	1,094	366	794	9.7
1980-81	63	225	.524	55	.640	673	170	507	8.0
Totals	984	4,369	.509	1,883	.633	13,769	3,822	10,624	10.8

Notes: Boldface indicates statistical leader. GP = games played; FGM = field goals made; FG% = field goal percentage; FTM = free throws made; FT% = free throw percentage; Reb. = rebounds; Ast. = assists; TP = total points; PPG = points per game

1967, 523 points and 533 rebounds; and in 1967-1968, 645 points and 513 rebounds. For these performances, Wes made *The Sporting News* All-America Second Team in 1967 and 1968.

Among the Louisville records Unseld set are the all-time scoring average (20.6 points per game) and rebounding average (18.9 rebounds per game). Wes also set the record for most points scored in a game (45 against Georgetown University in 1967) and became one of only a few Louisville players to accumulate more than 1,000 points and 1,000 rebounds.

The Emerging Champion

Wes had serious career plans to become a schoolteacher, but being named number-one draft choice and being picked second overall by the Baltimore Bullets of the National Basketball Association (NBA) in 1968 made him reconsider.

In the 1968-1969 season, Wes was named both Rookie of the Year and the league's most valuable player. The only other person to be so honored was Wilt Chamberlain. In addition, Wes made the All-NBA First Team that year.

In his thirteen years as a professional player, Wes became the seventh all-time rebounder in the league's history (13,769 rebounds) and became one of four players to score more than 10,000 career points and collect more than 10,000 rebounds. He was named to the All-Star team five times and set Bullets records for most minutes played and most rebounds.

The highest point in Wes's Bullet career came in the 1977-1978 season when he led his team to the NBA championship and was named the series' most valuable player. The statistics behind this achievement are significant. For the 1977-1978 playoffs and championship series, Wes played 677 minutes, made 71 field goals, made 27 free throws, took a total of 216 rebounds, made 79 assists, and scored a total of 169 points.

Continuing the Story

While a player, Wes Unseld had always been noted for his generosity off the court. He received the first NBA Walter Kennedy Citizenship Award for volunteer work in the neighborhoods of Baltimore, Maryland, and Washington, D.C., in 1975. When he retired as an active player in 1981, he continued to volunteer his time to worthy public service activities.

Yet that was only half the story. In 1981, Wes was hired as vice president of the Capital Center and the Washington Bullets. In 1987, Wes became an assistant coach for the Bullets, and in January of 1988, he replaced Kevin Loughery as head coach.

In his first season as head coach, Wes directed the Bullets to thirty wins, twenty-five losses, and the playoffs. In spite of their success that season, the Bullets lost to the Detroit Pistons in the first round of the 1988 playoffs.

During the 1988-1989 season, Wes had to readjust his offense because of the trade of key player Moses Malone. The team went without a center most of the season, so a new motion offense brought out the best in the veterans on his squad. Although they struggled at times, the Bullets still managed to post a record of forty wins and forty-two losses.

The style of unselfish play that Wes maintained as a player became the style of play he emphasized as a coach. The number of assists by his top players numbered in the hundreds each season. What former teammate Mike Riordan said of Wes, in a *Sports Illustrated* article by Pat Putnam, can be applied to him as a coach as well: "[He's] totally unselfish. He keeps the ball moving so much everybody gets a piece of the action. Guys love playing with him. He makes everybody else look good. . . . Most people are impressed by scoring statistics. The players are more impressed by all the other things he does. . . . And you have to remember—this guy isn't a superstar just on the court. He's a superstar in life, too."

At the end of the 1993-1994 season, Wes stepped down as the Bullets' coach, having compiled a 202-345 record with a mediocre team. After working as a color analyst on national broadcasts of NBA games during the 1994-1995 season, Wes became the executive vice president and general manager of the Bullets in 1996, a job that he maintained after the Bullets changed their name to the Wizards. Many basketball experts believe that Wes is the most important person in the history of the Washington Bullets/Wizards franchise.

Having been an incredibly proficient passer, rebounder, and team player, Wes received the ultimate honor in basketball when he was inducted to the Naismith Memorial Basketball Hall of Fame in 1988. Former Boston Celtics coach Red Auerbach labeled Wes as the best outlet passer to ever play in the NBA. As part of the celebration of the golden anniversary of the NBA during the 1996-1997 season, Wes was selected as a member of the NBA's 50 Greatest Players of All Time

HONORS AND AWARDS

1967-68	Consensus All-American
1969	NBA most valuable player All-NBA Team NBA Rookie of the Year NBA All-Rookie Team
1969, 1971-73, 1975	NBA All-Star Team
1975	Kennedy Citizenship Award
1978	NBA Finals most valuable player
1988	Inducted into Naismith Memorial Basketball Hall of Fame
1996	NBA 50 Greatest Players of All Time Team Uniform number 41 retired by Washington Bullets

Team. Wes and his wife, Connie, had a daughter, Kimberly, and a son, Westley, Jr.

Summary

One of the most exciting players in University of Louisville history, Wes Unseld took his record-breaking potential to the NBA and fulfilled expectations. As a player, he led the Washington Bullets to a world championship, and as a coach, he developed an exciting, crowd-pleasing style of play. The five-time professional All-Star also became an all-star citizen, donating his services and talents to his community.

Rustin Larson

Additional Sources:

Bjarkman, Peter C. *The Biographical History of Basketball.* Chicago: Masters Press, 1998.

Dolin, Nick, Chris Dolin, and David Check. *Basketball Stars: The Greatest Players in the History of the Game.* New York: Black Dog and Leventhal, 1997.

Mallozzi, Vincent M. *Basketball: The Legends and the Game.* Willowdale, Ont.: Firefly Books, 1998.

Sachare, Alex. *One Hundred Greatest Basketball Players of All Time.* New York: Simon and Schuster, 1997.

GREAT ATHLETES

Sport Index

James Worthy **8**-3089
Babe Didrikson Zaharias **8**-3134

 BEACH VOLLEYBALL
Dain Blanton **1**-259
Eric Fonoimoana **1**-259

 BILLIARDS
Willie Mosconi **5**-1944

 BOBSLEDDING
Eddie Eagan **2**-728

 BODYBUILDING
Tommy Kono **4**-1494
Steve Reeves **6**-2284
Eugen Sandow **6**-2442
Arnold Schwarzenegger **7**-2486

 BOWLING
Earl Anthony **1**-73
Don Carter **2**-415
Marion Ladewig **4**-1534
Floretta Doty McCutcheon **5**-1715
Carmen Salvino **6**-2422
Lisa Wagner **8**-2923
Dick Weber **8**-2967
Walter Ray Williams, Jr. **8**-3049

 BOXING
Muhammad Ali **1**-38
Alexis Arguello **1**-88
Henry Armstrong **1**-98
Max Baer **1**-125
Riddick Bowe **1**-306
Julio César Chávez **2**-454
Billy Conn **2**-506
Oscar de la Hoya **2**-638
Jack Dempsey **2**-648
Roberto Duran **2**-724
Eddie Eagan **2**-728
George Foreman **3**-856
Bob Foster **3**-862
Joe Frazier **3**-880
Rocky Graziano **3**-1012
Marvin Hagler **3**-1082
Thomas Hearns **3**-1152
Larry Holmes **4**-1215
Evander Holyfield **4**-1219
Jack Johnson **4**-1319
Roy Jones, Jr. **4**-1370
Sugar Ray Leonard **4**-1600

Lennox Lewis **4**-1607
Joe Louis **5**-1671
Rocky Marciano **5**-1792
Archie Moore **5**-1923
Laszlo Papp **6**-2135
Floyd Patterson **6**-2152
Sugar Ray Robinson **6**-2339
Felix Savon **7**-2448
Max Schmeling **7**-2466
Teófilo Stevenson **7**-2646
Dick Tiger **7**-2768
Felix Trinidad **7**-2813
Gene Tunney **7**-2828
Mike Tyson **7**-2840

 CANOEING/KAYAKING
Greg Barton **1**-172
Jon Lugbill **5**-1688

 CHESS
Bobby Fischer **3**-829
Anatoly Karpov **4**-1405
Garry Kasparov **4**-1411

 CRICKET
Donald G. Bradman **1**-318
Learie Constantine **2**-528

 CYCLING
Lance Armstrong **1**-102
Connie Carpenter **2**-409
Bernard Hinault **3**-1191
Miguel Indurain **4**-1259
Greg LeMond **4**-1588
Jeannie Longo **5**-1654
Eddy Merckx **5**-1859
Connie Paraskevin-Young **6**-2137
Major Taylor **7**-2721
Bobby Walthour **8**-2940
Sheila Young **8**-3122

 DECATHLON
Bruce Jenner **4**-1304
Rafer Johnson **4**-1346
Bob Mathias **5**-1825
Dan O'Brien **6**-2053
Bob Richards **6**-2300
Daley Thompson **7**-2747
Jim Thorpe **7**-2756
Bill Toomey **7**-2786

 DISCUS THROW
Olga Connolly **2**-522
Al Oerter **6**-2062
Mac Wilkins **8**-3024

 DIVING
Klaus Dibiasi **2**-657
Fu Mingxia **3**-893
Gao Min **3**-902
Micki King **4**-1471
Sammy Lee **4**-1579
Greg Louganis **5**-1668
Pat McCormick **5**-1709
Cynthia Potter **6**-2226
Laura Wilkinson **8**-3027

 EQUESTRIAN
Raimondo D'Inezeo **2**-671
Lis Hartel **3**-1123
David O'Connor **6**-2059
Hans Winkler **8**-3062

 FENCING
George Charles Calnan **1**-385
Laura Flessel-Colovic **3**-842
Nedo Nadi **5**-1998
Peter Westbrook **8**-2979

 FIELD HOCKEY
Betty Shellenberger **7**-2535
Anne Barton Townsend **7**-2798

 FIGURE SKATING
Tenley Albright **1**-29
Tai Babilonia **1**-122
Brian Boitano **1**-277
Dick Button **1**-382
Robin Cousins **2**-546
John Curry **2**-582
Christopher Dean **7**-2794
Peggy Fleming **3**-839
Randy Gardner **1**-122
Ekaterina Gordeeva **3**-992
Sergei Grinkov **3**-992
Dorothy Hamill **3**-1093
Scott Hamilton **3**-1096
Carol Heiss **3**-1162
Sonja Henie **3**-1170
Midori Ito **4**-1271
David Jenkins **4**-1298
Hayes Jenkins **4**-1301
Nancy Kerrigan **4**-1441
Michelle Kwan **4**-1528

V

Country Index

This index lists athletes by the countries—including some dependencies—with which they are most closely associated by virtue of their citizenship, residence, or membership on national teams. Many names are listed under more than one country, but some athletes are not listed under the countries in which they were born because they have no other meaningful ties with those countries. The index is intended to serve only as a guide and not be a definitive list of nationalities or birthplaces.

XIV

XVI

XIX

Name Index